T0145268

Quantum Computer Music

Eduardo Reck Miranda
Editor

Quantum Computer Music

Foundations, Methods and Advanced
Concepts

 Springer

Editor
Eduardo Reck Miranda ⓘ
Interdisciplinary Centre for Computer
Music Research
University of Plymouth
Plymouth, UK

ISBN 978-3-031-13911-6   ISBN 978-3-031-13909-3   (eBook)
https://doi.org/10.1007/978-3-031-13909-3

This Springer imprint is published by the registered company Springer Nature Switzerland AG
The registered company address is: Gewerbestrasse 11, 6330 Cham, Switzerland

Foreword

An art aims, above all, at producing something beautiful which affects not our feelings but the organ of pure contemplation, our imagination

Eduard Hanslick

Music is sounds organised in space and time

Eduardo Miranda

In 2015 I took part in a debate about quantum computing in front of a packed house at the Cambridge Union Society ("CUS"). The motion being debated was "Quantum Computers, whilst scientifically of interest, will not have an impact on humanity during our lifetime".

The debate was very enjoyable, not the least of the reasons being that the motion was easily defeated, with over 90% of the audience supporting me as my debating partner, Aram Harrow from MIT, and I argued that not only will quantum computers be of immense scientific interest, but that they will surely have an enormous impact on our lives during our lifetimes.

Arguably the debate was as much a bit of fun as a serious "peek" into the future, but what might seem surprising from today's vantage point is that the motion, as unlikely as it might seem, was supported by one of the UK's leading venture-capitalists and seconded by a professor of quantum computing from a leading UK academic institution. Both of them were utterly confident that quantum computing would remain a niche area of scientific interest during our lifetimes.

The venerable CUS building was packed with over 600 people in an audience that included Prof. Stephen Hawking, a Nobel laureate from quantum physics, and a whole set of interested parties from different industrial and research groups related to quantum technologies, as well as the usual Cambridge cohort of CUS members. It was also a very enlightened audience that voted overwhelmingly against the motion. In the seven years that have passed since the debate, it is clear that Quantum Computers are already impacting us, and as this book demonstrates, this impact is across many more areas than simply remote academic research.

What pleases me personally even more than convincing the audience back in 2015 that the supporters of the motion were wrong is that there is now, in 2022, a clear informed consensus that quantum computers will indeed have a meaningful impact on our lives. This consensus also holds that commercially relevant quantum computers are still a few years away, and the globally active (and rapidly growing) community of quantum computing companies, researchers and organisations who are engaged in this sector keenly track and monitor engineering advances on both the hardware and software (algorithmic) side.

Not surprisingly, when we try to imagine how quantum computers will affect us, our pre-disposition as a society is to start to think about "commercial" applications rather than other areas and certainly not in applications in music or art. This is perhaps not surprising since almost all new technologies that emerge from the "lab" and end up being funded for commercial purposes are backed by capital (in the form of investment) that needs to make significant returns, and those returns are measured in terms of the value of the company that is advancing the technology. When I say value, I mean of course $$$.

If there is a lesson to be learned from the past 70 years of technology innovation, it is that we almost always end up underestimating their impact on society as a whole, which is a consequence of the fact that we typically cannot forecast the "use cases" until talented people from diverse backgrounds are exposed to the technology as it matures. In fact, I cannot personally recall a successful technology where the ways in which we can use and benefit from that particular advance are clear at the outset.

The two most obvious such examples in relatively recent times are the Internet and mobile telephony. I am not sure that anyone in the early days of mobile phone availability would have thought that we would be carrying around small devices with the computational power equivalent to a supercomputer of just a few years ago, or how quickly transistors would be miniaturised, or how effectively collateral components and enabling technologies such as batteries and operating systems could enhance our experience of the humble telephone.

Even more telling is the way that we use the Internet, both for good and bad purposes, that far outweighs anything that we might have imagined in the mid-1990s when the concept of the world wide web started to become more widespread.

And so, it will be with quantum computing. The advent of quantum computing is largely made up of a community of pioneers who, try as they might, are unable to look beyond the obvious application of quantum technologies to areas such as sensing, metrology, material discovery and possibly even Artificial Intelligence (AI).

There are however exceptional people who don't conform to the "norm".

Eduardo Miranda, the editor of this book and a contributing author, and Bob Coecke, my colleague, close friend and a Chief Scientist of Quantinuum, (who is a co-author of one of the chapters in this book) are two very bright shining lights that find ways to look around corners that block the view for the rest of us. Bob has pioneered the development of quantum computers for Natural Language Processing —coining the phrase "Quantum Natural Language Processing ("QNLP")—and Eduardo is an accomplished composer and an emerging quantum information theorist, who is pioneering the development of quantum computers for Music. The fact that Bob also plays in a band might account for a consonant similarity in a mindset that facilitates the ability to look around corners.

The most pleasing thing about the publication of *Quantum Computer Music: Foundations, Methods and Advanced Concepts* is that it represents a noteworthy change in the balance of research and dialogue away from an almost exclusive focus on commercial and scientific applications of quantum computers, to a consideration of the impact on arts and society as a whole. I do not want to neglect the commercial and financial importance of computing technology and ultimately quantum computers to the music industry but what excites me more than anything else is how something as deeply fundamental to our nature as music can be exploited in ways that are as novel and almost (but not quite) disturbingly unfamiliar as any innovation in music in the broadest sense, in the past millennium.

Quantum Computers are sometimes described as "computing the way that nature computes". This description is essentially a riff on Feynman's positioning of a quantum computer as the only way to simulate quantum systems, which in turn are the basic tools that will allow us, finally, to design and create new materials in areas such as medicine, nitrogen fixation, batteries and carbon sequestration to name just a few.

Feynman famously also quipped that no one really understands quantum computers, and together with the now mythological status of the Einstein-Bohr debates, this quip has added to the aura of mystery that surrounds quantum computing. It seems that no self-respecting YouTube video or popular article about quantum computing can be complete unless it refers to and takes full advantage of the sense of mystery that is undoubtedly still present.

Feynman, and pretty much everyone else with the ability to comment meaningfully on this topic, concedes that whilst we understand the "what" of quantum mechanics, as evidenced by the fact that the theory may well be the most experimentally proven of all physics theories, we still do not understand the "why".

Attempts to capture and explain the reason for the continuing mystery of quantum mechanics are not easy. Different commentators choose to highlight different aspects of quantum mechanics to exemplify the lack of progress on the "why" as opposed to the "what".

Superposition, entanglement, wave-particle duality, the measurement problem, contextuality or Heisenberg's uncertainty principle all vie for being the most often cited examples of why Quantum Mechanics is hard or just weird. My own favourite popular explanation is the one used by Rovelli in his book "Helgoland" where $px - xp = i(\hbar)$ is used to explain the central and fundamental difference between the quantum world and the world that we regularly inhabit and intuit.

The truth of course is that any and all examples are inadequate to capture the fact that quantum computing, when making use of the laws of quantum mechanics via quantum information theory, taps into the true nature of reality and provides access to a realm of computation that surely is best described as "computing the way that nature computes" thus shifting the boundaries of what might have been, until now, computationally possible.

In fact, the mystery of quantum mechanics is very often cited as being a motivation for physicists who are working in the field. When asked why they are excited by quantum computing, a large percentage of what I would describe as quantum native researchers will reply by stating their hope that a fully universal fault-tolerant quantum processor will help us to understand the nature of reality. That we can then not only understand the "what" but also the "why" of quantum mechanics.

I share that hope.

Space and time are ineluctably mysterious in their own way and are invoked by Eduardo Miranda in his wonderfully simple but deep definition of music. Neither time nor space is easy to define. In fact, time is impossible to describe, and space is almost as difficult. Trying to define them using words brings to mind Wittgenstein and his now infamous dictum "whereof one cannot speak one must remain silent".

Music is not that different. Trying to explain music or describe a musical experience is well-nigh impossible using words. And yet music occupies such an important part of the human experience. As far as we can tell, music, and all that it implies, is uniquely human, and our attempts to describe or even capture what it means for music to be "beautiful" tend to end up being forlorn. As the chapters in this book collectively show, however, there is more than simply intuition to support the idea that quantum computers will bring something different to the table not only in terms of music production and composition but also to our understanding of just what it means for a sound or a series of sounds to be organised in space and time.

I will close this foreword with a little controversy. I am firmly in the camp of philosophers such as Eduard Hanslick and Peter Kivy who decry and vehemently oppose the easy option of giving the music the quality of a feeling. It is without question a fact that music can invoke feelings, just as poetry or any other art form might do so. But the music itself is not a feeling and carries no intrinsic meaning that we can define or describe using human language. On the other hand, however, syntax and semantics play a role—and depending on your point of view, that role dominates the art (or science) of what we might call music-making.

In a seminal essay titled "Music Science and Semantics", Kivy digs impressively deeply into the reasons why semantic and propositional meaning cannot be uncovered in music. I am in danger here of touching upon a raw nerve for all those proponents of the science of music who construct schemes to compose music using what can only be described as the rules of language. I raise this point, in closing, not in order to debate the typical construct of a computational toolkit for composing music (of which there are literally hundreds) but to note my hope that just as with language, where the exploitation of Hilbert space will uncover spatial and topo-logical components of human speech that fail miserably to be attained using classical computers, we may also, with quantum computers, recognise and find a whole new perspective about music. Perhaps even some new sounds in space and time?

Quantinuum, London, UK   Ilyas Khan

Preface: Music with quantum computing, a natural progression, but a potentially revolutionary one

Quantum computing has been on my radar for over two decades, owing to my forays into Unconventional Computing (UC) in the early 2000s; I have been harnessing biological organisms (e.g., Mycetozoa) to develop living music processors in vitro [2, 6, 7, 8]. At the time, the idea of actual quantum computing chips, with real qubits, and so on, sounded rather theoretical to me. But all of a sudden, quantum computing sprang out from the largely underestimated and underfunded UC research circles to the realms of national strategic research priorities and copious industrial investments, all over the globe. Quantum computing is mushrooming.

If you are reading this preface because you got, or are considering getting, a copy of this book, then I assume that you would no longer need to be persuaded that quantum computing is a fascinating development, which is bound to have an impact on how we will create, perform and listen to music in time to come. My pet theory goes like this: computers are ubiquitous in the music industry. Quantum computers are an emerging new computing technology. Therefore, quantum computers will, in one way or another, be useful for music. Hence my rationale for putting this book together.

As early as the 1840s, Ada King, countess of Lovelace, in England, predicted that computers would be able to compose music. Daughter of famed poet Lord Byron studied mathematics and logic and is often cited as the first-ever computer programmer. On a note about Charles Babbage's Analytical Engine, she wrote:

Supposing, for instance, that the fundamental relations of pitched sounds in the science of harmony and musical composition were susceptible to such expression and adaptations, the Engine might compose elaborate and scientific pieces of music of any degree of complexity or extent. ([5], p. 21)

At about the same time, at the apex of the first Industrial Revolution, steam-powered machines controlled by stacks of punched cards were being engineered for the textile industry. Musical instrument builders promptly recognised that punch-card stacks could be used to drive automatic pipe organs. Such initiatives revealed a glimpse of an unsettling idea about the nature of the music they produced: it emanated from information, which could also be used to control all sorts of machines. The idea soon evolved into mechanical pianos and several companies began as early as the 1900s to manufacture self-playing pianos, generally known as "pianolas".

Self-playing pianos enabled musicians to record their work with great fidelity: the recording apparatus could punch thousands of holes per minute on a piano roll, enough to store all the notes that a fast virtuoso could play. Because a piano roll stored a set of parameters that represented musical notes rather than sound recordings, the performances remained malleable: the information could be manually edited, the holes re-cut and so on. This sort of information technology gained much sophistication during the twentieth century and paved the way for the development of programmable electronic computers.

People seldom connect the dots to realise that the field of *Computer Music* has been progressing in tandem with *Computer Science* since the invention of the computer. Musicians started experimenting with computers far before the emergence of the vast majority of scientific, industrial and commercial computing applications in existence today. As an example of this, as early as the 1940s, researchers at Australia's Council for Scientific and Industrial Research (CSIR) installed a loudspeaker on their Mk1 computer to track the progress of a program using sound (Fig. 1). Shortly after, Geoff Hill, a mathematician with a musical background, programmed this machine to playback a tune in 1951 [3]. Essentially, they programmed the Mk1 as if they were punching a piano roll for a pianola.

Then, in the 1950s, Lejaren Hiller and Leonard Isaacson, at the University of Illinois at Urbana-Champaign, USA, programmed the ILLIAC computer to compose a string quartet entitled *Illiac Suite* (Fig. 2). The *Illiac Suite* consists of four movements, each of which uses different methods for generating musical sequences [4]. The innovation here was that the computer was programmed with instructions to *create* music rather than simply reproduce encoded music. The rest is history.

Fig. 1 CSIRAC computer used to playback a tune in the early 1950s. The loudspeaker can be seen on the right-hand door of the console. (Image published with the kind permission of Prof Paul Doornbusch.)

Fig. 2 Composer and Professor of Chemistry, Lejaren Hiller, in the University of Illinois at Urbana-Champaign's Experimental Music Studio. (Image courtesy of the University of Illinois at Urbana-Champaign.)

University-based research organisations and companies have been welcoming musicians to join their laboratories ever since. A notable early example is AT&T's Bell Laboratories, in New Jersey, where in the early 1960s composer Max Mathews developed MUSIC III: a system for synthesising sounds on the IBM 7094 computer. Descendants of MUSIC III, such as Csound [1], are still used today; see Chap. 16 in this volume for an example.

Interestingly, it seems that history is repeating itself. The current stage of quantum computing hardware development is somewhat comparable with the early days of classical digital computers (Fig. 3). They also were unportable, unreliable, high-maintenance, expensive and required unusual (at the time) specialist skills to be handled. Indeed, quantum computing companies and research laboratories are also starting to welcome musicians on their premises; IBM Quantum in the USA,

Fig. 3 State-of-the-art quantum computers at IBM Quantum. (Reprint Courtesy of IBM Corporation © (2022))

Quantinuum in the UK and the Center for Quantum Technologies and Applications (CQTA) at Desy in Germany come to mind.

Before we dive in, let us ponder this: in 2010, I took a personal computer to the stage (Fig. 4) at Queen Elizabeth Hall (Southbank Centre, London) to perform my symphony *Sacra Conversazione* with the BBC Concert Orchestra. That machine held inside it the equivalent of the whole studio used by Prof. Hiller in the 1950s (Fig. 2) and much more. Now, 12 years later, I am composing a new symphony, *Multiverse Symphony*, which I will also perform on stage with a computer as my instrument. But this time, my device will be connected to a quantum computer over the Internet. I shall be producing sounds interactively with it. We tend to take it for granted how significantly computer music technology evolved in just about 60 years. What will it be like in the next 60 years?

I often hear the CEO of Quantinuum, Ilyas Khan, saying that quantum computing is a driving force for a new Industrial Revolution that is taking place right now. This book is to inspire, inform and empower you to embrace this revolution. It is not intended to bring you answers. The field is just born, and we are still learning which questions should be asked. Rather, it brings fresh ideas and a plethora of unresolved problems, which will certainly be addressed as research evolves. I am most honoured to have the privilege to feature in this book the work of pioneering authors in the newborn field of *Quantum Computer Music*. In the following pages,

Fig. 4 A computer as an instrument of the orchestra

you will find chapters discussing ways in which the quantum-mechanical nature of quantum computing might be leveraged to compose, perform, analyse and synthesise music and sound.

Eduardo Reck Miranda
ICCMR, University of Plymouth
Plymouth, UK
eduardo.miranda@plymouth.ac.uk

References

1. Boulanger, R. (Ed.) (2000). *The Csound Book: Perspectives in Software Synthesis, Sound Design, Signal Processing, and Programming.* The MIT Press. ISBN: 9780262522618.
2. Paul-Choudhury, S. (2017). The slime mould instruments that make sweet music. *NewScientist.* 3 August 2017. Online: https://www.newscientist.com/article/2142614-the-slime-mould-instruments-that-make-sweet-music/
3. Doornbusch, P. (2004). Computer Sound Synthesis in 1951: The Music of CSIRAC. *Computer Music Journal* 28:1(10-25).
4. Hiller, L. A. and Isaacson, L. M. (1959). *Experimental Music: Composition with an Electronic Computer.* McGraw-Hill. Available online, https://archive.org/details/experimentalmusi00hill/page/n5/mode/2up (Accessed on 07 May 2021).

5. Manabrea, L. F. (1843). *Sketch of the Analytical Engine invented by Charles Babbage.* Translated by Ada Lovelace. R. and J. E. Taylor, London. Available online, http://johnrhudson.me.uk/computing/Menabrea_Sketch.pdf (Accessed on 03 Apr 2020).
6. Miranda, E. R., Braund, E. and Venkatesh, S. (2018). Composing with Biomemristors: Is Biocomputing the New Technology of Computer Music? *Computer Music Journal*, 42(3): 28–46.
7. Miranda, E. R. (Ed.) (2017) Guide to Unconventional Computing for Music Springer. ISBN: 9783319498805.
8. Miranda, E. R., Adamatzky, A. and Jones, J. (2011). Sounds Synthesis with Slime Mould of Physarum Polycephalum. *Journal of Bionic Engineering*, 8:107–113. arXiv:1212.1203v1 [nlin.PS]

Contents

Introduction to Quantum Computing for Musicians

1

Eduardo Reck Miranda and James L. Weaver

Abstract

This chapter introduces the basics of quantum computing deemed necessary to follow the topics discussed in this book. It begins with a concise introduction to gate-based quantum computing and follows with an overview of the book's content. It provides a glimpse of pioneering research that is taking place worldwide, which is laying the foundations of the emerging field of *Quantum Computer Music* research.

1.1 Introduction

The objective of this chapter is to provide a basic introduction to gate-based quantum computing and present a bird's eye view of the emerging field of *Quantum Computer Music*. The reader is referred to [1,4,6,8] for more detailed explanations.

1.1.1 History Repeating Itself

In the early days of digital computing, computers such as the ENIAC shown in Fig. 1.1 were so large that they filled up whole rooms. They also had limited amounts of memory (bits), and the instruction sets for programming them were very unique.

E. R. Miranda (✉)
ICCMR, University of Plymouth, Plymouth, UK
e-mail: eduardo.miranda@plymouth.ac.uk

J. L. Weaver
IBM Quantum Computation Center, Poughkeepsie, NY, USA
e-mail: james.weaver@ibm.com

Fig. 1.1 ENIAC computer circa 1947. *Source* Wikipedia.org/wiki

It is very interesting and exciting that history is repeating itself! For the past several years, radically new kinds of computers known as quantum computers have been built that fill rooms, have limited amounts of quantum bits (qubits), and their instruction sets are certainly unique. Figure 1.2 shows a quantum computer from these early days of quantum computing.

1.1.2 Raison d'être

As Fig. 1.3 represents, some problems are feasible on classical computers, but some problems will never be solved with them. The main reason for building and using quantum computers is to (hopefully) solve problems that are impossible with classical computers.

For example, the ability to simulate large molecules would facilitate drug discovery, but the best classical supercomputer in the world can only simulate a 40–50 electron orbital system. This is because every additional quantum particle to be modeled doubles the amount of memory required. A 300 electron orbital system, for example, would require more floating point numbers to model than there are atoms in the visible universe.

Fig. 1.2 A quantum computer at IBM Quantum in 2022. Reprint Courtesy of IBM Corporation © (2022)

Fig. 1.3 Some problems will never be solved with classical computers

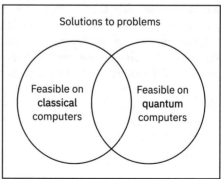

Simply put, quantum computers hold and operate upon quantum particles which could represent quantum particles in the molecule to be modeled. This is what Richard Feynman meant when he proposed the idea of creating a quantum computer[1] :

> Nature isn't classical, dammit, and if you want to make a simulation of nature, you'd better make it quantum mechanical, and by golly it's a wonderful problem, because it doesn't look so easy.

As Feynman prescribed, quantum computers make direct use of quantum-mechanical phenomena, such as superposition, interference and entanglement, to perform operations on data.

Other problem domains in which quantum computing will potentially provide an advantage include optimization, financial portfolios, machine learning, and of course, making music.

1.2 Computing Quantum-Mechanically

Classical computers manipulate information represented in terms of binary digits, each of which can value 1 or 0. They work with microprocessors made up of billions of tiny switches that are activated by electric signals. Values 1 and 0 reflect the on and off states of the switches.

In contrast, a quantum computer deals with information in terms of quantum bits, or *qubits*. Qubits operate at the subatomic level. Therefore, they are subject to the laws of quantum physics.

At the subatomic level, a quantum object does not exist in a determined state. Its state is unknown until one observes it. Before it is observed, a quantum object is said to behave like a wave. But when it is observed it becomes a particle. This phenomenon is referred to as the wave-particle duality.

Quantum systems are described in terms of wave functions. A wave function represents what the particle would be like when a quantum object is observed. It expresses the state of a quantum system as the sum of the possible states that it may fall into when it is observed. Each possible component of a wave function, which is also a wave, is scaled by a coefficient reflecting its relative weight. That is, some states might be more likely than others. Metaphorically, think of a quantum system as the spectrum of a musical sound, where the different amplitudes of its various wave-components give its unique timbre. As with sound waves, quantum wave-components interfere with one another, constructively and destructively. In quantum physics, the interfering waves are said to be coherent. As we will see later, the act of observing waves decoheres them. Again metaphorically, it is as if when

---

[1] https://quotes.yourdictionary.com/author/richard-feynman/158361.

listening to a musical sound one would perceive only a single spectral component; probably the one with the highest energy, but not necessarily so.

Qubits are special because of the wave-particle duality. Qubits can be in an indeterminate state, represented by a wave function, until they are read out. This is known as superposition. A good part of the art of programming a quantum computer involves manipulating qubits to perform operations while they are in such indeterminate state. This makes quantum computing fundamentally different from digital computing.

A qubit can be implemented in a number of ways. All the same, the qubits of a superconducting quantum computer need to be isolated from the environment in order to remain coherent to perform computations. Quantum coherence is a *sine qua non* for the operation of quantum processors. It is what maintains qubits in superposition. Yet, coherence is doomed to fall apart—i.e., to decohere—before any nontrivial circuit has a chance to run to its end. The promising advantages of quantum computers are crippled by decoherence, which leads to fatal processing errors. Metaphorically, think of keeping qubits coherent as something like balancing a bunch of coins upright on an unstable surface, where any movement, even the tiniest vibration, would cause them to fall to head or tail. In short, any interaction with the environment causes qubits to decohere. But it is extremely hard, if not impossible, to shield a quantum chip from the environment.

In order to picture a qubit, imagine a transparent sphere with opposite poles. From its centre, a vector whose length is equal to the radius of the sphere can point to anywhere on the surface. In quantum mechanics this sphere is called Bloch sphere and the vector is referred to as a state vector. The opposite poles of the sphere are denoted by $|0\rangle$ and $|1\rangle$, which is the notation used to represent quantum states (Fig. 1.4).

A qubit's state vector can point at anywhere on the Bloch sphere's surface. Mathematically, it is described in terms of polar coordinates using two angles, θ and φ. The angle θ is the angle between the state vector and the z-axis (latitude) and the angle φ describes vector's position in relation to the x-axis (longitude).

Fig. 1.4 Bloch sphere.
Source Smite-Meister,
https://commons.wikimedia.
org/w/index.php?
curid=5829358

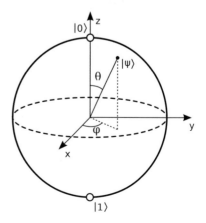

It is popularly said that a qubit can value 0 and 1 at the same time, but this is not entirely accurate. When a qubit is in superposition of $|0\rangle$ and $|1\rangle$, the state vector could be pointing anywhere between the two. However, we cannot really know where exactly a state vector is pointing to until we read the qubit. In quantum computing terminology, the act of reading a qubit is referred to as 'observing', or 'measuring' it. Measuring the qubit will make the vector point to one of the poles and return either 0 or 1 as a result.

The state vector of a qubit in superposition state is described as a linear combination of two vectors, $|0\rangle$ and $|1\rangle$, as follows:

$$|\Psi\rangle = \alpha |0\rangle + |1\rangle, \quad \text{where} \quad |\alpha|^2 = 0.5 \quad \text{and} \quad |\beta|^2 = 0.5 \tag{1.1}$$

The state vector $|\Psi\rangle$ is a superposition of vectors $|0\rangle$ and $|1\rangle$ in a two-dimensional complex space, referred to as Hilbert space, with amplitudes α and β. Here the amplitudes are expressed in terms of Cartesian coordinates; but bear in mind that these coordinates can be complex numbers.

In a nutshell, consider the squared values of α and β as probability values representing the likelihood of the measurement return 0 or 1. For instance, let us assume the following:

$$|\Psi\rangle = \alpha |0\rangle + |1\rangle, \quad \text{where} \quad |\alpha| = \frac{1}{2} \quad \text{and} \quad |\beta| = \frac{\sqrt{3}}{2} \tag{1.2}$$

In this case, $|\alpha|^2 = 0.25$ and $|\beta|^2 = 0.75$. This means that the measurement of the qubit has a 25% chance of returning 0 and a 75% chance of returning 1 (Fig. 1.5).

Quantum computers are programmed using sequences of commands, or quantum gates, that act on qubits. For instance, the 'not gate', performs a rotation of 180 degrees around the x-axis. Hence this gate is often referred to as the '**X** gate' (Fig. 1.6). A more generic rotation **Rx**(θ) gate is typically available for quantum programming, where the angle for the rotation around the x-axis is specified. Therefore, **Rx**(180)

Fig. 1.5 An example of superposition, where the state vector has a 25% chance of settling to $|0\rangle$ and a 75% chance of settling to $|1\rangle$ after the measurement

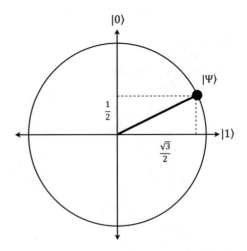

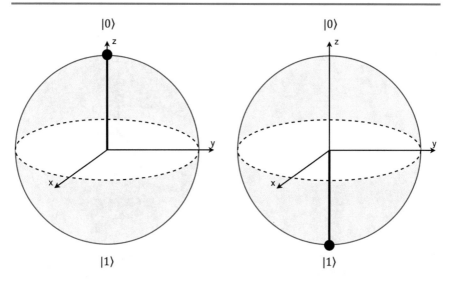

Fig. 1.6 The **X** gate rotates the state vector (pointing upwards on the figure on the left) by 180° around the x-axis (pointing downwards on the figure on the right)

applied to $|0\rangle$ or $|1\rangle$ is equivalent to applying **X** to $|0\rangle$ or $|1\rangle$. Similarly, also there are **Rz**(φ) and **Ry**(θ) gates for rotations on the z-axis and y-axis, respectively. As **Rz**(180) is widely used in quantum computing, various programming tools provide the gate **Z** to do this. An even more generic gate is typically available, which is a unitary rotation gate, with 3 Euler angles: **U**$(\theta, \varphi, \lambda)$.

In essence, all quantum gates perform rotations, which change the amplitude distribution of the system. And in fact, any qubit rotation can be specified in terms of **U**$(\theta, \varphi, \lambda)$; for instance **Rx**$(\theta) = $ **U**$(\theta, -\frac{\pi}{2}, \frac{\pi}{2})$.

An important gate for quantum computing is the Hadamard gate (referred to as the '**H** gate'). It puts the qubit into a balanced superposition state (pointing to $|+\rangle$) consisting of an equal-weighted combination of two opposing states: $|\alpha|^2 = 0.5$ and $|\beta|^2 = 0.5$ (Fig. 1.7). For other gates, please consult the references given at the introduction.

A quantum program is often depicted as a circuit diagram of quantum gates, showing sequences of gate operations on the qubits (Fig. 1.8). Qubits typically start at $|0\rangle$ and then a sequence of gates are applied. Then, the qubits are read and the results are stored in standard digital memory, which are accessible for further handling. Normally a quantum computer works alongside a classical computer, which in effect acts as the interface between the user and the quantum machine. The classical machine enables the user to handle the measurements for practical applications.

Quantum computation gets really interesting with gates that operate on multiple qubits, such as the conditional **X** gate, or '**CX** gate'. The **CX** gate puts two qubits in entanglement.

Entanglement establishes a curious correlation between qubits. In practice, the **CX** gate applies an **X** gate on a qubit only if the state of another qubit is $|1\rangle$. Thus, the

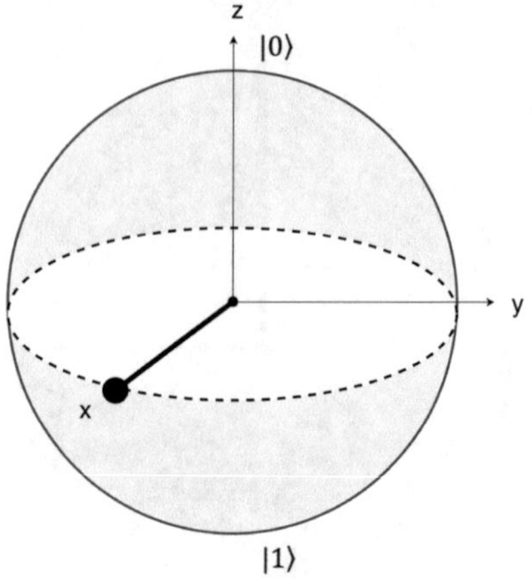

Fig. 1.7 The Hadamard gate
puts the qubit into a
superposition state halfway
two opposing poles

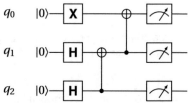

Fig. 1.8 A quantum
program depicted as a circuit
of quantum gates. The
squares with dials represent
measurements, which are
saved on classic registers

CX gate establishes a dependency of the state of one qubit with the value of another
(Fig. 1.9). In practice, any quantum gate can be made conditional and entanglement
can take place between more than two qubits.

The Bloch sphere is useful to visualize what happens with a single qubit, but it
is not suitable for multiple qubits, in particular when they are entangled. Entangled
qubits can no longer be thought of as independent units. They become one quantum
entity described by a state vector of its own right on a hypersphere. A hypersphere is
an extension of the Bloch sphere to 2^n complex dimensions, where n is the number
of qubits. Quantum gates perform rotations of a state vector to a new position on
this hypersphere. Thus, it is virtually impossible to visualize a system with multiple
qubits. Hence, from now on we shall use mathematics to represent quantum systems.

The notation used above to represent quantum states ($|\Psi\rangle$, $|0\rangle$, $|1\rangle$), is referred
to as Dirac notation, which provides an abbreviated way to represent a vector. For
instance, $|0\rangle$ and $|1\rangle$), represent the following vectors, respectively:

$$|0\rangle = \begin{bmatrix} 1 \\ 0 \end{bmatrix} \quad \text{and} \quad |1\rangle = \begin{bmatrix} 0 \\ 1 \end{bmatrix} \tag{1.3}$$

Fig. 1.9 The **CX** gate
creates a dependency of the
state of one qubit with the
state of another. In this case,
q_1 will be flipped only if q_0
is $|1\rangle$

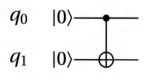

And quantum gates are represented as matrices. For instance, the simples gate of them all is the, 'I gate', or Identity gate, which is represented as an identity matrix:

$$\mathbf{I} = \begin{bmatrix} 1 & 0 \\ 0 & 1 \end{bmatrix} \tag{1.4}$$

The **I** gate does not alter the state of a qubit. Thus, the application of an **I** gate to $|0\rangle$ looks like this:

$$\mathbf{I}(|0\rangle) = \begin{bmatrix} 1 & 0 \\ 0 & 1 \end{bmatrix} \times \begin{bmatrix} 1 \\ 0 \end{bmatrix} = \begin{bmatrix} 1 \\ 0 \end{bmatrix} = |0\rangle \tag{1.5}$$

In contrast, the **X** gate, which flips the state of a qubit is represented as:

$$\mathbf{X} = \begin{bmatrix} 0 & 1 \\ 1 & 0 \end{bmatrix} \tag{1.6}$$

Therefore, quantum gate operations are represented mathematically as matrix operations; e.g., multiplication of a matrix (gate) by a vector (qubit state). Thus, the application of an **X** gate to $|0\rangle$ looks like this:

$$\mathbf{X}(|0\rangle) = \begin{bmatrix} 0 & 1 \\ 1 & 0 \end{bmatrix} \times \begin{bmatrix} 1 \\ 0 \end{bmatrix} = \begin{bmatrix} 0 \\ 1 \end{bmatrix} = |1\rangle \tag{1.7}$$

Conversely, the application of an **X** gate to $|1\rangle$ would therefore is written as follows:

$$\mathbf{X}(|1\rangle) = \begin{bmatrix} 0 & 1 \\ 1 & 0 \end{bmatrix} \times \begin{bmatrix} 0 \\ 1 \end{bmatrix} = \begin{bmatrix} 1 \\ 0 \end{bmatrix} = |0\rangle \tag{1.8}$$

The Hadamard gate has the matrix:

$$\mathbf{H} = \begin{bmatrix} \frac{1}{\sqrt{2}} & \frac{1}{\sqrt{2}} \\ \frac{1}{\sqrt{2}} & -\frac{1}{\sqrt{2}} \end{bmatrix} = \frac{1}{\sqrt{2}} \begin{bmatrix} 1 & 1 \\ 1 & -1 \end{bmatrix} \tag{1.9}$$

As we have seen earlier, the application of the H gate to a qubit pointing to $|0\rangle$ puts it in superposition, right at the equator of the Bloch sphere. This is notated as follows:

$$\mathbf{H}(|0\rangle) = \frac{1}{\sqrt{2}}(|0\rangle + |1\rangle) \tag{1.10}$$

As applied to $|1\rangle$, it also puts it in superposition, but pointing to the opposite direction of the superposition shown above:

$$\mathbf{H}(|1\rangle) = \frac{1}{\sqrt{2}}(|0\rangle - |1\rangle) \tag{1.11}$$

In the preceding equations, the result of $\mathbf{H}(|0\rangle)$ and $H(|1\rangle)$ could written as $|+\rangle$ and $|-\rangle$, respectively. In a circuit, we could subsequently apply another gate to $|+\rangle$ to $|-\rangle$, and so on; e.g. $\mathbf{X}(|+\rangle) = |+\rangle$.

The Hadamard gate is often used to change the so-called *computational basis* of the qubit. The z-axis $|0\rangle$ and $|1\rangle$ form the standard basis. The x-axis $|+\rangle$ and $|-\rangle$ form the so-called *conjugate basis*. As we saw earlier, the application of $\mathbf{X}(|+\rangle)$ would not have much effect if we measure the qubit in the standard basis: it would still probabilistically return 0 or 1. However, it would be different if we were to measure it in the conjugate basis; it would deterministically return the value on the opposite side where the vector is aiming to.

Another commonly used basis is the *circular basis* (y-axis). A more detailed explanation of different bases and their significance to computation and measurement can be found in [1]. What is important to keep in mind is that changing the basis on which a quantum state is expressed, corresponds to changing the kind of measurement we perform, and so, naturally, it also changes the probabilities of measurement outcomes.

Quantum processing with multiple qubits is represented by means of tensor vectors. A tensor vector is the result of the tensor product, represented by the symbol $\otimes$ of two or more vectors. A system of two qubits looks like this $|0\rangle \otimes |0\rangle$, but it is normally abbreviated to $|00\rangle$. It is useful to study the expanded form of the tensor product to follow how it works:

$$|00\rangle = |0\rangle \otimes |0\rangle = \begin{bmatrix} 1 \\ 0 \end{bmatrix} \otimes \begin{bmatrix} 1 \\ 0 \end{bmatrix} = \begin{bmatrix} 1 \times 1 \\ 1 \times 0 \\ 0 \times 1 \\ 0 \times 0 \end{bmatrix} = \begin{bmatrix} 1 \\ 0 \\ 0 \\ 0 \end{bmatrix} \qquad (1.12)$$

Similarly, the other 3 possible states of a 2-qubits system are as follows:

$$|01\rangle = |0\rangle \otimes |1\rangle = \begin{bmatrix} 1 \\ 0 \end{bmatrix} \otimes \begin{bmatrix} 0 \\ 1 \end{bmatrix} = \begin{bmatrix} 1 \times 0 \\ 1 \times 1 \\ 0 \times 0 \\ 0 \times 1 \end{bmatrix} = \begin{bmatrix} 0 \\ 1 \\ 0 \\ 0 \end{bmatrix} \qquad (1.13)$$

$$|10\rangle = |1\rangle \otimes |0\rangle = \begin{bmatrix} 0 \\ 1 \end{bmatrix} \otimes \begin{bmatrix} 1 \\ 0 \end{bmatrix} = \begin{bmatrix} 0 \times 1 \\ 0 \times 0 \\ 1 \times 1 \\ 1 \times 0 \end{bmatrix} = \begin{bmatrix} 0 \\ 0 \\ 1 \\ 0 \end{bmatrix} \qquad (1.14)$$

$$|11\rangle = |1\rangle \otimes |1\rangle = \begin{bmatrix} 0 \\ 1 \end{bmatrix} \otimes \begin{bmatrix} 0 \\ 1 \end{bmatrix} = \begin{bmatrix} 0 \times 0 \\ 0 \times 1 \\ 1 \times 0 \\ 1 \times 1 \end{bmatrix} = \begin{bmatrix} 0 \\ 0 \\ 0 \\ 1 \end{bmatrix} \qquad (1.15)$$

We are now in a position to explain how the **CX** gate works in more detail. This gate is defined by the matrix:

$$\mathbf{CX} = \begin{bmatrix} 1 & 0 & 0 & 0 \\ 0 & 1 & 0 & 0 \\ 0 & 0 & 0 & 1 \\ 0 & 0 & 1 & 0 \end{bmatrix} \qquad (1.16)$$

Table 1.1 The **CX** gate table, where q_1 changes only if q_0 is $|1\rangle$. Note, by convention $|q_1 q_0\rangle$

Input	Result
$|00\rangle$	$|00\rangle$
$|01\rangle$	$|11\rangle$
$|10\rangle$	$|10\rangle$
$|11\rangle$	$|01\rangle$

Fig. 1.10 The Toffoli gate creates a dependency of the state of one qubit with the state of two others

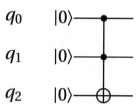

Table 1.2 Toffoli gate table. Note, by convention $|q_2 q_1 q_0\rangle$

Input	Result
$|000\rangle$	$|000\rangle$
$|001\rangle$	$|001\rangle$
$|010\rangle$	$|010\rangle$
$|011\rangle$	$|111\rangle$
$|100\rangle$	$|100\rangle$
$|101\rangle$	$|101\rangle$
$|110\rangle$	$|110\rangle$
$|111\rangle$	$|011\rangle$

The application of **CX** to $|10\rangle$ is represented as:

$$\mathbf{CX}\,|10\rangle = \begin{bmatrix} 1 & 0 & 0 & 0 \\ 0 & 1 & 0 & 0 \\ 0 & 0 & 0 & 1 \\ 0 & 0 & 1 & 0 \end{bmatrix} \times \begin{bmatrix} 0 \\ 0 \\ 1 \\ 0 \end{bmatrix} = \begin{bmatrix} 0 \\ 0 \\ 0 \\ 1 \end{bmatrix} = \begin{bmatrix} 0 \\ 1 \end{bmatrix} \otimes \begin{bmatrix} 0 \\ 1 \end{bmatrix} = |1\rangle \otimes |1\rangle = |11\rangle \quad (1.17)$$

Table 1.1 shows the resulting quantum states of **CX** gate operations, where the first qubit flips only if the second qubit is 1. Figure 1.9 illustrates how the **CX** gate is represented in a circuit diagram. Note that in quantum computing qubit strings are often enumerated from the right end of the string to the left: $\ldots |q_2\rangle \otimes |q_1\rangle \otimes |q_0\rangle$. (This is the convention adopted for the examples below.)

Another useful conditional gate, which appears on a number of quantum algorithms, is the **CCX** gate, also known as the Toffoli gate, involving three qubits (Fig. 1.10). Table 1.2 shows resulting quantum states of the Toffoli gate: qubit q_2 flips only if both q_1 and q_0 are $|1\rangle$.

The equation for describing a 2-qubits system $|q_1\rangle$ and $|q_0\rangle$ combines two state vectors $|\Psi\rangle$ and $|\Phi\rangle$ as follows. Consider:

$$|\Psi\rangle = \alpha_1 |0\rangle + \alpha_2 |1\rangle \text{ for } q_0$$

(1.18)

$$|\Phi\rangle = \beta_1 |0\rangle + \beta_2 |1\rangle \text{ for } q_1$$

Then:

$$|\Psi\rangle \otimes |\Phi\rangle = \alpha_0\beta_0 |00\rangle + \alpha_0\beta_1 |01\rangle + \alpha_1\beta_0 |10\rangle + \alpha_1\beta_1 |11\rangle \qquad (1.19)$$

The above represents a new quantum state with four amplitude coefficients, which can be written as:

$$|D\rangle = \delta_0 |00\rangle + \delta_1 |01\rangle + \delta_2 |10\rangle + \delta_3 |11\rangle \qquad (1.20)$$

Consider this equation:

$$|\Psi\rangle = \frac{1}{4} |00\rangle + \frac{1}{4} |01\rangle + \frac{1}{4} |10\rangle + \frac{1}{4} |11\rangle \qquad (1.21)$$

The above is saying that each of the four quantum states have equal probability of 25% each of being returned.

Now, it should be straightforward to work out how to describe quantum systems with more qubits. For instance, a system with four qubits looks like this:

$$\begin{aligned}
|B\rangle = {} & \beta_0 |0000\rangle + \beta_1 |0001\rangle + \beta_2 |0010\rangle + \beta_3 |0011\rangle + \\
& \beta_4 |0100\rangle + \beta_5 |0101\rangle + \beta_6 |0110\rangle + \beta_7 |0111\rangle + \\
& \beta_8 |1000\rangle + \beta_9 |1001\rangle + \beta_{10} |1010\rangle + \beta_{11} |1011\rangle + \\
& \beta_{12} |1100\rangle + \beta_{13} |1101\rangle + \beta_{14} |1110\rangle + \beta_{15} |1111\rangle
\end{aligned} \qquad (1.22)$$

A linear increase in the number of qubits extends the capacity of representing information on a quantum computer exponentially. With qubits in superposition, a quantum computer can consider many possible values of some input data simultaneously. This technique is known as quantum parallelism. However, we do not have access to the information until the qubits are measured.

Quantum algorithms require a different way of thinking than the way one normally approaches programming; for instance, it is not possible to store quantum states on working memory for accessing later in the algorithm. This is due to the non-cloning principle of quantum physics: it is impossible to make a copy of a quantum system. It is possible, however, to move the state of a set of qubits to another set of qubits, but in effect, this deletes the information from the original qubits. To program a quantum computer requires manipulations of qubits so that the states that correspond to the desired outcome have a much higher probability of being measured than all the other possibilities.

Decoherence is problematic because it poses limitations on the number of successive gates we can use in a circuit (a.k.a. the circuit depth). The higher the number of gates sequenced one after the other (i.e., circuit depth) and the number of qubits used (i.e., circuit width), the higher the likelihood of decoherence occurring. At the time of writing, quantum processors struggle to maintain a handful of qubits coherent for more than a dozen successive gates involving superposition and entanglement.

One way to mitigate errors is to run the algorithms many times and then select the result that appeared most. Additional post-processing on the measurement outcomes that tries to undo the effect of the noise by solving an inverse problem can also be carried out. The development of sophisticated error correction methods is an important research challenge.

1.3 Leveraging Quantum Computing for Making Music

Chapter 3 and following of this book represent the state of the art in leveraging quantum computers to create music. Each of these chapters focuses on innovative approaches that leverage the quantum-mechanical nature of quantum computing described in the previous section. Any additional theory required for understanding a given approach is supplied in the respective chapter, and plenty of references are also provided. Here is a glimpse of what is in store as you explore the balance of this book.

Chapter 3, *Quantum Computer Music: Foundations and Initial Experiments*, lays the foundations of the new field of Quantum Computer Music. It begins with an introduction to algorithmic computer music and methods to program computers to generate music, such as Markov chains. Then, it presents quantum computing versions of those methods. The discussions are supported by detailed explanations of quantum computing concepts and walk-through examples. A novel bespoke generative music algorithm in presented, the *Basak-Miranda algorithm*, which leverages a property of quantum mechanics known as constructive and destructive interference to operate a musical Markov chain.

Chapter 4, *Making Music Using Two Quantum Algorithms*, complements Chap. 3 with a further discussion on the potential impact of quantum physics and technology on music. It introduces the application of two quantum algorithms to generate music: quantum walks and Grover's algorithm, respectively. The algorithms and the methods developed to use them for generating music and sound are introduced in detail. In quantum computing, Grover's algorithm, also known as 'quantum search algorithm', refers to a quantum algorithm for unstructured search that finds with high probability the unique input to a black-box function. It produces a particular output value with quadratic speedup compared to other classical search methods. Here the authors envisage applications of Grover's algorithms as a musical search problem.

Chapter 5, *Exploring the Application of Gate-type Quantum Computational Algorithm for Music Creation and Performance*, introduces approaches to music creation based on quantum gate circuits, referred to as the analogue and the digital approaches, respectively. The analogue approach applies the time evolution of the wave function of a qubit, which changes with quantum gate operation, directly to the musical expressions in analogue ways. This approach basically relies on the use of full information of quantum states. Therefore, it is assumed that it uses a quantum computer simulator, rather than real quantum processors. Conversely, the digital approach applies the result of quantum measurements of quantum states associated with quantum gate operations. This implies wave function collapse and requires real quantum computing hardware.

Chapter 6, *Cellular Automata for Musical Composition: from Classical to Quantum*, leverages Quantum Cellular Automata to create music. Cellular Automata (CA) are abstract computational systems that have proved useful both as general models of complexity and as more specific representations of non-linear dynamics. They have been widely employed for musical composition due to the fact that they can generate evolving patterns of data, which are converted into music and/or sound. Quantum Cellular Automata (QCA) are quantum implementations of CA, whereby the properties of superposition and interference are harnessed for the development of distributed quantum computation. This chapter introduces approaches to making music with QCA. And presents PQCA, a Python library developed by the authors, which is freely available through GitHub.

Chapter 7, *QuiKo: A Quantum Beat Generation Application*, discusses a quantum music generation application called QuiKo. QuiKo combines existing quantum algorithms with data encoding methods from Quantum Machine Learning to build drum and audio sample patterns from a database of audio tracks. QuiKo leverages the physical properties and characteristics of quantum computers to generate what can be referred to as 'soft rules'. These rules take advantage of noise produced by the quantum devices to develop flexible rules and grammars for quantum music generation. These properties include qubit decoherence and phase kickback due to controlled quantum gates within the quantum circuit. QuiKo attempts to mimic and react to external musical inputs, similar to the way that human musicians play and compose with one another. Audio signals (ideally rhythmic in nature) are used as inputs into the system. Feature extraction is then performed on the signal to identify its harmonic and percussive elements. This information is then encoded onto QuiKo's quantum algorithm's quantum circuit. Then measurements of the quantum circuit are taken providing results in the form of probability distributions for external music applications to use to generate new drum patterns.

Chapter 8, *QAC: Quantum-Computing Aided Composition*, begins with a discussion around the role of quantum computing in music composition from a composer's point of view. The author contemplates how quantum computing can be integrated with music technology to serve the creative practice. It starts by considering the different approaches in current computer music and quantum computing tools, as well as reviewing some previous attempts for integrating them. Then, it reflects on the meaning of this integration and presents what is referred to as QAC (Quantum-computing Aided Composition) as well as an early attempt at realizing it. The chapter will also introduce The QAC toolkit Max Package and analyze the performance of two of its main objects. Lastly, the chapter explores one simple real use case scenario of QAC in the author's composition of *Disklavier Prelude #3*. The QAC toolkit was partially developed as part of the QuTune Project at the University of Plymouth, UK, and is freely available through GitHub.

Chapter 9, *Quantum Music Playground Tutorial*, introduces the Quantum Music Playground system. This is an educational tool for learning quantum computing concepts through music. It enables users to compose music while gaining intuition about quantum computing and algorithm design with circuits and states. It is implemented as a Max for Live device in the Ableton Live 11 digital audio workstation (DAW) and includes a MicroQiskit quantum simulator.

Chapter 10, *Quantum Representations of Sound: From Mechanical Waves to Quantum Circuits*, discusses methods for the quantum representation of audio signals. The chapter presents the state of the art in quantum audio. Quantum audio is still a very young area of study, even within the quantum signal processing community. Currently, no quantum representation strategy claims to be the best one for audio applications. Each one presents particular advantages and disadvantages. It can be argued that quantum audio will make use of multiple representations targeting specific applications. The authors also discuss how sound synthesis methods based on quantum audio representation may yield new types of musical instruments.

Chapter 11, *Experiments in Quantum Frequency Detection Using Quantum Fourier Transform*, introduces an approach to extracting pitch from audio files using Quantum Fourier Transform (QFT). In quantum computing, QFT is a linear transformation on quantum bits and is considered the quantum analogue of the inverse discrete Fourier transform. The quantum Fourier transform is a part of many quantum algorithms, notably Shor's algorithm for factoring and computing the discrete logarithm, the quantum phase estimation algorithm for estimating the eigenvalues of a unitary operator, and algorithms for the hidden subgroup problem. The authors present and discuss the results of experiments, which demonstrate the advantages of QFT over discrete Fourier transform, not only in terms of speed but also accuracy.

Chapter 12, *Sing and Measure: Sound as Voice as Quanta* presents a quantum mechanics approach to studying the human voice. The authors leverage quantum mechanics to analyze and improvise vocal sequences. From vocal imitations to opera singing, studies of voice have fascinated generations of scientists. Following the pioneering contribution by Dennis Gabor, who first proposed a description of sound informed by quantum mechanics, this chapter develops the basics of Quantum Vocal Theory of Sound (QVTS). QVTS is a quantum-based analysis of sound using the human voice as a probe. After the presentations of QVTS core ideas, two case studies are discussed, an improvised vocal sequence and the performance of *Sequenza III* composed by Luciano Berio for solo soprano.

Chapter 13, *A Quantum Natural Language Processing Approach to Musical Intelligence*, explores the relationship between music and language. Indeed, several generative music models of music have been developed based on linguistic ones. The burgeoning field of Quantum Natural Language Processing (QNLP) is developing computational linguistic models that are deemed quantum-native. Methods developed to represent quantum mechanics are used to represent linguistic processes. This chapter explores how this research can contribute to the development of models of music processing that are quantum-native. Quantum-native music generative methods are a natural progression for the development of linguistic-inspired music systems with quantum computing. An example of quantum machine learning of musical styles using a QNLP model is presented.

Chapter 14, *Adiabatic Quantum Computing and Applications to Music*, presents an approach to making music with a type of quantum computing known as *adiabatic computing*. It begins with an introduction to adiabatic computing with examples of classical analogues. Then it expands on quantum adiabatic computing, adiabatic runtimes, and quantum annealing to give background on an example approach to making music by using D-Wave's quantum annealers and the Python package Mingus. The chapter introduces a piece of software referred to as *Algorhythms*: a music generation program to be used on D-Wave quantum annealers.

Chapter 15, *Applications of Quantum Annealing to Music Theory*, introduces three applications to quantum annealing in music: composition, counterpoint generation and music arrangement. As discussed in the previous chapter, quantum annealing is different from gate-based quantum computing. The main aim here is to optimize an objective function based on some constraints. For that purpose, the first thing one should do is to identify a function needed to optimize and encode the problem into this objective. For music composition, the authors consider rules from harmony to generate polyphonic melodies. They use Markov Chain transition probabilities to calculate the probabilities of the next notes in the sequence, based on an initial music piece. In the end, what one ends up with is a new piece of music, which mimics the original piece in the sense of transition between the notes. In counterpoint generation, the authors follow a similar approach to the one for composition, but this time uses the rules of counterpoint. In music arrangement, specific focus is given to reducing a multitrack piece into two tracks. The main challenge here is to select the phrases that are most relevant for the reduction. This problem is also related to an NP-Hard problem called k-track assignment.

Chapter 16, *Making Sound with Light: Sound Synthesis with a Photonic Quantum Computer*, reports on the initial results of the authors' research on developing sound synthesizers with photonic quantum computers. More specifically, it introduces three systems that render sounds from the results of processing photons using Gaussian Boson Sampling (GBS). Essentially, a GBS algorithm normally includes three modules: squeezers, interferometers and photon detectors. In a nutshell, the squeezers prepare the inputs, the interferometer operates on the inputs, and the photon detectors produce the results. Pulses of laser light are input to an array of squeezers. What a squeezer does is crush light into a bunch of photons in a state of superposition, referred to as a squeezed state. Next, squeezed states are relayed to the interferometer. The interferometer provides a network of beam splitters and phase shifters, which are programmed with operations to manipulate the photons. It is expected to produce highly entangled quantum states encoding the processed quantum information. These are subsequently channelled to detectors that count how many photons are within each stream of squeezed states. The results of the computation are encoded in the statistics of this photon counting. The photon-counting data are used as control parameters for bespoke sound synthesizers.

Chapter 17, *New Directions in Quantum Music: Concepts for a Quantum Keyboard and the Sound of the Ising Model*, explores ideas for generating sounds and eventually music by using quantum devices in the NISQ era with quantum circuits. In particular, this chapter first considers a concept for the *Qeyboard*; that is, a quantum keyboard, where the real-time behaviour of expectation values using a time-evolving quantum circuit can be associated to sound features like intensity, frequency and tone. Then, it examines how these properties can be extracted from physical quantum systems, taking the Ising model as an example. This can be realized by measuring physical quantities of the quantum states of the system, e.g. the energies and the magnetization obtained via variational quantum simulation techniques.

Chapter 18, *Superconducting Qubits as Musical Synthesizers for Live Performance*, introduces a live performance with superconducting instruments. This is achieved by using quantum computer prototypes in the Yale Quantum Institute laboratories cooled to nearly absolute zero as if they were musical instruments. The authors performed on two of the circuits running within dilution refrigerators in a live performance. During the performance, their used data which were acquired from the superconductive devices and converted the data into signals, which were processed and performed live. Using pre-recorded data, the authors processed and performed the data and mixed the three audio signals to create a coherent composition. The audio signal went through an EMT plate for reverberation and was sent to Firehouse 12, the concert hall speakers. The range of sounds produced by the superconductive instruments is remarkable. It includes moments of intense noise, intercut by melodies in turns diatonic, ominous, or almost imperceptible.

But first, Chap. 2, *Music Fundamentals for Computer Programmers: Representation, Parametrization and Automation*, lays the musical groundwork by introducing the fundamentals of music, including approaches to representation and parametrization for computer processing. This chapter is intended to introduce musical concepts to engineers and computer programmers who are not conversant with musical concepts that were developed since the 1950s and respective approaches that have been developed to compose music algorithmically.

1.4 Final Remarks

Quantum computers are emerging as potentially disruptive devices built on the principles of quantum mechanics. As for the time of writing, there is a global race for developing fully-fledged quantum computers [5]. Quantum processors have been built using different technologies such as solid-state systems (e.g., electron spins in semiconductors and nuclear spins in solids) and atomic and optical systems (e.g., nuclear spins in molecules and hyperfine and Rydberg states in atoms and photons) [3].

Computers are absolutely essential for the music economy. Therefore, quantum computing is bound to have an impact on the way in which we create and distribute music in time to come. Hence emerging research into quantum computing applications in music—*Quantum Computer Music*—is a natural progression for music technology.

Quantum computing promises to bring unprecedented higher speed and optimisation for running algorithms that would take a prohibitive amount of time on current digital computers. Of course, this will benefit the music industry in one way or another. However, one common thread that runs through this book, and which is very exciting, is that new technologies have always yielded new approaches to musical creativity. Make no mistake: quantum computing is going to be no exception!

It is a fact that computing technology has always been influencing how musicians create music [7]. There are styles of music today that would have never existed without computers [2]. For example, nowadays there is a genre of music, referred to as live coding, whereby the audience watches musicians programming live on stage as if they were playing musical instruments. At nightclubs, DJs have been writing code live in addition to spinning records [9]. And the so-called *laptop orchestras* are commonly found; e.g. FLO,[2] PLOrk,[3] SLOrk[4] and Swansea Laptop Orchestra,[5] to cite but four. See Chap. 5 in this volume, for an idea for a 'quantum live coding' system, and Chap. 18 for an example of an actual live performance using data from superconducting devices. We anticipate that new ways of thinking boosted by quantum programming practices, and the modelling and simulations afforded thereof, are bringing new paradigms for musical creativity, which would not exist otherwise. The remaining chapters in this book give inspiring glimpses of what is to come. The reader is invited to jump on the bandwagon and pave the way for the music of the future with us.

References

1. Bernhardt, C. (2019). *Quantum computing for everyone*. The MIT Press. ISBN: 978-0262039253.
2. Baramishvili, L. (2019). Live coding and algorave. *Medium*. https://lukabaramishvili.medium.com/live-coding-and-algorave-9eee0ca0217f.
3. Gibney, E. (2020). Quantum computer race intensifies as alternative technology gains steam. *Nature*. https://www.nature.com/articles/d41586-020-03237-w.
4. Grumbling, E., & Horowitz, M., (Eds.). (2019). *Quantum computing: Progress and prospects*. National Academies Press. ISBN: 9780309479691. https://doi.org/10.17226/25196.
5. Leprince-Ringuet, D. (2021). The global quantum computing race has begun. What will it take to win it? *ZD Net*. https://www.zdnet.com/article/the-quantum-computing-race-has-begun-what-will-it-take-to-win-it/.

---

[2] https://femalelaptoporchestra.wordpress.com (Accessed on 30 Apr 2022).
[3] https://plork.princeton.edu (Accessed on 30 Apr 2022).
[4] https://slork.stanford.edu (Accessed on 30 Apr 2022).
[5] https://www.swansealaptoporchestra.com (Accessed on 30 Apr 2022).

6. Rieffel, E., & Polak, W. (2011). *Quantum computing: A gentle introduction*. The MIT Press. ISBN: 9780262015066.

7. Roads, C. (2015). *Composing electronic music: A new aesthetic*. Oxford University Press. ISBN: 978-0195373240.

8. Sutor, R. S. (2019). *Dancing with qubits: How quantum computing works and how it can change the word*. Packt. ISBN: 9781838827366.

9. Tiffany, M. (2019). DJs of the future Don't Spin records—They write code. *Wired*. https://www.wired.com/story/algoraves-live-coding-djs/.

Music Fundamentals for Computer Programmers: Representation, Parametrization and Automation

2

Eduardo Reck Miranda

Abstract

As it turns out, the great majority of research into computer music technology is developed by engineers and computer programmers who are passionate about music. Albeit very knowledgeable, it is often the case that their knowledge of music is limited to classical thinking that pre-dates contemporary approaches to music. This limitation is prone to restrict the imagination of those who are pioneering the development of new music technologies, in particular for music composition. In these cases, the research community may as well end up with new pieces of technology but for the same old kind of music, or problem. The objective of this chapter is to present an introduction to several topics of interest for those who are not conversant with contemporary music theory, in particular theory that has been evolving since the 1950s. These include approaches to music representation and parametrization for computer processing and modern composition practices that influenced the development of generative music techniques.

2.1 Introduction

The objective of this chapter is to present an introduction to contemporary music thinking for engineers and computer programmers. For those interested in developing research into novel quantum computing applications to music, it is important to be aware of approaches to music beyond classical tonal theory.

E. R. Miranda (✉)
ICCMR, University of Plymouth, Plymouth, UK
e-mail: eduardo.miranda@plymouth.ac.uk

E. R Miranda (ed.), *Quantum Computer Music*,
https://doi.org/10.1007/978-3-031-13909-3_2

This introduction is by no means exhaustive. It uncovers only the tip of an iceberg immersed in a sea of different theories, aesthetic preferences and viewpoints.[1]

The fact that we are inherently musical is a significant trait that differentiates humans from other animals [7]. Our compulsion to listen to and appreciate sound arrangements beyond the mere purposes of linguistic communication is extraordinary. But what is music?

As a working definition of music, let us propose this: *music is sounds organised in space and time*.

Our ability to create and appreciate the organisation of sounds in space and time insinuates the notion that musical compositions carry *abstract structures*. This notion is relevant for computer musicians because they address issues that are at the fringe of two allegedly distinct domains of our musical intelligence: the domain of abstract subjectivity (e.g., musical composition and artistic imagination) and the domain of abstract objectivity (e.g., logical operations and mathematical thought). There is no dispute that a computer is a tool of excellence for the latter domain. But these domains are not disconnected; they support each other.

2.2 Representation

2.2.1 Abstraction Boundaries

The idea that musical compositions carry abstract structures implies the notion of *abstraction boundaries*. The definition of abstraction boundaries is of primary importance for composers working with computers because it determines the compositional blocks—or components—that will form a piece of music.

As a starting point for discussion, let us establish three levels of abstraction:

- the microscopic level
- the note level
- the building-block level.

At the microscopic level, composers work with microscopic sound features, such as frequencies and amplitudes of the individual sound partials; that is, the spectral components of sounds. Here, composers normally have access to fine timing control of sounds, often in the order of milliseconds. Obviously, in this case, there is no score, in the traditional sense of the term, with musical notes for musicians to perform on acoustic instruments. Instead, a score here contains instructions in a sound synthesis programming language or lists of numerical values for digital sound synthesis instruments. For instance, below is a Frequency Modulation (FM) synthesiser

---

[1] This chapter contains materials adapted from the book *Composing Music with Computers* by this author, published in 2001 by Focal Press, which is now out of print.

programmed in Csound [4]. And then, there is a score, with parameter values for the instrument. Each line beginning with the code **i1** produces a two-second long sound. The musician has access to minutiae sound control here.

```
;
; Frequency Modulation (FM) Synthesiser
;
sr = 44100
kr = 4410
ksmps = 10
nchnls = 1
;
instr 1
; p4 = frequency deviation (d)
; p5 = modulator frequency (fm)
; p6 = carrier amplitude (ac)
; p7 = offset carrier frequency (fc)
;
kenv linen  1,0.1,p3,0.05
amod oscil p4,p5,1
acar oscil p6, amod+p7, 1
out  acar*kenv
endin
;
```

```
;
; Score for FM Instrument
;
f 1  0   4096  10   1
i1  0    2  220.0  110.0  20000  196.0
i1  2    2  220.0  110.0  20000  246.94
i1  4    2  220.0  110.0  20000  185.00
i1  6    2  220.0  110.0  20000  196.00
i1  8    2  220.0  110.0  20000  0.00
i1  10   2  0.0    110.0  20000  196.00
i1  12   2  220.0  55.0   20000  196.00
e
;
```

Conversely, the atomic element of music at the note level is the musical note. Music theory traditionally has a well-defined boundary of abstraction for characterising a musical note in terms of four main attributes: pitch, duration, dynamics and the instrument (or timbre) that plays the note. Tempo, which adds depth and further expression to sequences of notes is a complementary attribute. But tempo is not a single-note attribute.

At the note level, composers are encouraged to think of a musical piece as structures of notes considering their attributes. In this case, a composition is often written

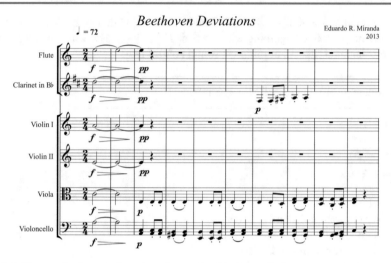

Fig. 2.1 The atomic element of music at the note level is the musical note

in a score by means of symbols representing note arrangements, and performers interpret the score by relating those symbols to actions on musical instruments. The inner acoustic features of a note are not directly represented on a score. There are no obvious symbols here to explicitly represent, for example, the spectrum of individual notes. Figure 2.1 shows an example of a score representing music as the note level.

To cut it short, at the note level musicians work with a conceptual model of individual instruments whose boundary of abstraction gives very little room for significant manipulation of the inner workings of the timbre of the notes. It is given by default that different timbres can be obtained through the combination of different instruments.

At the building-block level, composers work with larger musical units lasting several seconds, such as rhythmic patterns, melodic themes and sampled sound sequences. Figure 2.2 shows a template for musical form, which was generated by a quantum cellular automaton for my composition *Multiverse Symphony*; please refer to Chap. 6 for more details. The template, which is for 12 instruments (one instrument per line) was then completed with materials that I composed with other means. At this level, the content of the blocks is not important. What is important is how the blocks are organised in space (vertically) and time (horizontally).

Composition design at the building-block level started to gain popularity with the appearance of electroacoustic music in the 1950s, where pieces were composed by literally cutting, pasting and mixing sections of pre-recorded sounds and/or short musical snippets. Digital sampling and MIDI systems, as well as recorded sound libraries and MIDI files, are widely available to anybody wishing to compose with pre-fabricated sections of music; an example of such systems, amongst many others, is Ableton Live.[2]

---

[2] https://www.ableton.com.

Fig. 2.2 Template generated my a quantum cellular automaton for 12 instruments

To summarise, the microscopic level deals directly with physical sound attributes, such as frequency, amplitude, spectrum, and so on, which are mainly used for synthesis and sound processing. At the note level, we bundle certain sound attributes together and think of them as a note. Aggregates such as phrases, motives and structures constitute the building blocks for composition at a higher level of abstraction. In this book, Chaps. 10, 11 and 16, for example, discuss systems at the microscopic level, whereas the system presented in Chap. 13 works at the building-block level. Chapters 3, 4, and most of the remaining ones, present systems that work at the note level.

It must be said, however, that nowadays musicians working with technology often compose with all three levels of abstraction, in particular when writing pieces combining acoustic instruments and electronically generated and/or manipulated sounds. There are programming tools for music, such as Max,[3] which greatly facilitate this hybrid approach. Chapter 8 introduces a Max package to program and run quantum circuits and music algorithms under the same umbrella.

2.2.2 Time-Domain Hierarchies

Complementing the notion of abstraction boundaries introduced above, let us now introduce the notion of *time-domain hierarchies*. There are four distinct but interconnected musical domains, hierarchically organised with respect to our perception of time: *timbre*, *frequency*, *pulse*, and *form* [21].

2.2.2.1 Timbre

Timbre has the finest resolution of the four hierarchical time domains: it is a complex entity formed by a number of components (or partials) that are characterised by frequency relationships and relative amplitudes.

Composer Richard Orton [21] suggested that the first aspect of a sound to which we respond is its timbre. We seem to react to timbre even before we have the chance

---

[3] https://cycling74.com.

to fully process the sounds we hear. This is probably a legacy of a natural survival mechanism that emerged during the early stages of our evolution: sounds can indicate threat or danger. It is vital to be able to identify the source quickly and to react to what is causing it. In addition, we also have the ability to track the changes in the spectrum of a sound as it unfolds. It is believed that this ability was fundamental for the evolution of our linguistic as well as musical capacity [11].

Composers working at the microscopic level of abstraction have direct access to the domain of immediate perception. To many classical contemporary music composers, timbre is the ultimate frontier of music that has only recently begun to be explored systematically. This trend is very noticeable in the music of the end of the twentieth century, where composers tended to overemphasise the timbral crafting of their compositions [2].

2.2.2.2 Frequency

The notion of frequency refers to a sequence of repetitive patterns. In the case of a sound, frequency refers to a sequence of repetitive waveform patterns. Tied to the notion of frequency is the notion of the period, that is, the time it takes to repeat the pattern. Frequency and period are reciprocally related: Frequency $= \frac{1}{\text{Period}}$ and so Period $= \frac{1}{\text{Frequency}}$.

Sound frequencies are measured in cycles per second (cps) or Hertz (Hz). On average, the human ear is capable of perceiving frequencies between 20 and 18,000 Hz (or 18 kHz). However, this may vary from person to person and with age; the older we get the less we are able to hear frequencies above 8 kHz. Music rarely uses pitches higher than 4 kHz.

The pitch of musical notes operates in proportional cycles called octaves. For example, when the frequency of note A at 220 Hz is doubled to 440 Hz, one still perceives the same note A, but one octave higher. Conversely, if the frequency is halved to 110 Hz, then the note is perceived one octave lower (Fig. 2.3). Our hearing system deals with sound frequencies according to a logarithmic law. Thus, the phenomenon we perceive as pitch intervals is defined by a logarithmic process; for example, the distance from 110 to 440 Hz is two octaves, but the frequency ratio actually is quadrupled.

The notion of the octave is said to have been conceived in ancient Greece, where it was discovered that by halving the length of the string of the monochord (a one-stringed instrument that was used by the Greeks to explain musical concepts) one could double the octave of the tone. Pythagoras (560–490 BC) is credited for having put forward the notion that a musical scale can be naturally derived within the octave by dividing the string at various points using simple whole-number ratios: 2:1 the octave, 3:2 the perfect fifth, 4:3 the perfect fourth, 5:4 the major third, and so on. These ratios are known as the Pythagorean ratios of musical consonance and they are still respected today.

For Pythagoras, numbers and geometry were imbued with mystical connotations. The correlations discovered between whole-number ratios and the musical consonances were seen in terms of a divine revelation of universal harmony. However, in

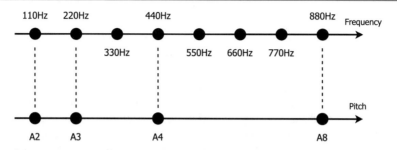

Fig. 2.3 The pitches of musical notes operate in proportional cycles called octaves. The phenomenon we perceive as pitch interval is defined by a logarithmic process

Fig. 2.4 The scale of equal temperament is one of the most used musical scales of our time

practical terms, the Pythagorean method is not the only method for defining musical scales. Scale systems have emerged and have fallen into disuse as musical styles evolved all over the world. Indeed, non-Western musical scales, for example, operate in completely different ways. For the purposes of this chapter, it suffices to know that one of the most frequently used scale systems today is the scale of equal temperament, which emerged in Europe in the nineteenth century. In this scale, the octave is divided into twelve equally-spaced notes (Fig. 2.4).

2.2.2.3 Pulse

Composer Karlheinz Stockhausen is known for having proposed that both pitch and rhythm can be considered as one continuous time-domain phenomenon. In an article entitled *Four Criteria of Electronic Music*, he described an interesting technique for producing synthetic tones [25]. He recorded individual pulses on tape, from an electronic generator. Then he cut the tape and spliced the parts together so that the pulses could form a particular rhythm. Next, he made a tape loop of this rhythm and sped it up until he could hear a tone. Different tones were produced by varying the speed of the loop and different rhythms on the tape produced different timbres. The components of the rhythmic sequence determined the spectrum according to their individual cycle on the tape loop.

Stockhausen's technique has encouraged composers to work with rhythm and pitch within a unified time domain. It should be noted, however, that the transition from rhythm to pitch is not perceived precisely. Hence the reason why the domain of pulse is considered here at a higher level in the time-domain hierarchy. Whilst Stockhausen's unified time domain makes perfect sense in quantitative terms, it fails to address the qualitative nature of the human ear: we can hear a distinct rhythm up to approximately 10 cycles per second but a distinct pitch does not emerge until approximately 16 cycles per second. It is not entirely by chance that the categorical differentiation between rhythm and pitch has remained firmly entrenched throughout history.

The domain of pulse, therefore, lies below the rate of approximately 10 cycles per second but we seem to deal more comfortably with rates that are close or related to the human heartbeat. The extremes of the heart-beat range from approximately 30 beats per minute up to 240 beats. In terms of Hz, a very fast heartbeat would be equivalent to 4 Hz ($240 \times \frac{1}{60}$). Conversely, a very slow heartbeat would be equivalent to 0.5 Hz ($30 \times \frac{1}{60}$). Musical rhythms generally fall within this bandwidth; i.e., from four pulses per second (4 Hz) to one pulse every two seconds (0.5 Hz).

The term 'beat' denotes regular stress or accent that usually occurs in a composition. The notion of tempo (a term borrowed from Italian which means time) is associated with the ratio of beat to pulse rate. Until the beginning of the nineteenth-century composers indicated this only vaguely on a musical score, using terms such as *adagio* (Italian for slow), *vivace* (Italian for lively), *andante* (Italian for at a walking pace), and so forth. With the invention of Maelzel's metronome in the 1810s, a clock-like device that produces a click according to a specific pre-set rate, the tempo indication became more precise. The scale of measurement is in terms of a number of beats per minute and in a musical score this is shown by the abbreviation M.M. (for Maelzel's Metronome) and a number; for instance, M.M. 72 indicates a tempo of 72 beats per minute (Fig. 2.1).

Beats can be sub-divided and grouped. The grouping of beats is called meter and it is indicated on the score by vertical bar-lines on the staves. At the beginning of the score, there is usually a pair of numbers indicating the meter of the piece: the top number indicates the number of beats in a bar and the lower number indicates the reference unit for the beat (Fig. 2.1).

2.2.2.4 Form

The domain of form involves the placing of musical materials in space and time; normally the focus is on time. As with the previous domains of frequency and pulse, the domain form also can be thought of as a cyclic succession of events. The first metaphor that comes to mind here is our breath cycle: a succession of inspirations and expirations that seem to drive the course of our motor and cognitive activities.

The human mind has an incredible ability to impose order on auditory information. Psychologists suggest that we employ mental schemes that guide our auditory system in order to make sense of incoming streams of auditory data such as speech and music [18]. There are controversies as to which of these schemes are genetically hard-wired in our brains and which ones are culturally shaped as we grow up, but we should not need to worry too much about this debate here. We will come back to the domain of form when we introduce the notion of cognitive archetypes below.

2.3 Thinking Composition: Top-Down Versus Bottom-Up

To what extent do composers think differently when composing with computers as opposed to earlier compositional practices, such as the classical picture of the composer working on the piano with a pencil and sheets of music? When engineers use a computer to calculate complex equations or to prototype artefacts, the machine certainly frees their minds to concentrate on the problem at hand, rather than dwelling on the particulars of the equations or drawings. This also applies to musicians to a great extent. However, there are surely other issues to be considered in the case of musical composition because composers have been using computers to perform creative decision-making tasks as well [17].

There are two major approaches to working with a computer as an active partner for composition: the bottom-up and the top-down approaches. One approach is to engage in improvisation and experimentation with the machine and store promising musical materials. Then at a later stage, these materials are developed into larger passages, musical structures and so forth. This is the bottom-up approach because these smaller sections, created by or with the computer, function as the foundation for building larger musical sections. Higher-level musical sections are composed—with or without the aid of the computer—by extending these smaller segments to form the entire piece.

Conversely, composers might prefer a top-down approach, that is, to start by developing an overall compositional plan and proceed by refining this plan. This approach forces the composer to be creative within self-imposed formal constraints; for example, the number of sections, the length and character of each, types of generative processes for each section, and so on. Of course, a composer may or may not choose to honour the limits.

In most cases, algorithmic composition software tends to support the bottom-up approach whereas computer-aided composition software tends to support the top-down approach. Exceptions to this rule, however, abound. All the same, as each approach has its pros and cons, composers tend to combine both approaches.

2.4 Cognitive Archetypes

2.4.1 Metaphorical Associations

Our cognitive capacities do not work in isolation from one another. Whilst our ability to infer the distance of a sound source is tied to our notion of timing and space, our tendency to associate colours with temperatures (e.g., red and blue with high and low temperatures, respectively) seems to be tied to our notions of fire and ice, to cite but two examples. In this context, music may be regarded as the art of invoking cognitive phenomena at one of the deepest and most sophisticated levels of human intelligence: the level of *metaphorical associations*.

One of the most important metaphors evoked by music is the notion of motion. We suggested earlier that a musical piece is the result of the dynamical unfolding of various musical attributes at different levels, namely levels of timbre, frequency, pulse and form. Here we build upon this notion by conjecturing that our ears naturally take in this dynamic unfolding as sequences of sonic events that seem to move from one lapse of time to another. When we engage in more sophisticated listening experiences we probably employ a number of cognitive strategies that are similar to those we employ to understand the events that take place during the course of our lives.

Comparable strategies also are employed when we read a text. Although of a significantly different nature, a piece of music and a novel, for example, are both multi-layered systems in which sequences of signs are used to convey emotions, ideas, and so on, according to specific conventions; e.g., harmony and counterpoint rules in music, and grammars and lexicon in natural language. Hence, it comes as no surprise that music and literature appear to share similar underlying structural principles [14], at least in the Western music tradition.

Due to the fact that music does not have the extra-textual referents of literature, the musical materials themselves must somehow enable listeners to infer syntagmatic and associative values from groups of sonic events at various levels. Music is not just any random sound arrangement; sound arrangements need something else to sound musical. After the work of composers such as John Cage and the like [23], this argument may appear to be adding insult to injury, but let us adopt a more pragmatic attitude here: the ultimate challenge for composers is to identify what this 'something else' actually is. What is it that makes an arrangement of sounds interesting?

Most composers would agree with me that musically meaningful sound events, or musical syntagms, should convey cues that enable listeners to infer organisational structures from them. These cues are normally associated with the style of the piece: a listener who is familiar with the style relies upon associative evaluations to group musical syntagms according to listening strategies that have proven successful for other pieces. The criteria by which people normally group these syntagms are based upon tonality, texture, timbre and rhythmic pattern, and these often occur in combination.

A musical style thus defines a system of syntagmatic relations in musical material that helps listeners to infer their musical structures. The grouping of smaller musical units is the first stage of the process that leads the listener to mentally build components of large scale musical forms. Both narrative texts and musical compositions are processes that are presented in small discernible units, strung together in a way that leads the listener to mentally build larger sub-processes at the syntagmatic level, resulting eventually in the creation of a complex structure in time. In this sense, one could think of a composition as a musical structure that conveys some sort of narrative whose plot basically involves transitions from one state of equilibrium to another. Equilibrium here is meant in the Cybernetic sense [26]: it describes a stable but not static relation between musical elements. Two states of equilibrium are separated by a stage of imbalance (Fig. 2.5).

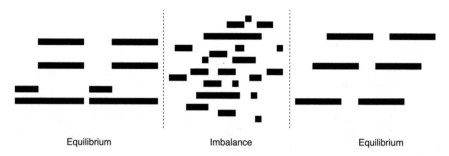

Fig. 2.5 A visual representation of a musical passage whereby two moments of equilibrium are separated by a stage period of imbalance

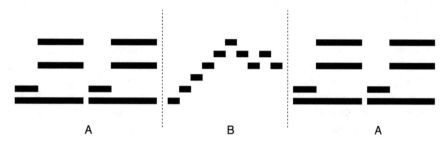

Fig. 2.6 The form A-B-A was very common in the music of the Baroque period

Composers wishing to develop complex musical forms and large-scale pieces need to devise strategies in order to provide reference points for the listener to hold on to the piece, otherwise, it may lose its sense of unity. Different styles and different composers have developed their own methods. In the Baroque period, for example, identical repetition of passages in ternary form A-B-A was very common (Fig. 2.6). Perhaps one of the most sophisticated forms of classical music is the sonata form, as perfected by eighteenth-century composer, Joseph Haydn, and still used today.

The importance of structure, syntagmatic relations and associative values in music is highly debatable. With regard to these notions, there is a school of thought in musicology purporting that in order to understand and appreciate music one must be able to naturally parse it and understand its structure: notes, phrases, motives, voice and so on. Readers who are interested in studying these themes further are invited to refer to the work of Meyer [19], and Lerdahl and Jackendoff [16].

2.4.2 Elementary Schemes

Paul Larivaille [15] proposed a five-stage elementary scheme for narrative in literature which is a useful starting point to study musical forms. The five stages are:

- initial equilibrium
- disturbance
- reaction
- consequence
- final equilibrium.

In a tonal musical context, for example, the initial equilibrium would correspond to the initial section at the tonic key. The arrival of elements that conflict with the tonic key, such as a dissonant note, would then introduce a disturbance in the initial state of equilibrium. A disturbance is invariably followed up by a reaction, such as modulation to the dominant key, for example. The arrival at the dominant key is the consequence of the action and the settlement at this key establishes the final equilibrium. However, pieces of music would seldom end here. The final equilibrium could indeed be disturbed again, thus recommencing the whole cycle, and so forth. In works of greater structural complexity, these elementary sequences can be combined to form various layers, which could follow the same type of narrative form. For instance, a sonata would normally have an exposition of a theme in the tonic key (an initial meta-equilibrium) followed by a dominant section (the meta-disturbance), the development section of the sonata (a meta-reaction) and the recapitulation section (the meta-consequence). The classical sonata regularly ends with a coda (the final meta-equilibrium).

Needless to say, interesting forms can be created by extrapolating the sequential nature of Larivaille's stages. One could create embedding forms, by inserting a second sub-sequence during a pause in the main sequence, and/or alternating schemes, by maintaining more than one sequence simultaneously with or without interruptions, to cite but two examples. What is important to bear in mind here is that the succession of sound events in a piece should give the listener a sense of direction.

As mentioned earlier, music psychologists suggest that our sense of musical direction may be prescribed by schemes of auditory expectation that we employ to predict which sound event will occur next in a musical sequence [12]. These schemes embody predetermined groupings that join elements into well-formed units in the listener's brain. These musical schemes are probably culturally shaped phenomena that emerge from the various kinds of associations that people make between music and extra-musical contexts, such as the associations between colour and temperature mentioned earlier.

There are however some schemes that are less culturally dependent than others, which can be found in the music of almost every culture on earth [22]. Examples of those schemes are:

- responsorial expectation
- convex curve
- principle of intensification.

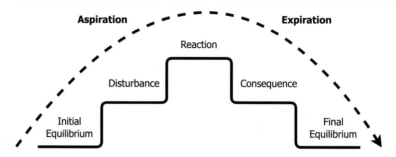

Fig. 2.7 The overall archlike shape of the breath metaphor follows a five-stage elementary scheme

2.4.2.1 Responsorial Expectation

One of the most typical musical schemes we seem to employ in musical listening is the responsorial auditory expectation scheme whereby people normally seek to identify musical passages in which sound events seem to call and answer one another. Most interestingly, this phenomenon often manifests itself in a convex arch-like shape, which possibly mirrors the rising and falling patterns of breath.

The breath metaphor also applies to the relationship between various simultaneous voices and their harmonic organisations. In Renaissance music, for example, polyphonic melodies have their own shape and rhythm, but the individual voices contribute to the overall harmonic convex structure. This structure normally follows Larivaille's stages previously mentioned (Fig. 2.7). The interplay between melodic phrases and harmonic structure that began to appear in Renaissance music fostered a number of composition techniques throughout musical history; for example time-displacement of musical phrases (an effect known as musical canon) and note progression in different proportions (two voices start together but the time displacement occurs gradually).

2.4.2.2 Convex Curve

The arch-like convex curve scheme provides an intuitive guide by which one can predict the evolution of given parameters in a music sequence: there is normally one stage where the music ascends towards a climax, followed by a descending stage (Fig. 2.8). Both the ascending and descending stages should normally evolve smoothly and at gradual intervals. Smaller intervals here often succeed large ones during the ascending phase and the reverse occurs during the descent. This scheme may apply to all domains of music, ranging from the domain of timbre to the domain of form. Historically, however, it has been consciously used by composers in the domain of form: one of the first composition techniques that aspiring composers study at the Conservatory is to construct musical phrases in the style of Palestrina[4]

---

[4] An Italian Renaissance composer of sacred music.

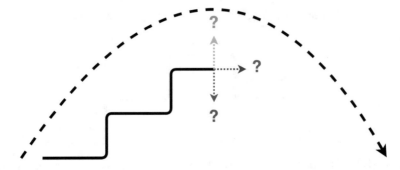

Fig. 2.8 The convex archlike scheme is one of the strategies that people employ for predicting the fate of musical sequences

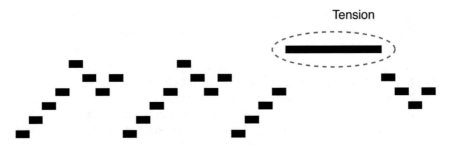

Fig. 2.9 Unfulfilled predictions often cause musical tension

by starting with slow notes at the low-pitch register, moving towards faster notes at higher-pitches and then conclude with slow and low-pitched notes.

Convexity is a means to achieve well balanced musical passages and can be used to forge those moments of equilibrium mentioned earlier. The opposite of convexity should thus produce moments of tension: linearity (i.e., no changes), sudden changes, abrupt zig-zags, concavity, are but a few examples that can produce tension in a piece of music (Fig. 2.9).

2.4.2.3 Principle of Intensification

As for the principle of intensification, it is commonly employed by composers to create tension and to give a sense of direction to the musical unfolding. The principle of intensification may apply to various time spans and may be expressed in various ways in different parameters through contrasts within a continuous scale ranging from the few to the many, low to high, non-rhythmic to rhythmic, slow to fast, small density to large density and so on (Fig. 2.10).

Intensification is normally used to build tension towards a climax, prompting the rise of a convex curve which may or may not be resolved. Some non-Western musical cultures often employ intensification to forge convexity.

Fig. 2.10 An example of the principle of intensification

2.5 Parametrization and Automation

The emergence of parametrical thinking in music has been of paramount importance for the development of computer-based composition systems. Parametrical thinking in general is a natural consequence of the increasing trend towards computer-oriented systematisations of our time and it is highly inspired by Cybernetics [26]. In Cybernetics, a parameter is one of the variables that control the outcome of a system. In our case, the output is music and the parameters refer to controllable musical attributes whose values can vary within upper and lower limits. As an example of a Cybernetic musical system, imagine a musical box furnished with a number of buttons that can be turned from one extreme of the dial to another; each button controls a specific attribute of the composition (pitches, tempo, etc.) and these buttons can be combined to form meta-buttons, and so on.

The parametrical approach to composition has led composers to think in terms of parametrical boundaries and groupings that probably would not have been conceived otherwise. Classic examples of parametrical thinking can be found in the work of composer Iannis Xenakis [28], in particular the algebraic method he devised for composing *Herma*, for piano [27]; more on Xenakis to follow.

It may be difficult for a computer musician to imagine how composers of the previous centuries could operate without thinking parametrically, but in a sense, we could say that parametrical thinking goes back to medieval music where rhythms and note sequences were created separately and then combined at a later stage. For example, pitches could be assigned to a text, forming what was referred to as colour, and then the notes were made to fit a rhythmic pattern, referred to as telea.

The range of attributes available in a musical system is an important aspect to consider in a composition because it contributes to the type of unfolding one wishes to imprint onto the piece. The smaller the inventory of all possible intervals, chords, rhythms, and so on, the lesser the combinatorial possibilities. The lesser the combinatorial possibilities, the easier it is for a composer to handle the material, but the outcome will tend to be either short or repetitive. The range of possibilities can of course be augmented by increasing the inventory, but the larger the inventory the greater the chances of producing pieces beyond the human threshold of comprehension and enjoyment. For instance, it is perfectly within our hearing capacity to use scales of 24 notes within an octave but more than this would only create difficulties for both the composer and listener.

Regardless of musical style, an increase of focus on certain parameters in a musical passage should be accompanied by a decrease in focus on others. The human mind has an attention threshold, beyond which music is most likely to be perceived as lacking order or direction. For instance, if the intention is to focus on melodic lines, then one should refrain from making too many contrasting timbre variations while the melodies are unfolding, otherwise, the timbre may distract attention away from the pitch. However, melody alone would not normally keep the listener's attention for long because a piece of music needs some variety and contrasting elements from time to time. One of the most difficult issues in the practice of composition is to find the right balance between repetition and diversity: a well-balanced piece of music should unfold naturally to listeners. In most Western musical styles, this unfolding results from a network of relationships between musical attributes that combine in different ways to create situations where contrasts can take place. Such contrasts are normally preceded by a preparatory stage, which builds upon the listener's expectations.

The main problem with the parametrical approach to music is that the correlation between the parameters, their values and the musical effect heard is not always obvious. Moreover, the role of a single parameter is often dependent on many different musical attributes that have subtle, and occasionally unknown, interrelationships. For instance, imagine that the Cybernetic musical box mentioned earlier allows us to speed up a melody simply by tweaking a tempo button: this would imply changes not only to the triggering time of the notes but also to their duration, articulation, phrasing and so forth.

2.5.1 The Legacy of Arnold Schoenberg

In the early 1920s, composer Arnold Schoenberg proposed a method for music composition known as *dodecaphony*, also referred to as *twelve-tone serialism* [5,24].

Schoenberg proposed that the standard twelve musical notes should be treated by the composer as having equal importance in relation to each other, as opposed to the hierarchical organisation of tonal musical scales, where some notes are considered to be more important than others. In practice, he wished to abolish the idea of using tonal scales (C major, C minor, etc.) by favouring the idea of a series of twelve notes organised according to principles other than the ones given by classical harmony. This may sound obvious to a twentieth first-century musician, but Schoenberg's ideas were revolutionary at the time [13].

A series of twelve notes functions here as the blueprint for the entire composition. Basically, there is only one principle to be strictly observed in Schoenberg's method: each note of the series should be used in the same order in which they occur in the series, all way through the piece. Furthermore, there can be no repetition of a note before all the notes of the series have been used. However, the particular sequence of notes that forms a series is entirely arbitrary. Figure 2.11 illustrates an example of a series.

It is not difficult to realise that a composition where the series is repeated over and over might become dull after a few moments. Of course, Schoenberg was aware of this

Fig. 2.11 An example of a 12-tone series

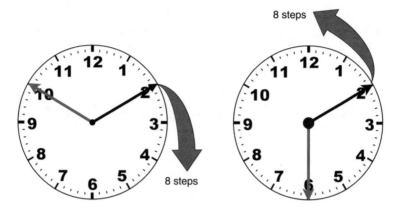

Fig. 2.12 In music, playing something upside down is technically called 'inversion'. A clock face is a good example to illustrate inversion: if the original interval moves forward eight steps (or notes) on the clock, from two to ten, then the inversion moves backwards eight steps from two to six

and cleverly allowed for some transformations on the twelve notes of the series: the series can be played forwards, backwards (or retrograde), upside-down (Fig. 2.12) or backwards upside-down (Fig. 2.13).[5] Furthermore, Schoenberg's method also made use of transposition; i.e., the series could start on a different pitch, provided it maintained the same sequence of intervals between the notes.

A notable twelve-tone piece by Schoenberg is *Variations*, for orchestra, Op. 31. As it stands, Schoenberg's dodecaphony in itself is just the beginning of a more radical idea: *total serialism*, which was subsequently developed by his pupils and other sympathisers, most notably Anton Webern and latterly by Pierre Boulez [6].

Originally, Schoenberg proposed serialism as a method for organising only notes; to a large extent, the other aspects of his pieces followed standard practices and forms. Webern, however, introduced other organisation principles in his music and prepared the ground for Boulez and others to extend the serial method technique to organise musical parameters other than notes, such as duration, dynamics and modes of attack. In the early 1950s, Boulez wrote a piece for two pianos called *Structures*, which is perhaps the first totally serial piece ever composed. The serial processes defined by Boulez could generate the piece almost automatically: the piece is in perpetual transformation and no pitch recurs with the same duration, dynamic or

---

[5] Coincidentally or not, this was the very same type of treatment that Medieval composers applied to musical modes in order to add variety to their compositions.

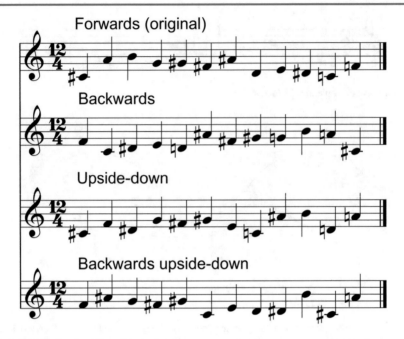

Fig. 2.13 The four versions of the series

mode of attack. In addition to the pitch series, he defined a duration series, a dynamics series (from *pianissississimo* to *fortississimo*) and modes of attack (*staccato*, *mezzo staccato*, etc.) series. The serial processes determined the overall structure of the composition, ordering the different series in a combinatorial-like fashion.

A serial piece of music such as *Structures* might perhaps never be loved by the wider audience, but nevertheless, the legacy of using formal and explicit rules to generate pieces of music is undeniably important for anyone intending to use computers to compose music. This piece is the paramount example of parametrical thinking.

2.5.2 The Legacy of Iannis Xenakis

The radical serialism fostered by Pierre Boulez and others in Europe naturally had many opponents. John Cage in the USA is a notorious example: rather than tie his pieces to a serial kernel, Cage preferred to toss a coin or play ancient divination games for generating musical material [23]. However opposed, both trends have lead to new ways of thinking about music, which emphasise the generative processes that underlie the origins of a piece, be they random or highly controlled.

Composer Iannis Xenakis proposed an interesting approach to composition, which is neither strictly serial nor loosely playful. Xenakis has inspired many of today's computer musicians: his approach embodies statistics principles. Scientists use statistics to make general predictions concerning a mass of random fluctuations, such as

Fig. 2.14 A vector representing a point in a three-dimensional space: $v_m = \{0.5, 0.5, 0.25\}$

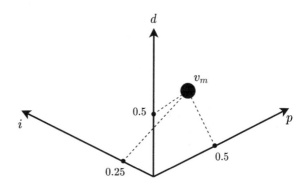

the overall speed and trajectory of the molecules in a cloud of gas. Xenakis purported that a similar rationale could be applied to large numbers of musical events, such as the sound of a mass of strings in different glissando ranges. To my mind, Xenakis's concepts are very inspiring for developing quantum computing approaches to music; e.g., [1,29].

Although Xenakis is commonly cited as being a pioneer in using probabilities for composing music, the aspect of his work that is of interest here is the abstract formalism that underlines his musical thought. The following example embodies a musical formalism based on set theory, inspired by the theoretical framework introduced by Xenakis in his book *Formalized Music* [28].

Let us define three sets of natural numbers, P, D and I, corresponding to pitch intervals, duration and intensity, respectively; these sets are ordered.

A general law of composition for each of these sets may be established as follows: Let v_m be a vector of three components, p_n, d_n and i_n, such that $p_n \in P$, $d_n \in D$ and $i_n \in I$, respectively, arranged in this order $v_m = \{p_n, d_n, i_n\}$. In this context, a vector is a point in a three-dimensional space, whose co-ordinates are given by p_n, d_n and i_n (Fig. 2.14). The particular case of the vector in which all the components are zero is referred to as the zero vector, v_0, that is, the origin of the co-ordinates.

Considering the algebraic properties of sets introduced earlier, let us define two *compositional laws* for vector v_m: the additive and the multiplication laws.

The additive law:

$(v_i = \{p_m, d_n, i_o\}) + (v_j = \{p_x, d_y, i_z\}) \Rightarrow (v_i + v_j) = \{(p_m + p_x), (d_n + d_y)(i_o + i_z)\}$

Multiplication law (c is a natural number):

$c \times (v_i = \{p_m, d_n, i_o\}) \Rightarrow c \times v_i = \{c \times p_m, c \times d_n, c \times i_o\}$

An additional constraint to be observed is that p_n, d_n and i_n should not take arbitrary values, but values within the audible range. For the purpose of this example, the default vector for the origins of the coordinates is defined as $v_0 = \{60, 4, 64\}$. The elements of set P are represented in terms of MIDI-note semitones, the elements of set D are represented in terms of metric beats and the elements of I in proportional terms from silence to *fortissimo* whose values range from 0 to 127. The origins of

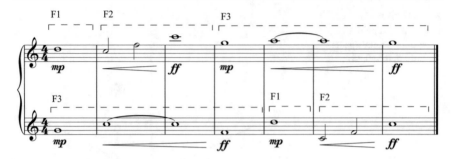

Fig. 2.15 A musical passage automatically generated by the generative musical score

the coordinates are, therefore: the note $C3$, a duration of one metric beat (in a $\frac{4}{4}$ measure) and an intensity equal to *mezzo piano*.

We are now in a position to define some generative rules for generating musical events. The following statements define three vector generators; np means n units above the origin of p, whereas $-np$ means n units below the origin p:

$$\begin{cases} v_1 = \{14p, 4d, i\} \\ v_2 = \{(X+12)p, Yd, Zi\} \\ v_3 = \{(X-4)p, Yd, Zi\} \end{cases}$$

The F_n statements below define the formation of sequences of vectors:

$$\begin{cases} F_1 = [v_1] \\ F_2 = [v_2, v_2, (2 \times v_2)] \\ F_3 = [v_3, (v_1 + v_3), v_3] \end{cases}$$

As implemented on a computer, suppose that each F_n statement has been implemented as functions that generate the vectors; in this case F_2 and F_3 receive the list of parameters for v. This could be denoted as $F_n(x, y, z)$, where x, y and z are lists of values for the variables of v.

A generative score could then be given to the system which in turn would produce the passage portrayed in Fig. 2.15 as follows:

Top stave: $\{F_1, F_2[(0, 2, 32), (5, 2, 48), (0, 2, 32)], F_3[(24, 4, 0), (12, 4, 48), (24, 4, 64)]\}$

Bottom stave: $\{F_3[(12, 4, 0), (0, 4, 48), (10, 4, 64)], F_1, F_2[(-12, 2, 32), (-7, 2, 48), (0, 2, 32)]\}$

Note that F_1 does not need any input parameter because v_1 needs no variable to function; v_1 always produces the same note: $\{14p, 4d, i\}$.

2.6 Final Remarks

An argument that pops up in almost every chapter of this book is that quantum computing is a disruptive technology with the potential to bring new paradigms for musical creativity, which would not exist otherwise.

Ideally, new music technologies ought to be developed collaboratively between musicians and engineers; see for instance the work introduced in Chaps. 4 and 18 in this volume. But this seldom happens in practice. Most often, developments are galvanised either by musicians with a good grasp of engineering, or engineers with a good knowledge of music.

The field of quantum computing is incipient and still requires skills that are difficult for musicians to learn. In gross terms, programming a quantum computer today still is comparable to having to program a digital computer using assembly language: one has to write code that operates at the level of qubits. This is changing rapidly, as the industry is making impressive progress in developing high-level programming tools, such as Quantinuum's TKET, to cite but one example.[6] Another problem that also needs to be addressed is the fact that quantum mechanics is rather unintuitive to grasp in relation to our daily physical reality. This makes the task of imaging algorithms that makes use of quantum mechanics to solve problems difficult.

Until higher-level programming tools and suitable learning resources become more widely available for musicians, with a few exceptions, it is engineers and quantum computer programmers who are conducting research into musical applications of quantum computing. This can be problematic.

Of course, one cannot expect engineers to be totally aware of new trends in musicology. But a lacking of awareness of contemporary musical thought is destined to limit their imagination when it comes to leveraging quantum-mechanical computing for creative musical applications. If the applications landscape remains the same as the one for which there are plenty of solutions already, it is likely that proposed new quantum developments for music might end up simply reinventing the wheel.

This chapter is a contribution to alleviating this problem. It introduced a few topics of interest for those who are not conversant with contemporary thinking, in particular, approaches to music representation and parametrization for computer processing and modern composition practices that influenced the development of generative music techniques. However, there is so much more to be discussed. Aspiring quantum computer music researchers and developers are strongly encouraged to become familiar with contemporary musical thinking[7] and the burgeoning field of computer music, including developments in Artificial Intelligence for music [3,8–10,20]. There is a fantastic opportunity here to develop new paradigms for musical creativity with quantum computers and to create new economic niches. But as the French chemist, Louis Pasteur, allegedly said: "Where observation is concerned, chance favours only the prepared mind".

---

[6] https://github.com/CQCL/tket (Accessed on 16 May 2022).
[7] https://www.oxfordmusiconline.com/page/essential-20th-century-reading-list/essential-20thcentury-reading-list (Accessed on 30 Apr 2022).

References

1. Arsenault, L. M. (2002). Iannis Xenakis's achorripsis: The matrix game. *Computer Music Journal, 26*(1), 58–72.
2. Barrière, J.-B. (Ed.). (1991). *Le timbre, métaphore pour la composition.* Christian Bourgois - Ircam. ISBN: 978-2267008081.
3. Beil, R., & Kraut, P. (Eds.). (2012). *A house full of music: Strategies in music and art.* Hatje Cantz Verlag. ISBN: 978-3775733199.
4. Boulanger, R. (2000). *The Csound book: Perspectives in software synthesis, sound design, signal processing, and programming.* The MIT Press. ISBN: 978-0262522618.
5. Boss, J. (2016). *Schoenberg's twelve-tone music: Symmetry and the musical idea.* Cambridge University Press. ISBN: 978-1107624924.
6. Boulez, P. (1963). *Penser la musique aujourd'hui.* Gallimard. ISBN: 978-2070709014.
7. Brown, S., Merker, B., & Wallin, N. L. (Eds.). (1999). *The origins of music.* The MIT Press. ISBN: 978-0262731430.
8. Dean, R. T. (Ed.). (2012). *The Oxford handbook of computer music.* Oxford University Press. ISBN: 978-0199792030.
9. Dogde, C., & Jersey, T. A. (1997). *Computer music: Synthesis.* Composition and Performance Schirmer. ISBN: 978-0028646824.
10. Hall, M. (1996). *Leaving home: Conducted tour of 20th century music.* Faber and Faber. ISBN: 978-0571178773.
11. Honing, H. (2018). *The origins of musicality.* The MIT Press. ISBN: 978-0262538510.
12. Huron, D. (2008). *Sweet anticipation: Music and the psychology of expectation.* The MIT Press. ISBN: 978-0262582780.
13. Haimo, E. (1992). *Schoenberg's Serial Odyssey: The evolution of his twelve-tone method, 1914–1928.* Clarendon Press. ISBN: 978-0198163527.
14. Jordan, R., & Kafalenos, E. (1994). Listening to Music: Semiotic and Narratological Models. In M. G. Boroda (Ed.), *Musikometrika* (vol. 6). Brockmeyer.
15. Larivaille, P. (1974). L'Analyse (morpho)logique du récit. *Poétique, 19,* 368–388.
16. Lerdhal, F., & Jackendoff, R. (1983). *A generative theory of tonal music.* The MIT Press. ISBN: 978-0262120944.
17. Manning, P. (1985). *Electronic and computer music.* Oxford University Press. ISBN: 978-0195170856.
18. McAdams, A. (Ed.). (1987). Music and psychology: A mutual regard. In *Contemporary music review* (vol. 2, Part 1). Gordon and Breach.
19. Meyer, L. (1961). *Emotion and meaning in music.* University of Chicago Press. ISBN: 978-0226521398.
20. Miranda, E. R. (Ed.). (2021). *Handbook of artificial intelligence for music: Foundations, advanced approaches, and developments for creativity.* Springer. ISBN: 978-3030721169.
21. Orton, R. (1990). *Music fundamentals.* Department of Music, University of York, Unpublished lecture notes.
22. Reck, D. (1997). *Music of the whole earth.* Da Capo Press.
23. Revill, D. (2014). *The roaring silence.* Arcade Publishing. ISBN: 978-1611457308.
24. Schoenberg, A. (1967). *Fundamentals of musical composition.* Faber and Faber. ISBN: 978-0571196586.
25. Stockhausen, K. (1991). Four criteria of electronic music. In R. Maconie (Ed.), *Stockhausen on music.* Marion Boyars. ISBN: 978-0714529189.
26. Wiener, N. (1961). *Cybernetics: Or control and communication in the animal and the machine.* The MIT Press. ISBN: 978-0262730099.
27. Xenakis, I. (1967). *Herma, musical score.* Boosey and Hawkes Music Publishers.
28. Xenakis, I. (1992). *Formalized music.* Pendragon Press. ISBN: 978-1576470794.
29. Xenakis, I., & Brown, R. (1989). Concerning time. *Perspectives of New Music, 27*(1), 84–92.

Quantum Computer Music: Foundations and Initial Experiments

3

Eduardo Reck Miranda and Suchitra Basak

Abstract

Quantum computing is a nascent technology, which is advancing rapidly. There is a long history of research into using computers for music. Nowadays computers are absolutely essential for the music economy. Thus, it is very likely that quantum computers will impact in the music industry in the future. This chapter lays the foundations of the new field of *Quantum Computer Music*. It begins with an introduction to algorithmic computer music and methods to program computers to generate music, such as Markov chains and random walks. Then, it presents quantum computing versions of those methods. The discussions are supported by detailed explanations of quantum computing concepts and walk-through examples. A novel bespoke generative music algorithm in presented, the *Basak-Miranda algorithm*, which leverages a property of quantum mechanics known as *constructive and destructive interference* to operate a musical Markov chain.

3.1 Introduction

As mentioned in the Preface for this volume, the first uses of computers in music were for composition. The great majority of computer music pioneers were composers interested in inventing new music and/or innovative approaches to composition. They focused on developing algorithms to generate music. Hence the term 'algorithmic

E. R. Miranda (✉) · S. Basak
ICCMR, University of Plymouth, Plymouth, UK
e-mail: eduardo.miranda@plymouth.ac.uk

S. Basak
e-mail: suchitra.basak@plymouth.ac.uk

© The Author(s), under exclusive license to Springer Nature Switzerland AG 2022   43
E. R Miranda (ed.), *Quantum Computer Music*,
https://doi.org/10.1007/978-3-031-13909-3_3

computer music'. Essentially, the art of algorithmic computer music consists of (a) harnessing algorithms to produce patterns of data and (b) developing ways to translate these patterns into musical notes or synthesised sound.

Nowadays, computing technology is omnipresent in almost every aspect of music. Therefore, forthcoming alternative computing technology, such as biocomputing and quantum computing will certainly have an impact on the way in which we create and distribute music in time to come.

This chapter introduces pioneering research into exploring emerging quantum computing technology in music. We say "emerging" because quantum computers are still being developed. There is some hardware already available, even commercially, but detractors say that meaningful quantum computers, that is, quantum machines that can outperform current classical ones, are yet to be seen. Nevertheless, research and development are progressing fast.

The chapter begins with an introduction to algorithmic computer music and methods to program computers to compose music, such as Markov chains and random walks [12]. Then, it discusses how to implement quantum computing versions of those methods. For didactic purposes, the discussions are supported by detailed explanations of basic quantum computing concepts and practical examples. A novel generative music algorithm in presented, which leverages a property of quantum mechanics known as *constructive and destructive interference* [1] to operate Markov chains [14] representing rules for sequencing music.

3.2 Algorithmic Computer Music

An early approach to algorithmic computer music, which still remains popular to date, is to program a machine with rules for generating sequences of notes. Rules derived from classic treatises on musical composition are relatively straightforward to encode in a piece of software. Indeed, one of the movements of the *Illiac Suite* string quartet mentioned earlier was generated with rules for making musical counterpoint[1] from a well-known treatise entitled *Gradus ad Parnassum*, penned by Joseph Fux in 1725 [8].

Rules for musical composition can be represented in a number of ways, including graphs, set algebra, Boolean expressions, finite state automata and Markov chains, to cite but five. For an introduction to various representation schemes and algorithmic composition methods please refer to the book *Composing Music with Computers* [12].

As an example, consider the following 12-tone series derived from a chromatic scale starting with the pitch E: {E, F, G, C♯, F♯, D♯, G♯, D, B, C, A, A♯}; please refer to Chap. 2 for an introduction to serial music. Unless stated otherwise, the musical examples presented in this chapter assume the notion of 'pitch classes'. A pitch class

---

[1] In music, counterpoint is the art of combining different melodic lines in parallel.

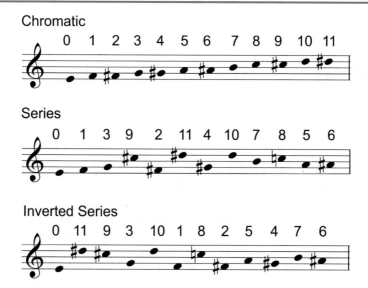

Fig. 3.1 Deriving a 12-tone series and its inverted version from a chromatic scale

encompasses all pitches that are related by an octave or enharmonic equivalence. For instance, pitch-class G♯ can be on any octave. Moreover, it sounds identical to pitch class A♭; e.g., think of the piano keyboard where the same black key plays G♯ and A♭.

Figure 3.1 shows our 12-tone series in musical notation, its chromatic scale of origin and its inverted version, which will be used in the example that follows. The inverted version of a series is produced by reversing the intervals between the notes in the sequence; that is, going in the opposite direction of the original. For example, a rising minor third (C → E♭) becomes a falling minor third (C → A). For clarity, the numbers above each note in Fig. 3.1 indicate its position in the chromatic scale.

Now, let us define a bunch of sequencing rules. These are represented in Table 3.1. The 12-tone series is laid on the horizontal axis and its inverted version on the vertical one. The rules are inspired by a composition method referred to as *serialism*, popularised in the second half of the 20th century by composers such as Karlheinz Stockhausen and Pierre Boulez [13]. The details of this method are not important to discuss here. What is important to observe is that for each note of the inverted series (in the vertical axis), there is a rule establishing which notes of the 12-tone series (in the horizontal axis) can follow it. For instance, the first row states that only an F or a D♯ can follow an E.

The rules are formalised as follows (the symbol ∨ stands for "or"):

- Rule 1: if E ⟹ F ∨ D♯
- Rule 2: if D♯ ⟹ E ∨ C♯ ∨ F♯ ∨ G♯
- Rule 3: if C♯ ⟹ G ∨ F♯ ∨ D♯
- Rule 4: if G ⟹ F ∨ C♯ ∨ D

- Rule 5: if D $\Longrightarrow$ F $\vee$ G $\vee$ G♯ $\vee$ B
- Rule 6: if F $\Longrightarrow$ E $\vee$ G $\vee$ D $\vee$C
- Rule 7: if C $\Longrightarrow$ F $\vee$ F♯, B $\vee$ A
- Rule 8: if F♯ $\Longrightarrow$ C♯ $\vee$ D♯ $\vee$ C $\vee$ A
- Rule 9: if A $\Longrightarrow$ F♯ $\vee$ G♯ $\vee$ C $\vee$ A♯
- Rule 10: if G♯ $\Longrightarrow$ D♯ $\vee$ D $\vee$ B $\vee$A
- Rule 11: if B $\Longrightarrow$ G♯ $\vee$ D $\vee$ C $\vee$ A♯
- Rule 12: if A♯ $\Longrightarrow$ B $\vee$ A.

One way to implement those rules in a piece of software is to program algorithms to produce notes according to probability distributions, which are equally weighted between the notes allowed by a respective rule. For instance, in Rule 2, each of the allowed 4 notes has a 25% chance of occurring after D♯. Thus, we can re-write Table 3.1 in terms of such probability distributions. This forms a Markov chain (Table 3.2).

Markov chains are conditional probability systems where the likelihood of future events depends on one or more past events. The number of past events that are taken into consideration at each stage is known as the order of the chain. A Markov chain that takes only one predecessor into account is of the first order. A chain that considers the predecessor and the predecessor's predecessor is of the second order, and so on. We will come back to our 12-tone Markov chain later.

For now, let us have a look at how to generate music with a method known as *random walk*. Imagine a system that is programmed to play a musical instrument with 12 notes, organised according to our 12-tone series. This system is programmed in such a way that it can play notes up and down the instrument by stepping only one note at a time. That is, only the next neighbour on either side of the last played note can be played next. If the system has a probability p to hit the note on the left side of the last played note, then it will have the probability $q = 1 - p$ to hit the one on the right. This is an example of a simple one-dimensional random walk.

A good way to visualize random walk processes is to depict them as directed graphs, or digraphs (Fig. 3.2). Digraphs are diagrams composed of nodes and arrows going from one node to another. Digraphs are widely used in computing to represent relationships in a network, such as roads linking places, hyperlinks connecting web pages, and so on.

As a matter of fact, the random walk depicted in Fig. 3.2 can be represented as a Markov chain with non-zero entries immediately on either side of the main diagonal, and zeros everywhere else. This is illustrated in Table 3.3. Note that in this case, we replaced the vertical axis of the previous tables with the same series as the one laid on the horizontal axis. Figure 3.3 shows an example of a sequence generated by our imaginary system. (Rhythmic figures were assigned manually.) Starting with pitch C♯, a virtual die decided which one to pick next: G or F♯. For this example, G was selected. Then, from G there were two options, and C♯ was selected. And so on and so forth.

Table 3.1 Visual representation of sequencing rules. Columns are the notes of the series and rows are notes of the inverted series

	E	F	G	C♯	F♯	D♯	G♯	D	B	C	A	A♯
E		■				■						
D♯	■			■	■		■					
C♯			■		■	■						
G		■		■				■				
D		■	■				■		■			
F	■		■				■			■		
C		■			■				■		■	
F♯			■			■				■	■	
A				■		■				■		■
G♯						■		■	■	■		
B							■	■		■		■
A♯								■		■		

Table 3.2 Sequencing rules represented as a Markov chain

	E	F	G	C♯	F♯	D♯	G♯	D	B	C	A	A♯
E		0.5				0.5						
D♯	0.25			0.25	0.25		0.25					
C♯			0.33		0.33	0.33						
G		0.33		0.33				0.33				
D		0.25	0.25				0.25		0.25			
F	0.25		0.25				0.25			0.25		
C		0.25			0.25				0.25		0.25	
F♯			0.25			0.25				0.25	0.25	
A				0.25		0.25				0.25		0.25
G♯						0.25		0.25	0.25	0.25		
B							0.25	0.25		0.25		0.25
A♯								0.5		0.5		

3.3 Musical Quantum Walks

This subsection introduces two preliminary ideas for making music with quantum versions of random walk processes. A comprehensive introduction to the basics of quantum computing and gate operations is beyond the scope of this chapter. Please refer to Chap. 1 in this volume and [15] for a more detailed introduction.

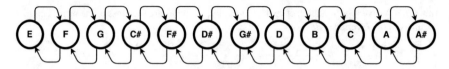

Fig. 3.2 Digraph representation of the simple random walk scheme depicted in Table 3.3

Fig. 3.3 A composition with pitches generated by the random walk depicted in Fig. 3.2, using the series in Fig. 3.1. A number above each note indicates its position in the chromatic scale. Rhythmic figures were assigned manually.

Table 3.3 Markov chain representation of a simple one-dimensional random walk process (Empty cells are assumed to hold zeros)

	E	F	G	C♯	F♯	D♯	G♯	D	B	C	A	A♯
E	**0.0**	1.0										
F	0.5	**0.0**	0.5									
G		0.5	**0.0**	0.5								
C♯			0.5	**0.0**	0.5							
F♯				0.5	**0.0**	0.5						
D♯					0.5	**0.0**	0.5					
G♯						0.5	**0.0**	0.5				
D							0.5	**0.0**	0.5			
B								0.5	**0.0**	0.5		
C									0.5	**0.0**	0.5	
A										0.5	**0.0**	0.5
A♯											1.0	**0.0**

3.3.1 One-Dimensional Musical Quantum Walk

A quantum implementation of the one-dimensional quantum walk depicted in Table 3.3 is shown in Fig. 3.4.

Given an initial musical note from our 12-tone series (Fig. 3.4 (1)), the system plays this note (4) and runs a binary quantum die (2, 3). The result is used to pick from the Markov chain the next note to play. If the result is equal to 0, then it picks

Fig. 3.4 One-dimensional quantum walk generative music system

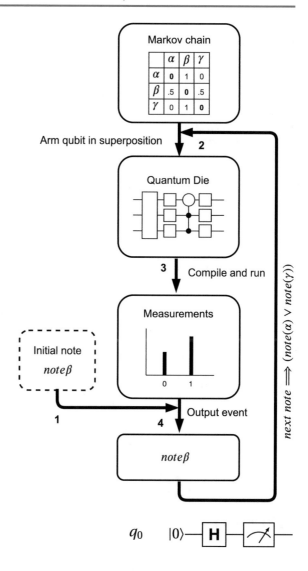

Fig. 3.5 Circuit for a quantum die

q_0 $|0\rangle$ —[**H**]—[📐]—

the note on the left side of the last played note, otherwise, it picks the one on the right side; see Fig. 3.2. Next, the circuit is re-armed (2) and run again to pick another note. This process is repeated a pre-specified number of times.

The quantum binary die is implemented with a single qubit and a Hadamard, or H, gate (Fig. 3.5). The H gate puts the state vector $|\Psi\rangle$ of the qubit in an equally weighted combination of two opposing states, $|0\rangle$ and $|1\rangle$. This is represented on the Bloch sphere in Fig. 3.6. Mathematically, this is notated as follows: $|\Psi\rangle = \alpha |0\rangle + \beta |1\rangle$ with $|\alpha|^2 = 0.5$ and $|\beta|^2 = 0.5$. That is to say, there is a 50% chance of returning 0 or 1 when the qubit is measured.

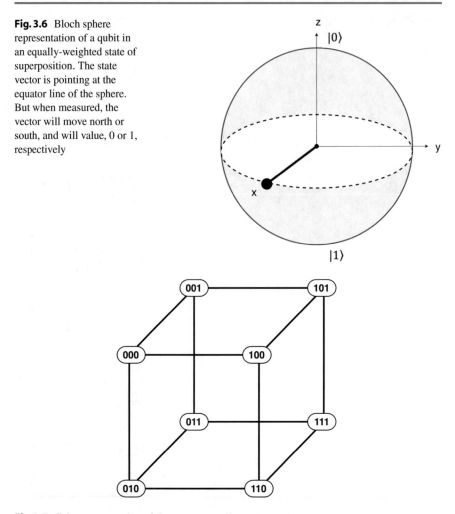

Fig. 3.6 Bloch sphere representation of a qubit in an equally-weighted state of superposition. The state vector is pointing at the equator line of the sphere. But when measured, the vector will move north or south, and will value, 0 or 1, respectively

Fig. 3.7 Cube representation of the quantum walk

3.3.2 Three-Dimensional Musical Quantum Walk

Let us take a look at a random walk scheme with more than two travel options. As an example, consider that the vertices of the cube shown in Fig. 3.7 represent the nodes of a graph. And its edges represent the possible routes to move from one node to another. From, say, node 100 the walker could remain on 100, or go to 000, 110 or 101.

In a classical random walk, a "walker" inhabits a definite node at any one moment in time. But in the quantum walk, it would be in a superposition of all nodes it can possibly visit in a given moment. Metaphorically, we could say that the walker would stand on all viable nodes simultaneously until it is observed, or measured.

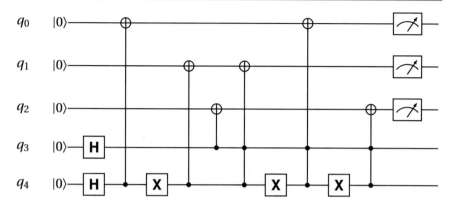

Fig. 3.8 Quantum walk circuit

The quantum circuit in Fig. 3.8 moves a walker through the edges of the cube. The circuit uses five qubits: three (q_0, q_1, and q_2) to encode the eight vertices of the cube $\{000, 001, \ldots, 111\}$ and two (q_3 and q_4) to encode the possible routes that the walker can take from a given vertex, one of which is to stay put.

The circuit diagram shows a sequence of quantum operations, the first of which are two Hadamard gates applied to q_3 and q_4, followed by a controlled-NOT gate with q_4 as a control to flip the state vector of q_0, and so on. We refer to the first three qubits as *input qubits* and the last two as *dice qubits*. The dice qubits act as controls for NOT gates to invert the state vector of input qubits.

For every vertex of the cube, the edges connect three neighbouring vertices whose codes differ by changing only one bit of the origin's code. For instance, vertex 111 is connected to 011, 101 and 110. Therefore, upon measurement the system returns one of four possible outputs:

- the original input with flipped q_0
- the original input with flipped q_1
- the original input with flipped q_2
- the original input unchanged.

The quantum walk algorithm runs as follows: the input qubits are armed with the state representing a node of departure and the two dice qubits are armed in a balanced superposition (Hadamard gate). Then, the input qubits are measured and the results are stored in a classical memory. This causes the whole system to decohere. Depending on the values yielded by the dice qubits, the conditional gates will change the state of the input qubits accordingly. Note that we measure and store only input qubits; the values of the dice can be lost. The result of the measurements is then used to arm the input qubits for the next step of the walk, and the cycle continues for a

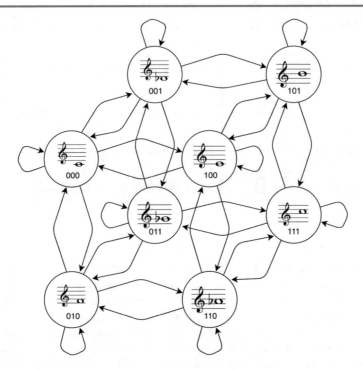

Fig. 3.9 Digraph representation of the quantum walk routes through musical notes. Notes from the so-called Persian scale on C are associated to the vertices of the cube shown in Fig. 3.7.

number of steps.[2] The number of steps is established at the initial data preparation stage.

As a trace table illustration, let us assume the following input: 001, where q_0 is armed to $|0\rangle$, q_1 to $|0\rangle$ and q_2 to $|1\rangle$. Upon measurement, let us suppose that the dice yielded $q_3 = 0$ and $q_4 = 1$. The second operation on the circuit diagram is a controlled-NOT gate where q_4 acts as a conditional to invert q_0. Thus, at this point the state vector of q_0 is inverted because $q_4 = 1$. As the rest of the circuit does not incur any further action on the qubits, the system returns 101. Should the dice have yielded $q_3 = 0$ and $q_4 = 0$ instead, then the third operation, which is a NOT gate, would have inverted q_4, which would subsequently act as a conditional to invert q_1. The result, in this case, would have been 011.

We implemented a demonstration system that runs each cycle of the quantum walk twice: once to generate a pitch and once again to generate a rhythmic figure. Take it that the system walks through two separate cubes in parallel. One of the cubes, the *pitch-cube*, encodes pitches on its vertices. The other, the *rhythm-cube*, encodes rhythms. Figure 3.9 shows a digraph representation of the pitch-cube, where each

---

[2] In fact, each step is run for thousands of times, or thousands of shots in quantum computing terminology. The reason for this will be clarified later.

Fig. 3.10 Rhythmic figures associated with the notes of the cube shown in Fig. 3.7

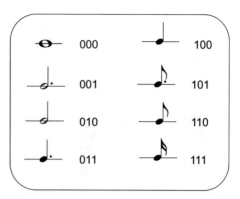

vertex is associated with a pitch; the respective binary code is also shown. The eight pitches form a musical scale known as the Persian scale on C: {C4, D♭4, E4, F4, G♭4, A♭4, B4, C5}. Figure 3.10 shows the rhythmic figures associated with the vertices of the rhythm cube. The system holds different musical dictionaries associating vertices with different sets of pitches and rhythmic figures.[3]

To generate a musical sequence, the system starts with a given note[4]; for instance, a crochet C4, whose codes for pitch and rhythm are 000 and 100, respectively. Then, for every new note, the system runs the quantum walk circuit twice, once with input qubits armed with the code for pitch and then armed with the code for rhythm. The results from the measurements are then used to produce the next note. For instance, if the first run results in 000 and the second results in 000, then the resulting note is another C4, but as a semibreve. The measurements are used to re-arm the circuit for the next note and so on (Fig. 3.11).

An example of a composition generated by the system is shown in Fig. 3.12. In this case, the system ran for 29 steps. The initial pitch was C4 (code = 000) and the initial rhythmic figure was as crochet (code = 100). Below each note on the score in Fig. 3.12 is a number indicating the step that generated it. Table 3.4 shows the codes generated at each step of the walk.

As mentioned in footnote 2 due to the statistical nature of quantum computation, it is necessary to execute a quantum algorithm for multiple times, or shots, in order to obtain results that are statistically plausible. This enables one to inspect if the outcomes reflect the envisaged amplitude distribution of the quantum states. And running a circuit multiple times helps to mitigate the effect of errors. For each shot, the measurements are stored in standard digital memory, and in the case of our quantum walk algorithm, the result that occurred more frequently is selected. Figure 3.11 shows histograms for four steps, for 40 shots each, for generating rhythms. Starting on 100, then the walker moves to 000 in step 1, to 010 in step

---

[3] The length of the composition and the dictionaries are set up by the user. It is possible to change dictionaries automatically while the system is generating the music.

[4] This initial note is input by the user.

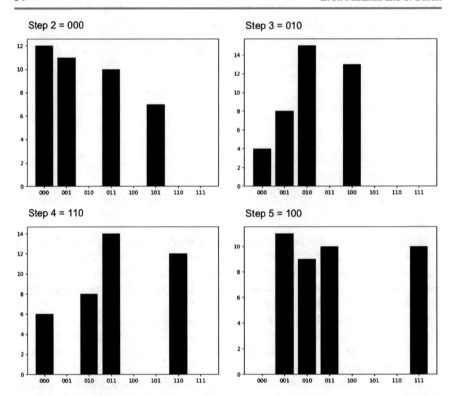

Fig. 3.11 Histograms for four steps of the quantum walk algorithm for generating rhythms. The vertical coordinate is the number of times an item listed on the horizontal coordinate occurred. For each step, the system selects the result that occurred more frequently. Note that the digits on the plots are in reverse order; this is due to the way in which the qubits are normally ordered in quantum programming

2, to 110 in step 3, and 100 in step 4. As we generated the example on a quantum computing software simulator,[5] 40 shots for each step were sufficient to obtain the expected results.

3.4 Basak-Miranda Algorithm

Throwing a one-qubit quantum die to select between two allowed choices on a Markov chain representing simple one-dimensional random walks works well. But this would not work for a chain representing more complex sequencing rules, such as the one in Table 3.2.

---

[5] For this example we used Rigetti's Quantum Virtual Machine (QVM), implemented in ANSI Common LISP.

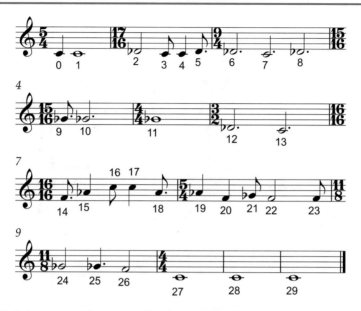

Fig. 3.12 A short composition generated by the quantum walk system

Table 3.4 Results from running the quantum walk algorithm 30 times

Step	Pitch	Rhythm	Step	Pitch	Rhythm
0	000	100	15	110	100
1	000	000	16	111	110
2	001	010	17	111	100
3	000	110	18	110	101
4	000	100	19	110	100
5	001	101	20	010	100
6	001	001	21	011	110
7	000	001	22	010	010
8	001	001	23	010	110
9	011	101	24	011	010
10	011	001	25	011	011
11	011	000	26	010	010
12	001	001	27	000	000
13	000	001	28	000	000
14	010	101	29	000	010

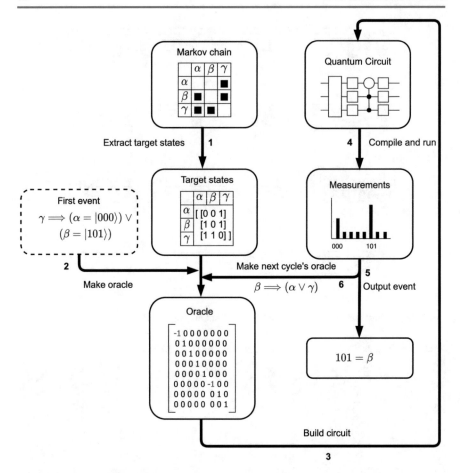

Fig. 3.13 The Basak-Miranda algorithm

To tackle this, we designed a novel algorithm: the *Basak-Miranda algorithm*. This algorithm exploits a fundamental property of quantum physics, known as *constructive and destructive interference* [4], to select sequencing options on a Markov chain.

The flow diagram of the Basak-Miranda algorithm is shown in Fig. 3.13. Let us first have a bird's-eye view of the algorithm by means of a table trace example. Then, we will dive deep into some of its important details.

Given the Markov chain representing the sequencing rules shown in Table 3.2, the algorithm builds a matrix $\mathscr{T}$ of *target states* (Fig. 3.13 (1)), as follows:

$$\mathscr{T} = \begin{bmatrix} 0&1&0&0&0&1&0&0&0&0&0&0 \\ 1&0&0&1&1&0&1&0&0&0&0&0 \\ 0&0&1&0&1&1&0&0&0&0&0&0 \\ 0&1&0&1&0&0&0&1&0&0&0&0 \\ 0&1&1&0&0&0&1&0&1&0&0&0 \\ 1&0&1&0&0&0&0&1&0&1&0&0 \\ 0&1&0&0&1&0&0&0&1&1&0&0 \\ 0&0&0&1&0&1&0&0&0&1&0&1 \\ 0&0&0&0&1&0&1&0&0&1&0&1 \\ 0&0&0&0&0&1&0&1&1&0&1&0 \\ 0&0&0&0&0&0&1&1&0&1&0&1 \\ 0&0&0&0&0&0&0&0&1&0&1&0 \end{bmatrix} \tag{3.1}$$

In fact, Table 3.1 comes in handy to clearly visualise what this matrix represents: a black square is a target state, or a digit 1 in the matrix.

Next, the algorithm extracts from the matrix the row for the respective rule to be processed. This rule is designated by the last generated note. For instance, if the last note was a D♯, then Rule 2 is to be processed. Therefore, the algorithm extracts the second row, which gives the target states for this rule: $R2 = [1\,0\,0\,1\,1\,0\,1\,0\,0\,0\,0\,0]$.

Then, the extracted row is converted into a quantum gate, which is referred to as an *oracle* (Fig. 3.13 (2)). The notion of an oracle will be discussed in more detail later.

Mathematically, quantum states are notated as vectors and quantum gates as matrices. In a nutshell, the oracle is expressed by an identity matrix, whose columns are tensor vectors corresponding to quantum states. Columns corresponding to target states are marked as negative.

The resulting oracle for Rule 2 is shown below. The target states $|0\rangle_4$, $|3\rangle_4$, $|4\rangle_4$, $|6\rangle_4$ (or pitches E, C♯, F♯ and G♯, respectively) are in bold, for clarity.[6]

$$\mathscr{O}(R2) = \begin{bmatrix} \mathbf{-1}&0&0&\mathbf{0}&\mathbf{0}&0&\mathbf{0}&0&0&0&0&0&0&0&0&0 \\ \mathbf{0}&1&0&\mathbf{0}&\mathbf{0}&0&\mathbf{0}&0&0&0&0&0&0&0&0&0 \\ \mathbf{0}&0&1&\mathbf{0}&\mathbf{0}&0&\mathbf{0}&0&0&0&0&0&0&0&0&0 \\ \mathbf{0}&0&0&\mathbf{-1}&\mathbf{0}&0&\mathbf{0}&0&0&0&0&0&0&0&0&0 \\ \mathbf{0}&0&0&\mathbf{0}&\mathbf{-1}&0&\mathbf{0}&0&0&0&0&0&0&0&0&0 \\ \mathbf{0}&0&0&\mathbf{0}&\mathbf{0}&1&\mathbf{0}&0&0&0&0&0&0&0&0&0 \\ \mathbf{0}&0&0&\mathbf{0}&\mathbf{0}&0&\mathbf{-1}&0&0&0&0&0&0&0&0&0 \\ \mathbf{0}&0&0&\mathbf{0}&\mathbf{0}&0&\mathbf{0}&1&0&0&0&0&0&0&0&0 \\ \mathbf{0}&0&0&\mathbf{0}&\mathbf{0}&0&\mathbf{0}&0&1&0&0&0&0&0&0&0 \\ \mathbf{0}&0&0&\mathbf{0}&\mathbf{0}&0&\mathbf{0}&0&0&1&0&0&0&0&0&0 \\ \mathbf{0}&0&0&\mathbf{0}&\mathbf{0}&0&\mathbf{0}&0&0&0&1&0&0&0&0&0 \\ \mathbf{0}&0&0&\mathbf{0}&\mathbf{0}&0&\mathbf{0}&0&0&0&0&1&0&0&0&0 \\ \mathbf{0}&0&0&\mathbf{0}&\mathbf{0}&0&\mathbf{0}&0&0&0&0&0&1&0&0&0 \\ \mathbf{0}&0&0&\mathbf{0}&\mathbf{0}&0&\mathbf{0}&0&0&0&0&0&0&1&0&0 \\ \mathbf{0}&0&0&\mathbf{0}&\mathbf{0}&0&\mathbf{0}&0&0&0&0&0&0&0&1&0 \\ \mathbf{0}&0&0&\mathbf{0}&\mathbf{0}&0&\mathbf{0}&0&0&0&0&0&0&0&0&1 \end{bmatrix} \tag{3.2}$$

---

[6] The subscript 4 next to the ket indicates the number of qubits required to represent the respective decimal number in binary form.

In principle our oracle would not need more than 12 quantum states, or columns, since our Markov chain specifies transitions between 12 pitches. However, we need 4 qubits to encode these 12 states because 3 qubits can encode only up to 8 states. Hence we need a 16×16 matrix to express our oracle.

The oracle is the first component of the quantum circuit that will select the next note. The other component is the so-called *amplitude amplification* (or amplitude remixing); again, this will be explained in more detail below. The algorithm then assembles the circuit, compiles it and runs the program (Fig. 3.13 (3) (4)).

The result will be a target state corresponding to one of the notes allowed by Rule 2: E, C♯, F♯, or G♯. Then, the algorithm outputs the respective note (Fig. 3.13 (5)), which in turn designates the rule for generating the next note. Next, it builds a new oracle (Fig. 3.13 (6)), assembles the quantum circuit, and so on. This cycle continues for as long as required to generate a composition.

3.4.1 Constructive and Destructive Interference

Interference, together with superposition and entanglement, are important characteristics of quantum computing, which make it different from traditional computing.

Interference is explained here in the context of an algorithm devised by Lov Grover in 1997 [5]. Grover's algorithm has become a favoured example to demonstrate the superiority of quantum computing for searching databases. However, this application is a little misleading. To perform a real quantum search in a database, the data would need to be represented as a superposition of quantum states. Moreover, this representation needs to be created at nontrivial high speeds and be readily available for processing through some sort of quantum version of random access memory (RAM). Although the notion of quantum random access memory (QRAM) has been proposed [3], they are not practically available at the time of writing.

Grover's algorithm is better thought of as an algorithm that can tell us whether something is in a dataset or not. Metaphorically, think of the puzzle books *Where's Wally?* (or *Where's Waldo?* in the USA) [6]. The books consist of illustrations depicting hundreds of characters doing a variety of amusing things in busy scenarios. Readers are challenged to find a specific character, named Wally, hidden in the illustrations. Assuming that it would be possible to represent those illustrations as quantum states in superposition, then Grover's algorithm would be able to tell us rather quickly whether or not Wally is in there.

3.4.1.1 Oracle

Mathematically, the *Where's Wally* puzzle can be formalised as a problem of finding the unique input(s) to a given function that produces a required result.

Let us formalise a simple musical example: assuming that the following binary string $s = 10100101$ represents the musical note A5, the function $f(x)$ returns 1 when $x = s$, and 0 otherwise:

$$f(x) = \begin{cases} 1 & \text{if } x = 10100101 \equiv A5 \\ 0 & \text{if otherwise} \end{cases} \tag{3.3}$$

For quantum computing, the function above is best represented as:

$$f(|\Psi\rangle) = \begin{cases} |1\rangle & \text{if } |\Psi\rangle = |10100101\rangle \equiv |A5\rangle \\ |0\rangle & \text{if otherwise} \end{cases} \tag{3.4}$$

In order to use a quantum computer to find out if, say, a musical composition contains the note A5, all of its notes would need to be provided in superposition to the function.

The standard method for conducting a search for note A5 is to check every note one by one. However, a quantum computer running Grover's algorithm would be able to return a result with a considerably lower number of queries.

Suppose that the composition in question has 1,000 notes. The best-case scenario would be when the first note that the system checks is the one it is looking for. Conversely, the worse case would be when the note it is looking for is the last one checked. In this case, the system would have made 1,000 queries to give us an answer. On average, we could say that the system would have to make $N/2$ queries; that is, with $N = 1000$, then $1000/2 = 500$ queries. Conversely, Grover's algorithm would require $\sqrt{N}$ queries; i.e., $\sqrt{1000} \approx 31$ queries. This is significantly faster.

In practice, for a quantum computer we need to turn $f(|\Psi\rangle)$ into a quantum gate $\mathbf{U}_f$ describing a unitary linear transformation.

$$\mathbf{U}_{f(|\Psi\rangle)} |x\rangle_7 = \begin{cases} -|y\rangle_7 & \text{if } |x\rangle_7 = |y\rangle_7 \ (\text{which is to say}, f(|y\rangle_7) = 1 \text{ for A5}) \\ |x\rangle_7 & \text{if otherwise} \end{cases}$$

$$\tag{3.5}$$

The gate $\mathbf{U}_f$ is what we referred to earlier as an oracle. Note that the oracle marks the target state by flipping the sign of the input that satisfies the condition. The rest is left unchanged. The reason for doing this will become clearer below. Effectively, the oracle $\mathcal{O}(R2)$ in Eq. 3.2 yields a $\mathbf{U}_f$ with 4 target states.

3.4.1.2 Amplitude Remixing

As a didactic example to illustrate how amplitude amplification works, let us consider a two-qubit quantum system $|\phi\rangle$, which gives 4 states on the standard basis, corresponding to 4 possible outcomes:

$$|00\rangle = \begin{bmatrix} 1 \\ 0 \\ 0 \\ 0 \end{bmatrix}, \quad |01\rangle = \begin{bmatrix} 0 \\ 1 \\ 0 \\ 0 \end{bmatrix}, \quad |10\rangle = \begin{bmatrix} 0 \\ 0 \\ 1 \\ 0 \end{bmatrix}, \quad |11\rangle = \begin{bmatrix} 0 \\ 0 \\ 0 \\ 1 \end{bmatrix} \tag{3.6}$$

If we put the qubits in balanced superposition, then the amplitudes of all possible states will be equally distributed; i.e., $1/\sqrt{2^2}$ each, which gives $\left| 1/\sqrt{2^2} \right|^2 = 0.25$.

Fig. 3.14 Two-qubit system
in balanced superposition

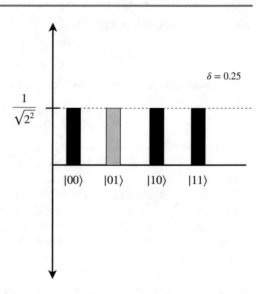

In other words, we would end up with an equal probability of 25% of obtaining any
of the outcomes:

$$\mathbf{H}^{\otimes 2}\,|\phi\rangle \Rightarrow |\phi_1\rangle = \left[\frac{1}{\sqrt{2^2}}\,|00\rangle + \frac{1}{\sqrt{2^2}}\,|01\rangle + \frac{1}{\sqrt{2^2}}\,|10\rangle + \frac{1}{\sqrt{2^2}}\,|11\rangle\right] \quad (3.7)$$

The graph in Fig. 3.14 depicts a visual representation of this balanced superposi-
tion. The variable δ is the squared average amplitude: $\delta = \left|1/\sqrt{2^2}\right|^2 = 0.25$.

In more detail:

$$\mathbf{H}^{\otimes 2} = \mathbf{H} \otimes \mathbf{H} = \frac{1}{\sqrt{2}}\begin{bmatrix} 1 & 1 \\ 1 & -1 \end{bmatrix} \otimes \frac{1}{\sqrt{2}}\begin{bmatrix} 1 & 1 \\ 1 & -1 \end{bmatrix} = \frac{1}{\sqrt{2^2}}\begin{bmatrix} 1 & 1 & 1 & 1 \\ 1 & -1 & 1 & -1 \\ 1 & 1 & -1 & -1 \\ 1 & -1 & -1 & 1 \end{bmatrix} \quad (3.8)$$

Therefore:

$$\mathbf{H}^{\otimes 2}\,|00\rangle = \frac{1}{\sqrt{2^2}}\begin{bmatrix} 1 & 1 & 1 & 1 \\ 1 & -1 & 1 & -1 \\ 1 & 1 & -1 & -1 \\ 1 & -1 & -1 & 1 \end{bmatrix}\begin{bmatrix} 1 \\ 0 \\ 0 \\ 0 \end{bmatrix} = \frac{1}{\sqrt{2^2}}\begin{bmatrix} 1 \\ 1 \\ 1 \\ 1 \end{bmatrix} \quad (3.9)$$

Let us suppose that the target state that we are looking for is $|01\rangle$. The oracle $\mathscr{O}$
to mark this target would look like this:

$$\mathscr{O} = \begin{bmatrix} 1 & 0 & 0 & 0 \\ 0 & -1 & 0 & 0 \\ 0 & 0 & 1 & 0 \\ 0 & 0 & 0 & 1 \end{bmatrix} \quad (3.10)$$

Fig. 3.15 The oracle inverts the amplitude of the target state

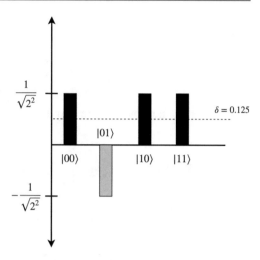

If the apply the oracle $\mathcal{O}$ to mark the target on $|\phi_1\rangle$ (Eq.3.7), then the target's signal will be flipped. That is, its amplitude will be reversed:

$$\mathcal{O}\,|\phi_1\rangle \Rightarrow |\phi_2\rangle = \left[\frac{1}{\sqrt{2^2}}\,|00\rangle \left(-\frac{1}{\sqrt{2^2}}\,|01\rangle\right) + \frac{1}{\sqrt{2^2}}\,|10\rangle + \frac{1}{\sqrt{2^2}}\,|11\rangle\right]$$

(3.11)

$$|\phi_2\rangle = \frac{1}{\sqrt{2^2}}\,[|00\rangle - |01\rangle + |10\rangle + |11\rangle]$$

The graph in Fig. 3.15 illustrates the effect of reversing the amplitude. The squared average has halved: $\delta = \left|1/\sqrt{2.82^2}\right|^2 \approx 0.125$.

In more detail:

$$\mathcal{O}\,|\phi_1\rangle \Rightarrow |\phi_2\rangle = \begin{bmatrix} 1 & 0 & 0 & 0 \\ 0 & -1 & 0 & 0 \\ 0 & 0 & 1 & 0 \\ 0 & 0 & 0 & 1 \end{bmatrix} \frac{1}{\sqrt{2^2}} \begin{bmatrix} 1 \\ 1 \\ 1 \\ 1 \end{bmatrix} = \frac{1}{\sqrt{2^2}} \begin{bmatrix} 1 \\ -1 \\ 1 \\ 1 \end{bmatrix} \text{ or } \begin{bmatrix} 1/\sqrt{2^2} \\ -1/\sqrt{2^2} \\ 1/\sqrt{2^2} \\ 1/\sqrt{2^2} \end{bmatrix}$$

(3.12)

Obviously, reversing the amplitude of the target still does not change the equal chance of obtaining any of the 4 outcomes. It is at this stage that amplitude amplification is put into action. What it does is unbalance the amplitudes of the quantum system: it will augment the amplitude of the marked target state and decrease the amplitudes of all others so that when measuring the system we would almost certainly obtain the target. Hence, we propose to refer to this procedure as *amplitude remixing* rather than amplitude amplification.

An amplitude remixer is defined as a unitary linear transformation, or gate $\mathbf{U}_\varphi$, as follows:

$$\mathbf{U}_\varphi = \mathbf{H}^{\otimes n}\,\mathbf{S}\,\mathbf{H}^{\otimes n}$$

(3.13)

The operator $\mathbf{S}$ acts as a conditional shift matrix operator of the form:

$$\mathbf{S} = \begin{bmatrix} 1 & 0 & 0 & 0 \\ 0 & e^{i\pi} & 0 & 0 \\ 0 & 0 & e^{i\pi} & 0 \\ 0 & 0 & 0 & e^{i\pi} \end{bmatrix} = \begin{bmatrix} 1 & 0 & 0 & 0 \\ 0 & -1 & 0 & 0 \\ 0 & 0 & -1 & 0 \\ 0 & 0 & 0 & -1 \end{bmatrix} \tag{3.14}$$

Thus, the application of $\mathbf{U}_\varphi$ to $|\phi_2\rangle$ looks like this:

$$\mathbf{U}_\varphi |\phi_2\rangle \Rightarrow \mathbf{H}^{\otimes n} |\phi_2\rangle \rightarrow |\phi_3\rangle = \frac{1}{\sqrt{2^2}} \begin{bmatrix} 1 & 1 & 1 & 1 \\ 1 & -1 & 1 & -1 \\ 1 & 1 & -1 & -1 \\ 1 & -1 & -1 & 1 \end{bmatrix} \frac{1}{\sqrt{2^2}} \begin{bmatrix} 1 \\ -1 \\ 1 \\ 1 \end{bmatrix} = \frac{1}{\sqrt{4^2}} \begin{bmatrix} 2 \\ 2 \\ -2 \\ 2 \end{bmatrix} = \frac{1}{\sqrt{2^2}} \begin{bmatrix} 1 \\ 1 \\ -1 \\ 1 \end{bmatrix}$$

$$\mathbf{S} |\phi_3\rangle \rightarrow |\phi_4\rangle = \begin{bmatrix} 1 & 0 & 0 & 0 \\ 0 & -1 & 0 & 0 \\ 0 & 0 & -1 & 0 \\ 0 & 0 & 0 & -1 \end{bmatrix} \frac{1}{\sqrt{2^2}} \begin{bmatrix} 1 \\ 1 \\ -1 \\ 1 \end{bmatrix} = \frac{1}{\sqrt{2^2}} \begin{bmatrix} 1 \\ -1 \\ 1 \\ -1 \end{bmatrix}$$

$$\mathbf{H}^{\otimes n} |\phi_4\rangle \rightarrow |\phi_5\rangle = \frac{1}{\sqrt{2^2}} \begin{bmatrix} 1 & 1 & 1 & 1 \\ 1 & -1 & 1 & -1 \\ 1 & 1 & -1 & -1 \\ 1 & -1 & -1 & 1 \end{bmatrix} \frac{1}{\sqrt{2^2}} \begin{bmatrix} 1 \\ -1 \\ 1 \\ -1 \end{bmatrix} = \frac{1}{\sqrt{4^2}} \begin{bmatrix} 0 \\ 4 \\ 0 \\ 0 \end{bmatrix} = 1 \begin{bmatrix} 0 \\ 1 \\ 0 \\ 0 \end{bmatrix}$$

$$\tag{3.15}$$

So, $|\phi_5\rangle = 1.0 |01\rangle$, which gives $|1|^2 = 1$, or in other words, there is now a 100% chance for outcome $|01\rangle$. The graph in Fig. 3.16 shows what happened with the amplitudes of our a two-qubit system. The quantum computing literature often refers to this effect as an *inversion about the mean*.

To summarize, the transformation $\mathbf{U}_{f(|\Psi\rangle)} \mathbf{U}_\varphi |\phi\rangle$ transforms $|\phi\rangle$ towards a target state $|\Psi\rangle$. This worked well for the above didactic two-qubit system. But

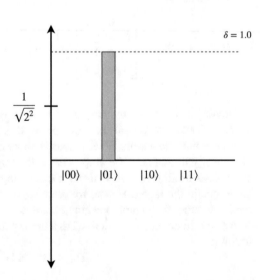

Fig. 3.16 There is now a 100% chance for outcome $|01\rangle$

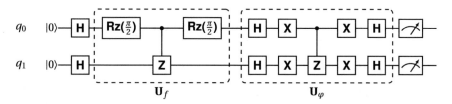

Fig. 3.17 Quantum circuit implementation of the $\mathbf{U}_f\mathbf{U}\varphi\,|\phi\rangle$ interference transformation ($\mathbf{Z}$ is $\mathbf{Rz}(\pi)$)

for systems with higher number of qubits it is necessary to apply the transformation a number of times. The necessary number of iterations is calculated as:

$i = \lfloor \frac{\pi\sqrt{\frac{2^n}{T}}}{4} \rfloor \approx \lfloor 0.7854\sqrt{\frac{2^n}{T}} \rfloor$, where n is the number of qubits and T is the number

of targets. Thus, for 2 qubits and 1 target, $i = \lfloor 0.7854\sqrt{\frac{2^2}{1}} \rfloor = \lfloor 0.7854\sqrt{4} \rfloor = 1$. And also, $i = 1$ for the Basak-Miranda algorithm example for Rule 2, with 4 target

states, as discussed earlier: $i = \lfloor 0.7854\sqrt{\frac{2^4}{4}} \rfloor = 1$. (We use the floor of i, generally because the floor requires a shallower circuit. In case of $i < 1$ then $i = 1$.) Should the example above have required more iterations, the "Oracle" and "Quantum Circuit" stages of the block diagram in Fig. 3.13 would have to be repeated accordingly.

A quantum circuit implementing the transformation $\mathbf{U}_f\mathbf{U}\varphi\,|\phi\rangle$ discussed above is shown in Fig. 3.17. The same architecture applies to the Basak-Miranda algorithm depicted in Fig. 3.13. One just needs to stack two additional qubits to the circuit. And, of course, the oracle $\mathbf{U}_f$ is replaced each time a different rule is evaluated.

3.4.2 An Example

An example of an outcome from the Basak-Miranda algorithm acting on Table 3.2 is shown in Fig. 3.18. In this example, rhythm is not considered; hence all notes are of the same duration.

Consider the histograms in Fig. 3.19, showing four cycles of the algorithm. As with the 3-D musical random walk example, 40 shots for each cycle were sufficient here to obtain plausible results.[7]

The initial pitch is D♯. Therefore, the system starts by processing Rule 2, which stipulates that one of these four pitches is allowed next: E, C♯, F♯ or G♯. That is, the target states are $|0\rangle_4$, $|3\rangle_4$, $|4\rangle_4$ and $|6\rangle_4$. In this instance the algorithm picked pitch E, because this is the option that would have been measured most frequently; i.e., the winner is $|0\rangle_4$, represented as 0000 on the histogram (Fig. 3.19, Cycle 1).

Now, the current pitch is E. So, the rule to be processed next is Rule 1. According to this rule, only pitches F or D♯ can follow E. The target states are $|1\rangle_4$ and $|5\rangle_4$.

---

[7] For this example we used IBM Quantum's QASM simulator.

Fig. 3.18 Musical output yielded by the the Basak-Miranda algorithm

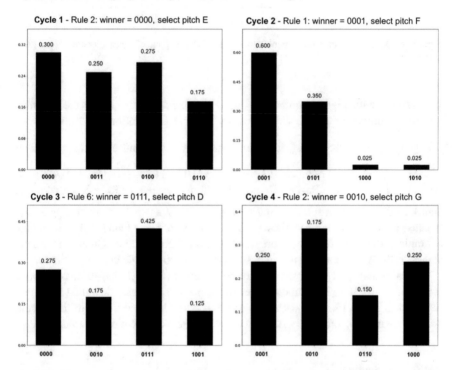

Fig. 3.19 Histograms from running the Basak-Miranda algorithm for 4 cycles. The vertical coordinate is the percentage of times an item listed on the horizontal coordinate occurred

And in this case, the system picked pitch F, because the winner state would have been $|1\rangle_4$ (0001 on the histogram in Fig. 3.19, Cycle 2).

Next, the current pitch is F. And so, the system processes Rule 6, which specifies 4 possible pitches: E, G, D or C. That is, the target states are $|0\rangle_4$, $|2\rangle_4$, $|7\rangle_4$ and $|9\rangle_4$. The winner state is $|7\rangle_4$, or 0111 on the histogram (Fig. 3.19, Cycle 3). And so on.

3.5 Concluding Discussion

Quantum computing is a nascent technology. But one that is advancing rapidly.

There is a long history of research into using computers for making music. Nowadays, computers are absolutely essential for the music economy. Therefore, it is very likely that quantum computers will impact the music industry in time to come. A new area of research and development is emerging: *Quantum Computer Music*. This chapter laid the foundations of this new exciting field.

In many ways, in terms of the development stage, it is fair to compare state-of-the-art quantum computers with the computer mainframes of the 1950s. It is hard to imagine what computers will be like in 2090, in the same way, that it must have been hard for our forefathers of the 1950s to imagine how computers look like today. But in contrast to 70 years ago, today's musicians are generally conversant with computing technology. Hence we believe that the time is ripe to start experimenting with quantum computers in music [9].

A sensible entryway in this fascinating field is to revisit tried-and-tested computer music methods and repurpose them for quantum computing. As one becomes increasingly more acquainted with core concepts and techniques, new quantum-specific algorithms for music will emerge. An example of this is the Basak-Miranda algorithm introduced above, probably the first-ever bespoke rule-based quantum algorithm for generating music.

Still, it is important to note, however, that the Basak-Miranda algorithm presents two important caveats, that one needs to bear in mind when using it. Firstly, if the number of desirable results is equal to half of the number of all possible states, then we get a circuit with an equal superposition of all states; that is, including the states that we do not want as results. And secondly, if the number of desirable results is higher than half of the number of all possible states, then undesirable results will get higher counts in the measurements. Thus, as a rule of thumb, the number of desirable results must be less than half the number of possible states.

As compared to an ordinary laptop computer, it must be acknowledged that there is absolutely no advantage to running the systems introduced in this chapter on a quantum computer. The problems are somewhat trivial. And quantum computing hardware is not yet available to tackle complex music problems. Indeed, all the examples above were run on software simulations of quantum hardware. At this stage, we are not advocating any quantum advantage for musical applications. What we advocate, however, is that the music technology community should be quantum-ready for when quantum computing hardware becomes more sophisticated, widely available, and possibly advantageous for creativity and business. Nevertheless, we propose that quantum computing is bringing two benefits to music: (a) a new paradigm for creativity and (b) algorithm speed-up.

It is a fact that computing has always been influencing how musicians create music [16]. For instance, there are certain styles of music that would have never been created if programming languages did not exist. Indeed, as was already mentioned in Chap. 1 in this volume, there are music genres nowadays where the audience watches musicians programming live on stage (as if they were playing musical instruments), and nightclubs where the DJs write code live instead of spinning records [2]. We anticipate that new ways of thinking boosted by quantum programming, and the modelling and simulations afforded by quantum computing, will constitute a new paradigm for creativity, which would not have been emerged otherwise. An example of this is the composition *Zeno* by the first author [10,11].

As for algorithm speed-up, it is too early to corroborate any hypothesis one could possibly make at this stage. It has been argued that quantum walk on real quantum hardware would be faster than classical random walk to navigate vast mathematical spaces [7]. Quantum walk is an area of much interest for computer music.

Moreover, we hypothesise that the Basak-Miranda algorithm would work faster on quantum computers than on classical ones for considerable large chains and a higher number of target states. As discussed earlier, the interference technique is at the core of Grover's algorithm. To check for an element in an unstructured set of N elements, a brute-force classic algorithm would scan all elements in the set until it finds the one that is sought after. In the worst-case scenario, the element in question could have been the last one to be checked, which means that the algorithm would have made N queries to find it. Grover's algorithm would be able to find a solution with $\sqrt{N}$ queries. Thus, the algorithm provides a quadratic speedup. Theoretically, this benchmarking is applicable to assess the Basak-Miranda algorithm. But this must be verified in practice when suitable hardware becomes available, as there might be other factors to be considered; e.g., the extent to which ancillary classical processing is required alongside quantum processing to implement a practical system.

References

1. Bernhardt, C. (2019). *Quantum computing for everyone*. The MIT Press. ISBN: 978-0262039253.
2. Calore, M. (2019). DJs of the future don't spin records—They write code. Wired. https://www.wired.com/story/algoraves-live-coding-djs/. Accessed 08 May 2021.
3. Giovannetti, V., Lloyd, S., & Maccone, L. (2008). Quantum random access memory. *Physical Review Letters, 100*(16), 501–504. https://doi.org/10.1103/PhysRevLett.100.160501
4. Griffiths, D. J., & Schroeter, D. F. (2018). *Introduction to quantum mechanics*. Cambridge University Press. ISBN: 9781107189638.
5. Grover, L. K. (1997). Quantum mechanics helps in searching for a needle in a haystack. *Physical Review Letters, 79*(2), 325–328. https://doi.org/10.1103/PhysRevLett.79.325
6. Handford, M. (2007). *Where's wally?*. Walker Books. ISBN: 978-1406305890.
7. Kendon, V. M. (2006). A random walk approach to quantum algorithms. *Philosophical Transactions of the Royal Society, 364*, 3407–3422.
8. Mann, A., (Trans.). (1965). The Study of Counterpoint: From Johann Fux' Gradus ad Parnassum. W. W. Norton and Company. ISBN: 978-0393002775.
9. Miranda, E. R. (2021). Quantum computer: Hello, Music!. In E. R. Miranda (Ed.), *Handbook of artificial intelligence for music: Foundations, advanced approaches, and developments for creativity*. Springer International Publishing. ISBN: 9783030721152. arXiv:2006.13849 [cs.ET].
10. Miranda, E. R. (2020). Creative quantum computing: Inverse FFT, sound synthesis, adaptive sequencing and musical composition. In A. Adamatzky (Ed.), *Handbook of unconventional computing* (pp. 493–523). World Scientific. ISBN: 9789811235030. arXiv:2005.05832 [cs.SD].
11. Miranda, E. R. (2020). The arrival of quantum computer music. The Riff. https://medium.com/the-riff/the-arrival-of-quantum-computer-music-ed1ce51a8b8f. Accessed 08 May 2021.
12. Miranda, E. R. (2001). *Composing music with computers*. Elsevier Focal Press. ISBN: 9780240515670.

13. Perle, G. (1972). *Serial composition and atonality*. University of California Press. ISBN: 9780520019355.
14. Privault, N. (2013). *Understanding markov chains: Examples and applications*. Springer Singapore. ISBN: 9789814451512.
15. Rieffel, E., & Polak, W. (2011). *Quantum computing: A gentle introduction*. The MIT Press. ISBN: 9780262015066.
16. Roads, C. (2015). *Composing electronic music: A new aesthetic*. Oxford University Press. ISBN: 9780195373240.

Making Music Using Two Quantum Algorithms

4

Euan J. Allen, Jacob F. F. Bulmer, and Simon D. Small

Abstract

Computers have and continue to shape the sound and music landscape that we experience. Whether that be as tools to make music with or inspiration for writing and composing music, the impact of computation in a sound generation is not difficult to find. This chapter provides the background and specific details of a collaboration formed in 2021 between the Quantum Engineering Technology Labs—a quantum computing and technology research group at the University of Bristol—and music artist, producer and audio engineer Simon Small. The goal of the collaboration was to explore how the data and concepts used in the research at the university could be 'sonified' to create sounds or even make music.

4.1 Introduction

Quantum computers are a new type of device that completes computational tasks in a very different way to the (classical) computers we experience in everyday life. Utilising aspects of quantum physics, such as entanglement and superposition, quantum

E. J. Allen (✉)
Centre for Photonics and Photonic Materials, Department of Physics, University of Bath, Bath BA2 7AY, UK
e-mail: ea901@bath.ac.uk

E. J. Allen · J. F. F. Bulmer
Quantum Engineering Technology Labs, H. H. Wills Physics Laboratory, Department of Electrical and Electronic Engineering, University of Bristol, Bristol BS8 1FD, UK

S. D. Small
Tunnel of Reverb, London, UK
URL: https://www.tunnelofreverb.com/

© The Author(s), under exclusive license to Springer Nature Switzerland AG 2022
E. R Miranda (ed.), *Quantum Computer Music*,
https://doi.org/10.1007/978-3-031-13909-3_4

computers are able to solve problems which are very difficult for a classical computer to complete.

The manner in which quantum computers work is distinct from classical computers. It is therefore of interest to explore what impact this technology could have on future sound and music generation, much like the impact conventional computers had in the early 20th century. Conversely, it is also of interest to explore how sound and music might help in disseminating concepts of quantum physics and computing to a wider audience—an audience that will likely feel the impact of this technology at some point in the future.

Quantum computers work and process quantum information, typically stored in quantum bits (qubits), whilst classical machines process classical information, typically stored in binary bits taking a value of 0 or 1. Whilst there are examples of quantum versions of sound or acoustic waves (phonons) [1], all music and sound that is processed by the human ear in day-to-day life can be understood as being entirely classical. It is an interesting task to work out which quantum concepts or computational algorithms have a sufficiently interesting classical output during or at the end of the computation to make them audibly distinct or interesting in contrast to a classical machine. This is part of the task of exploring quantum computing music.

This chapter provides the background and specific details of a collaboration formed in 2021 between the Quantum Engineering Technology Labs [2]—a quantum computing and technology research group at the University of Bristol—and music artist, producer and audio engineer Simon Small [3]. The goal of the collaboration was to explore how the data and concepts used in the research at the university could be 'sonified' to create sounds or even make music.

The project focused on two key concepts for a sound generation: quantum random walks and Grover's search algorithm. These two quantum algorithms formed the basis for sound and music generation, the culmination of which resulted in two full musical compositions. This chapter is split into three key sections. The first two provide a technical introduction to both quantum random walks and Grover's algorithm, covering how the algorithms work and how to produce data from them that can be used to generate sound. The final section covers how to take this data and use it for musical composition. Details of other techniques used in the collaboration, such as audio samples from the laboratory, are also detailed in the final section.

The audio outcomes of the collaboration can be heard at the following Refs. [4,5]. These links include the final pieces, audio samples, and a full musical pack for other musicians to utilise the data and sounds generated from this work.

4.2 Random Melodies from Quantum Walks

A random walk is a great example of a place where there is a clear difference in the behaviour of quantum and classical physics [6]. It is therefore frequently used as a thought experiment to teach the concepts of quantum mechanics, but has also been used to inspire quantum algorithms [7], and has been realised in experiments [8]. This section investigates how we can use the difference between classical and quantum random walks to create contrasting musical melodies.

We first describe how we define a quantum random walk, and show how measurement can lead to classical dynamics. We then discuss how we simulate these systems. Although there are a wide variety of excellent quantum simulation libraries, we chose to implement our simulation using only Python and NumPy. This allows us to clearly see how all of our operations are defined and implemented. Our code can be found at: https://github.com/jakeffbulmer/random_walks.

4.2.1 Quantum Random Walks

We will define our random walk as follows, imagine that every time you want to take a step, you toss a coin. If it lands on heads, you step to the left. If it lands on tails, you step to the right. We add a further rule of a *periodic boundary condition*, which can be described by saying that we have a fixed number of sites to stand on, if you reach the left edge, and need to step to the left, you move to the right edge and vice versa. This is equivalent to arranging our sites in a circle where if you go all the way around the circle you end up back where you started.

We wish for our sites to neatly correspond to musical notes in a scale, so we choose to use 14 sites, labelled from 0 to 13, which can then be turned into notes from 2 octaves of an 8-note scale.

If we assume that the state of our coin, and the site our walker is standing on are prepared independently from each other, our quantum system can be defined as shown in Eq. (4.1).

$$|\psi\rangle = |C\rangle \otimes |S\rangle \tag{4.1}$$

$|C\rangle$ is the wavefunction describing the coin and $|S\rangle$ is the wavefunction describing the site. The symbol "$\otimes$" is a tensor product, which here we can just think of as a symbol which shows that we are taking the two systems $|C\rangle$ and $|S\rangle$ and thinking of them as one system. We define coin basis states: $|\text{heads}\rangle$ and $|\text{tails}\rangle$, and site basis states $|j\rangle$ where j can take any value from 0 to 13 ($j \in \{0, 1, 2, \ldots, 13\}$).

The operation we apply to simulate a coin toss is a Hadamard rotation. This maps the coin states as shown in Eqs. (4.2) and (4.3).

$$|\text{head}\rangle \rightarrow \frac{|\text{heads}\rangle + |\text{tails}\rangle}{\sqrt{2}} \tag{4.2}$$

$$|\text{tails}\rangle \rightarrow \frac{|\text{heads}\rangle - |\text{tails}\rangle}{\sqrt{2}} \tag{4.3}$$

These two states are equal superposition states between heads and tails, with a phase difference between the two. We also need an operation which will move the site of the walker, depending on the outcome of the coin. We call this the *move* operator, $\hat{M}$.

$$\hat{M} = |\text{heads}\rangle\langle\text{heads}| \otimes \sum_{j=0}^{13} |(j+1)\text{mod } 14\rangle\langle j|$$

$$+ |\text{tails}\rangle\langle\text{tails}| \otimes \sum_{j=0}^{13} |(j-1)\text{mod } 14\rangle\langle j| \tag{4.4}$$

By inspecting Eq. (4.4), we can see that when this operator is applied to a state $|\psi\rangle$, the walker will move to an adjacent site. For a term containing a $|\text{heads}\rangle$ coin state, this will be a site to the right $(+1)$ and for $|\text{tails}\rangle$, it the left (-1).

Also notice the "mod 14" operation. This modulo division means that if we try to step to position $j = 14$, we move to $j = 0$, since 14 mod 14 = 0. Likewise, if try to move to $j = -1$, we move to $j = 13$. This is what allows us to encode the periodic boundary and put the sites in the circle configuration.

To implement our quantum walk, we alternate between applying Hadamard operations to the coin, and then the move operation to our coin and walker system. The move operation generates entanglement between the site of the walker and the state of the coin. Eventually, the state $|\psi\rangle$ will have support across the whole Hilbert space, which exists in $2 \times 14 = 28$ dimensions.

As an example, we will work out the state of the system explicitly after the first steps. Let us imagine that we started in position $j = 7$, and we initialise our coin in $|\text{heads}\rangle$.

$$|\psi\rangle = |\text{heads}\rangle \otimes |7\rangle \tag{4.5}$$

We apply the Hadamard operation to the coin.

$$\hat{H} \otimes \mathbf{1} |\psi\rangle = \frac{(|\text{heads}\rangle + |\text{tails}\rangle) \otimes |7\rangle}{\sqrt{2}} \tag{4.6}$$

Here, $\mathbf{1}$ is the identity operation (i.e. the do-nothing operation) acting on the walker. Then we apply the move operation to the system.

$$\hat{M}(\hat{H} \otimes \mathbf{1}) |\psi\rangle = \frac{|\text{heads}\rangle \otimes |8\rangle + |\text{tails}\rangle \otimes |6\rangle}{\sqrt{2}} \tag{4.7}$$

The resulting state, shown in Eq. (4.7), is now *entangled*, as we can no longer consider the coin and the walker state separately. If we were to measure position of the walker, and see it was at position 8, we would know that the coin was showing heads.

If we apply the coin flip then the move operation several times before we measure, we would have a much more complicated state. However, all of the terms in the state would contain either a heads of a tails outcome. If we want to know the probability of the walker being in a particular position, but we do not care about the state of the coin, we can sum together the heads and tails probabilities associated with that position.

$$p(j) = p(j, \text{heads}) + p(j, \text{tails}) \tag{4.8}$$

$p(j)$ is the probability of the walker being in position j, and $p(j, \text{heads/tails})$ is the probability of a walker being in position j with the coin in a state heads/tails respectively.

To get these probabilities, we just have to apply the *Born rule*. This tells us that the probabilities of measuring a quantum state is given by the absolute-square of the amplitude of the state.

For example, we see below that the probability for measuring the state in Eq. (4.7) in position $j = 6$ is $1/2$.

$$p(j = 6) = p(j = 6, \text{heads}) + p(j = 6, \text{tails}) \tag{4.9}$$

$$= 0 + \left| \frac{1}{\sqrt{2}} \right|^2 \tag{4.10}$$

$$= 1/2 \tag{4.11}$$

However, an important fact of quantum mechanics is that we disturb a system when we measure it. If we perform a measurement of the position of the walker, we collapse it to the result of the measurement. In the case above, we would end up with $|S\rangle = |6\rangle$.

So, we had a 50% chance of seeing the tails outcome and moving to the left. We see this movement, and we now know that we are in position 6. If we consider repeating this process every step, we see that measurement at each step collapses our random walk into completely classical dynamics.

We wish to also probe the quantum dynamics of our system, and so we give ourselves some abilities which cannot be achieved in real-world quantum experiments: we let ourselves look *inside* the state. In simulation, we can see the probability of a given measurement from occurring without needing to perform the measurement. It is this ability which we harness to generate data for our quantum walk.

We could actually replicate the dynamics of looking inside the state in an experiment by making some changes to the rules. Here, what we would have to do is after each measurement, we start the walk again from the beginning. Before we make the next measurement, we let the walker take one more step than in for the previous measurement before we take the next measurement.

4.2.2 The Walker's Journey

When we simulate the random walk we are returned with a sequence of integers. In our simulation, we can choose whether or not our measurement collapses the state. As discussed above, collapsing the state at each measurement recovers the dynamics of the classical random walk. We see that both classical and quantum start returning numbers close to the starting position, gradually drifting apart. The classical version only can take one step to the left or right each time, whereas the quantum version can take larger steps. This is reminiscent of how a quantum wavefunction spreads out over time. Importantly, this creates clearly noticeable differences to the melodies created from the data.

4.3 Grover's Algorithm

Grover's search algorithm is one of the most well know algorithms that can be run on a quantum computer. It was first introduced by Lov Kumar Grover in 1996/7 [9, 10] and tackles a problem known as an 'unstructured search'. We introduce this specific problem in Sect. 4.3.1 and discuss how a quantum computer may offer an improvement in implementing such an algorithm. The specific details of the algorithm and how it can be implemented on a quantum computer are discussed in Sect. 4.3.2. Data outputs are provided from the algorithm at various points.

4.3.1 An Unstructured Search

The problem that Grover's algorithm can be applied to is that of searching through a list or database of entries to find a particular value of interest. An example would be searching for a particular piece of music in a database. In particular, the problem of interest is applied to an *unstructured* list, whereby the entries in the database are listed randomly (rather than, for example, in alphabetical order). Whilst this type of problem seems a simple one, searching for an entry in a database is a fundamental feature of many computational tasks and most of that data is unsorted [11].

In order to be able to say that the quantum (Grover's) algorithm is better than the classical one, we need to assess how difficult it is to complete the unstructured search task classically. If we consider a database with N entries in a completely random order, then the task is to search through the list to find a particular song title. A simple method would be to just go through the entries, searching until you find the title you want. If N is large, then the initial probability of finding the entry is very small. As you check more and more titles, the probability of finding the one you want increases. Eventually, after checking half the entries $(N/2)$ you will have a 50% chance of finding the track you want. That's to say, that if you want a 50% chance of finding the correct entry, you will have to check $N/2$ times.

Note that if we double the size of our database, then the number of entries we have to check to get a 50% probability also doubles. Similarly, if the database gets a million times larger, it takes a million times longer to find the result. This is an indication of how the algorithm *scales* and is predicted entirely by the dependence of the algorithm on N (in this case, a linear dependence). Sometimes, the scaling of the algorithm with N is the only bit of information that is relevant to the comparison. In this case, the algorithm is said to scale as $\mathcal{O}(N)$ or 'with a leading order linear in N'. Note that whilst we have discussed here a very particular method of searching the database classically, one actually finds that any classical algorithm will complete the search task $\mathcal{O}(N)$ [9].

In contrast to classical methods, Grover derived an algorithm using a quantum computer that is able to complete the task with only $\mathcal{O}(\sqrt{N})$ accesses to the database [9, 10]. What this means is that if the database doubles in size, then the quantum algorithm only takes $\sqrt{2}$ longer, or about 1.4 times. If it goes up by a factor of one million, then the quantum algorithm only needs one thousand times longer. If we assume that to check each track title in the database takes a certain fixed amount of time, then the quantum algorithm will be able to search much faster than the classical one—particularly for very large lists. Even in the case where the quantum algorithm is slower at checking entries than the classical one, there will always be a value of N (a size of database) where the quantum algorithm outperforms the classical one and can complete the task is less time.

4.3.2 Structure of the Algorithm

This section will give a surface level overview of Grover's algorithm and how it is implemented on a quantum computer. We will give particular focus to aspects of the algorithm that are relevant to later sections. A more detailed description of how the algorithm works can be found in Refs. [9, 10, 12].

Suppose we want to search through a list of eight entries, which we label using binary encoding: 000, 001, 010, 011, 100, 101, 110, 111, or alternatively from 0 to 7. These can be encoded using three qubits $|q_1 q_2 q_3\rangle$ with any measurement of q_1, q_2, or q_3 taking a value of 0 or 1. The goal of the quantum algorithm is to take in a set input qubit register of qubits in the state $|000\rangle$, perform some kind of manipulation and computation on the qubits, and then (ideally) output the qubit values which correspond to the entry we are searching for. For this example we consider the entry we are searching for to be $|110\rangle$, or entry 6, but in principle the algorithm works for any of the eight possible outcomes.

The operations performed on the qubits during any algorithm are defined by quantum gates. The arrangement of quantum gates for Grover's algorithm are shown in Fig. 4.1. Each horizontal line or 'rail' corresponds to a qubit (q_1, q_2, and q_3), with operations or gates defined by any square or circle drawn on the rail, running in order from left to right. In this case, the quantum gates required to perform the algorithm include the Hadamard (H), Pauli X (X), and control-NOT (control node •, 'NOT' node ⊕) gate. These gates in total perform the algorithm as desired. A more detailed description of why this arrangement of quantum gates performs Grover's algorithm can be found in the following Refs. [9, 10, 12, 13].

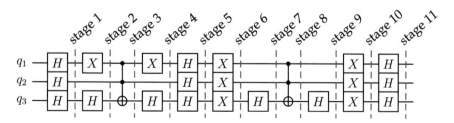

Fig. 4.1 A three qubit Grover's algorithm implementation. Each horizontal line (or 'rail') corresponds to an individual qubit q_x with boxes on that rail representing quantum gates acting on each qubit. The gates displayed include the Hadamard (H), Pauli X (X), and control-NOT (control node •, 'NOT' node ⊕). The algorithm runs from left to right

As we have stated previously, at the start of the algorithm the qubits are initiated in the state $|000\rangle$. The first action of the algorithm is to apply a Hadamard gate (H) to each qubit. The action of this gate on an initial state $|0\rangle$ can be described as $|0\rangle \xrightarrow{H} \frac{|0\rangle+|1\rangle}{\sqrt{2}}$, and so a Hadamard generates an equal superposition of $|0\rangle$ and $|1\rangle$. When a Hadamard is applied to all three initial qubit states, the quantum state generated is an equal superposition across all possible qubit outcomes: $|000\rangle \xrightarrow{H} \frac{|000\rangle+|001\rangle+|010\rangle+\cdots+|111\rangle}{\sqrt{8}}$. The amplitude of the quantum wavefunction is equally split between all possible measurement outcomes. Practically, what this means is that at stage 1 in the algorithm, any measurement of the qubits has an equal chance of outputting any of the eight possible binary output values. In a sense, at this point in the algorithm the particular value we are looking for is completely unknown. Asking the algorithm which entry in the list is the one we are looking for (by measuring the state of the qubits at this point), will randomly output any of the possible entries.

The complete randomness of stage 1 is in complete contrast with the end of the algorithm (stage 11) which, as we have already stated, will ideally always output 110 and therefore has all of its quantum amplitude in the state $|110\rangle$. In practice, the end of the algorithm manipulates *most* of the quantum amplitude to the state $|110\rangle$ because of small details in how the algorithm works or noise in the quantum machine completing the computation. It is the goal of the applied gates/the algorithm to redistribute the wavefunction to place the maximal amount in the correct output. This means that at the end of the computation, we have the greatest chance to measure the correct qubit output values and therefore find our entry. This contrast between the complete randomness of the start of the algorithm, and the complete (or near-complete) determinism of the end of the algorithm is why it was of interest for music generation. The journey between these two stages is also of interest and gives insight into the inner workings of Grover's algorithm.

4.3.3 Simulating Grover's Algorithm

There are a number of publicly available tools to simulate Grover's algorithm. Here we focus on QuTech's Quantum Inspire Home Platform [14] which allows users to simulate the algorithm and measure qubit outcomes after processing. Simulating the algorithm allows a user to generate lists of measurement outcomes at each stage in the algorithm which can then but used as source material for sound and music generation.

Each measurement of the qubit values is probabilistic, with the probability of measuring any particular outcome described by the wavefunction amplitude of that qubit outcome at that point in the algorithm. This means that preparing the qubits in the state $|000\rangle$, processing to a particular stage of the algorithm, and then measuring the qubits will produce a different output if you repeat it multiple times. For example, at stage 1, a set of ten measurements could produce the following outcome (where we have not converted back from binary to numerical values, e.g. 010 = 2): 1, 0, 3,

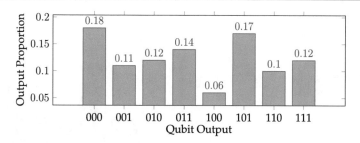

Fig. 4.2 Histogram plot of the qubit measurement outcomes for stage 4 in the algorithm as defined by Fig. 4.1. The numbers relate to the proportion of measurement outcomes of that particular value for 100 measurements of the qubit state at stage 4

2, 4, 7, 2, 2, 6, 2. Similarly, a set of ten measurements at stage 11 of the algorithm produces the following output: 6, 6, 3, 5, 6, 6, 6, 6, 6, 6. These two lists demonstrate the contrast discussed before between the complete randomness of stage 1 and the (near) deterministic output of stage 11—always outputting our correct entry value '6'. By completing a tally of the proportion of each output we measure, each stage can also be displayed graphically. This is complete for 100 measurements of stage 4 in the algorithm in Fig. 4.2.

The Quantum Inspire Home Platform [14] allows one to simulate all stages of the algorithm and make multiple measurements of the state at each stage. Completing this process and making 100 measurements at each stage produces 11 lists of 100 numbers. The proportion of each measurement outcome at each stage of the algorithm completed using this platform is presented in Table 4.1 and Fig. 4.3. This list of numbers, documenting the state of the qubits at each point in the algorithm, can be

Table 4.1 The proportion of measurement outcomes generated for 100 measurements of the qubit state at all 11 stages of Grover's algorithm

Stage	Proportion of measurement outcomes							
	000	001	010	011	100	101	110	111
1	0.19	0.16	0.08	0.12	0.07	0.12	0.14	0.12
2	0.20	0.09	0.10	0.13	0.16	0.07	0.15	0.10
3	0.10	0.10	0.10	0.17	0.13	0.09	0.19	0.12
4	0.18	0.11	0.12	0.14	0.06	0.17	0.10	0.12
5	0.25	0.25	0.03	0.00	0.03	0.06	0.03	0.35
6	0.04	0.05	0.03	0.30	0.03	0.23	0.03	0.29
7	0.11	0.14	0.09	0.12	0.00	0.00	0.00	0.54
8	0.03	0.02	0.04	0.02	0.25	0.36	0.23	0.05
9	0.12	0.64	0.06	0.00	0.07	0.00	0.11	0.00
10	0.00	0.00	0.16	0.11	0.11	0.14	0.48	0.00
11	0.00	0.01	0.02	0.02	0.01	0.02	0.92	0.00

Fig. 4.3 Proportion of each
qubit outcome measured at
different stages of Grover's
algorithm. The data
presented here is also
displayed in Table 4.1

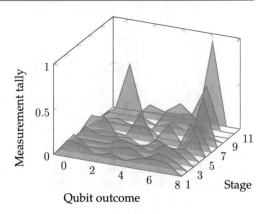

used as a seed for sound and music generation. This is described in the following
section, where the numbers for each stage were used to define the pitch of the melody
at different points in the piece.

4.4 Making Music Using Quantum Algorithms

In this section, the process of taking raw data from Grover's algorithm and the
quantum random walk and translating it into an appropriate format for making music
is discussed. Section 4.4.1 explains how the MAX MSP programming language
turns this data into MIDI and then transmits it for musical hardware and software to
interpret. Cycling 74's MAX MSP is a visual programming language for music and
multimedia. Section 4.4.2 discusses the musical nature of the data and the audible
differences between the algorithms. Section 4.4.3 features a quote from the composer,
Simon Small, about the composition process and he discusses the emotional reaction
to the quantum-data driven melodies.

4.4.1 Raw Data and Processing into MIDI

Once raw data is simulated from the random walks and Grover algorithms, processing
it into data that could be understood by musical hardware and software can begin. An
obvious choice for this is the MIDI protocol, the industry standard for communicating
data to hardware and software alike. This can be achieved using a patch in Max MSP.
This process is discussed in the following text and summarised in Fig. 4.4.

The patch works by importing a text file containing data from each algorithm's
simulation, cycling through the numbers at a set tempo and outputting them as MIDI
data. A simple tempo object is used to drive the data from the text file, pushing it
through the sequence of numbers at a set tempo. The makenote object outputs a MIDI
note-on message paired with a velocity value (i.e., a value for the loudness of the

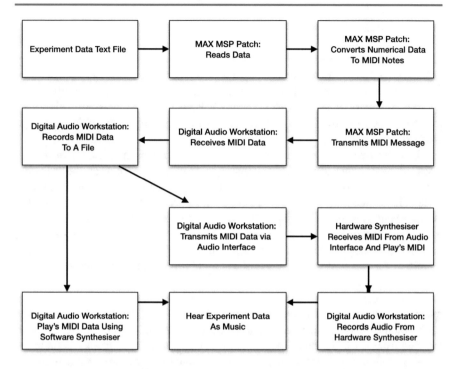

Fig. 4.4 Workflow diagram of the processing of quantum data into a format that can be used for sound generation

note) followed by a note-off message after a specified amount of time. In this patch, a fixed amount of time between a note on and note off is used, but this can also be tempo relative. Using a fixed time allows the user to hear the experimental output as a fixed flow of notes. The numbers from the text files are input into this object to designate the pitch. It is worth noting that the pitched notes are transposed an octave up before hitting the makenote object as in their raw form they are extremely low and almost inaudible. A midiformat object was used to pack the data into a MIDI message, which is then transmitted to a specific MIDI port with midiout.

With the MIDI data transmitting from MAX MSP, the user can then route it as needed. Routing into the digital audio workstation is simple using this setup, and the data can be recorded into a MIDI track in real-time. Ableton Live 11 Suite is excellent for this task as it has brilliant MIDI capability and a simple nature in which it can be used to integrate MIDI, Audio and live synthesis. Once the MIDI data is recorded into Ableton Live 11 Suite, there is a file to play and can be listened to via a VST plug-in or hardware synthesiser.

4.4.2 Musicality of the Data

A simple sine wave was used to hear the data initially, picked for its clarity and pure sound which makes it easy to hear definitive notes so the focus can be placed on the relationship between each note. The raw data is atonal in nature, but differences between the quantum and classical random walks are clear, as is Grover's algorithm and how it changes over time and reduces down to just one note (finds the correct answer).

There are two main differences which can be heard in the music between the classical and the quantum walk. The first is that in the classical walk, the note only ever moves up or down by one step, making the melody sound quite similar to playing a scale. In the quantum walk, there are large jumps because the position of the walker is spread out over many positions at once. Another feature that can be heard is that in the quantum walk is that the notes move away from the starting point (the first note in the melody) faster than in the classical walk. This is because of an important feature of the classical versus quantum walk—if you want to get somewhere fast, it helps to be quantum!

The first step in making the data more musical and 'pleasant' to listen to was to quantise the notes to follow a musical key. C minor was chosen for this, specifically the harmonic minor scale. From a creative point of view, this felt musically fitting to the data from the laboratory. This choice was inspired by how the data sounded in its original atonal state—there was something about the movement of the notes that also inspired the choice to go with a minor key. After cycling through some different choices—C sounded the most appropriate. The next step is transposing the octave of the created melodies, in their raw form they are extremely low and are essentially inaudible. By shifting them up to three octaves they are in a usable range.

4.4.3 Composition Process

The quote below covers the composition process of the two finished pieces as documented by the composer Simon Small.

> After spending some time listening to the melodies created by the classical and quantum walks and Grover's algorithm, I found myself interpreting emotion and drawing inspiration from their raw forms. Grover's algorithm was a constant build to me, a crescendo, caused by the data honing in on its final destination. This led me to begin composing a track that in its essence is one large crescendo, building intensity as the algorithm progresses. Listening to the random Walks together made me want to compose a track to showcase their differences but also show how they can harmoniously play together. Keeping them as the main feature of the piece was important. The melody and harmony created really reminded me of early synthesiser music, specifically the works of Georgio Morodor. This influenced me to create a piece inspired by Morodo's synthesiser work and including drums from a drum machine as opposed to an acoustic instrument.
>
> Aside from using the melody and harmony created by the experiment data, I also used fragments of the data with hardware synthesisers to create textural layers in the tracks. This

was made incredibly simple by having the data available in the MIDI format. I wanted the entire piece to be influenced by data rather than a melody bolted onto an unrelated song. This was also achieved by using recorded audio samples from the Physics Laboratory at the University of Bristol. Samples were recorded using an Apple iPhone by Euan Allen as I was unable to attend due to the Covid-19 pandemic. Equipment such as the lab's key card access point, cryostat, compressor and lab doors were recorded. They were used to create percussion, drones and textures within the compositions. This was an important creative point for me as again I wanted the whole composition to be created by and influenced by the data and the surroundings used in its creation.

4.5 Conclusion

In this chapter, we have covered just two ways in which quantum computers can be utilised for musical composition. The pieces of music generated from the collaboration apply simulated data from real quantum processes, namely a random quantum walk and Grover's algorithm, to seed the music generation process. Concepts behind the two algorithms also provided inspiration in the creative process of composing the two pieces, demonstrating that the impact of quantum computing in music can be both literal and emotional.

The extent to which the musical pieces can be utilised as pedagogical tools to help get across concepts of quantum physics and computing has yet to be explored in full. However, the distinction between the classical and quantum inputs in both pieces does allow a listener to distinguish between the two computational modes. During the project collaboration, this contrast assisted the understanding for those involved from a non-technical quantum background.

The techniques described here may be applied to the many quantum algorithms that available and known in the literature. With an increasing number of both simulation and physical quantum computing resources publicly available, the barrier to utilising these concepts for musicians and artists is low and so we may begin to see increasing interest in using quantum concepts in art and music generation.

References

1. Satzinger, K. J., Zhong, Y., Chang, H.-S., Peairs, G. A., Bienfait, A., Chou, M.-H., et al. (2018). Quantum control of surface acoustic-wave phonons. *Nature, 563*(7733), 661–665.
2. (2021). Quantum Engineering Technology Labs. https://www.bristol.ac.uk/qet-labs/. Accessed 01 Dec 2021.
3. Small, S. (2021). Tunnel of reverb. https://www.tunnelofreverb.com/. Accessed 01 Dec 2021.
4. Quantum Music, University of Bristol School of Physics. (2021). https://www.bristol.ac.uk/physics/research/quantum/engagement/quantum-music/. Accessed 01 Dec 2021.
5. Bohm Electronic Collective Bandcamp. (2021). https://bohmelectronic.bandcamp.com/. Accessed 01 Dec 2021.

6. Aharonov, Y., Davidovich, L., & Zagury, N. (1993). Quantum random walks. *Physical Review A, 48*(2), 1687.
7. Childs, A. M., Cleve, R., Deotto, E., Farhi, E., Gutmann, S., & Spielman, D. A. (2003). Exponential algorithmic speedup by a quantum walk. In *Proceedings of the Thirty-Fifth Annual ACM Symposium on Theory of Computing* (pp. 59–68).
8. Schreiber, A., Cassemiro, K. N., Potoček, V., Gábris, A., Mosley, P. J., Andersson, E., et al. (2010). Photons walking the line: A quantum walk with adjustable coin operations. *Physical Review Letters, 104*(5), 050502.
9. Grover, L. K. (1996). A fast quantum mechanical algorithm for database search. In *Proceedings of the Twenty-Eighth Annual ACM Symposium on Theory of Computing* (pp. 212–219).
10. Grover, L. K. (1997). Quantum mechanics helps in searching for a needle in a haystack. *Physical Review Letters, 79*(2), 325.
11. Gandomi, A., & Haider, M. (2015). Beyond the hype: Big data concepts, methods, and analytics. *International Journal of Information Management, 35*(2), 137–144.
12. Nielsen, M. A., & Chuang, I. (2002). Quantum computation and quantum information.
13. Qiskit Grover's Algorithm. (2021). https://qiskit.org/textbook/ch-algorithms/grover.html. Accessed 23 Oct 2021.
14. QuTech Quantum Inspire. (2021). https://www.quantum-inspire.com/. Accessed 01 Dec 2021.

Exploring the Application of Gate-Type Quantum Computational Algorithm for Music Creation and Performance

5

Satofumi Souma

Abstract

We are interested in developing approaches to making music using gate-type quantum algorithms. We propose various principles and models to apply quantum gate circuits for music creation. In considering how we can connect between musical notes and qubits, and associate musical progression with quantum gate operations, we propose two distinct approaches: the *wavefunction-based* approach and the *measurement-based* approach. The former approach is intended to translate the quantum wavefunction directly to the musical expression and provide a scheme to perform a new improvisational live performance, referred to as *quantum live coding*. The latter is based on the quantum gate circuits' measurement results, enabling various music creation schemes, including the quantum phase modulation model and the quantum game theoretical model.

5.1 Introduction

The role of computers in modern society is increasing in importance not just as a basis for information and communication technology, but also as a means of supporting different social activities relating to the human senses, such as art and entertainment. In particular, computers have played an essential role in various algorithmic compositions, recording and performances of music. Additionally, now, with a growing interest in an essentially new computing principle, that is quantum computing, thereby

S. Souma (✉)

Department of Electrical and Electronic Engineering, Kobe University, 1-1 Rokkodai Nada, Kobe 657-8501, Japan

e-mail: ssouma@harbor.kobe-u.ac.jp

E. R Miranda (ed.), *Quantum Computer Music*,
https://doi.org/10.1007/978-3-031-13909-3_5

the prospect of music production unique to quantum computing is also expected. Several projects and conferences have been held in an attempt to apply quantum mechanical concept to music creation. For example, the proposal of conceptual correspondence between quantum mechanics and musical expression Putz and Svozil [17], Putz and Svozil [18] and pioneering experimental and theoretical works by the University of Plymouth group Kirke and Miranda [9], Kirke [8], Miranda [11], and Chap. 3, in this volume. The application of gate quantum computing to counterpoint composition Weaver [20], the application of quantum network to beat-making performance Oshiro and Hamido [16], an interesting discussion between musicians and physicists in a project called *Quantum Music* in Serbia Ser [1], and the recent symposium *International symposium on Quantum Computing and Musical Creativity* organized by QuTune project isq [2].

In this chapter, we present our recent proposals for developing a music creation system applying quantum gate circuit, mainly conducted as FY2018 MITOU target program (gate-type quantum computing division) that Information-technology Promotion Agency, Japan (IPA) provided. We investigated the music application of quantum computing in this project by proposing a music creation principle using the quantum gate circuit and developing the quantum gate composition software based on the proposed principle. Our research is composed of two distinct issues, as follows:

- Consideration of the music creation principle using the quantum gate circuit, which is essential to answer the non-trivial question on how we can connect between the musical note and the qubit and associate musical progressions with quantum gate operations.
- Developing software that enables us to do the quantum gate composition comprehensively.

We propose two different music creation approaches based on quantum gate circuits, as follows:

- An approach that applies the time evolution of the wave function of a qubit, which changes with the quantum gate operation, directly to musical expressions in an analogue way. This approach relies on the use of full information from the quantum wavefunction. Therefore, we do not presume the use of an actual quantum computer unless the full information from the wavefunction is made available through quantum tomography, and instead, offer our unique simulator-based music creation and performance system. This scheme is referred to as the wavefunction-based approach. As we explain later, this wavefunction-based approach can provide an interesting framework for a new musical performance, referred to as *quantum live coding*.
- An approach that applies the result of measurement (wavefunction collapse) for the quantum state associated with quantum gate operation to the musical expressions digitally. This is a measurement-based approach. Therefore, we can assume the use

of real quantum computers here. This scheme is referred to as the measurement-based approach hereafter.

5.2 Wavefunction-Based Approaches and Quantum Live Coding

5.2.1 Basic Principles of Music Generation Based on the Wavefunction-Based Approach

First, we describe the details of the first approach: (1) The analogue approach, in which one musical note is represented by one qubit or multiple qubits. More specifically, the musical pitch is represented by one qubit, and optionally other note-related quantities such as the note value can be represented by additional qubits. Keeping in mind that the quantum state $|\Psi\rangle$ of a single qubit, given by the equation

$$|\Psi\rangle = \cos\left(\frac{\theta}{2}\right)|0\rangle + e^{i\phi}\sin\left(\frac{\theta}{2}\right)|1\rangle \qquad (5.1)$$

can be visualized using the Bloch sphere shown in Fig. 5.1, we propose that the angle ϕ within the x-y plane of the Bloch sphere is made to correspond to the note name within one octave. Here the discrete values in $\pi/6$ increments of ϕ correspond to the pitches (or notes) on a piano keyboard (Fig. 5.1). The other continuous angles between the above discrete values do not apply to the piano keyboard but can be used to express microtonal pitches.   Based on this primitive idea of pitch-qubit correspondence, we propose using a multiple qubit system for music progression, such as in Fig. 5.2, where we use five qubits in total. In Fig. 5.2 we assume that two of the qubits are note qubits (qubits used to describe musical note information), while the remaining three qubits are observation (or audience) qubits (qubits that are not directly converted into the musical note). Then, for each qubit, various single-qubit gates (e.g., Hadamard gate, phase rotation gate, etc.) are applied. Two qubits gates such as controlled-NOT (CNOT) gate and controlled phase gates are also provided sequentially between any two observation qubits or between one note qubit and one observation qubit. Here we assume that the quantum gate placement is designed such that the two note-qubits are not entangled with each other and can be represented as the direct products of two note-qubits states as

$$
\begin{array}{cc}
\overbrace{\phantom{(a_{000}|0\rangle + b_{000}|1\rangle)(c_{000}|0\rangle + d_{000}|1\rangle)}}^{\text{Note qubits}} & \overbrace{}^{\text{Observation qubits}}
\end{array}
$$

$$
\begin{aligned}
|\Psi\rangle = \;& (a_{000}|0\rangle + b_{000}|1\rangle)(c_{000}|0\rangle + d_{000}|1\rangle)\;|000\rangle \\
& + (a_{001}|0\rangle + b_{001}|1\rangle)(c_{001}|0\rangle + d_{001}|1\rangle)|001\rangle \\
& + \cdots \\
& + (a_{111}|0\rangle + b_{111}|1\rangle)(c_{111}|0\rangle + d_{111}|1\rangle)|111\rangle .
\end{aligned} \qquad (5.2)
$$

Then, two note-qubits are represented as two independent Bloch spheres and two musical notes can be defined according to the above mentioned pitch-qubit correspondence. This operation (placing quantum gates) corresponds to one of the processes of composition or the improvised performance of music.

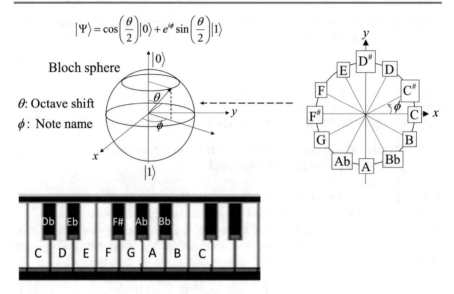

Fig. 5.1 Schematic illustration of the correspondence between the note name and quantum bit state in the wavefunction-based (analogue) approach. The angle ϕ in the Bloch sphere (left top) is made to correspond to note names as illustrated in the right top panel, where the discrete values in $\pi/6$ increments of ϕ correspond to each note of the piano keyboard (left bottom panel). The other continuous angles between the above discrete values do not apply to a piano keyboard but can be used to express the microtonal pitch. The angle θ is made to correspond to the octave shift

In Fig. 5.2, the quantum state (including note and observation qubits) changes each time it passes through each gate, and then the resulting change in the note qubit is converted (translated) to the change in the musical note according to the above-mentioned rule, based on the Bloch sphere, resulting in real-time music generation. An interesting feature of the proposed "note qubit—observation qubit system" is as follows: by providing CNOT gates between the note qubit and the observation qubit, quantum entanglement can be brought about between the note qubit and the observation qubit. Then, in general, the quantum state of the note qubit differs depending on the state of the observation qubit (eight different states from $|000\rangle$ to $|111\rangle$ if three qubits are used as observation qubits), so the music we can hear will differ depending on which frame is selected as the state of the observation (audience) qubit. Furthermore, when there are two qubits categorized as note qubits as shown in Fig. 5.2, these two notes are used to form chords.

In our implementation, these quantum gates are placed at will by the user (i.e., the performer) on a live-coding system based on SuperCollider McCartney [10] + Fox-Dot Kirkbride [7]. Figure 5.3 shows the screenshot of an example of a quantum live coding system actually developed based on SuperCollider + FoxDot. The left panel is the FoxDot coding screen to be shown to the audience, where the quantum gates are arranged in real-time (write the codes or put the prepared codes and execute). The Bloch spheres of the note qubits associated with the executed gate are designed

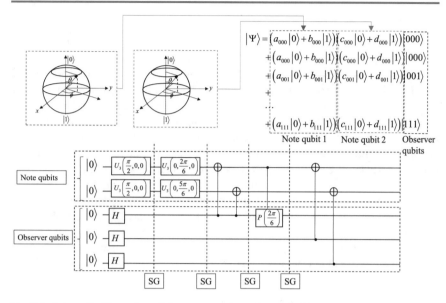

Fig. 5.2 Schematic illustration of the correspondence between the quantum gate operation and music progression in the wavefunction-based approach. This illustration is for the two note-qubits + three observer-qubits case. Sound generation is performed at the positions of vertical dashed bars indicated as SG (sound generation) through the proposed wavefunction

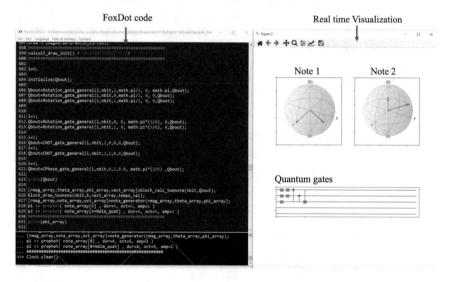

Fig. 5.3 Screenshot of quantum live coding system developed based on FoxDot. The left part is the quantum live coding screen of FoxDot, the right top part is the real-time visualization of Bloch spheres, and the right bottom part is the real-time visualization of quantum gate circuit schematics

to be automatically drawn in the upper right panel in a real-time manner, and the quantum circuit diagram is also drawn automatically in real-time in the lower right. The Bloch sphere were drawn using the QuTiP library Johansson, Nation, and Nori [5], Johansson, Nation, and Nori [6], and the quantum circuit diagram was drawn using Tkinter library (standard GUI library of Python). In this quantum live coding environment, various improvisational performances are possible. After the note qubit and the observation qubit form a quantum entanglement, for example, the quantum state of the note qubit can be modified by adding a phase rotation gate to the observation qubit (note–to–observer controlled phase rotation gate in the case of multiple note qubits), where non-local properties in quantum mechanics can play an important role. Furthermore, for a two-note qubit and a three-observation qubit, it is possible to obtain music reproduction with a change by selecting a different state from eight superposition states each time and performing loop playback. This means that, even if the gate arrangement as a score is the same, different music can be generated by selecting the frame at the time of measurement, which means that the audience can actively intervene in the way of enjoying the performance participatively.

5.2.2 Example of Music Generation Based on the Wavefunction-Based Approach

Below we present one specific simple example of music generation based on FoxDot.

Here we consider three qubits system for simplicity, composed of two note-qubits and one observation-qubit. Initially these qubits are initizlized to $|000\rangle$, which is given in the following FoxDot code by the one-dimensional array Qbit = $[1, 0, 0, 0, 0, 0, 0, 0]$ in the basis represented in Eq. (5.2). Subsequently, the following FoxDot code is performed (complete source code is available on GitHub Souma [19]):

$$Qbit = \text{Rotation\_gate}(2, pi/2, 0, pi, Qbit) \tag{5.3}$$

$$Qbit = \text{Rotation\_gate}(0, pi/2, 0, 0, Qbit) \tag{5.4}$$

$$Qbit = \text{Rotation\_gate}(1, pi/2, 0, 0, Qbit) \tag{5.5}$$

$$\text{Sound\_generator}(Qbit) \rightarrow [CC] \tag{5.6}$$

$$Qbit = \text{Rotation\_gate}(0, 0, pi * (2/6), 0, Qbit); \tag{5.7}$$

$$Qbit = \text{Rotation\_gate}(1, 0, pi * (5/6), 0, Qbit); \tag{5.8}$$

$$\text{Sound\_generator}(Qbit) \rightarrow [DF] \tag{5.9}$$

$$Qbit = \text{CNOT\_gate}(2, 0, Qbit); \tag{5.10}$$

$$Qbit = \text{CNOT\_gate}(2, 1, Qbit); \tag{5.11}$$

$$\text{Sound\_generator}(Qbit) \rightarrow [DF] |0\rangle / [B^{\flat}G] |1\rangle \tag{5.12}$$

$$Qbit = \text{CPhase\_gate}(0, 2, pi * (2/6), Qbit) \tag{5.13}$$

$$\text{Sound\_generator}(Qbit) \rightarrow [DF] |0\rangle / [CG] |1\rangle . \tag{5.14}$$

This code is illustrated in Fig. 5.2 (up to the 4th SG in Fig. 5.2). In this code Rotation_gate$(i, \theta, \phi, \xi,$ Qbit$)$ is the general rotation gate defined by

$$U_3 (\theta, \varphi, \xi) = \begin{pmatrix} \cos(\theta/2) & -e^{i\xi} \sin(\theta/2) \\ e^{i\phi} \sin(\theta/2) & e^{i(\phi+\xi)} \cos(\theta/2) \end{pmatrix}, \quad (5.15)$$

applied to the ith qubit component of Qbit, and CNOT_gate$(i_c, i_t,$ Qbit$)$ is the CNOT gate with i_cth and i_tth being the control and target qubits, respectively. Similarly CPhase_gate$(i_c, i_t, \phi,$ Qbit$)$ is the controlled phase rotation gate with ϕ being the phase rotation angle within the x-y plane of Bloch sphere. Now let us take a look at the above code line by line. In Eq. (5.3) the Hadamard gate $H = U_3 (\pi/2, 0, \pi)$ is applied to the observation (third) qubit to obtain $|00\rangle (|0\rangle + |1\rangle) /\sqrt{2}$. In Eqs. (5.4 and 5.5) the two note-qubits' phases are rotated to $(\theta, \phi) = (\pi/2, 0)$, giving rise to the wavefunction $(|0\rangle + |1\rangle) (|0\rangle + |1\rangle) (|0\rangle + |1\rangle) /\sqrt{2^3}$ and the notes' name [CC], subsequently in Eqs. (5.7 and 5.8) they are further rotated by $\phi = 2\pi/6$ and $5\pi/6$, respectively, giving rise to the wavefunction $\left(|0\rangle + e^{i2\pi/6} |1\rangle\right) \left(|0\rangle + e^{i5\pi/6} |1\rangle\right) (|0\rangle + |1\rangle) /\sqrt{2^3}$ and the notes' name [DF]. We note that in Eqs. (5.4–5.8) the wavefunction of the three qubits system can be written in general as $(a |0\rangle + b |1\rangle) (c |0\rangle + d |1\rangle) (|0\rangle + |1\rangle) /\sqrt{2}$ with a, b, c, and d being the complex number coefficients. Next in Eqs. (5.10) and (5.11), CNOT gates (controlled by the observer-qubit and targeted to two note-qubits) are applied. Then, in the above wavefunction $|0\rangle$ and $|1\rangle$ in the note-qubits are interchanged only when the observer qubit is $|1\rangle$, and the wavefunction becomes $(a |0\rangle + b |1\rangle) (c |0\rangle + d |1\rangle) |0\rangle /\sqrt{2} + (b |0\rangle + a |1\rangle) (d |0\rangle + c |1\rangle) |1\rangle /\sqrt{2}$, meaning that the note-qubits and observation-qubit are entangled with each other. Here, the note-qubits' states in the 2nd term can be interpreted as being rotated as $\theta \rightarrow \theta - \pi$ and $\phi \rightarrow \pi - \phi$ in the Bloch sphere ($\phi \rightarrow -\phi$ change when projected to the x-y plane of Bloch sphere) compared with the 1st term. In the note name representation this entangled state is written as $|DF\rangle |0\rangle + |B^b G\rangle |1\rangle$. Therefore depending on which state ($|0\rangle/|1\rangle$) the observer choose, the different sounds ([DF]/ [B^{b}G]) are produced. Finally in Eq. (5.13) the controlled phase rotation gates (the 1st note-qubit is the control qubit and the observer-qubit is the target bit) with the phase $\phi = 2\pi/6$ is applied. This gate operation gives the phase rotation in the 1st *note-qubit* by the phase $\phi = 2\pi/6$ only when the *observer-qubit* is $|1\rangle$ through the phase kickback mechanism, resulting into the quantum state in the note name representation as $|DF\rangle |0\rangle + |CG\rangle |1\rangle$.

The note name modulation by the controlled phase rotation gates introduced here enables us to modulate the note name in a way depending on the states of the observation qubits within the quantum superpositioned states. This is the key issue to generating wider variety of music progression patterns forming quantum superpositioned states, especially when there are multiple observation qubits.

5.3   Measurement-Based Approach

In this section, we present the principle and examples of the measurement-based approach and describe how the measurement result for the quantum state associated with quantum gate operation is applied to musical expressions.

5.3.1   Stochastic Note Generation Model

As a way to express the note name in the measurement-based approach, we first propose to make the measurement axis of one qubit correspond to a user-determined specific direction (angle) in the circle of fifths (Fig. 5.4a), so that the probabilistic realization of ↑ and ↓ along the measurement axis is translated to the probabilistic realization of two different notes that differs by the angle π in the circle of fifth. We propose a method for obtaining stochastic note sequences from the measurement results of the quantum gate circuit shown in Fig. 5.4b as one of the most simple possible application examples based on this scheme.

In Fig. 5.4b, the measurement axis of the each ith note is set by the phase θ_i of the phase rotation gate provided before the measurement for each qubit; this is the information given by the user, which corresponds to a part of the composition.

In the example shown in Fig. 5.4b, quantum entanglement is generated by the CNOT gate between adjacent sounds (adjacent qubits). Here, since the qubits connected by the CNOT gate are only between two consecutive qubits, one can reduce the total number of required qubits to two as shown in Fig. 5.4c regardless of the

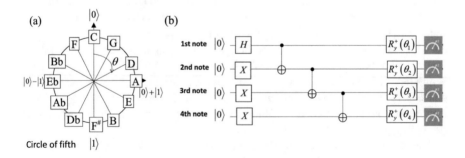

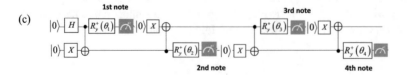

Fig. 5.4   a Circle of fifth. **b** An example of quantum gate circuit to generate stochastic music with entanglement. **c** Reduced quantum gate circuit

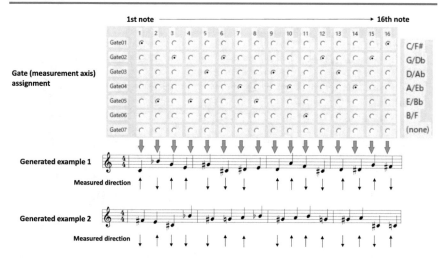

Fig. 5.5 Graphical user interface (GUI) screen to assign the measurement axes required for all the notes (top). Two different examples of the actual generated note sequences (bottom)

total number of notes, where the qubits are once measured they are initialized to $|0\rangle$ and used again to describe the next note.

In Fig. 5.5, we show a part of the graphical user interface (GUI) developed for this purpose, where users must first assign measuring axes information to all the notes. Then the assigned information is sent to Qiskit (an open-source software development kit for quantum computing) qis [3]. Once the quantum computation is done, the measurement results are in turn sent to another software Takt: a text-based music programming language Nishimura [14] Nishimura [15] Nishimura [13] to playback the generated music and optionally, generate the MIDI file. The bottom panel of Fig. 5.5 shows two different examples of the actual generated note sequences. We note that every time the measurement is performed, the different measurement results, and thus different note sequences are generated. The arrow in the bottom panel of Fig. 5.5 indicates the direction in each note was measured along the pre-assigned measurement axis. Here, adjacent notes are entangled in the quantum mechanical sense.

As an extension of this method, we next consider the model to take into account not only the note name but also the note value in the quantum gate composition. In this model, we use two qubits for one of each note, where one is used for the note name, and the other is used for the note value, as illustrated in Fig. 5.6. Regarding the qubit representing the note value, a quarter note is assigned when the measured result of the note value bit is $|0\rangle$, while a half note is assigned when the measured result of the note value bit is $|1\rangle$. As shown in Fig. 5.6, the note value of one note is intended to be entangled with the note name of the next note. Here, the quarter and the half notes are generated in a seemingly random form with some entangled correlation. An actual measurement example is shown in Fig. 5.7.

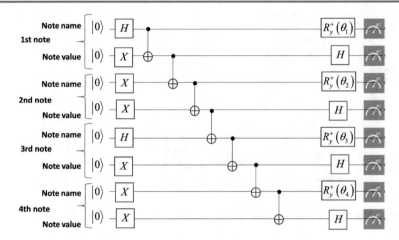

Fig. 5.6 Quantum gate circuit for two qubits—one note correspondance model, where one qubit is for the note name and the other one for the note value (note length)

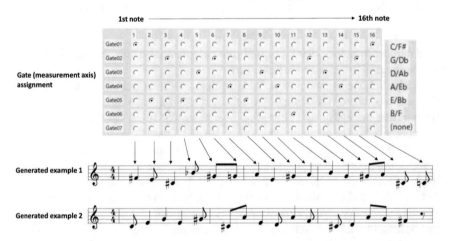

Fig. 5.7 GUI screen to assign the measurement axes in the two qubits—one note correspondence model (top). Two different examples of the actually generated note sequences (bottom)

5.3.2 Note-Expression Model

We next consider another possible note-expression model within the measurement-based approach, called the digital note-expression model.

As shown in Fig. 5.8 (left), one note name is represented by three qubits. The 1st, 2nd, and 3rd digits correspond to the raising or lowering of the note at intervals of V, II, and III degrees, respectively. Here the order of notes is based on the concept of the circle of fifth (right panel), which is a way of organizing the 12 chromatic pitches as a sequence of perfect fifths. This scheme makes it possible to generate music quantum mechanically compatible with the standard theory of tonal music. For example, we

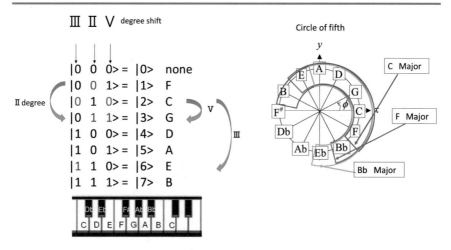

Fig. 5.8 Digital note expression (left) and circle of fifth (right). One of the advantages of using the concept of the circle of fifth for the qubits–note name correspondence is that the same algorithm can be used in different keys (for example, C major and F major) as depicted in the right panel

can use the same quantum gate algorithm for different keys in accordance with the circle of fifth shown in Fig. 5.8 (right).

5.3.2.1 Diatonic Chord Generation Model

Based on the note-name expression model introduced above, we devised quantum gate circuit models that can create a superpositioned state of each diatonic chord tone (four notes chords), and developed a program to generate probabilistic phrases that match a given chord progression pattern. Figure 5.9 shows the quantum gates that produce chord tones of seven major diatonic chords. When a measurement of three qubits is made for the state of passing through these gates, the result is measured in one of the four chord tones if there is no noise. For example, as shown in Fig. 5.10, after giving (determining) the chord progression: C_{M7}-V_7-A_{m7}-E_{m7}-F_{M7}-C_{M7}-F_{M7}-G_7, the quantum gates are arranged corresponding to the chord progression of each bar, and the measurement is performed sequentially for each bar. If the measurement is performed several times (for example, three times) and recorded, and the recorded results for three measurements are simultaneously played, the progression of the chord can be obtained as in the top pattern of Fig. 5.10. This top panel is the case when the input state is exactly prepared in $|000\rangle$, but if the input state slightly deviates from $|000\rangle$ (corresponding to noise), the measurement result also slightly deviated from the perfect chord tone, as shown in the middle and bottom pattern of Fig. 5.10. However, the deviation can give the music a unique tension and depth as a musical tension. Aiming and obtaining such a tension sound (as a gate operation) is an issue for the future research, but since it is desirable that the tension sound also appears

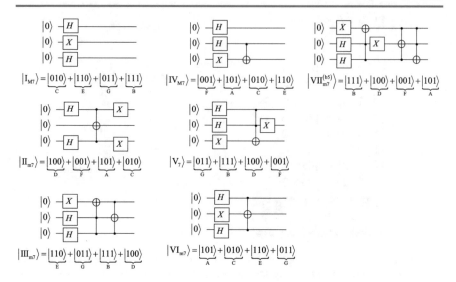

Fig. 5.9 Possible example of the quantum gate circuit that can produce chord tones of various diatonic codes

Initial qubits are all set to $|0\rangle$

Initial qubits are rotated from $|0\rangle$ to x direction by 0.1π

Initial qubits are rotated from $|0\rangle$ to x direction by 0.2π

Fig. 5.10 Generation examples of chord tones corresponding to the given chord progression. The top one is the generation example following the given chord progression in the absence of noise, while the bottom two case are in the presence of the noise. Notes indicated by the arrow are out of the diatonic chord

at an appropriate frequency, the noise as obtained in Fig. 5.10 is preferable to some extent.

5.3.2.2 Phase-Modulated Music Generation Model

We next propose a phase-modulated music generation model using the note-name expression and phase estimation quantum algorithm. In this model, the three qubits representing one note (initially initialized to $|000\rangle$) are first passed through the Hadamard gate, and then the phase evolution (phase rotation gate R_ϕ) corresponding to the note name aimed at each digit of the three qubits is performed. Finally, by passing through the inverse quantum Fourier transform, the quantum state corresponding to the desired note name can be obtained resonantly. The actual quantum gate and the conceptual explanation of the phase's role in this model are shown in Figs. 5.11 and 5.12, respectively.

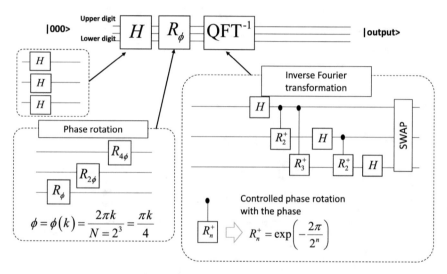

Fig. 5.11 Basic unit of the quantum gate circuit used in the phase-modulated music generation model and its conceptual explanation especially on the role of phase in this circuit

It is possible to determine the note-name sequence in a non-independent manner by using this basic mechanism and changing the phase of the next note by the output of the quantum state of one previous note by the control phase gate as shown in Fig. 5.13. Here, the basic flow of note names is determined by the phase rotation gate R_ϕ (located immediately after the Hadamard gate) given inside the three-qubit system that constitutes each note. However, the existence of a control phase gate from one note to the next plays the role of disturbing this predetermined basic flow of note names (original song). In other words, the original song is the theme, and the song modulated by the control phase gate can be regarded as a variation of the theme. Fig. 5.14 shows an example in which a certain theme is given and a variation is obtained with a controlled rotation gate. The topmost note sequence in Fig. 5.14 is the theme (given note sequence), and the other cases below are phase modulated patterns (variations), where the modulation strength q is the largest for the bottom pattern. Here we note that different variations can be obtained for each measurement

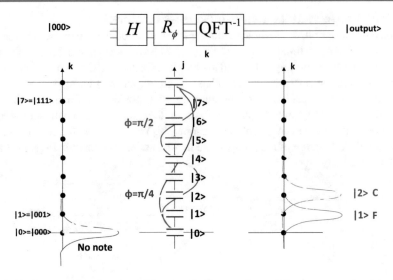

Fig. 5.12 Conceptual explanation of the phase implementation and the note generation principle

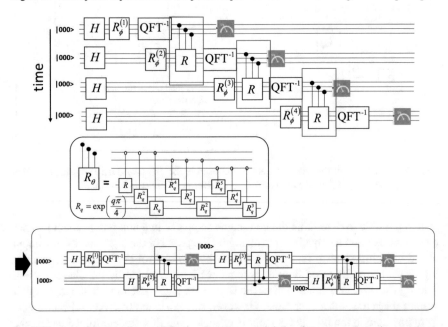

Fig. 5.13 A music generation model using the phase modulation from one note to the next (top). The bottom panel is the reduced (equivalent) circuit model. When the value of the phase in the inter-note controlled phase rotation gate (middle panel) is $q = 1$, one note $|k\rangle$ adds the value k to the next note in the decimal expression. For example, if the original sequence pattern is $|k_1\rangle \rightarrow |k_2\rangle$, the modulation with $q = 1$ results in the sequence pattern $|k_1\rangle \rightarrow |k_2 + k_1\rangle$

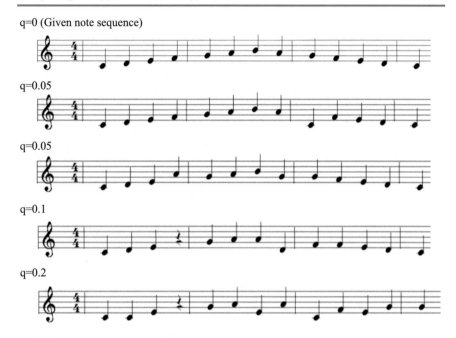

Fig. 5.14 Examples of the generation of the variation for a given theme, where the quantum phase modulation model is employed. The topmost note sequence is the theme (given note sequence), and the other cases below are phase modulated pattern (variations), where the modulation strength q is largest for the bottom pattern

even with the same degree of modulation strength q (see the results for $q = 0.05$ in Fig. 5.14). Since the deviation from the original theme increases as the modulation is strengthened, it is possible to control how much the given theme changes by changing the modulation strength. Furthermore, since the phase modulation in this scheme is applied from one note to the next note, the deviation from the original theme increases as the music progresses in general as demonstrated in Fig. 5.14.

5.3.2.3 Two Players Model Based on Quantum Game Theory

So far, our proposals have assumed the creation and performance of music by a single player. In this subsection, we consider the possibility of extending the basic principle of quantum mechanical music creation to the case of the multiple players model by employing the concept of quantum game theory. Game theory studies mathematical models of strategic interactions among rational agents. It has a long history of research, which began in 1944 with the book *The Theory of Games and Economic Behavior*, by John von Neumann and Oscar Morgenstern von Neumann and Oscar [12]. One of the classic representative examples analyzed by the game theory is the prisoner's dilemma, a paradox in decision analysis in which two individuals acting in their self-interests does not produce the optimal outcome. We first explain the

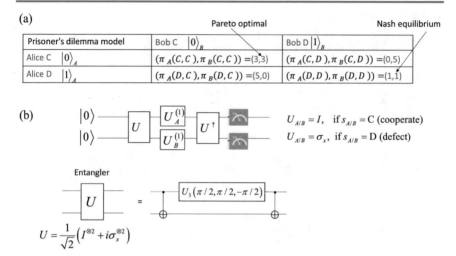

Fig. 5.15 Schematic explanation of the classical and quantum game theory scheme. **a** Is the payoff table of the prisoner's dilemma. **b** Is the quantum gate circuit model used in the quantum version of the prisoner's dilemma (see the text for detail)

essence of the classical prisoner's dilemma briefly and later consider its quantum generalization with the reference to Grabbe [4]. Suppose that there are two players: Alice and Bob, and they can choose one of two strategies: cooperate (C) or defect (D). When Alice's move is s_A and Bob's move is s_B with s_A and s_B are C or D, the payoff value to Alice and Bob are given as $\pi_A(s_A, s_B)$ and $\pi_B(s_A, s_B)$, respectively. Here the actual values of $\pi_A(s_A, s_B)$ and $\pi_B(s_A, s_B)$ are given in the table in Fig. 5.15. Then the Nash equilibrium is defined by the strategy (s_A^*, s_B^*) which satisfies the conditions $\pi_A(s_A^*, s_B^*) \geq \pi_A(s_A, s_B)$ and $\pi_B(s_A^*, s_B^*) \geq \pi_B(s_A, s_B)$ simultaneously. From Fig. 5.15 we can see that the Nash equilibrium is established when both of Alice's and Bob's moves are defect so that $(s_A, s_B) = (D, D)$, while actually the strategy $(s_A, s_B) = (C, C)$ is optimal for both players, called the Pareto optimal. Now let us consider this classical prisoner's dilemma from the viewpoint of the quantum formulation. To do this, we consider the quantum gate circuit depicted in Fig. 5.15a, which is composed of the entangler U, disentangler $U^\dagger$, and the single-qubit gates U_A and U_B for Alice and Bob, respectively. Here the two qubits gate U is given as given by

$$U = \frac{1}{\sqrt{2}} \left(I^{\otimes 2} + i\sigma_x^{\otimes 2} \right), \qquad (5.16)$$

while the single qubit gate $U_{A/B}$ is given as $U_{A/B} = I$ if $s_{A/B} = C$(cooperate) and $U_{A/B} = \sigma_x$ if $s_{A/B} = D$(defect). Then one can calculate the final output quantum state $|\Psi_f(s_A, s_B)\rangle = U(U_A \otimes U_B)U^\dagger$, and the expectation values of the payoffs for Alice and Bob becomes

$$\bar{\pi}_A = 3\left|\langle 00 \mid \Psi_f \rangle\right|^2 + 0\left|\langle 01 \mid \Psi_f \rangle\right|^2 + 5\left|\langle 10 \mid \Psi_f \rangle\right|^2 + 1\left|\langle 11 \mid \Psi_f \rangle\right|^2$$
$$\bar{\pi}_B = 3\left|\langle 00 \mid \Psi_f \rangle\right|^2 + 5\left|\langle 01 \mid \Psi_f \rangle\right|^2 + 0\left|\langle 10 \mid \Psi_f \rangle\right|^2 + 1\left|\langle 11 \mid \Psi_f \rangle\right|^2 \quad (5.17)$$

for any combinations of s_A and s_B. For example, when $(s_A = \sigma_x, s_B = \sigma_x)$ we obtain

$$\left|\Psi_f \left(s_A = \sigma_x, s_B = \sigma_x\right)\right\rangle = |11\rangle$$
$$\rightarrow \bar{\pi}_A = 3\left|\langle 00 \mid \Psi_f \rangle\right|^2 + 0\left|\langle 01 \mid \Psi_f \rangle\right|^2 + 5\left|\langle 10 \mid \Psi_f \rangle\right|^2 + 1\left|\langle 11 \mid \Psi_f \rangle\right|^2 = 1$$
$$\rightarrow \bar{\pi}_B = 3\left|\langle 00 \mid \Psi_f \rangle\right|^2 + 5\left|\langle 01 \mid \Psi_f \rangle\right|^2 + 0\left|\langle 10 \mid \Psi_f \rangle\right|^2 + 1\left|\langle 11 \mid \Psi_f \rangle\right|^2 = 1$$
$$(5.18)$$

in consistent with the values in the table in Fig. 5.15a. The payoff values for other values of (s_A, s_B) are also calculated similarly Grabbe [4]. In the case of the quantum version of the prisoner's dilemma, the single-qubit gate $U_{A/B}$ is generalized to

$$U_{A/B}(\theta, \varphi) = U_3(\theta, \varphi, \pi) = \begin{pmatrix} \cos(\theta/2) & \sin(\theta/2) \\ e^{i\varphi}\sin(\theta/2) & -e^{i\varphi}\cos(\theta/2) \end{pmatrix}. \quad (5.19)$$

We note that $U_{A/B}(0, \pi) = I$ (C) and $U_{A/B}(\pi, 0) = \sigma_x$ (D) correspond to the classical strategies. However, other angles are neither C nor D and are quantum strategies. Some special cases of the quantum strategies are $U_{A/B}(\pi/2, 0) = H$ (Hadamard gate) and $U_{A/B}(0, 0) = \sigma_z$ (Z gate). For example, when Alice's strategy is σ_z (quantum move) and Bob's strategy is σ_x (D), the output state becomes $\left|\Psi_f(s_A = \sigma_z, s_B = \sigma_x)\right\rangle = |10\rangle$, so that Alice's actual move is D and Bob's actual move is C, meaning that Bob's actual move was changed from his original strategy D. Similarly, when Alice's move is σ_x (D) and Bob's move is σ_z (quantum move), the output state becomes $\left|\Psi_f(s_A = \sigma_z, s_B = \sigma_x)\right\rangle = |01\rangle$, so that Alice's actual move is C and Bob's actual move is D, where Alice's actual move was changed from her original strategy D. Therefore, when one's strategy is quantum, the other's actual move can be changed from his/her original strategy. More details of the quantum game theory itself are referred to in the reference Grabbe [4]. With the above understanding of the quantum prisoner's dilemma problem, we next consider how we can apply this concept to the music creation.

In our proposal of the quantum game-based music creation principle, the above-mentioned quantum game unit $U(U_A \otimes U_B)U^\dagger$ is used to generate one pair of musical notes, which is composed of two notes played by Alice and Bob. Then the measured results (either $|0\rangle$ or $|1\rangle$) of each Alice's and Bob's qubits are made correspond to musical notes following the pre-assigned qubit–note name correspondence. For example, in Fig. 5.15a, $|0\rangle$ and $|1\rangle$ of Alice's qubit are made to correspond to C and $F^\sharp$, respectively, which are π difference in a circle of fifth. Similarly, Bob's qubit is made to correspond to G and $D^\flat$, respectively. The note measurement axis in the circle of fifth (e.g., C-$F^\sharp$ axis and G-$D^\flat$ axis in the above example) is intended to be pre-assigned manually for each note timing as a part of the composition process, as illustrated in Fig. 5.16. It is also possible to place optionally CNOT gates connecting between one note slot to the next, as in Fig. 5.16, by which if the quantum state of one note is $|1\rangle$ the initial state of the next note is changed from $|0\rangle$ to $|1\rangle$. In Figs. 5.17

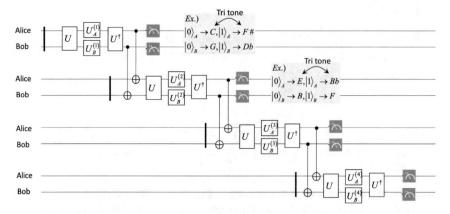

Fig. 5.16 Two players model of music creation based on quantum game theory. The music progresses from the top to the bottom, where two players (Alice and Bob) are intended to make their sound according to their own strategies. Correspondence between $|0/1\rangle$ and note name for each i-th note is pre-assigned as one of the composition processes. The quantum gates U_A and U_B (strategies) for the i-th note are composed by players A and B, respectively

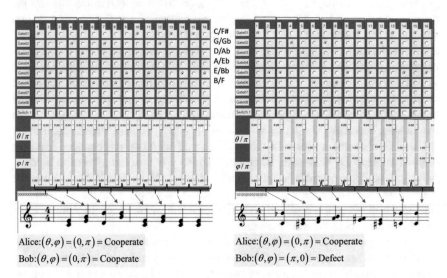

Fig. 5.17 Examples of the composition applying the quantum game theory. In the left panel, Alice's and Bob's strategy is both cooperative, while in the right panel Alice's strategy is to cooperate and Bob's strategy is to defect. These are both classical strategies

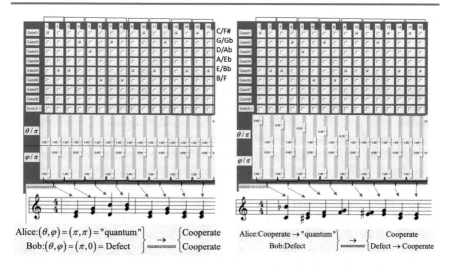

Fig. 5.18 Examples of the composition applying the quantum game theory. In the left panel Alice's strategy is $(\theta, \phi) = (\pi, \pi)$ (one of quantum strategies) and Bob's strategy is defect. After the measurement the Bob's move is turned to "cooperate", while the Alice's move is also cooperate. In the right panel Alice's strategy is gradually changed from cooperate (classical) to $(\theta, \phi) = (\pi, \pi)$ (quantum), while the Bob's strategy is defect. After the measurement, Bob's result (move) is gradually changed from defect to cooperate, while Alice's move is to cooperate

and 5.18, we show an examples of the composition by applying the quamtum game theory. In this example Alice's and Bob's measurements of $|0\rangle$ and $|1\rangle$ states produce the prepared melodies in C major and F$^\sharp$ major scale, respectively, as shown in the GUI interface shown in Figs. 5.17 and 5.18. In the left panel of Fig. 5.17 Alice's and Bob's strategy is both cooperating, making harmony on the C major scale. On the other hand, in the right panel Alice's strategy is to cooperate and Bob's strategy is to defect, resulting in unharmony. We note that these are both classical strategies.

We next consider the quantum strategy. In the left panel of Fig. 5.18, Alice's strategy is $(\theta, \phi) = (\pi, \pi)$ (one of quantum strategies) and Bob's strategy is defect. After the measurement is performed, Bob's move is turned to "cooperate", while Alice's move is cooperative, thereby making harmony in C major scale, meaning that one player's quantum strategy can change the other player's original strategy to make harmony. In the right panel, we assume that Alice's strategy is gradually changed from cooperation (classical) to $(\theta, \phi) = (\pi, \pi)$ (quantum), while the Bob's strategy is defect. After the measurement, Bob's result (move) is gradually changed from defect to cooperate, while Alice's move is cooperative. Then the transition from inharmony to harmony can be obtained as shown in Fig. 5.18.

5.4 Closing Summary and Acknowledgements

This chapter presented the latest outcomes from our research into creating music with gate-type quantum algorithms. We considered various principles and models to apply the quantum gate circuits for music creation. In considering how we can connect between musical notes and qubits, and associate musical progression with quantum gate operations, we proposed two distinct approaches: the wavefunction-based approach and the measurement-based approach. In the former approach, we translated the quantum wavefunction directly to the musical expression and proposed a new improvisational live performance, called the quantum live coding. In the latter approach, the measurement results of the quantum gate circuits are used to create music and we proposed various music creation schemes, including the quantum phase modulation model and the quantum game theoretical model. This research was supported in FY2018 MITOU Target Program that Information-technology Promotion Agency, Japan (IPA) provided. The author would like to thank Enago (www.enago. jp) for the English language review.

References

1. (2018). *International Interdisciplinary Conference, Quantum music (and beyond). Music and New Technologies in the 21st century (Mar 21–22, 2018).* http://quantummusic.org/2018/03/26/quantum-music-conference/.
2. (2021). *International Symposium on Quantum Computing and Musical Creativity (Nov 19–20, 2021).* https://iccmr-quantum.github.io/1st_isqcmc/.
3. (2021). *Qiskit: An open-source software development kit for quantum computing.* https://qiskit.org/.
4. Grabbe, J. O. (2005). An introduction to quantum game theory. arXiv:quant-ph/0506219.
5. Johansson, J. R., Nation, P. D., & Nori, F. (2012). QuTiP: An open-source Python framework for the dynamics of open quantum systems. *Computer Physics Communications, 183*, 1760–1772.
6. Johansson, J. R., Nation, P. D., & Nori, F. (2013). QuTiP 2: A Python framework for the dynamics of open quantum systems. *Computer Physics Communications, 184*, 1234.
7. Kirkbride, R. (2016). FoxDot: Live coding with python and supercollider. In *Proceedings of the International Conference of Live Interfaces* (pp. 194–198).
8. Kirke, A. (2019). Applying quantum hardware to non-scientific problems: Grover's algorithm and rule-based algorithmic music composition. arXiv:1902.04237.
9. Kirke, A., & Miranda, E. R. (2017). Experiments in sound and music quantum computing. In *Guide to unconventional computing for music.* Springer International Publishing.
10. McCartney, J. (2016). Rethinking the computer music language: Supercollider. *Computer Music Journal, 26*, 61–68.
11. Miranda, E. R. (2020). Quantum computer: Hello, music! arXiv:2006.13849.
12. von Neumann, J., & Oscar, M. (1944). *The theory of games and economic behavior.* Wiley.
13. Nishimura, S. (1998). PMML: A music description language supporting algorithmic representation of musical expression. In *Proceedings of the 1998 International Computer Music Conference* (pp. 171–174).
14. Nishimura, S. (2014a). *Takt: A text-based music programming language.* http://takt.sourceforge.net/.

15. Nishimura, S. (2014b). Takt: A read-eval-play-loop interpreter for a structural/procedural score language. In *Proceedings of the 2014 International Computer Music Conference, 2014* (pp. 1736–1741).
16. Oshiro, S., & Hamido, O. C. (2020). A quantum-classical network for beat-making performance. *Journal of Network Music and Arts, 2,* 1.
17. Putz, V., & Svozil, K. (2017). Quantum music. *Soft Computing, 21,* 1467.
18. Putz, V., & Svozil, K. (2021). Quantum music, quantum arts and their perception. arXiv:2108.05207.
19. Souma, S. (2022). https://github.com/ssouma3/qumusic.
20. Weaver, J. L. (2018). *Jamming with a quantum computer.* https://medium.com/rigetti/jamming-with-a-quantum-computer-bed05550a0e8.

Cellular Automata Music Composition: From Classical to Quantum

6

Eduardo Reck Miranda and Hector Miller-Bakewell

Abstract

We are interested in developing cellular automata systems to support the creation of original music. Cellular automata are of interest to musicians because they generate visual patterns that can be translated into musical ones. It could be said that cellular automata evolve time-based patterns, resembling how composers sometimes develop variations on musical forms. Emerging quantum technology is already opening new avenues for exploring musical composition using quantum cellular automata. The chapter begins with a brief introduction to cellular automata focusing on one-dimensional and two-dimensional discrete automata for classical computing. It briefly shows how they can be leveraged to generate music. Then, it moves on to quantum cellular automata. To develop a technique that is meaningfully non-classical, we use partitioned quantum cellular automata (PQCA) instead of regular, classical cellular automata. PQCA are intrinsically universal, capable of simulating all of the various quantum extensions of cellular automata that have been proposed to date. After an introduction to PQCA, the chapter presents the methods we have been developing for generating music with PQCA and shows practical examples.

E. R. Miranda (✉) · H. Miller-Bakewell
ICCMR, University of Plymouth, Plymouth, UK
e-mail: eduardo.miranda@plymouth.ac.uk

H. Miller-Bakewell
e-mail: h.millerbakewell@gmail.com

6.1 Introduction

The great majority of Artificial Intelligence (AI) systems developed to compose music to date focus on replicating well-known types of music [26]. They are either programmed with rules to compose in a certain style or can allegedly learn to generate tunes that sound like the examples given in a training set. From an academic perspective, this AI practice is favoured because it facilitates evaluating how well a system can achieve what it was programmed to do: people can simply listen to the outputs and compare them against the originals.

From a creative perspective, however, we are interested in developing systems to support the creation of original music rather than pastiches of existing repertoires. One plausible approach to achieve this is to program computers with models believed to express compositional processes of some sort and adapt them to generate new music. Various composers have programmed computers to generate music using set theory, probabilistic methods, chaos, fractals, and so on [6,14,36,37]. In the same vein, Artificial Life (or A-Life) models have been developed to generate music [24,27]. A-Life models are computational models that display some form of emergent behaviour resembling natural phenomena; e.g., cellular automata and genetic algorithms [16].

We believe that emerging quantum computing technology is certain to open new avenues for the aforementioned creative perspective. Whereas much research is being conducted into harnessing quantum computing for machine learning [30], which may, of course, be useful for music, the *stochastic tradition* championed in the last century by composer Iannis Xenakis [37] and many others [17] is bound to enjoy a fertile renaissance with quantum computing. Indeed, Xenakis is known for having explored cellular automata to compose a piece for orchestra entitled *Horos*, dated 1986. He used the states of a cellular automaton to assign instruments of the orchestra to play given notes [12].

The first co-author has been composing with cellular automata for nearly three decades [19–21,25]. In many ways, music composition can be thought of as being based on pattern propagation and manipulation of its parameters. Cellular automata are useful for musical composition because they can produce a variety of patterned data, which evolve in time (e.g., Figs. 6.2 and 6.4). The crux of using cellular automata to make music is the design of suitable methods to render music from the patterns they generate. A few examples of this will be discussed in this chapter.

The chapter begins with a brief introduction to cellular automata, focusing on one-dimensional and two-dimensional discrete automata for classical computing. As an example of a musical application, it briefly introduces a system, which uses a well known two-dimensional cellular automaton known as the Game of Life. Then it focuses on quantum cellular automata. We describe *partitioned quantum cellular automata* (subsequently referred to by its acronym, *PQCA*), which has been formulated as a plausible way forward to developing quantum cellular automata. Then, we present the methods that we developed for generating music using PQCA. Concluding the chapter is a discussion of the use of PQCA systems as aides for music composition, including examples produced for a composition for orchestra and electronically produced sounds, entitled *Multiverse Symphony*.

6.2 Classical Cellular Automata

Cellular Automata (CA) are discrete[1] dynamical systems that are often described as a counterpart to partial differential equations, which have the capability to represent continuous dynamical systems [34]. CA reframe a large system governed by complex equations as many small systems, the interactions between which can be expressed using simple equations. They are useful tools to model systems that change some features with time. They have been applied in a considerable variety of fields, such as image processing [29], ecology [13], biology [8], sociology [7], and indeed music [2,3,23].

Cellular automata were conceived by Stanislaw Ulam and John von Neumann in the 1960s to model self-reproducing machines; that is, machines that automatically construct a copy of themselves [5]. They built a model consisting of a two-dimensional grid of cells. Each cell could assume several states, representing the components from which they built a self-reproducing machine. Completely controlled by a set of simple rules, the machine was able to make identical copies of itself at other locations on the grid.

In practice, a cellular automaton is usually implemented as an arrangement of identical units—or cells—that can only interact with other, nearby, cells. This arrangement usually forms either a one-dimensional string of cells or a two-dimensional grid. But it can be in any number of dimensions. Most often the cells are arranged as a simple, regular grid. However, sometimes other arrangements, such as honeycomb-style lattices, are adopted. Importantly, these structures determine which cells are considered to be each other's neighbours.

The key properties of a cellular automaton are the states that each cell can assume at each time step and the update mechanism that determines each cell's next state, based solely on its own state and the states of its neighbours. The set of available states might simply be the two states *on* and *off*, but can be of any size, and can represent any number of different objects, properties, or processes. For instance, if each cell stands for a portion of a landscape, then the state might represent the number of animals at different locations or the type of vegetation that is growing in the area.

A neighbourhood is the set of cells that a single cell interacts with. On a grid, these normally are the cells physically closest to, or surrounding, the cell in question. An algorithm expressing transition rules operates on all cells *simultaneously* to alter their states. These rules often take into account the states of the neighbourhood

---

[1] The meaning of 'discrete' here is that space, time and properties of the automata can have only a finite, countable number of states.

around each cell. The functioning of a cellular automaton is normally monitored on a computer screen as a sequence of changing patterns of coloured square cells, according to the *tick of an imaginary clock*, like an animated film.

6.2.1 One-Dimensional Cellular Automata

By way of an introductory example, Fig. 6.1 shows an example from a collection of one-dimensional cellular automata, referred to here as *Wolfram's elementary cellular automata* [18]. It consists of a bar of cells, each of which can have the value either zero or one, represented by the colours white or black respectively. From given initial values, the states of all cells change simultaneously at each tick t of the imaginary clock. An example of a rule could be given as follows: if the current value of a cell is equal to one and if both neighbours are equal to zero, then this cell flips its value to zero at the clock's next tick.[2]

Figure 6.2 illustrates the pattern that would arise if our initial bar in Fig. 6.1 contained a few more cells, for twelve ticks of the imaginary clock. The checked pattern is a result of the automaton's *emergent behaviour*. It is important to note that the rules are concerned with the interactions between parts of the system. They do not explicitly encode any emerging global trend.

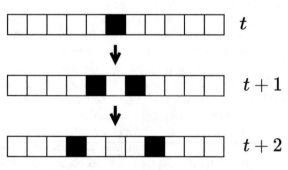

Fig. 6.1 An example of an one-dimensional cellular automaton consisting of an array of 11 cells

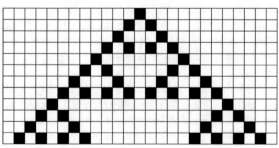

Fig. 6.2 One-dimensional cellular automaton consisting of 25 cells running for 12 cycles

---

[2] To create a cellular automaton the transition function must know how to act on every combination of states. We have only stated one of the rules used in our example automaton.

Fig. 6.3 Elementary
Wolfram's rule set number
90

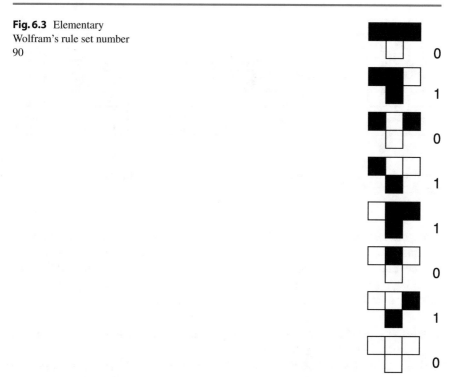

The evolution of Wolfram's elementary cellular automata is described by a set of eight rules that define the value that a given cell will have in the next tick of the clock. The rules consider the value of the cell to the left side, the value of the cell in question and the value of the cell to the right side. Therefore, there are $2 \times 2 \times 2 = 2^3 = 8$ possible situations, each of which must be handled by a rule. This gives us a total of $2^8 = 256$ rule sets [33]. For example, rule set number 90, which generated the pattern in Fig. 6.2, is depicted in Fig. 6.3. Please refer to [18] for more information about Wolfram's elementary automata and their rulesets.

6.2.2 The Game of Life: A Two-Dimensional Cellular Automaton

The Game of Life is a two-dimensional cellular automaton invented by mathematician John Conway in the 1970s [10]. It is praised for resembling real-life processes; for instance, the rise, fall and alterations of living organisms—hence, its name.

Theoretically, the automaton is defined on an infinite square lattice. In practice, however, it is normally implemented as a finite $m \times n$ array of cells, each of which can be in one of two possible states: 'alive' represented by the number 1, or 'dead' represented by the number 0. The right edge of the array wraps around to join the left edge and the top edge wraps around to join the bottom edge. On a computer screen,

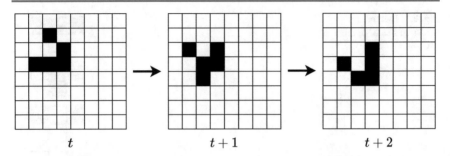

t $t+1$ $t+2$

Fig. 6.4 An example of the game of life cellular automaton consisting of a lattice of 64 cells, running for 3 cycles

living cells are normally coloured black and dead cells are coloured white (Fig. 6.4); but this is, of course, arbitrary, as any colour can be used to represent a state.

The state of a cell as time progresses is determined by its own state, and the state of its eight surrounding cells. There are four rules, referred to as (2, 3, 3, 3), that determine the fate of the cells at the next tick of the clock:

- **Death by loneliness**: A cell that is alive at time t will die at time $t + 1$ if it has fewer than 2 living neighbours at time t
- **Death by overcrowding**: A cell that is alive at time t will die at time $t + 1$ if more than 3 neighbours are alive at time t
- **Birth**: A cell that is dead at time t becomes alive at time $t + 1$ if exactly 3 of its neighbours are alive at time t
- **Survival**: A cell that is alive at time t will remain alive at time $t + 1$ only if it has either 2 or 3 living neighbours at time t.

There are a few well-known initial conditions for the Game of Life, which produces interesting results. Three examples are shown in Fig. 6.5.

Several alternative rules other than (2, 3, 3, 3) could be defined, which would, consequently, produce different behaviours. The general form for such rules is (E_{min}, E_{max}, F_{min} and F_{max}) where $E_{min} \leq E \leq E_{max}$ and $F_{min} \leq F \leq F_{max}$. Whilst the 'environment', represented as E, is defined as the number of living neighbours that

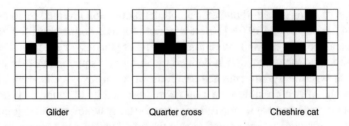

Glider   Quarter cross   Cheshire cat

Fig. 6.5 Examples of interesting initial states for the game of life

surround a particular live cell, a 'fertility' coefficient, represented as F, is defined as the number of living neighbours that surround a particular dead cell. In the case of the rules above, we could say that the life of a currently living cell is preserved whenever $2 \leq E \leq 3$ and a currently dead cell will be reborn whenever $3 \leq F \leq 3$.

6.3 A Classical Cellular Automata Music System: CAMUS

As an example of using cellular automata to compose music, we will show the system CAMUS [20,21]. It uses two types of cellular automata, one of which is the Game of Life introduced above. Here we focus on how the Game of Life generates sequences of musical notes.

CAMUS uses a Cartesian model to represent an ordered set of three notes, that may or may not sound simultaneous. These sets are referred to as *triples*. They are defined in terms of the distances between their notes, or *intervals*. The first note of the triple is given, with the remaining two notes determined by the intervals between the first and second, and then the second and third, notes. The horizontal coordinate of the Cartesian model represents the interval between the first and the second note, and the vertical coordinate represents the interval between the second and the third note (Fig. 6.6).

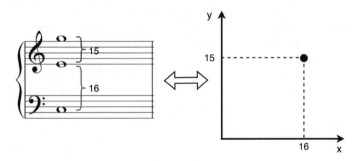

Fig. 6.6 A point in a x-y space represents an ordered set of three notes

To begin the music generation process, the cells of the automaton are set up with an initial configuration of states, which is defined by the user. Then, the automaton is set to run. The living cells of the automaton at a time t produce sets of three notes each; n living cells, therefore, produce n triples.

The coordinates of a living cell (in terms of $m \times n$ cells in the array) are taken to determine the set of three notes. From a given reference note (the 'fundamental note'), the system uses the x-y coordinates to calculate the second and the third note. The unit for calculating the intervals is a musical semitone (Fig. 6.7). For instance, if $m = 1$, then add 1 semitone to the fundamental note to generate the second note; if $m = 2$, then add 2 semitones, and so forth. The system uses a uniform distribution

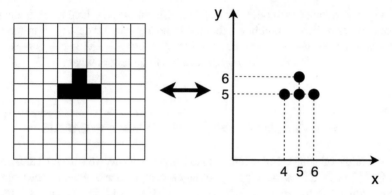

Fig. 6.7 Living cells are mapped onto x and y coordinates. Each point in this space represents a set of three of notes

function to select a fundamental note from a set predefined by the user. CAMUS reads the columns top-to-bottom and then left-to-right.

When CAMUS plays the notes of a triple, they are not necessarily simultaneous. CAMUS uses the states of neighbouring cells to determine how to distribute those notes in time. This is calculated locally, for each cell.

The states of the eight surrounding neighbours of a cell define its timing template, according to a set of 'temporal codes' (Fig. 6.8). A more detailed explanation of CAMUS' method to calculate the temporal codes can be found in [20,21]. As a brief illustration, let us assume that the timing template for the cell at coordinates 5×5 is the one illustrated in Fig. 6.9. The musical rendering that would have been generated for this single cell is shown in Fig. 6.10.

A three-dimensional version of CAMUS and other developments, such as the use of a Markov chain to generate rhythms is discussed in [19]. A recording of a composition for orchestra, entitled *Entre l'Absurde et le Mystère*, which was entirely generated by CAMUS is available online [22].

6.4 Towards Quantum Cellular Automata

Quantum Cellular Automata (QCA) are the quantum version of cellular automata. They were introduced as an alternative paradigm for quantum computation and were shown to be universal, meaning that "QCA can efficiently simulate quantum Turing machines"[3] (Farrelly, p. 17) [9]. A comprehensive theoretical discussion about QCA and universal computation is available in [9].

Translating classical cellular automata algorithms to their quantum counterparts is a plausible starting point from an educational point of view. But the transition

---

[3] But note, this is a subtly different notion of universal to the one about to be discussed below.

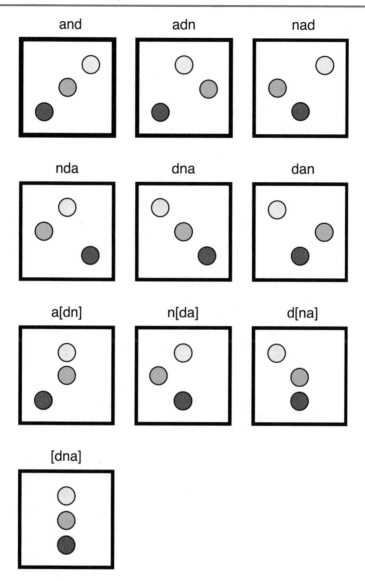

Fig. 6.8 Temporal codes define timing templates for the notes of a triple

Fig. 6.9 Example of timing template using codes 'nad' and 'a[dn]'

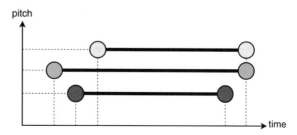

Fig. 6.10 Musical rendering of the example shown in Fig. 6.9

from classical cellular automata to their quantum counterparts is not straightforward to implement with the currently available quantum computing hardware technology. The difficulty lies in updating each cell of the quantum cellular automaton simultaneously. In practice, for a quantum version of a classical algorithm, we would need to keep a copy of the original state of a cell to update the others. This is not allowed in a quantum setting because of the no-cloning theorem [35], which states that it is impossible to create an independent and identical copy of an arbitrary unknown quantum state. A number of approaches have been proposed to get around this problem [1,9,15], one of which is Partitioned Quantum Cellular Automata, or PQCA. PQCA are capable of efficiently simulating other proposed quantum extensions of cellular automata [9].

6.5 Partitioned Quantum Cellular Automata: PQCA

This section introduces the basics of PQCA. A rigorous theoretical discussion is beyond the scope of this chapter. Please refer to [1,15] for such discussion, in particular, to learn more about the reasoning behind PQCA's non-classical behaviour. Here we focus on the practical aspects of implementing PQCA and show the methods that we developed to generate music with them.

To recapitulate, a cellular automaton at a certain time t is characterized by two properties: its current state and an update step that establishes its state at time $t + 1$. Thus, a quantum cellular automaton should iteratively apply an update circuit to some initial state.

In PQCA, a partition scheme splits the cells into tessellating *supercells*. A *global update circuit* is built from update frames. Update frames are built using the partitions and *local update circuits*.

To illustrate the concept of tessellation, let us assume an example PQCA characterised by a lattice of 21 qubits: seven wide and three tall. This is depicted in Fig. 6.11.

Figures 6.12 and 6.13 show two examples of tessellation, one which partitions the lattice into horizontal strips, and the other into vertical strips, respectively. Effectively,

q_0	q_1	q_2	q_3	q_4	q_5	q_6
q_7	q_8	q_9	q_{10}	q_{11}	q_{12}	q_{13}
q_{14}	q_{15}	q_{16}	q_{17}	q_{18}	q_{19}	q_{20}

Fig. 6.11 A lattice of 7×3 qubits

Fig. 6.12 A lattice of 7×3 qubits partitioned into vertical strips

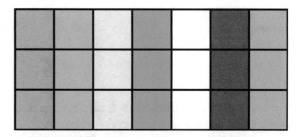

Fig. 6.13 A lattice of 7×3 qubits partitioned into horizontal strips

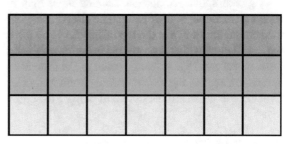

Fig. 6.12 constitutes seven supercells, each of which is formed by three qubits. And Fig. 6.13 has three supercells, each of which is formed by seven qubits.

6.5.1 One-Dimensional PQCA

Consider the one-dimensional PQCA shown in Fig. 6.14. It is composed of a line of twelve qubits, which has been partitioned into six cells, two qubits long each. Let us notate this as follows: [[0,1], [2, 3], [4,5], [6,7], [8,9], [10,11]]. Note that a tessellation can be shifted to form another tessellation, for instance [[1,2], [3, 4], [5,6], [7,8], [9,10], [11,0]].

Next, let us consider a local updating quantum circuit, as shown in Fig. 6.15. It has one Hadamard gate (labelled H) and one CNOT gate (which acts on both qubits at once). This updating circuit is for two qubits because each supercell of the partition

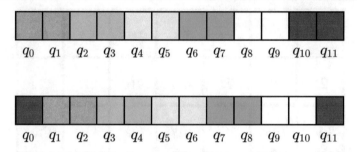

q_0 q_1 q_2 q_3 q_4 q_5 q_6 q_7 q_8 q_9 q_{10} q_{11}

q_0 q_1 q_2 q_3 q_4 q_5 q_6 q_7 q_8 q_9 q_{10} q_{11}

Fig. 6.14 At the top is a line of ten qubits partitioned into five supercells, two qubits long each. At the bottom is a shifted version of the partition

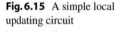

Fig. 6.15 A simple local updating circuit

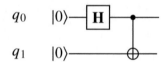

is composed of two qubits. This local circuit is then tessellated through the other supercells of the line, forming an update frame.

A global update circuit can include more than one update frame. Figure 6.16 shows an example of a global update circuit using two update frames, one based on the tessellation shown at the top of Fig. 6.14 and the other using a shifted version of the tessellation, which is shown at the bottom of the figure. An example showing four iterations of this PQCA from a given initial state at $t = 0$ is shown in Fig. 6.17. The automaton applies the global update circuit to its current state, and then overwrites its state with the measured output to prepare the qubits for the next cycle, and so on.

6.5.2 Two-Dimensional PQCA

In the same spirit as one-dimensional PQCA, but now for two-dimensional ones, a lattice of $m \times n$ qubits is partitioned into supercells to form tessellations. Then, respective local circuits are applied to the supercells of the tessellations to form update frames. Two-dimensional examples were already seen above in Figs. 6.12 and 6.13.

Note that each update frame should have a different tessellation of supercells and respective local circuits. Thus, a global update circuit can embody a combination of these.

Let us examine an example PQCA, which uses two different tessellation schemes and two local update circuits, one for each of the tessellations. Figure 6.18 shows a lattice of 9×4 qubits partitioned vertically into supercells consisting of two qubits each and Fig. 6.19 shows the same lattice partitioned horizontally into supercells consisting of three qubits each.

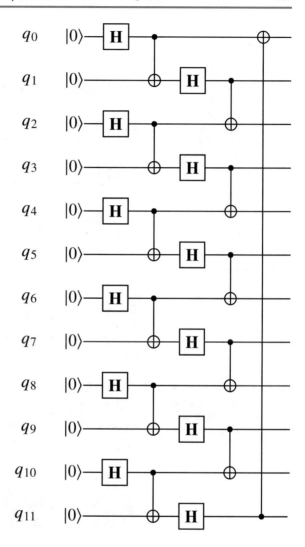

Fig. 6.16 An example of a global quantum circuit

Local quantum circuits for the two and three qubits tessellations are shown in Figs. 6.20 and 6.21, respectively. They yield two update frames, which combined result in the global update circuit for the 36 qubits of the automaton, as shown in Fig. 6.22.

An example of a pattern generated with the example above is shown in Fig. 6.23. Different tessellation arrangements, local circuits, and update frames will, of course, produce different patterns.

Fig. 6.17 An example of five cycles of a one-dimensional PQCA. *Note* The colours of the squares, or 'qubits', stand for the measured state of the automaton rather than partitions. A black cell represents the number 1 and a white one the number 0

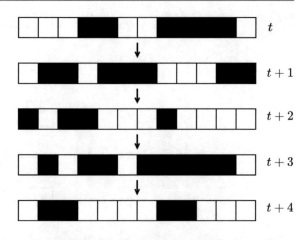

Fig. 6.18 A lattice of 36 qubits is partitioned vertically with supercells consisting of two qubits each

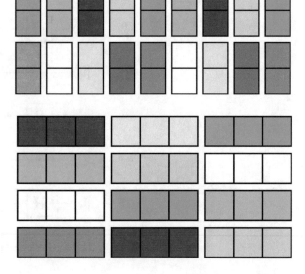

Fig. 6.19 The same lattice of Fig. 6.18, but partitioned horizontally with supercells consisting of three qubits each

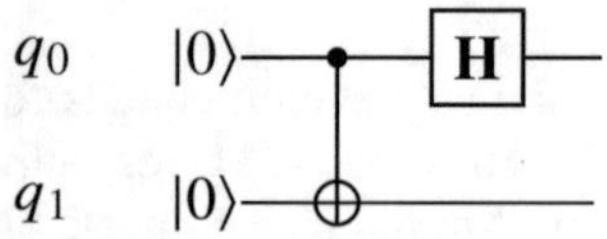

Fig. 6.20 Local circuit for the tessellation with supercells made of two qubits

Fig. 6.21 Local circuit for the tessellation of cells made of three qubits

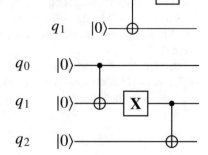

Fig. 6.22 A global update circuit resulting from the combination of two update frames

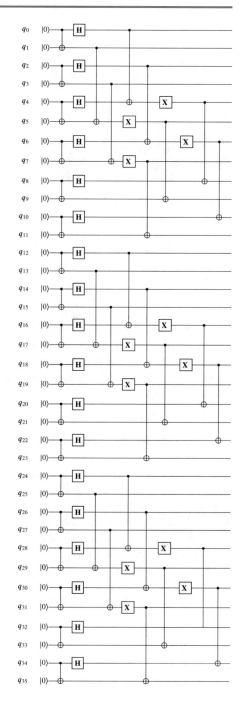

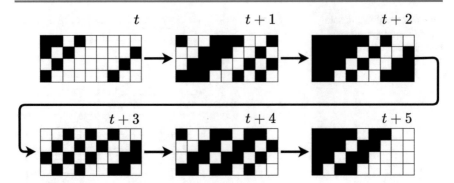

Fig. 6.23 An example of a generated pattern

6.6 Rendering Music from PQCA

The art of generating music with cellular automata hinges on the methods to convert the outputs—or measurements—into music parameters; e.g., notes, rhythms, melodies, chords, phrases, and so on. An example of a method for doing this was briefly shown earlier for the CAMUS system. As the measured outputs of CA and PQCA are of identical nature, any method that renders music from CA would, in principle, also work for PQCA. Here we present two methods that we developed for making music with PQCA: one using one-dimensional PQCA and another using two-dimensional ones.

6.6.1 Music from One-Dimensional PQCA

Here we introduce a method to generate sequences of chords, which we developed for the one-dimensional PQCA shown in Fig. 6.14, with circuits Figs. 6.15 and 6.16.

Each cycle, therefore, produces a twelve-bit long bitstring that is converted into either a cluster of notes or a rest. A cluster is a group of notes arranged vertically; they sound simultaneous. In this case, the cluster can have up to eight notes. A musical rest is when zero notes are played.

In order to encode musical information, a bitstring is split into four parts (Fig. 6.24). Each part constitutes a code representing a parameter for building a musical event, as follows (bit order is from the left to the right of the bitstring):

- Code A (bit 0) = is a flag to indicate whether this cluster should be played, or instead play a rest
- Code B (bit 1) = indicates whether this event is short or long
- Code C (bits 2 and 3) = specifies which scale will be used by Code D
- Code D (bits from 4 to 11) = specifies which notes to use; these notes are taken from the scale specified by Code C.

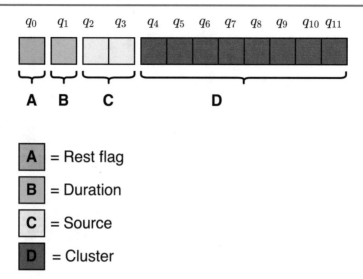

Fig. 6.24 From bits to a chord of notes

Fig. 6.25 Four musical scales starting at a given pitch. From top to bottom, the scales: Neapolitan major (starting from D3), harmonic minor (starting from G3), Lydian (starting from E3) and major (starting from A3)

If the rest flag (code **A**) is equal to 0, then the event will be a rest; i.e., there will be no notes. A musical event here can last for two types of durations: if code **B** = 0, then the event will last for an eighth-note (a.k.a. a quaver). If code **B** = 1, then the event will last for a quarter-note (a.k.a. a crotchet). The scales (represented by code **C**) are sequences of eight pitches, which are used to form the cluster. For this example, we defined four scales: D Neapolitan major (**C** = 00), G harmonic minor (**C** = 01), E Lydian (**C** = 10) and A major (**C** = 11) as shown in Fig. 6.25. Needless to say, the durations and sources are customisable.

11

Fig. 6.26 An example of a PQCA-generated musical cluster

Fig. 6.27 An example of a sequence of clusters generated with 20 cycles of the automaton

Note that the musical scales comprise eight notes each. The last eight bits of the bitstring (from 4 to 11) define which notes of a respective scale will constitute the cluster. For instance, code 01100100 will pick the second, third and sixth notes of the respective scale (in this case, let us assume the A major scale, code 11 in Fig. 6.25) to build the cluster (Fig. 6.26). Of course, if the first left-most bit (of the whole string) is equal to 0, then the system outputs a rest, respective to the duration of the cluster. An example of a PQCA-generated cluster sequence is shown in Fig. 6.27.[4]

6.6.2 Music from Two-Dimensional PQCA

Now, let us examine a method for generating music with two-dimensional PQCA, which is a variation of the one presented earlier for CAMUS. Consider the 9 × 4 lattice shown in Figs. 6.18 and 6.19. Similar to the idea of splitting a one-dimensional PQCA bitstring to encode musical information, we also split the lattice into zones here. Each of these zones represents parameters to generate music.

Each cycle of the automaton generates groups of triples. The number of triples produced in a cycle of the automaton is given by the number of qubits that are measured equal to 1 in the relevant zone (in this case, zone **B**). The lattice is split as follows (Fig. 6.28):

- Zone **A**: the first column defines a reference pitch for building the triples

---

[4] This music was not generated from the output shown in Fig. 6.17. It comes for a different run of 20 cycles.

Fig. 6.28 The two-dimensional grid for representing musical forms

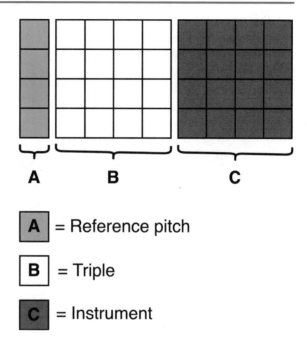

A = Reference pitch

B = Triple

C = Instrument

- Zone **B**: the next four columns define triples
- Zone **C**: the final four columns allocate instruments to play the triples.

The reference pitch is determined by the four bits of zone **A**, reading from top to bottom. These four bits give us sixteen values, each of which represents a number of semitones above a given default base pitch: $C4$. For example, the code [0011] corresponds to three semitones above $C4$, which results in $D\sharp 4$.

Zone **B** is formed by the second to fifth columns of the lattice (Fig. 6.28). Each live cell in this zone will be turned into a triple as follows (Fig. 6.29):

- The x coordinate of the cell in this zone defines the interval between the reference pitch and the second pitch of the triple
- The y coordinate of the cell in this zone defines the interval between the first pitch and the second pitch of the triple.

For example, given $D\sharp 4$ as a reference note, the living cell at coordinates (3, 2) in Fig. 6.29 would yield the triple: $[D\sharp 4, F\sharp 4, G\sharp 4]$, where $F\sharp 4$ sits at three semitones above $D\sharp 4$ and $G\sharp 4$ sits at two semitones above $F\sharp 4$.

The codification scheme designed for one-dimensional PQCA assumes that all the notes of a cluster are played simultaneously. In contrast, in our two-dimensional PQCA, the notes of a triple are not necessarily played all at the same time. Zone **B** also encodes separate timings for each note of a triple. For this, we consider the values of neighbours around a triple's cell. We also need to specify what happens if

Fig. 6.29 Scheme for
generating triples. The x and
y coordinates are considered
from the top-left cell of the
zone

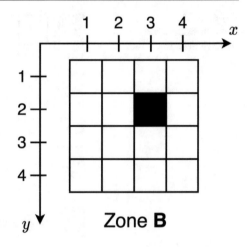

Fig. 6.30 Neighbourhood
code

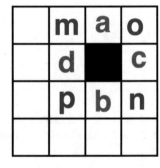

we look up a cell outside the range of our grid, and in these instances, the system
simply returns the value 0. Let us establish a nomenclature for the neighbourhood
of a cell as follows (Fig. 6.30):

- **a** is North
- **b** is South
- **c** is East
- **d** is West
- **m** is North-West
- **n** is South-East
- **o** is North-East
- **p** is South-West.

We follow from the original CAMUS notion of 'temporal morphologies' [23],
which are timing templates indicating where a note starts and stops in a bar of music.
Similarly, we form two four-bit codes using the neighbours [a, b, c, d] and [m, n, o,

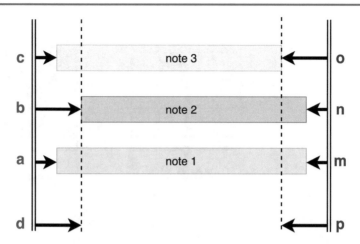

Fig. 6.31 The temporal morphology for two-dimensional pqca

p], respectively, to represent the starting and ending points of the notes of a triad, in the following way (Fig. 6.31):

- **a** indicates whether the bottom note of the triple starts on the first beat of the bar or waits for a while
- **b** indicates whether the middle note of the triple starts on the first beat of the bar or waits for a while
- **c** indicates whether the upper note of the triple starts on the first beat of the bar or waits for a while
- **d** determines how long the wait is. If this is equal to 1, then the wait is the equivalent of a quaver note, if equal to 0 then wait for the equivalent of a crotchet.

- **m** indicates whether the bottom note of the triple goes to the end of the bar or finishes early
- **n** indicates whether the middle note of the triple goes to the end of the bar or finishes early
- **o** indicates whether the upper note of the triple goes to the end of the bar or finishes early
- **p** determines the precise value of 'finishing early'. If this is equal to 1 then it ends the equivalent of a quaver early; if it is equal to 0, then it ends the equivalent of a crotchet early.[5]

A neighbourhood scheme is also used to select a musical instrument to play the notes of a triple. When a cell is alive in zone **B**, the same coordinates in zone **C**

---

[5] Of course, you, the user, are free to make your own choices.

Fig. 6.32 The
instrumentation scheme

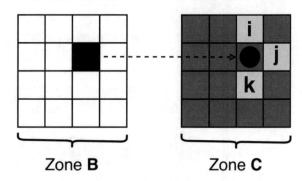

determine which instruments will play the respective notes (Fig. 6.28). One of two
different instruments (e.g., flute or violoncello) or classes thereof (e.g., strings or
woodwinds) is assigned to play a note, according to the scheme shown in Fig. 6.32,
as follows:

- If neighbour **i** is alive, then the bottom note of the triad is played by the flute,
  otherwise it is played by the violoncello
- If neighbour **j** is alive, then the middle note of the triad is played by the flute,
  otherwise it is played by the violoncello
- If neighbour **k** is alive, then the middle note of the triad is played by the flute,
  otherwise it is played by the violoncello.

As an example of musical rendering, Fig. 6.33 shows the music yielded by the
PQCA example shown in Fig. 6.23. This example takes into account only one cycle
of the automaton at $t + 4$. The ten cells that are alive in zone **B** generated ten bars of
music, each of which has its own temporal morphology and instrumentation. In this
case, the instrumentation is defined by two classes of instruments: 0 = woodwinds
(flute, clarinet and bassoon) and 1 = strings (violin and viola).

6.7 Concluding Discussion

In this chapter, we introduced the basics of cellular automata and briefly reviewed
an example of a system that generates music using the Game of Life automaton.
We stated that we are interested in developing systems that generate new kinds of
music rather than imitate existing music. And we discussed the usefulness of cellular
automata for building such systems.

Cellular automata are interesting for music because they produce sequences of
evolving patterns. Along the same lines, music can be thought of as sequences of
auditory patterns. The art of making music with cellular automata depends on con-

Fig. 6.33 An example of musical output from a two-dimensional PQCA

structing the automaton, and the method for translating the automaton's patterns into musical patterns.

Our research is exploring the potential of *quantum* cellular automata for music. To enable this, we developed a Python module for the easy creation and execution of partitioned quantum cellular automata (PQCA). It includes tools, tutorials and examples for translating outputs into music. The PQCA package and accompanying tutorials are available on GitHub: https://github.com/iccmr-quantum/pqca and https://github.com/iccmr-quantum/PQCA_Tutorial.

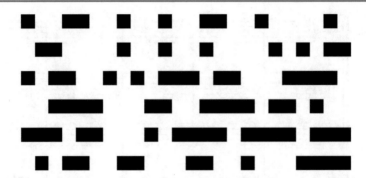

Fig. 6.34 An example of musical form generated with a one-dimensional PQCA. In this case, the line of qubits, or cells, are dispositioned vertically. The automaton evolution is displayed from the left to the right

The techniques described above to translate PQCA outputs into music are, of course, arbitrary; they were proposed here as starting points for further developments. And so are the tessellations and update circuits.

Currently, we are developing many more additional translation techniques, tessellations and update circuits to generate sections for the orchestral composition *Multiverse Symphony* mentioned earlier. One characteristic of PQCA that we are already started to explore musically is the fact that, although the rules are deterministic, quantum computing measurements are stochastic. We can generate slightly different musical sequences by running the same program multiple times. Depending on the translation method, this can emulate the well-known practice known as the recapitulation of a musical section to compose classical sonatas [11].

We also have been exploring PQCA to control music at abstract levels of representation other than the note level; please, refer to Chap. 2 in this volume for a discussion on abstraction boundaries. We have been using PQCA to control parameters for sound synthesisers and also musical form. Figure 6.34 shows a form produced for *Multiverse Symphony*, using a one-dimensional PQCA.

Current quantum computing hardware struggles to perform gates exactly, leading to small errors called *noise*. Noise adds even more unpredictability to the already unpredictable nature of measuring the outcomes of quantum computations. Considerable research is being conducted to develop error mitigation strategies; e.g., [28, 31, 32]. However, whereas mitigation of noise is a sine qua non for the robustness of quantum computing, controlled degrees of noise would be acceptable for creative applications of PQCA. For the composition of *Multiverse Symphony*, we implemented a virtual potentiometer to control the level of acceptable noise expected from a backend quantum processor. This enables us to generate musical variations but based on the same underlying PQCA rules.

In terms of further work, there are a few inspiring unexplored quantum-specific behaviours that we plan to experiment with PQCA. For instance, the entanglement of qubits leads to interesting global correlations (such as are visible in Fig. 6.23) despite the rules being explicitly local. Einstein referred to this phenomenon as "spooky action at a distance" [4] and this behaviour cannot be achieved with classical cellular automata.

Acknowledgements This project was funded by the QuTune Project. QuTune kick-started in the Spring of 2021 thanks to funding kindly provided by the UK National Quantum Technologies Programme's QCS Hub: [https://iccmr-quantum.github.io/].

References

1. Arrighi, P., & Grattage, J. (2010) Partitioned quantum cellular automata are intrinsically universal. arxiv:1010.2335.
2. Beyls, P. (1989). The musical universe of cellular automata. In *Proceedings of the International Computer Music Conference (ICMC)* (pp. 34–41). USA.
3. Bilotta, E., Pantano, P., Talarico, V. Synthetic harmonies: An approach to musical semiosis by means of cellular automata. In *Artificial Life VII: Proceedings of the Seventh International Conference on Artificial Life* (p. 200). The MIT Press. https://doi.org/10.7551/mitpress/1432.001.0001.
4. Brubaker, B. (2021). How bell's theorem proved 'spooky action at a distance' is real. *Quanta magazine*. https://www.quantamagazine.org/how-bells-theorem-proved-spooky-action-at-a-distance-is-real-20210720.
5. Burks, A. W. (Ed.). (1971). *Essays on cellular automata*. University of Illinois Press. ISBN: 9780252000232.
6. Dodge, T., & Jerse, T. A. (1985). *Computer music: Synthesis, composition and performance*. Schirmer Books.
7. Epstein, J. M., & Axtell, R. (1996). *Growing artificial societies: Social sciences from the bottom up*. The MIT Press. ISBN: 978-0262550253.
8. Ermentrout, G. B., & Edelstein-Keshet, L. (1993). Cellular automata approaches to biological modeling. *Journal of Theoretical Biology, 160*.
9. Farrelly, T. (2020). A review of quantum cellular automata. *Quantum, 4*. https://doi.org/10.22331/q-2020-11-30-368.
10. Gardner, M. (1970). The fantastic combinations of john Conway's new solitaire game "life". *Scientific American, 223*(4), 120–123. https://doi.org/10.1038/scientificamerican1070-120
11. Hepokoski, J., & Darcy, W. (Eds.). *Elements of sonata theory: Norms, types, and deformations in the late-eighteenth-century sonata*. Oxford University Press. ISBN: 9780195146400.
12. Hoffmann, P. (2002). Towards an automated art: Algorithmic processes in Xenakis' compositions. *Contemporary Music Review, 21*(2–3), 121–131.
13. Hogeweg, P. (1988). Cellular automata as a paradigm for ecological modeling. *Applied Mathematics and Computation, 27*.
14. Hsü, K. J., & Hsü, A. J. (1990). Fractal geometry of music. *Proceedings of the National Academy of Sciences, Physics, 87*, 938–941.
15. Inokuchi, S., & Mizoguchi, Y. (2003). Generalized partitioned quantum cellular automata and quantization of classical ca. arxiv:quant-ph/0312102.
16. Kelemen, J., & Sosik, P. (Eds.). (2001). *Advances in artificial life—Lecture notes in artificial intelligence* (Vol. 2159). Springer.
17. Loy, G. (2011). *Musimathics: The mathematical foundations of music* (Vol. 1). The MIT Press. ISBN: 978-0262516556.
18. MathWorld. Wolfram mathworld. (1999). https://mathworld.wolfram.com/ElementaryCellularAutomaton.html. Accessed 19 Feb 2022.

19. McAlpine, K., Miranda, E., & Hoggar, S. (1999). Making music with algorithms: A case-study system. *Computer Music Journal, 23*(3).

20. Miranda, E. R. (1993). Cellular automata music: An interdisciplinary project. *Interface, 22*(1).

21. Miranda, E. R. (1995a). Granular synthesis of sounds by means of cellular automata. *Leonardo, 28*(4), 297–300.

22. Miranda, E. R. (1995b). Entre l'absurde et le mystère. https://soundcloud.com/ed_miranda/entre-labsurde-et-le-mystere. Accessed 05 Mar 2022.

23. Miranda, E. R. (2007). Cellular automata music: From sound synthesis to musical forms. In E. R. Miranda & J. A. Biles (Eds.), *Evolutionary computer music*. Springer. https://doi.org/10.1007/978-1-84628-600-1_8.

24. Miranda, E. R. (2011). *A-life for music: Music and computer models of living systems*. A-R Editions. ISBN: 978-0-89579-673-8.

25. Miranda, E. R. (2014). *Thinking music: The inner workings of a composer's mind*. University of Plymouth Press.

26. Miranda, E. R., (Ed.). (2021). *Handbook of artificial intelligence for music foundations, advanced approaches, and developments for creativity*. Springer International Publishing. https://doi.org/10.1007/978-3-030-72116-9.

27. Miranda, E. R., & Biles, J. A. (2007). *Evolutionary computer music*. Springer.

28. Nachman, B., Urbanek, M., de Jong, W. A., & Bauer, C. W. (2020). Unfolding quantum computer readout noise. *npj Quantum Information,* (6). https://doi.org/10.1038/s41534-020-00309-7.

29. Preston, K., & McDuff, M. J. B. (1984). *Modern cellular automata: Theory and applications*. Springer. ISBN: 9781489903952.

30. Schuld, M., & Petruccione, F. (2021). *Machine learning with quantum computers*. Springer. ISBN: 9783030830984.

31. Shaib, A., Naim, M. H., Fouda, M. E., Kanj, R., & Kurdahi, F. (2021). Efficient noise mitigation technique for quantum computing. https://doi.org/10.48550/arXiv.2109.05136.

32. Shaw, A. (2021). Classical-quantum noise mitigation for NISQ hardware. https://doi.org/10.48550/arXiv.2105.08701.

33. Wolfram, S. (1983). Statistical mechanics of cellular automata. *Reviews of Modern Physics, 55*, 601–644.

34. Wolfram, S. (1984). Cellular automata as models of complexity. *Nature, 311*, 419–424.

35. Wootters, W. K., & Zurek, W. H. (1982). A single quantum cannot be cloned. *Nature, 299*, 802–803. https://doi.org/10.1038/299802a0

36. Worral, D. (1996). Studies in metamusical methods for sound image and composition. *Organised Sound, 1*(3), 183–194.

37. Xenakis, I. (1971). *Formalized music*. Indiana University Press.

QuiKo: A Quantum Beat Generation Application

7

Scott Oshiro

Abstract

In this chapter, a quantum music generation application called QuiKo is introduced. QuiKo combines existing quantum algorithms with data encoding methods
from Quantum Machine Learning to build drum and audio sample patterns from a
database of audio tracks. QuiKo leverages the physical properties and characteristics of quantum computing to generate what can be referred to as soft rules. These
rules take advantage of noise produced by quantum devices to develop rules for
music generation. These properties include qubit decoherence and phase kickback
to controlled quantum gates within the quantum circuit. QuiKo attempts to mimic
and react to external musical inputs, like the way that human musicians play and
compose with one another. Audio signals (ideally rhythmic in nature) are used as
inputs into the system. Feature extraction is performed on the signal to identify
its harmonic and percussive elements. This information is then encoded onto a
quantum circuit. Then, measurements of the quantum circuit are taken providing
results in the form of probability distributions. These distributions are used to
build a new rhythmic pattern.

7.1 Introduction

Artificial intelligent (AI) music generation systems have been exciting developments
in the fields of machine and deep learning, but are limited to the data set(s) that they
are given. As a result, these systems lack a sense of organicness, or intuition, in their

S. Oshiro (✉)
CCRMA, Stanford University, Stanford, USA
e-mail: soshiro@ccrma.stanford.edu

responses to external musical events. It has been speculated that quantum computing can be leveraged to go beyond just the imitation of a provided data set to the system. But concrete methods and results have not yet been presented to support this concept. However, Quantum Machine learning (QML) algorithms [1] can be dissected and adapted to begin developing algorithms that could possibly give these AI music generation systems the organic touch that they need.

In this chapter, a quantum music generation application called QuiKo will be discussed. It combines existing quantum algorithms with data encoding methods from QML [1] to build drum and audio sample patterns from a database of audio tracks. QuiKo leverages the physical properties and characteristics of quantum computers to generate what can be referred to as *soft rules* [2]. These rules take advantage of noise produced by the quantum devices to develop flexible rules and grammars for quantum music generation. These properties include qubit decoherence and phase kickback due to controlled quantum gates within the quantum circuit.

QuiKo builds upon the concept of soft rules in quantum music generation and takes it a step further. It attempts to mimic and react to external musical input, similar to the way that human musicians play and compose with one another. Audio signals (ideally rhythmic in nature) are used as inputs into the system. Feature extraction is then performed on the signal to identify its harmonic and percussive elements. This information is then encoded onto QuiKo's quantum algorithm's quantum circuit. Measurements of the quantum circuit are taken providing results in the form of probability distributions for external music applications to use to build new drum patterns.

The chapter begins with the system overview of the QuiKo application followed by a walk through of several quantum algorithms that act as the building blocks for the application. Next, it outlines in detail the inner workings of QuiKo along with two different encoding methods. Then, it presents results and analysis of the performance of the QuiKo application. The chapter also discusses initial experiments in building out the whole application in one quantum application. The final section discusses future work.

7.2 System Overview

Quiko, developed using IBM's quantum framework, Qiskit [3], has three main components (1) Preprocessing (2) Quantum Circuit (3) Beat Construction. Elements within these components are flexible and can be modified by the user, but we will stick to specific methods presented in this chapter.

First, the pre-processing component takes in an audio file, containing a piece of music, and extracts specific features from it. This provides a guide for how the system should aim to generate the new beat. It acts as a sort of influence or template for the system to use. To do this, the input audio file is fed into a filter bank producing filtered versions of the original audio based on a specific sub-band mapping. For simplicity, we will be using three filters. One for low-frequency content (low pass),

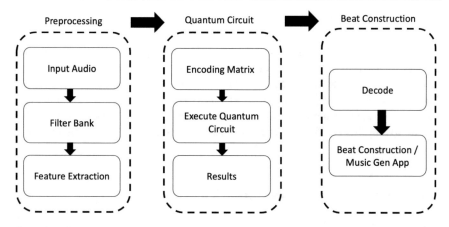

Fig. 7.1 QuiKo architecture

one for mid-frequency (bandpass) content and one for high frequency (high pass) content giving a total of three bands. The purpose of this step will become more clear in later sections. The system then performs feature extraction for collecting specific musical data for each measure and subdivision in the audio file (Fig. 7.1).

We then move to the second component of the system, which is the encoder. Here the features extracted in the pre-processing module are encoded onto the quantum circuit using controlled Unitary quantum gates (U gates), which we will discuss in future sections. First, the encoder organizes the data into an encoding matrix in order to easily access and encode the extracted features onto their corresponding Unitary gates for a specific subdivision. It then builds out the core quantum circuit to be used in the generation of a new beat. Here we will discuss two methods, static encoding and phase kickback sequencing encoding (PKBSE). The circuit is initialized and measured 1024 times (shots). The results are obtained and recorded for each shot.

The third and final component includes the decoder and beat constructor. After we have collected the results from running our quantum circuit, this component parses out the results for each subdivision and compares the states of the input audio to the states associated with the audio files in the database. From there, the system can determine which audio files (samples) in the database are more or less correlated with the quantum state of the input audio file. This information is then fed into a music generation application, developed in another computer music framework or DAW such as WebAudio API, MAX MSP, Abelton, Logic Pro, etc, to build out the final beat. Currently, separate circuits are needed to be run for each audio file in the database to obtain their resulting probability distributions. Thus, the comparison between the audio files in the database and the input audio is performed classically. However, in the future work section, designs and findings are presented from initial experiments in combining the quantum circuit and comparison process into one quantum circuit.

7.3 Algorithm Building Blocks

Before we dive into the specifics of the design for this application, we first need to discuss the underlying quantum algorithms and properties that are being utilized. These primarily include the Quantum Fourier Transform (QFT) [4] and Quantum Phase Estimation (QPE) [4]. These will be used to handle the rhythmic elements of the output beat, while the timbre and spectral elements will be handled using methods similar to amplitude and phase encoding used in quantum machine learning (QML) [1].

7.3.1 Quantum Fourier Transform (QFT)

The Quantum Fourier Transform (QFT) lies at the heart of many different quantum algorithms such as phase estimation along with Shor's factoring and period finding algorithms [4]. Essentially, the QFT transforms our states from the computational basis to Fourier Basis. We can gain some intuition about this by studying the Bloch sphere in Fig. 7.2. If we assume the qubit is initialized in the ground state $|0\rangle$ and we then apply a Hadamard gate to the qubit to transform its state from $|0\rangle$ to a state of equal superposition between 0 and 1. In other words, we rotate our state vector from the north pole of the Bloch sphere to the equator. This changes our basis states from $|0\rangle$ and $|1\rangle$ to $|+\rangle$ and $|-\rangle$ in the Fourier basis. The following examples and equations are based on those outlined in [4].

Mathematically, we can express this transform for a single qubit as follows:

$$|\tilde{X}\rangle = QFT\,|X\rangle = \frac{1}{\sqrt{N}} \sum_{k=0}^{N-1} \omega_N^{jk} \, |k\rangle \tag{7.1}$$

where $\omega_N^{jk} = e^{\frac{2\pi i x y}{N}}$. If we were to apply this to the single qubit case we would get:

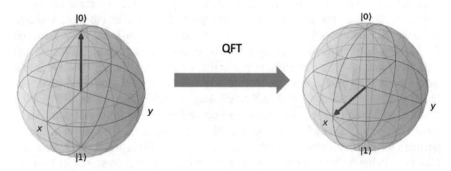

Fig. 7.2 Single Qubit QFT (Bloch Spheres generated using Qiskit [3])

$$|\tilde{0}\rangle = QFT\,|0\rangle = \frac{1}{\sqrt{2}}\sum_{k=0}^{N-1}\omega_N^{jk}\,|k\rangle = \frac{1}{\sqrt{2}}(e^{\frac{2\pi i(0)(0)}{2}}\,|0\rangle + e^{\frac{2\pi i(0)(1)}{2}}\,|1\rangle)$$
$$\frac{1}{\sqrt{2}}(|0\rangle + |1\rangle)$$

$$|\tilde{1}\rangle = QFT\,|1\rangle = \frac{1}{\sqrt{2}}\sum_{k=0}^{N-1}\omega_N^{jk}\,|k\rangle = \frac{1}{\sqrt{2}}(e^{\frac{2\pi i(1)(0)}{2}}\,|0\rangle + e^{\frac{2\pi i(1)(1)}{2}}\,|1\rangle) = \frac{1}{\sqrt{2}}(|0\rangle + e^{\pi i}\,|1\rangle$$

$$= \frac{1}{\sqrt{2}}(|0\rangle - |1\rangle)$$

The implementation of the QFT becomes more complex as we scale up to more qubits due to the fact we have more states to deal with. After we put all qubits in equal superposition we can then encode different values within their phases. We can encode information by rotating the state of each qubit by a different amount around the equator of the Bloch sphere. The rotation of each qubit depends on the angle of rotation of the other qubits. For example, to encode some state $|\tilde{x}\rangle$ on three qubits we will need to rotate the least significant bit (LSB) by $\frac{x}{2^n}$, which in this case would be $\frac{x}{2^3} = \frac{x}{8}$ full turns. The next qubit would then have to rotate twice as much, and so on and so forth depending on the number of qubits. As a result, the circuit for the QFT is going to implement a series of controlled Z gates in order to appropriately entangle the qubits being transformed to the Fourier basis.

This process may seem a little intimidating, but mathematically, we can break it down into individual qubit parts to make it easier for us to understand. If we have

$$n$$

qubits then we have $N = 2^n$ states. Let us say for example we have three qubits, $n = 3$, and as a result have $N = 2^3 = 8$ states. Our states on the computational basis are going to look like this:

$$|y_1 y_2 ... y_n\rangle = 2^{n-1}y_1 + 2^{n-2}y_2 + \cdots + 2^0 y_n = \sum_{k=1}^{n} y_k 2^{n-k} \qquad (7.2)$$

Which is just how we would represent a specific state in binary such as $|\tilde{7}\rangle = |1\tilde{1}1\rangle$. Each y_n represents a single bit in the binary string. If we plug this into the QFT equation we defined earlier we get:

$$|\tilde{x}\rangle = \frac{1}{\sqrt{N}}\sum_{y=0}^{N-1} e^{i2\pi x \sum_{k=1}^{n} y_k 2^{n-k}}\,|y_1 y_2 ... y_n\rangle = \frac{1}{\sqrt{N}}\sum_{y=0}^{N-1}\prod_{y=0}^{n} e^{\frac{2\pi i x y_k}{2^k}}\,|y_1 y_2 ... y_n\rangle$$

$$(7.3)$$

$$|\tilde{x}\rangle = \frac{1}{\sqrt{N}}(|0\rangle + e^{\frac{2\pi i x}{2^1}}\,|1\rangle)\otimes(|0\rangle + e^{\frac{2\pi i x}{2^2}}\,|1\rangle)\otimes(|0\rangle + e^{\frac{2\pi i x}{2^3}}\,|1\rangle)\otimes...\otimes(|0\rangle + e^{\frac{2\pi i x}{2^n}}\,|1\rangle)$$

$$(7.4)$$

We can know to expand out the Eq. (7.3) so that we have the tensor products of qubit rotating at the specific angle that we have specified in relation to the other qubits as seen in Eq. (7.4). We can think of the first parenthesis as the LSB while the elements in the last parenthesis represent the state of the qubit in the MSB position. Also, we can also observe that the rotations are applying a global phase on each of the individual qubits as the $e^{\frac{2\pi i x}{2^n}}$ elements.

Looking at Eq. (7.4), we can build out the circuit for the QFT on a multi-qubit system as follows (Fig. 7.3).

However, if we were to measure the circuit as is, after the forward QFT we would get results identical to the equal superposition case of all qubits in the register. This is because all qubits are in a state of equal superposition of $|0\rangle$ and $|1\rangle$. If we want to make this useful we would have to encode a specific state onto the phase of the qubit register in the phase domain (Fourier basis) and then apply what is called in the inverse QFT or $QFT^\dagger$. This transforms the Fourier basis back into the computational basis. This circuit can be implemented simply by reversing the QFT operation. The quantum circuit is illustrated in Fig. 7.4.

The $QFT^\dagger$ is useful in quantum algorithms that need to perform operations in a Fourier basis such as addition and multiplication as presented in [5]. More commonly, the practical use of the $QFT^\dagger$ is used within the quantum phase estimation algorithm.

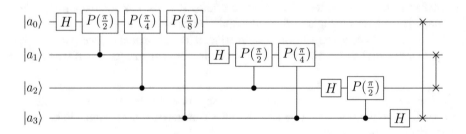

Fig. 7.3 Quantum circuit for quantum fourier transform (QFT) [4]

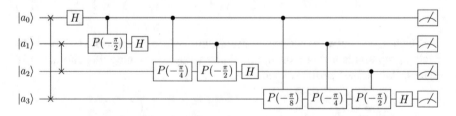

Fig. 7.4 Quantum circuit for inverse quantum fourier transform $QFT^\dagger$ [4]

7.3.2 Quantum Phase Estimation

Quantum Phase Estimation demonstrates the practical use cases for the QFT and $QFT^\dagger$. This algorithm estimates the amount of phase that a unitary gate applies to a qubit. Let's consider the following quantum circuit below as an example. This example is outlined the Qiskit textbook [4]

This controlled unitary gate, U-gate, applies a specific amplitude and phase to the target qubit. However, the phase applied by the U-gate to the target qubit also gets kicked back and applied to the control qubit. This effect is called *phase kickback*. In order to estimate the phase of the unitary, we need to apply full turns on the MSB. We will use cascading controlled phase gates (P gates) to create these rotations. This circuit is illustrated in Fig. 7.5. We use an auxiliary qubit a_3 to apply the P gates while the phases of those gates are kicked back to their control qubit. The circuit above shows that we rotate LSB by $\pi/4$ and then a_1 by $\pi/2$ and a_2 by π due to the phase kickback. This is similar to what we have seen in the previous section on the QFT. The circuit then applies the $QFT^\dagger$ on qubit a_0, a_1 and a_2 and then measures those three qubits. This particular circuit estimates a generic T-gate. This example is outlined in [4] as well. A T-gate rotates the qubit by $\pi/4$, with a matrix of:

$$T = \begin{bmatrix} 1 & 0 \\ 0 & e^{\frac{i\pi}{4}} \end{bmatrix}$$

If we apply the T-gate to a qubit in the $|1\rangle$ state we get:

$$T|1\rangle = \begin{bmatrix} 1 & 0 \\ 0 & e^{\frac{i\pi}{4}} \end{bmatrix} \begin{bmatrix} 0 \\ 1 \end{bmatrix} = e^{\frac{i\pi}{4}}|1\rangle$$

This means that we get get a phase applied to the qubit equal to $e^{\frac{i\pi}{4}}$. Since the generic phase of qubit is $e^{2i\pi\theta}$ we can say that θ is $\theta = \frac{1}{8}$. As result, when we execute the quantum phase estimation for the T-gate we should get a result of $\theta = \frac{1}{8}$. When we run this circuit we run it for multiple shots, or measurements. For this circuit we will run it for shots = 1024.

On the left side of Fig. 7.6, we see that there is a 100% chance that we get the bit string '001'. However, if we rotate the qubit by an odd amount, such as $\pi/3$ we will

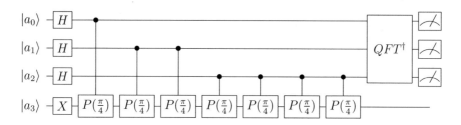

Fig. 7.5 Quantum phase estimation quantum circuit [4]

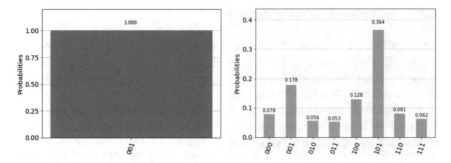

Fig. 7.6 Phase estimation results: (left) Aer-simulator, (right) IBMQ-Manhattan

get less accurate phase estimations of the gate. As a result, there will be a certain percentage of states other than the true value of the phase that is present. Here is where we take advantage of this phenomenon to create a responsive music system using the physical properties of the quantum computer. Not only is the property of phase kickback utilized to create a more flexible distribution of states within the phase domain but the noise from the real devices can be utilized to provide more variation in the states represented. This is illustrated on the right side of Fig. 7.6, where the phase estimation circuit is run on both the simulator and on IBMQ Manhattan off the IBMQ net hub. We observe that we expect to see 100% of measuring the state '001'. This means that we are estimating the gate to apply the phase of

$$\theta = \frac{y_n}{2^n} = \frac{1}{2^3} = \frac{1}{8}$$

In general, we not only have to consider the incorrect or mixed phases being applied. Rather, we have to deal with the noise of these devices. As result, we will have to study how these two elements interact with one another.

7.4 Pre-processing and Mapping Audio Signals to Qubits

We want our system to use specific musical features from different sub-bands of our audio files to generate a new beat out of our samples from our database. To do this, we will take inspiration from the work presented in [6] where a speech coding system is proposed using biological processes in the auditory nervous system (AN). In this work, speech signals are represented solely using the zero-crossing metric from different sub-bands (i.e. low, mid and high-frequency content) of the signals. For each sub-band, a spike is used to represent a positive zero crossing event resulting in a sequence of impulses. This results, in a representation that requires a low bit rate, and even though this compression algorithm is still lossy, the lost data is perceptually irrelevant. A similar method was implemented for QuiKo. A filter bank is applied to the input and database audio files creating filtered versions of each one. We will look at a simple case of dealing with just three sub-bands. Eventually, we will want to scale up to the full 25 sub-bands, roughly corresponding to the critical bands in the human hearing mechanism [7]. For now, however, we will apply a low pass, bandpass, and high pass filter to create three filtered versions of the signals. They will then be placed within a matrix to be encoded on the QuiKo Circuit which will be discussed in the next section.

Music Producer Timbaland states "Everything is not a theory bruh...It's a feeling" [8]. As a result, the QuiKo methodology overall does not take on a rule-based approach. It is based on the sonic content of audio samples being chosen and combined together. This application is focused on implementing an organic approach to generating music, attempting to give the system a sense of intuition, a "gut feeling". Quantum computing is well suited for this due to the fact that it can consider many different possibilities and outcomes simultaneously as do human musicians in the music creation process. This is the fundamental concept behind QuiKo's process for music generation in which we will call this approach as *organic rule-based*.

7.4.1 Drum Sample Database Preparation

First we need to prepare a database of audio samples to be used in the construction of the newly generated beat. We will gather a collection of audio samples; that is, single drum hits and long melodic and harmonic patterns and progressions. We then apply the filter bank as specified previously to each of the samples in the database. There should be a low, mid and high version of each sample. For each of the samples' filtered versions, the Harmonic Percussive Source Separation (HPSS) algorithm from the Python Librosa library [9] is then applied to extract harmonic and percussive features of the signals. The algorithm returns two signals via median filtering [9]: (1) the percussive part where the transients and onsets of the signal are more pronounced and (2) the harmonic part where the tonal and spectral content is more defined. These resulting signals are shown in Fig. 7.7. For the percussive part shown in Fig. 7.7a, the values of the peaks (spikes) in the signal are identified and are summed together. This sum is then divided by the value of the maximum peak, which will become our λ angle for the unitary gates used in the quantum circuit. The parameters and matrix for the U gate (U3 gate in Qiskit) are expressed in Eq. (7.5) [4].

For the harmonic part of the signal, shown in Fig. 7.7b, the Fast Fourier Transform (FFT) is performed. From there the highest three peaks are identified within the spectrum, and the weighted average of these values is calculated. This will be our θ parameter for the U-gates. Finally, the spectral centroid is also calculated from the harmonic part which will define our ϕ parameter.

$$U(\theta, \phi, \lambda) = \begin{pmatrix} \cos\frac{\theta}{2} & -e^{i}\lambda sin\frac{\theta}{2} \\ e^{i}\phi \sin\frac{\theta}{2} & e^{i}(\phi + \lambda) \cos\frac{\theta}{2} \end{pmatrix} \tag{7.5}$$

$$\phi = \frac{\sum_{k=0}^{N/2} k \cdot |X(k)|}{\sum_{k=0}^{N/2} |X(k)|} \tag{7.6}$$

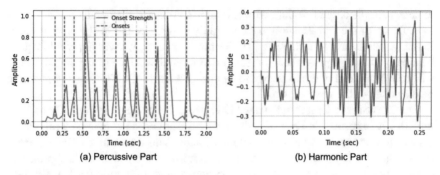

(a) Percussive Part   (b) Harmonic Part

Fig. 7.7 Percussive and harmonic parts of the audio signal

$$\lambda = \frac{\sum\limits_{n=0}^{N} f(n)_{onset}}{\max\{f(n)_{onset}\}} \tag{7.7}$$

$$\theta = \arg\max_{x=s}\left\{\sum_{n=0}^{N-1} x_n e^{\frac{-i2\pi kn}{N}} k = 0, \ldots, N-1\right\} \tag{7.8}$$

Equation (7.5) expressed the U-gate operation in matrix form [4]. Also, it defines the parameters that are encoded onto each U-gate in the quantum circuit. Methods for this encoding will be discussed in further detail in the following sections. Also, keep in mind that any set of features can be extracted and used as the parameter for these gates (Fig. 7.8).

7.4.2 Sample Database, Quantum Circuit and States

The calculations in the previous section will be done for each of the filtered versions of the original samples. The values in Eqs. (7.6), (7.7) and (7.8) will be encoded onto U-gates and applied to specific qubits [10,11]. The angles calculated in (3) for the low version of the sample will be mapped to q_0 using a U3 gate in Qiskit [3]. The angles for the mid will be mapped to q_1, and the high one will be mapped to q_2.

The circuit in Fig. 7.9 is then executed for 1024 shots. The resulting probability distribution for each audio track is then stored for future use. This process is repeated for each audio sample in the database.

7.5 The Quantum Circuit (QuiKo Circuit)

The process for preparing the database is similar to that of the input audio file that we want our output beat to be influenced by. The input audio file is filtered through

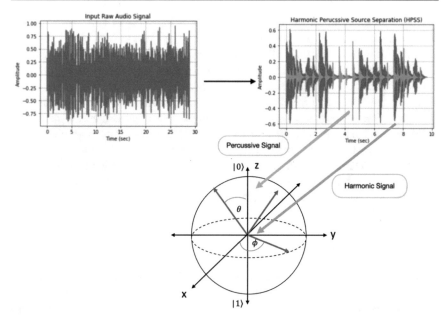

Fig. 7.8 HPSS qubit encoding

Fig. 7.9 Quantum circuit for database audio file features

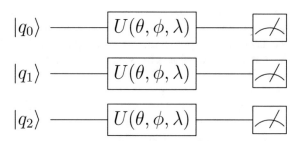

the same filter bank that was used for the audio files in the database. So in this case we will get three filtered versions (low, mid and high bands) of the input audio file. Then, as we did for the database, we applied the HPSS algorithm to each filtered version getting two separate signals (the percussive part and the harmonic part) for each.

The percussive and harmonic parts are then segmented into subdivisions depending on the number of qubits available in our circuit. Here we will allocate 3 qubits for our subdivision register which we will call our spinal cord register. Since we have 3 qubits in our register we will divide the parts into 8 subdivisions corresponding to eight notes. For each subdivision between the first eighth note and the last eighth note, we will apply a U-gate with the same feature set that we extracted from the database audio files. In other words, the averaged onset strengths of the percussive part of the input signal will map to θ, the weighted average of the 3 highest frequency peaks in the spectrum of the harmonic part of the input signal will map to ϕ, and the spectral centroid of the harmonic part will be mapped to λ of our U-gates for each subdivision. Again, this will be done for each filtered version of the input audio file. Once these features have been extracted for each subdivision of each filtered version of the signal and encoded as parameters on our U-gates, we need to associate each U-gate with a specific subdivision. The way this is done is through entangling another register of qubits, where we will apply the encoded U-gates, to the spinal cord register. This will entangle a particular U-gate to its corresponding subdivision.

This can be done in various ways. In this section, we will discuss two methods of encoding this musical feature onto qubit registers and entangling them with their corresponding subdivision information. These methods include (1) Encoding Static (2) Phase Kickback Sequencing Encoding.

7.5.1 Static Encoding

This method is based on the QRDA [12] and FQRDA [13] quantum representations of audio signals; refer to Chapter 10 in this volume for an introduction to quantum audio representation. In general, the extracted musical features per sub-band are encoded onto the quantum circuit and are entangled with its corresponding subdivision. Breaking down Fig. 7.5 we see that the circuit is divided into two-qubit registers timbre register and the spinal cord register. We first prepare both qubit registers in equal superposition by applying a single Hadamard gate to each qubit in the circuit so that we have an equal probability of getting each subdivision. All these initial gates on both registers are referred to as the internal pulse of the system. Metaphorically, this is analogous to a musician's personalized sense of 'groove' or rhythm based on their past musical experiences. For now, we will only deal with the equal superposition case as we want to see how the system will perform with an equal probability of getting each eight-note subdivision.

Next, we set up a series of cascading multi-controlled Unitary gates. Each of these U3 gates is applied depending on the subdivision to which the spinal cord register collapses to. Note that the controls represented as closed black filled dots are checking to see if the qubit happens to collapse to '1', and the controls represented as empty dots are checking to see if the qubit collapses to '0'. For example, in Fig. 7.5 the multi-controlled U-gate U_5 has a closed black filled control on the first and the third qubits, and an empty control on the second qubit in the spinal cord register. This means that the U-gate U_5 will be applied to the timbre register if the spinal cord register collapsed to $|101\rangle$, or the 5th subdivision in the measure (Fig. 7.10).

Each of the multi-controlled U-gates in Fig. 7.5 contains three separate multi-controlled U3 gates. Each corresponds to a different sub-band on a particular subdivision. We can also see that for each gate on each sub-band we see the parameters associated with the musical feature we extracted for a corresponding subdivision. Qubit q_0 is allocated for parameters in the low band, q_1 is allocated for parameters in the mid-band, and q_2 is allocated for parameters in the high band. As a result, the

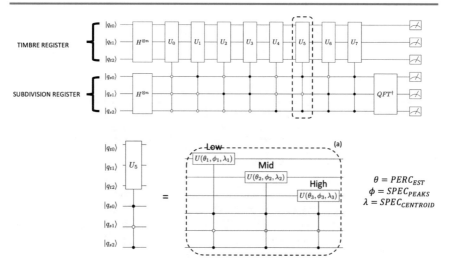

Fig. 7.10 Static encoding circuit

timbre register will collapse to a three-bit binary string, and thus when we measure it many times we get a probability distribution associated with a particular subdivision.

As each of these multi-controlled U-gates is applied to the timbre register, depending on the collapsed state of the spinal cord register, the phase of the corresponding U-gate is kicked back to the spinal cord register. Thus, if we consider the case of U_5 again, the phase associated with those set of gates will be pushed into the spinal cord register thus changing is a state in the Fourier basis. In other words, the state it was upon triggering the U_5 is now offset in the Fourier basis. Thus, if we measure the spinal cord on the Fourier basis we will obtain a different subdivision than that the resulting timbre code was originally entangled with. To do this, phase estimation is performed on the spinal cord register by applying the $QFT^\dagger$ to the spinal cord register and then measuring it.

7.5.2 Phase Kickback Sequencing

Static encoding, however, is very expensive to implement as multi-controlled qubit gates (containing more than one control) do not correspond to the cost of the number of controls and targets. For example, a controlled X (cx) gate would have a cost equal to 2 for the target and the control qubits [14]. Any more than one control qubit would need to decompose into a larger circuit as shown for the multi-controlled U-gate with two controls in Fig. 7.11. As a result, if we want to design our algorithms to deal with subdivisions any small than eight notes, the circuit cost would drastically increase. Alternative, cheaper methods are needed if we want to scale our system for more detail and resolution.

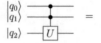

Fig. 7.11 Multi-controlled U-gate decomposition

Here we propose a method in order to reduce the cost associated with static encoding. This method is called Phase Kickback Sequence Encoding (PKBSE). In previous sections, we discussed the effects of phase kickback produced by controlled quantum gates and how to estimate the amount of phase that gets kicked back into the control qubit register (in this case the spinal cord register).In order to reduce the cost of the static encoding circuit, we need to replace the multi-controlled U-gates with single controlled U-gates and sequence them in a way that applies parameters of a specific subdivision. Figure 7.12 outlines the logic behind this method. This has a number of steps:

1. Split the measure in half with half the subdivisions on one side (starting with 0 in binary) and the other on the right side (subdivisions starting with 1 in binary).
2. Calculate and/or extract the desired feature for each subdivision on the left and right side of the measure.
3. For one side of the measure (the '0' side or the '1' side) sum the features associated with each subdivision with the same type of features in previous subdivisions. This is done to reflect the behaviour of a human musician in which their musical response is based on the current and previous musical events from other performing entities.
4. Multiplies all the feature summations by -1 if they are not associated with the final subdivision for each half of the measure.
5. Repeat this process for the other side of the measure.
6. Organize the data into a PKBSE encoding matrix as at the bottom of Fig. 7.12.

We negate all summed other than the last subdivision within the respective halves of the measure due to the fact that they cover the entire segment. If we sum all the parts together for a particular sub-band we get a sequence-dependent on the qubits themselves being 0 or 1 and remove the smaller segments from the total feature value from the higher segment layers. After we have done this for each feature we organize it into an encoding matrix shown at the bottom of Fig. 7.12 in order to organize our parameters to encode onto our quantum circuit. Since we are dealing with a low, mid and high band along with three separate parameters, our PKBSE encoding matrix

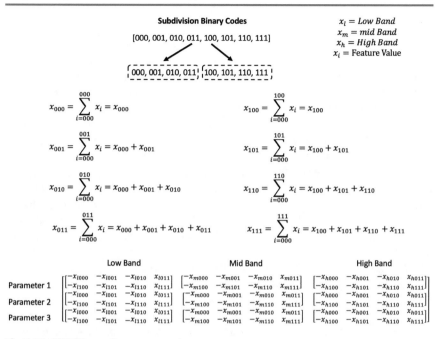

Fig. 7.12 PKBSE encoding representation

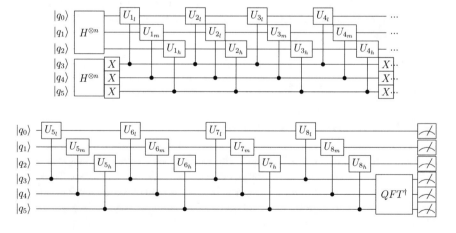

Fig. 7.13 The circuit for the PKBSE encoding method

will be 3×3. Each element of this matrix will be a 2×4 matrix containing each of the summed features for each subdivision.

Figure 7.13 shows the quantum circuit for the PKBSE encoding method. The spinal cord and timbre registers are set up in the same way that they were in static encoding. Each qubit in the timbre register represents one of the sub-band of the input audio signal, while the spinal cord register represents the different subdivisions that are being considered. This is done by entangling the two registers in a particular way. We will use the concept presented in [15] which states that human musicians perceive the attack times of instruments with lower frequency content with less resolution than that of instruments with high-frequency content. Here we can say that parameters associated with the low sub-band, encoded on to q_0, will be entangled with the most significant qubit in the spinal cord register, q_3. This is due to the fact that the rate at which q_3 changes is less frequent than the other qubits in the register. Following suit, q_1 which deals with mid-sub-band sequence parameters will be entangled with the next significant qubit q_4, and so on and so forth.

The separation between the sequences for the first and the second half of the measure can be observed in the circuit as well. The first half of the measure (as stated previously) is defined by '0' in the most significant spinal cord qubit, and thus its U-gate sequence is enclosed by X gates on the spinal cord register. This sequence of gates will be triggered if any of the spinal cord qubits happen to be '0'. On the other hand, if any of these qubits happen to be '1' then the gate sequence outside of the X gates will be triggered. The encoding process of mapping the extracted features of the signal to parameters on their corresponding controlled U-gates is identical to that for static encoding. However, in the PKBSE circuit, we will get a direct phase kickback from the U-gates that were applied to the timbre register, and thus elements from the original signal should have a more direct impact on the states for the spinal cord register. Also in contrast to the static encoding method where we considered the effects of features for one subdivision at a time, the PKBSE method allows the system to consider the effects of groups of subdivisions at the same time in superposition.

7.6 Results

7.6.1 Decoding and Beat Construction

Once the core quantum algorithm has been executed on either a simulator or a real device, we want to decode the results in order to construct the final beat. To do this we need to compare the probability distributions generated by executing the quantum circuits for our audio files for each subdivision of the input signal. To compare the different quantum states the fidelity between the state of the input track and the database tracks is calculated. Fidelity measures how close two quantum states are to each other [16], and thus will identify which audio files in the database are most (and least) similar to the input audio file.

$$F(\rho, \sigma) = (tr(\sqrt{\rho}\sigma\sqrt{\rho}))^2 = |\langle \psi_\rho | \psi_\sigma \rangle|^2 \qquad (7.9)$$

After the fidelity is calculated for all the database and the input audio files, the audio samples in the database are organized into layers based on the value of each sample's fidelity. A layer is a group of audio samples that occupy a single subdivision.

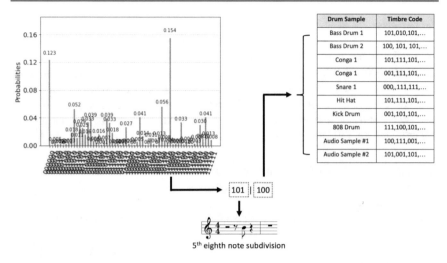

Fig. 7.14 Results for spinal cord qubit register

(a)

	Sample 1	Sample 2
Subdiv 1	samp16.wav	samp6.wav
Subdiv 2	samp16.wav	samp6.wav
Subdiv 3	samp16.wav	samp6.wav
Subdiv 4	samp16.wav	samp6.wav
Subdiv 5	samp16.wav	samp6.wav
Subdiv 6	samp16.wav	samp6.wav
Subdiv 7	samp16.wav	samp6.wav
Subdiv 8	samp16.wav	samp6.wav

(b)

	Sample 1	Sample 2	Sample 3	Sample 4	Sample 5
Subdiv 1	bass5.wav	samp2.wav	bass7.wav	bass8.wav	samp4.wav
Subdiv 2	samp1.wav	hihat5.wav	samp10.wav	samp19.wav	drum2.wav
Subdiv 3	samp1.wav	hihat5.wav	samp10.wav	samp19.wav	drum2.wav
Subdiv 4	bass7.wav	bass8.wav	conga12.wav	crash0.wav	samp14.wav
Subdiv 5	samp14.wav	drum2.wav	bass6.wav	samp4.wav	bongo4.wav
Subdiv 6	samp1.wav	hihat5.wav	samp10.wav	samp19.wav	drum2.wav
Subdiv 7	cymb1.wav	snare1.wav	samp15.wav	samp17.wav	snare6.wav
Subdiv 8	samp1.wav	samp1.wav	samp11.wav	hihat4.wav	conga4.wav

(c)

	Sample 1	Sample 2	Sample 3	Sample 4	Sample 5
Subdiv 1	snare2.wav	samp18.wav	hihat3.wav	samp14.wav	conga6.wav
Subdiv 2	snare3.wav	samp18.wav	samp4.wav	hihat3.wav	samp14.wav
Subdiv 3	snare5.wav	samp14.wav	snare6.wav	samp18.wav	conga4.wav
Subdiv 4	samp12.wav	samp18.wav	samp4.wav	bass3.wav	samp14.wav
Subdiv 5	snare5.wav	samp18.wav	samp14.wav	conga4.wav	snare6.wav
Subdiv 6	snare.wav	samp18.wav	samp14.wav	conga4.wav	snare4.wav
Subdiv 7	snare5.wav	samp18.wav	hihat0.wav	samp14.wav	conga6.wav
Subdiv 8	samp12.wav	samp4.wav	samp18.wav	bass3.wav	samp14.wav

(d)

	Sample 1	Sample 2	Sample 3	Sample 4	Sample 5
Subdiv 1	conga7.wav	conga5.wav	snare0.wav	samp19.wav	conga3.wav
Subdiv 2	drum1.wav	hihat4.wav	conga8.wav	bongo4.wav	samp8.wav
Subdiv 3	cymb0.wav	samp19.wav	conga7.wav	conga5.wav	samp11.wav
Subdiv 4	conga3.wav	conga8.wav	hihat4.wav	bongo4.wav	drum1.wav
Subdiv 5	cymb0.wav	snare2.wav	conga7.wav	samp19.wav	conga3.wav
Subdiv 6	snare1.wav	samp7.wav	conga3.wav	samp3.wav	conga1.wav
Subdiv 7	bass0.wav	samp11.wav	drum1.wav	samp19.wav	cymb0.wav
Subdiv 8	conga8.wav	conga3.wav	bongo4.wav	hihat4.wav	conga1.wav

Fig. 7.15 Sample results of static and PKBSE encoding decoded layer tables. **a** Static encoding maximum fidelity. **b** Static encoding minimum fidelity. **c** PKBSE encoding maximum fidelity. **d** PKBSE encoding minimum fidelity

After some subjective listening and experimentation, this author found that high fidelity values led to more pulsating and repeating audio sample sequences. Layers further away from the input audio signal begin to present more rhythmic patterns and sequences with more variation. An example of this is illustrated in Figs. 7.14 and 7.15. There is a trade-off between consistent spectral content and the rhythmic variation in the input audio signal.

7.6.2 Analysis

To understand how our system behaves for a wide variety of input signals a matrix of random parameters is used as input to the system for a number of trials. We compare the performance of these two methods by looking at their flexibility with respect to choosing different audio samples from the database. In addition, we measure the impact that phase kickback and noise associated with real quantum devices have on the newly generated beat patterns. We utilize the expressibility measure proposed in [17]. This measure is primarily used to indicate the degree that which a quantum circuit can explore Hilbert space. However, in this case, we will adapt it to measure how well our Static and PKBSE quantum circuits can explore our audio database. We will take the following steps:

1. Generate a matrix of random parameters values to encode onto the quantum circuits used to generate the probability distributions associated with audio files within the audio sample database.
2. Generate a uniformly random matrix and encode it onto our quantum circuit for Static and PKBSE methods.
3. For each subdivision calculates the fidelity between the resulting state of the input and the states of the audio tracks in the database.
4. Repeat to collect 50 samples.
5. Record the probability distribution of how often a particular layer occurs (layer with identical samples in it).
6. After the distribution of the layer occurrence is generated, generate a uniform distribution of the layers.
7. Repeat this process for each layer of samples.

Figure 7.16 plots the expressibility curve for both the static and PKBSE methods, executed on the simulator and IBMQ Manhattan backend. The x-axis shows the layer number, the y-axis shows the expressibility value for the layer, while the plot on the left depicts the expressibility of running the quantum circuits on Qiskit's Aer-simulator. The plot on the right depicts the expressibility results after running the quantum circuits on the real device from the IBMQ net hub. Looking at these graphs we can see that the overall expressibility for the simulator is high for the static encoding method in comparison to the lower layers. The higher the expressibility value the less it can explore the database for a variety of inputs.

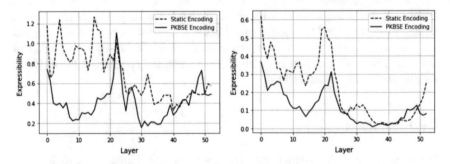

Fig. 7.16 PKBSE encoding circuit: Aer-simulator (Right), real device (Left)

For the results obtained from running on the Aer simulator, it is observed that the lowest layer has a 70% higher expressibility that the PKBSE. As the layer number increases the PKBSE decreases to a local minimum around layer 10. A spike in the expressibility curve then occurs between layers 20 and 25, approximately matching the expressibility value of the static encoding. We then see another local minimum at layer 30, with expressibility of approximately 0.2. After this, the curve begins to increase again starting at layer 35 and the static and PKBSE expressibility begin to converge. However, for static encoding, the local minimums are not as pronounced as they are for the PKBSE method. There is more of a gradual decline for the static encoding method with oscillations about the general shape of the curve. The two expressibility curves for the static and PKBSE encoding then begin to converge with each other after layer 40.

For results obtained from running on IBMQ hadrware, both curves take on a gradual declining shape with a pronounced spike around layer 20. Here a more noticeable difference can be observed between the spike of the static and PKBSE expressibility curves. These spikes are also offset from one another by a layer. The curves then begin to converge to very low expressibility values until they diverge again after layer 40. This shape shows that the noise introduced by the real device lowers the expressibility value and in the case of the static encoding smooths out the curve. The oscillations associated with the static encoding method are now minimized and begin to look similar to the shape of the PKBSE curve. In contrast, the PKBSE expressibility curve maintains the same shape that was observed from the simulator. The noise introduced from the real quantum device scales the PKBSE curve down by a factor of 2 (approximately).

What we can conclude is that static and PKBSE encoding theoretically behave differently for various input values for a single database of audio samples. However, with the noise introduced by the real devices, we see that they then begin to behave more similarly. In addition, it can also be concluded from analyzing these plots that the layers with the highest expressibility (least flexibility) for a randomized database are the lowest, the highest and the layers halfway between the highest and lowest layers. Figure 7.17 shows the expressibility curves of the system for both static and PKBSE circuits for a real audio sample database (non-randomized). When

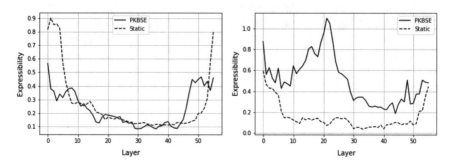

Fig. 7.17 PKBSE encoding circuit: Aer-simulator (Right), real device (Left)

executed on the simulator, the results obtained are in line with what we found for the randomized database run on IBMQ hardware with the exception that no spike within the mid-layers occurred for either method. Overall, for this database, it is expected that the PKBSE has a lower expressibility (more flexibility) than the static encoding. The Static encoding, however, has steeper slopes near the ends of the curves allowing for more flexibility with more of the inner layers. At the time of running the system for the results in Fig. 7.17, IBMQ Manhattan had been retired and all circuits needed to be run on a different device, IBMQ Toronto. The Static encoding expressibility curve for this database on IBMQ Toronto keeps its same shape as seen for running on the simulator. But the expressibility curve for the PKBSE shows a massive spike, surpassing a value of 1.0 at layer 20, and spanning layers between 10 and 30. Thus, what has been observed is that the noise from the real devices can cause the expressibility curves to smooth out, scale down or scale up from the shape of the expected results. As result, various types of databases with audio samples varying in timbres and spectral content need to be further studied.

When encoding the musical information onto quantum circuits the perfect reconstruction of the musical data is not the primary concern. We can prepare the state of the qubit register so that different voices of the musical information can be generalized and operated on as a single object. When a musician is improvising in the moment they are less concerned with the transcription of the music but rather how to react. So when the system is measured without any additional operations applied, it should produce a very flexible but still related interpretation of the original musical content, rather than replicating it.

7.6.3 Phase Kick Back Results and Analysis

The expressibility metric primarily considers only the timbre and spectral aspects of the audio signals. However, we also need to analyze the other critical element of our system, phase kickback. As stated previously, phase kickback contributes to the rhythmic response of the system. To analyze it we need to look at the effects that phase kickback has on the spinal cord register of our quantum circuit. We will follow a similar method as we did with the expressibility metric. We will take 50 samples of randomly generated parameters for both encoding methods, and then will obtain averaged probability distributions for the spinal cord qubit register when the circuits are executed. The results will then be compared to the distribution showing an equal superposition of each eighth-note subdivision. This will be done by computing the Kullback-Leibler Divergence (KLD) [18] between the averaged distributions of each of the encoding methods against the equal superposition produced by the quantum circuit in Fig. 7.18.

Figure 7.18 shows the results for the spinal cord register for both the simulator and IBMQ Manhattan quantum computer for both the Static and PKBSE encoding methods. Distributions for the circuit are included to compare and observe the impact that phase kickback and noise introduced from the real device had on the results for both encoding methods. Let's first take a look at the simulator. In the upper left-

Fig. 7.18 Quantum circuit for equal superposition for 3 qubits

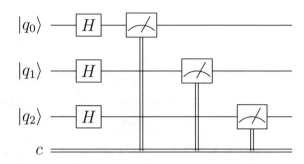

hand corner of Fig. 7.19, we see the distribution for equal superposition executed on the simulator. The distribution in the upper centre of Fig. 7.19 shows the results for the static encoding circuit, which produced a decrease in the probability that subdivisions '000' or '111' would occur. It shifted energy from these subdivision to subdivisions '001', '011', '100' and '110', while '010' and '101' stayed the same. These are similar results observed for the PKBSE method.

If we look at the results from the real device, we see that the static and the PKBSE averaged distributions for the spinal cord registers are now different. The phase introduced by the static encoding circuit on the spinal cord register caused the results to slightly skew right. The median shifts from '011' (subdivision 4), as seen in the simulator, to '010' (subdivision 3). This causes the first three subdivisions to increase their probability of occurring, with the exception of '100' (subdivision 5), which has the highest probability to be selected within the measure. Comparing the KLDs calculated (Table 7.1) for the simulator and IBMQ Manhattan for the static encoding, the KLD for the simulator case is 38.6% smaller than KDL in the real device case. This means that the phase kickback and noise associated with IBMQ Manhattan had a greater impact than expected from the simulator.

For the PKBSE there is a decrease in the right and left ends of the distribution in comparison to the equal superposition case for results obtained from the simulator and IBMQ Manhattan. However, the results for the real device are more consistent among groups of subdivisions. There is a decrease in amplitude at '011' (subdivision 4) causing the distribution to take on a bi-modal shape, with a median of '100' (subdivision 5). The three most likely subdivisions that the PKBSE will select occur on the left side of the measure at '100' (subdivision 5), '101' (subdivision 6) and '110' (subdivision 7). For the right side of the measure, PKBSE will more likely choose '001' (subdivision 2) and '010' (subdivision 3). The KLD values for the PKBSE are also shown in Table 7.1 and are very similar to the values for the Static encoding method.

If we listen to the PKBSE generated beats we get more of a pulsating marching sound than we do with the beats generated from the static encoding. This is consistent with the groups of subdivisions that increased in amplitude due to the noise from the real device and phase kickback. As a result, we can say that the characteristics of the noise being introduced by real quantum devices are a significant influence on the rhythmic aspects of the system. This could lead to encoding internal rhythms, grooves

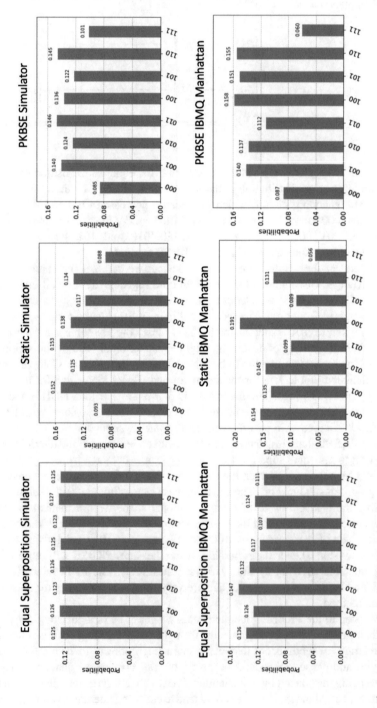

Fig. 7.19 Results for spinal cord qubit register

Table 7.1 The KLD table

	Static KLD	PKBSE KLD
Aer simulator	0.017	0.013
IBMQ Manhattan	0.044	0.045

and feels into the system. This possibly could give quantum computers the ability to feel and understand the concepts of style, groove and personality and creativity in computer/algorithmic music generation.

7.7 Initial Steps to A Complete Quantum Application

So far we have compared and contrasted the distributions of the database circuits to the results of the timbre register of the input audio track classically. If we increase the number of qubits in our circuit, or in other words use a larger device we can do this comparison on a quantum computer! The circuit below outlines how this can be done.

Figure 7.19 shows the case of comparing one track from the audio database to the output of the input audio track for a specific subdivision. To recap, we put the qubits q_0 through q_5 in superposition by applying $H^{\otimes n}$ Hadamard gates. We then apply the QuiKo circuit (Static or PKBSE encoding methods) to qubits q_0 through q_5. We then apply the circuit set-up for one track discussed earlier. After this, a syndrome measurement is implemented to act as a comparator between the QuiKo circuit and each audio database circuit. This will flag a match between the output of the timbre register and the collapsed value of the database circuit. We then see that the qubits on the syndrome measurement are then measured and recorded in a classical register. The spinal cord register on the QuiKo circuit is also measured to record which subdivision the match is associated with.

Once the matches on the syndrome qubit register are measured then we store the results in a larger classical bit register in their assigned position within the classical bit string. In this case of Fig. 7.20, the first three bits will be allocated to the syndrome measure between the QuiKo timbre register and the state of the first audio track quantum register. The next three bits will be for the next syndrome measure with the QuiKo circuit and the second audio track in the database, and so on and so forth. The last three bits of the classical register will be allocated for the subdivision the comparison is happening on, so when we do the post-processing or parsing of the results we know how to associate which comparison distribution goes with which subdivision in the measure.

The syndrome measurement (Fig. 7.20) [4] is implemented here as an alternative to the more expensive comparators used in various applications for quantum audio signal processing [12, 13]. Here compare register is initialized in $|0\rangle$ and then uses a

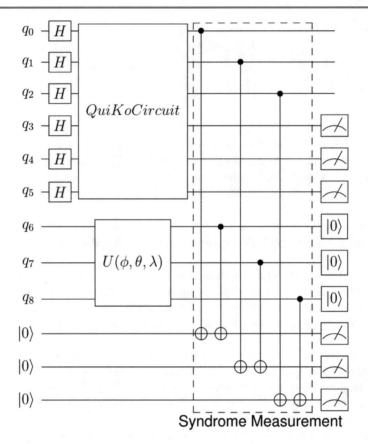

Fig. 7.20 Quantum circuit for comparing the output of the input audio track to the audio tracks in the database

CNOT gate to entangle q_0 and q_9. If q_0 happens to be '1' then q_9 will flip to '1', and if q_6 happens to match then it will flip it back to 0. This also occurs if both q_0 and q_9 are matching '0's since the CNOT will not trigger. As a result, if we follow this logic for all the qubits in the comparator if we get the compare register to be '000' then the input and the audio track have a match for that particular shot, and since we measure the compare register right after we can reuse it to compare another audio track. We also have to reset the audio track qubits after measurement of the comparator if we want to reuse it for another audio track in the database. Figure 7.21 illustrates an example of a full circuit implementation of comparing from the database.

If we compare the expressibility metric with the one obtained classically we see that it generally shares the same shape. However, we do see for both the static and PKBSE methods that it hits a maximum around layer 45 and then maintains a constant expressibility value of 4.0, which tells us that there is only one outcome for a variety of input parameters. In other words, the system is no longer flexible between layers 45 and 61. This is due to the decoherence and quantum volume of the actual device

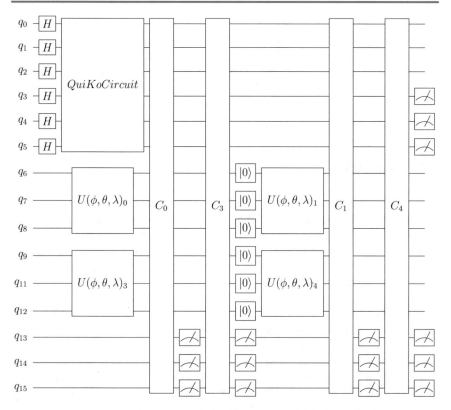

Fig. 7.21 Quantum circuit for comparing four audio tracks to the input track

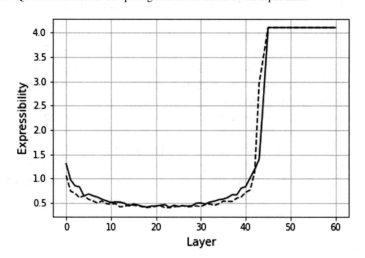

Fig. 7.22 Expressibility results for the full circuit including database selection

(IBMQ Brooklyn). This becomes a factor due to the fact that we are implementing the circuit in Fig. 7.20 for 61 audio tracks. This makes our full circuit very large and the number of gates and time it takes to process probably approaches or exceeds the quantum volume of IBMQ Brooklyn. In addition, since the qubits in the timbre register are not being reset, the qubits within the register decohere over time, which explains why we see a constant flat top after the 45th layer in Fig. 7.22.

7.8 Future Work

This experiment has only taken the initial steps in using quantum computers in creating responsive beats. Keep in mind here we only conducted this experiment with one kind of database containing a limited number of samples and variability. In future studies, this experiment should be repeated with databases of different samples, lengths and instruments/timbres to truly get a better picture of how these algorithms are performing.

The experiments performed in this chapter only dealt with initially setting both qubit registers in equal superposition. Further investigation is required to know how the system would perform if the initial states of the qubits are not equal. These initial states will be referred to as the internal pulse of the system. Different functions and probability distributions can be used as internal pulse states, thus allowing for real-world musical rhythms and grooves (e.g., Afro-Cuban Rhythms, Funk and Swing) to be encoded into the system. Figure 7.23 illustrates the change from initializing the timbre and spinal cord registers from superposition to different states.

In addition, the downside of our method is that we still classically compare and contrast the different quantum states from the database. Further research will investigate how to design this process to work within one quantum circuit, and will also look into applying Quantum Access Memory (QRAM) [19] to better store the quantum states of the audio files. It will also be extended to generate segments larger than one measure at a time and to study how to take advantage of elements such as decoherence for musical purposes.

Finally, further studies will need to be conducted to increase the resolution of the system. So far we have only dealt with eight-note subdivisions. The number of qubits will have to be scaled up to account for anything shorter than an eighth note. Initial experiments have been attempted to run these algorithms for more qubits allowing for more sub-bands and subdivisions to be considered. However, as the size of the qubit registers scaled up so did the run time and it became very inefficient. As a result, the method presented in this chapter will have to be adapted for these larger high definition circuits.

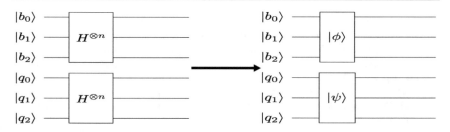

Fig. 7.23 Internal bounce states

References

1. LaRose, R., & Coyle, B. (2020). Robust data encodings for quantum classifiers. *Physical Review A, 102*(3).
2. Kirke, A. (2019). Applying quantum hardware to non-scientific problems: Grover's algorithm and rule-based algorithmic music composition. *International Journal of Unconventional Computing,* (Old City Publishing) (Accepted). arXiv:1902.04237v3 [cs.AI].
3. Hector, A., et al. (2019). Qiskit: An open-source framework for quantum computing. https://doi.org/10.5281/zenodo.2562110, https://qiskit.org/textbook/preface.html.
4. Asfaw, A., et al. (2020). Learn quantum computation using qiskit. https://qiskit.org/textbook. Accessed 11 June 2021.
5. Ruiz-Perez, L., & Garcia-Escartin, J. C. (2017). Quantum arithmetic with the quantum Fourier transform. *Quantum Information Processing, 16*(6).
6. Pahar, M., & Smith, L. (2020). Coding and decoding speech using a biological inspired coding system. In *2020 IEEE Symposium Series on Computational Intelligence (SSCI)*. https://doi.org/10.1109/SSCI47803.2020.9308328.
7. Bosi, M., & Goldberg, R. E. (2003). *Introduction to digital audio coding and standards.* Springer, US.
8. CLA Woo. (Mar 6, 2021). Timbaland on why music theory is not necessary. YouTube, [Video file]. https://www.youtube.com/watch?v=Lk8XUxcf0Cs. Accessed 7 Oct. 2021.
9. McFee, B., Raffel, C., Liang, D., Ellis, D., McVicar, M., Battenberg, E., Nieto, O. (2015). Librosa: Audio and music signal analysis in python. In *Proceedings of the 14th Python in Science Conference*.
10. Verfaille, V., Arfib, D., Keiler, F., von dem Knesebeck, A., & Zölzer, U. (2011). Adaptive digital audio effects. *DAFX: Digital Audio Effects*, 321–391. https://doi.org/10.1002/9781119991298.ch9.
11. Verfaille, V., Holters, M., & Zölzer, U. (2011). Introduction. *DAFX: Digital Audio Effects*, 1–46. https://doi.org/10.1002/9781119991298.ch1.
12. Wang, J. (2016). QRDA: Quantum representation of digital audio. *International Journal of Theoretical Physics, 55*(3), 1622–1641. https://doi.org/10.1007/s10773-015-2800-2 Mar.
13. Yan, F., Iliyasu, A. M., Guo, Y., & Yang, H. (2018). Flexible representation and manipulation of audio signals on quantum computers. *Theoretical Computer Science, 752*, 71–85.
14. Lee, S., Lee, S. J., Kim, T., Lee, J. S., Biamonte, J., & Perkowski, M. (2006). The cost of quantum gate primitives. *Journal of Multiple-Valued Logic and Soft Computing, 1*, 12.
15. Rottondi, C., Chafe, C., Allocchio, C., & Sarti, A. (2016). An overview on networked music performance technologies. *IEEE Access, 4*, 8823–8843.
16. Liang, Y.-C., Yeh, Y.-H., Mendonça, P. E., Teh, R. Y., Reid, M. D., & Drummond, P. D. (2019). Quantum fidelity measures for mixed states. *Reports on Progress in Physics, 82*(7), 076001. https://iopscience.iop.org/article/10.1088/1361-6633/ab1ca4.

17. Sim, S., Johnson, P. D., & Aspuru-Guzik, A. (2019). Expressibility and entangling capability of parameterized quantum circuits for hybrid quantum-classical algorithms. *Advanced Quantum Technologies, 2*(12), 1900070. https://doi.org/10.1002/qute.201900070.
18. Ji, Z. Z., Ying, S., Wang, L., Zhao, X., & Gao, Y. (2020). Kullback-Leibler divergence metric learning. *IEEE Transactions on Cybernetics.*
19. Asaka, R., Sakai, K., Yahagi, R. (May 2021). Quantum random access memory via quantum walk. *Quantum Science and Technology, 6*(3). https://iopscience.iop.org/article/10.1088/2058-9565/abf484/pdf.

QAC: Quantum-Computing Aided Composition

8

Omar Costa Hamido

Abstract

In this chapter I will discuss the role of quantum computing in computer music and how it can be integrated to better serve the creative artists. I will start by considering different approaches in current computer music and quantum computing tools, as well as reviewing some previous attempts to integrate them. Then, I will reflect on the meaning of this integration and present what I coined as QAC (Quantum-computing Aided Composition) as well as an early attempt at realizing it. This chapter will also introduce *The QAC Toolkit* Max package, analyze its performance, and explore some examples of what it can offer to realtime creative practice [1]. Lastly, I will present a real case scenario of QAC in the creative work *Disklavier Prelude #3*.

8.1 Computer Music and Quantum Computing Tools

Recent literature exploring the intersection of Quantum Computing (QC) with creative music practice, of which this book is a prime example, have welcomed the potential increase in speed and computational power offered by future fault tolerant QC machines. In the context of Computer Music (CM), a need for more powerful machines is evident in the limitations that classical machines still present for the realtime (or near realtime) control of compositional processes [2].

O. C. Hamido (✉)
ICCMR, University of Plymouth, Plymouth, UK
URL: https://omarcostahamido.com

Several research projects have already proposed proof-of-concept implementations that integrate QC with music practice, in simulation or with current hardware. However, there is still no consistency between the tools, and approaches undertaken in these explorations, and current CM practice. More importantly, a disconnect between scientific research and creative practice, may only serve to maintain a gap between scientists and artists. My proposed line of inquiry here intends to bridge that gap by focusing on the tools used and how they articulate with realtime creative music practices.

Modern Computer Music tools and Quantum Computing tools have been shaped by their main users in their practice in such a way that each might currently be regarded as capable of drawing their own self-contained world of practice and practitioners (Fig. 8.1). CM tools include score engravers, Digital Audio Workstations (DAW), and visual programming environments, like Musescore [3], Ableton Live [4], and Max/MSP[1] [5], respectively. The use of these three categories of tools is deeply embedded in the creative practice of writing musical scores, recording and producing a track, and developing new interactive instruments as well as enabling realtime control of compositional processes.

On the other hand, current QC tools seem to inherit greatly from code-based programming practices, where the majority of its user base is found. These include the different QC programming frameworks[2] like Qiskit [6], Cirq [7], and pyQuil [8], which are accessed using a terminal or a Jupyter notebook, as well as some web applications that allow the design of circuits online like Strangeworks [9], IBM Quantum Experience [10], and QPS [11].[3]

These QC tools, based on a more traditional computer programming paradigm, can still be regarded as inheriting the *punch card* computation paradigm. In it, the user is faced with the clearly delineated step sequence of writing the code, submitting the code to be executed, and waiting for the results to come back. On the other hand, within the CM tools sphere, it is often seen the predominance of a realtime computation paradigm, where the program is being changed as it is being executed.

It is worth noting that, while I offer these simple categories here, painting the landscape with large brushstrokes, there are examples of practices that challenge these broad boundaries. Such is the case with *live coding* [14], as mentioned in previous chapters in this volume, where performer-composers can be found programming music live using code-based languages, and often projecting their code on a screen on stage alongside them.

Computer Music practice, in its broadest sense, is strongly informed by this realtime computation paradigm. From listening to notes as they are being dropped on a score, to tuning audio effects while a song is playing, and algorithmically generating tones and melodies that respond to a live input on the fly.

---

[1] From now on, in this chapter, simply referred to as Max.
[2] Most of them are based in the Python programming language.
[3] For a more complete list of current Quantum Computing tools see [12, 13].

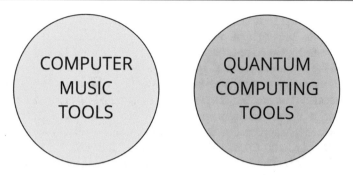

Fig. 8.1 Computer music tools and quantum computing tools

8.2   Previous Attempts for an Integration

Given that only recently QC has become more available to the larger community of researchers and enthusiasts worldwide, in both tools and learning references, the first initiatives to integrate QC with Music Composition mostly came from researchers with a Computer Science background. Unsurprisingly, these attempts have relied heavily on QC code-based tools, meant for non-artistic practice. Such is the case with Hendrik Weimer's *quantenblog*, where he presents some musical examples that were built with his C library for QC simulation, libquantum [15]. As early as 2014, I attempted to integrate the (then very obscure) QCL programing language[4] with my compositional practice and electroacoustic setup, with no practical success.

A second generation can be found expressed in the work published by researchers with stronger artistic considerations. The integration strategies present in these works are mostly characterized by more complex systems that include higher software stack requirements, or simply the proposal of a new CM dedicated application altogether. The first generation of the *Quantum Synthesizer* [17], a Max-based synthesizer making use of QC, can illustrate this.

In this first generation of the *Quantum Synthesizer*, a 48 h hackathon project at the Qiskit Camp Europe, in September 2019 [18], Max is used as a frontend where the user changes selected parameters that are passed to a backend Python environment via OSC.[5] In turn, this Python environment, that can be running on the same machine or somewhere else in the local area network, is configured with Qiskit and running several Python scripts that account for the network information exchange and to programmatically build quantum circuits based on the parameters

---

[4] The first quantum computing programming language by Ömer [16].

[5] Open Sound Control, a mostly music related, udp-based, networking protocol.

received from Max. These circuits are then simulated locally (with or without a noise model) or sent to real quantum computer hardware in the cloud. After retrieving the execution results, these are returned to Max, via OSC, which changes the state of the synthesizer accordingly (Fig. 8.2).

A similar strategy is explored by Eduardo Reck Miranda in his interactive quantum vocal system architecture (Fig. 8.3). In it, there is also a CM system that is connected to a Python environment, within a networked software architecture. However, Miranda's approach relies more heavily on the direct use of Python and Jupyter notebooks, with Csound scripts being triggered from the Python environment [19, 20, p. 17]. The musical output, in this case, is managed through a more code-based interface, which was intended to work more seamlessly with the QC framework. This is at the cost of a higher learning curve, and a *less* realtime CM environment.

Another approach, taken by James Weaver, has been to create an entirely new CM application environment from scratch. In his web application, *Quantum Music Composer*, Weaver creates a new interface that allows the user to generate third species counterpoint melodies, based on melody and harmony matrices [21]. The software generates output as Lilypond code, that can be rendered as a readable musical score using the Lilypond music score engraver [22]. Though it has a cleaner interface, its use is also more restricted than in the previous examples.

It is clear from most of these examples that more visual user interfaces, that are not simply just a terminal window, are more inviting to musicians and creative users. However, it is also clear that most of these implementations still relied on rather complex software infrastructures that are not easy to set up and modify during the creative process. Weaver's system requires considerable non-CM and non-QC skills to modify it and use it to achieve a different compositional goal. Miranda's system requires more knowledge of code-based practices. And my own initial version of the *Quantum Synthesizer*, even in the more inviting user interface that was explored shortly after its hackathon conception (Fig. 8.4), requires different software pieces to be running at the same time and be launched in the correct order.

At this point, there is both a need for more musician-friendly interfaces as well as to rethink what is to be expected of this integration and what it should look like. On the one hand, it seems that reducing code-based language barriers is one avenue,

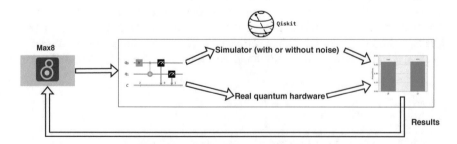

Fig. 8.2 Architecture of *quantum synth*. From [17]

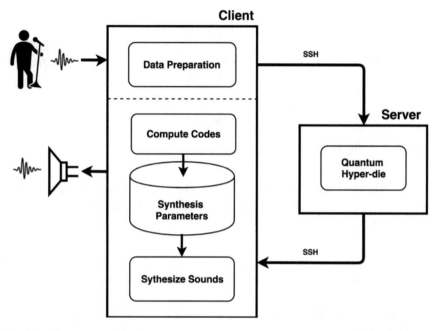

Fig. 8.3 The interactive quantum vocal system architecture. Reproduced by permission from Eduardo Reck Miranda [20]

Fig. 8.4 Second GUI for the *quantum synth* presented in [23]

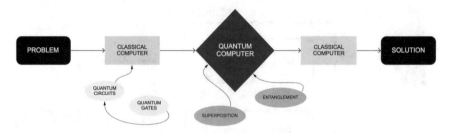

Fig. 8.5 Overview of computing a problem with QC. From [25]

on the other hand, simplifying the deployment/setup/configuration process of these systems is equally important to make it a more practical tool. For the rest of this chapter, I will give an account of my own work to this effect.

8.3 A New Quantum-Computing Aided Composition

When exploring the integration of QC with Music, it is important to have a clear idea of what it is that QC can offer, and set the proper expectations. There are some popular misconceptions about QC that need to be avoided, as the idea of it replacing all the current classical computers when, in reality, as Scott Aaronson and science communication outlets like Quanta articulate, "quantum computers aren't the next generation of supercomputers—they're something else entirely" [24]. They are different in the way they function, making use of quantum mechanics phenomena to compute, which requires a different approach to articulate a problem to be computed. QC uses quantum information, but we build and send the set of instructions for the computation (the computing job) using classical machines, and classical information. And, most importantly, what we retrieve from a quantum computer is, in fact, classical information—that is the result of measurement operations that collapse the quantum states into readable classical information (Fig. 8.5).

As music is composed of sound, and sound is the result of a (classical) mechanical force, pulling and pushing air particles around, there will be no "quantum sound" one will be able to hear at some point. QC can enter the world of music in assisting the compositional process, similar to what has been happening with classical computers for the past century. Computer Aided Composition[6] (CAC) has a long tradition, with different approaches to using computers for sound and music [26], and a new Quantum-computing Aided Composition (QAC) should refer to it.[7]

---

[6] Also mentioned in some references as "Computer Assisted Composition."

[7] The term "QAC" was first coined in 2019, in the context of the research found in [27]. It was intentionally not abbreviated to qCAC or QCAC to make it clear that it is not simply an addition to

In effect, creating music that draws analogies with quantum mechanics (QM) is a practice that predates, by several decades, the actual use of QC in music. This calls for a necessary distinction where the former can still be represented by the term "Quantum Music," adopted by some early creative practitioners,[8] while the latter might be better suited under the term "Quantum Computer Music." Furthermore, as it will become clear during the rest of the chapter, the QAC concept further articulates a distinction under this umbrella where, as the name implies, QC must support or help the progress of creative practice. For QAC, the creative practice must be the driving force for the integration of QC.

When talking about IBM's roadmap for QC's near and long-term future, Gambeta refers back to the importance of pursuing QC as a way to tackle seemingly impossible problems "with fresh eyes," and explains the motivation for their hardware and software improvements. Ending his presentation, he states that "[...] if developers can eventually do all this, with a few simple lines of code, using their existing tools, we've succeeded." [29]. This corroborates an important point that I am bringing up in my writing. To advance QC, with diverse communities such as the one represented by creative artists, a balance must be found between stimulating thought within a new (computational) paradigm and lifting language barriers. With my work, I propose that using existing creative tools is a way to cross that barrier or, better yet, to expand the current creative vocabulary and stimulate thought in this new paradigm more easily.

A modern-day generation of tools for QAC must emerge from within the CM sphere and allow more seamless integration with music composition workflows. These may have to be simple enough so that the musician should not need to worry about the underlying software (and hardware) framework. But they also need to be complex enough so that the musician can dive deeper into them and use them to accomplish different compositional tasks. In practical terms, one might still be tempted to devise two approaches at this point. One approach would be to extend current algorithmic music composition libraries in Python, like music21 [30], Abjad [31], or SCAMP [32],[9] which would still require considerable effort in articulating them with the rest of CM tools, and lending them simpler interfaces. The other approach, the one I took, is to make the new tools emerge within an already well-known environment and well-articulated with the different CM practices, like the Max visual programming environment.

In my research and creative practice, I already use Max quite extensively and I find it to be accessible to musicians and artists working with technology at different levels, and coming from different backgrounds.[10] The ability to quickly create simple interfaces and the strong direct integration with the Ableton Live DAW,

---

CAC. On the same token, as will become clear in the next paragraph, it was intentionally not translated to simply "Quantum Aided Composition."

[8] A recent collective manifestation of that can be found in [28].

[9] For more context about these tools see, for example, Tymoczko's review of music21 [33], and Evanstein's comparison between algorithmic composition tools in [34].

[10] Another programming environment worth considering for this type of work is Pure Data [35].

makes it the perfect candidate for developing tools for QAC.[11] In the next section I will give an account of the early attempts for the creation of these tools.

8.4   Early Attempts for QAC

As it started to become clear to me what needed to be articulated with QAC and what its contributions to the artistic community would be, it also started to become clear what were the strategies to explore its implementation. It was very important to be able to abstract away all the underlying software infrastructure setup required to simulate quantum circuits, and to eventually communicate with real quantum hardware in the cloud. And all this in a CM environment already familiar to musicians. The creation of a Max for Live device, using the integration of Max in the Ableton Live DAW, available since 2012 [37], was already a clear goal in order to make it available for a larger community of non-programmer electronic musicians. But another integration made available in late 2018, the Node for Max [38], turned out to be equally important in clarifying the path to get there.

In early 2019 I devised several experiments to explore this integration of QC using Node.js, and ended up working very closely with the (now archived) Qiskit.js node module [39]. Even as an experimental module, I was able to incorporate it into Max and successfully deploy a simple Max for Live device called **och.qc-circ-2q**.[12] This was a MIDI device that can be simply drag-and-dropped into a MIDI track chain to add it to the Live session. On the right side of the device the user is presented with a set of four sliders that represent the expected probabilities for measuring each of the four possible states that two qubits can represent: |00>, |01>, | 10>, and |11>. These probabilities change depending on the quantum circuit being used. The left side of the device displays the 3 different ways to load a quantum circuit. The first two involve loading Qasm code from either a file on disk or from the clipboard. The third possibility is to read the MIDI clip names in the track (Fig. 8.6).

Qasm, or OpenQasm, stands for "Open Quantum Assembly Language" and it was proposed as a simple language for describing quantum circuits that can be written or decoded by several of the modern quantum computing frameworks [40]. It is also accepted by different quantum hardware backends and given its flexibility it was very clear early on that I should articulate a way to integrate Qasm into the device. However, because the generation of the Qasm code can be non-trivial at times, I also decided to implement a new minified circuit notation that I invented for

---

[11] A similar approach was taken by the Magenta team at Google, where they decided to build Max for Live devices to reach a wider audience of music practitioners [36].

[12] The new Max devices, objects, and abstractions will be highlighted in bold for ease of identification while reading.

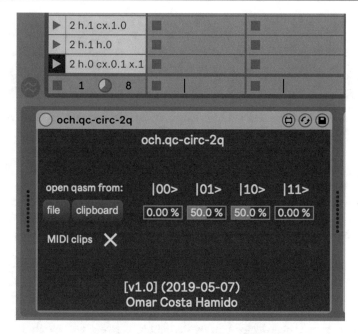

Fig. 8.6 Earlier generation of fully integrated device. From Hamido [27]

this occasion. This notation, as illustrated in the top portion of Fig. 8.6, consists of a list of strings, starting with the number 2 (for two qubits), defining which quantum gates to apply to which qubits.

Once the quantum circuit is read, and the probabilities are calculated, displaying the results on the sliders, the user can map each slider value to control other parameters in the Live session.[13] In this case, I used multiple **och.Param2Param** devices to map the slider values to different **och.probGate** devices in several chains of a drum rack. A drum rack in Ableton Live is a virtual instrument that splits incoming MIDI notes to trigger different samples (usually percussive sounds, as part of a drum kit); and **och.probGate** simply serves as a gate that will either block or allow MIDI notes to pass through the chain and play the sample (Fig. 8.7).

Internally, after receiving the quantum circuit instruction, **och.qc-circ-2q** calculates the quantum statevector[14] and translates that into the predicted probabilities for retrieving each of the possible computational-basis states that two qubits can offer. The reason for hardcoding two qubits in this system is that performance

---

[13] Mapping one parameter value to another parameter value is a recurring practice when working with DAWs. Ableton Live comes with a couple devices that allow this, and several more can be found in [41].

[14] "Statevector" (one word) is in effect a "state vector" (two words), but the former, influenced by its code-based notation, has been largely adopted in the QC world to directly refer to the quantum state, that is, the mathematical description of the internal state of a quantum system.

Fig. 8.7 Example device chain using och.qc-circ-2q together with a drum rack, och. Param2Param, and och.probGate. From Hamido [27]

started to be affected when using a slightly higher number of qubits. With two qubits it was still fast enough to be usable in realtime, swapping quantum circuits with no noticeable delay. Some of the factors for this could include the ever-increasing library dependencies, sometimes not working perfectly with each other, which made the compilation of this device take more than 10 min at some point.

Another important limitation of this device was the fact that it only provided access to the quantum statevector. QC is a probabilistic means of computation, meaning that one only obtains results by running the quantum circuit multiple times and aggregating its results (counts). The distribution of these results should resemble the inner statevector but, by definition, it rarely will be able to express those *clean* values that are calculated mathematically. The actual quantum statevector is, thus, not something that can be retrieved in real quantum computation, but only in simulation. Other factors explaining the variation on the results obtained from real quantum hardware include the noise that disturbs the system and measurement.[15]

The insights gained during these early experiments ultimately meant that I had to abandon this specific approach. Though very important milestones were achieved at this stage while trying to realize QAC, the instability of the underlying framework, a project that was even shut down at some point, as well as the limitations described above, dictated that I had to explore a different approach. It was clear to me that I needed to find a way to implement something much more performant, that would not be limited to an extremely reduced number of qubits and would still allow the use in a realtime creative practice context.

8.5 Introducing *The QAC Toolkit*

One of the things that also became clear, after my early attempts for QAC, was that I needed to learn more about how QC frameworks work to find the minimum viable implementation that would be less prone to instability. As I started learning more

---

[15] As explored in [17], there are multiple *outputs* in QC that can be explored: statevector calculation, simulation, simulation with noise models, and real hardware.

about how the Max environment works, and how to actually write new native objects for this environment, I also became more active in the QC community, participating in hackathons and becoming more involved with IBM researchers and the Qiskit Advocates community, to whom I presented QAC and QAD as well [42–44].

As it will become clear in the next pages of this chapter, this interaction with the community revealed to be very important for the development of my proposed work. By November 2019, I started building my own quantum computing simulator, inspired by the work of Christine Corbett Moran [45, 46] and James Wootton [47]. And between December 2019 and December 2020 I was able to work with James Wootton on creating a new version of the MicroQiskit library in C++ [48] that ultimately enabled me to complete a quantum simulator natively integrated in the Max environment. This new generation of tools, to allow musicians and artists to build, simulate, and run quantum circuits inside Max, gave birth to the software package that I called *The QAC Toolkit* (Fig. 8.8).

The QAC Toolkit is a package for Max that is available directly from the Max package manager, and it includes some externals and abstractions for working with QC in Max. This package includes examples for learning about quantum gates and

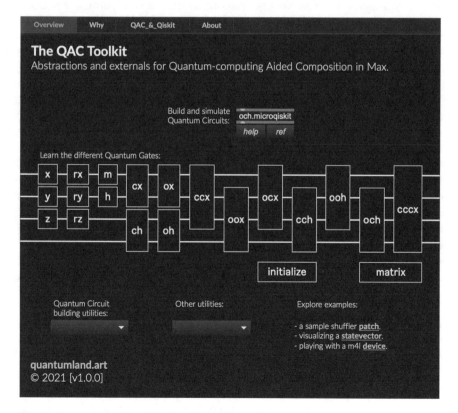

Fig. 8.8 Screenshot of *The QAC Toolkit* overview patch

the new workflow directions that these tools enable, as well as several objects to help streamline working with it. One of the main objects, **och.microqiskit**, implements circuit building and simulation functions in Max.[16]

8.5.1 och.microqiskit

As the name suggests, **och.microqiskit** is very much inspired by the MicroQiskit framework, even sharing several of the method names. However, as a Max object the user interacts with it using Max messages instead of running scripts or using the command line. It should be noted that, besides creating a new object box in the Max patch and typing its name, there is nothing more that is required to set up—no Node modules, no Python packages. This object contains in itself all the required resources to build and simulate valid quantum circuits, as well as to retrieve other information from it.

There are two main *entities* (or classes) in **och.microqiskit**, one is the *QuantumCircuit*, representing the definition of a quantum circuit as a group of quantum gates and the number of qubits and classical bits allocated. The other is the *Simulator*, which makes use of the *QuantumCircuit* definition to perform a series of different tasks, including simulation, retrieving the statevector, and converting the circuit definition to other code-based language definitions. All the messages to interact with **och.microqiskit** will always refer to either a *QuantumCircuit* or a *Simulator*. And one instance of this object can hold multiple quantum circuits and simulators.

In Fig. 8.9 we can see a simple example patch using **och.microqiskit**.[17] On the top portion of the patch there are two groups of messages, one for creating and changing the quantum circuit, and another for creating and firing the simulator. The first message "QuantumCircuit qc 1 qw 1 1" creates two new *QuantumCircuits* named *qc* and *qw*; the first with 1 qubit, and the second with 1 qubit and 1 classical bit. The second message "qc h 0, qw m 0 0" actually sends two consecutive messages,[18] one adds a Hadamard gate on qubit 0 to the *qc* circuit, and the other adds a measurement gate between qubit 0 and classical bit 0 on the *qw* circuit. The third message on this left column simply adds the contents of the circuit *qw* to the *qc* circuit.

On the group of messages on the top right, the first message "Simulator sim qc 127" creates a new *Simulator* named *sim* with the contents of the *qc* circuit and sets

---

[16] All the objects start with "och." because the original short name of the toolkit package is och. This also reflects a recurring practice in object crafting among the Max developer community. Still, some object mappings are available as well: e.g. *och.microqiskit* can also be initialized simply by typing *microqiskit*.

[17] This Max patch is available for download in [49].

[18] In Max, multiple messages can be grouped in one message box by separating them with a comma. The result is that when the message box is triggered both messages will be sent out individually, one immediately after the other.

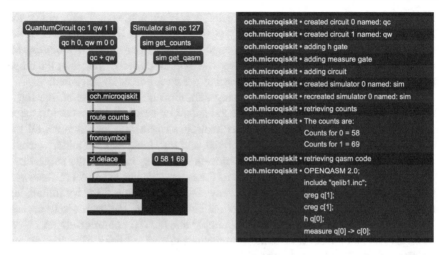

Fig. 8.9 och.microqiskit object example patch, on the left, and its console output, on the right

its configuration to use 127 shots.[19] The second message "sim get_counts" requests a simulation to be run and retrieve the counts of that simulation. In fact, every time this message is triggered a new simulation is executed and new results retrieved. The third message "sim get_qasm" will not run a simulation but will instead convert the quantum circuit into a Qasm definition and output it. By default, **och.micro-qiskit** will print to the console information regarding each action that was taken (see right side of Fig. 8.9),[20] and by doing that the learning process of using it becomes easier. By the same token, it will also print error messages to the console every time there was an incorrect message sent to the object.[21]

The lower portion of this patch shows an example of using the results retrieved from the quantum simulation to change the state of a *multislider* object. When asked to retrieve the counts, **och.microqiskit** will output a message that contains the word *counts* followed by a symbol (string) containing the list of states and its respective counts. We use the *route* object to allow only messages starting with *counts* to pass, and we use the *fromsymbol* object to transform the symbol back into a list—the contents of the message at this point are shown on the connected message box. The *zl.delace* object simply splits a list into two lists with every other

---

[19] One "shot" is the same as one execution of the quantum circuit. As explained in the previous sections, QC needs to execute a quantum circuit multiple times to derive enough information to more faithfully represent the computed solution.

[20] Unless the *console_output* attribute is set to 0. See, for example, how och.microqiskit is used in the next section.

[21] For example, if the user tries to call a circuit with a name that has not been previously set on this object instance, it will reply with an error message on the console. The object will also post error messages if, for example, the user tries to add a gate to a circuit on a qubit that is outside of range, tries to run a simulation without measurement gates, or tries to add measurement gates on circuits without classical bits to store them. This helps to make sure that only valid quantum circuit definitions are generated.

item, that are output separately on the left and right outlets. At this point, the message coming from the right outlet only contains a list of counts (without the states) and this is all that is needed to change the state of two sliders in a *multislider* object: note that the *multislider* object was configured to receive values in the range of 0–127, which is the number of times that the circuit is being executed.

This is a very simple example of using **och.microqiskit**. Because all the interactions with this object only require using standard objects in the Max environment, it is very easy to integrate it with other workflows in Max. For example, all the messages can be programmatically generated, and may include placeholder values[22] that can interactively change the quantum circuit being built. At the same time, there is some flexibility in the structure of the messages. For example, the user can create new quantum circuits by giving it any single word name,[23] opt for initializing it with only qubits, or with both qubits and classical bits, and even create several circuits in one go, as illustrated in the example above. The **och.microqiskit** object itself can be initialized with some arguments that will already give it a *QuantumCircuit* and *Simulator* already defined.[24]

The *Simulator* memory contains the *QuantumCircuit* definition as it was when it was passed to the simulator, but this can be changed if the *sim_update* attribute is set equal to 1, which will automatically update the simulator whenever its corresponding quantum circuit changes. And once the simulator is defined, we can retrieve different results like the aggregated counts using *get_counts*, the statevector using *get_statevector*, or each individual shot result using *get_memory*.[25] The resemblance of the notation used with that of Qiskit, MicroQiskit, and some other QC frameworks, is not accidental. This includes the short names used for the quantum gates, like x for the NOT gate, h for the Hadamard gate, m for the measurement gate, cx for the controlled-NOT gate, etc.[26]

Given this object running natively in Max, and with all the concerns that went into making it work seamlessly, I devised a test to evaluate how well it performed when compared the original QC tools, in Python—more specifically against Qiskit, and MicroQiskit, in a Python terminal. The experiment consisted of running a very small circuit—one qubit and one classical bit with one Hadamard gate followed by one measurement gate—for different numbers of shots, in simulation. The experiment was run for 2,000 shots (Fig. 8.10), 20,000 shots (Fig. 8.11), and 1,000,000 shots, which is the maximum number of shots that Qiskit allows for a single experiment execution (Fig. 8.12).

---

[22] For example, in Max, a message box can have the $1 symbol that is replaced by an incoming value.

[23] This is similar to what is already practiced in Max to initialize and refer back to jitter matrices.

[24] As an example, see the patch in Fig. 8.13.

[25] For a complete list of methods for the och.microqiskit object, please refer to the help patch and reference page included in the distributed Max package.

[26] See the full list of available gates in the overview patch (reproduced in Fig. 8.8) and each individual help patch. General good quick sources for understanding different quantum gates include [50, Chap. 7 Quantum Gates and Circuits], [51, 52].

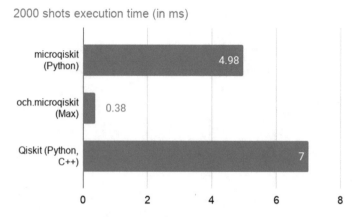

Fig. 8.10 Comparing MicroQiskit, och.microqiskit, and Qiskit simulating 2,000 shots. From Hamido [27]

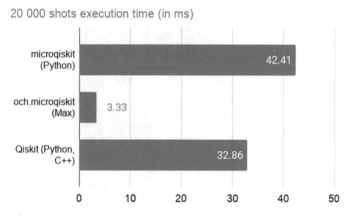

Fig. 8.11 Comparing MicroQiskit, och.microqiskit, and Qiskit simulating 20,000 shots. From Hamido [27]

The results, plotted in the figures above, were very surprising. The **och.microqiskit** implementation was consistently ten times faster than the original MicroQiskit in Python. This can be attributed to the fact that **och.microqiskit** is itself written in C++, which is much more efficient than Python, as has been noted repeatedly for decades [53–55]. For 2,000 shots, MicroQiskit is around 40% faster than Qiskit, something that other members in the Qiskit community have also noticed for simple circuits. However, by the time we are executing 20,000 shots, Qiskit is faster than MicroQiskit. This can be due to the fact that Qiskit actually includes some high-performance components also written in C++. At 1,000,000 shots Qiskit is about 70% faster than MicroQiskit, and **och.microqiskit** is still ten times faster than MicroQiskit and eight times faster than Qiskit.

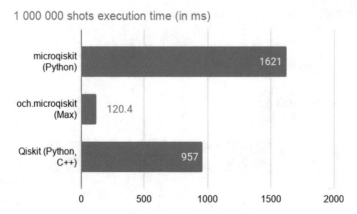

Fig. 8.12 Comparing MicroQiskit, och.microqiskit, and Qiskit simulating 1,000,000 shots. From Hamido [27]

Fig. 8.13 och.qisjob object example patch. From Hamido [27]

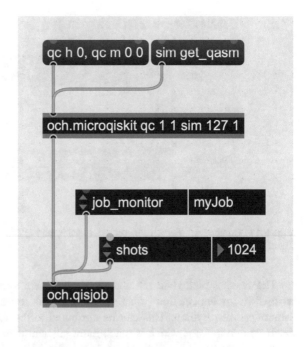

Being able to simulate QC efficiently is an important step to understanding how QC can integrate current creative practices and learning how to eventually get an advantage from the real quantum hardware. As it stands, these tools are already very important for QAC as they are usable in a realtime creative practice context, which was the motivation for pursuing this work in the first place.[27] It should still be noted that it is not possible to prove that computing a problem using QC simulation will be necessarily faster than any other strategy for computation using classical machines. If we consider this idea, finding ways to connect with real quantum hardware will still be an important avenue to pursue, in order to allow creative artists to be ready to benefit from the quantum advantage in the (hopefully near) future.

8.5.2 och.qisjob

The possibility to connect to real quantum hardware was impossible to achieve with the tools and resources used in the early attempts for QAC (see previous section), and even the original MicroQiskit framework has that limitation. By extension, **och. microqiskit** also does not include in itself the resources to establish that direct connection. However, it does have some features in place that are important to achieve it. To address this challenge of connecting with real quantum hardware in the cloud I considered recreating the Qiskit library components that allow the remote connection, but the number of necessary dependencies makes it a very arduous task. Proof of that is the fact that, up until the time of this writing, I have not met anyone else that would be interested in doing it too.

Connecting to full Qiskit (in Python) in some way seemed unavoidable. During my explorations, I experimented with very old Max objects that should be able to interface with Python directly, but most of them would either only work with older versions of Python, which are not supported by the modern QC frameworks, or they would still need the user to have Python configured on his/her machine anyway. Other strategies considered included deploying a web server with a Qiskit configuration, to relay the jobs to the real machines,[28] but concerns about scalability and managing potential sensitive access credentials cautioned me not to pursue this path on my own.

Once again, I turned to the community in search of ideas for this seemingly small problem of simplifying the process of submitting a job to real quantum hardware. It so happened that my former hackathon partner Jack Woehr already had a project that he also started in early 2019 that addressed just that: a simpler command-line interface for submitting jobs to quantum computing hardware [57]. A job is simply the set of instructions to run on the quantum computer, which include the quantum circuit definition, the number of shots, and some other required information that is compiled by a QC framework in order to successfully submit it. Woehr's QisJob is a program that only requires the user to pass an OpenQasm file (or a Python script file with a circuit defined in Qiskit) and automatically executes all the necessary Python and Qiskit functions to successfully submit the job. In effect, it is able to do so because it includes a version of Qiskit as a module in its code.

---

[27] For more about the discussion on the advantages of QC for the creative practices, please see [27, Chap. 3: QAD and more].

[28] A process similar to one I explored in my QC-enabled interactive story in 2019 [56].

Between late 2020 and early 2021 I contributed to Jack's project while, at the same time, started exploring the possibility of compiling it into a single application that could connect directly with the Max environment. The **och.qisjob** object emerged from this exploration.[29] This is a two-part object where it includes an OS-specific application, running in the background, and a Max object that automatically starts that application and connects directly to it. This approach still removes the need for creative artists to manually set up a Python environment and establish the necessary connections between both environments. Furthermore, this approach also works well with the previous objects and what they already offer.

The **och.microqiskit** object already offers the possibility to retrieve the Qiskit or Qasm code definitions for a quantum circuit—using the *get_qiskit* and *get_qasm* methods, respectively.[30] This is very useful when working with **och.qisjob** since we can take advantage of the circuit building capabilities introduced earlier. Figure 8.13 shows an example of what it looks like to work with this new object. On the top portion of this patch the **och.microqiskit** object is initialized with some arguments that define a *QuantumCircuit* named *qc*, with 1 qubit and 1 classical bit, as well as a *Simulator* named *sim*, using 127 shots and with auto update enabled (also known as the *sim_update* attribute). The first message "qc h 0, qc m 0 0" adds a Hadamard gate to the *qc* circuit on qubit 0, and also adds a measurement gate between qubit 0 and classical bit 0. The "sim get_qasm" message requests the *Simulator sim*, holding the *QuantumCircuit qc*, to translate the circuit definition into Qasm code.

The Qasm code generated is sent directly to the **och.qisjob** object that, in this example, also shows two *attrui* objects connected that allow both inspecting and changing the *job_monitor* and *shots* attributes. As an object whose sole purpose is to manage and submit jobs to different backends and retrieve its results, it can also offer the possibility to keep track of the progress of a job using a job monitor function that is offered by Qiskit. The *job_monitor* attribute simply defines the name of the job monitor that will appear in the console window, when it starts reporting back on the job. This is especially useful since most of the publicly available quantum hardware machines use queues to manage all the incoming jobs; with the job monitor the user can know on which place in the queue the job is, when it is being executed, and when it is reading the results.

There are other messages to interact with the **och.qisjob** object to determine which backends to use, as well as to load the necessary credentials to access them. For the purpose of this chapter however, instead of providing a very detailed description of all the functionalities of this object, which is still under development, I will present the performance measurements and some insights obtained from it. Given that this object appears as a response to the previous strategies described in

---

[29] Note that, as of this writing, och.qisjob is still experimental, and only available in closed beta.

[30] Internally, och.microqiskit does not use qiskit or qasm code to simulate the quantum circuit. Calling these methods triggers a translation of the internal quantum circuit memory. Furthermore, when simulating, the internal representation of the quantum system is a statevector; calling the *get_statevector* method can retrieve the most direct reading of this object's inner computed state.

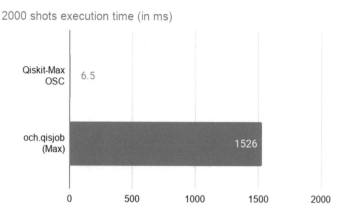

Fig. 8.14 Comparing Qiskit-Max OSC architecture and och.qisjob simulating 2,000 shots. From Hamido [27]

Sect. 8.2, the most direct comparison will be between this object and a Qiskit Python environment connected to Max via OSC.[31]

While devising the test to evaluate the performance of these two strategies, it became clear that there was no way to guarantee that each iteration would spend the exact same amount of time in the queue, when waiting to be executed by the real quantum hardware. For the sake of consistency, I ended up performing these tests using the high-performance simulator found in Qiskit that is accessible to both, as a type of backend to request. Using a similar circuit to the one presented above, this experiment was run for 2,000 shots (Fig. 8.14), then 20,000 shots (Fig. 8.15), and finally 1,000,000 shots (Fig. 8.16).

The results, plotted in the figures above, were once again very surprising. Even though both strategies ultimately used the same underlying backend system, the high-performance simulator provided by Qiskit, their execution times differ greatly. The **och.qisjob** object was consistently worse than the Qiskit-Max OSC strategy. A closer inspection of these results reveals the additional execution time for running the experiment with a higher number of shots increases in the same exact proportion. Somewhere along the way, the current implementation of **och.qisjob** is spending roughly 1.5 s every time it is activated.

Debugging so far has suggested that the major bottleneck may be directly related to the fact that, with each new job, **och.qisjob** launches the compiled QisJob application every time, to run in the background, something that takes time given the amount of resources that need to be loaded. This does not happen in the Qiskit-Max OSC strategy explored, since the Python environment needs to be continuously running prior to start receiving the OSC messages that trigger the backend simulation.

---

[31] For simplicity, it will be referred to as "Qiskit-Max OSC" in the next pages. It consists of a Python environment with both Qiskit and OSC installed where, upon receiving a message from Max via OSC, it will trigger the circuit execution and then return the results to Max, via OSC.

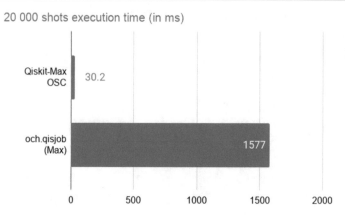

Fig. 8.15 Comparing Qiskit-Max OSC architecture and och.qisjob simulating 20,000 shots. From Hamido [27]

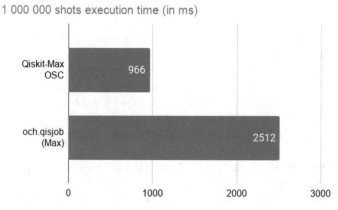

Fig. 8.16 Comparing Qiskit-Max OSC architecture and och.qisjob simulating 1,000,000 shots. From Hamido [27]

Figure 8.17 combines all the results retrieved from the different tests run. It becomes evident that the Qiskit-Max OSC strategy returned practically identical results to only running Qiskit in the Python terminal, as their lines overlap, which was to be expected since their setups were very similar. It also becomes clear that, among the implementation strategies evaluated here, **och.microqiskit** runs faster than anything else, and **och.qisjob** runs slower than anything else. Further work will be pursued to reduce the execution time of **och.qisjob**. And in the meantime, creative artists that are familiar with working with Python may want to consider using a project like OSC-Qasm: in effect a Qiskit-Max OSC system, inspired by QisJob and **och.qisjob**, offering a python module, a max abstraction, and respective documentation, as the minimum viable product for setting up this type of system [58].

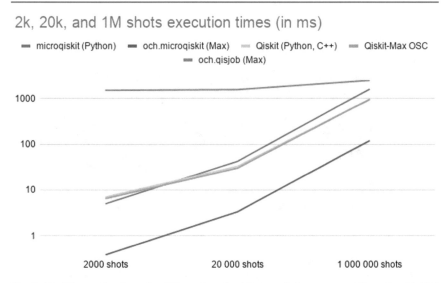

Fig. 8.17   All execution times for all the tools and architectures being compared. From Hamido [27]

In any case, it is important to consider that, when working with real quantum hardware, most users will be faced with a fair-share queue access system, as described, for example, in [59]. Keeping that in mind, the current 1.5 s of execution time overhead in **och.qisjob** might not be that concerning in a real use case scenario. Jobs submitted to be executed on real quantum hardware will always have to wait in a queue, somewhere between several seconds to several minutes.[32] For what they were meant to be, the tools presented in this chapter were very successful in addressing the main concerns. They emerge from within the CM sphere to allow creative artists to integrate QC in their practice, without the need to set up additional environments or be forced to take a traditional code-based approach. With the development of these tools being informed by realtime creative practices, it is equally important the fact that they are fast enough to be used in that context (even more so than some of the alternatives).

Going back to the two conceptual spheres for CM and QC, articulated earlier in this chapter, we can now visualize the place of the different systems and integration strategies in it (Fig. 8.18). The same way Qiskit and MicroQiskit inhabit the QC tools sphere, **och.microqiskit** and **och.qisjob** will inhabit the CM tools sphere. As for the previous attempts for an integration, which include works by me, Miranda, and Weaver, they stand somewhere in the middle with one part in each sphere, as well as a portion outside of both, representing the required work that is not directly related to neither practice. Even though it still needs some work ahead, **och.qisjob**

---

[32] There might be providers that can offer to schedule dedicated access time to a machine that can reduce the roundtrip time, but for the majority of users their jobs will have to sit in some sort of a queue for a shared machine. One can anticipate a major revolution when "personal quantum computers" will become widely available.

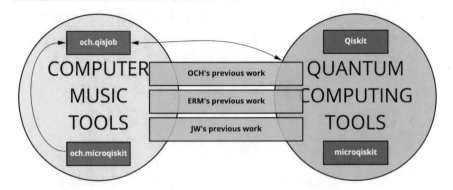

Fig. 8.18 Computer Music Tools and Quantum Computing Tools, with some specific tools being compared, in context. From Hamido [27]

seems to be unique in pointing to a suitable direction to offer a direct connection between these two spheres. Considering this more conceptual and purely technical presentation of how QAC is currently implemented by *The QAC Toolkit*, I will present next a more thorough practical example, showing how a quantum computing algorithm can be implemented.

8.6 Implementing BMA with the QAC Toolkit

In this section I will dive deeper into using *The QAC Toolkit* by exploring my implementation of the Basak-Miranda algorithm.[33] The BMA is an algorithm proposed by Basak and Miranda in Chap. 13, in this volume, where they create a first-order Markov chain pitch sequencing system making use of quantum computing. Given a pitch transition table, each iteration of the algorithm will extract a row from it and modify an identity matrix based on the possible target pitches, which are translated here into quantum states. The state with highest number of counts, upon execution and measurement of the quantum circuit, is then translated back into the MIDI pitch domain, played on a MIDI instrument device, and used to retrieve the next row of the transition table [60].

Together with their theoretical explanation, Basak and Miranda also released Jupyter notebooks containing the Python code to implement BMA using Qiskit [61]. The rest of this section follows some of the strategies in that example code, sharing function names for some clarity, whenever possible. In Fig. 8.19 we can see the main Max patch that displays the overall structure of this implementation as well as the few objects that the user interacts with.[34]

---

[33] From now on referred to as BMA.
[34] This patch is available for download in [49].

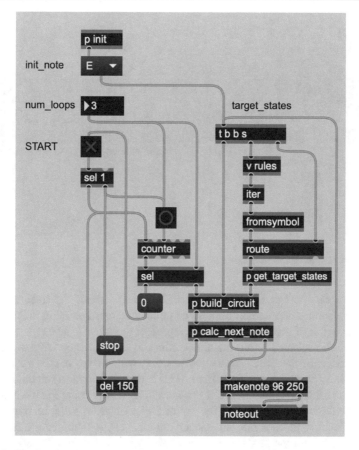

Fig. 8.19 The Basak-Miranda algorithm running natively in Max with *The QAC Toolkit*

On the top left of the main patch, the three user interface objects allow selecting the initial pitch, the number of iterations to run, and toggle the start of the process, with the *umenu*, *numbox*, and *toggle* box, respectively. The *init* patcher object above the *init_note* menu contains the complete transition table and labels, as defined in the example provided by Basak and Miranda (Fig. 8.20). These are stored in two value objects, *next_notes* and *rules*, which are accessed remotely from other sections of the patch. In effect, as soon as the user selects a pitch from the *umenu* box, the patch will retrieve all the *rules*, from a value object, and route the one that starts with the selected pitch name to the *get_target_states* patcher.

The *get_target_states* patcher simply transforms every non-zero value from the selected transition table row into a value equal to 1 (Fig. 8.21). This tiny patch includes another subpatcher of its own, named *warn*, that simply serves as an aid to let the user know that BMA, as initially described,[35] will work as intended only

---

[35] As of the pre-print available in [60] at the time of this writing.

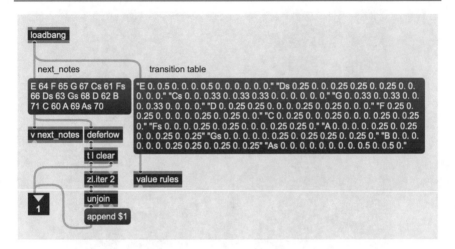

Fig. 8.20 Contents of *init* patcher

when the total number of target states is less than half of the total number of possible states that the current number of qubits can represent (Fig. 8.22).

This new list of zeros and ones, that represent the target pitches (or states) that can follow the selected initial pitch, according to the transition table provided, is then passed onto the *build_circuit* patcher that will, as the name suggests, programmatically build the quantum circuit. This is perhaps the most important patcher in this whole implementation, and it is where I am mostly using the tools provided by *The QAC Toolkit* (Fig. 8.23). The list of target states will first be translated by the *states2qubits* patcher into an integer number that is equal to the number of qubits required to represent the number of states in our list. In this case, we have twelve pitches, so we will need four qubits to be able to represent them. Looking at this patch as being organized in seven horizontal layers, we can see that this calculated number of required qubits is temporarily stored in mostly message boxes on the fourth horizontal layer[36] that will be triggered next.

The *bang* triggering the actual automatic circuit building is coming from the *trigger* object in the main patch that will fire a *bang* as the last action after receiving the initial note from the *umenu*. This *bang* is then split into eleven different *bangs* that are fired consecutively, by the large *trigger* object inside the *build_circuit* patcher on the third horizontal layer. In turn, these *bangs* are directly responsible for generating all the messages to control the **och.microqiskit** object using the different objects in the fifth horizontal layer, in the right to left order. The first message is setting up (or recreating) a *QuantumCircuit* named *qc* with the same number of qubits and classical bits (determined by the number received on its inlet), as well as

---

[36] Here I am counting these horizontal layers from the top. As a related note, in Max the order of operations happens from top to bottom, from right to left.

Fig. 8.21 Contents of
get_target_states patcher

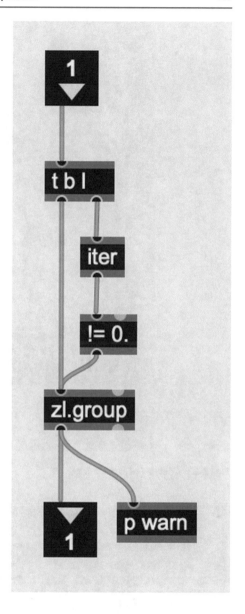

creating a *Simulator* named *sim* with 100 shots that will hold the circuit named *qc* and auto-update its memory when *qc* changes.

Following the definition of BMA, a series of Hadamard gates is created covering the entire range of qubits in the circuit, and we use **och.hset** to make this process faster. Giving an argument to this object that is the name of the *QuantumCircuit* in question, in this case *qc*, and sending it an integer number, representing the number

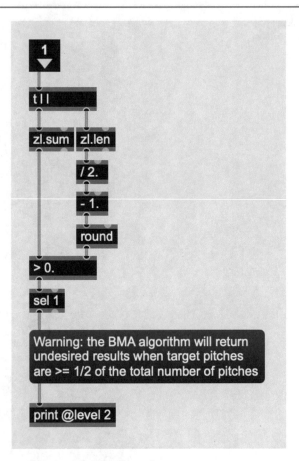

Fig. 8.22 Contents of *warn* patcher

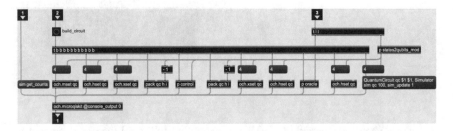

Fig. 8.23 Contents of *build_circuit* patcher

of qubits of the circuit, this object will automatically generate a series of messages that will fit our need - i.e. "qc h 0," "qc h 1," "qc h 2," and "qc h 3." The **och.xset** and **och.mset** objects, that are found later in this patch, work exactly the same way.

The oracle portion of BMA is built next (Fig. 8.24). This is entirely generated using only the transition table row transformed by the *get_target_states* patcher before. After creating an identity matrix of the required size using **och.identity-matrix** object, the patch starts iterating through its multiple rows at the same time that it is reading each of the values from the transition table row above. When the value for the transition table row evaluates to 1, then the corresponding row from the identity matrix is opened and have its value multiplied by −1. This process goes on until the transition table row reading is complete, and all the resulting iterations and modifications are grouped together into a new matrix.

Again, given that the total number of pitches in the original transition table might be less than the number of possible states that the qubits can represent, the patch will still need to stitch together a *tail* of an identity matrix long enough to complete the full matrix—see the trio of *zl* objects at the bottom right section of the patch.[37] All throughout this patch, matrices take the form of a list of symbols, where each symbol is itself a list of values. In order to request **och.microqiskit** to create a unitary gate from a matrix, though, the standard message format must be maintained: *QuantumCircuit* name, quantum gate type, and list of arguments. Therefore the final complete matrix is transformed into a long list of single values before it is passed to the last message at the bottom of the patch.

The rest of the circuit building will either repeat or use very similar strategies for programmatically generating the required messages. Only the *control* subpatcher will offer three different options for its generation (Fig. 8.25). At some point in BMA there is a controlled-NOT gate, or multi-controlled-NOT gate, being applied to the quantum circuit. As it stands, my implementation is prepared to select the appropriate gate when the number of qubits of the quantum circuit is between two and four. It should be noted that a one qubit version of BMA cannot exist: if we have a transition table between two pitches, it may seem that we only need one qubit to represent the required states but, as noted above, by design BMA will not retrieve the desired results if targeting one state out of two possible ones. Again, the proportion between target states and total number of possible states needs to be less than one half.

With the quantum circuit defined for the initial pitch selected on the main patch, all that is left is running the actual program and retrieving some results. The *start* toggle on the main patch initiates a loop that will repeat several times determined by the *num_loops* number box. The *counter* and *select* objects are keeping track of the repetitions, and as long as the maximum number of repetitions isn't reached, it will keep sending *bangs* to the first inlet of *build_circuit*. Because at this point the *QuantumCircuit* and *Simulator* is already completely defined, all that is left to do is request **och.microqiskit** object to simulate the circuit and retrieve the counts - this is done by the "sim get_counts" message.

---

[37] In this case, the 12 pitches require 4 qubits, and the 4 qubits can represent 16 states. We need to complete the 12×12 matrix in order to become a full 16×16 matrix that can be applied to the quantum circuit covering the full range of qubits.

Fig. 8.24 Contents of *oracle* patcher

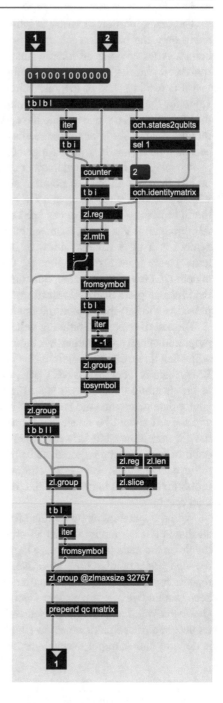

Fig. 8.25 Contents of
control patcher

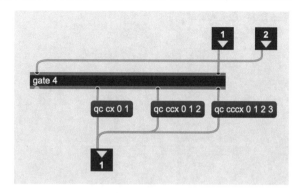

The counts are then passed to the *calc_next_note* patcher that will unpack the list of results, sort them, and select the bitstring for the state with the highest number of counts (Fig. 8.26). This bitstring is then converted into a decimal number with the **och.binstr2dec** object, and this number is used to retrieve both the MIDI note number as well as pitch name from the initial list of labels that was stored in the *next_notes* value object at the start. The MIDI note number is sent out via the third outlet to a MIDI instrument synthesizer, and the pitch name is sent via the second outlet back into the *trigger* object, on the main patch, that is responsible for programmatically generating the quantum circuit, as described in detail in this section.[38] After that, a final *bang* is sent out via the first inlet and will trigger, 150 ms later, the next iteration of the loop.

This patch is available in [49] and I invite the reader to explore it, including changing the initial rules and labels that are defined at the start. As was explained in this section, rather than hardcoding the exact example provided by Basak and Miranda, this patch took several steps in consideration to make it somewhat flexible and able to adapt to different transition tables which might have different sizes, and thus also produce different quantum circuits. In the next section, I will explore a different approach to QAC, still making use of *The QAC Toolkit*, in the context of the creative work *Disklavier Prelude #3*.

8.7 QAC in *Disklavier Prelude #3*

In a nutshell, *The QAC Toolkit* is what I wish would exist back in the early 2010s when I first became aware of quantum computing, and especially when I was struggling to understand and integrate QCL. But this process does not end here. Now, given that there is such a toolkit, I can create compositional devices that make use of it but don't necessarily require me to interact with them at the level of

---

[38] Note that a different pitch name entering this trigger object will result in the extraction of a different row from the transition table and, consequently, in the generation of a different quantum circuit.

Fig. 8.26 Contents of
calc_next_note patcher

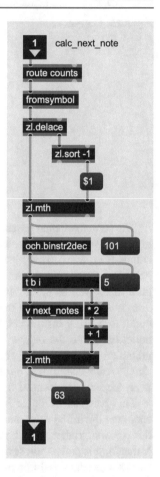

programming patches with Max objects and messages. One of the main advantages of using Max, as mentioned before, is the ability to quickly deploy plugin-like Max for Live devices that act as ready-to-use plugins in the DAW environment Ableton Live. When using the DAW, I am mostly working in a *creative mode* and less of a *programmer mode*.[39] The ability to quickly put together a set where I can connect virtual and acoustic instruments and make use of both traditional techniques and new QC-based ones, is truly invaluable.

One of the first devices of this kind, to include and make use of *The QAC Toolkit* objects under the hood, is **och.qc-superposition**.[40] This Max for Live device presents the user with a simple interface that abstracts away the process of writing the actual quantum circuit (Fig. 8.27). On the bottom portion, there is a visualization of the counts retrieved from running a quantum circuit, as a histogram. And on the top portion, there is a number box to determine the number of qubits (and

---

[39] By the same token, it also makes these tools more accessible to non-programmers.

[40] This device is included in *The QAC Toolkit* Max package [1].

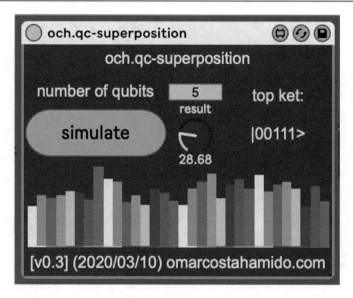

Fig. 8.27 The och.qc-superposition Max for Live device, using *The QAC Toolkit*. From Hamido [27]

classical bits) to allocate, a *Simulate* button to trigger the simulation, and a text field that declares the top ket (as in the wining computational basis state), and a map-pable *result* knob that reflects the state with the highest number of counts too.

Internally, **och.qc-superposition** creates a simple circuit with a Hadamard gate and a measurement gate applied to each qubit, effectively putting all qubits in a state of equal superposition. By changing the number of qubits, the total number of possible states increases. In practical terms, this change is noticeable as a change in resolution of the *result* knob, that will be able to output finer variations as the number of qubits increases: its range is divided by $2^{(\text{number of qubits})}$ parts. This device represents a fundamental departure from the constraints encountered pre-viously with **och.qc-circ-2q**. At the same time, it also represents QC more faith-fully, as a probabilistic means of computation. Instead of simply retrieving a statevector, we are simulating a circuit, and that drives the change in this device.

One of the music compositions that make use of this device is *Disklavier Pre-lude #3*.[41] This is a work for Disklavier, dancer, and lights that explores the concept of virtual particles, QC, man-machine interaction, and social media (Fig. 8.28). All the way through the piece, the Disklavier plays major seventh chords that are transposed up and down based on the result of the **och.qc-superposition** device. At some point during the piece, the lampshade that the dancer is wearing falls off, and the dancer becomes aware of her surroundings and the controlling light. At this point the Disklavier adds a melodic line to the arpeggiated chords that creates a

---

[41] Part of the work *4 Disklavier Preludes*, presented in the film-recital *The Gedanken Room* (2021) [62].

Fig. 8.28 Still frame of *Disklavier Prelude #3*. From Hamido [62]

dialogue with the dancer. The melodic line, that appears to be trying to communicate with the dancer, is composed of streams of notes from a pentatonic scale being transposed together with the chords, and being driven by another **och. qc-superposition** device.

Figure 8.29 illustrates in more detail the compositional process involving the use of this device. There is a MIDI clip with arpeggiated major seventh chords driving the Disklavier that includes two automation lanes for triggering each of the **och. qc-superposition** device instances. The first automation lane only triggers a new simulation at the end of the clip, on a device instance configured with a high qubit count in order to achieve a finer resolution while controlling the transposition. The devices were modified here to include an interpolation time, to smooth out the transitions. In the first instance, interpolation is set to 0 because those changes should take effect immediately. The actual transposition is achieved simply by mapping the *result* knob to the *pitch* knob, on a *Pitch* device, that transposes the MIDI information being sent to the Disklavier.

The second automation lane, which is enabled later in the piece when the lampshade falls off, is responsible for controlling the melodic stream of notes. This automation triggers, every bar, a second **och.qc-superposition** device configured with a lower qubit count and a much higher interpolation time. The *result* knob then slowly transitions between results every time it is triggered, and this movement is mapped to an instance of Yehezkel Raz's *Jazz me* device that generates a stream of notes in a major pentatonic mode. These notes are guaranteed to stay in tune with the arpeggiated chords because they are also being transposed by the first automation lane chain.

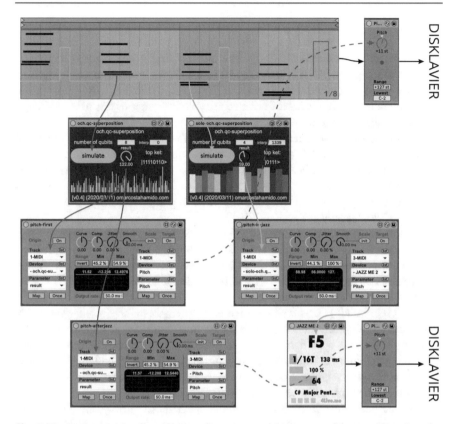

Fig. 8.29 One automation line triggers och.qc-superposition to control transposition, the other automation line triggers another och.qc-superposition to control a stream of notes on *Jazz me*. From Hamido [27]

This complex network of interdependencies, including in the synchronized lights, allowed to express a very controlled scenario of a seemingly unknown outcome. Since the QC process is relying on a simple circuit with qubits in equal superposition, any possible value is equally likely. The predetermined automation lanes, resembling the control pulse automations generated from quantum circuits when passed to quantum computers,[42] depict these tensions between control and uncertainty. And, in turn, the repeating rhythmic motif was also very important in order to be able to articulate well with the dancer, by allowing her to express the constraints, as well as break free from them, and freely explore this creative environment.

---

[42] The quantum circuit, as a set of instructions, is actually converted in a series of pulses to control the real quantum hardware. Pulse scheduling is involved in the actual implementation of each quantum gate, and it is one of the avenues where researchers attempt to optimize QC and mitigate noise.

8.8   Closing Remarks

In this chapter I presented QAC (Quantum-computing Aided Composition) as a proposal to integrate QC in creative practice. This is a contribution emerging from the *Adventures in Quantumland* research [27].[43] In particular, QAC proposes to draw a framework that places the creative artist at the center of this new landscape, revealed in the exploration of the paradigm introduced by QC.

It is important to understand the context and the relations between CM and QC, as well as to know what QC is and what can be expected from it. The fact that there is no real (perceptible) *quantum sound* may lead to the question of whether an audience member will ever be able to determine if some sound, or music, was produced using QC—perhaps only the composer or performer using the system will be able to know, really.

Previous attempts for an integration of QC with music practice tend to favor code-based languages and require a skillset that only the more programmer-inclined creative artists possess. Being informed by realtime creative practices, QAC places the emphasis on the creative process, and interaction with performers, rather than in exclusively computer-driven artwork.

The QAC Toolkit [1], as well as some early attempts before it, emerged within this context to empower creative artists to use quantum gates as logical operations in their practice. As a modern attempt to put QAC into practice, it provides new tools integrated into the Max visual programming environment with a performance that, even though it might not be relevant to the computer scientist, may enable new prospects for realtime creative practice with QC.

Still, the **och.microqiskit** object includes methods to retrieve the circuit definition in Qasm, using *get_qasm*, and Qiskit Python code, using *get_qiskit*, offering the possibility to explore and reuse the current circuits in other environments.[44] With this, and during the research process involved in the creation of these tools, there were some contributions to the QC community. For example, the version of MicroQiskit that I have worked on is the only one to include multi-qubit gates other than crx and cx.

Furthermore, the examples described in this chapter demonstrated how these tools can be used when creating new patches, implementing algorithms, building plugin-like devices, and composing a new musical work. The ability to abstract away the underlying QC process inside the self-contained devices makes it accessible to non-programmers and a wider audience of creative practitioners.

It is my intent that the tools, concepts, and perspectives shared here will be inspiring to both the creative and scientific community, promoting dialogues about their respective practices and possible intersections.

---

[43] Where I also proposed QAD (Quantum-computing Aided Design).

[44] These can be easily copied from a popup text box that appears when the method is called in a message that includes the keyword textbox (e.g. "sim get_qiskit textbox").

References

1. Hamido, O. C. (2021). *The QAC toolkit.* https://www.quantumland.art/qac. Accessed 06 Dec 2021.
2. Bouche, D., Nika, J., Chechile, A., & Bresson, J. (2017). Computer-aided composition of musical processes. *Journal of New Music Research, 46*(1), 3–14. https://doi.org/10.1080/09298215.2016.1230136.
3. MuseScore. https://musescore.org/en. Accessed 22 Feb 2021.
4. *Ableton Live.* Ableton, 2021. https://www.ableton.com/. Accessed 22 Feb 2021.
5. *Max.* Cycling '74, 2021. https://cycling74.com/. Accessed 22 Feb 2021.
6. Gambetta, J., et al. (2021). *Qiskit/qiskit: Qiskit 0.23.6.* Zenodo. https://doi.org/10.5281/zenodo.4549740.
7. Gidney, C. et al. (2021). *Cirq.* The Cirq Developers. https://github.com/quantumlib/Cirq. Accessed 11 Feb 2019.
8. Karalekas, P., et al. (2021). *PyQuil: Quantum Programming in Python.* Rigetti Computing. https://github.com/rigetti/pyquil. Accessed 22 Feb 2021.
9. Strangeworks | Quantum Computing Ecosystem. (2021). *Strangeworks.* https://strangeworks.com/. Accessed 22 Feb 2021.
10. IBM Quantum Experience. *IBM Quantum Experience.* https://quantum-computing.ibm.com/. Accessed 22 Feb 2021.
11. Quantum Programming Studio. (2018). https://quantum-circuit.com/. Accessed 22 Feb 2021.
12. Vogt-Lee, D. (2021). *Awesome quantum computing.* https://github.com/desireevl/awesome-quantum-computing. Accessed 22 Feb 2021.
13. *Open-Source Quantum Software Projects.* Quantum Open Source Foundation (2021). https://github.com/qosf/awesome-quantum-software. Accessed 22 Feb 2021.
14. Collins, N., McLEAN, A., Rohrhuber, J., & Ward, A. (2003). Live coding in laptop performance. *Organised Sound, 8*(3), 321–330. https://doi.org/10.1017/S135577180300030X
15. Weimer, H. (2020). Listen to quantum computer music. http://www.quantenblog.net/physics/quantum-computer-music. Accessed 26 Mar 2021.
16. Ömer, B. (2014). QCL—A programming language for quantum computers. http://tph.tuwien.ac.at/~oemer/qcl.html. Accessed 18 May 2020.
17. Hamido, O. C., Cirillo, G. A., & Giusto, E. (2020). Quantum synth: A quantum-computing-based synthesizer. In *Proceedings of the 15th International Conference on Audio Mostly* (pp. 265–268). USA. https://doi.org/10.1145/3411109.3411135.
18. IBM Corp. (2019). Qiskit Camp Europe. https://qiskit.org/events/europe/. Accessed 22 Feb 2021.
19. Csound Community. https://csound.com/. Accessed 23 Feb 2021.
20. Miranda, E. R. (2020). Quantum computer: Hello, Music!. arXiv:2006.13849. Accessed 22 Jan 2021.
21. Weaver, J. (2018). *Quantum Music Composer for IBM Quantum Computers.* https://github.com/JavaFXpert/quantum-toy-piano-ibmq. Accessed 28 Oct 2019.
22. Daniels, T., et al. (2021). *LilyPond.* https://lilypond.org/. Accessed 23 Feb 2021
23. Festival della Tecnologia - Musica con un Computer Quantistico. (2019). https://www.festivaltecnologia.it/sessioni/musica-con-un-computer-quantistico. Accessed 20 Oct 2019.
24. Aaronson, S. (2021). Quantum computers, explained with quantum physics. *Quanta Magazine.* https://www.quantamagazine.org/videos/quantum-computers-explained-with-quantum-physics/. Accessed 03 Feb 2022.
25. Hamido, O. C. (2021). *Intro to Quantum Computer Music pt1 [1st ISQCMC].* Accessed 06 Dec 2021. https://www.youtube.com/watch?v=-vq_bELlhrI.
26. Dean, R. T. (2011). The Oxford Handbook of Computer Music. *Oxford University Press.* https://doi.org/10.1093/oxfordhb/9780199792030.001.0001
27. Hamido, O. C. (2021). Adventures in quantumland. UC Irvine. Accessed 01 Oct 2021. https://escholarship.org/uc/item/93c1t8vx.

28. Quantum Music—Pilot Project (2015–18). *Beyond quantum music.* http://quantummusic.org/about-us/. Accessed 29 Mar 2021.
29. Wehden, K., Faro, I., & Gambetta, J. (2021). IBM's roadmap for building an open quantum software ecosystem. *IBM Research Blog.* https://www.ibm.com/blogs/research/2021/02/quantum-development-roadmap/. Accessed 22 Feb 2021.
30. Cuthbert, M. S., & Ariza, C. (2010). music21: A toolkit for computer-aided musicology and symbolic music data. *Michael Cuthbert.* https://dspace.mit.edu/handle/1721.1/84963. Accessed 03 Feb 2021.
31. Bača, T., et al. (2021). *Abjad.* Abjad. https://github.com/Abjad/abjad. Accessed 24 Feb 2021.
32. Evanstein, M. (2021). *SCAMP.* https://github.com/MarcTheSpark/scamp. Accessed 21 Feb 2021.
33. Tymoczko, D. (2013). Review of Michael Cuthbert. *Music21: A Toolkit for computer-aided musicology.* http://web.mit.edu/music21/.; *Music Theory Online, 19*(3). https://mtosmt.org/issues/mto.13.19.3/mto.13.19.3.tymoczko.html. Accessed 25 Mar 2021.
34. Evanstein, M. (2020). *Cooking Up Some Music in SCAMP!.* https://www.youtube.com/watch?v=vpv686Rasds. Accessed 25 Mar 2021.
35. Puckette, M. Pure data (Pd): Real-time music and multimedia environment. http://msp.ucsd.edu/software.html. Accessed 22 Feb 2021.
36. Magenta Studio. *Magenta.* https://magenta.tensorflow.org/studio/. Accessed 17 Apr 2020.
37. Max for Live | Ableton. https://www.ableton.com/en/live/max-for-live/. Accessed 23 Feb 2021.
38. Grosse, D. (2019). Node for max intro—Let's get started!. https://cycling74.com/articles/node-for-max-intro-%E2%80%93-let%E2%80%99s-get-started. Accessed 23 Feb 2021.
39. Rubio, J., et al. (2019). *Qiskit.js.* Qiskit Community. https://github.com/qiskit-community/qiskit-js. Accessed 24 Feb 2021.
40. Cross, A. W., Bishop, L. S., Smolin, J. A., & Gambetta, J. M. (2017). Open quantum assembly language. arXiv:1707.03429. Accessed 09 Mar 2019.
41. Max for Live Community Resource. https://maxforlive.com/. Accessed 05 Feb 2022.
42. Qiskit. Qiskit Advocates. https://qiskit.org/advocates. Accessed 08 Mar 2021.
43. Hamido, O. C. (2019). *Computer Music and QAC/QAD with Omar Costa Hamido.* https://www.youtube.com/watch?v=GrD_eUrmcqM. Accessed 22 Mar 2020.
44. IBM Corp. (2019). Qiskit Camp Africa. https://qiskit.org/events/africa/ Accessed 17 Mar 2021.
45. Moran, C. C. (2016a). 5-qubit quantum computing simulator. *codeXgalactic.* https://codexgalactic.com/2016/05/21/5-qubit-quantum-computing-simulator/. Accessed 01 Mar 2021.
46. Moran, C. C. (2016b). Quintuple: A Python 5-qubit quantum computer simulator to facilitate cloud quantum computing. arXiv:1606.09225. Accessed 01 Mar 2021.
47. Wootton, J. (2019). *MicroQiskit for Python.* https://github.com/qiskit-community/MicroQiskit. Accessed 01 Mar 2021.
48. Hamido, O. C., & Wootton, J. (2021). *MicroQiskit C++.* https://github.com/qiskit-community/MicroQiskit/tree/master/versions/C%2B%2B. Accessed 22 Feb 2021.
49. Hamido, O. C. (2022). QAC [book chapter supplementary materials]. *Zenodo.* https://doi.org/10.5281/zenodo.5988942
50. Bernhardt, C. (2019). *Quantum computing for everyone.* The MIT Press.
51. Asfaw, A., et al. (2020). Learn quantum computation using qiskit. http://community.qiskit.org/textbook.
52. Koch, D., Wessing, L., & Alsing, P. M. (2019). Introduction to coding quantum algorithms: A tutorial series using Qiskit. arXiv:1903.04359. Accessed 19 Mar 2019.
53. Prechelt, L. (2000). An empirical comparison of seven programming languages. *Computer, 33*(10), 23–29. https://doi.org/10.1109/2.876288
54. Fourment, M., & Gillings, M. R. (2008). A comparison of common programming languages used in bioinformatics. *BMC Bioinformatics, 9*, 82. https://doi.org/10.1186/1471-2105-9-82

55. Jain, S. B., Sonar, S. G., Jain, S. S., Daga, P., & Jain, R. S. (2020). Review on Comparison of different programming language by observing it's advantages and disadvantages. *Research Journal of Engineering and Technology, 11*(3), 133–137. https://doi.org/10.5958/2321-581X.2020.00023.9

56. Huang, J., Hamido, O. C., & Campo, A. D. (2020). *Wolfiverse*. https://github.com/HuangJunye/Wolfiverse. Accessed 17 Mar 2021

57. Woehr, J., & Hamido, O. C. (2021). *QisJob*. Zenodo. https://doi.org/10.5281/zenodo.4554481.

58. Hamido, O. C., & Itaboraí, P. (2022). *OSC-Qasm: v1.0.0*. Zenodo. https://doi.org/10.5281/zenodo.5920428.

59. Fair-share queuing. *IBM Quantum*. https://quantum-computing.ibm.com/services/docs/services/manage/systems/queue/. Accessed 07 Feb 2022.

60. Miranda, E. R., & Basak, S. T. (2021a). Quantum computer music: Foundations and initial experiments. arXiv:abs/2110.12408v1. Accessed 03 Feb 2022.

61. Miranda, E., & Basak, S. (2021b). *iccmr-quantum/Miranda_Basak_Demos*. https://github.com/iccmr-quantum/Miranda_Basak_Demos. Accessed 01 Feb 2022.

62. Hamido, O. C. (2021). *The Gedanken Room*. https://www.imdb.com/title/tt14443510/.

Quantum Music Playground Tutorial

9

James L. Weaver

Abstract

This chapter introduces the Quantum Music Playground system. This introduction is the form of a tutorial, which walks the reader through the functionalities of the system. This is an educational tool for learning quantum computing concepts through music. It enables users to compose music while gaining intuition about quantum computing and algorithm design with circuits and states. It is implemented as a Max for Live device in the Ableton Live 11 digital audio workstation (DAW) and includes a MicroQiskit quantum simulator.

9.1 Introduction

Quantum Music Playground represents one of many possible approaches for leveraging quantum computing to compose music. It is implemented as a Max for Live device in Ableton Live 11 and includes a MicroQiskit quantum simulator. It is Apache 2.0 licensed open-source software, freely available; see conclusion for the weblink to access it.

Quantum Music Playground takes the approach of rendering beats and melodies from statevectors that model quantum states. For example, Fig. 9.1 shows a four-qubit quantum circuit in the IBM Quantum Circuit Composer. The basis state amplitudes (denoted by the heights of the bars) from the resultant quantum state are all equivalent. The phases of the basis states (denoted by the shading of the bars) differ, however, progressing from 0 radians to 15 $\pi/8$ radians.

J. L. Weaver (✉)
IBM Quantum, Yorktown Heights, NY, USA
e-mail: james.weaver@ibm.com

© The Author(s), under exclusive license to Springer Nature Switzerland AG 2022   197
E. R. Miranda (ed.), *Quantum Computer Music*,
https://doi.org/10.1007/978-3-031-13909-3_9

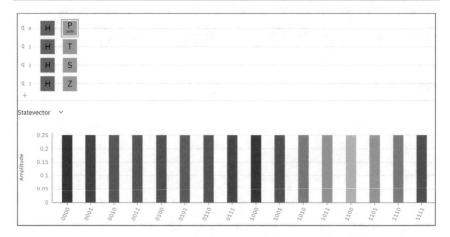

Fig. 9.1 Representing a sequence of phases in IBM quantum circuit composer

The quantum circuit and state shown in Fig. 9.1 may also be created in the Quantum Music Playground as shown in Fig. 9.2. The notes corresponding to each of the basis states are played in sequence. The amplitude of a given basis state controls the likelihood that the basis state will be played, and its phase controls the pitch played.

Quantum Music Playground is not only a tool for composing music, but it is also an enjoyable way of gaining intuition about quantum circuits and states in the process. As an example, Fig. 9.3 shows an Ableton Live Session View that contains MIDI clips that play an arrangement of the well-known tune entitled *Twinkle Twinkle Little Star*.

The song is played using Piano, Bass and various percussion instruments, and the clips are expressed using quantum circuits.

At the bottom of Fig. 9.3 is the Quantum Music Playground device, shown here expressing the kick drum part contained in the **Kick** clip in one of the tracks labelled **808 Core Kit**. In the centre of the device is a quantum circuit, shown by itself in Fig. 9.4.

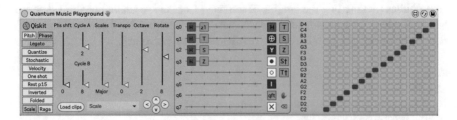

Fig. 9.2 Representing a sequence of pitches in quantum music playground

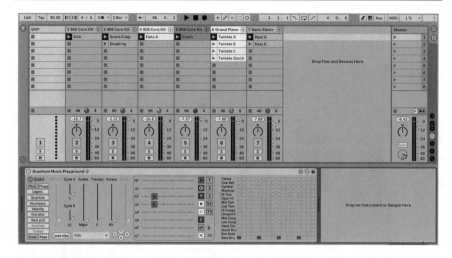

Fig. 9.3 *Twinkle Twinkle Little Star* programmed in quantum music playground

Fig. 9.4 Expressing Twinkle
Twinkle's kick drum

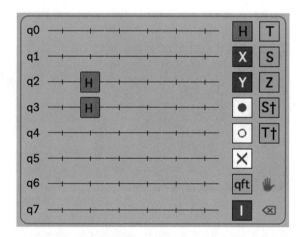

On the right side of the quantum circuit is a toolbox with quantum operations that may be placed on the quantum circuit. For the kick drum part, we are using a couple of **H** gates on the wires labelled **q2** and **q3**. The result is that the **Bass Drum** will play the four on the floor drum pattern shown in the sequence grid in Fig. 9.5. This sequence grid represents one measure in 4/4 time, and each column represents a sixteenth note. The bass drum is playing on each of the four beats in the measure.

The logic by which a couple of **H** (Hadamard) gates resulted in this drum pattern can be explained using some basic math.

First off, the wires labelled as **q0**–**q7** on the quantum circuit represent the least significant digit through the most significant digit of a binary value. The reason that there are 16 columns in the previous grid is that **q3** (the fourth wire) is the highest wire on which a gate is present. This defines a range of 16 binary numbers from

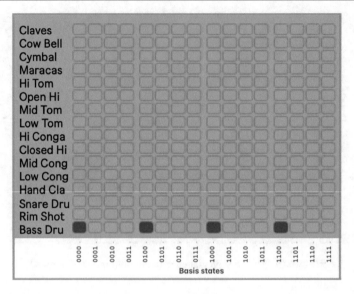

Fig. 9.5 Sequence grid representing one measure in 4/4 time

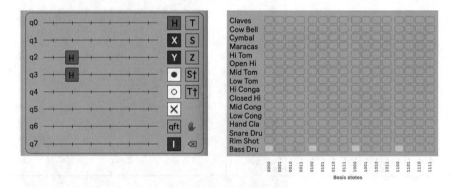

Fig. 9.6 Quantum circuit and corresponding sequence grid

0000 to 1111 and is labelled **Basis states** across the bottom of the previous image. Each *basis state* represents a step in our musical sequence.

To calculate which of these sequence steps the bass drum will play, take a look at the quantum circuit and the sequence grid together in Fig. 9.6 while reading the explanation that follows.

Each of the wires in the quantum circuit contains an initial value of 0.

- Because there are no gates on wire **q0**, the drum may only play on basis states whose 0 (least significant) position contains 0.
- Because there are no gates on wire **q1**, the drum may only play on basis states whose 1 position contains 0.

- Because there is an **H** gate on wire **q2**, the drum may play on basis states whose 2 position contains either 0 or 1. This is because the **H** gate puts the wire into a combination of 0 and 1.
- Because there is an **H** gate on wire **q3**, the drum may play on basis states whose 3 position contains either 0 or 1.

Putting that all together, the bass drum will play on all of the basis states whose 0 and 1 positions contain 0, which are 0000, 0100, 1000 and 1100.

You may be wondering why the bass drum, and not the other percussion instruments, are played as a result of this quantum circuit. The short answer is that the Quantum Music Playground chooses instruments and pitches based upon the phase angles mentioned earlier. The next section contains a more complete and satisfying explanation.

9.1.1 A Bit About Basis States

A basis state sometimes referred to as a *computational basis state*, is a concept used in quantum computing to represent a component of a quantum state. In this example, the quantum circuit defines a quantum state that is comprised of 16 basis states. Each basis state contains a complex number from which two important values may be derived:

- The *probability amplitude* that represents the likelihood that this basis state will be the result when measuring the quantum state, and
- the *phase angle* of this basis state.

Both concepts will be revisited at appropriate times. For now, it is important to understand that there is one binary digit in each basis state for each wire in a quantum circuit, where the number of wires is determined by the highest wire on which a gate is present. It is also necessary to know that the rightmost binary digit of each basis state corresponds to the topmost wire, labelled **q0**.

9.2 Choosing Instruments and Pitches

Up to this point, we have created a simple bass drum beat pattern by placing Hadamard gates on a quantum circuit. Now we're going to choose a different instrument to provide a cymbal crash at the beginning of each measure. As before, at the bottom of Fig. 9.7 is the Quantum Music Playground device, now expressing the cymbal part contained in the **Crash** clip in another one of the tracks labelled **808 Core Kit**. You may navigate to that clip by selecting **Crash** from the drop-down list to the right of the **Load clips** button in the Quantum Music Playground device.

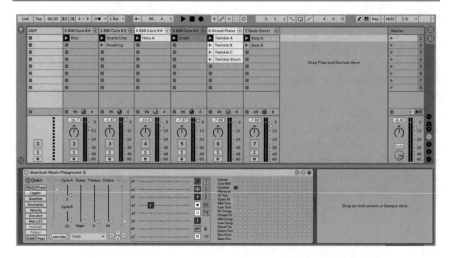

Fig. 9.7 Expressing the cymbal part contained in the Crash clip

Let's examine the Quantum Music Playground device by itself in Fig. 9.8.

The quantum circuit in this **Crash** clip contains just one gate, namely the **I** (Identity) gate. The **I** gate doesn't alter the state of a wire, but it's used here to set the number of basis states, and therefore steps, to 16 for this clip. The length of this **Crash** clip is now the same length as the **Kick** clip, so as each clip is playing in a loop, the cymbal and the bass drum will play together on the downbeat of the measure, followed by the bass drum playing on the remaining three beats.

To see why the **Cymbal**, rather than the **Bass Drum**, will be played, take a look at the disabled **Phs shft** slider and notice the value of 13 at the bottom. This indicates that the global phase angle shift, often referred to as *global phase shift*, of the quantum state is $13\pi/8$ radians (292.5°). This happens to correspond with the value of 13 to the right of the **Cymbal** row in Fig. 9.9.

As mentioned previously, each individual basis state contains a phase angle. Shifting the global phase by $\pi/8$ radians (22.5°) shifts each individual phase by $\pi/8$ radians, which results in moving the notes up one instrument or pitch.

9.2.1 Shifting the Phase Angles of Basis States

To create an interesting beat pattern or melody, it is usually necessary to shift the phase angles of various basis states. A common way to accomplish this is to follow an **H** gate with a *phase* gate. To demonstrate this, we'll play hi-hat cymbals, shifting back and forth from open to closed hi-hats. The bottom of Fig. 9.10 shows the Quantum Music Playground device, now expressing the hi-hat part contained in the **Hats A** clip in yet another one of the tracks labeled **808 Core Kit**.

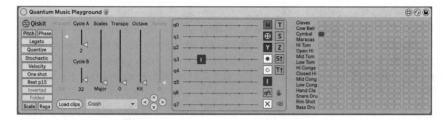

Fig. 9.8 Zooming in on the cymbal part contained in the Crash clip

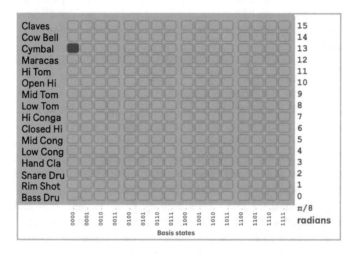

Fig. 9.9 Using global phase shift to play the Cymbal

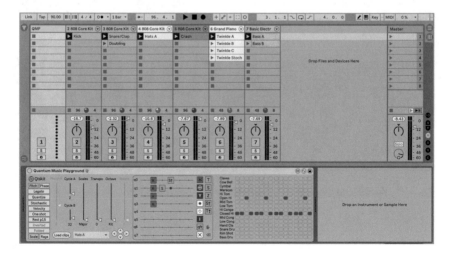

Fig. 9.10 Expressing the Hi-hat part contained in the Hats A clip

Now we will examine the Quantum Music Playground device by itself in Fig. 9.11. The quantum circuit in this **Hats A** clip contains a column of four **H** gates on wires **q0–q3**, which defines one measure with a beat pattern full of sixteenth notes. The circuit also contains two of the *phase gates* obtained from the right column of the toolbox, and a *control gate modifier* taken from the toolbox's left column.

We will discuss phase gates and control gate modifiers shortly but let us analyze the results of progressively adding gates to this circuit. Figure 9.12 shows the Quantum Music Playground device after placing only the **H** gates.

As with the **Kick** clip earlier, the **H** gates play a beat pattern on the **Bass Drum**. Next, Fig. 9.13 shows the **Phase** button selected and the **Phs shft** slider adjusted so that the **Closed Hi-hat** is played with the same beat pattern, having been shifted by a global phase.

To play the **Open Hi-hat** on the third sixteenth note of every beat, we employ one of the *phase gates*, specifically the **S** gate, as shown in Fig. 9.14.

The **S** gate rotates the phase on a wire by $4\pi/8$ radians, which rotates the phase on each of the basis states whose corresponding position contains a number one. This is seen more clearly in Fig. 9.15, in which the rotation is performed on every basis state whose bit in position one is equal to one.

Finally, to play the **Open Hi-hat** on the fourth sixteenth note of every beat, we employ another one of the *phase gates*, specifically the **S†** gate, in conjunction with the control gate modifier. This is shown in Fig. 9.16.

The **S†** gate rotates the phase on a wire by $12\pi/8$ radians. However, when a control gate modifier is placed in the same column, the **S†** gate only operates when the control wire has a value equal to on. This rotates the phase on each of the basis states whose positions corresponding to the **S†** gate and the control gate modifier both contain a number 1. This is seen more clearly in Fig. 9.17, in which the rotation is performed on every basis state whose bits in positions zero and one are both equal to one.

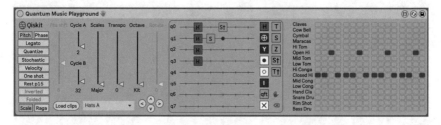

Fig. 9.11 Zooming in on the Hi-hat part contained in the Hats A clip

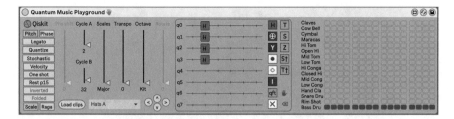

Fig. 9.12 Status after placing only the H gates

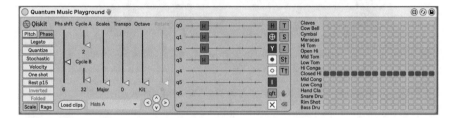

Fig. 9.13 Status after shifting global phase

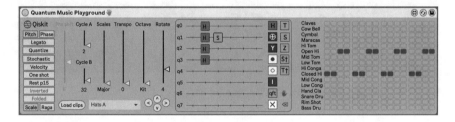

Fig. 9.14 Using a phase gate to play the open Hi-hat

9.3 Playing with Rhythm

So far, the rhythms that we created consisted of instruments playing at consistent time intervals. For example, our **Kick** clip played the bass drum on the four beats of the measure, and the **Hats A** clip played the hi-hats on each sixteenth note. Now we will discuss how to create syncopated rhythms, beginning with playing on the off beats. To demonstrate this, we will play the snare drum on beat two of a measure, and a hand clap on beat four of the measure, but neither will be played on beats one and three. The bottom of Fig. 9.18 shows the Quantum Music Playground device, now expressing the **Snare Drum** and **Hand Clap** parts contained in the **Snare/Clap** clip in another one of the tracks labelled **808 Core Kit**.

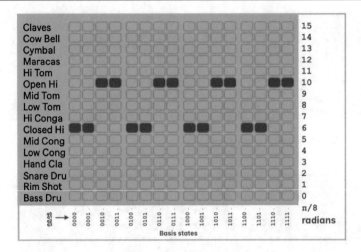

Fig. 9.15 Zooming in on using a phase gate to play the open Hi-hat

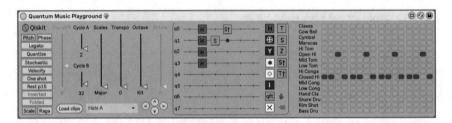

Fig. 9.16 Tweaking the sequence with a controlled-S† gate

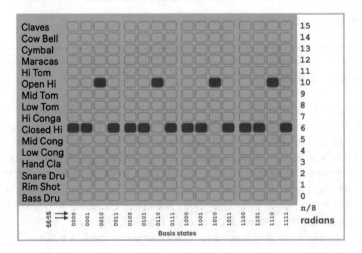

Fig. 9.17 Zooming in on the effects of using the controlled-S gate

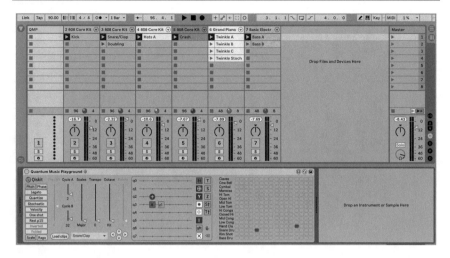

Fig. 9.18 Expressing the snare drum and hand clap parts

Looking at Fig. 9.19, we see that there are some similarities to the previous example in which open and closed hi-hats were played, but there are some differences to point out as well.

One difference is that the Phase gate on the quantum circuit is labelled **z1**, but there is no **z1** gate in the toolbox. This is because out of the 16 possible phase gates that rotate multiples of π/8 radians, only five of them (**T**, **S**, **Z**, **S†** and **T†**) have names. The rest are expressed in Quantum Music Playground with a lower-case **z** and the number of π/8 radians by which they rotate the phase. When a gate is placed or selected on the quantum circuit with the hand tool (i.e., the hand symbol near the bottom right in the toolbox), it may be rotated by adjusting the **Rotate** slider, or clicking and dragging the gate vertically.

Another difference from the previous example is that an **X** gate, (or *NOT* gate) or a *bit-flip* gate, is leveraged on wire **q2** to make the instruments play on the off-beats. This is seen more clearly in Fig. 9.20, where the notes appear on some basis states whose bit in position two is one because the **X** gate flipped that wire to have a value of one.

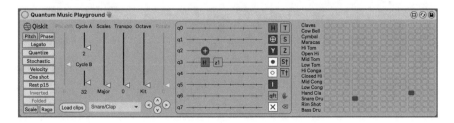

Fig. 9.19 Zooming in on the snare drum and hand clap parts

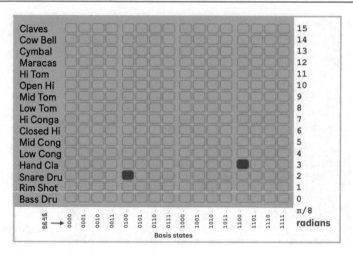

Fig. 9.20 Making instruments play on the off-beats

9.3.1 Leveraging the CNOT Gate for More Syncopation

Let's discuss how to create more syncopated rhythms, leveraging the CNOT gate. This gate is also known as the *controlled-NOT* gate, as well as the *controlled-X gate*. To demonstrate this technique, we'll play a simple bass line in a syncopated fashion. The bottom of Fig. 9.21 shows the Quantum Music Playground device, now expressing the note pitches to be played by the bass guitar in the **Bass B** clip of the track labeled **Basic Electr**.

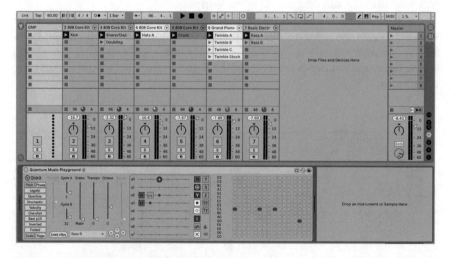

Fig. 9.21 Using C-NOT gate for syncopation

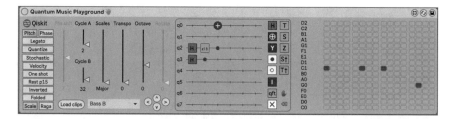

Fig. 9.22 Zooming in on using C-NOT gate for syncopation

Looking at Fig. 9.22, you'll notice that note pitches are specified rather than percussion instruments. The main point of this example, however, is the use of the control gate modifier with the **X** gate, turning it into a *CNOT* gate. Notice that the bit is flipped only when the control wire has a value equal to one. This flips the bit in the position on which the **X** gate is placed, but only on the basis states whose position corresponding to the control gate modifier contains a number one.

This is seen more clearly in Fig. 9.23, in which the notes appear on some basis states whose bit in position zero is equal to one because the **X** gate conditionally flipped that wire to have a value of one.

9.3.2 Manipulating Rhythms with Controlled-H Gates

We have leveraged **H** gates quite a bit to create rhythm patterns so far. Now we will add control gate modifiers to **H** gates for more rhythmic control. In the **Doubling** clip in Quantum Music Playground shown in Fig. 9.24, notice the use of control

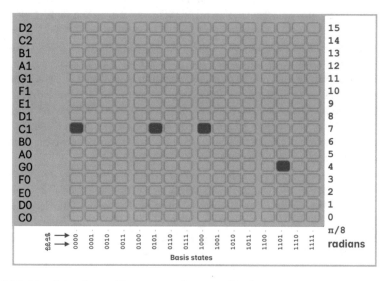

Fig. 9.23 Examining the resulting sequence in terms of basis states

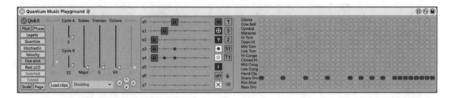

Fig. 9.24 Using controlled-H gates to achieve a doubling tempo

gate modifiers with some of the **H** gates to implement a well-known drum pattern in electronic dance music. This doubling pattern is achieved in part by making the **H** gate on wire **q0** conditional on whether the final eight out of 32 steps in the pattern are being played. Note that we're using two control gate modifiers in that column, in this case making the **H** gate active only on those of the 32 basis states (numbered 00000 through 11111) that begin with 11.

Notice that the **One shot** button is selected, which causes the clip to play just once, rather than looped.

Now that we discussed multiple ways of creating patterns, let us introduce ways to drop notes out of a pattern so as to prevent them from being played.

9.3.3 Dropping Notes Out of a Pattern

Creating a rhythm is as much about the notes that are *not* played as the notes that are played. Therefore, an important part of rhythm is inserting rests. There are several techniques for doing so with Quantum Music Playground, with the first method being turning down the *probability amplitude* of their basis states. To demonstrate this, we will play the 'up above the world so high, like a diamond in the sky' phrase of the melody in *Twinkle Twinkle Little Star*. The bottom of Fig. 9.25 shows the Quantum Music Playground device, now expressing the note pitches to be played by the piano in the **Twinkle B** clip of the track labelled **Grand Piano**.

Taking a closer look at Quantum Music Playground in Fig. 9.26, you'll notice a column of gates on the left side of the quantum circuit that are labeled **y1**.

These are examples of the more general **RY** gate, which is defined by its amount of rotation on the Y-axis of a Bloch sphere. Except for the **Y** gate itself, the RY gates are expressed in Quantum Music Playground with a lower-case **y** and the number of $\pi/8$ radians by which they rotate the on the Y-axis.

An effect of rotating a wire with an RY gate is that its probability amplitude may increase or decrease. We leverage this effect in Quantum Music Playground by making the MIDI velocity proportional to the probability amplitude. Consequently, the volumes of the notes vary according to their probability amplitudes.

Note that this default behaviour may be turned off by de-selecting the **Velocity** toggle button, which causes all notes to be played at the same velocity.

Additionally, there is a probability amplitude threshold below which a given basis state's note will not be played. By applying certain RY gates on one or more

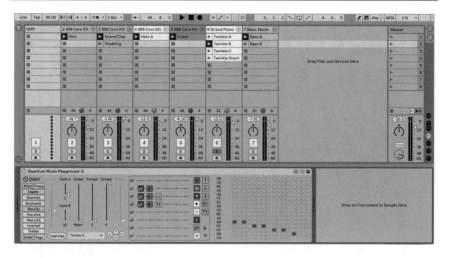

Fig. 9.25 Decreasing probability amplitudes to drop out notes

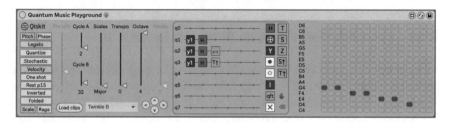

Fig. 9.26 Using RY gates to decrease probability amplitudes

wires, corresponding notes may be directed not to play. In the **Twinkle B** example, we are applying slight Y rotations on wires **q1–q3**, which has the effect of dropping out the notes on the basis states that begin with 111. This is illustrated in Fig. 9.27.

In general, the following technique may be used to express basis states to drop out, putting the RY gates to the left of the H gates.

- To drop out all basis states that have a number one in *one* given position, use a **y3** gate.
- To drop out all basis states that have a number zero in *one* given position, use a **y13** gate.
- To drop out all basis states that have some combination of one and zero bits in *two* given positions, use **y2** and **y14** gates, respectively.
- To drop out all basis states that have some combination of one and zero bits in *three* or *four* given positions, use **y1** and **y15** gates, respectively.

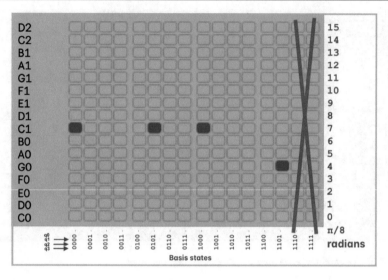

Fig. 9.27 Dropping out notes on basis states beginning with 111

9.3.4 Dropping Out a Note by Putting It in Pitch 15

Another way to drop out a note is to select the **Rest 15** toggle button and use some method (usually a phase gate) to make the desired note appear on the top row of the sequence grid. This technique is demonstrated in Fig. 9.28, where the top row of the sequence grid is now labeled **REST**.

This example leverages multiple control gate modifiers. In this case, the **T†** gate will only be rotated for basis states whose bits corresponding to **q2** and **q3** are both equal to one. We'll explore control gate modifiers in more detail next.

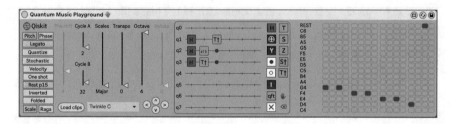

Fig. 9.28 Using the rest p15 toggle button to drop out notes

Fig. 9.29 Using an anti-control gate modifier

9.4   Understanding Control Gate Modifiers

We've used control gate modifiers with various gates in several of the examples, so let us gain a deeper understanding of them. Figure 9.29 shows the **Bass A** clip, in which you can see the use of control gate modifiers in some of the ways discussed previously. In addition, notice that in the third column of wire **q4** the control gate modifier is an empty circle. This is an *anti-control* gate modifier, and its behaviour is the opposite of its filled-circle counterparts. Specifically, the corresponding bit must be 0 for the gate it is modifying to operate. Therefore, the **z13** phase gate in the third column will only operate on sequence steps whose basis states contain zero and one in bit positions corresponding to **q4** and **q3**, respectively.

Table 9.1 shows which gates in Quantum Music Playground may have control (and anti-control) gate modifiers, as well as how many modifiers may be used with the gate.

Please note that if a column on a quantum circuit contains more than one of these gates, each will share the same control gate modifiers in the column. For example, if a column contains one **X** gate, one **H** gate, and one control gate modifier, the **X** gate will become a CNOT gate, and the **H** gate will become a controlled-H gate. Now that we've discussed how to express melodic and rhythmic sequences with quantum circuits, let's explore additional musical functionality available in Quantum Music Playground.

Table 9.1 Gates and maximum number of control modifiers

Gate	Max control modifiers
H gate	2
X gates: ×0 ×7, X, ×9 ×15	2
Y gates: y0–y7, Y, y9–y15	2
Phase gates: z0, z1, T, z3, S, z5–z7, Z, z9–z11, S†, z13, T†, z15	5

Fig. 9.30 Additional musical functionalities in quantum music composer

9.5 Exploring Additional Musical Functionality

Up to this point, focused on creating quantum circuits to select instruments and pitches, and to express rhythm patterns. When composing a song, of course, there are countless choices involving things such as instrument banks, octaves, musical scales, and time signatures. These choices help implement abstract musical sequences expressed by your quantum circuits. They are on the left side of the Quantum Music Playground device, shown in Fig. 9.30.

9.5.1 Selecting Musical Octaves

In Ableton Live, a track may contain either a rack of instruments (e.g., a drum kit) or an instrument that plays pitches. In the former case, a MIDI note selects an instrument, and in the latter case, a MIDI note selects a note pitch. In Fig. 9.31, showing the previous example of the **Hats A** clip, the vertical slider labelled **Octave** has **Kit** selected.

The instrument names displayed in the column to the left of the musical sequence grid are from the drum kit placed on the same track as the **Hats A** clip resides. The MIDI note values generated when **Kit** is selected range from 36 through 51, which often correspond to the main instruments in an instrument rack.

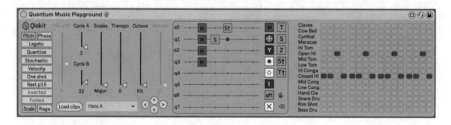

Fig. 9.31 Selecting an instrument from a rack or kit

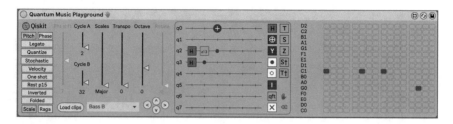

Fig. 9.32 Selecting a pitch from an instrument

By contrast, in the previous example of the **Bass B** clip, the vertical slider labelled **Octave** has **0** selected. This is shown in Fig. 9.32.

Available octave number selections are −**1**, **0**, **1**, **2**, **3** and **4**. Selecting an octave number normally causes the lowest pitch in the musical sequence grid to be the note C in the corresponding octave. For example, in the **Bass B** clip, selecting **Octave 0** causes the lowest pitch in the musical sequence grid to be **C0**.

9.5.2 Changing Musical Scales

By default, the musical scale known as **Major** is selected in the **Scales** slider. Several other scales and modes (e.g., NatMinor and Dorian) are available by selecting them in the slider. As shown in Fig. 9.33, when the scale or mode is changed the musical pitches in the column to the left of the musical sequence grid change appropriately.

9.5.3 Transposing Musical Pitches

By default, the lowest note in the musical sequence grid is C, playing in the key of C. To play in another musical key, select the number of semitones to transpose in the **Transpo** slider. As shown in Fig. 9.34, when the key is transposed the musical pitches in the column to the left of the musical sequence grid change accordingly.

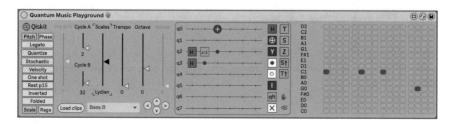

Fig. 9.33 Selecting a musical scale

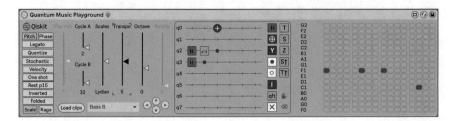

Fig. 9.34 Transposing the musical key

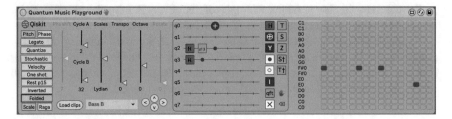

Fig. 9.35 Folding a musical scale

9.5.4   Folding a Musical Scale

When using a diatonic scale, it is sometimes convenient for the pitches to range from a tonic to the tonic an octave above, for a total range of eight pitches. To achieve that result, the **Folded** toggle button may be selected. As shown in Fig. 9.35, the pitches in the column to the left of the musical sequence grid change accordingly.

9.5.5   Inverting a Musical Scale

The pitches in the musical sequence grid may be inverted by selecting the **Inverted** toggle button. As shown in Fig. 9.36, the pitches in the column to the left of the musical sequence grid change accordingly.

9.5.6   Playing Notes Legato

Notes play for a duration of one-quarter note by default. To make notes play with a legato technique (held until the following note begins), and select the **Legato** toggle button.

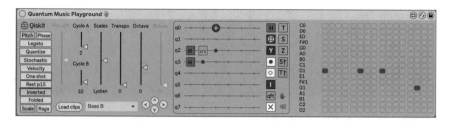

Fig. 9.36 Inverting a musical scale

9.5.7 Playing Harmonic Intervals and Chords

By default, notes are played melodically (one after another). Notes may be played harmonically by selecting the **Quantize** toggle button, producing intervals or chords. In the example shown in Fig. 9.37, a jazzy chord progression is played harmonically, as their individual notes are quantized into chords.

In this example the quantization occurs among basis states whose bit in position 3 are the same. Consequently, the following groups of notes are played harmonically:

- the C major seventh chord in basis states 00000–00111
- the D minor seventh chord in basis states 01000–01111
- the E minor seventh chord in basis states 10000–10111
- the F major seventh chord in basis states 11000–11111.

Similarly, the example in Fig. 9.38 demonstrates playing intervals harmonically.

In this example, the quantization occurs among basis states whose bits in position two are the same. Consequently, the following pairs of notes are played harmonically:

- the **E1–C2** interval in basis states 00000–00011
- the **F1–D2** interval in basis states 00100–00111
- the **G1–E2** interval in basis states 01000–01011
- the **A1–F2** interval in basis states 01100–01111
- the **B1–G2** interval in basis states 10000–10011
- the **C2–A2** interval in basis states 10100–10111

Fig. 9.37 Playing chords harmonically

Fig. 9.38 Playing intervals harmonically

- the **D2–B2** interval in basis states 11000–11011
- the **E2–C3** interval in basis states 11100–11111.

In each example, the bit position to use for quantization is ascertained by adding two to the position of the lowest occupied wire. In the first example, the lowest occupied wire is one, so quantization occurs among basis states whose bit in position three is the same. In the second example, the lowest occupied wire is equal to zero, so quantization occurs among basis states whose bit in position two is the same.

9.5.8 Implementing Time Cycles

Some of the most common time signatures and loop lengths in music are some power of 2. When other time cycles are desired (e.g., playing in 5/4 time signature, or in some Indian classical time cycles), a different length may be selected. For example, Fig. 9.39 shows part of the *Twinkle Twinkle Little Star* melody in clip **Twinkle A** being played in 7/8 time.

This is achieved by selecting 14 in the **Cycle A** slider, which removes all musical steps after the 14th up to the end of the next power of 2. This is visually represented by a column of blue cells wherever a step is removed. The **Cycle B** slider may be used in conjunction with **Cycle A** when two cycles are nested, as is required by some complex time cycles in Indian classical music.

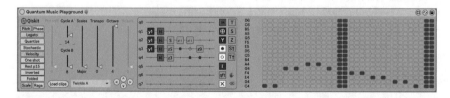

Fig. 9.39 Playing in 7/8 time

9.5.9 Generating Stochastic Pitches

All of the Quantum Music Playground functionality covered so far has been deterministic, which leverages the fact that we have access to the probability amplitudes and phases of the basis states in a quantum state. We only have access to this information because Quantum Music Playground uses a quantum simulator. Using a real quantum computer, information about an underlying quantum state is opaquer, and may only be glimpsed via repeated measurements. To introduce some quantum measurement randomness, select the **Stochastic** toggle button as shown in Fig. 9.40.

As a visual indication that pitches have been generated via measurement, notes in the musical sequence grid are bright green. The musical sequence contains the same number of notes and temporal spacing as before. However, the generated pitches result from taking one measurement of the quantum circuit for each of the notes and using the pitch that corresponds to the basis state resulting from each measurement.

When a clip has the **Stochastic** toggle selected, new pitches will be generated each time the clip is loaded. If the user modifies the quantum circuit or any other setting, the clip will toggle out of **Stochastic** mode.

9.6 Indian Classical Music Related Functionality

Quantum Music Playground contains some limited functionality that supports composing Indian classical music. This functionality includes the ability to select ragas instead of western scales and to control the lengths of complex time cycles.

9.6.1 Selecting Ragas

Figure 9.41 shows the first of the fundamental sequences (Sarali Varisai 1), used to teach Carnatic music. It is played in the Mayamalavagowla raga, which is number 15 in the Melakarta ragas. To select this raga, first press the **Raga** button, after which the **Scales** slider becomes a **Ragas** slider. Then select **Raga15** from the **Ragas** slider.

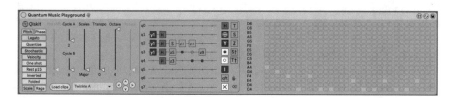

Fig. 9.40 Playing pitches stochastically

Fig. 9.41 Selecting a Carnatic Raga

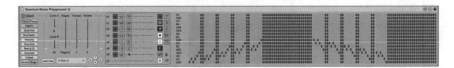

Fig. 9.42 Implementing nested time cycles

9.6.2 Controlling Lengths of Time Cycles

As discussed previously, Quantum Music Playground supports nested time cycles, such as required by the multi-cycle sequences in Carnatic lessons known as Alankaras. In the example shown in Fig. 9.42, the **Cycle B** slider is used in conjunction with **Cycle A** to implement the time cycles for Alankara 3.

9.7 Miscellaneous Functionalities

Quantum Music Playground contains functionality not directly related to music composition, such as loading and selecting MIDI clips, and moving all gates on the quantum circuit.

9.7.1 Loading MIDI Clips

When the Quantum Music Playground device starts, it identifies all of the clips contained in all of the MIDI tracks of the current set. The dropdown list to the right of the **Load clips** button is populated with these clip names. When you add, rename, duplicate, move or delete a MIDI clip, pressing the **Load clips** button will update the dropdown list appropriately.

9.7.1.1 QMP Metadata in MIDI Clips
MIDI clips in Ableton Live store MIDI data that includes note pitches, start times, and durations. In addition to the playable notes in a clip, Quantum Music Playground stores metadata in the MIDI clip that expresses the quantum circuit, slider

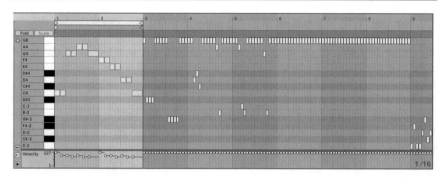

Fig. 9.43 QMP metadata in MIDI clips

values, and button toggle states. This may be seen in the Ableton MIDI Clip View for the **Twinkle A** clip (Fig. 9.43), whose measure numbers across the top will now be used as we discuss their contents.

For reference during this discussion, please also refer to Fig. 9.44 containing the **Twinkle A** clip in Quantum Music Playground. In the previous image, measures number one and two contain the MIDI notes for the notes to be played. Measures number three, four and five contain a MIDI representation of the quantum circuit, beginning with the first column, with each note encoding either a blank cell or operation. Measure number six contains slider values, with its final MIDI notes encoding the binary states of the toggle buttons. Should you be interested to learn more about this, please consult the Quantum Music Playground source code.

9.7.2 Selecting a MIDI Clip

To select a different MIDI clip in Quantum Music Playground, click the dropdown list located to the right of the **Load clips** button, and press the desired clip.

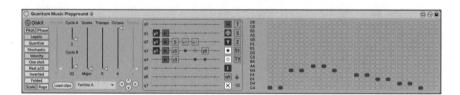

Fig. 9.44 The Twinkle A clip in quantum music playground

9.7.3   Moving All Operations on the Quantum Circuit

It is often desirable to move all the operations in a quantum circuit to the left or right in order to make room for a column of operations. It is also desirable to move all of the operations in a quantum circuit up or down, as that halves or doubles the number of steps in the musical sequence, changing its speed relative to other clips. Provided the appropriate row or column is empty, the left, right, up and down buttons, labeled "<", " >", "^" and "v" respectively, may be used for those purposes.

9.8   Conclusion

This chapter presented a tutorial on the Quantum Music Playground, which represents just one approach for leveraging quantum computing to compose music. For more information, including videos that contain examples in this tutorial, visit the Quantum Music Playground repository through the following weblink: qisk.it/qmp.

Quantum Representations of Sound: From Mechanical Waves to Quantum Circuits

10

Paulo Vitor Itaboraí and Eduardo Reck Miranda

Abstract

This chapter discusses methods for the quantum representation of audio signals. Quantum audio is still a very young area of study, even within the quantum signal processing community. Currently, no quantum representation strategy claims to be the best one for audio applications. Each one presents advantages and disadvantages. It can be argued that quantum audio will make use of multiple representations targeting specific applications. The chapter introduces the state of the art in quantum audio. It also discusses how sound synthesis methods based on quantum audio representation may yield new types of sound synthesizers.

10.1 Introduction

Sounds and images share common grounds. From the point of view of information processing, both are just signals. But obviously, we perceive them differently.

Most signal processing methods used for sounds are applicable to images and vice-versa. Their main difference is with respect to dimensionality. For instance, whereas sound is a one-dimensional (1D) signal in the time domain, image is a two-dimensional (2D) one. From a mathematical perspective, the higher the dimension of a signal, the more complex to represent and process it. Therefore, it is logical first to learn how 1D signal representation and processing methods work and then

P. V. Itaboraí · E. R. Miranda (✉)
ICCMR, University of Plymouth, Plymouth, UK
e-mail: paulo.itaborai@plymouth.ac.uk

E. R. Miranda
e-mail: eduardo.miranda@plymouth.ac.uk

extrapolate to 2D (images), 3D (videos), and beyond. By and large, this is how textbooks on audio and visual signal processing introduce the subject; e.g., [1,2].

Thus, from a historical perspective, it would seem reasonable to expect that quantum representations and potential algorithms for sound would have appeared in research avenues before the appearance of those for images and video. Surprisingly, this is not the case. An avid interest in developing quantum algorithms for image processing (primarily for facial recognition and similar applications) produced methods for quantum image representations and processing rapidly, leaving the case of 1D sound behind by almost a decade. This gap is unexpected, given the importance of speech technology to the electronics industry. Even more, if bearing in mind the relatively long-standing desire to develop quantum computing for natural language processing [3].

The first papers describing how to represent an image on a quantum processor theoretically were published in 2003 [4] and 2005 [5]. In comparison, the first papers proposing quantum representation methods for sound are from 2016 [6] and 2018 [7]; they are based on a method for images proposed in 2013 [8]. Indeed, most quantum signal processing algorithms designed to date are for image applications. The quantum sound community needs to catch up. Hence the motivation for this chapter.

The chapter is structured as follows: firstly, Sect. 10.2 contains a short introduction that delineates essential aspects and concepts of sound, analogue and digital audio representations that will be used later. It generally explains how the original sound content is transformed from one media to another. The concepts shown in this section will propel us toward the quantum territory with better intuition. This introductory section concludes by giving an initial idea of how quantum information logic will be applied to audio signals.

The introduction is followed by a short Sect. 10.3 that explains how time information is generally encoded in a quantum state. The following note Sect. 10.3.2 identifies some confusion problems present in the nomenclatures used by the literature for quantum audio. It proposes a new naming system to unify and clarify the different strategies used to encode audio information.

Then, the two subsequent sessions dive into various definitions and schemes proposed for representing audio in quantum machines using the previously proposed naming system. For instance, Sect. 10.4 explores Coefficient-Based representations, whereas Sect. 10.5 focuses on State-Based ones.

Section 10.6 summarizes the representations shown in the previous sections. It discusses some obstacles that should be accounted for when considering building and running quantum audio circuits for state-of-the-art quantum hardware.

Section 10.7 details some basic quantum signal processing operations and circuit design, such as quantum audio addition and concatenation, as well as sample-by-sample comparison.

The last Sect. 10.8 introduces some potential artistic applications in the short and near term. Specifically, there is a case study exploring wavetable synthesis and simple effects that make use of configurable parameters of coefficient-based representations.

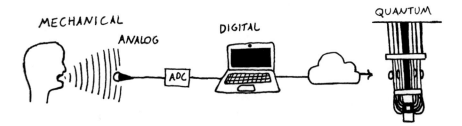

Fig. 10.1 The signal path from mechanical sound to quantum sound

10.2 From Mechanical to Quantum

The main objective of this section is to review how sound is represented in digital computers and electronic devices in general. It will provide the foundations to understand how sound can be represented for quantum computation.

In order to store a given sound in a quantum computer (i.e., by the time of writing), one would need to record the sound as analogue audio and make an analogue-to-digital conversion. Then, the digital audio needs to be translated into a quantum audio representation of some kind (Fig. 10.1). Let us go through each of these stages in more detail.

10.2.1 From Mechanical to Analog

In the most general sense, waves are physical entities that carry information about disturbances in a particular medium. For instance, electromagnetic waves carry information about disturbances in an electromagnetic field. Sound, however, is a mechanical wave. It can be generated by providing energy to a set of coupled vibrating systems in an acoustic medium, such as air.

Upon reaching a microphone, vibrating air pressure—that is, sound—becomes electric voltage. This is *analogue audio*. There are many ways to do this mechanic-to-electric conversion. One of the first techniques ever developed to do this can still be found in dynamic microphones today.

A dynamic microphone has three main elements: a thin diaphragm, a cylindrical magnet and a wire coil. The coil is wrapped around the magnet, but it does not touch it. It can move freely on the cylinder's axis. The diaphragm is coupled to one end of the coil. So, the vibrating sound will move the diaphragm back and forth. As a consequence, the coil will oscillate through the magnet—or, from the perspective of the coil, the magnet will oscillate through it. In an oversimplified way, Faraday's Law teaches us that when a magnet is moving through a conductive coil, it will induce an electric current. This movement will result in a measurable voltage. So, an oscillating coil will induce an oscillating voltage at its terminals. Thus, the mechanical sound has been converted into a varying electric voltage signal which is, by definition, analogue audio.

10.2.1.1 Audio Encoding

Analogue audio creates a direct connection between mechanical and electrical media. We could say that it *represents sound*.

Analogue audio imposes itself as a new technique for propagating and manipulating sound, which was not possible before its invention. For instance, a singer could try to sing louder or even scream, attempting to reach listeners located far away and still not be heard. Alternatively, this singer could convert her voice into audio and then transmit the signal through conductive wires or electromagnetic waves until it reaches the listener. The audio would then be converted back into sound through loudspeakers. The caveat is that transmission, reception and conversion are prone to noise and errors.

Attempts to reduce noise and errors during long transmissions (for example, radio transmissions) are what motivated the first audio encoding schemes as effective ways of representing electric audio information. The three most widely used analogue audio encoding schemes are Amplitude Modulation (AM), Frequency Modulation (FM) and Phase Modulation (PM) [9]. In these cases, the raw analogue signal is encoded by means of a measurable variation of a *signal parameter*, such as the frequency, amplitude (i.e., power), or phase.

10.2.2 From Analogue to Digital

A digital computer is unable to process a continuous stream of audio, which contains voltage information at all possible points in time. There are infinitely many of them inside an audio signal. Thus, analogue information needs to be digitized. This is done by means of an ADC (Analogue-to-Digital Converter) device, which converts an analog signal into a digital signal. How is this done? How to turn continuous time and amplitude information into discrete binary codes?

This section introduces the notions of *sampling* and *quantization*, which are discretizations of time and amplitude, respectively.

Audio sampling is the action of taking snapshots of a continuous signal and storing them (i.e., the values captured by the snapshots) as time-indexed *samples* (Fig. 10.2).

As shown in Fig. 10.2, the snapshots of a signal are conventionally taken in equally spaced time lapses. The speed of lapses is referred to as the *sampling rate* or *sampling frequency*. In other words, the sampling rate establishes how many samples are taken per unit of time. Good quality audio systems use a sampling rate of 44,100 Hz (or 44,100 snapshots per second). The sampling rate has the role of translating an index $k = 0, 1, 2, ...$ into a respective instant in time t_k. That is, the sampling rate S_R is the constant responsible for carrying the conversion between the moment of the snapshot (in time units) and an index of time (dimensionless) (Eq. 10.1). The index k can be represented in binary form and thus stored in a classical computer.

$$t_k = \frac{k}{S_R} \tag{10.1}$$

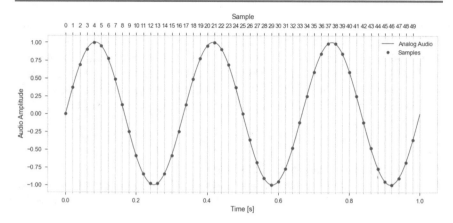

Fig. 10.2 A sampled sine wave

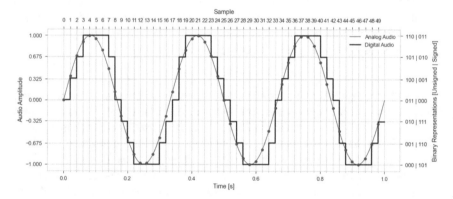

Fig. 10.3 An analogue wave and its respective quantization

Now, let us look at the quantization step. Bear in mind that the notion of quantization here has nothing to do with quantum mechanics. Here, quantizing means *to restrict a continuous range to a prescribed set of values*.

Let us examine how the amplitude of an analogue signal, usually represented in the −1 to 1 range, can be quantized into binary numbers (Fig. 10.3).

Quantization is, in some ways, similar to sampling, but it operates alongside the vertical axis. The main difference is that the values can be negative. Nevertheless, we can rescale and shift the whole signal to make it fall entirely in the positive domain without any loss of generality. This is a resourceful operation in audio signal processing.

The way to shift a signal along a determined axis is by adding or subtracting a defined quantity on all signal values. In our case, we would like to shift the entire signal up by 1, so we add 1 to every amplitude value. After doing this, the amplitudes range from 0 to 2 instead of −1 and 1. The range is already positive, but we can further improve this by rescaling the signal to the 0–1 range; this will be relevant to our quantum audio discussion later. The rescaling is done by multiplication and division, and of course, for our case, we divide the amplitudes by 2. With this *unitary* range, we can do the quantization scheme more easily. If we have n-bit words to store each amplitude, we will perform 2^n subdivisions in our range. Then, the voltage values are rounded to fit the closest binary value afforded by the subdivision scheme.

Hence, we have successfully digitized our audio by putting them on a grid, as shown in Fig. 10.3.

10.2.2.1 Two's Complement Scheme

The quantization scheme presented above is perfectly valid and general for any type of signal in a positive range. However, we have seen that audio signals have negative values as well.

Of course, this is not a problem in itself. We showed above how to shift audio to a positive domain. However, this shifting procedure can often render the audio unsuitable for specific manipulations. A concerning example would be amplitude multiplication. Shifting a value to the strictly positive domain could drastically alter the result of a simple multiplication (as indicated in Eq. 10.2).

$$(a_1 + shift)(a_2 + shift) \neq a_1 a_2 + shift \tag{10.2}$$

This absence of negative numbers may also prove to be at least inconvenient. Consider, for instance, the task of adding two audio signals. The way to add digitized audio waves is by summing their amplitudes, term-by-term. Specifically, imagine an oversimplified digital noise cancellation algorithm. It relies on negative numbers. First, some unwanted noise in an audio signal is received. Then, it generates a copy of the noise with inverted polarity (In other words, all amplitudes are multiplied by -1). Finally, the inverted signal is added to the original. Each amplitude is added to a negated version of itself, meaning they cancel each other, and the noise disappears. This phenomenon is nominally called *destructive interference*.[1] Even though there might be an elaborate way of achieving the desired result with only positive numbers, a less laborious alternative is desirable.

A viable solution—which is the one that is generally used for representing audio signals—is to use another interpretation of the binary integers. One that could enable us to represent negative numbers and facilitate binary addition arithmetic. This solution is referred to as the *Two's Complement* scheme.

It is important to understand the underlying logic of representing negative numbers in binary, as this will also be useful for quantum audio representations.

The main idea of the Two's Complement encoding scheme is to divide the binary words into two sets. Half of them would represent negative numbers and the other half positive ones. This can be made by using the *Most Significant Bit* (i.e., the

---

[1] This also appears in the context of the quantum theory, since quantum systems also show wave-like behaviour and thus have wave-like properties such as superposition and interference, among others. But do not be misled. A classical wave and a quantum particle-wave still are fundamentally different, even if they have similar mathematical properties.

leftmost bit), or MSB, as a *signing bit*. If the MSB is 0, then the number is positive. Otherwise, it is negative (Eq. 10.3).

$$0010... \longrightarrow \overset{(+\text{ or}-)}{0} \quad \overset{(\text{number})}{010...} \tag{10.3}$$

However, just the signing bit by itself is not enough for having a 'good' negative number. For it to be useful, it needs to comply with binary addition properties.

Let us consider a computer with a 4-bit architecture and then use the MSB to indicate the signal of the following 3 bits without applying any other logic. Now, let us try to add 2 and -2 using this new interpretation. Consider the simplified binary addition rules in Eq. 10.4, and see what happens when we add the numbers (Eq. 10.5).

$$\begin{aligned} 0 + 0 &= 0 \\ 0 + 1 &= 1 + 0 = 1 \\ 1 + 1 &= 10 \quad \{\text{The bit to the left is added by }1\} \end{aligned} \tag{10.4}$$

$$2 \to 0010; \quad -2 \to 1010 \ \therefore \ 0010 + 1010 = 1\,100 \to -4\ (?) \tag{10.5}$$

What is shown in Eq. 10.5 clearly does not work. But this can be solved. We can apply another condition to our encoding scheme. That is: $x + (-x) = 0$. This condition would interestingly and conveniently change the representation of the negative numbers completely, as shown in Eq. 10.6. Now we can verify in Eq. 10.7 that the addition works perfectly.

$$\begin{matrix} \text{Regular Integer} & & \text{Two's Complement Integer} \\ \begin{bmatrix} 15 \\ 14 \\ \ldots \\ 8 \end{bmatrix} \begin{bmatrix} 1\,111 \\ 1\,110 \\ \ldots \\ 1\,000 \end{bmatrix} & & \begin{bmatrix} 0\,111 \\ \ldots \\ 0\,001 \\ 0\,000 \end{bmatrix} \begin{bmatrix} 7 \\ \ldots \\ 1 \\ 0 \end{bmatrix} \\ = & \searrow & = \\ \begin{bmatrix} 7 \\ \ldots \\ 1 \\ 0 \end{bmatrix} \begin{bmatrix} 0\,111 \\ \ldots \\ 0\,001 \\ 0\,000 \end{bmatrix} & & \begin{bmatrix} 1\,111 \\ 1\,110 \\ \ldots \\ 1\,000 \end{bmatrix} \begin{bmatrix} -1 \\ -2 \\ \ldots \\ -8 \end{bmatrix} \end{matrix} \tag{10.6}$$

$$2 \to 0010; \quad -2 \to 1\,110 \ \therefore \ 0010 + 1\,110 = 0\,000 \to 0 \tag{10.7}$$

10.2.2.2 Digital Audio as an Array

After being digitized, the audio's binary information is stored in a data structure. The most common structure for digital audio is an array vector, visualized in Fig. 10.4. The time information becomes an index to a specific position of an array, and the respective amplitude becomes the variable stored in that position. In this way, one can retrieve the amplitudes by having the time index.

In order to efficiently represent, store and transmit binary data structure as a stream of audio information, a digital audio encoding scheme is typically used. Similar to the analogue case shown above, the digital domain provides some parameters that

Fig. 10.4 Audio array visualization

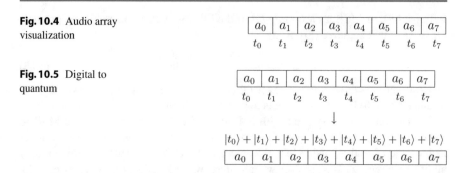

Fig. 10.5 Digital to quantum

can be controlled (or modulated) to represent information. For example, we could represent a stream of digital information using *pulses* that are precisely controlled by piezoelectric crystals. The representation that has dominated the music industry is the PCM audio or Pulse Code Modulation. PCM has become a standard in digital audio due to its reliable lossless storage and transmission capacities. Furthermore, it is less prone to noise and errors compared to other pulse representations such as Pulse Amplitude Modulation (PAM), Pulse Position Modulation (PPM), and Pulse Width Modulation (PWM) [9].

We should note at this stage that the two's complement digital audio is used in a wide variety of applications. However, modern 32-bit and 64-bit operating systems, as well as high-level programming languages like Python, further improve the representation of the quantized audio amplitudes by using *floating-point numbers*. A good approximation of Real ($\in \mathbb{R}$) numbers can be stored with floating-point numbers, with high precision and significant decimal figures. Thus, instead of storing an integer representing the middle number of a quantization range, we could add a new pre-processing layer and store a good approximation of the number itself, using the flexibility of floating-point numbers to process the signal in the digital medium. However, this requires a considerable amount of space and computing power. As we will see in the remainder of this chapter, we are still far from similar schemes for quantum computer audio. But imaginable nevertheless.

10.2.3 From Digital to Quantum

Gaining an intuitive understanding of quantum audio representation is straightforward, in the sense that Dirac's notation can clearly show how the audio information (time and amplitude) can be translated into quantum states (Fig. 10.5). Of course, the underlying quantum computing paradigm can be counter-intuitive. However, this intuitive bird's-eye view understanding of the organizational structure of quantum audio gives us an end goal and provides a guiding thread for us to cross the uncertain quantum algorithmic roads. On this path, we shall explore how these representations of quantum audio are prepared and measured, as well as potential near-term and long-term applications.

It is important to state that quantum audio is still a very young area of study, even under the quantum signal processing umbrella. Therefore many fundamental questions remain open for discussion. There is no audio representation strategy that we could argue to be the best one for audio applications. Each of them presents particular advantages and disadvantages. It can be argued that quantum audio will make use of multiple representations targeting specific applications.

10.3 Preparation and Retrieval of Quantum Audio

The near-term prospects of quantum technology indicate that quantum computers will not replace classical computers in many ways. Rather, they will co-exist, creating hybrid classical-quantum processing environments. This already occurs in current working quantum systems, many of which are accessible via cloud services and interact with classical machines. It is not going to be different for near-term quantum audio applications. These applications rely strongly on classical computers, not only to provide a digital audio file to be prepared but also to post-process quantum circuit measurement results. There are well-known classical programming languages for this part; e.g. Python and MatLab. In the following sections, we will look in detail at quantum audio representations that have been proposed to date. We will examine how quantum audio is prepared, measured, and envisage possible applications. Let us start by introducing the connection between time indexes and quantum superpositions.

10.3.1 Encoding Time Information

As mentioned previously, a qubit is a 2-state quantum system that can be measured to value either 0 or 1. It can also be put in a superposition of states, written as shown in Eq. 10.8, where $|\alpha|^2$ and $|\beta|^2$ are the probabilities that a measurement of this state results in 0 or 1, respectively. Since the sum of the probabilities of all possible outcomes needs to be 1, it means that $|\alpha|^2 + |\beta|^2 = 1$.

$$|\Psi\rangle = \alpha |0\rangle + \beta |1\rangle \qquad (10.8)$$

For 2-qubit states, a similar equation can be written, considering all possible outcomes, as shown in Eq. 10.9.

$$|\Psi\rangle = a |00\rangle + b |01\rangle + c |10\rangle + d |11\rangle ; \qquad |a|^2 + |b|^2 + |c|^2 + |d|^2 = 1 \quad (10.9)$$

Since we have few letters in the alphabet to represent many of these probability amplitudes, it might be better to change the notation slightly and use the same letter with a subscript. For instance, a 3-qubit state written this way is shown in Eq. 10.10.

$$\begin{aligned} |\Psi\rangle = {} & a_{(000)} |000\rangle + a_{(001)} |001\rangle + a_{(010)} |010\rangle + a_{(011)} |011\rangle \\ & + a_{(100)} |100\rangle + a_{(101)} |101\rangle + a_{(110)} |110\rangle + a_{(111)} |111\rangle \end{aligned} \qquad (10.10)$$

At this point, we ought to make another helpful change to the notation for improving our intuitiveness. Sometimes, it is convenient (and conventional) to interpret the numbers inside the 'kets' not as a sequence of states of individual qubits in a register—but as a classical binary bit string associated with an integer number.

Before we do so, it is imperative to remind us that these zeros and ones inside the 'kets' *are not numbers*. Kets are a simplified notation for writing *vectors*. Therefore, whatever is written inside the ket, is just a conventionalized *label* that refers to a vector: $|label\rangle$. We use numbers as labels to reduce the level of abstraction of those mathematical entities and provide some insight into their use inside a system. In other words, the interpretation above is not changing the state in mathematical terms. Instead, it is just a change of notation. It is essential to have this clear and fresh in our minds to avoid confusion as we introduce the representations next.

Thus, by interpreting the qubit states as binary numbers, we can write a particular 3-qubit state of Eq. 10.10 as shown in Eq. 10.11.

$$|\Psi\rangle_{3-\text{qubit}} = \frac{1}{\sqrt{8}}\left[|0\rangle + |1\rangle + |2\rangle + |3\rangle + |4\rangle + |5\rangle + |6\rangle + |7\rangle \right] \qquad (10.11)$$

All of the quantum audio representations presented in this text share the same encoding strategy for time information. They use a quantum register to create a superposition of all the possible time indexes associated with each audio sample. This is called a *time register*. Each state will be an index, indicating a position in time, similar to a classical array.

Any information related to this state will encode the respective sample using different strategies (Eq. 10.12). For instance, it could use the probability amplitude or another coupled quantum register.

$$(\text{Amplitude}) \, |t_k\rangle \qquad (10.12)$$

Note the necessity of a 2^n-sized signal for all of the representations. We can use zero padding for using audio with different sizes. We will explore in more detail below how amplitude information is represented in the different schemes.

10.3.2 Note on Nomenclature

Before we proceed, let us clarify the nomenclature used to refer to the various Quantum Audio Representation (QAR) methods that will be reviewed below. For the sake of clarity and systematization, we propose slight adaptations to the names given in the research papers where these methods were originally introduced.

The representation methods can be grouped into two categories related to how they encode the audio amplitude information and retrieve it back to the classical realm through measurements. The first group contains what is referred to as 'Probabilistic' or 'Coefficient-Based' representations—due to its probabilistic nature when retrieving information classically. The second group include 'Deterministic' or 'State-Based' methods.

As mentioned earlier, quantum audio representation methods are derived from methods developed for representing images rather than sound. The research literature introduced methods such as Quantum Representation of Digital Audio (QRDA), Flexible Representation of Quantum Audio (FRQA), and Quantum Representation of Multichannel Audio (QRMA), which are all State-Based. However, there also are some Coefficient-Based methods for images that can (and will in this chapter) be easily adapted for audio representation.

Also, this chapter intends to reach the signal processing community, and in this endeavour, we will be proposing a new nomenclature system for the already proposed representations. The intention is to correlate, integrate or unify these representations with classic representations in the future. For that, we will use the term 'Modulation' as a central spine. This means that we will propose to rename, for example, the Flexible Representation of Quantum Audio (which by itself already has some confusion problems in relation to quantum images[2]) into Quantum State Modulation (QSM), based on the fact that amplitude information is stored in a multi-qubit state. This naming system also paves the way for other coefficient-based audio representations, such as the Quantum Probability Amplitude Modulation (QPAM).

10.4 Coefficient-Based Representations

Suppose that we have some digital audio A, with $N = 2^n$, $n \in \mathbb{Z}^*$ samples, with each sample quantized to $[-2^{q-1}, -2^{q-1} + 1, ..., 2^{q-1} - 1]$. That is, 2^q possible values.

We can induce that the easiest way to represent those samples in a quantum state $|A\rangle$ would be first to create a superposition of all of its possible states t (encoding time). Then, each time state would be weighted by their respective probability amplitude (encoding the sample value) in a way that resembles an array, but in a quantum superposition (Eqs. 10.13 and 10.14).

$$\boxed{a_n}\, t_n \longrightarrow \alpha_i\, |t_i\rangle \tag{10.13}$$

$$|A\rangle_{(3-qubit\,Array)} = \alpha_0\,|0\rangle + \alpha_1\,|1\rangle + \alpha_2\,|2\rangle + \alpha_3\,|3\rangle + \alpha_4\,|4\rangle + \alpha_5\,|5\rangle + \alpha_6\,|6\rangle + \alpha_7\,|7\rangle \tag{10.14}$$

---

[2] It would feel logical to induce that the Flexible Representation of Quantum Audio (FRQA) was derived from the Flexible Representation of Quantum Images (FRQI). Unfortunately, this is not the case, since the FRQI is a Coefficient-Based Representation, and the FQRA is a State-Based one, derived from the Novel Enhanced Quantum Representation for digital images (NEQR). The choice to name the FQRA as such is unclear and might have been made for historical reasons. The FRQI was one of the pioneering representations for images (like FRQA) and probably the first to be widely studied in the literature with a variety of applications.

10.4.1 Quantum Probability Amplitude Modulation: QPAM

More generally, we could write an arbitrary quantum audio of size N, with n (or $\lceil \log N \rceil$) qubits and build an encoding scheme where each possible amplitude value of the audio is mapped onto a probability amplitude (Eq. 10.15).

$$|A_{QPAM}\rangle = \sum_{i=0}^{N-1} \alpha_i \,|i\rangle \qquad (10.15)$$

Quantum computing theory usually presents the upper bound of the sum showing the number of qubits explicitly, like $(2^n - 1)$. Instead, we chose to use $N = 2^n$ as our primary notation, as this will make more sense to the reader with an audio digital signal processing background.

With Eq. 10.15, we achieved a simple but still very useful QAR. We refer to this method as Quantum Probability Amplitude Modulation representation of audio, or QPAM. It is a convenient name, as the amplitude information is encoded as probability amplitudes of each quantum state.

10.4.1.1 Mapping the Digital Amplitudes to QPAM

Now, let us examine how to convert a digital signal representation to QPAM representation and vice-versa.

The audio amplitudes a_n are not equal to the probability amplitudes α_i of measuring each sample state. Instead, there is a specific *mapping* between them, which makes this encoding scheme possible. Let us see how this works using the hypothetic snippet of audio depicted in Fig. 10.6.

In Quantum Mechanics, we can affirm that given an arbitrary qubit $|\phi\rangle = \alpha \,|0\rangle + \beta \,|1\rangle$ the probability of measuring the state $|0\rangle$ is $|\alpha|^2$, with the proviso that:

- Probabilities are numbers ranging between 0 and 1
- The sum of probabilities of all possible states should be equal to 1.

Digital audio amplitudes in Fig. 10.6, however, are numbers ranging between -1 and 1. Their sum does not necessarily add to 1 at all. So, in order to go from digital to quantum, we need to take the following steps to *normalize* the amplitudes:

- Step 1: add 1 to all amplitudes a_n
- Step 2: divide the amplitudes by 2
- Step 3: divide again, by the sum of all of the amplitudes
- Step 4: take the square root of the result.

Consider the amplitudes of our example listed before the down arrow in Fig. 10.7. The approximate normalized values are shown after the down arrow. Firstly, we shifted the amplitude values to the positive domain by adding 1 to every value. At this point, the amplitudes range between 0 and 2. Next, we scaled them to fit the range between 0 and 1. Then, we summed all their values and divided every value

Fig. 10.6 Hypothetic audio

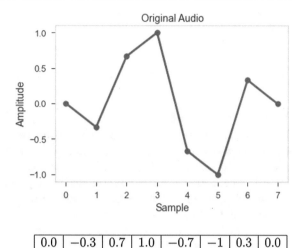

Fig. 10.7 Normalization process

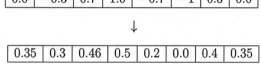

by the result of the sum. At this point, the sum of all amplitudes should be equal to 1.

The last step is to turn these amplitudes into probability values by taking their square root (Eq. 10.16).

$$\alpha_i = \frac{1}{\sqrt{g}}\sqrt{\frac{(a_i + 1)}{2}}; \qquad g = \sum_k \frac{(a_k + 1)}{2} \tag{10.16}$$

10.4.1.2   QPAM Preparation

The QPAM representation is the most straightforward to prepare. As the information is stored in the probability amplitudes, we just need to initialize the quantum audio at the desired quantum superposition. This can be done by using the probability amplitudes to calculate a unitary gate. Alternatively, one could create a quantum circuit that maps a set of qubits initialized in the $|0000...\rangle$ state into the arbitrary state. Fortunately, we do not need to worry about calculating these matrices and circuits in a more practical sense. Most quantum computing programming tools available nowadays provide commands to initialize qubit states. So, it suffices to assume that any arbitrary superposition of states can be initialized by providing a set of probability amplitudes to the respective command (Fig. 10.8). Consequently, for preparing a QPAM quantum audio, we would only need to convert the digital samples into probability amplitudes.

Thus, preparing an arbitrary n-qubit state usually requires $\mathcal{O}(n)$ simple operations, which implies that QPAM preparation needs $\mathcal{O}(\lceil \log N \rceil)$ operations.

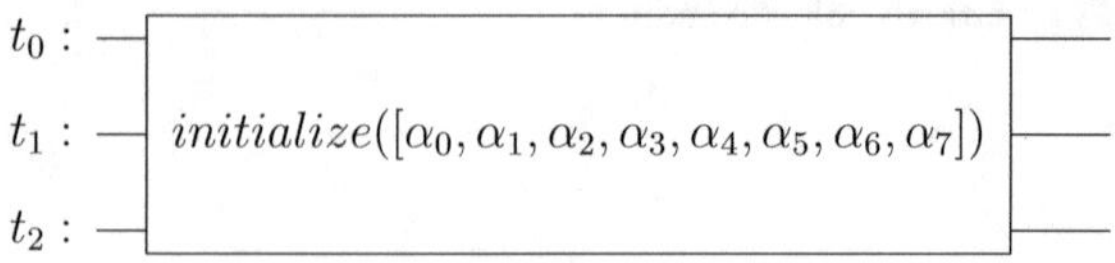

Fig. 10.8 Initializing qubit states for QPAM

t_0 : ———

t_1 : ——— $initialize([\alpha_0, \alpha_1, \alpha_2, \alpha_3, \alpha_4, \alpha_5, \alpha_6, \alpha_7])$ ———

t_2 : ———

10.4.1.3 QPAM Retrieval

Retrieving information from the quantum domain means taking measurements from our quantum system. Measuring a quantum system means that only one of the possible state outcomes of that system will be 'materialized' in our measurement apparatus. In other words, once we measure our time registers, the superpositions will be 'destroyed', and only one of the possible time states will be returned.

Figure 10.9 portrays a hypothetical QPAM representation (i.e., histogram of amplitudes) of the audio shown in Fig. 10.6. Furthermore, Fig. 10.10 shows the respective audio reconstructed by retrieving measurements with an allegedly perfect quantum machine. Let us look into this in more detail.

The Probabilistic representations have this name precisely because of their retrieval strategy. Retrieving audio requires that we prepare many identical quantum versions of the said audio and make a statistical analysis of the result of all measurements. The analysis will return a histogram of the measurements (e.g., Fig. 10.9), from which we can assess the approximate probability of measuring each state. When considering how the system was prepared in the first place, it indicates that the histogram itself is already a scaled and shifted version of a digital audio. We just need to scale the audio back to its original range, using an inverted version of Eq. 10.16 for a_i, shown in Eq. 10.17.

$$a_i = 2g|\alpha_i|^2 - 1 \tag{10.17}$$

There are two critical aspects of Eq. 10.17 to be noticed. First, the previous sum in Eq. 10.16 is a defined constant value, which is referred to as g. Second, the

Fig. 10.9 A hypothetical QPAM representation

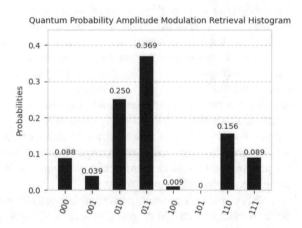

Quantum Probability Amplitude Modulation Retrieval Histogram

Fig. 10.10 Reconstructed audio from QPAM in Fig. 10.9

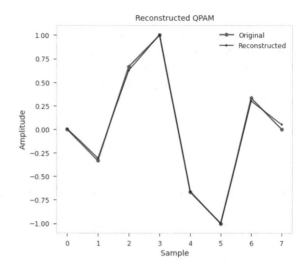

addition of a "||" on α_i. We need to be careful with α_i because it is, rigorously, a complex number ($\alpha_i^2 \neq |\alpha_i|^2$). Nevertheless, the valuable information lies in its absolute value squared, which corresponds to the probability $p_i = |\alpha_i|^2$ of $|i\rangle$ being measured. After completing the measurements, a histogram bin will not return p_i, but rather an approximation $\tilde{p}_i$.

By replacing Eq. 10.17 with $\tilde{p}_i$, the final post-processing step for retrieving a digital audio is achieved, as shown in Eq. 10.18.

$$a_i = 2g\,\tilde{p}_i - 1 \tag{10.18}$$

10.4.1.4   A Caveat

The constant g in Eq. 10.16 presents an important caveat. The equation contains terms related to digital amplitudes a_k. What is the caveat?

Let us consider the preparation stage. The constant g is the denominator, meaning that the sum over the terms $\frac{(a_i+1)}{2}$ cannot be equal to 0. This condition occurs if all values of a_i were equal to -1, which is a perfectly valid audio signal.

From a retrieval perspective, there is another consideration. The presence of g makes the normalization of the original input necessary for retrieving a QPAM representation. However, in more general terms, one could consider g to be any arbitrary constant, which would define the overall *amplitude range* of the signal.

This arbitrariness of choice for g can be a problem if not properly assessed. It undesirably changes the amplitude range for the retrieved audio. Let us imagine a thought experiment to illustrate this.

Consider a QPAM audio signal with 8 samples. All sample values are equal to 0. Equation 10.16, confirms that $g = 4$. Then, suppose that a certain quantum algorithm transforms this signal into the measured waveform shown in Fig. 10.9. The signal will be reconstructed using Eq. 10.17. Particularly, consider the peak value of the histogram. Applying Eq. 10.17 will result in $2g|0.369|^2 - 1 = 0.089288$. Moreover, when a low probability sample is picked: $2g|0.009|^2 - 1 = -0.999352$. Therefore, the amplitude range is *compressed*.

A possible approach to this reconstruction problem may be to use the normalization of the output to calculate a new g, as shown in Eq. 10.19.

$$g = \sum_k \tilde{p}_k \tag{10.19}$$

10.4.2 Single Qubit Probability Amplitude Modulations: SQPAM

Another coefficient-based quantum audio representation instance can be derived from an image representation scheme known as Flexible Representation of Quantum Images or FRQI [10]. We propose calling this method *Single Qubit Probability Amplitude Modulation*, or SQPAM.

SQPAM works similarly to QPAM. However, instead of using the raw probability amplitudes, it uses $\lceil \log N \rceil + 1$ qubits. It improves the logic to encode the samples in the probability amplitudes of one extra, *dedicated* qubit, added as a new register, $|\gamma_i\rangle$, using trigonometric functions. It is a more reliable and editable encoding scheme than QPAM (Eq. 10.22).

$$a_n \longrightarrow |\gamma_i\rangle = \cos\theta_i |0\rangle + \sin\theta_i |1\rangle \tag{10.20}$$

$$
\begin{aligned}
|A\rangle_{3-\text{qubit}} = \frac{1}{\sqrt{8}}\Big[&(\cos\theta_0 |0\rangle + \sin\theta_0 |1\rangle) \otimes |0\rangle + (\cos\theta_1 |0\rangle + \sin\theta_1 |1\rangle) \otimes |1\rangle + \\
&(\cos\theta_2 |0\rangle + \sin\theta_2 |1\rangle) \otimes |2\rangle + (\cos\theta_3 |0\rangle + \sin\theta_3 |1\rangle) \otimes |3\rangle + \\
&(\cos\theta_4 |0\rangle + \sin\theta_4 |1\rangle) \otimes |4\rangle + (\cos\theta_5 |0\rangle + \sin\theta_5 |1\rangle) \otimes |5\rangle + \\
&(\cos\theta_6 |0\rangle + \sin\theta_6 |1\rangle) \otimes |6\rangle + (\cos\theta_7 |0\rangle + \sin\theta_7 |1\rangle) \otimes |7\rangle \Big]
\end{aligned}
\tag{10.21}
$$

Generalizing for a N-sized audio, he have:

$$|A_{\text{SQPAM}}\rangle = \frac{1}{\sqrt{N}} \sum_{i=0}^{N-1} (\cos\theta_i |0\rangle + \sin\theta_i |1\rangle) \otimes |i\rangle \tag{10.22}$$

10.4.2.1 Mapping the SQPAM Audio Amplitudes

Similarly to the previous representation, there are some pre-processing steps for mapping the amplitudes to a normalized scope. Trigonometric functions are often used to represent probability amplitudes since their absolute value ranges from 0 to

1, and the relation between the cosine and sine functions satisfies the normalization requirement perfectly.[3]

Essentially, this describes a simple change of variables, where $\alpha_i = \cos \theta_i$ and $\beta_i = \sin \theta_i$. Notice how only real numbers are being considered, analogous to QPAM.

The introduction of an extra qubit $|\gamma_i\rangle$ significantly improves the representation in terms of both encoding and retrieval of the audio. The first improvement is that the encoding scheme does not rely on the entirety of the audio size content (the total number of states on the superposition and their relative amplitudes) anymore. It is encoded locally in the new qubit and therefore could be independently manipulated, using *rotation matrices* as gates. This opens a new range of possibilities.

The function that maps the audio amplitudes a_i into angles θ_i is displayed in Eq. 10.23. This mapping can also be conceived as the following set of instructions:

- Step 1: Add 1 to all amplitudes a_n.
- Step 2: Divide the amplitudes by 2.
- Step 3: Take the square root.
- Step 4: Evaluate the *Inverse Sine* of the result (The *Inverse Cosine* is also applicable, as long as the same convention is followed throughout the implementation).

$$\theta_i = \sin^{-1}\left(\sqrt{\frac{a_i + 1}{2}}\right) \tag{10.23}$$

The mapped array of angles will enable the preparation of the SQPAM quantum audio state.

10.4.2.2 Preparation

The SQPAM state preparation requires n qubits for encoding time (like QPAM) and 1 qubit for the amplitude (γ_i). They can all be initialized in the $|0\rangle$ state, as denoted in Eq. 10.24.

$$|000...\rangle \equiv |0\rangle \otimes |0\rangle \otimes |0\rangle \otimes ... \equiv |0\rangle^{\otimes n+1} \equiv \underset{(\gamma_i)}{|0\rangle} \otimes |0\rangle^{\otimes n} \tag{10.24}$$

The qubits of the time register are put in a balanced superposition by applying Hadamard gates in each one of them (Fig. 10.11). The resulting quantum state is written in Eq. 10.25.

$$|\Psi\rangle = \frac{1}{\sqrt{N}}\left[|0\rangle \otimes |0\rangle + |0\rangle \otimes |1\rangle + |0\rangle \otimes |2\rangle + ... + |0\rangle \otimes |N-1\rangle\right] \tag{10.25}$$

At this stage, we should discuss the particular strategy for transforming the amplitude qubit into the desired form ($|0\rangle \rightarrow |\gamma_i\rangle$). There is a perfect quantum gate for

---

[3] $\cos(\theta)^2 + \sin(\theta)^2 = 1$.

Fig. 10.11 Circuit segment
with Hadamard gates applied
to a 3-qubit time register

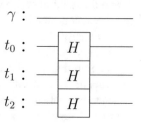

the task, called R_y. It applies rotations in the y axis of a Bloch Sphere (Eq. 10.26[4]).

$$R_y(2\theta) = \begin{pmatrix} \cos\theta & -\sin\theta \\ \sin\theta & \cos\theta \end{pmatrix} \tag{10.26}$$

Let us take a look at what happens when we apply $R_y(2\theta)$ to the state $|0\rangle$. Reminding that quantum states represent vectors, this will resolve in a matrix-vector multiplication (Eq. 10.27).

$$R_y(2\theta_i)|0\rangle = \begin{pmatrix} \cos\theta_i & -\sin\theta_i \\ \sin\theta_i & \cos\theta_i \end{pmatrix} \begin{pmatrix} 1 \\ 0 \end{pmatrix} = \begin{pmatrix} \cos\theta_i \\ \sin\theta_i \end{pmatrix} = \cos\theta_i|0\rangle + \sin\theta_i|1\rangle = |\gamma_i\rangle \tag{10.27}$$

Lastly, there should be a way to, somehow, *loop* through the different indexes of the time register for applying a particular $R_y(2\theta_i)$ to them. As a result, the angles $|\gamma_i\rangle$ would be entangled to their respective states $|i\rangle$. How to access and correlate specific states if they are in a superposition?

The desired correlations can be achieved by controlling our value setting gate R_y using a *multi-controlled* version of R_y. Let us explore the effect of controlled gates on a quantum state.

Imagine a 1-qubit length audio example. Assume that a superposition was created in the time register by following the first preparation step. The quantum state would be described by Eq. 10.28.

$$|\phi_0\rangle = \frac{1}{\sqrt{2}}\Big[|0\rangle|0\rangle + |0\rangle|1\rangle\Big] \tag{10.28}$$

Then, a controlled $R_y(2\theta)$ gate is applied. By analyzing the circuit in Fig. 10.12, we could conclude that the R_y gate will only be applied if the time qubit is 1. Equation 10.29 shows the resulting state.

$$|\phi_1\rangle = cR_{y[t_0]}|\phi_0\rangle = \frac{1}{\sqrt{2}}\Big[|0\rangle|0\rangle + R_y(2\theta)|0\rangle|1\rangle\Big] \tag{10.29}$$

Now, let us place an X gate before and after R_y (Fig. 10.13). What is the effect? If the time qubit happens to be in the $|0\rangle$ state, it will be flipped to $|1\rangle$. Consequently,

---

[4] $R_y(2\theta)$ has the same form of a 2D rotation matrix, found in many Linear Algebra textbooks. The main difference is that the angle theta rotates twice as fast in a Bloch Sphere compared to a regular Euclidean space.

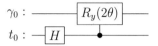

Fig. 10.12 Application of a controlled $R_y(2\theta)$

Fig. 10.13 Inverting the control condition using two X gates

it triggers the control condition, which leads to Eq. 10.30. Then, it is flipped back to $|0\rangle$. Notice that it would not trigger the controlled gate otherwise.

$$|\tilde{\phi_1}\rangle = (I \otimes X)cR_{y[t_0]}(I \otimes X)|\phi_0\rangle = \frac{1}{\sqrt{2}}\Big[R_y(2\theta)|0\rangle|0\rangle + |0\rangle|1\rangle\Big] \quad (10.30)$$

The X gates create a strategy for effectively switching the control condition, triggering when the qubit is in the $|0\rangle$ state instead of $|1\rangle$. This is denoted by a white circle at the control position, as shown on the right side of Fig. 10.13.

For two-qubit systems, the same strategy can be used to access particular indexes. In this case, there are two control conditions to verify simultaneously. For instance, the address for the third sample- θ_2 - is $|10\rangle$. Hence, the control condition on t_0 (the rightmost bit) is "$|0\rangle$", whereas t_1 is "$|1\rangle$". Equation 10.31 demonstrates that $R_y(2\theta_2)$ is only being applied to the third position.

By using four 2-controlled $R_y(2\theta_i)$ gates, each amplitude can be addressed and stored accordingly (Fig. 10.14).

$$|\phi_0\rangle = \frac{1}{2}\Big[|0\rangle|00\rangle + |0\rangle|01\rangle + |0\rangle|10\rangle + |0\rangle|11\rangle\Big] \therefore$$

$$|\phi_{\theta_2}\rangle = (I \otimes X \otimes I)(ccR_{y[t_0t_1]}(2\theta_2))(I \otimes X \otimes I)|\phi_0\rangle \quad (10.31)$$

$$= \frac{1}{2}\Big[|0\rangle|00\rangle + |0\rangle|01\rangle + R_y(2\theta_2)|0\rangle|10\rangle + |0\rangle|11\rangle\Big]$$

By generalizing this strategy, we arrive at an algorithm for the second preparation step of the SQPAM audio. For each time state,

- Have a binary version of the state's label stored in a classical variable.
- If a bit in a given position of the string is zero, apply an X gate at the respective qubit.
- Apply the $R_y(2\theta)$ gate.
- Apply another X gate, following the second instruction.

Notice how this strategy depends on classical numbers. Depending on the programming language of the framework, this can be easily done while constructing the circuit, using a classical 'for loop'.

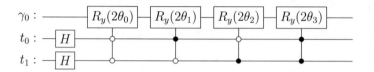

Fig. 10.14 Preparation of a SQPAM representation using Value-Setting operations with R_y gates

This preparation strategy (using multi-controlled gates) can be called *Value-Setting Operation*. This operation will be applicable to other representations as well.

This preparation process applies $\lceil \log N \rceil$ Hadamard gates, and N N-controlled $R_y(2\theta)$ gates. Since the N-controlled $R_y(2\theta)$ have $\mathcal{O}(N)$ of basic operations, this means that $\mathcal{O}(N^2)$ operations are needed for preparing a SQPAM audio.

10.4.2.3 Retrieval

Figure 10.15 shows what to expect of a SQPAM retrieval histogram. Each sample is encoded in complementary sine and cosine pairs embedded in $|\gamma_i\rangle$ probabilities (Eq. 10.32). Hence, 16 bins instead of 8.

In Eq. 10.23, there is a arcsin function. Therefore, the audio's profile appears if the sine components ($p_{\gamma_i}(|1\rangle)$) are picked.

Then, it suffices to use Eq. 10.33 to reconstruct the signal.[5] Figure 10.16 shows a signal reconstruction using the histogram in Fig. 10.15 and Eq. 10.33.

$$p_{\gamma_i}(|0\rangle) = (\cos(\theta_i))^2 \quad ; \quad p_{\gamma_i}(|1\rangle) = (\sin(\theta_i))^2 \tag{10.32}$$

$$a_i = \frac{2p_{\gamma_i}(|1\rangle)}{p_{\gamma_i}(|0\rangle) + p_{\gamma_i}(|1\rangle)} - 1 \tag{10.33}$$

10.5 State-Oriented Representations

In the previous section, the quantum audio representation schemes stored the time domain into a superposition of multi-qubit states and the amplitudes into probability amplitudes. In this section, the main difference is that the audio amplitudes will also be stored in a multi-qubit state. This new quantum register will produce a set of time-amplitude pairs of *entangled information* when put together with the time register.

---

[5] Consider using the cosine term ($p_{\gamma_i}(|0\rangle)$) in the nominator of Eq. 10.33. What would happen? The complementarity of the trigonometric functions would result in a reconstructed audio with *inverted polarity*.

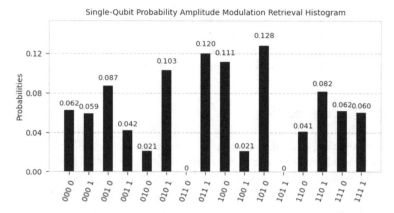

Fig. 10.15 Hypothetical SQPAM representation

Fig. 10.16 Reconstructed audio from SQPAM in Fig. 10.15

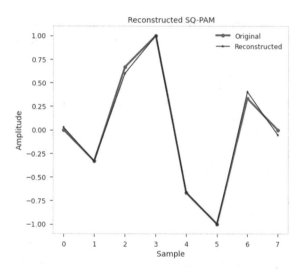

Put another way, if a given time sample t_i is measured, there will be a correlated state that will provide the respective amplitude once measured.

It can be seen as an evolutionary branch of the previous representations (regarding the quantum image representation timeline). For instance, they can *potentially* be manipulated in more detail and used in a wider range of applications. Of course, this needs to be discussed on a case-by-case basis. There is no way to know which representation type is more adequate for different audio and musical applications yet. This will be further discussed in the next section.

The consequence of these "finer" capabilities is that they might increase the amount of space required to represent and manipulate the audio. In other words, there is a trade-off between the number of qubits required to store the quantum audio and the amount of known potential applications.

In addition, another historical motivation to develop the following representation strategies is related to their preparation complexity (e.g. the number of instructions needed for encoding). Furthermore, the logic of storing the audio amplitudes as binary quantum states align with the quantized digital amplitudes of Sect. 10.2.2.

10.5.1 QSM and uQSM

The two following quantum audio representations were derived from the Novel Enhanced Quantum Representation of Images, or NEQR [8]. They were the first proposed quantum representations of audio, namely, QRDA (Quantum Representation for Digital Audio) and FRQA (Flexible Representation of Quantum Audio). Both are identical from a notation standpoint, but there is a slight difference in the interpretation of the qubit states. Respectively, they are read as either *unsigned* or *signed* integers.

The QRDA [6] was the first quantum audio representation proposed in the literature. It was responsible for indicating the path towards its preparation and retrieval techniques, bringing many of the primary foundations of a State-Oriented Representation. In Sect. 10.2.2, we discussed how the analogue amplitudes were converted into digital. The samples were approximated to the closest binary integer of the quantization scheme. The same quantized amplitudes will be used in this section to prepare multi-qubit states.

The QRDA has a dedicated quantum register that encodes the sample using strictly positive integers (directly inherited from the NEQR Image that encoded Gray colour information ranging from 0 to 1). The FRQA, or Flexible Representation of Quantum Audio, on the other hand, uses the Two's Complement scheme to interpret the amplitudes (Sect. 10.2.2.1).

The signed integer makes audio mixing extremely convenient since only a regular bit-wise adder algorithm is needed. This indicates that the FRQA's interpretation of the states is more suitable for quantum audio than QRDA.

Apart from the variable class interpretation, the logics of preparation and retrieval are identical. These similarities suggest merging their names onto our proposed naming system: Quantum State Modulation, or QSM. Whenever a specific application requires unsigned integers explicitly (QRDA), we could indicate that with a lower case 'u' before the acronym (uQSM). This terminology can be extended to fit other variable types in the future, like fixed-point (Sect. 10.5.3) or floating-point numbers.

10.5.2 QSM

Consider a digital audio file with 8 samples and amplitude values quantized in a 3-bit depth two's complement scheme. Let us assume that the seventh sample of the signal was represented by the following integer bit string: "001". In possession of this string, we somehow prepare an analogous 3-qubit string on a dedicated amplitude register by initializing it in the ground state and then flipping the rightmost qubit.

This amplitude state can be later entangled with a respective state of the time register, in this case, t_7, as described in Eq. 10.34.

$$(a_7, t_7) \equiv (001, 110) \longrightarrow |001\rangle \, |110\rangle \equiv |a_7\rangle \otimes |t_7\rangle \qquad (10.34)$$

Applying this structure for all of the samples would result in the superposition shown in Eqs. 10.35 and 10.36. More generally, the QSM could be written as in Eq. 10.37.

$$\begin{aligned} \overset{\text{binary notation}}{|A_{\text{QSM}}\rangle} = \frac{1}{\sqrt{8}}\Big[& |000\rangle \otimes |000\rangle + |111\rangle \otimes |001\rangle + |010\rangle \otimes |010\rangle + \\ & |011\rangle \otimes |011\rangle + |110\rangle \otimes |100\rangle + |101\rangle \otimes |101\rangle + \\ & |001\rangle \otimes |110\rangle + |000\rangle \otimes |111\rangle \Big] \end{aligned}$$

$$(10.35)$$

$$\begin{aligned} \overset{\text{decimal notation}}{|A_{\text{QSM}}\rangle} = \frac{1}{\sqrt{8}}\Big[& |0\rangle \otimes |0\rangle + |-1\rangle \otimes |1\rangle + |2\rangle \otimes |2\rangle + |3\rangle \otimes |3\rangle + \\ & |-2\rangle \otimes |4\rangle + |-3\rangle \otimes |5\rangle + |1\rangle \otimes |6\rangle + |0\rangle \otimes |7\rangle \Big] \end{aligned}$$

$$(10.36)$$

$$|A\rangle = \frac{1}{\sqrt{N}} \sum_{i=0}^{N-1} |S_i\rangle \otimes |i\rangle \qquad (10.37)$$

The time register uses n qubits (audio length), and the amplitude register needs q qubits (qubit-depth).

As previously mentioned, this strategy has some foreseeable advantages. The multi-qubit register for amplitude directly relates to the digital audio. This similarity suggests that some quantum algorithms could be developed to apply the same operations as known digital signal processing. From there, developers could explore if the quantum media would improve, extend or optimize some of them. This "intuition" layer contributes to the instant popularity of the State-Based representations compared to the less explored Coefficient-Based ones.

10.5.2.1 Preparation

The same strategy mentioned in the SQPAM case will be used here: a Value-Setting Operation. In this case, instead of using $R_y(2\theta_i)$, the operation will use multi-controlled CNOT gates for flipping the qubit states of the amplitude register. As a result, the algorithm will access and entangle specific amplitude states with their respective time states.

Value-Setting Operation: For each time state,

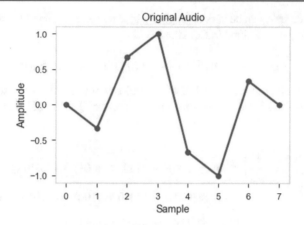

Fig. 10.17 Example audio used to prepare the QSM circuit

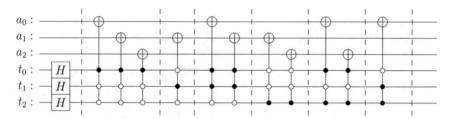

Fig. 10.18 Preparation of a QSM representation using value-setting operations

- Step 1: Have a binary form of the time state's label stored in a classical variable.
- Step 2: Have the binary form of the quantized audio sample at the same index.
- Step 3: If a bit in a given position of the time variable is zero, apply an X gate at the respective qubit. Verify all bits.
- Step 4: If a bit in a given position of the audio sample is 1, apply a multi-controlled CNOT gate. Verify all bits.
- Step 5: Repeat the third instruction to reset the control condition.

Figures 10.17 and 10.18 exemplify a preparation circuit for an audio with 8 samples and 3-bit depth

Compared with SQPAM ($R_y(2\theta_i)$), the preparing circuit for the audio in Fig. 10.17 will apply N value-setting operations, demanding $\mathcal{O}(q + \log N)$ basic instructions. In conclusion, the preparation circuit for the QSM is exponentially faster, requiring $\mathcal{O}(qN \log N)$ simple operations.

10.5.2.2 Retrieval

The interesting part of retrieving a state-based quantum audio is that it can be seen as *deterministic*. It guarantees a perfect reconstruction of the digital audio. This is assured since the sample is represented as a binary state.

In the coefficient-based version, the samples were statistical quantities that needed to be approximated through many measurements and statistical analysis. There will always be an intrinsic statistical error whenever the amount of measurements is finite. It is a trade-off between lying an error inside some tolerance range (depending on musical, psychoacoustic, perceptual factors) and time consumption (mainly the number of times a circuit will be prepared and measured).[6]

In the case of state retrieval, we would only need to measure all valid time-amplitude pairs to retrieve the audio. Each time state is entangled to an amplitude state. So this theoretically assures that a given time state would certainly measure its correlated amplitude; there is no other combined state possible.

That being the case, we could in principle measure each time state just once, enabling the retrieval of all respective amplitudes. Unfortunately, it is potentially impossible to devise a method that could guarantee only one measurement per sample based on a quantum time state in a superposition. In other words, *controlled measurements* (only measuring a quantum state based on another quantum state) are *non-unitary* instructions and cannot be written as a set of quantum gates.[7]

With that said, the strategy for retrieving the QSM will be similar in many ways to the previous ones: preparing several copies, making measurements, and analyzing a histogram. Enough measurements are needed to assure a sufficient probability of having all possible states measured. Then, the histogram is analyzed and the *valid* measured states are parsed into digital amplitudes and time indexes. This analysis is also a good strategy for dealing with quantum error in real-life quantum processors. Making enough measurements to separate noise from a signal. In an ideal situation, a state-modulated representation will have a balanced superposition of the possible states (states containing the audio amplitudes and their time index), meaning they should be equally likely to be measured (Fig. 10.19). Moreover, the measured states of the amplitude register are decoded into the correspondent digital amplitudes using the Two's Complement scheme (Fig. 10.20).

The QSM framework is powerful due to its relatability with digital representations. It looks like PCM audio in a superposition. It promptly awakes the idea of comparing the computational efficiency of known classical DSP algorithms (of course, even if quantum parallelism helps with computational complexity, we need to consider the preparation and retrieval time consumption as well).

---

[6] In his paper about generative quantum images using a coefficient based image representation, James Wootton [11] states that he measured the n-qubit image state 4^n times before considering it was a good approximation for his application. This number can be much higher for reliable retrieval, and it scales exponentially.

[7] We can build circuits that use the result of measurements for controlling quantum gates (due to the *deferred measurement principle*). But only unitary instructions.

Fig. 10.19 Hypothetical QSM histogram

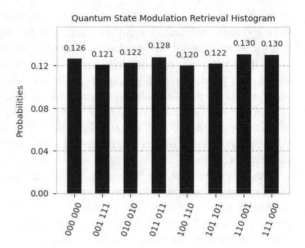

Fig. 10.20 Reconstructed audio from QSM in Fig. 10.19

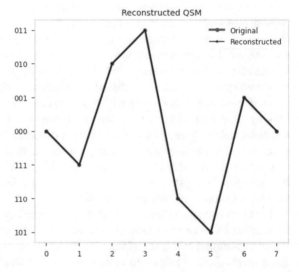

10.5.3 Fixed Point QSM

Preparation complexity and quantum states interpreted as integers made QSM (FRQA) well known. Nevertheless, it raises the question: why stop at integers? We could easily interpret the qubit registers as fixed (or floating) point numbers and use the same state structure of the QSM. A fixed point, QSM-based representation was formalized by Li et al. [12] and was named QRDS (Quantum Representation of Digital Signals). For the terminology purposes of this text, this representation could be named fixed-point QSM or fpQSM.

It essentially divides the q qubits used to represent integers into three parts: one sign bit, m integer bits and $q - m - 1$ fractional bits,[8] as shown in Eq. 10.38.

$$|A\rangle = \frac{1}{\sqrt{N}} \sum_{i=0}^{N-1} |\text{fixed}_i\rangle \otimes |i\rangle = \frac{1}{\sqrt{N}} \sum_{i=0}^{N-1} |x_i^m, x_i^{m-1} \cdots x_i^0 . x_i^{-1} \cdots x_i^{q-m-1}\rangle \otimes |i\rangle$$

$$(10.38)$$

10.5.4 Multichannel Audio

The QRMA (Quantum Representation of Multi-Channel Audio), proposed by [13] extends the logic of a state-oriented representation for quantum audio. In our naming system, it is called Multichannel Quantum State Modulation (MQSM). It furthers the QSM implementation logic by introducing a new quantum register in the circuit: the *channel register* (Eq. 10.39). With this new register, we can address, for example, left ($|0\rangle$) and right ($|1\rangle$) channels of a stereo audio (Eq. 10.40). Also, it enables efficient storage of multichannel audio in the same quantum state (or a soundbank with multiple mono tracks with the same length).

$$(a_{n,m}, t_{n,m}, c_m) \longrightarrow |c_j\rangle \otimes |a_{i,j}\rangle \otimes |t_{i,j}\rangle \tag{10.39}$$

$$|A_{\text{Stereo}}\rangle = \frac{1}{\sqrt{2N}} \begin{bmatrix} |L\rangle \otimes \big(|0\rangle |0\rangle + |0\rangle |1\rangle + |0\rangle |2\rangle + |0\rangle |3\rangle + ...\big) \\ |R\rangle \otimes \big(|0\rangle |0\rangle + |0\rangle |1\rangle + |0\rangle |2\rangle + |0\rangle |3\rangle + ...\big) \end{bmatrix} \tag{10.40}$$

$$|A_{\text{MQSM}}\rangle = \frac{1}{\sqrt{NC}} \sum_{i=0}^{N-1} \sum_{j=0}^{C-1} |c_j\rangle \otimes |a_{i,j}\rangle \otimes |t_{i,j}\rangle \tag{10.41}$$

The general equation of the MQSM is shown in Eq. 10.41, where $C = 2^c$ is the number of channels used. Similar to N, if the number of channels is not a power of two, the remaining possible channels would be zero-padded before preparing the state.

Correspondingly, a channel register could be added to Coefficient-Based representations. As exemplified in the next section, it can become a valuable tool for feature extraction algorithms. For instance, A Multichannel version of the SQPAM could be derived as shown in Eq. 10.42.

$$|A_{\text{MSQPAM}}\rangle = \frac{1}{\sqrt{NC}} \sum_{i=0}^{N-1} \sum_{j=0}^{C-1} |c_j\rangle \otimes (\cos\theta_i |0\rangle + \sin\theta_i |1\rangle) \otimes |i\rangle \tag{10.42}$$

---

[8] The $q - m - 1$ was adapted to our notation. In the original notation, the text uses $n + 1$ qubits instead of q.

Table 10.1 Comparison between quantum representations of audio

Representation	Original acronym	Basic structure	Amplitude mapping	Space required	Preparation complexity	Retrieval
QPAM	–	$\alpha_n \lvert t_n \rangle$	Normalized, strictly positive vector	$\lceil \log N \rceil$	$\mathcal{O}(N)$	Probabilistic
SQPAM	–	$(\cos \theta_n \lvert 0 \rangle + \sin \theta_n \lvert 1 \rangle) \lvert t_n \rangle$	Angle vector	$\lceil \log N \rceil + 1$	$\mathcal{O}(N^2)$	Probabilistic
uQSM	QRDA	$\lvert U_n \rangle \lvert t_n \rangle$	Unsigned integer vector	$\lceil \log N \rceil + q$	$\mathcal{O}(qN \lceil \log N \rceil)$	Deterministic
QSM	FRQA	$\lvert S_n \rangle \lvert t_n \rangle$	Signed integer vector	$\lceil \log N \rceil + q$	$\mathcal{O}(qN \lceil \log N \rceil)$	Deterministic
fpQSM	QRDS	$\lvert F p_n \rangle \lvert t_n \rangle$	Fixed point integer vector	$\lceil \log N \rceil + q$	$\mathcal{O}(qN \lceil \log N \rceil)$	Deterministic
MQSM	QRMA	$\lvert c_i \rangle \lvert S_n \rangle \lvert t_n \rangle$	Multiple signed integer vectors	$\lceil \log N \rceil + q + \lceil \log C \rceil$	$\mathcal{O}(CqN \lceil \log N \rceil)$	Deterministic

10.6 Summary

Different strategies for encoding audio in quantum systems were developed from quantum image representations. A change in the quantum audio representation terminology was also proposed (which could be extended to images and other signals in the future). The key pieces of information and features discussed are compared in Table 10.1.

When progressing down the table, the representations require more and more qubit space to store all of the information. As a result, the probabilistic representations are capable of storing larger samples in the same hardware. This is also true for bit depth: since the probability amplitudes are continuous variables, they can store as much amplitude resolution as classical computers can provide after the retrieval process. In comparison, the state-based representations use qubit binary words, which require significantly more quantum space to achieve a comparable resolution. Also, the bit depth q has a role in the preparation complexity of the state modulation.

On the other hand, the amount of instructions necessary to prepare the SQPAM state considering only the audio size N is significantly worse than the deterministic representations for larger audio samples.

These comparisons are essential for imagining near-term applications of music-quality audio on quantum hardware. Imagine that a composer wants to process two different audio samples in a quantum machine for some hypothetical artistic reason. The first sample may be coming from a real-time audio signal processing language, with a block of 64 samples that needs to run on a brand-new quantum audio effect. The second one is stored on a computer and has approximately 1.5 s of audio, containing $2^{16} = 65536$ samples that will be fed to a large quantum sound database. Both samples have CD quality: A sample rate of 44,100 Hz and a 16-bit resolution. We will compare three representations: QPAM, SQPAM and QSM.

According to Table 10.1, QPAM will require 6 qubits and ~64 instructions for storing the first sample; 7 qubits and ~4096 instructions for SQPAM. QSM will need to allocate 16 more qubits for achieving the necessary amplitude resolution, with a total of 22 qubits and ~6144 instructions.

For the second audio, things scale up in the time register. QPAM will use 16 qubits and ~65 thousand instructions; SQPAM, 17 qubits and a surprising amount of ~4.3 billion instructions. Finally, QSM will need 32 qubits and ~16 million instructions.

A noticeable result of this comparison is that SQPAM might be better suited for processing small signal samples or segmented blocks of audio, useful for algorithms for information retrieval). QSM, on the other hand, would handle large sounds effectively. Also, QPAM needs the lowest amount of resources for preparation, which is very useful for near-term applications.

10.6.1 Running on Real Hardware

This chapter focuses on surveying and consolidating a smooth and didactic theoretical transition path between digital audio and the new field of quantum audio, underlying potential problems of the computational level, proposing a more unified terminology, and finally glimpsing at potential artistic applications. This approach is why the chapter focuses on a high-level discussion, assuming that the qubits are perfect and perfectly manipulable, referred to as a *logical qubit*. Even so, it is worth saying something about running these algorithms on real hardware. The state-of-the-art computers that are publicly available at the time of writing have a range of three to sixteen rather noisy *physical qubits*. It is possible to correct potential errors for a better approximation of a logical qubit. For that purpose, multiple physical qubits can be combined into a *fault-tolerant* qubit. This field is known as Quantum Error Correction [14]. The state-of-the-art machines and their qubits are not fault-tolerant.

A real-world qubit is prone to a myriad of errors and noises. For example, its state can be flipped spontaneously due to external electromagnetic interference. It also tends to lose energy and go to a lower energy level state. Furthermore, a quantum system might lose coherence as time evolves. Also, each gate or instruction applied to a qubit has a chance of failing or being inaccurate, introducing more noise and potentially leading to incorrigible errors. Additionally, qubits might interfere with each other in different ways, depending on their displacement on the actual quantum chip.

Unfortunately, the depth of the circuits necessary to prepare quantum audio representations might be too high for near-term, fault intolerant machines (as previously shown in the last section). The more instructions present in a fault-intolerant machine (and the more physical qubits you have), the less reliable the result will be.[9] This technological barrier has propelled the quantum audio community towards theory

---

[9] While this limitation may be true, it can be seen as an advantage inside a sensible noise/degraded aesthetic for artistic purposes.

Fig. 10.21 Test audio with 8 samples

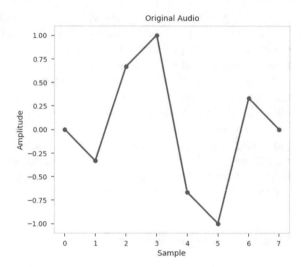

and simulations rather than real-hardware experiments on state-of-the-art technology.

As a reference for future analysis and comparison, this text underlines how some of the presented encoding schemes (QPAM, SQPAM, QSM) perform in state-of-the-art hardware. An experiment was made using IBM Q hardware [15]. Specifically, a 7-qubit (32 Quantum Volume) chip called *ibmq_casablanca*. These experiments (along with results and simulations in the following sections) were run by using quantum audio modules implemented in Python and Qiskit, within the scope of the QuTune Project [16]. The QuTune module was used to map and generate the quantum audio circuits from a signal (shown in Fig. 10.21). Then, the circuit was fed to the IBMQ system. Finally, the resulting histograms—shown in Figs. 10.22, 10.24 and 10.26—were retrieved and post-processed. The reconstructed audio signals are shown in Figs. 10.23, 10.25 and 10.27.

QPAM (Figs. 10.23 and 10.22) had the lowest preparation complexity (approximately 8 instructions and 3 qubits). It seems to retain most of the original information.

The SQPAM (Figs. 10.24 and 10.25), on the other hand, introduced value-setting operations, which are more expensive. The retrieved audio lost most of its amplitude range (notice the values in the y axis) but retained some of the original profile.

In contrast, QSM (Fig. 10.26) produced an interesting result. Surprisingly, its resemblance with the original file was gone. This was probably caused by the amount of multi-controlled instructions for preparation and the time required for the operations. Moreover, some qubits might have flipped to a lower energy state. Even though it has a guarantee of exact retrieval, the reconstruction process relies on the states that are most likely to be measured. At this stage of loss of information, the QSM audio was irrecoverable Fig. 10.27.[10]

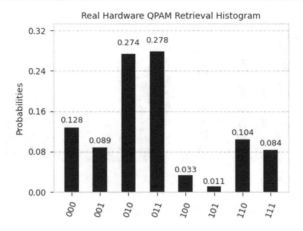

Fig. 10.22 QPAM histogram retrieved from IBMQ

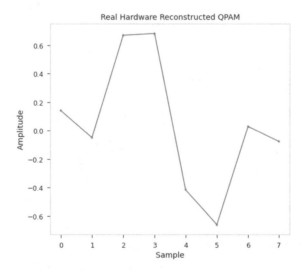

Fig. 10.23 Reconstructed audio from Fig. 10.22

10.7 Processing Audio Signals in Quantum Computers

Current digital audio signal processing (DSP) algorithms can perform a wide range of applications. Among them, identifying and classifying sound objects, generating speech from text, applying artistic effects in a real-time performance. However, these algorithms have depended on decades of development and experimentation in hard-

---

[10] Still, in the QSM histogram Fig. 10.26, there is a slight emergence of periodicity on the qubit sequencing. Can it be used artistically?

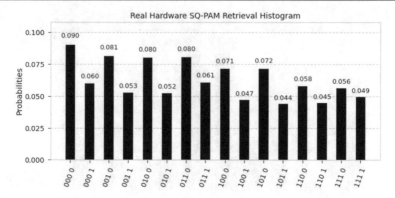

Fig. 10.24 SQPAM histogram retrieved from IBMQ

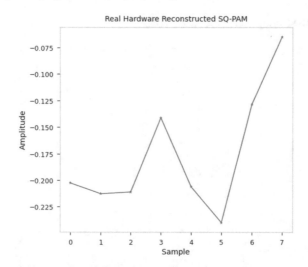

Fig. 10.25 Reconstructed audio from Fig. 10.24

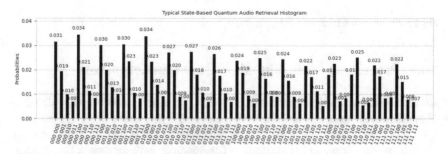

Fig. 10.26 QSM histogram retrieved from IBMQ

Fig. 10.27 Reconstruction attempt from Fig. 10.26

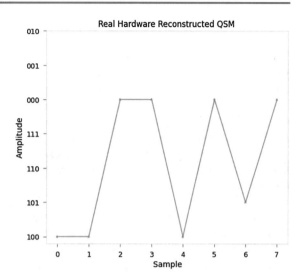

ware and software. Quantum hardware and algorithms will face similar challenges. They will start crawling first before eventually walking and running.

Since Quantum Audio is a very recent research field, there is much to be studied in terms of quantum audio signal processing (QSP). As far as the authors are aware, the literature about signal processing applied to audio is more propositive and theoretical. In other words, it is more focused on formalization and quantum circuit design.

The popularity and consolidation of the QSM (FRQA) representation in the literature implied that the majority of the QSP algorithms today use QSM. Hence, the focus will be on this representation while exploring some basic structures of quantum signal processing.

As noted in Sect. 10.6.1, there is still a technical barrier that hinders QSP testing on physical hardware. The problem is worsened when considering longer manipulations on one or multiple quantum audio states. Furthermore, state-based representations (such as QSM) use several qubits to store amplitude information.

For example, a simple simulation of a signal addition algorithm (as explained in Sect. 10.7.1) would initially need to allocate space for preparing and storing two quantum audio. Then, there should be space for any ancillary qubit necessary for computing the operation—which in this case almost doubles the qubit requirement. In summary, the circuits are too large.

Additionally, it is also difficult to simulate these circuits in classical computers. Simulating the application of quantum gates involve huge matrix multiplications. Their size grows exponentially for every additional simulated qubit. Therefore, it requires a significant amount of both RAM and CPU power.

The following sections will explain some fundamental quantum audio signal processing algorithms. The presentation, accompanied by equations, should elucidate the effect of some gates on the signal and some circuit design strategies.

10.7.1 Signal Addition

In a digital and analogue audio environment, signals are constantly added and mixed. Learning how to add audio signals in the quantum domain is probably one of the essential building blocks for enabling complex signal processing operations. This section intends to overview the circuit proposed by Yan et al. [7] for adding two QSM audio, $|A_x\rangle$, $|A_y\rangle$ (Eq. 10.43). The focus will be on the computational thinking behind complex quantum gates and circuits.

The QSM is a great representation candidate for this task for two main reasons: firstly, its encoding allows for negative amplitudes using the two's complement scheme.

Secondly, having separate registers for the amplitude and the time information gives more control over the sample-by-sample manipulation (compared to QPAM), which was already explored while preparing the audio signals.

In order to design a quantum mixer for two QSMs, we should first make some assumptions. For example, both audio need to have the same length and bit resolution. A previous circuit should have already prepared them on the machine as well. Then, we separate the problem into parts.

$$|A_x\rangle\,|A_y\rangle\,|000..\rangle \longrightarrow |A_x\rangle\,|A_y\rangle\,|A_x + A_y\rangle = |A_x\rangle\,|A_y\rangle\,|A_z\rangle \qquad (10.43)$$

The addition of audio is essentially a term-by-term sum of respective samples. Therefore, the macroscopic quantum addition logic can be conceived by two general blocks. There should be an "addition" block for summing two amplitude registers. Also, a term-by-term block, ensures that the correct samples are being added. A good way of matching timestamps might be achieved with some kind of comparison in the time register. That is, the amplitudes will be added if and only if the timestamps match.

With these basic concepts, a circuit could be sketched, as shown in Fig. 10.28. A *Comparator* gate would receive both time registers as input and then trigger an ancillary qubit, indicating whether they match or not. This same qubit would act as a control qubit for a *Controlled-Adder* gate. Fortunately, the Comparator and the Adder gates are algorithms that can be found in the literature [17, 18].

Bear in mind that the operations are being applied on superpositions. In other words, gates are being computed in parallel on all audio samples by the quantum processor.

Fig. 10.28 Sketch of a signal addition circuit

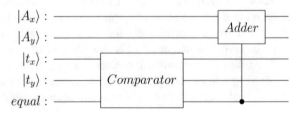

Of course, control conditions will restrict the effect of the gates on specific states. This parallelism calls attention to the particularities of this kind of algorithm. There is an assumption that this circuit will be run (and measured) several times on the processor. The executions will span possible state configurations. Only then the information can be fully retrieved to the digital realm, in the form of a histogram.

10.7.1.1 Adding Two Qubit Sequences

Let us start dissecting the signal addition circuit by understanding how to perform addition.

The addition of two single-qubit registers is one of the most fundamental circuits in quantum computing, known as the quantum half-adder.

The half-adder circuit is a 4-qubit gate that adds two qubits and is composed of two CNOT gates and one Toffoli gate, as shown in Fig. 10.29. The table shows how different inputs are computed by this circuit.

The first two qubits are the terms of the addition. The third qubit computes the result of the sum. The fourth handles overflowing issues and can be used to carry the sum to the next digits. The intuition behind the half-adder is simple: it flips the qubit that computes the sum whenever one of the qubits is in the $|1\rangle$ state. If both qubits are 1, the sum overflows, and the last qubit is flipped. In this case, the *sum* qubit is flipped two times, resulting in the expected behaviour ($1 + 1 = 10$).

In order to add larger numbers, we need to consider that the resulting sum of a binary digit is carried to the next digit, as exemplified in Eq. 10.44.

$$
\begin{array}{r}
^{1\ 1}1\ 1 \\
+\ 1\ 1 \\
\hline
1\ 1\ 0
\end{array}
\tag{10.44}
$$

For that reason, the Quantum Plain Adder circuit uses two different gates in its operation: a Carry gate (Fig. 10.31 and a Sum gate (Fig. 10.30)).

As the quantum computing field evolves, the algorithms for plain addition (and comparison) of two qubit sequences get more efficient and optimized, using fewer elementary gates for its calculation and ancillary qubits. Vedral et al. [17] described a circuit for plain addition, in which he replaces one of the operand registers with

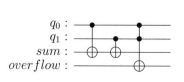

q_0	q_1	$overflow$	sum
0	0	0	0
0	1	0	1
1	0	0	1
1	1	1	0

Fig. 10.29 Half-adder circuit and its I/O table

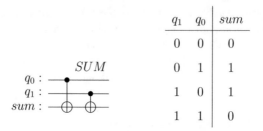

q_1	q_0	sum
0	0	0
0	1	1
1	0	1
1	1	0

Fig. 10.30 Sum operation circuit and its I/O table

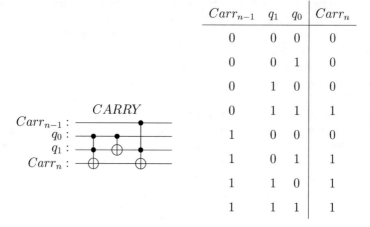

$Carr_{n-1}$	q_1	q_0	$Carr_n$
0	0	0	0
0	0	1	0
0	1	0	0
0	1	1	1
1	0	0	0
1	0	1	1
1	1	0	1
1	1	1	1

Fig. 10.31 Carry operation circuit and its I/O table

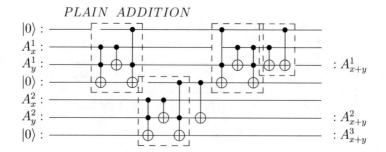

Fig. 10.32 Example of a 2-qubit plain addition circuit

the result of the sum. An example of such a circuit for 2-qubit addition is shown in Fig. 10.32.

For a more detailed explanation of the plain multi-qubit addition circuit and other basic operations please refer to [17].

Fig. 10.33 Sign Extension
circuit and its I/O table

q_1	q_0	$|0\rangle$
0	0	0
0	1	1
1	0	1
1	1	0

$$EXT$$

q_0 :
q_1 :
$|0\rangle$:

There is one final detail for completing this module for the QSM: a gate that
ensures the correct sign qubit of the two's complement integer scheme. In the FRQA
paper [7], this gate is named as the Sign Extension module (Fig. 10.33).

It will look at the Most Significant Bit of each number and check if any of them
is negative, propagating this information to the overflowing qubit. We now have a
circuit for adding the amplitude register of a QSM.

10.7.1.2   Comparing two Qubit Sequences

For the comparison part, Yan et al. used a serial-based quantum comparator described
by Wang et al. [18]. It allocates $2q$ ancillary qubits (where q is the size of the register),
two of which—(e_0, e_1)—are used as the operation's output. They compute whether
a multi-qubit state is smaller (1, 0), bigger (0, 1) or equal (0, 0) to another multi-qubit
state. A 2-qubit example is shown in Fig. 10.34.

Notice that when $|a\rangle$ and $|b\rangle$ are equal, none of the control conditions are satisfied
and $|e_1 e_0\rangle = |00\rangle$.

10.7.1.3   Adding Two QSMs

Finally, there is enough material to perform a QSM addition. For didactic purposes,
we will walk through a toy example combining the circuits shown previously.

Let us consider two QSM quantum audio signals, $|X\rangle$ and $|Y\rangle$, with 2-bit amplitude
resolution and 4 samples, prepared in advance on a quantum machine, as described
in Eqs. 10.45 and 10.46. The circuit for adding these audio is depicted in Fig. 10.35.

Fig. 10.34 2-qubit example
of a serial-based quantum
comparator circuit

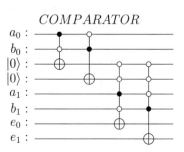

$COMPARATOR$

a_0 :
b_0 :
$|0\rangle$:
$|0\rangle$:
a_1 :
b_1 :
e_0 :
e_1 :

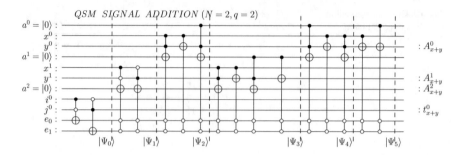

Fig. 10.35 Circuit segment that performs a QSM signal addition operation (2-qubit length, 2-qubit depth)

$$|X\rangle \otimes |Y\rangle = \frac{1}{2}\sum_{i=0}^{1}|x_i\rangle|i\rangle \otimes \frac{1}{2}\sum_{j=0}^{1}|y_i\rangle|j\rangle = \frac{1}{2}\sum_{i=0}^{1}|x_i^1 x_i^0\rangle|i^0\rangle \otimes \frac{1}{2}\sum_{j=0}^{1}|y_j^1 y_j^0\rangle|j^0\rangle$$
$$(10.45)$$

$$\frac{1}{4}\left[|x_0^1 x_0^0\rangle|0\rangle + |x_1^1 x_1^0\rangle|1\rangle\right] \otimes \left[|y_0^1 y_0^0\rangle|0\rangle + |y_1^1 y_1^0\rangle|1\rangle\right] \qquad (10.46)$$

$$= \frac{1}{4}\left[|x_0^1 x_0^0\rangle|0\rangle|y_0^1 y_0^0\rangle|0\rangle + |x_0^1 x_0^0\rangle|0\rangle|y_1^1 y_1^0\rangle|1\rangle + |x_1^1 x_1^0\rangle|1\rangle|y_0^1 y_0^0\rangle|0\rangle + |x_1^1 x_1^0\rangle|1\rangle|y_1^1 y_1^0\rangle|1\rangle\right] \quad (10.47)$$

For simplifying the notation and increasing visibility, the order of the qubits will be changed as shown in Eq. 10.48. Then, ancillary qubits will be included (Eq. 10.49). In this way, the order of the qubits will match the one shown in the circuit (Fig. 10.35), from top to bottom. As a result, we will be able to compute each instruction of the circuit on the expanded quantum state by following the diagram.

$$\frac{1}{4}\left[|x_0^1 y_0^1 x_0^0 y_0^0\rangle|00\rangle + |x_0^1 y_1^1 x_0^0 y_1^0\rangle|01\rangle + |x_1^1 y_0^1 x_1^0 y_0^0\rangle|10\rangle + |x_1^1 y_1^1 x_1^0 y_1^0\rangle|11\rangle\right]$$
$$(10.48)$$

$$\frac{1}{4}\left[|x_0^1 y_0^1 x_0^0 y_0^0\rangle|00\rangle + |x_0^1 y_1^1 x_0^0 y_1^0\rangle|01\rangle + |x_1^1 y_0^1 x_1^0 y_0^0\rangle|10\rangle + |x_1^1 y_1^1 x_1^0 y_1^0\rangle|11\rangle\right] \otimes |a^2 a^1 a^0\rangle|e^1 e^0\rangle$$

$$= \frac{1}{4}[|a^2 x_0^1 y_0^1 a^1 x_0^0 y_0^0 a^0\rangle|00 e^1 e^0\rangle + |a^2 x_0^1 y_1^1 a^1 x_0^0 y_1^0 a^0\rangle|01 e^1 e^0\rangle + |a^2 x_1^1 y_0^1 a^1 x_1^0 y_0^0 a^0\rangle|10 e^1 e^0\rangle +$$
$$|a^2 x_1^1 y_1^1 a^1 x_1^0 y_1^0 a^0\rangle|11 e^1 e^0\rangle] \qquad (10.49)$$

Now, the toy example will be prepared by substituting the amplitudes with numbers and the ancillae with zeroes (all initially prepared in the $|0\rangle$ state). Suppose that $X = [1, -1]$, $Y = [1, 0]$. The binary values, using two's complement would be the sets $X = [01, 11]$ and $Y = [01, 00]$. The expected result would then be $X + Y = [010, 111] \equiv [2, -1]$. Let us start by replacing the example values into Eq. 10.49, leading to Eq. 10.50.

$$|X\rangle |Y\rangle = \frac{1}{2} [|0000110\rangle |0000\rangle + |0000100\rangle |0100\rangle + |0100110\rangle |1000\rangle + |0100100\rangle |1100\rangle]$$
(10.50)

Then, instructions are applied. The circuit in Fig. 10.35 was cut down into six sets of instructions. The resulting quantum state after each set is depicted by Eqs. 10.51 through 10.56.

The first set is the Comparator gate, composed of two instructions. The first can be interpreted as the following pseudo-code: "*If $i^0 = |1\rangle$ and $j^0 = |0\rangle$, then flip e_0*". The second instruction states the opposite, but flipping e_1 instead. The result is $|\Psi_0\rangle$ (Eq. 10.51). The comparator gate, in a way, has just "synchronized" both time registers. We can see that whenever $|e_1 e_0\rangle = |00\rangle$, both $|i\rangle$ and $|j\rangle$ have the same value.

$$|\Psi_0\rangle = \frac{1}{2} [|0000110\rangle |0000\rangle + |0000100\rangle |0110\rangle + |0100110\rangle |1001\rangle + |0100100\rangle |1100\rangle] \quad (10.51)$$

Then, the EXT function is applied, ensuring the adequate addition operation with two's complement. If only one of the numbers is negative (meaning that one of the sign bits is 1) and $|e_1 e_0\rangle = |00\rangle$, flip a^2. The result is $|\Psi_1\rangle$ (Eq. 10.52).

$$|\Psi_1\rangle = \frac{1}{2} [|0000110\rangle |0000\rangle + |0000100\rangle |0110\rangle + |0100110\rangle |1001\rangle + |1100100\rangle |1100\rangle] \quad (10.52)$$

The next steps apply CARRY, CNOT and SUM operations to perform the full addition:

- $|\Psi_2\rangle$ (Eq. 10.53): Carries the LSB partial sum to the MSB.
- $|\Psi_3\rangle$ (Eq. 10.54): Carries the MSB partial sum to overflow and compute MSB sum.
- $|\Psi_4\rangle$ (Eq. 10.55): Undo Carry operation.
- $|\Psi_5\rangle$ (Eq. 10.56): Compute LSB sum.

$$|\Psi_2\rangle = \frac{1}{2} [|0001100\rangle |0000\rangle + |0000100\rangle |0110\rangle + |0100110\rangle |1001\rangle + |1100110\rangle |1100\rangle] \quad (10.53)$$

$$|\Psi_3\rangle = \frac{1}{2} [|0011100\rangle |0000\rangle + |0000100\rangle |0110\rangle + |0100110\rangle |1001\rangle + |1110110\rangle |1100\rangle] \quad (10.54)$$

$$|\Psi_4\rangle = \frac{1}{2} [|0010110\rangle |0000\rangle + |0000100\rangle |0110\rangle + |0100110\rangle |1001\rangle + |1110100\rangle |1100\rangle] \quad (10.55)$$

$$|\Psi_5\rangle = \frac{1}{2} [|0010100\rangle |0000\rangle + |0000100\rangle |0110\rangle + |0100110\rangle |1001\rangle + |1110110\rangle |1100\rangle] \quad (10.56)$$

After the circuit has been applied, the ancilla qubits (e_1, e_0, a^1) and a^0 can be hidden again for simplification. However, a^2 is now the sign qubit of the sum. Thus, it is now considered as y^2 (Eq. 10.57). Then, the qubit order can be rearranged back to an "audio-readable" form (Eqs. 10.58, 10.59 and 10.60).

$$\frac{1}{2} \left[|00110\rangle \, |0000\rangle + |00010\rangle \, |0110\rangle + |01011\rangle \, |1001\rangle + |11111\rangle \, |1100\rangle \right] \quad (10.57)$$

$$\frac{1}{2} \left[|01\rangle \, |010\rangle \, |00\rangle \, |00\rangle + |01\rangle \, |000\rangle \, |01\rangle \, |10\rangle + |11\rangle \, |001\rangle \, |10\rangle \, |01\rangle + |11\rangle \, |111\rangle \, |11\rangle \, |00\rangle \right] \quad (10.58)$$

$$= \frac{1}{2} \left[(|01\rangle \, |010\rangle \, |00\rangle + |11\rangle \, |111\rangle \, |11\rangle) \, |00\rangle + |11\rangle \, |001\rangle \, |10\rangle \, |01\rangle + |01\rangle \, |000\rangle \, |01\rangle \, |10\rangle \right] \quad (10.59)$$

$$= \frac{1}{2} \left[(|01\rangle \, |0\rangle \, |010\rangle \, |0\rangle + |11\rangle \, |1\rangle \, |111\rangle \, |1\rangle) \otimes |00\rangle + |11\rangle \, |1\rangle \, |001\rangle \, |0\rangle \otimes |01\rangle + |01\rangle \, |0\rangle \, |000\rangle \, |1\rangle \otimes |10\rangle \right] \quad (10.60)$$

Finally, by hiding the qubits respective to $|X\rangle$ in our notation, The sum $|X + Y\rangle$ emerges in Eq. 10.61.

$$\frac{1}{2} \left[(|010\rangle \, |0\rangle + |111\rangle \, |1\rangle) \otimes |00\rangle + |001\rangle \, |0\rangle \otimes |01\rangle + |000\rangle \, |1\rangle \otimes |10\rangle \right]$$

$$\frac{1}{2} \left[|X + Y\rangle \otimes |00\rangle + |001\rangle \, |0\rangle \, |01\rangle + |000\rangle \, |1\rangle \, |10\rangle \right] \quad (10.61)$$

In conclusion, if the signal addition circuit is applied, then whenever $|e_1 e_0\rangle$ is at the state $|00\rangle$, the qubits (a^2, y^1, y^0, j^0) will be in a QSM state representing the sum of X and Y.

To exemplify how these circuits scale with respect to the audio size and bit depth, we invite the reader to examine how the circuit in Fig. 10.36 performs a signal addition of two 3-bit, 8-sample QSM audio.

10.7.2 Concatenation

Another basic operation that is desirable in a quantum signal processing environment is the concatenation of sounds. Wang et al. [6] propose a circuit for concatenating two uQSMs (QRDAs) with the same length. Essentially, the circuit allocates enough qubits to encode the output which has twice the length (e.g., has a time register with one additional qubit). Then, it performs Value-Setting Operations, similar to the preparation circuits shown previously Sect. 10.5.2.1. In detail, it applies fine-tuned multi-controlled CNOT gates for each time state to prepare the amplitude register at the respective samples.

However, in this case, the circuit is not using classical audio as a reference for conditioning the respective control qubits. Instead, it uses the amplitudes from the original uQSMs as control qubits. By taking advantage of the signal addition circuit

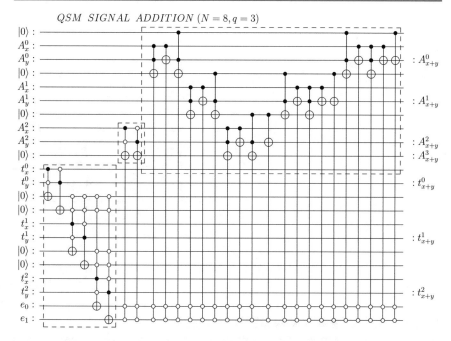

Fig. 10.36 Example of a larger QSM signal addition circuit (3-qubit length, 3-qubit depth)

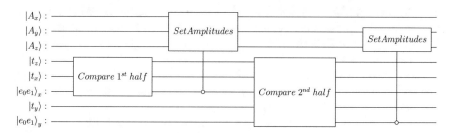

Fig. 10.37 Sketch of a signal concatenation circuit

of the previous section, a comparator gate will be incorporated into the concatenation circuit as an improvement to the one proposed in [6]. The comparator will be responsible for syncing the audio, similar to the addition of audio (Fig. 10.37).

A circuit for concatenating two QSMs, with 2-bit amplitude depth and 2 samples in size, producing a 2-bit depth and 4-sized output is represented in Fig. 10.38.

In a general look, it would initially sync $|A_x\rangle$ with the first half of the output audio $|A_z\rangle$. Then, it would apply the Value-Setting operations (whenever a qubit in the amplitude register of $|A_x\rangle$ is 1, it will flip the corresponding qubit in $|A_z\rangle$). Finally, it will repeat the circuit, but now syncing and populating the second half of $|A_z\rangle$ with $|A_y\rangle$.

A similar toy example, as made in the previous section, is left as an exercise.

Fig. 10.38 Example of a QSM signal concatenation using comparator gates (1-qubit length, 2-qubit depth)

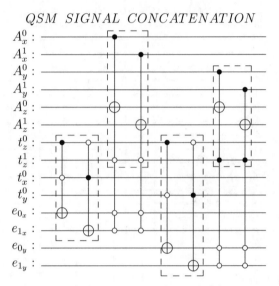

10.7.2.1 Considerations for QSM Operations

It is worth noting that these QSP algorithms, such as addition and concatenation (and possibly other state-based signal operations) could affect the superpositions. That is, it might alter the relative probabilities of the originally balanced QSM audio states. Subsequently, larger or more extensive operations might introduce unwanted errors. For instance, the probability of a valid QSM state could get close to zero and be confused with noise.

As an illustrative example, Fig. 10.39 shows the histogram of a simulation result. The concatenation was applied on two identical QSM audio with 8 samples each (the same signal from Fig. 10.17) [6].

There is another foreseeable concern. Equation (10.60) asserts that the result of the QSP algorithm ($|X + Y\rangle$) is stored within the full quantum state. It is entangled with the ancilla qubits (e_0, e_1) at state $|00\rangle$. However, the result of the operation is not the only measurable state. The reconstruction process needs to account for unwanted states and filter the desired result.

Therefore, the post-processing might depend on specificities and previous knowledge of the quantum circuit mathematical structure. This is an example of a dependency relation that quantum algorithms have with classical machines.

10.7.3 A Simple Similarity Metric for Making Parallel Comparisons with Multiple SQPAM

At the beginning of this chapter, we mentioned that the quantum representations of audio were derived from quantum image encoding schemes. Also, the quantum audio literature has been focusing solely on the QSM (NEQR) encoding technique.

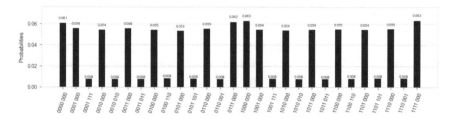

Fig. 10.39 Result of a concatenation of two QSM audio

This chapter suggested that coefficient-based techniques needed to be rescued and included in the mix. Consequently, it led to the formalization of QPAM (Based on Qubit Lattice) and SQPAM (Based on FRQI)—even though they do not appear anywhere else on these terms yet. To put forward these representations for computer music applications, we further developed a potential algorithm originally proposed for FRQI images [19]: a parallel pixel-by-pixel comparison that arrives at a simple distance metric. This could be used to measure the similarity between multiple signals.

The 1D version of this circuit would achieve a sample-by-sample distance-based similarity metric for quantum audio, that can calculate all of the respective distances in parallel using only one Hadamard gate and one measurement instruction.

The main idea of the algorithm is to use an additional register to index (prepare) multiple SQPAM audio in a superposition. This was briefly discussed while examining Multichannel audio in Sect. 10.5.4. Then, the algorithm takes advantage of a clever probability amplitude arithmetic. The metric is computed once a Hadamard gate is applied to the channel register, creating a superpositioned mix of all the quantum audio.

The multiple audio superposition is shown in Eqs. 10.62 and 10.63. They are similar to Eq. 10.42.

$$|S\rangle = \frac{1}{\sqrt{L}} \sum_{s=0}^{L-1} [|\text{SQPAM}_s\rangle] \otimes |s\rangle \tag{10.62}$$

$$= \frac{1}{\sqrt{L}} \sum_{s=0}^{L-1} \frac{1}{\sqrt{N}} \sum_{i=0}^{N-1} [(\cos\theta_{i,s}\,|0\rangle + \sin\theta_{i,s}\,|1\rangle) \otimes |i\rangle] \otimes |s\rangle \tag{10.63}$$

For this purpose, let us compare two audio files, meaning $L = 2$. The the soundbank $|S\rangle$ could be written as in Eq. 10.64.

$$|S\rangle = \frac{1}{\sqrt{2}}\,|\text{SQPAM}_0\rangle\,|0\rangle + \frac{1}{\sqrt{2}}\,|\text{SQPAM}_1\rangle\,|1\rangle \tag{10.64}$$

Suppose a Hadamard gate is applied in the $|s\rangle$ register (Eq. 10.65). If a sum (or difference) of two SQPAM audio is expanded (Eq. 10.66), an interesting result appears. It is noticed that the SQPAM probability amplitudes are being added or subtracted. These operations are somehow related to the addition or subtraction of the angles, therefore, the encoded amplitudes.

$$I \otimes H(|S\rangle) = \frac{1}{2}[|SQPAM_0\rangle\,|0\rangle + |SQPAM_0\rangle\,|1\rangle + |SQPAM_1\rangle\,|0\rangle - |SQPAM_1\rangle\,|1\rangle]$$

$$= \frac{1}{2}[(|SQPAM_0\rangle + |SQPAM_1\rangle)\,|0\rangle + (|SQPAM_0\rangle - |SQPAM_1\rangle)\,|1\rangle] \quad (10.65)$$

$$|SQPAM_0\rangle \pm |SQPAM_1\rangle = \frac{1}{N}\sum_{i=0}^{N-1}[(\cos\theta_{i,0} \pm \cos\theta_{i,1})\,|0\rangle + (\sin\theta_{i,0} \pm \sin\theta_{i,1})\,|1\rangle] \otimes |i\rangle$$

$$(10.66)$$

Consequently, once $|s\rangle$ is measured, the result will depend on the relation between θ_0 and θ_1. The result will be a single qubit histogram.

Consider the probability of $|s\rangle = |1\rangle$ in Eqs. 10.67, 10.68 and 10.69 (after some trigonometric substitutions[11]). In conclusion, the probability $\text{Prob}(|1\rangle)_s$ depends entirely on sample-wise differences between both audio:

$$\text{Prob}(|1\rangle)_s = \frac{1}{N^2}\sum_{i=0}^{N-1}[(\cos\theta_{i,0} - \cos\theta_{i,1})^2 + (\sin\theta_{i,0} - \sin\theta_{i,1})^2] \quad (10.67)$$

$$\text{Prob}(|1\rangle)_s = \frac{1}{4}\frac{1}{N^2}\sum_{i=0}^{N-1}4(\sin^2\frac{\theta_{i,0}+\theta_{i,1}}{2} + \cos^2\frac{\theta_{i,0}+\theta_{i,1}}{2})\sin^2\frac{\theta_{i,0}-\theta_{i,1}}{2} \quad (10.68)$$

$$\text{Prob}(|1\rangle)_s = \frac{1}{2} - \frac{1}{2N^2}\sum_{i=0}^{N-1}\cos\theta_{i,0} - \theta_{i,1} \quad (10.69)$$

In other words, If $\forall i$, $\theta_{i,0} = \theta_{i,1}$ (identical), then $\cos\theta_{i,1} - \theta_{i,1} = 1$ and $\text{Prob}(|1\rangle)_s = 1$. But if instead $\theta_{i,0} = \theta_{i,1} + \frac{\pi}{2}$ (complete opposites), then $\cos\theta_{i,1} - \theta_{i,1} + \frac{\pi}{2} = 0$ and $\text{Prob}(|1\rangle)_s = 0$.

From that measure, a simple similarity metric for SQPAM is achieved. It is the normalized sum of the cosine of sample-by-sample differences. All realized with a "multichannel-like" SQPAM preparation step and one Hadamard gate.

---

[11] $\cos a - \cos b = -2\sin\frac{a+b}{2}\sin\frac{a-b}{2}$; $\sin a - \sin b = 2\cos\frac{a+b}{2}\sin\frac{a-b}{2}$; $\sin^2 x = \frac{1-\cos 2x}{2}$.

10.7.4 Other Proposed Signal Processing Algorithms

Beyond the circuits discussed in this chapter, there are other signal processing algorithms (mostly for QSM) that were already proposed in the literature, knowingly [7]:

- QSM Signal Inversion (inverts the integers on the amplitude register)
- QSM Signal Reversal (applies X gates on the time register)
- QSM Delay (uses the adder module to shift the time register by some integer unit and then sets the first samples to 0)
- QSM Circular Convolution [12].

Other algorithms being proposed in the literature are security-related; e.g., Quantum Audio Steganography [20] and Quantum Audio Watermarking Schemes [21,22].

10.8 Potential Applications

After enumerating a number of quantum audio representations and exemplifying some fundamental QSP algorithms, it is time to speculate on potential applications to music and art in general.

The state-based representations of quantum audio propose a framework for dealing with quantum signals that are closer to digital signal processing strategies. There are similarities in the perspective of the signal structure, using binary words that can be addressed, flipped, and interpreted as integers, among others. Hence, there is more intuition when translating known classical algorithms to quantum computers.

So far, these translations are made (despite expectations) without any strong guarantee that quantum computers will *concretely* improve speed and efficiency—or even be of use for known signal processing algorithms. Still, it is at the very least a worthwhile exercise that deepens our understanding of new technologies and provides a fertile and more accessible environment for developing new tools for future artists and technicians.

Nevertheless, we encourage the reader to think of the potential of quantum audio's less intuitive coefficient-based representations. Its probabilistic nature will likely provide new perspectives of viewing, representing and processing audio that could be unique to quantum computers and convenient to artistic thinking. This exercise is more challenging and requires more collaboration and abstraction.

The QPAM representation is a great starting point for coefficient-based signal processing exploration and a space to learn common quantum algorithms. The fact is: The QPAM is effectively *interpreting* the information present in the probability amplitudes as rescaled audio amplitudes (Eq. 10.16). Many algorithms in the quantum computing literature operate over these superpositions; e.g., Grover's, Shor's, Teleportation Algorithms, the Quantum Fourier Transform (QFT) and others.

10.8.1 A Brief Note About Quantum Audio and the Quantum Fourier Transform

The Discrete Fourier Transform (DFT) [2] is a well-known algorithm in the digital audio community. It is used to compute the frequency spectrum of a given sound and consequently applied for audio analysis and synthesis, detection, classification, information retrieval, effects, and more. The impact of modern and contemporary electronic music is unprecedented. It is logical for a person from a signal processing or electroacoustic music background to be interested in understanding the potentials of a Quantum Fourier Transform (QFT) algorithm, and have high expectations, considering early theoretical results that showed an exponential improvement in the computational complexity of the transformation [23]. It is also being extensively used to optimize quantum operations (basic mathematical operations; for example, [24]). However, one needs to be cautious about the expectations of its potential for quantum audio.

If we compare the definitions of the Inverse Discrete Fourier Transform and the Quantum Fourier Transform, we will notice that both will operate the coefficients of the signal very similarly:

$$\text{Inverse Discrete Fourier Transform} \longrightarrow x_m = \frac{1}{\sqrt{N}} \sum_{k=0}^{N-1} e^{\frac{2\pi i m k}{N}} X_k \qquad (10.70)$$

$$\text{Quantum Fourier Transform} \longrightarrow QFT \left| x \right\rangle = \frac{1}{\sqrt{N}} \sum_{k=0}^{N-1} e^{\frac{2\pi i x k}{N}} \left| k \right\rangle \qquad (10.71)$$

This equation induces the idea that we could apply the QFT to a quantum signal as a way of extracting Fourier coefficients of them. If applied to a QPAM audio, the QFT would still preserve periodicities present in the signal (but also potentially change the relative amplitudes of some coefficients). However, this direct frequency-domain intuition of the Quantum Fourier Transform fades away with more complex quantum representations. If a QFT is applied on a QSM, it will Not extract a frequency spectrum of the audio since the amplitudes are stored inside the registers. A proper algorithm to achieve this computation would need to apply multi-qubit multiplications on every step of the QFT, using large circuits similar to the convolution circuit mentioned in [12] (meaning multiplication gates applied term by term).

10.8.2 Quantum "Dithering"

Consider how a composer might wish to apply different quantum audio concepts and circuits more artistically. For instance, let us look at an example: a simple QPAM loopback circuit. That is, the QPAM state is prepared and then immediately retrieved back. A 3-qubit version of this algorithm (for audio with eight samples) is described in Fig. 10.40. Can this simple circuit be used artistically?

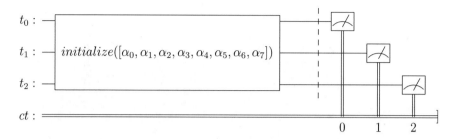

Fig. 10.40 3-qubit example of a QPAM loopback circuit (preparation + retrieval)

QPAM loopback:

- Choose a digital audio sample of preference
- Map the amplitudes to a normalized range (Eq. 10.16)
- Prepare a QPAM State in a Quantum circuit with enough qubits
- Measure the circuit
- Map the measurements back to a digital audio signal range.

Bear in mind that to retrieve quantum information through measurement, the quantum processor will prepare several identical copies of the circuit and then measure them independently. Then, the measurements are grouped into a histogram. The retrieved information is analyzed with a classical program. Finally, the reconstructed data can be interpreted as an audio signal.

During this process, it is possible to underestimate (on purpose) the number of *shots* (measurements of identical circuits) necessary to retrieve a sufficient approximation of the audio. The underestimated audio can be reconstructed and listened to. Let us consider this circuit as a potential quantum audio effect, parametrized by the number of shots. Figure 10.41 displays a 4-qubit example. What are the possible effects?

With subtle underestimations (remind that the reconstruction will not be perfect in this case), the presence of a faint white noise is perceived. This noise could loosely resemble the effect achieved with dithering or noise shaping algorithms. Therefore, the first result of this circuit is a Quantum Dithering effect. Figure 10.42 shows an example of a 15-qubit signal (in blue) submitted to a quantum dithering effect processor (in red).

10.8.3 Noise Transient Attack

As the *shots* parameter decreases, the reconstructed audio starts to fade from the original, while the white noise presence increases. Eventually, the noise dominates the space—until it reaches a new behaviour. With fewer and fewer parallel executions

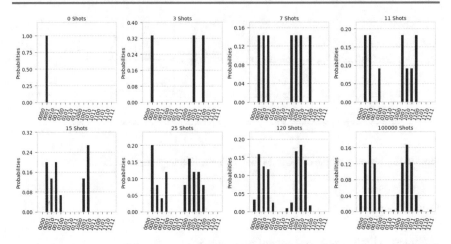

Fig. 10.41 Different retrievals of a 4-qubit QPAM loopback circuit with 1, 3, 7, 11, 15, 25, 120 and 100000 shots, respectively

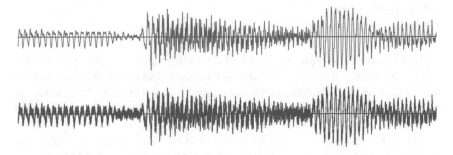

Fig. 10.42 Simulation of the quantum dithering effect on a 15-qubit audio

of the loopback circuit, the histogram starts to return isolated peaks. Finally, it arrives at 1 shot and a single-peak histogram.

By concatenating (classically) these different evolving stages in a sequence, another potential effect appears. A sharp transient attack for an oscillator or sound object.

An illustration of this application with is shown in Fig. 10.43. The signal used as input is a sine function with five periods, sampled in 7 qubits (128 values). First, there is a silent section to represent "0 shots". The silence is followed by a rapid, randomized sequence of impulses—a result extracted from a 1-shot and a 10-shot version. Then, there is a small section with saturated noise from a 100-shot experiment. From that point (500, 1000, 10000 and 1000000 shots), the signal progressively approximates the sinusoid wave.

Fig. 10.43 Example of a transient attack created with multiple retrievals of a 7-qubit QPAM sinusoid and a varying number of shots

10.8.4 The Geiger Counter Effect Using Wavetable Synthesis

When contemplating signals with 128 samples it is not useful to simply listen to the signal as raw audio data. Considering that a typical sample rate of an audio file is 48 kHz. Therefore, a file with 128 samples would contain a sound with a duration of $128/48000 = 0.0027$ s.

To further this logic, an artist could ponder possible mappings and sonifications to listen to the result. In other words, connections between data from a quantum computing framework (e.g., Pytket, Strawberry Fields, Qiskit and OpenQASM) and a synthesizer built on a music programming language (e.g., Supercollider, Pure Data, Csound, Max).[12]

A convenient and practical method to sonify short signals is the *wavetable synthesis* technique [25]. Essentially, a wavetable here consists of a fixed buffer or table, from which you can store short signals. The software synthesizer has a pointer that slides and loops through the table at a pre-determined speed. This pointer reads the value at its current position at audio sampling rates.

For instance, imagine that the pointer is at a fixed position and is not moving (the speed is zero). The value at that position is, for example, 0.25. Then, the synthesis would generate a constant 0.25 signal with 48 kHz sampling rate.

At another time, the pointer may be moving at sampling speed. That is, with each sample, the pointer moves to the next value in the table. If the speed is twice as fast, the pointer will skip an index and read the consequent value, and so on.

Fractional speeds are also possible. Suppose the pointer speed is half the sampling rate. Then, there will be times that the pointer is positioned between two samples. In this case, interpolation is applied, generating an intermediate value.

The plus side of using a wavetable synthesizer is that it can be updated in runtime. In other words, a quantum machine could process information, wait for the results and update the table without interrupting the sound. Let us revisit the example shown in (Fig. 10.43). Assume that there is a wavetable synthesis engine that will read a buffer with 128 values and synthesize the reconstructed histograms. Every second, a new histogram is calculated using an increasing amount of *shots*. Then, the new histogram updates the synthesis. We refer to this process as "the Geiger counter effect".

---

[12] Many possible connections between quantum and music software are made available in the QuTune Project repository [16].

Fig. 10.44 Spectrogram of a Geiger Counter effect on a sinewave

Figure 10.44 displays a spectrogram of this effect when applied to a 10-qubit table at a reading speed of 1 Hz. The audio content is one second of a 100 Hz sinewave.

Similarly to the previous effect, the sound starts silently. Then, a first measurement raises a peak, generating a click train pulse. With a few measurements, these clicks will get randomized and more complex. Eventually, a saturated noise emerges. The auditory result resembles the sound of a Geiger counter, a device that detects ionizing radiation in an environment. As more measurements are computed, the signal approximates the original audio form. The original sound appears smoothly and gains presence over the vanishing noise.

Despite the possibility of reproducing similar results using classical computers, there are some arguable advantages of going quantum on this audio effect. First, the very quantum logic of quantum machines (the probabilistic nature, the statistics related to retrieving quantum information) was the pavement that structured the idea of this artistic application in simple terms. Second, reproducing the Geiger counter effect on a classical machine would require generating pseudo-random variables that follow arbitrary probability density functions. This is not the most straightforward task for classical algorithms, but a trivial one, inherent to its hardware structure, for quantum. Third, this simple example might efficiently introduce correlated noises into a complex sound. Fourth, this application can be tested in state-of-the-art quantum processors.

10.9 Final Remarks

This chapter discussed various different approaches for quantum representation of audio that have been proposed to date. Quantum audio is still a very young field of study. Naturally, the different approaches presented here have advantages and disadvantages. At this stage, we are not in a position to foresee which of the method(s) discussed here, if any, might end up being adopted by the industry simply because the hardware to realize them is not available.

Nevertheless, as shown above, we can already start developing approaches and dream of interesting applications (e.g., a quantum electric guitar effects pedal) based on simulations and educated guesses about how quantum processors will evolve. An important caveat of quantum computing that needs to be addressed is the problem of memory. Essentially, quantum information cannot be stored and retrieved in the same way that digital information can with classical processors. The development of quantum random access memory (qRAM) technology would make a significant impact on quantum audio. A number of propositions for developing qRAM have been put forward (e.g., [26,27]), but a practical device for more general use is still not in sight yet.

Acknowledgements The authors acknowledge the support of the University of Plymouth and the QuTune Project, funded by the UK Quantum Technology Hub in Computing and Simulation.

References

1. Rabiner, L. R., & Gold, B. (1975). *Theory and application of digital signal processing.* Prentice-Hall.
2. Broughton, S. A., & Bryan, K. (2008). *Discrete Fourier analysis and wavelets: Applications to signal and image processing.* Wiley.
3. Meichanetzidis, K., Gogioso, S., De Felice, G., Chiappori, N., Toumi, A., & Coecke, B. (2021). Quantum natural language processing on near-term quantum computers. arXiv:2005.04147 [cs.CL].
4. Venegas-Andraca, S. E., & Bose, S. (2003). Storing, processing, and retrieving an image using quantum mechanics. In *Quantum information and computation* (Vol. 5105, pp. 137–147). International Society for Optics and Photonics.
5. Venegas-Andraca, S. E. (2005). Discrete quantum walks and quantum image processing.
6. Wang, J. (2016). QRDA: Quantum representation of digital audio. *International Journal of Theoretical Physics, 55*(3), 1622–1641.
7. Yan, F., Iliyasu, A. M., Guo, Y., & Yang, H. (2018). Flexible representation and manipulation of audio signals on quantum computers. *Theoretical Computer Science, 752,* 71–85.
8. Zhang, Y., Kai, L., Gao, Y., & Wang, M. (2013). NEQR: A novel enhanced quantum representation of digital images. *Quantum Information Processing, 12*(8), 2833–2860.
9. Ziemer, R. E., & William, H. T. (2014). *Principles of communications*, chapters 3–4. Wiley.
10. Yan, F., Iliyasu, A. M., & Venegas-Andraca, S. E. (2016). A survey of quantum image representations. *Quantum Information Processing, 15*(1), 1–35.
11. Wootton, J. R. (2020). Procedural generation using quantum computation. In *International Conference on the Foundations of Digital Games* (pp. 1–8).
12. Li, P., Wang, B., Xiao, H., et al. (2018). Quantum representation and basic operations of digital signals. *International Journal of Theoretical Physics, 57,* 3242–3270.
13. Şahin, E., & Yilmaz, İ. (2019). QRMA: Quantum representation of multichannel audio. *Quantum Information Processing, 18*(7), 1–30.
14. Lidar, D. A., & Brun, T. A., (Eds.). (2013). *Quantum error correction.* Cambridge University Press.

15. *IBM Quantum*. https://quantum-computing.ibm.com/. Accessed 01 Feb. 2022.
16. *QuTune Project—Quantum Computer Music Resources*. https://iccmr-quantum.github.io/, Accessed 01 Feb. 2022.
17. Vedral, V., Barenco, A., & Ekert, A. (1996). Quantum networks for elementary arithmetic operations. *Physical Review A, 54*(1), 147.
18. Wang, D., Liu, Z.-H., Zhu, W.-N., & Li, S. Z. (2012). Design of quantum comparator based on extended general Toffoli gates with multiple targets. *Computer Science, 39*(9), 302–306.
19. Yan, F., Iliyasu, A. M., Le, P. Q., Sun, B., Dong, F., & Hirota, K. (2013). A parallel comparison of multiple pairs of images on quantum computers. *International Journal of Innovative Computing and Applications, 5*, 199–212.
20. Chen, K., Yan, F., Iliyasu, A. M., & Zhao, J. (2018). Exploring the implementation of steganography protocols on quantum audio signals. *International Journal of Theoretical Physics, 57*(2), 476–494.
21. Chen, K., Yan, F., Iliyasu, A. M., & Zhao, J. A. (2018). Quantum audio watermarking scheme. In *2018 37th Chinese Control Conference (CCC)* (pp. 3180–3185). IEEE.
22. Chen, K., Yan, F., Iliyasu, A. M., & Zhao, J. (2019). Dual quantum audio watermarking schemes based on quantum discrete cosine transform. *International Journal of Theoretical Physics, 58*(2), 502–521.
23. Nielsen, M. A., & Chuang, I. (2002). *Quantum computation and quantum information* (pp. 216–221). American Association of Physics Teachers.
24. Şahin, Engin. (2020). Quantum arithmetic operations based on quantum Fourier transform on signed integers. *International Journal of Quantum Information, 18*(06), 2050035.
25. Miranda, E. R. *Computer sound design: Synthesis techniques and programming* (2nd edn.). Focal Press.
26. Chen, K. C., Dai, W., Errando-Herranz, C., Lloyd, S., & Englund, D. (2021). Scalable and high-fidelity quantum random access memory in spin-photon networks. *PRX Quantum, 2*, 030319.
27. Asaka, R., Sakai, K., & Yahagi, R. (2021). Quantum random access memory via quantum walk. *Quantum Science and Technology, 6*(3), 035004.

Experiments in Quantum Frequency Detection Using Quantum Fourier Transform

11

Rajiv Mistry and Jonathan Ortega

Abstract

In this chapter, we will walk through our experiments in utilizing the Quantum Fourier Transform (QFT) to analyze a single frequency audio file and a personal MIDI rendition of Bach's *Cello Suite Prelude, BWV-1007* on simulated and real IBM Quantum (IBM Q) backends. We will begin by giving a brief history of the famous Fourier Transform as well as the nomenclature surrounding its derivative forms. This will lead to some quantum computing basics and derivations of the QFT in different contexts. From there, we will give a breakdown of our testing methodologies and results. Finally, we will conclude by speaking on some of the potential musical and scientific applications of using the QFT for signal analysis.

11.1 Introduction

11.1.1 Fourier Analysis

Fourier analysis is named after Jean Baptiste Joseph Fourier (1768–1830), a French mathematician and physicist [8]. He is credited with highlighting the practicality of decomposing signals into harmonic waveforms. Sinusoids are particularly important due to sinusoidal fidelity. This attribute means that in a linear system, a sinusoidal input will have a sinusoidal output. Fourier was particularly interested in using these methods to analyse heat propagation, but his ideas were suppressed for nearly 50 years. This was primarily the doing of renowned mathematician Joseph

R. Mistry (✉) · J. Ortega
Pivotport, Inc, Chicago, USA
e-mail: rajiv@pivotport.com

J. Ortega
e-mail: jortega@pivotport.com

© The Author(s), under exclusive license to Springer Nature Switzerland AG 2022   275
E. R. Miranda (ed.), *Quantum Computer Music*,
https://doi.org/10.1007/978-3-031-13909-3_11

Louis Lagrange (1736–1813), due to the longstanding belief that Fourier's approach "could not be used to represent signals with *corners*, i.e., discontinuous slopes, such as in square waves" [8]. While this is technically true, under proper conditions Fourier analysis can lead to transforms that are exact signal decompositions (for discrete signals) or such good approximations (for continuous signals) that there is no practical difference.

11.1.2 Fourier Transforms

Historically, the Fourier Transform is a loosely used phrase which can refer to four distinct transformations. These distinctions are based on a combination of the signal's continuity (continuous or discrete) and periodicity (periodic or aperiodic). All these transforms decompose functions dependent on space or time into functions dependent on spatial or temporal frequency. This is most often referred to as going from the time domain to the frequency domain. The input and output of the transformation can be vectors of complex value,[1] where the output has two defining qualities. Firstly, the magnitude of the value is an indicator of how much of the frequency was in the input. Secondly, argument[2] corresponds to the phase offset of the sinusoid corresponding to the output frequency. With each Fourier Transform also exists an inverse Fourier Transform[3] which takes a function in the frequency domain and transforms it back into its original time-domain representation. The formulas for each will be given later, but for now, we will just touch on the fact that the Fourier Transform and Inverse Fourier Transform are very similar mathematically. So much so, that the domains of each are symmetrical. Each contains the exact same information, just represented in different bases. This symmetry is known as duality.

11.1.3 Mathematical Concepts

The principle of duality is an overarching one with many meanings across all of mathematics. In our case, it refers to the bilinear mapping of one complex vector onto another. An example of duality at play is shown with convolution. Convolution[4] is one of, if not the most, important operation used in digital signal processing. It also has countless applications in acoustics, engineering, physics, and statistics [2]. One of the most important consequences of Fourier Transform is

---

[1] For simplicity, some transforms are only defined here as $f : \mathbb{R} \to \mathbb{C}$. In the text, we will just refer to the domain and codomain as being complex since our main concern is with the Discrete Fourier Transform.

[2] The angle between the imaginary and real parts of a complex value. If we consider $c = a + bi$, then the argument is: $\arg(c) = \tan^{-1}(b/a)$. Also notice that these represent c in polar coordinates.

[3] In most real-life applications, such is not the case in pure mathematics.

[4] Consider functions $f(t)$ and $g(t)$, their convolution is $h(t)$ and the operation is denoted by an asterisk: $h(t) = f(t) * g(t)$. For reference, convolution is associative, commutative, and distributive.

drastically simplifying the computational complexity of convolving signals. We will not be getting into any proofs or derivations, but the operation of convolution becomes multiplicative in the frequency domain. The converse of this statement is also true, where convolution in the frequency domain is equivalent to multiplication in the time domain. This relation is an example of the duality between the Fourier Transform and its inverse [8]. Now we will touch on each transform.

11.1.3.1 Fourier Transform

Also referred to as the Continuous Fourier transform or Continuous-time Fourier Transform (CTFT), the Fourier Transform is used for signals which are continuous and aperiodic. An example of this would be exponential models, whether that be particle half-life, harmonic oscillations, or population change: the Fourier Transform is shown in Eq. 11.1 and the inverse Fourier Transform is in Eq. 11.2. We will be denoting Fourier transformed functions by $\hat{f}$, the imaginary number $\sqrt{-1} = i$, and the frequency by F.

$$\hat{f}(F) = \int_{-\infty}^{\infty} f(t)e^{-2\pi i F t} dt, \forall F \in \mathbb{R} \tag{11.1}$$

$$f(F) = \int_{-\infty}^{\infty} \hat{f}(t)e^{2\pi i F t} dF, \forall t \in \mathbb{R} \tag{11.2}$$

11.1.3.2 Fourier Series

The Fourier Series is used for signals which are continuous and periodic. This encapsulates the familiar regular trigonometric functions such as sin, cos, as well as square and triangle waveforms. The phrase Harmonic Analysis has also been used to refer to the study of this topic in general. The formula for the Fourier series of a complex function f, with an assumed period F of 2π, is shown in Eq. 11.3 is [11].

$$f_N(t) = \sum_{n=-N}^{N} \frac{1}{P} \int_P f(t)e^{-2\pi i n t/P} dx \cdot e^{2\pi i n t/P} = \sum_{n=-N}^{N} \frac{1}{2\pi} \int_{-\pi}^{\pi} f(t)e^{-int} dx \cdot e^{int} \tag{11.3}$$

11.1.3.3 Discrete-Time Fourier Transform (DTFT)

The Discrete-time Fourier Transform (DTFT) is used for signals which are discrete and aperiodic and can be interpreted as the limiting form of the DFT when N approaches infinity. The DTFT is shown in Eq. 11.4 and the inverse DTFT is shown in Eq. 11.5, as derived by [7]. In this instance, $\tilde{\omega}$ is the continuous normalized radian frequency, $j = \sqrt{-1}$, and $x(n)$ is the signal amplitude at n.

$$X(\tilde{\omega}) \triangleq \sum_{n=-\infty}^{\infty} x(n)e^{-j\tilde{\omega}n} \tag{11.4}$$

$$x(n) = \frac{1}{2\pi} \int_{-\pi}^{\pi} X(\tilde{\omega})e^{-j\tilde{\omega}n} \tag{11.5}$$

11.2 Discrete Fourier Transform and Beyond

11.2.1 Discrete Fourier Transform (DFT)

The Discrete Fourier Transform (DFT) is used for signals which are discrete and periodic. As stated before, the use of Fourier Analysis to decompose real signals has a couple of prerequisites. Firstly, computers have limited resources, therefore can only work with discrete waveforms. Secondly, for an aperiodic signal, exact decomposition would require an infinite number of constituent sine waves. Lastly, all these transforms are defined for infinite length signals, which would also require the constituent waveforms to be infinite in length. To get around all these mathematical infinities, the DFT is calculated by treating the entire signal as one period of an infinite-periodic signal. In contrast to the continuous transformations which have an input and output function, the remaining discrete transformations will have input and output vectors. The equation for DFT is given in Eq. 11.6 and its inverse in Eq. 11.7. (Note: classical Fourier transformed vectors are denoted with a tilde above the variable; e.g., $\tilde{x}$ in Eq. 11.6.)

$$\tilde{x}_k = \sum_{n=0}^{N-1} x_n e^{-2\pi ikn/N} \tag{11.6}$$

$$x_n = \frac{1}{N} \sum_{k=0}^{N-1} \tilde{x}_k e^{2\pi ikn/N} \tag{11.7}$$

11.2.2 Quantum Gates

The Hadamard gate is key in the ability of many quantum algorithms, it is responsible for setting qubits on the computational basis to a superposition of states. This superposition is known as the polar basis (with 'plus' basis vector shown in Eq. 11.8 and 'minus' basis vector in Eq. 11.9) and is used here because it is the simplest transformation in which qubits are superimposed and have an equal probability of being in either computational basis state. This single-qubit gate from the computational basis to the polar basis is equivalent to a Fourier Transform acting on two qubits [4].

$$\frac{1}{\sqrt{2}}(|0\rangle + |1\rangle) = |+\rangle \tag{11.8}$$

$$\frac{1}{\sqrt{2}}(|0\rangle - |1\rangle) = |-\rangle \tag{11.9}$$

The Hadamard gate in combination with the controlled phase gate makes up the Quantum Fourier Transform. The Hadamard gate for two qubits is depicted in Eq. 11.10 and the phase shift rotation gate for two qubits is in Eq. 11.11. The variable m in the controlled phase gate R_m (Eq. 11.11) is dependent on the number of qubits and how far along the circuit it is. The controlled phase gate applies successively larger pulses to each qubit. The DFT on 2^n amplitudes can be implemented with $O(n)^2$ Hadamard gates and controlled phase shift gates, where n is the number of qubits [5].

$$H = \frac{1}{2}\begin{bmatrix} 1 & 1 \\ 1 & -1 \end{bmatrix} \tag{11.10}$$

$$R_m = \begin{bmatrix} 1 & 0 \\ 0 & e^{2\pi i/2^m} \end{bmatrix} \tag{11.11}$$

11.2.3 Quantum Fourier Transform (QFT)

The Quantum Fourier Transform (QFT) is a transformation that acts on a quantum state and is the quantum analogue of the inverse DFT. It is the transform between the computational basis and the Fourier basis [12]. As you can see in Eq. 11.12 (QFT) and Eq. 11.12 (inverse QFT), QFT bears a lot of similarities to the classical DFT. The respective QFT matrix representation is shown in Eq. 11.14.

$$y_k = \frac{1}{\sqrt{N}}\sum_{n=0}^{N-1} x_n e^{\frac{2\pi i k n}{N}}, 0 \leq k \leq N-1 \tag{11.12}$$

$$x_n = \frac{1}{\sqrt{N}}\sum_{k=0}^{N-1} y_k e^{\frac{2\pi i k n}{N}}, 0 \leq n \leq N-1 \tag{11.13}$$

$$F_N = \frac{1}{\sqrt{N}} \begin{bmatrix} e^{2\pi i \cdot 0 \cdot 0/N} & \cdots & e^{2\pi i \cdot (N-1) \cdot 0/N} \\ \vdots & \ddots & \vdots \\ e^{2\pi i \cdot 0 \cdot (N-1)/N} & \cdots & e^{2\pi i (N-1)(N-1)/N} \end{bmatrix} \begin{pmatrix} 1 & \cdots & 1 \\ \vdots & \ddots & \vdots \\ 1 & \cdots & e^{2\pi i (N-1)^2/N} \end{pmatrix}$$

$$(11.14)$$

It has been demonstrated that Quantum Fourier Transform algorithms can achieve good results using at most $O(n\log(n))$ gates [3].

11.3 Experimental Framework

11.3.1 The Qubit

The primary building block of quantum systems is the qubit, or *quantum bit*, which can physically be any two-state system. These are the simplest quantum systems that quantum computer scientists work with.

In our experiments, we used IBM's chips, which use superconducting transmon qubits kept at around 15 millikelvins to reduce latent heat which could increase noise and decoherence [9]. The physical qubit is composed of two niobium/aluminium superconductors separated by a barrier (also known as a Josephson junction), whose state is determined by the tunnelling of superconducting Cooper pairs. This creates areas of no charge ($|0\rangle$) and excess charge ($|1\rangle$). It is worth mentioning that the potentials of several other forms of qubits are being realized at this time, utilizing photons, quantum dots and electrons, each with their unique scalability, error, and coherence time issues.

11.3.2 OpenQASM

OpenQASM is an imperative programming language for describing quantum circuits. It can describe universal quantum computing using the circuit model, measurement-based model, and near-term quantum computing experiments [1]. We will not be talking about OpenQASM in detail since its specifications would be outside the scope of this chapter. Although, we will touch on some distinctions between the quantum circuit and measurement-based quantum computing models. As you are likely familiar with, the quantum circuit model begins with an initialized register of known values which undergo a sequence of gates and measurements to perform a computation. In contrast, a computation in the measurement-based model (also known as the one-way quantum computing model) begins with a register of entangled qubits, which undergo single-qubit measurements whose classical values serve as input for further single-qubit measurements. Due to this model's use of measurement, a quantum computer using it is irreversible, hence the name one-way [10].

11.3.3 Qiskit Aer Provider and Visualization

The experiments reported below were developed using IBM Quantum (IBM Q) resources, which are accessible on the cloud. The experiments were implemented in Qiskit, which is a Python tool provided by IBM Q. The IBM Q system translates Qiskit to OpenQASM to run the circuits on their devices, or *backends*.

At the time of experimenting, IBM Q offered several backends of various sizes (up to 16 qubits) for free use.[5] We ran our experiments on IBM Q's quantum simulators (Qiskit Aer's QasmSimulator backend[6]) and quantum hardware backends.

Qiskit offers many built-in methods to work with and present data throughout experimentations, most of which make use of the Matplotlib package. Some notable ones used here were plot_histogram, plot_bloch_multivector, and circuit drawer for easily plotting data, visually representing Bloch sphere states for each qubit, and outputting circuit representations of algorithms, respectively.

To visualize the circuits, we also use Quirk [6], a drag-and-drop quantum circuit simulator, which is very useful for manipulating and exploring small quantum circuits. Quirk's visual style is intuitive and displays updates in real-time as one changes the circuit.

11.3.4 System's Flowchart

The flow chart shown in Fig. 11.1 shows the architecture of our experimental system. It depicts the iterative process to find the top n frequencies in an audio file used as an input. Here, n is a count of how many top frequencies are to be detected. It can involve simulator-based or real-device-based execution to debug the Python code used to build the Quantum Fourier Transform circuit.

Once the simulator executes without errors and can output results for small single-frequency audio files in Wav format, the same code can be used to submit a multi-frequency audio file such as a live sound signal or a recording to a real device.

Figure 11.2 shows a QFT circuit using 8-qubits, implemented in Quirk; the qubits are ordered from top to bottom. A Hadamard gate is applied to superpose each qubit with the next one, followed by successive fractional phase shifts for $\frac{\pi}{(n-1)}$ pulses, where n is the remaining number of qubits in any QFT circuit after each phase shift is applied to a given qubit.

Once all n qubits are subjected to this set of gates, swaps are applied, and observations are taken for the final state of each qubit. Quirk is useful to visualise circuits; it displays an animation to view the phase shifts, as the input traverses along the circuit.

---

[5] In testing, we used the ibmqx2, ibmq_quito, and ibmq_16_melbourne systems. At the time of writing, IBMQ freely offers Falcon and Canary processors which can utilize up to 5 qubits.

[6] This is now a legacy backend, please refer to Qiskit Aer Provider documentation for current API information https://qiskit.org/documentation/apidoc/aer_provider.html.

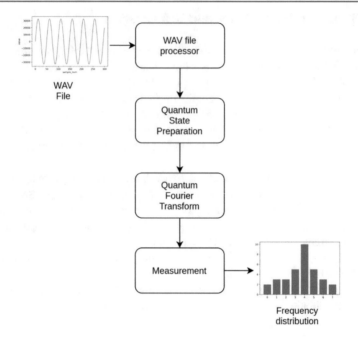

Fig. 11.1 System's flow chart

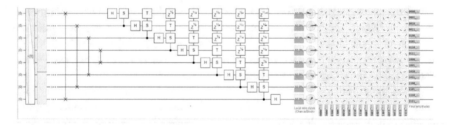

Fig. 11.2 A QFT circuit for eight qubits visualized with Quirk

11.3.5 Experimental Design

The aim of the experiments is to use QFT determine the top five frequencies in two monophonic audio files: a 900 Hz single frequency sinewave audio file lasting for 5 s and a 2 min, 54 s long audio sample from one of the Bach's *Six Cello Concertos* (BWV-1007, Prelude). Both files have a sample rate of 44.1 kHz and bit depth of 16 bits, though the concerto is dual channel, which doubles its bitrate.

Each audio file was run on simulation and hardware IBM Q backends, with varying counts of qubits. Due to limited space, we report below the results from the experiments using four, eight and twelve qubits. An example of a QFT circuit for four qubits, implemented in Qiskit is shown in Fig. 11.3.

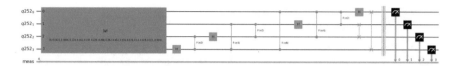

Fig. 11.3 A QFT circuit using four qubits

11.4   Results

11.4.1   Experiments with the Aer Simulation Backend

11.4.1.1   Simulated QFT of Audio with a Single 900 Hz Sinewave Using Four Qubits

Figure 11.4 is a plot of the first 16 values of a 900 Hz sine wave signal and Fig. 11.5 shows the probability distribution for QFT of audio with a single 900 Hz frequency using four qubits with 8192 shots.

With four qubits, the probability distribution is indicating a high likelihood of a single frequency, which is accurate since the input does have a single frequency. More specifically, the top five frequencies detected are as follows: 2756, 5512, 8268, 11025 and 16537 Hz. The respective probabilities distribution was calculated as 0.13, 0.023, 0.011, 0.005, 0.004. The peak is at 2756 Hz.

In this case, 4 qubits do not provide enough computational space to properly calculate the Fourier transform. This is fairly evident from the value plot not even being able to encode a full period of the sine wave and the QFT frequency resolution in Fig. 11.5 being much higher than 900 Hz.

Fig. 11.4 The first 16 samples of a 900 Hz sine wave signal

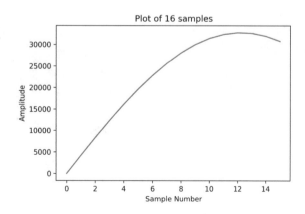

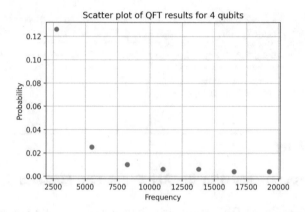

Fig. 11.5 Probability distribution from a four-qubits QFT applied to a single 900 Hz wav file

11.4.1.2 Simulated QFT of Audio with a Single 900 Hz Sinewave Using Eight Qubits

Figure 11.6 shows the plot of the first 256 samples of the sine waveform and Fig. 11.7 shows the obtained probability distribution for QFT of the single 900 Hz frequency using eight qubits and 8192 shots.

With eight qubits, the probability distribution showed a distinctive peak under 1000 Hz. The top five frequencies detected are as follows: 861 Hz, 1033 Hz, 689 Hz, 1205 Hz, and 516 Hz with probabilities: 0.82, 0.074, 0.029, 0.017, and 0.009 respectively.

In the case of eight qubits, Fig. 11.7 indicates good waveform depiction and peak frequency indication using 256 samples.

Fig. 11.6 Plotting 256 samples of a 900 Hz sine wave

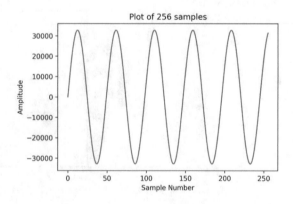

Fig. 11.7 Probability distribution from an eight-qubit QFT applied to a single 900 Hz

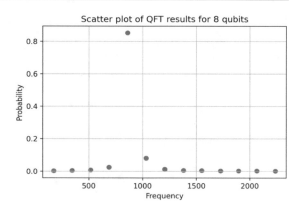

11.4.1.3 Simulated QFT of Audio with a Single 900 Hz Sinewave Using Twelve Qubits

Figure 11.8 shows a plot of the first 4096 samples of the signals and Fig. 11.9 shows the obtained probability distribution for QFT of audio with a single 900 Hz frequency using twelve qubits with 8192 shots.

With twelve qubits, the probability distribution shows a distinct peak within a 20 Hz range around 900 Hz. The top five frequencies detected are as follows: 904, 893, 915, 882, and 925 Hz. Their respective probabilities are: 0.563, 0.262, 0.051, 0.039, and 0.016.

For twelve qubits, a much higher sample count was used. As a result, the waveform is captured accurately but shows a higher gradient due to the image being scaled to fit the 4096 samples (Fig. 11.8). Regardless, the sharp peak around 900 Hz (Fig. 11.9) indicates an increasing accuracy of the frequency being detected.

The above experiments give a good indication that if we input an audio file consisting of several different frequencies, then we may have consistent results that would yield top n frequencies from the spectrum present, as well as capture a waveform with higher accuracy as the qubit count increases.

Fig. 11.8 Plot of a 900 Hz frequency wav file encoded into twelve qubits

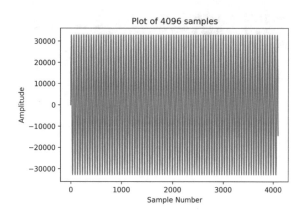

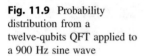

Fig. 11.9 Probability distribution from a twelve-qubits QFT applied to a 900 Hz sine wave

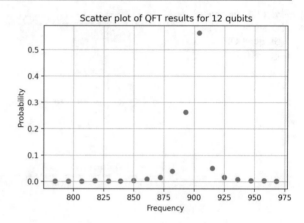

In the next set of simulations, we used an audio file with a guitar rendition of Bach's *Cello Suite* (BWV-1007 Prelude). This file was generated using the software Ableton Live Studio, from a MIDI file of Bach's piece.

11.4.1.4 Simulated QFT of Bach's Music Using Four Qubits

As with the single sinewave experiments presented above, we carried out QFT analyses using 4, 8, and 12 qubits to detect the top five frequencies present in the sound spectrum. Figure 11.10 plots the first 16 samples of our audio rendering of Bach's music and Fig. 11.11 shows the obtained probability distribution for a four-qubits QFT of 2 min, 54 s long excerpt from the audio rendering of Bach's music with 8192 shots (Figs. 11.12 and 11.13).

The top 5 detected frequencies are: 2756, 5512, 8268, 11025 and 13781 Hz. The respective probabilities were calculated to be: 0.207, 0.048, 0.021, 0.014 and 0.01.

Note that there was not any waveform accurately depicted in this experiment. The value plot Fig. 11.10 only contains 16 samples, which we know was not enough to accurately depict even a simple 900 Hz sine wave, so we don't expect any notable results from this exercise.

Fig. 11.10 Plot of 16 samples of our Bach music file

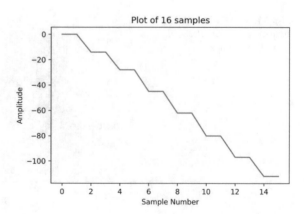

Fig. 11.11 Probability distribution from a four-qubits QFT applied to an excerpt of Bach's music

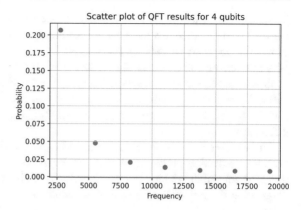

Fig. 11.12 Plot of 256 samples of our Bach music file

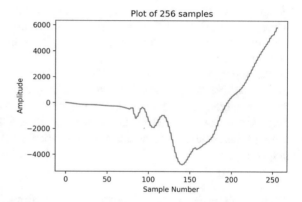

Fig. 11.13 Probability distribution from an eight-qubits QFT applied to an excerpt of Bach's music

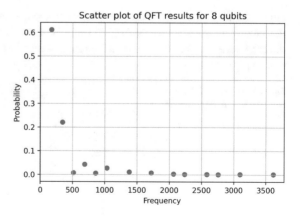

11.4.1.5 Simulated QFT of Bach's Music Using Eight Qubits

Figure 11.16 plots the results of the measurements from 8192 shots and Fig. 11.17 shows the obtained probability distribution for an eight qubits QFT of 2 min and 54 s long excerpt from the audio rendering of Bach's music.

In contrast to the previous experiment, the value plot (Fig. 11.16) for this eight qubit experiment is promising. We can begin to see actual details regarding the signals form, which means that we can begin to extract useful frequency information.

The top five detected frequencies are 172, 344, 689, 1033, and 1378 Hz. The obtained respective probabilities are as follows: 0.611, 0.221, 0.043, 0.028, and 0.011. Eight qubits yielded good results, with 2 distinct states (172 and 344 Hz) dominating the rest of the frequency probabilities.

11.4.1.6 Simulated QFT of Bach's Music Using Twelve Qubits

Figure 11.14 plots the relevant signal being encoded into our 12 qubit exercise while Fig. 11.20 shows the obtained probability distribution for a twelve qubits QFT of a 2 min and 54 s long excerpt from the audio rendering of Bach's music with 8192 shots (Fig. 11.15).

The top five frequencies are: 75 Hz, 32 Hz, 107 Hz, 43 Hz, and 118 Hz and their respective probabilities are: 0.468, 0.212, 0.076, 0.06, and 0.034. Very good results emerged again from the twelve qubits simulated run, with 3 or 4 notable frequency peaks being detected. The peaks at 32 and 43 Hz may correspond to a central value, which we do not have (in this experiment) the frequency resolution to pinpoint.

11.4.2 Experiments Using IBM Q's Hardware Backend

Due to ibmq system access changing between the beginning of experimentation and the time of writing, we are unable to replicate experiments of higher-order on real device backends and only have left archived results from eight qubit and twelve

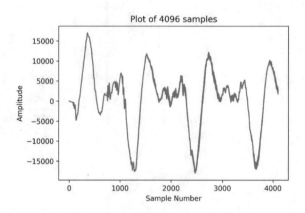

Fig. 11.14 Plot of 4096 samples of our Bach music file

Fig. 11.15 Probability distribution from a twelve-qubit QFT applied to an excerpt from Bach's cello suite

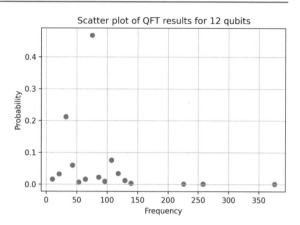

qubit experiments. Of those archived, we will only present the eight qubit QFT of Bach, since it is the most cohesive. In total, we will present 3 experiments running on real hardware: four qubit QFT of 900 Hz, four qubit QFT of Bach, and eight qubit QFT of Bach. All in all, we used the ibmqx2, ibmq_manila, ibmq_quito, and ibmq_16_melbourne backends. They yielded mixed results. The results were erratic at best. This was most probably due to noise and errors of the backends that were available for this work at the time. Most often, the cycle time was less than the time required to execute the complete number of gates on a given count of qubits in the quantum circuit. This resulted in incomplete jobs that yielded partial or no results at all.

With four and twelve qubits, the probability distribution on each state was low or at times unavailable for higher qubit counts, meaning that the certainty of the state observations was not likely to be true or did not execute successfully on the backend available.

Still, it is important to report these results here to highlight the fact that general access to robust quantum hardware is still problematic at the time of writing.

11.4.2.1 QFT of Audio with a Single 900 Hz Sinewave Using a Four-Qubits Hardware

Figure 11.16 shows a plot of the first 16 samples of the same 900 Hz sine wave and Fig. 11.17 shows the probability distribution for the QFT of the 900 Hz wave file using four qubits with 8192 shots.

The top 5 detected frequencies in this experiment are: 8268 Hz, 2756 Hz, 19293 Hz, 13781 Hz, and 11025 Hz and their probabilities: 0.182, 0.172, 0.159, 0.138, and 0.118 respectively. Even with the notable peak at 2756 Hz, similar to the simulated experiment earlier on, it is not the only one nor the largest. The real device noise contributed significantly, leaving us with effectively random data, negating any ability to make assumptions about the frequency spectrum of the signal.

Fig. 11.16 Probability
distribution from a four-qubits
QFT applied to a single
900 Hz, using a hardware
backend. This is the same as
Fig. 11.4

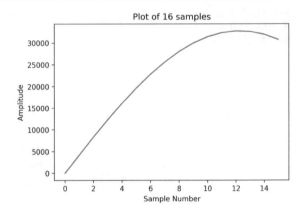

Fig. 11.17 Probability
distribution from a four-qubits
QFT applied to the 900 Hz
sine wave using a hardware
backend

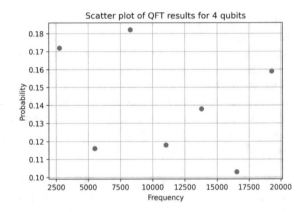

11.4.2.2   QFT of Bach's Music Using a Four-Qubits Hardware

Figure 11.18 plots the first 16 samples of our Bach cello concerto wav file and
Fig. 11.19 shows the probability distribution for QFT of Bach's music using four
qubits with 8192 shots.

The top 5 detected frequencies were: 11025 Hz, 5512 Hz, 2756 Hz, 16537 Hz,
and 8268 Hz and their probabilities: 0.176, 0.164, 0.128, 0.098, and 0.085
respectively. Similar to the results from our previous experiment, the four-qubit
QFT running on real hardware also produced seemingly random results for the
Bach cello concerto.

11.4.2.3   QFT of Bach's Music Using an Eight-Qubits on Real
Hardware

Figure 11.20 plots 256 samples of our Bach cello concerto file and Fig. 11.21
shows the probability distribution for QFT of Bach's music using eight qubits with
8192 shots.

Fig. 11.18 Plot of 16 samples of our Bach music file. This is the same as Fig. 11.10

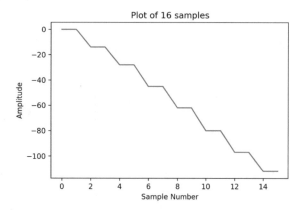

Fig. 11.19 Probability distribution from a four-qubit QFT applied to Bach's cello concerto using a hardware backend

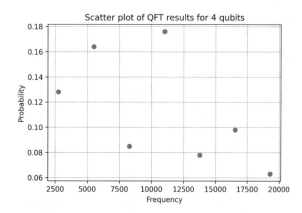

As stated at the beginning of this section, this experiment is a presentation of archived material, so Fig. 11.21 is more difficult to interpret than past probability distributions.

The top 5 frequencies are: 172, 344, 689, 1033, and 1378 Hz. The probabilities are unnormalized, but you can see qualitatively that we were able to achieve a probability distribution much like the simulated experiment done earlier. We will consider this run a success.

11.5 Discussion

Based on the results shown above, we can conclude the following from our experiments using the IBM Quantum resources that are freely available through the cloud as of the first half of 2021: simulator results were much more stable and repeatable but had a very limited number of qubits available to experiment with.

Fig. 11.20 Plot of 256 samples of our Bach music file. This is the same as Fig. 11.12

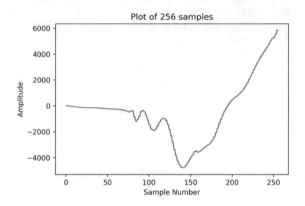

Fig. 11.21 Probability distribution from an eight-qubit QFT applied to Bach's cello concerto using a hardware backend

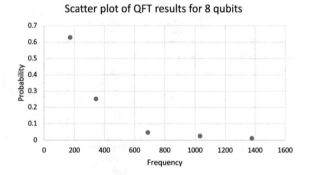

Results from hardware backends were unreliable with higher qubit counts to the point of complete failure in completing the required QFT execution using phase gates for fractional π rotations (Figs. 11.2 and 11.3).

Still, for both sets of results (single and multi-frequency audio file inputs), for completed executions, the top five frequencies were detected proving that this approach may be a quick way to detect top frequencies in any input audio file. This type of frequency detection can be a very useful feature in certain types of audio engineering applications. Below are two use cases that could benefit from faster QFT based top frequency detection in audio inputs.

11.5.1 Application for Final Mixdown in the Recording Studio

The ability to detect frequencies in an audio file is useful in the studio for final mixdown editing of recordings. In multitrack mixes, resonance driven amplification occurs unpredictably at times when two or more tracks happen to have frequencies that are close to each other but from different instruments.

In such cases, having the ability to detect top frequencies for audio clips taken from the mix and sent to a Quantum Frequency Detection job can return the offending frequency very quickly, allowing for rapid isolation and equalization of the individual tracks so that the resonant amplification is controlled before it results in unpleasant audio being heard.

Digital Audio Workstation software used in studios could have such an application integrated into the workflow with automation enabling features so that there is rapid analysis and suppression of offensive resonant frequencies when multitrack mixdown is done.

11.5.2 Application for Active Acoustics in Auditoriums

Live music performance venues can benefit from active frequency detection using live microphone placement during soundcheck as a pre-performance optimization of the audio quality delivered using recorded music from the performing group. Such pre-optimization can lead to easier dead zone elimination or over-equalization elimination to yield a balanced audible sound spectrum in local spots within the audience during a live performance of a concert. This can result in a more pleasing and enjoyable auditory experience across the width and depth of the audience in the auditorium. Typically, static speaker equalization and placement result in a static sound field in terms of loudness and audio spectrum during a concert. However, with active amplitude and frequency equalization, a balanced sound can be delivered using live quantum frequency detection to rapidly correct the sound field throughout the audience, reducing the decrease in the audio quality further away from the performance stage.

Multitrack feeds into the "front of house" mixing console can be connected to automatic quantum frequency detection execution using an application built into the console that would then be used to detect signals for each microphone placed across the performance venue compared to the remaining microphones to equalize the audio spectrum so that flat response approximation is delivered to all locations where microphones are placed to monitor the audio.

A closed-loop active response audio control system can also be developed with active movement of the dampening treatments to further improve the flat response characteristics of the performance venue for a specific type of music concert. Such a system would require very fast optimization once the quantum frequency detection executes, so quantum optimization, as well as quantum machine learning, would need to be coupled to the top frequencies detected to deliver control system commands for spatial and temporal changes to the damper controls within the auditorium walls and ceiling.

11.5.3 Application for Cardiac Anomaly Detection and Waveform Analysis

Much of the advantage of QFT over classical Fourier transform can be useful in such scenarios when large high-performance computing systems must be used for one-off custom calculations requiring engineering skills that are not easily developed. For example, when using classical fast Fourier transform (FFT) for cardiac waveform signal analysis, the operations require high-performance computing platforms that must be managed and administered painstakingly to deliver research outputs that inform cardiac anomaly detection. These calculations often take a time that is much longer than can be afforded for life-saving consequences in cardiac patients. Should QFT and quantum machine learning be applied here, it may yield a much faster turnaround time for decision support that can become meaningful in terms of real-time lifesaving consequences for cardiac patients.

11.6 Conclusion

As shown in this chapter, quantum frequency detection shows much promise in advancing recording quality in studios as well as delivering balanced auditory experiences at performance venues. There may be other applications that can be developed for acoustic dynamics in vehicle simulations as well. For example, acoustic engineering simulation within automotive cabin space is a field where finite element analysis is used to conduct simulation engineering studies in engine noise cancellation as well as enhancing musical acoustics for sound systems within cabins. Active interior dampening can result in tuneable cabin acoustics using quantum frequency detection to drive amplitude and frequency calibration in a dynamic instead of static manner, with the acoustics in the cabin being actively tuned to engine noise variation at various speeds of travel. Such active tuning can be only accomplished using a quantum frequency detector running in the vehicle using a quantum computer that can perform at ambient temperature and accept audio signals from microphonic detectors placed in the cabin. Further research needs to be focused on developing such applications only after the production scale quantum computing capabilities that allow noise and error-free, miniaturized quantum compute platforms are available to take on rapid workflows requiring fast quantum computing results.

The approach described in this chapter requires further work in terms of integration within applications that serve specific use cases, such as the ones described above to create hybrid applications that use classical computation surrounding quantum computation as a tightly integrated system.

References

1. Cross, A. W., Bishop, L. S., Smolin, J. A., & Gambetta, J. M. (2020). *OpenQASM Live Specification.* https://qiskit.github.io/openqasm/intro.html. Accessed 10 May 2022.
2. Diggle, P. (1985). A Kernel method for smoothing point process data. *Journal of the Royal Statistical Society: Series C, 34*(2), 138–147.
3. Hales, L., & Hallgren, S. (2000). An improved quantum fourier transform algorithm and applications. In *Proceedings 41st Annual Symposium on Foundations of Computer Science* (pp. 515–525).
4. IBM. (2021). *Quantum Fourier Transform.* https://qiskit.org/textbook/ch-algorithms/quantum-fourier-transform.html#8.2-General-QFT-Function. Accessed 10 May 2022.
5. Nielsen, M. A., & Chuang, I. L. (2000). *Quantum Computation and Quantum Information.* Cambridge University Press.
6. Quirk. (2022). *How to use Quirk.* https://github.com/Strilanc/Quirk/wiki/How-to-use-Quirk. Accessed 10 May 2022.
7. Smith, J. O. (2007). *Discrete-Time Fourier Transform (DTFT).* http://ccrma.stanford.edu/~jos/mdft/Fourier_Theorems_DFT.html. Accessed 10 May 2022.
8. Smith, S. W. (1997). The scientist and engineer's guide to digital signal processing. In S. W. Smith (Ed.), *The Scientist and Engineer's Guide to Digital Signal Processing* (pp. 141–161). California Technical Publishing.
9. The qubit. (2021). *IBM Quantum Composer.* https://quantum-computing.ibm.com/composer/docs/iqx/guide/the-qubit. Accessed 10 May 2022.
10. Walther, P., Resch, K. J., Rudolph, T., Schenk, E., Weinfurter, H., Vedral, V., & Zeilinger, A. (2005). Experimental one-way quantum computing. *Nature, 434*(7030), 169–176.
11. Wolfram, E. W. (2021). *Fourier Series.* https://mathworld.wolfram.com/FourierSeries.html. Accessed 10 May 2022.
12. Young, P. (2019). *The Quantum Fourier Transform and a Comparison with the Fast Fourier Transform.* Peter Young Physics USCS. https://young.physics.ucsc.edu/150/QFT-FFT.pdf. Accessed 10 May 2022.

Sing and Measure: Sound as Voice as Quanta

12

Maria Mannone and Davide Rocchesso

Abstract

The universal concept of a "music of the spheres" traverses the history of philosophy, science and art, from Pythagoras to Kepler and beyond. In modern times, a sphere in three dimensions—the Bloch sphere—is used to illustrate the state of a qubit, the basic unit of quantum information. On the same spherical surface, the fundamental components of voice production can be located, so that any utterance can be seen as the evolution of a unit two-dimensional vector having complex coefficients. Indeed, any sound can be analyzed and decomposed into overlapping sinusoidal components, broadband noises, and impulsive transients, which in turn can be associated to fundamental means of vocal sound production, such as phonation, turbulence, and slow myoelastic vibrations or pulses. The quantum sphere can be made to sing the universal sound.

M. Mannone (✉)
Department of Engineering, University of Palermo, Palermo, Italy
e-mail: mariacaterina.mannone@unipa.it

M. Mannone
Dipartimento di Scienze Ambientali, Informatica e Statistica (DAIS) and European Centre for Living Technology (ECLT), Ca' Foscari University of Venice, Venice, Italy
e-mail: maria.mannone@unive.it

M. Mannone · D. Rocchesso
Department of Mathematics and Computer Sciences, University of Palermo, Palermo, Italy
e-mail: davide.rocchesso@unipa.it

© The Author(s), under exclusive license to Springer Nature Switzerland AG 2022
E. R Miranda (ed.), *Quantum Computer Music*,
https://doi.org/10.1007/978-3-031-13909-3_12

12.1 Sound of The Quantum Sphere

The universal concept of the music of the spheres traverses the history of philosophy, science and art, from Pythagoras to Kepler and beyond. In modern times, a sphere in three dimensions—the Bloch sphere—is used to illustrate the state of a qubit, the basic unit of quantum information. On the same spherical surface, the fundamental components of voice production can be located [22], so that any utterance can be seen as the evolution of a unit two-dimensional vector having complex coefficients. Indeed, any sound can be analyzed and decomposed into overlapping sinusoidal components, broadband noises, and impulsive transients [23], which in turn can be associated with fundamental means of vocal sound production, such as phonation, turbulence, and slow myoelastic vibrations or pulses [8]. The quantum sphere can be made to sing the universal sound.

The human voice is embodied sound and, as such, it is a probe humans have to explore the sonic environment. Vocal imitations are used effectively by humans [13, 19] to communicate sounds from an early age, well before articulating words (Fig. 12.1). During the first artistic avant-garde, Italian futurism, vocal imitations and ono-matopoeic words have risen to the rank of poetry. In the work by Filippo Tommaso Marinetti (1876–1944), the words *Zang Tumb Tumb* imitate motor and war noises [16]. In the poem *La fontana malata* (The sick fountain), Aldo Palazzeschi used the words *Clof, clop, cloch* [20] to mimic the intermittent flow of water and the noise of falling drops. In a sense, onomatopoeia gives poetical dignity to vocal imitations. From a sound design perspective, vocal imitations give embodied sound imagination to the sound designer [7].

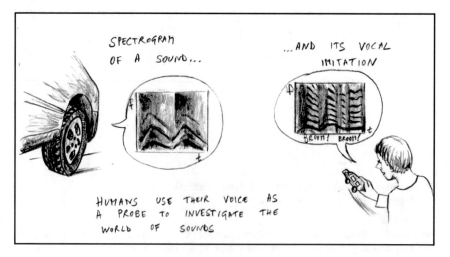

Fig. 12.1 Left: a car and its spectrogram; right: a kid producing a vocal imitation, and the corresponding spectrogram. Voice is catching essential features of the original sound. Drawing by M. Mannone

The Fourier formalism has been, for over two centuries, the main mathematical tool to investigate sound [11,12]. Fourier-related visual representations such as the spectrogram are everyday tools for audio scientists and engineers. However, this formalism is not very useful in everyday communications between laypersons, as it is far less immediate than vocal imitations. It is a fact that vocal imitations can be effective despite having a Fourier representation that is largely different from that of the reference sound, thus indicating that invariants must be looked for in a few features, such as the direction of sinusoidal glides, or the rate of slow pulsations, that characterize a variety of sound categories differently [14].

Research in phonetics of vocal imitations has shown that there are three principal classes of vocal production mechanisms: phonation, turbulence, and supraglottal myoelastic vibrations [8]. In phonation, the source is in the vocal folds. In turbulence, the source is in chaotic motion of inhaled or exhaled air. Supraglottal myoelastic vibrations include several kinds of low-frequency oscillations, pulse trains, or isolated pulses generated with different parts of the vocal apparatus, such as the lips or the tongue. We propose extending the adoption of this three-fold description of vocal sound production, called the *phon*, to the general universe of sound. Indeed, any audio recording and its spectrogram can be decomposed into sines, noise, and transients [4,23], thus making embodiment in terms of voice-related components practically possible.

The components of phonation, turbulence and myoelastic pulsation are often combined in superposition at the source, during vocal production. Human hearing, on the other hand, measures sources in superposition or mixes of sources through their acoustic manifestation, and auditory attention can collapse on different specific components at different moments in time. These observations suggest the possible quantum-theoretical modeling of sound phenomena, as superpositions of basis states or as mixed states, with temporal evolutions based on unitary dynamics and a context-dependent field of forces.

The idea that quantum theory may apply to sound and music phenomena date back to Gabor, who imagined sound analysis and synthesis based on acoustical quanta [10], or wavelets. His work is at the root of granular approaches to sound and music [21]. More recent studies in mathematics and music propose quantum modeling. For example, tonal attractions have been modeled as metaphorical forces [2], and quantum parallelism has been proposed to model music cognition [6]. Quantum superposition has been proposed to model the perceptual ambiguity between ascending and descending musical intervals of Shepard tones [9]. Quantum computing has been considered to control sound synthesizers and computer-generated music [5,17,18,24].

At the intersection of sound, voice, and quanta there are the core ideas of Quantum Vocal Theory of Sound (QVTS) [15,22]. It is a quantum-based approach to sound analysis, processing and synthesis, using human voice as a probe to investigate the world of sound. The chapter summarizes the basic formalism of QVTS in Sect. 12.2. In Sect. 12.3 we analyze a polyphonic vocal improvisation in the framework of QVTS, showing example evolutions of pure or mixed phons, that can be used to produce synthetic sound articulations that somehow shadow the original superposition or mixture. Infinitely many evolutions are indeed possible, each exploring one of the possible universes that are captured by a quantum listening process of repeated measurement and collapse.

12.2 The Quantum Vocal Theory of Sound

The Quantum Vocal Theory of Sound has been developed by drawing an analogy between vocal sound and the spin of a particle, both evolving in time under the effect of contextual forces [22]. In the QVTS, the three axes of the phonetic space are:

- z: phonation, periodic component with a pitch;
- x: turbulence, noise component with a spectral brightness;
- y: myoelasticity, impulsive component with a repetition rate.

Such three-dimensional space is sketched in Fig. 12.2, and the unit-radius sphere is called the Bloch sphere.

12.2.1 Phon and Measurement in the Computational Basis

In quantum computing, the computational basis is arranged along the z-axis, expressed as $|0\rangle, |1\rangle$. In QVTS, the z-axis represents phonation, $|0\rangle$ corresponds to pitch-up $|u\rangle$, and $|1\rangle$ corresponds to pitch-down $|u\rangle$. We can borrow the quantum formalism

Fig. 12.2 The Bloch sphere adapted to QVTS, to represent the phon space. Hand-made figure by D. Rocchesso

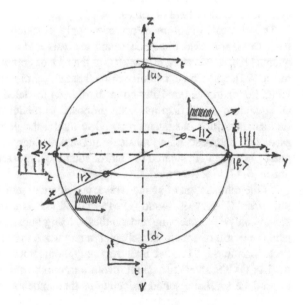

of Pauli matrices, projectors, and state superpositions. In particular, the pitch-up and pitch-down basis vectors are the eigenvectors of the Pauli matrix $\sigma_z = \begin{pmatrix} 1 & 0 \\ 0 & -1 \end{pmatrix}$:

$$\sigma_z \ket{u} = \ket{u}, \quad \sigma_z \ket{d} = -\ket{d}.$$

We can define the projectors

$$\Pi_u = \ket{u}\bra{u}, \quad \Pi_d = \ket{d}\bra{d},$$

and we can describe the generic phon as a superposition of pitch-up and pitch-down:

$$\ket{\psi} = \alpha_u \ket{u} + \alpha_d \ket{d}, \tag{12.1}$$

where $\alpha_u = \braket{u|\psi}$ and $\alpha_d = \braket{d|\psi}$ are the probability amplitudes, or complex numbers whose squares give the probability to measure pitch up and pitch down, respectively. The expectation value of pitch measurement is given by $\langle \sigma_z \rangle := \braket{\psi|\sigma_z|\psi}$.

12.2.2 Phon and Measurement in the Hadamard Basis

In quantum computing, the Hadamard basis is obtained from the computational basis through the application of a Hadamard gate: $H = \frac{1}{\sqrt{2}} \begin{pmatrix} 1 & 1 \\ 1 & -1 \end{pmatrix}$:

$$H \ket{0} = \frac{\ket{0} + \ket{1}}{\sqrt{2}}, \quad H \ket{1} = \frac{\ket{0} - \ket{1}}{\sqrt{2}}.$$

The Hadamard basis is indicated as $\ket{+}$, $\ket{-}$, and it is along the x-axis. In QVTS, the x-axis represents turbulence, and the basis is indicated as $\ket{r}$, $\ket{l}$, standing for high-frequency (right) and low-frequency (left) turbulence centroids, respectively. Making use of the Pauli matrix $\sigma_x = \begin{pmatrix} 0 & 1 \\ 1 & 0 \end{pmatrix}$, we have:

$$\sigma_x \ket{r} = \ket{r}, \quad \sigma_x \ket{l} = -\ket{l}.$$

Projectors and state superpositions are:

$$\Pi_r = \ket{r}\bra{r}, \quad \Pi_l = \ket{l}\bra{l}; \quad \ket{r} = \frac{1}{\sqrt{2}}(\ket{u} + \ket{d}), \quad \ket{l} = \frac{1}{\sqrt{2}}(\ket{u} - \ket{d}).$$

12.2.3 Phon and Measurement in the Complex Basis

Finally, there is the y-axis or the complex basis. In QVTS, the y-axis indicates myoelasticity, and the basis is indicated by $\ket{f}$, $\ket{s}$, with faster and slower (slow) myoelastic pulsations, respectively. The action of Pauli matrix $\sigma_y = \begin{pmatrix} 0 & -i \\ i & 0 \end{pmatrix}$ is:

$$\sigma_y \ket{f} = \ket{f}, \quad \sigma_y \ket{s} = -\ket{s},$$

and we have:

$$\Pi_f = \ket{f}\bra{f}, \quad \Pi_s = \ket{s}\bra{s}; \quad \ket{f} = \frac{1}{\sqrt{2}}(\ket{u} + i\ket{d}), \quad \ket{s} = \frac{1}{\sqrt{2}}(\ket{u} - i\ket{d}).$$

12.2.4 Non-commutativity

Given a vocal audio file, measuring phonation first and then the turbulence is not yielding the same result as doing the opposite. This can be easily shown with commutators. In fact, considering that $\langle r|u \rangle$ is a scalar, $\langle u|r \rangle$ is its complex conjugate, and that $|u\rangle \langle r|$ is generally non-Hermitian, we obtain a non-null commutator:

$$[M_r, M_u] = |r\rangle \langle r|u\rangle \langle u| - |u\rangle \langle u|r\rangle \langle r| =$$
$$= \langle r|u\rangle |r\rangle \langle u| - \langle u|r\rangle |u\rangle \langle r| \neq 0. \tag{12.2}$$

Thus, non-commutativity, a key-topic ingredient in quantum theory, is also present in QVTS [15,22].

12.2.5 The Density Operator

If the state can be expressed as a linear combination of basis vectors with complex coefficients as in Eq. 12.1, then the density matrix is

$$\rho = |\psi\rangle \langle \psi|,$$

and the state is called *pure*. If there is epistemic uncertainty about the state, so that it can be expressed as a probabilistic combination of possible states, each weighted by a probability coefficient p_j, then the density matrix is

$$\rho = \sum_j p_j |\psi_j\rangle \langle \psi_j|, \tag{12.3}$$

and the state is called *mixed*.

An ensemble of sound sources can be inspected and modeled through the density operator. We can make the pure states to correspond to the upper or the lower of the most salient pitches, and the completely mixed state corresponds to noise. Let p_u and p_d be the probabilities of $|u\rangle$ and $|d\rangle$, respectively, as encoded in the mixed state. A schematic re-mix can be obtained by superimposing the following ingredients: a noise with amplitude $\min(p_u, p_d)$, an upper pitch weighted by $p_u - \min(p_u, p_d)$, and a lower pitch weighted by $p_d - \min(p_u, p_d)$.

12.2.6 Time Evolution

In quantum theory, a general state evolves in time t according to

$$\rho(t) = \mathbf{U}^\dagger(t_0, t)\rho(t_0)\mathbf{U}(t_0, t). \tag{12.4}$$

Here we are not making any assumption on states (mixed or pure), and the only assumption on the time operator $\mathbf{U}$ is that it is unitary, i.e., $\mathbf{U}^\dagger\mathbf{U} = \mathbf{I}$, with $\mathbf{I}$ the identity matrix, and that it depends only on t and t_0. Under such assumption, pure states evolve along the unit surface of the Bloch sphere, and mixed states evolve within the sphere. For a closed and isolated system, the unitary operator takes the form

$$\mathbf{U}(t_0, t) = e^{-i\mathbf{H}(t-t_0)},$$

where H is a constant matrix called the Hamiltonian. In particular, for the spin in a magnetic field, the Hamiltonian takes the form

$$\mathbf{H} = \frac{\omega}{2} \begin{bmatrix} n_z & n_x - in_y \\ n_x + in_y & -n_z \end{bmatrix}, \tag{12.5}$$

and has energy eigenvalues $E_j = \pm\frac{\omega}{2}$, with energy eigenvectors $|E_j\rangle$. However, closed and isolated systems do not exist in physical reality and, similarly, there is no such thing as an isolated sound. The phon is immersed in a time-varying sonic context, as if it was a spin in a time-varying magnetic field. We consider restoring forces in sound, coming from the local temporal sound production context, in analogy with speech co-articulation.

By considering a piece-wise time dependency, we can introduce a time-dependent yet commutative Hamiltonian:

$$H(t) = e^{-kt}\mathbf{S}, \tag{12.6}$$

where k is a damping factor governing co-articulating features, and $\mathbf{S}$ is a time-independent Hermitian matrix.

In this way, if starting with pure pitch-down at time 0, the phon at time t is be given by:

$$|\psi(t)\rangle = e^{-i\int_0^t \mathbf{H}(\tau)d\tau} |d\rangle = \mathbf{U}(0, t) |d\rangle. \tag{12.7}$$

12.3 Evolutions of a Vocal Improvisation

We give two example evolutions, one of a pure state and one of a mixed state, of a polyphonic vocal improvisation obtained through layered recordings.[1] The monophonic signal, sampled at 44100 samples/s, is analyzed through Short-Time Fourier Transform with a 2048−sample Hann window, zero-padded to 4096 samples, and hop size of 512 samples. The resulting spectrogram is reported in Fig. 12.3 (top). The Essentia library [3] is used to extract the spectral peaks, perform sinusoidal analysis, separate sines from residual noise, extract the most salient pitches and the onsets. Two bands of noise (1–2 and 2–6 kHz) are extracted from the residual. The PitchSalienceFunction() is used to extract the most salient pitches and compute their salience. The Onsets() function is used to extract the onsets, or time instants of the most relevant transients, and these are divided into two sets, based on inter-onset interval (fast if less than 200 ms). Figure 12.3 shows the first and second most salient pitches superimposed on the spectrogram (top plot) as a red and a grey line respectively, and their saliences are reported in the second plot. The third plot of Fig. 12.3 shows the high (red) and low (grey) frequency noise energies. The fourth plot shows the fast (red) and slow (grey) onsets. These lines of salient pitches, noise energies in different bands, and fast and slow pulses can be used to

---

[1] https://shorturl.at/dsBS7.

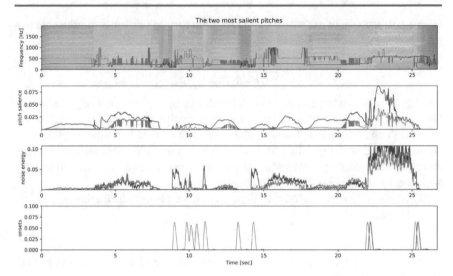

Fig. 12.3 Top plot: Spectrogram of a polyphonic vocal improvisation, overlayed with the first (red) and second (gray) most salient pitches. Second plot: Traces of the two most relevant pitch saliences. Third plot: Noise energies in the 2–6 kHz band (red) and in the 1–2 kHz band (gray). Fourth plot: Onsets with fast (red) and slow (gray) repetition rate

synthesize an abstract version of the original audio signal, a sort of skeleton that captures some of its relevant pitch, turbulence, and pulsation content.

12.3.1 Hamiltonian Evolution from Pitch-Down

The Hamiltonian represented in Eq. 12.5 is constructed by decimating and holding the values of pitch salience, noise energy, and onsets across frames:

```
decimation = 40 # PARAMETER: hold potential across frames
n_x = energyNoise1[::decimation]
n_x = np.repeat(n_x, decimation)[0:size(energyNoise1)] # turb. pot.
n_y = abs(totalOnsets1[::decimation] + totalOnsets2[::decimation])
n_y = np.repeat(n_y, decimation)[0:size(totalOnsets1)] # myo. pot.
n_z = totalSaliences1[::decimation]
n_z = np.repeat(n_z, decimation)[0:size(totalSaliences1)] # pitch pot.
S = np.array([[n_z, n_x - 1j*n_y], [n_x + 1j*n_y, -n_z]])
```

Exponential damping, as in Eq. 12.6, is introduced, and the resulting potential lines are shown in Fig. 12.4:

```
k = 0.1 # PARAMETER (damping)
et = exp(-k*np.arange(0,decimation))
et = np.tile(et,int(size(n_z)/decimation))
ett = np.pad(et,(0,size(n_z)-size(et)),'constant',constant_values=(0))
nzc = n_z*ett
nxc = n_x*ett
nyc = n_y*ett
H = np.array([[nzc, nxc - 1j*nyc], [nxc + 1j*nyc, -nzc]])
```

Fig. 12.4 Potentials for the considered improvised vocal sequence

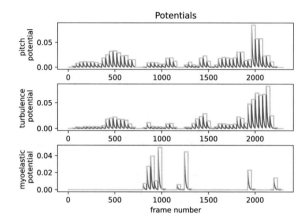

The Hamiltonian is integrated and exponentiated as in Eq. 12.7, so that, given the initial pitch-down state, all future state evolution can be computed:

```
intHc = np.cumsum(H, axis=2) # integral (cumulative sum)
Uc = intHc
for t in range(size(n_z)):
    Uc[:,:,t] = linalg.expm(-(1j)*intHc[:,:,t])
s0 = np.matrix([[0], [1]])
sT = np.zeros((2, size(n_z)), dtype=complex)
for t in range(size(n_z)):
    sT[:,[t]] = Uc[:,:,t] @ s0
```

Instead of letting the state evolve according to potentials, we can take sparse measurements and, at each measurement instant, peep the state and perform a different measurement/collapse according to how close the state is to being pitchy or turbulent. In particular, a pitch measurement is performed if the current state differs from an eigenvalue of σ_z by less than a threshold, and the collapse is to pitch-up or pitch-down based on probability amplitudes:

```
random.seed(1024) # for reproducibility
threshold = 0.3 # PARAMETER (pitchiness threshold)
hopCollapse = 20 # PARAMETER (decimation of collapses)
sigma_z = [[1, 0], [0, -1]]
sigma_x = [[0, 1], [1, 0]]
sigma_y = [[0, -1j], [1j, 0]]
traccia = zeros(size(n_z))
sbuffi1 = zeros(size(n_z))
sbuffi2 = zeros(size(n_z))
myo1 = zeros(size(n_z))
myo2 = zeros(size(n_z))
for t in range(size(totalFreqs1)):
    sdiff = norm(transpose(matrix(sT[:, t])) - \
                 sigma_z @ transpose(matrix(sT[:, t])))
    if (sdiff < threshold or sdiff > (2 - threshold)): # state is pitchy
        prob = np.square(abs(sT[0,t])) # collapse based on probability
        cstate = np.random.choice(np.arange(0, 2), p=[prob, 1-prob])
        if (cstate == 0):
            if (t%hopCollapse == 0):
                sT[0,t] = ONE # 1.0
                sT[1,t] = ZERO # 0.0
            traccia[t] = totalFreqs1[t] if (totalFreqs1[t] >= totalFreqs2[t])\
                                        else totalFreqs2[t]
        else:
```

```
        if (t%hopCollapse == 0):
            sT[0,t] = ZERO # 0.0
            sT[1,t] = ONE # 1.0
        traccia[t] = totalFreqs1[t] if (totalFreqs1[t] < totalFreqs2[t])\
                                    else totalFreqs2[t]
else: # state is turbulent or myo
    sdiff = norm(transpose(matrix(sT[:, t])) - \
                            sigma_y @ transpose(matrix(sT[:, t])))
    if (sdiff < threshold or sdiff > (2 - threshold)): # state is myo
        prob = abs(np.square(np.dot(sT[:,t],[1/sqrt(2),1j/sqrt(2)])))
        cstate = np.random.choice(np.arange(0, 2), p=[prob, 1-prob])
        if (cstate == 0):
            if (t%hopCollapse == 0): # collapse to |f>
                sT[0,t] = 1/sqrt(2)
                sT[1,t] = (1j)/sqrt(2)
            myo1[t] = totalOnsets1[t]
            traccia[t] = 20 # to highlight transients
        else:
            if (t%hopCollapse == 0): # collapse to |s>
                sT[0,t] = 1/sqrt(2)
                sT[1,t] = -(1j)/sqrt(2)
            myo2[t] = totalOnsets2[t]
            traccia[t] = 20
    else:                   # state is turbulent
        prob = abs(np.square(np.dot(sT[:,t],[1/sqrt(2),1/sqrt(2)])))
        cstate = np.random.choice(np.arange(0, 2), p=[prob, 1-prob])
        if (cstate == 0):
            if (t%hopCollapse == 0): # collapse to |r>
                sT[0,t] = 1/sqrt(2)
                sT[1,t] = 1/sqrt(2)
            sbuffi1[t] = energyNoise1[t]
        else:
            if (t%hopCollapse == 0): # collapse to |l>
                sT[0,t] = 1/sqrt(2)
                sT[1,t] = -1/sqrt(2)
            sbuffi2[t] = energyNoise2[t]
```

In Fig. 12.5 (top), the results of pitch measurement are reported as a green dotted line and superimposed on the most salient pitch lines. When the green dots are shown with zero value, that means that the measurement apparatus was turned toward turbulence or pulses. The remaining panels of Fig. 12.5 show the resynthesis of states that result from measurement/collapse in conditions of state close to turbulent ($|l\rangle$ and $|r\rangle$) or myoelastic pulsation ($|s\rangle$ and $|f\rangle$). There is much freedom in the choice of the ingredients for the resynthesis from the pitch turbulence, and myoelastic trajectories and amplitudes that result from Hamiltonian evolution and sparse measurements. A minimal choice would be to use a sine wave and bandlimited noises for the pitch and non-pitch components, respectively,[2] but nothing prevents using harmonic or inharmonic complexes for the pitch component and sound grains for the myoelastic component.

---

[2] Sound example evolutionDownBrr.wav. The recording is available at https://on.soundcloud.com/WL8AT.

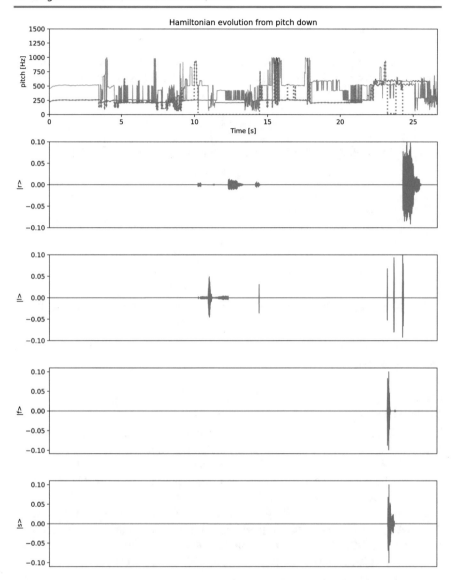

Fig. 12.5 Evolution from pitch-down with sparse measurement/collapse. Top plot: The two most salient pitches (red and gray lines) and the results of pitch measurements (green dotted line). Second and third plots: High- and low-frequency noise bursts. Fourth and fifth plots: Fast and slow myoelastic bursts

12.3.2 Evolution of a Mixed State

Considering the polyphonic vocal improvisation as before, assume we know the initial state only probabilistically. For example, we can consider the initial mixture of $\frac{1}{2}$ pitch-up and $\frac{2}{3}$ pitch-down. The density matrix

$$\rho = \begin{bmatrix} \frac{1}{3} & 0 \\ 0 & \frac{2}{3} \end{bmatrix}$$

is evolved according to Eq. 12.4, where the unitary operator is defined as

$$\mathbf{U}(t_0, t) = e^{-i \int_0^t \mathbf{H}(\tau) d\tau}.$$

```
H = np.array([[nzc, nxc - 1j*nyc], [nxc + 1j*nyc, -nzc]])
intHc = np.cumsum(H, axis=2)
Uc = intHc
for t in range(size(n_z)):
    Uc[:,:,t] = linalg.expm(-(1j)*intHc[:,:,t])
rho = np.matrix([[1/3, 0], [0, 2/3]])          # initial mixed state
rhoT = np.zeros((2, 2, size(n_z)), dtype=complex)
for t in range(size(n_z)): # density matrix at all future times
    rhoT[:,:,t] = (np.matrix(Uc[:,:,t])).getH() @ rho @ Uc[:,:,t]
```

When a pitch measurement is taken, the outcome is up or down according to

$$P[m = i|\rho] = Tr[\rho \Pi_i],$$

where the literal i stands for 'u' or 'd'. Similarly, a myoelastic measurement can be taken and give a fast or a slow outcome:

```
p_up = abs((rhoT[:,:,t] @ pi_up).trace())       # prob. of pitch-up
p_down = abs((rhoT[:,:,t] @ pi_down).trace())  # prob. of pitch-down
p_fast = abs((rhoT[:,:,t] @ my_fast).trace())  # prob. of myo-fast
p_slow = abs((rhoT[:,:,t] @ my_slow).trace())  # prob. of myo-slow
```

The density matrix can be made audible in various ways, thus sonifying the Hamiltonian evolution. For example, the completely chaotic mixed state, corresponding to the half-identity matrix $\rho = \frac{1}{2}\mathbf{I}$, can be made to sound as noise, and the pure states can be made to sound as the upper or the lower of the most salient pitches. These three components can be mixed for intermediate states. If p_u and p_d are the respective probabilities of pitch-up and pitch-down as encoded in the mixed state, the resulting mixed sound can be composed by a noise having amplitude min (p_u, p_d), by the upper pitch weighted by $p_u - \min (p_u, p_d)$, and by the lower pitch weighted by $p_d - \min (p_u, p_d)$. We can treat the myoelastic component similarly:

```
amplitude_noise[t] = min(p_up, p_down) # noise
amplitude_up[t] = p_up - amplitude_noise[t] # pitch-up
amplitude_down[t] = p_down - amplitude_noise[t] # pitch-down
amplitude_noise_p[t] = min(p_fast, p_slow) # myo
amplitude_fast[t] = p_fast - amplitude_noise_p[t] # myo-fast
amplitude_slow[t] = p_slow - amplitude_noise_p[t] # myo-slow
```

The density matrix that results from collapsing upon measurement is given by

$$\rho_{post}^{(i)} = \frac{\Pi_i \rho \Pi_i}{Tr[\rho \Pi_i]}.$$

Similarly to what we did for the evolution of a pure state, we can peep the state and perform a different measurement/collapse according to how close the state is to being pitchy:

Fig. 12.6 Amplitudes of two sinusoidal components and a noise component, resulting from the evolution of a mixed state with sparse measurement/collapse

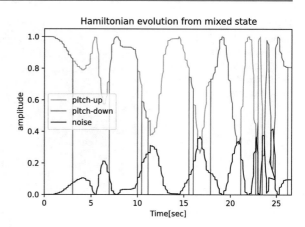

```
if (max(p_up, p_down) > threshold): # if pitchy
    cstate = np.random.choice(np.arange(0, 2), # measure phonation
                              p=[p_up, p_down]) # probabilistically
    if (cstate == 0):   # outcome up
        if (t%hopCollapse == 0): # collapse to pitch-up
            rhoT[:,:,t] = pi_up * rhoT[:,:,t] * pi_up / \
                          (rhoT[:,:,t] * pi_up).trace()
    else:               # outcome down
        if (t%hopCollapse == 0): # collapse to pitch-down
            rhoT[:,:,t] = pi_down * rhoT[:,:,t] * pi_down / \
                          (rhoT[:,:,t] * pi_down).trace()
else:                            # if not pitchy
    cstate = np.random.choice(np.arange(0, 2), # measure myoelasticity
                              p=[p_fast, p_slow]) # probabilistically
    if (cstate == 0):   # outcome fast
        if (t%hopCollapse == 0): # collapse to myo fast
            rhoT[:,:,t] = (my_fast @ rhoT[:,:,t] @ my_fast) / \
                          (rhoT[:,:,t] @ my_fast).trace()
    else:               # outcome slow
        if (t%hopCollapse == 0): # collapse to myo slow
            rhoT[:,:,t] = (my_slow @ rhoT[:,:,t] @ my_slow) / \
                          (rhoT[:,:,t] @ my_slow).trace()
```

According to the proposed Hamiltonian evolution, measurement/collapse and amplitude computation scheme, an example evolution of amplitudes for two sinusoidal components and a noise component is depicted in Fig. 12.6. The spectrogram of a possible minimalistic rendering,[3] including a high-frequency myoelastic component set at 2 kHz, is reported in Fig. 12.7.

---

[3] Sound example `mixed_lines_brr.wav`. The recording is available at https://on.soundcloud.com/tbkv3.

Fig. 12.7 Spectrogram of a "re-mix" of the polyphonic vocal improvisation, resulting from the evolution of a mixed state with sparse measurement/collapse

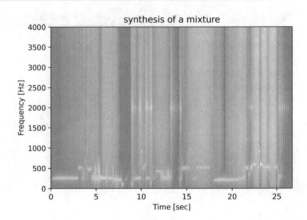

12.4 Conclusion and Perspective

From a whispered kind word to a shouted command, to a cry of terror, the human voice is a neverending source of inspiration for poets and scientists, and for non-empty intersections of these two sets. The vocal production mechanisms give us an embodied representation of found or imagined sounds, as the effectiveness of vocal imitations undoubtedly shows. In these pages, we summarized the key points of the Quantum Vocal Theory of Sounds, an analytic and creative approach to sound, represented in a space with voice-related axes, and based on the theoretical formalism and computational tools provided by quantum mechanics. We presented an example of analysis of a polyphonic improvised vocal sequence, ranging across the entire vocal space, encompassing pitch as well as noise as well as transient pulses.

The proposed example indicates a way of possible development in the direction of using QVTS as an analytical tool for purely-vocal pieces using extended techniques, such as *Sequenza III* by Luciano Berio [1], providing infinitely many listening pathways and schematic re-syntheses. But the QVTS can deal with sound at large, as the three-fold decomposition of sound is well supported by spectral processing techniques, thus allowing to analyze the sonic world through the embodied lenses (or earplugs) of the human voice. The QVTS framework offers the ground for new compositions and sonic creations, fostering new creative approaches based on vocal primitives and paths in the vocal space. Wandering around the Bloch sphere can in fact favor wonderful sonic encounters, for new music of the spheres.

References

1. Berio, L. (1968). *Sequenza III per voce femminile*. Universal Edition.
2. Blutner, R., & Beim Graben, P. Gauge models of musical forces. *Journal of Mathematics and Music* (2020). https://doi.org/10.1080/17459737.2020.1716404.

3. Bogdanov, D., Wack, N., Gómez Gutiérrez, E., Gulati, S., Herrera Boyer, P., Mayor, O., Roma Trepat, G., Salamon, J., Zapata González, J. R., & Serra, X. Essentia: An audio analysis library for music information retrieval. In *Proceedings of the 14th Conference of the International Society for Music Information Retrieval (ISMIR)* (pp. 493–498) (2013).
4. Bonada, J., Serra, X., Amatriain, X., & Loscos, A. (2011). Spectral processing. In U. Zölzer (Ed.), *DAFX: Digital audio effects* (pp. 393–445). Wiley.
5. Costa Hamido, O., Cirillo, G. A., & Giusto, E.: Quantum synth: A quantum-computing-based synthesizer. In *Proceedings of the 15th International Conference on Audio Mostly* (pp. 265–268) (2020).
6. Dalla Chiara, M. L., Giuntini, R., Leporini, R., Negri, E., & Sergioli, G. (2015). Quantum information, cognition, and music. *Frontiers in Psychology, 6*, 1583.
7. Delle Monache, S., Rocchesso, R., Bevilacqua, F., Lemaitre, G., Baldan, S., & Cera, A. (2018). Embodied sound design. *International Journal of Human-Computer Studies, 118*, 47–59.
8. Friberg, A., Lindeberg, T., Hellwagner, M., Helgason, P., Salomão, G. L., Elowsson, A., Lemaitre,G., & Ternström, S. Prediction of three articulatory categories in vocal sound imitations using models for auditory receptive fields. *The Journal of the Acoustical Society of America, 144*(3), 1467–1483 (2018).
9. Fugiel, B. Quantum-like melody perception. *Journal of Mathematics and Music* (2018). Retrieved from https://doi.org/10.1080/17459737.2022.2049383.
10. Gabor, D. Acoustical quanta and the theory of hearing. *Nature, 159*(4044), 591 (1947).
11. von Helmholtz, H. (1870). *Die Lehre von den Tonempfindungen als physiologische Grundlage-fürdie Theorie der Musik*. F. Vieweg und sohn.
12. Koenig, D. M., & Delwin, D. F. (2015). *Spectral analysis of musical sounds with emphasis on the Piano*. Oxford University Press.
13. Lemaitre, G., & Rocchesso, D. On the effectiveness of vocal imitations and verbal descriptions of sounds. *The Journal of the Acoustical Society of America, 135*(2), 862 (2014). Retrieved from https://iris.unipa.it/retrieve/handle/10447/370549/745030/1.4861245.pdf.
14. Lemaitre G., Houix O., Voisin F., Misdariis N., & Susini P. Vocal imitations of non-vocal sounds. *PLoS ONE, 11*(12), e0168167 (2016). Retrieved form https://doi.org/10.1371/journal.pone.0168167.
15. Mannone, M., & Rocchesso, D. Quanta in sound, the sound of quanta: A voice-informed quantum theoretical perspective on sound. In E. R. Miranda (Ed.), *Quantum computing in the arts and humanities*. Springer, Cham (2022) Retrived from https://doi.org/10.1007/978-3-030-95538-0_6.
16. Marinetti, F. T.: Zang tumb tumb. Milano, Edizioni futuriste di poesia (1914). Retrieved from http://parliamoitaliano.altervista.org/zang-tumb-tumb/.
17. Miranda, E. R. Quantum computer: Hello, Music! In E. Miranda (Ed.), *Handbook of artificial intelligence for music: Foundations, advanced approaches, and developments for creativity*. Springer Nature (2021)
18. Miranda, E. R.: Creative Quantum computing: Inverse FFT sound synthesis, adaptive sequencing and musical composition. In A. Adamatzky (Ed.), *Alternative computing*. World Scientific (2021).
19. Newman, F. (2004). *MouthSounds: How to whistle. Pop: Boing, and Honk... for All Occasions and Then Some*. Workman Publishing.
20. Palazzeschi, A. La fontana malata, from Poemi. Firenze, Cesare Blanc (1909). Retrieved from https://www.pensieriparole.it/poesie/poesie-d-autore/poesia-38384.
21. Roads, C. (2001). *Microsound*. MIT Press.
22. Rocchesso, D., & Mannone, M. (2020). A quantum vocal theory of sound. *Quantum Information Processing, 19*, 292. https://doi.org/10.1007/s11128-020-02772-9

23. Verma, T. S., Levine, S. N., & Meng, T. H. Transient modeling synthesis: A flexible analy-sis/synthesis tool for transient signals. In *Proceedings of the International Computer Music Conference* (pp. 48–51) (1997).
24. Weimer, H. Listen to quantum computer music. http://www.quantenblog.net/physics/quantum-computer-music. Accessed 02 Jan 2021 (2010).

A Quantum Natural Language Processing Approach to Musical Intelligence

13

Eduardo Reck Miranda, Richie Yeung, Anna Pearson, Konstantinos Meichanetzidis, and Bob Coecke

Abstract

There has been tremendous progress in Artificial Intelligence (AI) for music, in particular for musical composition and access to large databases for commercialisation through the Internet. We are interested in further advancing this field, focusing on composition. In contrast to current 'black-box' AI methods, we are championing an *interpretable compositional* outlook on generative music systems. In particular, we are importing methods from the Distributional Compositional Categorical (DisCoCat) modelling framework for Natural Language Processing (NLP), motivated by musical grammars. Quantum computing is a nascent technology, which is very likely to impact the music industry in time to come. Thus, we are championing a Quantum Natural Language Processing (QNLP) approach to develop a new generation of intelligent musical systems. This work follows previous experimental implementations of DisCoCat linguistic models on quantum hardware. In this chapter, we present *Quanthoven*, the first

E. R. Miranda (✉)
ICCMR, University of Plymouth, Plymouth, UK
e-mail: eduardo.miranda@plymouth.ac.uk

E. R. Miranda · R. Yeung · A. Pearson · K. Meichanetzidis · B. Coecke
Quantinuum, Oxford, UK

R. Yeung
e-mail: richie.yeung@cambridgequantum.com

Anna Pearson
e-mail: anna.pearson@cambridgequantum.com

Konstantinos Meichanetzidis
e-mail: k.mei@cambridgequantum.com

Bob Coecke
e-mail: bob.coeck@cambridgequantum.come

© The Author(s), under exclusive license to Springer Nature Switzerland AG 2022
E. R Miranda (ed.), *Quantum Computer Music*,
https://doi.org/10.1007/978-3-031-13909-3_13

proof-of-concept ever built, which (a) demonstrates that it is possible to program a quantum computer to learn to classify music that conveys different meanings and (b) illustrates how such a capability might be leveraged to develop a system to compose meaningful pieces of music. After a discussion about our current understanding of music as a communication medium and its relationship to natural language, the chapter focuses on the techniques developed to (a) encode musical compositions as quantum circuits, and (b) design a quantum classifier. The chapter ends with demonstrations of compositions created with the system.

13.1 Introduction

When people say that John Coltrane's *Alabama* is awesome or that Flow Composer's[1] *Daddy's car* is good, what do they mean by 'awesome music' or 'good music'? This is debatable. People have different tastes and opinions. And this is true whether the music is made by a human or a machine.

The caveat here is not so much to do with the terms 'awesome music' or 'good music', or whether it is made by humans or machines. The caveat is with the word 'mean'.

In the last 20 years or so, there has been tremendous progress in Artificial Intelligence (AI) for music. But computers still cannot satisfactorily handle meaning in music in controlled ways that generalise between contexts. There is AI technology today to set up computers to compose a decent pastiche of, say, a Beethoven minuet; e.g., there are connectionist (a.k.a., 'neural networks') systems for composition that have been trained on certain genres or styles. (For a comprehensive account of the state of the art of AI for music, please refer to [46].) However, it is very hard to program a computer to compose a piece of music from a request to, say, 'generate a piece for Alice's tea party'. How would it know what tea party music should sound like, or who Alice is? And how would it relate such concepts with algorithms to compose?

A challenging task is to design generative systems with enough knowledge of musical structure, and the ability to manipulate said structure, so that given requests for mood, purpose, style, and so on, are appropriately met. Systems that currently attempt to perform such tasks, especially for music recommendation systems, work in terms of finding and exploiting correlations in large amounts of human-annotated data; e.g., [2]. These for example would fill a preference matrix, encoding information such as 'likes' for songs, which are categorised already in certain genres by listeners.

Following an alternative route, which comes under the umbrella of *Compositional Intelligence* [15], we are taking the first steps in addressing the aforementioned

---

[1] Flow Composer is an AI lead sheet generator developed at Sony CSL Paris [53]. A lead sheet is a form of musical notation that specifies the essential elements (melody, lyrics, and harmony) of a song.

challenge from a Natural Language Processing (NLP) perspective, which adopts a structure-informed approach.

Providing domain-specific structure to intelligent systems in a controlled and scalable way is a nontrivial challenge: we would need to ensure that the system does not significantly lose the flexibility to adapt to different datasets. Nevertheless, having structure present in intelligent systems has potential benefits, such as increased interpretability. Another potential benefit is the need for fewer training parameters; in general, a learning system would need a set of free parameters so that it learns structure from scratch. But in our case, a structural approach is motivated by an analogy between grammar in language, and structure in musical compositions. Specifically to the present work, we are pioneering a Quantum Natural Language Processing (QNLP) approach to develop a new generation of intelligent musical systems. This in turn is motivated by our specific choice of mathematical grammar and a modelling framework for NLP, referred to as Distributional Compositional (DisCo). DisCo models are amenable to implementation on quantum computers due to a shared mathematical structure between grammar and quantum theory.

Our aim in this work is to train parameterised quantum circuits to learn to classify music conveying different meanings. And then, use the classifier to compose music that conveys such meanings via rejection sampling. Here, the notion of 'meaning' is defined as *perceived properties of musical compositions, which might holistically characterise different types of music*. This is the first step towards the ambition of being able to ask an autonomous intelligent system to generate bespoke pieces of music with particular meanings, required purposes, and so on.

Our classification system is trained on human-annotated examples. It scans given examples for musical elements, which we refer to as *musical snippets*. A snippet can be as small as a single musical note. But it can also be a melody, a bar of music, or a group of bars. The main assumption made by the system—known also as the *distributional hypothesis*—is that snippets that occur in similar contexts convey similar meanings. This is a hypothesis that regards the meanings of words in a text: words that appear in similar contexts convey similar meanings. Then, a combination of the meanings of all snippets determines the meaning of entire compositions, or sections thereof.[2] These combinations follow *grammatical* rules. Our aim is to input these rules into the machine along with meaning-encodings of the snippets, to allow it to identify different types of music. In the near future, we hope it will be able to use this knowledge to compose pieces, or sections thereof, conveying specific meanings. Towards the end of the chapter, we provide a glimpse of how this might be achieved.

Technically, the system assigns types to snippets, in analogy with a parser assigning grammatical part-of-speech tags to words, such as nouns, adjectives, verbs, and so on. Types follow specific compositional rules, and in the specific grammar model that we employ—that is, *pregroup grammar*—types obey algebraic relations.

---

[2] For large pieces of music, it is assumed that different sections may convey different meanings, in the same way, that sentences or paragraphs convey localised meanings within the overall narrative of a large text.

The rules induce a dependency structure onto a musical piece that is composed with snippets. Then, *meaning* enters the picture by sending types to vector spaces of specific dimensions. Snippet-meaning is encoded inside these vector spaces in terms of multilinear maps, i.e., *tensors*. The compositional rules represented by the dependency structure induce a pattern of tensor-contractions between the tensors.

The choice to embed meaning in vector spaces is motivated by a similar mathematical structure between the algebra of the types and the composition of tensors. Importantly, the tensors form a network, which reflects the dependencies as *inherited* by the grammatical structure of a piece of music. However, as we are encoding meaning in tensors, we realise that the computational cost of manipulating and composing tensors is prohibitive for large numbers of snippets, even for mainframe supercomputers, let alone your average desktop. These would require high dimensionality of vector spaces along with a highly connected dependency network.

Enter the quantum computer! Quantum processes constitute a powerful choice for a playground in which to encode meaning. After all, quantum theory can be formulated entirely in terms of complex-valued tensor networks. Specifically, quantum theory can be fully considered around one fundamental principle: the way quantum systems compose to form larger ones, and the mathematical operation that jointly describes multiple quantum systems is the tensor product.

Emerging quantum computing technology promises formidable processing power for some tasks. As it turns out, and we will see this below, the mathematical tools that are being developed in QNLP research are quantum-native, by yet another analogy between mathematical structures. That is, they enable direct correspondences between language and quantum mechanics, and consequently music. In this case, (a) the meaning of words can be encoded as quantum states and (b) grammars would then correspond to quantum circuits [12].

Despite the rapid growth in size and quality of quantum hardware in the last decade, quantum processors are still limited in terms of operating speed and noise tolerance. However, they are adequate to implement proof-of-concept experiments of our envisaged system.

In this chapter, we present *Quanthoven*, the first proof-of-concept ever built, which (a) demonstrates that it is possible to program a quantum computer to learn to classify music that conveys different meanings and (b) illustrates how such a capability might be leveraged to develop Artificial Intelligence systems able to compose meaningful pieces of music.

The remainder of this chapter is structured as follows:

- Section 13.2 explores our current understanding of music as a communication medium and its relationship to natural language, which motivates our research.
- Section 13.3 contextualises our work in relation to approaches to computational modelling of music and algorithmic composition.
- Section 13.4 introduces the very basics of quantum computing, just enough to follow the technical aspects of the quantum classifier (i.e., machine learning algorithm) discussed in this chapter.

- Section 13.5 introduces Distributional Compositional Categorical (DisCoCat) modelling, which uses Category Theory to unify natural language and quantum mechanics. It also shows how DisCoCat can model music.
- Section 13.6 describes the DisCoCat music model that we developed for this project, including the process by which musical pieces are generated using a bespoke grammar and converted into a quantum circuit. It delineates the machine learning algorithm and training methodology.
- Section 13.7 illustrates how the results from the classification can be leveraged to generate two classes of musical compositions.

The chapter ends with final remarks. A number of appendices provide complementary information.

13.2 Music and Meaning

It is widely accepted that instrumental music[3] is a non-verbal language. But what does music communicate? What is meaning in music?

Some advocate that music communicates nothing meaningful because it cannot express ideas or tell stories in the same way that verbal languages can. Music has no 'words' to express things like 'Bob', 'mussels and fries', 'beer', 'Bob loves mussels and fries with a beer', and so on. But this is a rather defeatist view.

Conversely, others advocate that music can communicate messages of some sort. For example, the imitation of cuckoo birds in Ludwig van Beethoven's Pastoral Symphony is often thought to signify 'springtime has arrived' [49]. But this is speculation. We do not know if Beethoven really wanted to communicate this.

There have been studies, however, suggesting that different types of chords, rhythms, or melodic shapes may convey specific emotions. For instance, the notion that a minor chord conveys sadness and a major one happiness has been demonstrated experimentally [4]. And brain imaging studies have identified correlations between perceived musical signs and specific patterns of brain activity associated with feelings. These studies support the notion that music conveys, if anything, affective states [18,33]. But still, there is no treatise to date on how to communicate a specific feeling in a composition. There are no universal rules for doing this.

Yet, it would be perfectly possible to have musical languages matching the expressive power of verbal languages. Creators of Esperanto-like verbal languages, such as Dothraki, made for the TV series *The Game of Thrones*, have developed fully-fledged musical languages [50,57]. It is just that *Homo sapiens* have not naturally evolved one as such. This is because we evolved musicality for purposes other than verbal communication. Thus, meaning in music is not quite the same as meaning in

---

[3] That is, music without singing. No lyrics. Only musical instruments.

verbal languages. But what is it? To tackle this question, we ought to examine how the brain makes sense of language and music.

13.2.1 Brain Resources Overlap

Music and verbal languages do have a lot in common. There is scientific evidence that the brain resources that humans deploy to process music and verbal languages overlap to a great degree [29]. Stefan Koelsch proposed an ambitious neurocognitive model of music perception supported by extensive research into the neural substrates shared by music and language [32]. Of course, there are differences too. For instance, whereas, the brain engages specialised areas for processing language (e.g., Broca's and Wernicke's areas), music processing tends to be distributed over a number of areas, which are not necessarily specialised for music.

Let us consider, for instance, the notion of narrative, in a text and in a piece of music; see also discussion in Chap. 2 in this volume. We seem to deploy cognitive strategies to make sense of music, which are similar to those employed to read a text. This is because verbal languages and music share similar intrinsic structures [54]. Or at least our brain thinks that this is the case. This is questionable. But it is a useful assumption, which is somewhat supported by experiments testing if musical cognitive functions can influence linguistic ones, and vice-versa.

Notable experiments highlighted the benefits of musical proficiency for the acquisition of linguistic skills, in particular learning a second language [40,55]. And Dawson et al. provided experimental evidence that native speakers of distinct languages process music differently [19]. This seems to be determined by the structural and phonological properties of their respective languages. For example, speakers of languages that has words whose meaning is determined by the duration of their vocalization tend to deal with rhythm more accurately than speakers of languages whose durations do not interfere with meaning.

13.2.2 Meaning is Context

In a similar fashion to a narrative in text, a musical narrative delineates relationships and changes in the state of affairs from event to event [30]. Auditory events in a piece of music acquire significance within a structure that our mind's ear imposes on them. Different types of music define systems of relations among these elements, which induce us to assign them structural impressions; or create categories. The more we listen to the music of certain styles, the more familiar the categories that define such styles become. And the higher the chances that those assigned impressions might be elicited when we listen to such kinds of pieces of music again and again.

Thus, we parse and interpret auditory streams according to our own made-up mental schemes. We might as well refer to such schemes as *musical grammars*. And the labels we give to impressions as *meanings*.

A piece of music may as well make one feel sad or happy, or remember Bob, or think of mussels and fries. And one might even hear Beethoven shouting from his grave that springtime has arrived. Thus, for instance, music with fast repetitive patterns might be categorised as 'rhythmic', 'energetic', or 'exciting'. In contrast, music composed of irregular successions of notes forming melodies and exquisite harmonies might be categorised as 'melodic', 'relaxing' or 'impressionistic'. But this is not as simple as it appears to be. What happens when a piece is prominently rhythmic but is also melodic; e.g., ballroom dance music? We could think of a new category. But what if yet another piece is only slightly more melodic than rhythmic? The boundaries of such categories are not trivial to establish.

Anyway, one thing is certain: the more culturally related a group of listeners are, the higher the chances that they might develop shared repertoires of mental schemes and impressions.

Incidentally, we learn verbal languages in a similar way to what we just described. We make up the meaning of words and learn how to assemble them in phrases from the context in which they are used. We do this as we grow up and continue doing so throughout our lifetime [21]. Perhaps the main difference is that meaning in verbal languages needs to be more precise than meaning in music. That is, meaning in music tends to be more fluid than in language. As stated above, however, one can construct musical natural languages if one attempts to.

13.3 Computational Modelling and Algorithmic Composition

Scholars from both camps (i.e., linguistics and musicology) have developed comparable models to study linguistic and musical structures, and respective mental schemes [5,10,24,35].

Not surprisingly, computational models of linguistic processes have been successfully used to model musical processes and vice-versa. David Cope harnessed transition networks grammars [16], which have been used for the analysis and synthesis of natural language [64], to develop systems to analyse and synthesise music. A system to generate music using stochastic context-free grammars was proposed by [56]. Indeed, Noam Chomsky's context-free grammar [27] proved to be relevant for music in many ways. In particular transformative grammars [9], which suit well the widely adopted method of composing music referred to as variations on a theme. And [42] created a system whereby a group of interactive autonomous software agents evolved a common repertoire of intonations (or prosodies) to verbalise words. The agents evolved this by singing to each other. Moreover, evolutionary models informed by neo-Darwinism [25] have been developed to study the origins of language and music almost interchangeably [7,48].

Generally, there have been two approaches to designing computer systems to generate music, which we refer to as the Artificial Intelligence (or AI) and the algorithmic approaches, respectively [41,44].

The AI approach is concerned with embedding the system with musical knowledge to guide the generative process. For instance, computers have been programmed with rules of common practice for counterpoint and voicing in order to generate polyphonic music. And machine-learning technology has enabled computers to learn musical rules automatically from given scores, which are subsequently used to generate music [17]. The linguistic-informed modelling mentioned above falls in this category.

Conversely, the algorithmic approach is concerned with translating data generated from seemingly non-musical phenomena onto music. Examples of this approach abound. Computers have been programmed to generate music with fractals [28] and chaotic systems [26]. And also with data from physical phenomena, such as particle collision [8], and DNA sequences [45].

Aesthetically, the algorithmic approach tends to generate highly novel and rather unusual music; some may not even consider the outputs as music. The AI approach tends to generate imitations of existing music; that is, imitations in the style of the music that was used to teach the AI system. Neither approach can, however, satisfactorily respond to sophisticated requests such as 'generate something for Alice's tea party' or 'compose a tune to make Bob feel energetic'. The QNLP approach that we are developing is aimed at improving this scenario.

13.4 Brief Introduction to Quantum Computing

A detailed introduction to quantum computing is beyond the scope of this chapter. This can be found in [12,51,62]; see also Chap. 1 in this volume. Nevertheless, in this section, we briefly introduce a few basic concepts deemed necessary to follow the discussions in the following sections.

Our starting point is a quantum bit, known as a *qubit*, which is the basic unit of information carrier in a quantum computer. Physically, it is associated with a property of a physical system; e.g., the spin of an electron up or down along some axis. A qubit has a state $|\psi\rangle$, which lives in a 2-dimensional complex vector space, referred to as Hilbert space. The orthonormal basis vectors $|0\rangle$ and $|1\rangle$, related to measurement outcomes 0 and 1, respectively, allow us to write the most general state of a qubit as a linear combination of the basis vectors known as *superposition*: $|\psi\rangle = \alpha |0\rangle + \beta |1\rangle$ with $\alpha, \beta \in \mathbb{C}$ and $|\alpha|^2 + |\beta|^2 = 1$.

An important aspect of quantum computers is that they are fundamentally probabilistic. This leads to the situation where even if one knows that a qubit is in a state $|\psi\rangle$, one can only obtain measurement outcomes $i = \{0, 1\}$ with probability given by the Born rule $P(i) = |\langle i|\psi\rangle|^2$, which gives the square of the norm of the so-called amplitude $\langle i|\psi\rangle \in \mathbb{C}$. So, $\langle i|$ is a quantum effect, also known as a 'bra' in Dirac notation, and is the dual vector of the state, or 'ket', $|i\rangle$. For the general single-qubit superposition in the paragraph above, $P(0) = |\alpha|^2$ and $P(1) = |\beta|^2$.

In order to picture a single qubit, imagine a transparent sphere with opposite poles. From its centre, a vector whose length is equal to the radius of the sphere can point

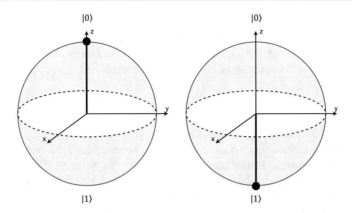

Fig. 13.1 The Pauli **X** gate rotates the state vector (pointing upwards on the figure on the left side) by 180 degrees around the x-axis (pointing downwards on the figure on the right)

to anywhere on the surface. This sphere is called the *Bloch sphere* and the vector is referred to as a *state vector* (Fig. 13.1). Before measurement, the evolution of a single qubit (that is, a qubit that is not interacting with any other qubits) is described by the transformation of its state vector with a unitary linear map U, so that $|\psi'\rangle = U |\psi\rangle$ (Fig. 13.2). However if a qubit interacts with other qubits, then things become a little more complicated; more about this below.

In simple terms, quantum computers are programmed by applying sequences of unitary linear maps to qubits. Programming languages for quantum computing provide a number of such linear maps, referred to as *gates*, which act on qubits. For instance, the 'not gate', rotates the state vector by 180° around the x-axis of the Bloch sphere (Fig. 13.1); that is, if the qubit vector is pointing to $|0\rangle$, then this gate flips it to $|1\rangle$, or vice-versa. This gate is often referred to as the 'Pauli **X** gate'. A more generic rotation **Rx**(θ) gate is typically available for quantum programming, where the angle for the rotation around the x-axis is specified. Obviously, **Rx**(π) applied to $|0\rangle$ or $|1\rangle$ is equivalent to applying **X** to $|0\rangle$ or $|1\rangle$. Similarly, there are **Rz**(φ) and **Ry**(θ) gates for rotations on the z-axis and y-axis of the Bloch sphere,

Fig. 13.2 Diagrammatic format showing the evolution of an isolated qubit in initial state $|\psi\rangle$ with unitary map U composed with effect $\langle 0|$. Taken from [36] and used with permission

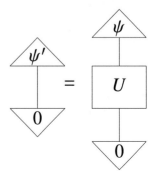

respectively. An even more generic gate is typically available, which is a unitary rotation gate, with 3 Euler angles: $U(\theta, \varphi, \lambda)$. Essentially, all single-qubit quantum gates perform rotations, which change the amplitude distribution of the system. And in fact, any qubit rotation can be specified in terms of $U(\theta, \varphi, \lambda)$; for instance $Rx(\theta) = U(\theta, -\frac{\pi}{2}, \frac{\pi}{2})$.

Quantum computation gets really interesting with gates that operate on multiple qubits, such as the controlled **X** gate, or **CX** gate; commonly referred to as the **CNOT** gate. The **CNOT** gate puts two qubits in *entanglement*.

Entanglement establishes a curious correlation between qubits. When considering its action on the computational states, the **CNOT** gate applies an **X** gate on a qubit only if the state of another qubit is $|1\rangle$. Thus, the **CNOT** gate establishes a dependency of the state of one qubit with the value of another. In practice, any quantum gate can be made conditional and entanglement can take place between more than two qubits.

An important gate for quantum computing is the Hadamard gate (referred to as the '**H** gate'). It puts the qubit into a balanced superposition state consisting of an equal-weighted combination of two opposing states:$|\alpha|^2 = 0.5$ and $|\beta|^2 = 0.5$.

A combination of **H** and **CNOT** gates enables the implementation of the so-called Bell states; a form of maximally entangled qubits, which is explored later on in this chapter to represent grammatical structures.

A quantum program is often depicted as a circuit diagram of quantum gates, showing sequences of gate operations on the qubits (Fig. 13.3). So, if one has n qubits, then their joint state space is given by the tensor product of their individual state spaces and has dimension 2^n. The evolution of many qubits interacting with each other is given by a (global) exponentially large unitary map acting on the entire joint exponentially large state space.

There are two ways of thinking of a quantum circuit. On an abstract level, it can be viewed as the application of a linear map to a vector, which computes the entire state of the system at a later time. As stated above, these complex-valued matrices and vectors are exponentially large in terms of the number of qubits required to encode them. Therefore, at least naive simulations of quantum systems are believed to be a

Fig. 13.3 Example of a quantum circuit of the kind used in our system: the Hadamard gate **H**, the X-rotation gate $Rx(\beta)$ by angle β, the controlled Z-rotation gate (i), part of which is a Z-rotation gate $Rz(\delta)$ by angle δ, and finally the **CNOT** gate. Taken from [36] and used with permission

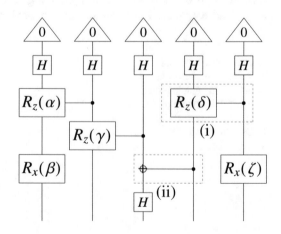

hard task for classical computers. And on a physical, or operational, level, a quantum circuit is a set of instructions for a quantum computer to execute.

In the circuit model of quantum computation, qubits typically start at easily preparable states, $|0\rangle$, and then a sequence of gates is applied. Next, the qubits are read and the results are stored in standard digital memory, which is accessible for further handling. In practice, a quantum computer works alongside a classical computer, which in effect acts as the interface between the user and the quantum machine. The classical computer enables the user to handle the measurements for practical applications.

Once a circuit has been physically implemented on a quantum computer, and once it has been run, the qubits are measured. For an n qubit circuit this gives n bits. As a quantum computer is probabilistic, the circuit must be run many times to give statistics to estimate outcome probabilities. The design of a circuit must be such that it encodes the problem in a way that the outcome probabilities are obtained to give the answer to what one wishes to solve.

Building and running a quantum computer is an engineering task on a completely different scale from that of building and running a classical computer. Not only must qubits be shielded from random errors picked up from the environment, but one must also avoid unwanted interactions between multiple qubits within the same device. In order to avoid such problems, the number of successive operations on qubits (i.e., 'circuit depth') is limited on current quantum hardware. It is expected that to give an advantage for large scale problems one must have many fault-tolerant qubits, which are obtained by error correction techniques. These involve encoding the state of a 'logical' qubit in the state of many 'physical' qubits. As this is a difficult engineering task, quantum computers with fault-tolerant qubits are not available at the time of writing. Current machines are known as Noisy Intermediate-Scale Quantum (NISQ) computers and at the time of writing, they typically have less than 100 physical qubits.

13.5 DisCoCat Modelling

Development in the growing new field of QNLP is greatly facilitated by the Distributional Compositional Categorical (DisCoCat) modelling of natural language semantics. In DisCoCat, grammar dictates the composition of word meanings to derive the meaning of a whole sentence [13].

DisCoCat is a natural framework to develop natural language-like generative music systems with quantum computing. At the core of DisCoCat, as the model was originally formulated, is Joachim Lambek's, algebraic model of pregroup grammar; the curious reader may refer to [14] for a more rigorous mathematical treatment.

At the core of DisCoCat, the compositional structure of language is captured by (symmetric) monoidal categories, a.k.a. *process theories*. This mathematical formalism comes equipped with a formal graphical notation in the form of *string diagrams*. Meaning is encoded by a mapping, which endows semantics on the diagram representing the grammatical structure of a text. This is in fact how DisCoCat was introduced in the first instance, by sending words to vectors, or in general, higher-order tensors, which are connected according to the grammatical dependencies to form a tensor network. Contracting the tensors along with the connections results in the derivation of the meaning of a text.

Categorical quantum mechanics (CQM) is a framework that reformulates quantum theory in terms of process theories. In this context, string diagrams describe quantum protocols involving quantum states, transformations, and measurements [1,12]. Low-level and fine-grained diagrammatic calculi, which build on the philosophy of CQM, such as ZX-calculus [11], are promising complementary—or even alternative—approaches to reasoning about quantum systems and processes. We see then that string diagrams provide a common language via which we can make the connection from language to quantum theory. After all, Hilbert spaces, which are where quantum states are encoded, are vector spaces. By analogy, many-body quantum states encode word meanings. And grammatical reductions correspond to processes such as quantum maps, quantum effects, and measurements.

To take advantage of this formal mathematical analogy, in order to perform grammar-based musical experiments on quantum processors, we employ DisCoPy [22], an open-source toolbox for manipulating string diagrams and implementing mappings to underlying semantics of our choosing. Among its features, DisCoPy includes tools for defining Context-Free Grammars (CFGs), Lambek's pregroup grammars [34], tensor networks [52], ZX-calculus, and other diagram-based reasoning processes, under the same compositional paradigm. In essence, and particular to this work, DisCoPy provides the means for mapping representations of musical systems into quantum circuits, encoding quantum processes, to be implemented on a quantum computer. For instance [38,39], used DisCoPy and Quantinuum's compiler t|ket⟩ [60] to develop and deploy a pioneering QNLP experiment on quantum hardware. Here the sentences were represented as parameterised quantum circuits and the parameters were trained to perform on a sentence-classification task. A larger-scale experiment of the same nature was reported by [36]. The models built for those experiments have been further developed into a Python library for QNLP known as lambeq [31], which is named in homage to Joachim Lambek. Indeed, part of the work reported in this chapter was conducted using an early version of lambeq.

13.5.1 A Musical DisCoCat Model

In pregroup grammar, the syntax of a sentence is captured by a finite product of words of different pregroup types. In our case, musical snippets will play the role of words, and musical compositions the role of sentences.

Let us define a musical composition σ as a finite product of musical snippets w as follows: $\sigma = \prod w_i$, where the product operation captures the sequential nature of the string representing a musical piece, in analogy with words being placed side by side in a sentence. Each snippet is assigned a pregroup type $t_w = \prod b_i^{k_i}$ comprising a product of basic types b_i from a set of types B. Basic types also have adjoints:

$k_i \in \{\ldots, ll, l, \_, r, rr, \ldots\}$. Then, the type of a given musical composition σ is simply the product of the types of its snippets.

A composition is deemed valid, that is, grammatically correct—or musical—if and only if its type reduces to a special type $s \in B$. These reductions take place by means of an algebraic process of pair-wise annihilations of basic types and their adjoints according to the following rules: $b^l \cdot b \rightarrow 1$, $b \cdot b^r \rightarrow 1$, $b^{ll} \cdot b^l \rightarrow 1$, $b^r \cdot b^{rr} \rightarrow 1$, ... To visualise this, let's go back to natural language and consider a sentence with a transitive verb: *Bob plays guitar*. Here, the transitive verb is a process that expects two input nouns of, say, type n, on each side, in order to output a sentence type s. The type of the transitive verb is therefore denoted as $n^r \cdot s \cdot n^l$. There exists a grammatical reduction following the algebraic rules of pregroup types:

$$n \cdot (n^r \cdot s \cdot n^l) \cdot n \rightarrow (n \cdot n^r) \cdot s \cdot (n^l \cdot n) \rightarrow 1 \cdot s \cdot 1 \rightarrow s \qquad (13.1)$$

The DisCoCat string diagram for Eq. 13.1 is shown in Fig. 13.4. They carry a type. The wires bent in a U-shape, or cups, represent the reductions. Complex networks of processes and relationships can be designed by connecting boxes with input and output wires and observing that the types are respected and are reducible as required.

Such pregroup modelling is directly applicable to music. For instance, consider the example shown in Fig. 13.5. Here we defined a relationship $n^r \cdot s \cdot n^l$ between two musical notes (type n): C4 and A4. The relationship states that note A4 follows note C4 (Fig. 13.6). In this particular example, *sequence* is not a verb but an actual action to be carried out by some hypothetical generative music system.

Figure 13.7 depicts an example of a pregroup diagram representing a short musical composition, which is shown in Fig. 13.8. In this case, there are five musical snippets (labelled as p4, p9, p7 and p5), each of which comprises several musical notes forming two entire musical bars each.

The semantic map is a functor $\mathcal{F}$ that sends basic types (n, s) to vector spaces (N, S). Take the example in Fig. 13.4, 'Bob plays guitar'. The DisCoCat diagram can be decomposed as diagram $= (\text{Bob} \otimes \text{plays} \otimes \text{guitar}) \circ \text{cups}$. The second word 'plays' is a transitive verb and has the pregroup type $n^r \cdot s \cdot n^l$, whilst 'Bob' and 'guitar' have pregroup type n. The functor $\mathcal{F}$ sends the diagram to vector space semantics

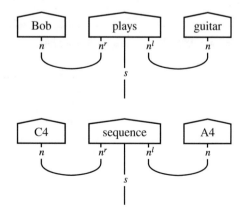

Fig. 13.4 Pregroup diagram for transitive the sentence 'Bob plays guitar'

Fig. 13.5 Pregroup diagram for musical form shown in Fig. 13.6

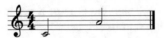

Fig. 13.6 A sequence of two notes: C4 and A4

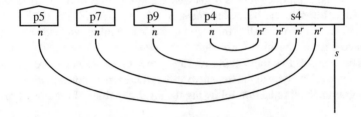

Fig. 13.7 Pregroup diagram for a musical composition form

by dropping the adjoints (l, r) and sending the pregroup type to the corresponding vector spaces. Based on their pregroup types, the words of the sentence will be sent to tensors of the corresponding vector space (Eq. 13.2).

$$\mathcal{F}(\text{Bob}), \mathcal{F}(\text{guitar}) \in \mathcal{F}(n) = N$$
$$\mathcal{F}(\text{plays}) \in \mathcal{F}(n^r \cdot s \cdot n^l) = N \otimes S \otimes N \tag{13.2}$$

Moreover, $\mathcal{F}$ translates all reductions cups to tensor contractions. Conceptually, the functor can be thought of as something that performs tensor contraction between the words and the cups to return a vector for the whole sentence (Eq. 13.3). In Sect. 13.6.4, we will relay the details of the corresponding mapping to quantum processes.

$$\mathcal{F}(\text{diagram}) = (\mathcal{F}(\text{Bob}) \otimes \mathcal{F}(\text{plays}) \otimes \mathcal{F}(\text{guitar})) \circ \mathcal{F}(\text{cups}) \in S \tag{13.3}$$

Exactly the same principles are applicable to music. For instance, assuming the example in Fig. 13.5, and a set of musical notes N, the relationship *sequence* acquires the meaning $s = C4 \cdot R \cdot A4$ with $\{C4, A4\} \in N$ and $R \in (N \otimes S \otimes N)$.

13.6 Machine Learning of Music

In this section we introduce our DisCoCat music model and the quantum machine learning algorithm that we built to differentiate between two categories of music. Example code for the machine learning process can be found at [https://github.com/CQCL/Quanthoven]. A schematic overview of the algorithm is shown in Fig. 13.9.

In a nutshell, the algorithm learns from corpora generated by a bespoke context-free grammar (CFG). However, the quantum machine learning algorithm needs to see the structure of the compositions in the form of parameterised quantum circuits. Thus, the system needs to transform its underlying CFG structures into quantum circuits. This is done by converting CFGs into pregroups diagrams, which are then

Fig. 13.8   A short musical composition corresponding to the pregroup diagram in Fig. 13.7

optimised before they are translated into quantum circuits. This optimisation is highly advisable because cups tend to produce more qubits than necessary when converting pregroup diagrams into a quantum circuit. The system then generates instructions for an appropriate quantum computer to run the circuit.

13.6.1   Generating a Training Corpus with a Context-Free Grammar

Here we define a Context-Free Grammar (CFG) to generate musical compositions for piano, which will be used to teach the machine learning algorithm. And *Quanthoven* will use this CFG to generate new pieces after it has learn to classify them.

   The lexicon of our CFG contains four types of musical snippets. As it was mentioned already, a snippet is the equivalent of a word in natural language. Whereas a word is formed by letters from an alphabet, a snippet is formed by notes from a pitch framework.[4] Likewise, whilst combinations of words form sentences, combinations of snippets form musical sequences; that is, musical compositions.

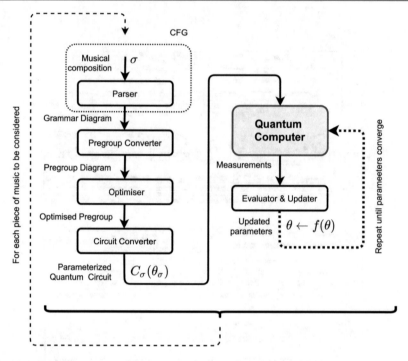

Fig. 13.9 Schematic overview of our quantum machine learning algorithm

As the second level of the Chomsky hierarchy, CFGs are expressive enough to model a vast portion of natural language. An informal, diagrammatic representation of a CFG is to draw words in the lexicon as boxes with one output wire. And production rules can be represented as boxes with multiple input wires and one output wire. Then, sequences can be built by freely composing these boxes. A more detailed explanation about combining CFGs with monoidal category theory can be found in Appendix A.1.

---

[4] In the context of this work, a musical pitch framework defines the notes that characterise a specific musical style or culture. An octave is defined by two notes, one having twice the pitch of another. Different pitch frameworks have their own way of subdividing the octave to create distinct scales of musical notes. Conventionally, there are 1,200 cents to the octave. Western European music normally subdivides the octave into 12 notes, equally spaced at 100 cents. This forms the so-called chromatic scale. However, some cultures subdivide the octave into notes with different spacings between one another. For example, Slendro Indonesian music subdivides the octave into five notes, spaced by 240 cents from each other. And most Middle Eastern music divides the octave into six notes spaced by 200 cents. Furthermore, no matter how an octave is divided, the notes can be played at different registers, or heights, depending on the instrument at hand. For instance, most pianos can produce 88 notes, accommodating seven octaves. That is, one can play seven different notes 'E' on the piano (or 'Mi' in traditional nomenclature). The snippets discussed in this article are made from the piano's 88 note-set.

Fig. 13.10 Diagrammatic representation of snippets

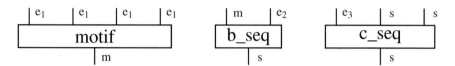

Fig. 13.11 Diagrammatic representation of musical sequences

Verbal languages have different *types* of words, such as nouns, verbs, adjectives, and so on. Grammatical rules then dictate how they are combined to form sentences. Similarly, our composition system contains four *types* of snippets: ground (g), primary (p), secondary (s) and tertiary (t) snippets. Some examples are shown in Fig. 13.12. These will be represented below as s, e_1, e_2 and e_3, respectively. We annotate the wires of the boxes with these types to enforce how the lexicon and production rules can be combined in a grammatical way to form musical compositions (Fig. 13.10).

Languages have different kinds of sentences; e.g., simple, compound, complex, and compound-complex sentence structures. By the same token, here we have three types of musical sequences: motif, basic (b_seq) and composite (c_seq) sequences , respectively (Fig. 13.11).

In a nutshell, a motif is composed of four primary snippets, and a basic sequence is composed of a motif followed by a secondary snippet. A composite sequence will always start with a tertiary snippet, followed by two elements. Each of them can be one of three options: a tertiary snippet, a basic sequence, or another composite one (Fig. 13.12).

Unlike natural languages, the productions rules of this musical grammar are defined explicitly. Therefore it is possible to implement a parser to recover the derivation from the sequence. In fact, our CFG is parsable by a LL(1) parser and hence is a LL(1) grammar [59]. In contrast, parsing natural language requires a contextual understanding of the words, so a statistical CCG parser [66] combined with a conversion from CCG to DisCoCat [65] is necessary. By explicitly implementing a parser, we show that the grammatical structure is recoverable from a sentence and need not be explicitly provided to the DisCoCat model: other models are welcome to take advantage of it.

Firstly, we generated a corpus of 100 compositions for piano. Then, we annotated the corpus according their meaning: *rhythmic* or *melodic*. As explained earlier, the overarching meaning of a composition describes an overall perceived property. Thus, compositions perceived as having prominent fast and loud rhythmic patterns were labelled as RIT (for rhythmic). Otherwise, those having above all successions of notes forming melodies and harmonies were labelled as MEL (for melodic).

Fig. 13.12 Examples of primary, secondary and tertiary snippets, respectively

The annotation of the corpus was carried out manually. The labellings were agreed upon by the authors after they independently listened to the 100 compositions and reached a consensus. Equation 13.4 shows how the corpus Σ of annotated compositions σ look like. The symbols $t3$, $g1$, $p3$, and so on, represent the snippets that form a respective composition.

$$\begin{aligned}
\Sigma = \{ & (1, \text{MEL}, [t3,\ g1,\ p3,\ p1,\ p3,\ p3,\ s3]), \\
& (2, \text{RIT}, [p4,\ p9,\ p7,\ p5,\ s1]), \\
& (3, \text{RIT}, [t3,\ g2,\ g2]), \\
& ...\}
\end{aligned} \tag{13.4}$$

The complete lexicon of musical snippets is provided in Appendix A.2. Although some snippets are more rhythmic than others, and vice-versa, we made sure there is a considerable overlap of snippets between the two categories. This ensures that the machine learning task is realistic. After annotation, the corpus is split into training, development, and test sets with a $50 + 25 + 25$ split, respectively. The compositions last for different durations, ranging for a few seconds to various minutes. A symbolic representation of the dataset is available in Appendix A.3[5]

---

[5] Audio files are available at [https://github.com/CQCL/Quanthoven/]. Note, these were synthesised from MIDI codes.

13.6.2 Pregroup Converter: From Context-Free Grammars to Pregroup Grammars

In this section, we give a functorial mapping from musical CFGs to pregroups. The DisCoCat model is more naturally suitable for pregroup grammars as they are lexicalised grammars. In DisCoCat, most of the grammatical information is stored in the lexicon instead of the grammatical production rules. This is not the case for CFGs. Hence the need to convert to pregroups.

In natural language, a transitive verb is a word that takes a noun on the left and a noun on the right to give a sentence, and so has the pregroup type $F(VP_{TV}) = n^r \cdot s \cdot n^l$. An adjective is a word that takes a noun on the right to give another noun, and so has the pregroup type $F(Adj) = n \cdot n^l$.

Let us reason with analogies here: first we fix the types ground and primary elements, s and e_1, to be the atomic types for our pregroup grammar. This is done by setting $F(s) = s$ and $F(e_1) = n$. Since a motif is made of four primary elements, we give it the pregroup type $F(m) = n \cdot n \cdot n \cdot n$. A secondary element takes a motif on the left to give a sentence, it has the pregroup type $F(e_2) = F(m^r \cdot s) = F(e_1 \cdot e_1 \cdot e_1 \cdot e_1)^r \cdot s = n^r \cdot n^r \cdot n^r \cdot n^r \cdot s$. Finally, a tertiary element takes two sentences on the right to give another sentence, and so it has the pregroup type $F(e_3) = s \cdot s^l \cdot s^l$.

Once we have used our functor to convert the CFG types into the appropriate pregroup types, the CFG production rules become pregroup contractions, which are represented as 'cups' (Fig. 13.13). An example of this conversion on an actual musical grammar can be found in Fig. 13.14.

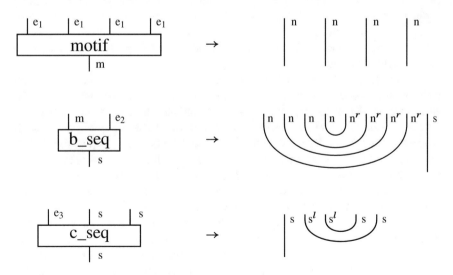

Fig. 13.13 Diagrammatic representation of pregroup contractions

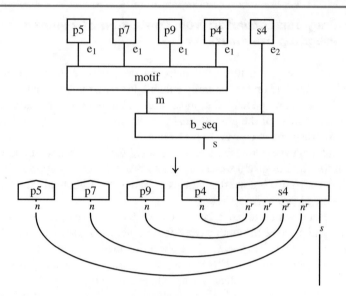

Fig. 13.14 Converting a CFG diagram into pregroup grammar

13.6.3 Optimiser: Diagrammatic Rewriting

Once a CFG diagram is converted into a pregroup grammar diagram, a circuit functor can be applied to transfer the pregroup diagram into a quantum circuit; this will be explained below, in Sect. 13.6.4. However, due the length of the compositions produced by our generation procedure, the resulting quantum circuit, after the functorial conversion has been applied, has too many qubits to be efficiently simulated before being executed on quantum hardware.

Furthermore, to perform the highly entangled qubit measurements—or Bell measurements—required by pregroup grammars, we need to use postselections. To perform a postselection on a qubit, one measures the qubit and then discards the circuits that do not have the desired outcome on the respective qubit. As a rough estimate, postselection halves the number of usable shots.[6] By performing n postselections, we reduce the number of usable shots by a factor of 2^n. For example, if a 12-qubit circuit requires 11 postselections, then we would expect approximately only 4 out of 8192 shots to be usable after postselection. This makes our results even more sensitive to the noise of a quantum computer.

One way to ameliorate both problems is to perform some diagrammatic rewriting. By rotating certain words in the pregroup diagram, we can eliminate the cups that correspond to Bell measurements using what we refer to as the snake equation. In terms of linear algebra, the rotation operation corresponds to taking the transpose. This rewriting technique, first used in [36], can also be applied to our musical pre-

---

[6] 'Shots' is a term used to refer to repeated runs of a circuit.

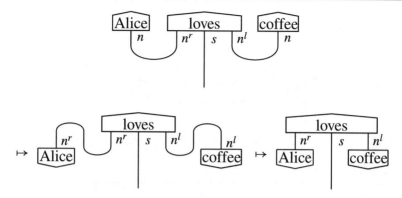

Fig. 13.15 Optimisation through rewriting

group diagrams. In Fig. 13.15, the number of postselections performed is halved from 8 to 4, so the number of useful shots has increased by a factor of 16.

By applying this rewriting technique to our diagrams, we reduce the worse-case circuit size in our training set from 25 qubits to 13 qubits. This is a reduction of 12 postselections. Thus, the number of shots required is reduced by a factor of 4096.

13.6.4 Circuit Converter: Translating Musical Compositions into Quantum Circuits

With DisCoCat, a string diagram for a musical composition σ (which is generated by a CFG and thus has a corresponding pregroup diagram) can be translated onto a parameterised quantum circuit $C_\sigma(\theta_\sigma)$ over a parameter set θ_σ. The translation assigns a number of qubits q_b to each wire carrying a type b. Therefore, Hilbert spaces are defined on the wires (Fig. 13.16).

The snippet-state of the η-th snippet in a string diagram is reinterpreted as a pure quantum state prepared from a given reference product-state by a circuit C_η (Eq. 13.5).

$$C_\eta(\theta_\eta)\,|0\rangle^{\otimes q_\eta} \ , \ \ q_\eta = \sum_{i=1}^{|\eta|} q_{b_i} \tag{13.5}$$

The width of a snippet-circuit depends on the number of qubits assigned to each of the $|\eta|$-many basic types $b \in B$ assigned to the snippet. Given a composition σ, the system firstly concatenates the snippet-states of the snippets as they appear in the composition. Concatenation corresponds to taking their tensor product (Eq. 13.6).

$$C_\sigma(\theta_\sigma)\,|0\rangle^{\otimes q_\sigma} = \bigotimes_{\eta_j} C_{\eta_j}(\theta_{\eta_j})\,|0\rangle^{\otimes q_{\eta_j}} \tag{13.6}$$

The circuit in Fig. 13.17 prepares the state $|\sigma(\theta_\sigma)\rangle$ from the all-zeroes basis states. A musical composition is parameterised by the concatenation of the parameters of its snippets: $\theta_\sigma = \cup_{\eta \in \sigma}\theta_\eta$, where θ_η defines the snippet-embedding $|\eta(\theta_\eta)\rangle$.

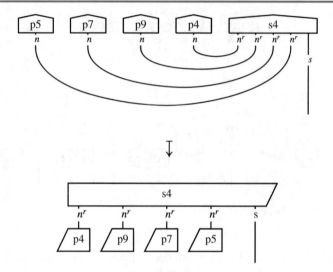

Fig. 13.16 The pregroup diagram in Fig. 13.14 rewritten by removing the caps

Then, Bell effects are applied, as determined by the cups representing pregroup reductions. Cups are interpreted as entangling circuits that implement a Bell effect by postselecting on a Bell state. This effect of grammar, denoted g, acts on the state of the composition and returns the state $g(|\sigma(\theta_\sigma)\rangle)$.

13.6.5 Training the System to Classify

Here we describe how we trained the system with the aforementioned musical dataset to distinguish between two categories of music: rhythmic and melodic.

As we are performing binary classification, we choose to represent the output of the system in one-hot encoding. This means that our two class labels are [0, 1] and [1, 0] corresponding to 'melodic' and 'rhythmic' music respectively. In the DisCoCat model, this can be conveniently achieved by setting the sentence dimension space (recall the whole circuit is represented by an open sentence wire) of our DisCoCat model to one qubit. The circuit C_σ for each composition σ is evaluated for the current set of parameters θ_σ on the quantum computer giving output state $|C(\theta_\sigma)\rangle$. The expected prediction $L^i_{\text{pred}}(\sigma, \theta)$ is given by the Born rule in Eq. 13.7, where $i \in \{0, 1\}$ and $\theta = \bigcup_{\sigma \in \Sigma} \theta_\sigma$.

$$L^i_{\text{pred}}(\sigma, \theta) := |\langle i|C_\sigma(\theta_\sigma)\rangle|^2 \qquad (13.7)$$

Fig. 13.17 The pregroup diagram in Fig. 13.16 converted to a quantum circuit, according to the IQP and Euler decomposition ansätze. Regions of the diagram and circuit have been coloured to illustrate the transformation of each part of the diagram into a quantum circuit

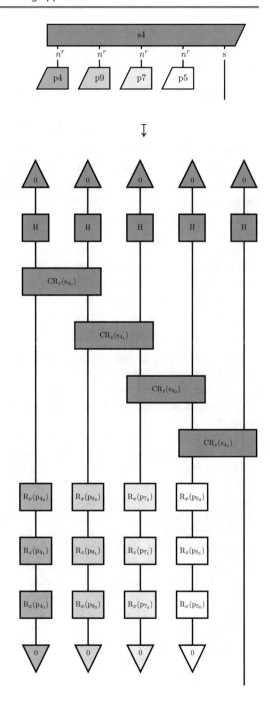

By running and measuring the outcome (either $[0, 1]$ or $[1, 0]$) of the circuit many times, the average outcome will converge towards this value. Then $L^i_{\text{pred}}(\sigma, \theta)$ is normalised to obtain a smooth probability distribution (Eq. 13.8).

$$l^i_{\text{pred}}(\sigma, \theta) := \frac{L^i_{\text{pred}}(\sigma, \theta) + \epsilon}{\sum_j \left(L^j_{\text{pred}}(\sigma, \theta) + \epsilon \right)} \tag{13.8}$$

The smoothing term is chosen to be $\epsilon = 10^{-9}$. The predicted label is obtained from the probability distribution by setting a decision threshold t on $l^0_{\text{pred}}(\sigma, \theta)$: if $t < l^0_{\text{pred}}(\sigma, \theta)$ then the predicted label is $[0, 1]$. And if $t \geq l^0_{\text{pred}}(\sigma, \theta)$ then the predicted label is $[1, 0]$. This threshold can be adjusted depending on the desired sensitivity and specificity of the system. For this chapter, the threshold $t = 0.5$ is selected.

To predict the label for a given snippet well, we need to use optimisation methods to find optimal parameters for our model. We begin by comparing the predicted label with the training label using a loss function. Since we are performing a classification task, the binary cross-entropy loss function is chosen (Eq. 13.9).

$$\text{BCE}(\theta) = \sum_\sigma \sum_{i \in \{0,1\}} l^i_{\text{label}}(\sigma, \theta) \log(l^i_{\text{pred}}(\sigma, \theta)) \tag{13.9}$$

A non-gradient based optimisation algorithm known as SPSA (Simultaneous Perturbation Stochastic Approximation) is used to minimise our loss function [61]. Alternatively, one could use gradient-based optimisation algorithms by differentiating the DisCoCat diagram [63]. However, SPSA was found to be sufficient for our purposes.

In order to minimise the loss function, the system learns to classify the compositions by adjusting the parameters of the musical snippets. Philosophically, this is in contrast to typical machine learning models—that is, neural networks—where the weights of the network are adjusted rather than the weights of the word embeddings. This is because pregroup grammars are lexical. And in lexical grammar, whilst words have parameters that can be changed, the grammatical structure cannot be changed.

Unfortunately, the training process cannot be performed entirely on a real quantum device at the time of writing. Access to quantum hardware still is limited, due to the demand for and the limited number of available quantum processors at the time of writing. This can be problematic for running variational tasks where circuits must be run for many iterations in order to get satisfactory results.

Therefore, we firstly pre-train the model parameters using the exact tensor contraction of the quantum circuits on a classical computer. We use Python's JAX library[7] for just-in-time compilation, which speeds up the pre-training. This speed-up allows us to efficiently perform grid search and find the best hyper-parameter settings for the SPSA optimiser. The results for such a classical simulation are shown in Fig. 13.18 for the final settings chosen for the subsequent training.

---

[7] https://jax.readthedocs.io/en/latest/.

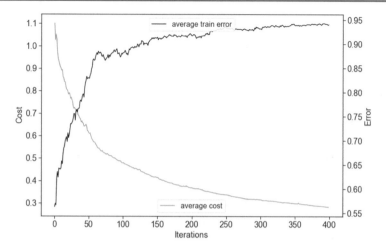

Fig. 13.18 Average over 20 different runs of a classical simulation of the training set showing the cost (green, left hand side axis) and the training error (black, right hand side axis)

Then, we simulate the quantum process on a classical machine. In order to do this, we need to take into account the statistical nature of experiments, which would involve running the same circuit thousands of times to obtain measurement statistics. And we also need to bear in mind the noise that is present in a real device. The parameters learnt from the exact pre-training are transferred to a model, which closely resembles the real quantum device, which includes noise simulation. This will ultimately improve testing performance on the real quantum device. So, the same circuit is simulated 8192 times with a noise model specific to the quantum device that will be used for testing. This process is carried out for each composition in the training set, for a chosen number of iterations. The train and development set results from the quantum simulations are shown in Fig. 13.19.

Once the pre-training phase is complete, and we are happy with the simulated results on the development set, then we take the parameters from the noisy quantum simulation and evaluate the test set on a real quantum computer. We used IBM Quantum's device ibmq_guadalupe, which is a 16-qubit superconducting processor with a quantum volume of 32. Despite the expected differences between a real experiment and a simulation, we can see that the model learns to classify compositions in the test set with an impressive final accuracy of 76%, as shown in Fig. 13.19.

13.6.5.1 Further Classification Tests

The results from the testing with quantum hardware (Fig. 13.19) exceeded our expectations. We conducted additional tests to probe the system further, which confirmed the system's positive performance.

For the new tests we ran our CFG to produce two additional datasets: one containing 60 compositions and another containing 90. As with the previous dataset, we

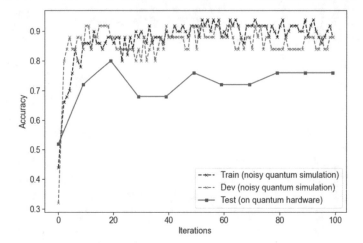

Fig. 13.19 Noisy quantum simulation to train the model (black), noisy quantum simulation of the development set (blue) and the test set run on on quantum hardware (red). The noise model used for the noisy simulation was that of the `ibmq_guadalupe` device, which is the hardware that we subsequently usedfor running the test set

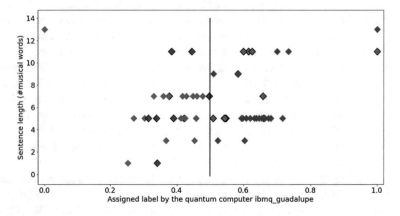

Fig. 13.20 Quantum computing classification of dataset with 60 compositions

auditioned and annotated the pieces manually. Again, both sets contain compositions of varying lengths. Then, we submitted the sets to the quantum classifier. Now we display the results from a different perspective than in Fig. 13.19.

Figure 13.20 shows that the system correctly classified 39 compositions from the set of 60. Melodic pieces correspond to a value plotted on the first element in the tuple of <0.5 (grey), whereas the Rhythmic ones correspond to a value ≥0.5 (red). Misclassified compositions have a black outline around them, as well as being the wrong colour for the side of the graph that they appear on. For clarity, Fig. 13.21 plots only those compositions that were classified correctly.

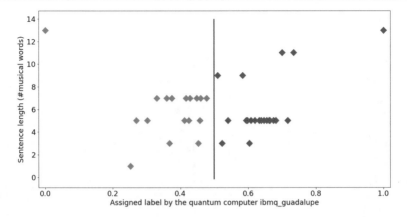

Fig. 13.21 A version of Fig. 13.20 plotting only those pieces that were classified correctly

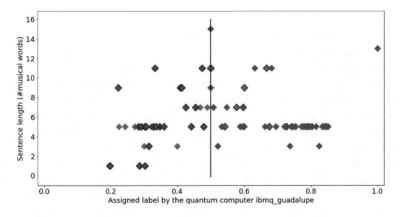

Fig. 13.22 Quantum computing classification of dataset with 60 compositions

Next, Fig. 13.22 shows that the system correctly classified 59 compositions from the set of 90. Again, Melodic (MEL) pieces corresponds to a value plotted on the first element in the tuple of <0.5 (grey), whereas the Rhythmic (RIT) ones corresponds to a value ≥0.5 (red). And Fig. 13.23 shows the same results, but plots only those compositions that were classified correctly.

13.7 *Quanthoven*: Leveraging the Quantum Classifier to Compose

Composer Lejaren Hiller, who also was a chemistry teacher, allegedly is a pioneer of programming computers to generate music. In 1957, he teamed up with Leonard Isaacson, also a chemist and composer, to program the ILLIAC I

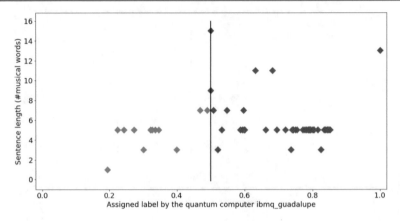

Fig. 13.23 A version of Fig. 13.22 plotting only those pieces that were classified correctly

(Illinois Automatic Computer)[8] at the University of Illinois, USA, to compose music. The computer produced materials for their string quartet, entitled *Illiac Suite*.[9]

In their initial experiments, they programmed the computer to do two things: (a) generate musical data[10] (pseudo-randomly), and (b) test if the data satisfied musical rules. Musical data that did not satisfy the rules were discarded. Conversely, those that satisfied the rules were kept for the ongoing composition. For instance, for the first movement of *Illiac Suite* they set the machine with rules from the famous treatise *Gradus ad Parnassum*, written by Joseph Fux in the 17th century [37].

Hiller's approach became an archetype for algorithmic music composition with computers, which is often referred to as the *generate-and-test* approach (Fig. 13.24). Various variants have been implemented, with increasingly sophisticated methods for generating musical data and probing them [20,41]. Such systems might generate notes that are checked one at a time, or generate phrases, larger sequences or even entire pieces. Human approval often takes place as well, whereby composers may further discard or amend computer-validated materials.

The generate-and-test approach also informed the development of Artificial Intelligence (AI) techniques for musical composition [23,46], including highly praised constraint-satisfaction methods [3]. Moreover, the generate-and-test method epitomises Evolutionary Computing techniques for music composition; e.g., using genetic algorithms [47]. Such systems generate new sequences using biologically inspired processes (e.g., genetic mating, reproduction and mutation) and then employ fitness measurements to evaluate them [43].

---

[8] This was the first von Neumann architecture computer built and owned by a university in the USA. It was put into service on September 22, 1952.

[9] Later retitled as "String Quartet No. 4".

[10] That is, sequences of symbols representing notes, rhythms and expressions such as 'pizzicato and 'arco', and so on.

Fig. 13.24 Archetypal
generate-and-test approach
to algorithmic music
composition

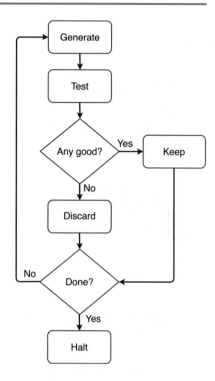

The quantum machine learning paradigm discussed above fits the generate-and-test approach to algorithmic music composition very nicely. To test this, we developed *Quanthoven*, a system for composition with the classifier presented above acting as the evaluator. In a nutshell, the CFG (Sect. 13.6.1) generates compositions and the trained classifier (Sect. 13.6.5) evaluates them (Fig. 13.24).

In the introduction, we mentioned that our ambition is to develop systems to aid musicians to compose 'music for Alice's tea party', or a 'tune to make Bob feel energetic'. In order to do this, the machine is required to handle the meaning of music; that is, the perceived properties of musical compositions, which holistically characterise their style. Our proof-of-concept gives a good hint about how this can be achieved.

Effectively, our machine learning algorithm learned what we mean by 'melodic' and 'rhythmic' music. The CFG can generate pieces with snippets combined in ways that may render a piece more melodic than rhythmic, or vice-versa. Some might be neither to our ears, others might be both. But the quantum classifier is able to suggest whether a CFG-generated piece is one or the other.

As a demonstration, we set ourselves the task of composing four pieces of music with *Quanthoven*: two for relaxing at a tea party and two aimed at inducing excitement. We set *Quanthoven* to generate two dozen pieces and save four, two for each category. The others were discarded on the spot; we do not even know what they sounded like.

Alice's Caffeine Rush

Quanthoven

-- CQ & ICCMR, Aug 2021 --

Fig. 13.25 First page of the composition *Alice's Caffeine Rush*

The saved pieces were encoded as MIDI files. Then, we uploaded these files into a music editor, formatted them, added titles and other details, and printed the scores. We hired a professional pianist to record them. The two pieces for relaxing at a tea party were entitled *Bob's Chamomile Slowdown* and *Alice's Mushroom Trip*. The ones aimed at making one feel excited were entitled *Bob's Cigar Buzz* and *Alice's Caffeine Rush*.

The score for *Alice's Caffeine Rush* is shown in Figs. 13.25 and 13.26. The eyes of a trained musician would immediately see patterns that characterise this piece as rhythmic, in particular, the section starting at bar 15. The scores for the other three pieces are provided in Appendix A.4.

Fig. 13.26 Second page of the composition *Alice's Caffeine Rush*

13.8 Final Remarks

Recordings of all four pieces are released in SoundClick [58]. You are invited to listen to the compositions and make your own mind whether you agree with *Quanthoven* or not. We are rather satisfied with the results. But of course, they are debatable.

This chapter started by saying that people have different tastes and opinions about music. And it is also noted that people perceive and react to music differently from each other. However, the five authors agreed on the 'meanings' here. And the aim was to teach the machine to classify the pieces according to our opinions. Objectively, the system does what it says on the tin.

We made the conscious decision of conducting this experiment with music generated from a CFG designed from the ground up, completely from scratch. Of course, we could have written a piece of software to extract a CFG from given corpora of musical scores; e.g., [6]. Ultimately, we would extract this information directly from audio recordings. However, we wanted to test our approach with something other than existing styles of music. Moreover, we wanted to ensure that, at this stage of our research, the two categories in question share the same grammatical structure. Effective annotation methods for a much larger database should also be developed; for instance, based on information extracted from social media.

As quantum computing hardware and error-correction technologies evolve, we will certainly continue pushing the boundaries in tandem, with compositions of increased sophistication, more instruments, longer durations, more categories (or 'meanings'), and so on. These will probably require generative mechanisms other than CFG, something along the lines of transformational-generative grammars. Also, an important next step would be to design an actual quantum generative music engine drawing directly from the classifier, as opposed to using the classifier as a filter.

Acknowledgements This project was developed during Miranda's research residency at Quantinuum (formerly Cambridge Quantum) in 2021, which was partially funded by the QuTune Project. QuTune kick-started in the Spring of 2021 thanks to funding kindly provided by the UK National Quantum Technologies Programme's QCS Hub: [https://iccmr-quantum.github.io/]. Coecke acknowledges support from Foundational Questions Institute (FQXi). Project entitled *Categorical Theories of Consciousness: Bridging Neuroscience and Fundamental Physics*: [https://fqxi. org]. The authors thank pianist, Lauryna Sableveciute, and recording engineers, John Lowndes and Manoli Moriaty, at Liverpool Hope University, for the recordings of *Bob's Chamomile Slowdown*, *Alice's Mushroom Trip*, *Bob's Cigar Buzz*, and *Alice's Caffeine Rush*.

A Appendices

A.1 Context-Free Grammars and Monoidal Category Theory

A context-free grammar (CFG) is typically defined with a set of terminal words T, non-terminal symbols N, and a set of production rules of the form A $\rightarrow$ α, where A $\in N$ is a non-terminal symbol and $\alpha \in (N \cup T)^*$ is a string of terminal words and non-terminal characters. Any sentence that can be produced by freely applying the production rules on the starting terminal symbol S is considered to be a grammatical sentence.

For example, below is a CFG which defines a collection of sentences:

$$\text{NP} \rightarrow \text{Adj NP, S} \rightarrow \text{NP V NP, NP} \rightarrow \text{N}$$

$$\text{N} \rightarrow n \in \{Alice, tea\}$$

$$\text{V} \rightarrow v \in \{drinks, likes, hates\}$$

Fig. 13.27 A diagrammatic representation of the CFG example (top) and a sentence built using it (bottom)

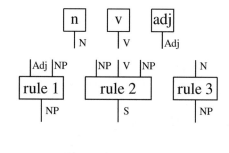

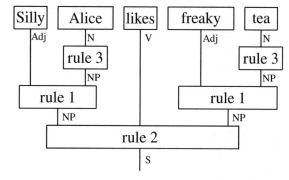

$$\text{Adj} \rightarrow adj \in \{funny, silly, freaky\}$$

The general framework of CFGs can be thought of as a freely generated monoidal category. In diagrammatic notation, a monoidal category consists of boxes with input and output wires. The 'types' of the wires are the generating objects of the monoidal category. Wires of matching types can be connected by extending the wire vertically.

In a free monoidal category, any diagram produced by freely composing the boxes is a valid diagram in the category. This resembles how CFGs allow free applications of the production rules.

Production rules in a CFG of the form $A \rightarrow \alpha$ are represented as a box with multiple input wires representing the string α and output wire representing the non-terminal A. Input wires representing terminal words in α are closed with boxes of type $I \rightarrow T$, where I is an auxiliary type for terminal types. For example, the CFG above can be described by freely composing the boxes in Fig. 13.27.

A.2 Lexicon of Musical Snippets

The lexicon for the music composition system presented in this chapter contains four types of snippets: ground (g), primary (p) secondary (s) and tertiary (t) snippets. Here, snippets are for music what words are for natural languages; languages have different types of words, such as nouns, verbs, and adjectives (Figs. 13.28, 13.29, 13.30 and 13.31).

Fig. 13.28 Ground snippets g1 and g2

Fig. 13.29 Primary snippets p1, p2, p3, p4, p5, p6, p7, p8, and p9

Fig. 13.30 Secondary snippets s1, s2, s3, and s4

Fig. 13.31 Tertiary snippets t1, t2 and t3

A.3 Musical Datasets

A.3.1 Training Data

$\Sigma_\alpha = \{(1, \text{MEL}, [t3, g1, g1]),$
$(2, \text{MEL}, [t3, p8, p1, p8, p1, s4, g1]),$
$(3, \text{RIT}, [t3, p9, p9, p5, p9, s4, g2]),$
$(4, \text{RIT}, [p9, p4, p4, p4, s3]),$
$(5, \text{RIT}, [p4, p9, p9, p9, s4]),$
$(6, \text{RIT}, [p5, p9, p4, p5, s1]),$
$(7, \text{RIT}, [t3, p9, p5, p7, p7, s1, g2]),$
$(8, \text{MEL}, [p1, p8, p2, p3, s4]),$
$(9, \text{MEL}, [p6, p1, p8, p3, s4]),$
$(10, \text{MEL}, [t2, g1, t1, g1, g1]),$
$(11, \text{RIT}, [p4, p5, p5, p7, s4]),$
$(12, \text{MEL}, [t2, t3, t2, g1, g1, g1, g1]),$
$(13, \text{MEL}, [p8, p1, p6, p2, s4]),$
$(14, \text{RIT}, [p5, p7, p7, p9, s2]),$
$(15, \text{RIT}, [p5, p7, p5, p9, s4]),$
$(16, \text{RIT}, [t3, g2, p9, p9, p7, p7, s1]),$
$(17, \text{MEL}, [p6, p2, p3, p2, s1]),$
$(18, \text{MEL}, [t1, g1, p3, p1, p1, p1, s2]),$
$(19, \text{RIT}, [p7, p7, p5, p7, s1]),$
$(20, \text{RIT}, [t3, p5, p9, p5, p7, s2, g2]),$
$(21, \text{RIT}, [p7, p4, p4, p9, s2]),$
$(22, \text{RIT}, [p5, p9, p5, p4, s1]),$
$(23, \text{RIT}, [p9, p9, p7, p9, s1]),$
$(24, \text{RIT}, [p7, p7, p9, p7, s1]),$
$(25, \text{RIT}, [p9, p4, p5, p7, s4]),$
$(26, \text{MEL}, [t3, p8, p6, p1, p2, s2, g1]),$
$(27, \text{MEL}, [t2, p6, p8, p8, p8, s1, g1]),$
$(28, \text{MEL}, [p6, p3, p6, p6, s2]),$
$(29, \text{MEL}, [p6, p8, p3, p1, s2]),$
$(30, \text{MEL}, [p1, p2, p6, p6, s4]),$
$(31, \text{MEL}, [p6, p1, p2, p8, s3]),$

(32, MEL, [p1, p1, p6, p3, s2]),
(33, RIT, [p4, p9, p7, p5, s1]),
(34, RIT, [t2, g2, p5, p4, p5, p4, s1]),
(35, RIT, [p9, p9, p9, p5, s3]),
(36, RIT, [p9, p9, p5, p5, s4]),
(37, MEL, [p6, p2, p6, p2, s1]),
(38, RIT, [p5, p5, p5, p5, s4]),
(39, MEL, [p6, p1, p1, p1, s1]),
(40, RIT, [p5, p7, p5, p4, s2]),
(41, MEL, [t2, g1, p1, p6, p2, p6, s2]),
(42, MEL, [p1, p6, p3, p8, s2]),
(43, RIT, [p4, p5, p7, p7, s1]),
(44, MEL, [p1, p6, p8, p1, s2]),
(45, MEL, [p6, p1, p2, p3, s1]),
(46, RIT, [t2, g2, t1, g2, p9, p5, p4, p9, s2]),
(47, MEL, [t3, t1, g1, g1, p8, p6, p6, p8, s4]),
(48, MEL, [p2, p3, p8, p6, s2]),
(49, RIT, [t1, g2, t1, p7, p4, p7, p7, s4, g2]),
(50, RIT, [t1, t2, g2, p4, p9, p4, p7, s4, g2])}

A.3.2 Development Data

$\Sigma_\beta = \{(51, MEL, [t1, g1, p8, p6, p8, p2, s4]),$
(52, MEL, [t1, p6, p8, p2, p8, s4, g1]),
(53, RIT, [p4, p5, p7, p4, s2]),
(54, MEL, [t2, p2, p8, p1, p6, s2, g1]),
(55, MEL, [p8, p2, p3, p1, s2]),
(56, MEL, [t3, p6, p2, p8, p2, s3, g1]),
(57, RIT, [p4, p9, p4, p9, s1]),
(58, RIT, [p7, p9, p5, p4, s4]),
(59, RIT, [t2, p7, p7, p4, p9, s1, g2]),
(60, RIT, [p9, p9, p7, p5, s4]),
(61, RIT, [p5, p9, p5, p7, s1]),
(62, RIT, [p4, p5, p4, p9, s2]),
(63, RIT, [p9, p4, p9, p9, s4]),
(64, RIT, [p4, p7, p5, p5, s3]),
(65, MEL, [p2, p1, p2, p2, s3]),
(66, RIT, [p7, p7, p9, p7, s4]),
(67, MEL, [p6, p3, p6, p6, s4]),
(68, RIT, [p9, p7, p9, p4, s3]),
(69, RIT, [p9, p9, p4, p5, s2]),
(70, MEL, [p8, p3, p2, p6, s2]),
(71, RIT, [p9, p4, p5, p4, s4]),
(72, MEL, [p6, p6, p2, p3, s4]),
(73, RIT, [p7, p7, p4, p5, s2]),

(74, MEL, [t3, g1, t3, g1, p1, p2, p2, p3, s2]),
(75, MEL, [t1, g1, g1])}

A.3.3 Testing Data

$\Sigma_\gamma = \{(76,$ RIT, [p9, p9, p9, p9, s1]),
(77, MEL, [p3, p6, p8, p2, s4]),
(78, RIT, [p4, p7, p5, p9, s1]),
(79, RIT, [p9, p9, p5, p5, s3]),
(80, RIT, [p7, p9, p9, p7, s2]),
(81, RIT, [t3, g2, p4, p4, p9, p9, s4]),
(82, RIT, [p4, p4, p7, p9, s2]),
(83, RIT, [p4, p5, p9, p4, s4]),
(84, MEL, [t3, p6, p6, p8, p3, s4, g1]),
(85, MEL, [p2, p6, p1, p8, s3]),
(86, MEL, [p6, p2, p8, p3, s4]),
(87, MEL, [p8, p3, p1, p2, s2]),
(88, MEL, [t1, g1, t3, g1, g1]),
(89, RIT, [p9, p7, p9, p9, s2]),
(90, RIT, [p9, p7, p7, p9, s3]),
(91, MEL, [t3, g1, p3, p1, p3, p3, s3]),
(92, MEL, [p3, p3, p1, p8, s3]),
(93, MEL, [t2, p2, p1, p3, p8, s3, g1]),
(94, MEL, [t3, g1, p3, p8, p3, p3, s2]),
(95, MEL, [p2, p1, p6, p6, s3]),
(96, RIT, [t1, p5, p9, p4, p9, s3, g2]),
(97, RIT, [t2, p9, p7, p5, p5, s4, g2]),
(98, MEL, [t2, p2, p1, p6, p1, s4, g1]),
(99, RIT, [t3, p9, p5, p9, p9, s1, t3, g2, g2]),
(100, MEL, [t2, g1, g1])}

A.4 Compositions

See Figs. 13.32, 13.33, 13.34, 13.35.

Fig. 13.32 The composition *Bob's Chamomile Slowdown*

Alice's Mushroom Trip

Quanthoven

-- CQ & ICCMR, Aug 2021 --

Fig. 13.33 The composition *Alice's Mushroom Trip*

Bob's Cigar Buzz

1

Quanthoven

-- CQ & ICCMR, Aug 2021 --

Fig. 13.34 First page of the composition *Bob's Cigar Rush*

Fig. 13.35 Second page of the composition *Bob's Cigar Rush*

References

1. Abramsky, S., & Coecke, B. (2008). Categorical quantum mechanics. In K. Engesser et al., (Eds.), *Handbook of quantum logic and quantum structures*. Elsevier. arxiv:0808.1023.
2. Adiyansjah, A., Gunawan, A. S., & Suhartono, D. (2019). Music recommender system based on genre using convolutional recurrent neural networks. *Procedia Computer Science, 157*, 99–109. https://doi.org/10.1016/j.procs.2019.08.146
3. Anders, T., & Miranda, E. R. (2009). Interfacing manual and machine composition. *Contemporary Music Review, 28*(2), 133–147. https://doi.org/10.1080/07494460903322422
4. Bakker, D., & Martin, F. H. (2014). Musical chords and emotion: Major and minor triads are processed for emotion. *Cognitive Affective and Behavioral Neuroscience, 15*(1), 15–31. https://doi.org/10.3758/s13415-014-0309-4
5. Baroni, M. (1999). Musical grammar and the study of cognitive processes of composition. *Musicae Scientiae, 3*(1), 3–21.
6. Bod, J. C. (2001). Probabilistic grammars for music. https://www.researchgate.net/publication/2402113_Probabilistic_Grammars_for_Music.
7. de Boer, B. (1999). Evolution and self-organisation in vowel systems. *Evolution of Communication, 3*(1), 79–103.
8. Cherston, J., Hill, E., Goldfarb, S., & Paradiso, J. A. (2016). Musician and mega-machine: Composition driven by real-time particle collision data from the ATLAS detector. In *Proceedings of NIME* (pp. 11–15).
9. Chomsky, N. (1975). *The logical structure of linguistic theory*. Springer.
10. Chomsky, N. (2006). *Language and mind*. Cambridge University Press.
11. Coecke, B., & Duncan, R. (2011). Interacting quantum observables: Categorical algebra and diagrammatics. *New Journal of Physics, 13*(4), 04301. arxiv:0906.4725.
12. Coecke, B., & Kissinger, A. (2017). *Picturing quantum processes: A first course in quantum theory and diagrammatic reasoning*. Cambridge University Press.
13. Coecke, B., Mehrnoosh, S., & Clark, S. (2010). Mathematical foundations for a compositional distributional model of meaning. *Linguistic Analysis, 36*(1–4), 345–384. arxiv:1003.4394.
14. Coecke, B., Grefenstette, E., & Sadrzadeh, M. (2013). Lambek versus Lambek: Functorial vector space semantics and strings diagrams for Lambek calculus. *Annals of Pure and Applied Logic, 164*, 1079–1100. https://doi.org/10.1016/j.apal.2013.05.009.
15. Coecke, B. (2021). Compositionality as we see it, everywhere around us. https://arxiv.org/abs/2110.05327
16. Cope, D. (1991). Recombinant music: Using the computer to explore musical style. *Computer, 24*(7), 22–28. https://doi.org/10.1109/2.84830
17. Cope, D. (2000). *The algorithmic composer*. A-R Editions.
18. Daly, I., Williams, D., Hallowell, J., Hwang, F., Kirke, A., Malik, A., Weaver, J., Miranda, E. R., & Nasuto, S. J. (2015). Music-induced emotions can be predicted from a combination of brain activity and acoustic features. *Brain and Cognition, 101*, 1–11. https://doi.org/10.1016/j.bandc.2015.08.003
19. Dawson, C., Aalto, D., Šimko, J., Vainio, M., & Tervaniemi, M. (2017). Musical sophistication and the effect of complexity on auditory discrimination in finnish speakers. *Frontiers in Neuroscience, 11*, 213. https://doi.org/10.3389/fnins.2017.00213.
20. Edwards, M. (2011). Algorithmic composition: Computational thinking in music. *Communications of the ACM, 54*(7), 58–67.
21. Eliot, L. (1999). *Early intelligence*. Penguin Books.
22. de Felice, G., Tuomi, A., Coecke, B. (2020). Discopy: Monoidal categories in python. In *Applied Category Theory 2020 Conference*. arxiv:2005.02975.
23. Fernandez, J. D., & Vico, F. (2013). Ai methods in algorithmic composition: A comprehensive survey. *Journal of Artificial Intelligence Research, 48*, 513–582.

24. Frank, S. L., Bod, R., & Christiansen, M. H. (2012). How hierarchical is language use? *Proceedings of the Royal Society B, 279*(1747), 4522–4531. https://doi.org/10.1098/rspb.2012. 1741
25. Gouyon, P.-Y., Henry, J.-P., & Arnould, J. (2002). *Gene avatars: The neo-Darwinian theory of evolution.* Kluwer Academic/Plenum Publishers.
26. Harley, J. (1995). Generative processes in algorithmic composition: Chaos and music. *Leonardo, 28*(3), 221–224.
27. Hopcroft, J. E., & Ullman, J. D. (1979). *Introduction to automata theory, languages, and computation.* Addison-Wesley.
28. Hsü, K. J., & Hsü, A. J. (1990). Fractal geometry of music. *Proceedings of the National Academy of Sciences, Physics, 87*, 938–941.
29. Jäncke, L. (2012). The relationship between music and language. *Frontiers in Psychology, 3*, 123. https://doi.org/10.3389/fpsyg.2012.001
30. Jordan, R., & Kafalenos, E. (1994). Listening to music: Semiotic and narratological models. *Musikometrik, 6*, 87–115.
31. Kartsaklis, D., Fan, I., Yeung, R., Pearson, A., Lorenz, R., Toumi, A., de Felice, G., Meichanetzidis, K., Clark, S., & Coecke, B. (2021). Lambeq: An efficient high-level python library for quantum NLP.
32. Koelsch, S. (2011). Toward a neural basis of music perception—A review and updated model. *Frontiers in Psychology, 2*, 110. https://doi.org/10.3389/fpsyg.2011.00110
33. Koelsch, S. (2014). Brain correlates of music-evoked emotions. *Nature Reviews Neuroscience, 15*, 170–180. https://doi.org/10.1038/nrn3666
34. Lambek, J. (1999). Type grammar revisited. In *Lecture notes in computer science* (Vol. 582, pp. 1–27). Springer.
35. Lerdhal, F., & Jackendoff, R. (1996). *A generative theory of tonal music.* The MIT Press.
36. Lorenz, R., Pearson, A., Meichanetzidis, K., Kartsaklis, D., & Coecke, B. (2021). QNLP in practice: Running compositional models of meaning on a quantum computer. arxiv:2102.12846.
37. Mann, A. (1965). *The study of counterpoint: From Johann Joseph Fux's Gradus ad Parnassum.* W. W. Norton and Company.
38. Meichanetzidis, K., Toumi, A., de Felice, G., & Coecke, B. (2020). Grammar-aware question-answering on quantum computers. arxiv:2012.03756.
39. Meichanetzidis, K., Gogioso, S., De Felice, G., Chiappori, N., Toumi, A., & Coecke, B. (2021). Quantum natural language processing on near-term quantum computers. *Electronic Proceedings in Theoretical Computer Science, 340*, 213–229. ISSN: 2075-2180. https://doi.org/10. 4204/eptcs.340.11.
40. Milovanov, R., & Tervaniemi, M. (2011). The interplay between musical and linguistic aptitudes: A review. *Frontiers in Psychology, 2*, 321. https://doi.org/10.3389/fpsyg.2011.00321
41. Miranda, E. R. (2001). *Composing music with computers.* Focal Press.
42. Miranda, E. R. (2008). Emergent songs by social robots. *Journal of Experimental and Theoretical Artificial Intelligence, 20*(4), 319–334. https://doi.org/10.1080/09528130701664640
43. Miranda, E. R. (2011). *A-life for music: Music and computer models of living systems.* A-R Editions. ISBN: 978-0-89579-673-8.
44. Miranda, E. R. (2014). *Thinking music: The inner workings of a composer's mind.* University of Plymouth Press.
45. Miranda, E. R. (2020). Genetic music system with synthetic biology. *Artificial Life, 26*(3), 1–27. https://doi.org/10.1162/artl_a_00325
46. Miranda, E. R. (Ed.). (2021). *Handbook of artificial intelligence for music foundations, advanced approaches, and developments for creativity.* Springer International Publishing. https:// doi.org/10.1007/978-3-030-72116-9.
47. Miranda, E. R., & Biles, J. A. (2007). *Evolutionary computer music.* Springer.
48. Miranda, E. R., Kirby, S., & Todd, P. (2010). On computational models of the evolution of music: From the origins of musical taste to the emergence of grammars. *Contemporary Music Review, 22*(3), 91–111. https://doi.org/10.1080/0749446032000150915

49. Monelle, R. (1992). *Linguistics and semiotics in music*. Harwood Academic Publishers.
50. Moore, J. (2019). The language of moss. https://web.archive.org/web/20090813110752, http://www.thelanguageofmoss.com/. Accessed 02 Apr. 2021.
51. Nielsen, M. A., & Chuang, I. L. (2011). *Quantum computation and quantum information: 10th anniversary edition* (10th ed.). Cambridge University Press. 10.7002176. ISBN: 978-1107002173.
52. Orus, R. (2014). A practical introduction to tensor networks: Matrix product states and projected entangled pair states. *Annals of Physics, 349*, 117–158. arxiv.org:1306.2164.
53. Pachet, F., Roy, P., & Carre, B. (2021). Assistive music creation with flow machines: Towards new categories of new. In E. R. Miranda (Ed.), *Handbook of artificial intelligence for music* (pp. 485–520). Springer. ISBN: 978-3-030-72115-2.
54. Patel, A., & Morgan, E. (2016). Exploring cognitive relations between prediction in language and music. *Cognitive Science: A Multidisciplinary Journal, 41*(S2), 303–320. https://doi.org/10.1111/cogs.12411
55. Patel, A. D. (2011). Why would musical training benefit the neural encoding of speech? The opera hypothesis. *Frontiers in Psychology, 2*, 142. https://doi.org/10.3389/fpsyg.2011.00142
56. Perchy, S., & Sarria, G. (2016). Musical composition with stochastic context-free grammars. In *Proceedings of 8th Mexican International Conference on Artificial Intelligence*. https://hal.inria.fr/hal-01257155. Accessed 05 Apr. 2021.
57. Peterson, D. (2015). *The art of language invention*. Penguin Random House.
58. Quanthoven. (2021). *Quantum computer music album*. SoundClick. www.soundclick.com/LudovicoQuanthoven.
59. Rosenkrantz, D. J., & Stearns, R. E. (1970). Properties of deterministic top-down grammars. *Information and Control, 17*(3), 226–256. https://doi.org/10.1016/S0019-9958(70)90446-8. https://www.sciencedirect.com/science/article/pii/S0019995870904468. ISSN: 0019-9958.
60. Sivarajah, S., Dilkes, S., Cowtan, A., Simmons, W., Edgington, A., & Duncan, R. (2020). t|ket?: a retargetable compiler for NISQ devices. *Quantum Science and Technology, 6*(1), 014003. https://doi.org/10.1088/2058-9565/ab8e92. ISSN: 2058-9565.
61. Spall, J. C. (1998). Implementation of the simultaneous perturbation algorithm for stochastic optimization. *IEEE Transactions on Aerospace and Electronic Systems, 34*(3), 817–823. https://doi.org/10.1109/7.705889
62. Sutor, R. S. (2019). *Dancing with qubits: How quantum computing works and how it can change the word*. Packt. ISBN: 978-1-838-82736-6.
63. Toumi, A., Yeung, R., & de Felice, G. (2021). Diagrammatic differentiation for quantum machine learning. *Electronic Proceedings in Theoretical Computer Science, 343*, 132–144. https://doi.org/10.4204/eptcs.343.7. ISSN: 2075-2180.
64. Woods, W. A. (1970). Transition networks grammars for natural language analysis. *Communications of the ACM, 13*(10). https://doi.org/10.1145/355598.362773.
65. Yeung, R., & Kartsaklis, D. (2021). A CCG-based version of the DisCoCat framework. https://arxiv.org/abs/2105.07720
66. Yoshikawa, M., Noji, H., & Matsumoto, Y. (2017). A* CCG parsing with a supertag and dependency factored model. In *Proceedings of the 55th Annual Meeting of the Association for Computational Linguistics* (Vol. 1, pp. 277–287). Association for Computational Linguistics. https://doi.org/10.18653/v1/P17-1026. http://aclweb.org/anthology/P17-1026.

Adiabatic Quantum Computing and Applications to Music

14

Jake M. Chuharski

Abstract

This chapter presents an approach to making music with Adiabatic Quantum Computing. We layout an introduction to the adiabatic algorithm with examples of classical analogues to our quantum problem. We expand on Adiabatic Quantum Computing, adiabatic runtimes, and Quantum Annealing to give background on an example approach to making music by using D-Wave quantum annealers and the Python package *Mingus*. We discuss in detail the software *Algorhythms*. We present how it works, why it works, and how it can be further expanded. Algorhythms is a first of its kind music generation program to be used on D-Wave quantum annealers. The results of our exploration have led to excitement about the potential applications and expansions of the technology to be used in creating quantum-inspired music.

14.1 Introduction

The idea of a computational device based on quantum mechanics was explored as early as the 1970s. By 1998 Neil Gershenfeld, Isaac Chuang, and Mark Kubinec created the first working two-qubit quantum computer. In order to create their model, they dissolved a large number of chloroform molecules ($CHCL_3$) in water at room temperature and applied a magnetic field to orient the spins of the carbon and hydrogen nuclei in the chloroform. A spin parallel to the external magnetic field was interpreted as a 1 and an antiparallel spin as 0. This allowed the hydrogen nuclei and carbon-13 nuclei to be run as a 2-qubit system. In addition to the external

J. M. Chuharski (✉)
Massachusetts Institute of Technology (MIT), Boston, USA
e-mail: chuharsk@mit.edu

magnetic field, radiofrequency pulses were applied to cause spin states to flip, allowing for superimposed parallel and antiparallel states. More pulses were applied to execute a simple algorithm and to examine the system's final state. Now, over 20 years later, quantum computers can be implemented on a much larger scale using superconducting electronic circuits. Many computing companies including D-Wave, Google, IBM, Intel, Quantinuum, Rigetti and IMEC are working on gate-based chips that apply the universal model of quantum computation. In October 2019 Google published an article demonstrating quantum supremacy using a chip with 53 superconducting qubits. In addition, D-Wave's quantum annealing systems use chips that have over 5,000 qubits.

Adiabatic Quantum Computing started as an approach to solving optimization problems and has evolved into an important universal alternative to the standard circuit model of quantum computing. Adiabatic Quantum Computing can be run on the D-Wave quantum annealing computers which give low energy solutions. The general strategy includes designing a Hamiltonian with a ground state that includes the solution of an optimization problem, preparing the ground state of a simple Hamiltonian, and interpolating slowly between them. These Hamiltonians can be structured as simple optimization problems that are read in their final state and translated into music.

14.2 Adiabatic Computation

Adiabatic Quantum Computation gets its name from the Adiabatic Theorem which was originally stated in *Beweis des Adiabatensatzes* (1928) as follows:

> A physical system remains in its instantaneous eigenstate if a given perturbation is acting on it slowly enough and if there is a gap between the eigenvalue and the rest of the Hamiltonian spectrum [1].

Put simply, if a given quantum mechanical system is subjected to gradually changing conditions (a slow perturbation) then the system will adapt its configuration, and its probability density will be modified by the process. When subjected to rapidly varying conditions, however, there is insufficient time for the functional form to adapt, so the spatial probability density will remain unchanged. This also means that if the system starts in an eigenstate of the determined initial Hamiltonian, it will end in the *corresponding* eigenstate of the final Hamiltonian.

Eigenstates can be understood from the example of a wave, or a guitar string and have their origins in German. The prefix eigen means "own" or "one's self." So, the eigenstate is the fixed value of its own state. When thinking of a guitar string for example the string gives a sound, and the eigenstates correspond with rather stable ways that the string oscillates with wavelengths that are integer fractions of the distance between the two connection points of the string. These are notes. Another example of an eigenstate might be flipping a fair coin. The two fixed states you can have when the coin is flipped are either heads or tails.

Let us also refresh our understanding of a Hamiltonian. In quantum mechanics, a system's Hamiltonian is an operator that represents the entire energy of the system. It corresponds to the sum of the kinetic energy plus potential energy for the system. Hamiltonians function as operators acting on the system. We can develop other operators using the basic ones. For example, let's consider a simple non-relativistic case. In classical mechanics we have:

$$H = \frac{1}{2}mv^2 + V(x)$$

Here the potential energy just depends on x. In quantum mechanics we have:

$$H = -\frac{\hbar^2}{2m}\frac{\delta^2}{\delta x^2} + V(x)$$

While they both represent the total energy of the system, depending on what you are defining you can have a different Hamiltonian spectrum.

14.2.1 Example: Simple Harmonic Oscillator

As an example of a system progressing adiabatically, consider a simple harmonic oscillator. In physics, a simple harmonic oscillator is something that has a characteristic repetitive movement through a central equilibrium position so that the maximum displacement on one side of this position is equal to the maximum displacement on the other side. The interval of time for each complete cycle is constant and does not depend on the maximum displacement. The cycle having constant time makes these oscillators great time keeping tools; a mechanical metronome is a perfect example.

Another good example of a simple harmonic oscillator is a pendulum hanging from the ceiling (incidentally, a metronome is also a pendulum). Imagine our ceiling pendulum has a small, balled weight on the bottom. If you start with the pendulum at rest and do not touch it, nothing changes, the pendulum stays still not very interesting. However, if you were to very slowly pull the pendulum upwards and release, it will have a nice arc through the air, smoothly swinging back and forth. This smooth swing is a good analogue to our adiabatic motion. The pendulum will eventually settle again and will do so gently and predictably. Instead, if you were to yank on the pendulum and/or try to throw it horizontally, you will end up with lots of jerky motion that is much harder to predict. The pendulum has experienced too rapid of a change in its condition and, as a result, it is no longer possible to determine the path of the pendulum from its starting position. Many physical systems behave as simple harmonic oscillators (when assuming no energy loss), such as: the pendulums discussed above, the electrons in a wire carrying alternating current, the vibrating particles of the medium in a sound wave and the motion of a compressed spring, to cite but two examples.

As an aside, the oscillators being classified as *harmonic* has their origins in music theory. The motion is called harmonic because many instruments vibrate to make music notes as sound. When playing a stringed instrument, in some way or another, the strings are vibrated to make the pitches we recognize.

How are these described in a way we can predict? The differential equation of motion for our simple harmonic oscillator is generally defined as:

$$-kx = m\frac{d^2x}{dt^2}$$

where k is a force constant, x is displacement, m is mass, and $\frac{d^2x}{dt^2}$ is acceleration. Simply, it shows that the force exerted on an oscillator is proportional to its displacement.

Now let use examine the force constant k. This time imagine a spring hanging from the ceiling: we will use this spring as our classical analogue to our quantum oscillator. All springs behave similarly but not all springs are made the same. Some springs are thick and hard to move, like those ones used in heavy machinery, and others, like a slinky, are light and very easy to move. The force constant k acts as a measure of how stiff our spring is. The higher our value for k, the stiffer the spring; this constant applies to all oscillators but is best imagined through a spring.

So, if we are to set our spring in motion, as the force constant k is increased, the effect is narrowing the potential energy curve of the system (Fig. 14.1), meaning that our spring becomes harder and harder to move as k increases. So in the quantum sense, if we were to increase k adiabatically ($\frac{\delta k}{\delta t} = 0$) then the oscillator, which is described by a single quantum number, will have that quantum number preserved. Our spring analogue will continue moving as k is increased but now it will just move the mass back and forth a little faster. For a rapidly changing constant k where the constant is increased diabatically ($\frac{\delta k}{\delta t} = \infty$), the final state will look identical to the initial state ($|\psi(t)|^2 = |\psi(0)|^2$). For our spring analogue this means that we made the spring too hard to move too fast which leaves us at our initial position. This is consistent with our definition above. The final state of this quantum oscillator will be composed of a linear superposition of many different eigenstates of the current Hamiltonian which sum to reproduce the form of the initial state.

14.2.2 Example: Two Hamiltonians

Now, if we were to backtrack to our initial list explaining the strategy for adiabatic computation, then we would have: first, design a Hamiltonian with a ground state that includes the solution of your optimization problem, then, prepare the ground state of a second, simple Hamiltonian, and finally, interpolating slowly between them. Let us start by imagining that you have two Hamiltonians. The first (H_0) we will define as a transverse field from the Ising model, and we know that H_0 will be in equal superposition at the lowest energy state.

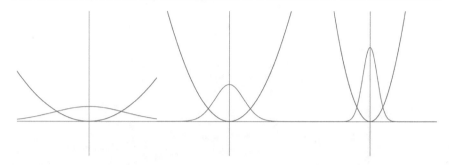

Fig. 14.1 Change in potential energy as k is increased. The red line represents potential energy, and the blue line is $|\psi(t)|^2$

$$H_0 = \sum_i \sigma_i^x$$

Our second Hamiltonian (H_1) can be defined by a classical Ising model [2].

$$H_1 = -\sum_{(i,j)} \exists_{i,j} \sigma_i^z \sigma_j^z - \sum_i \hbar_i \sigma_i^z$$

Now we have our two Hamiltonians. All that is left is interpolating slowly between them. Therefore, from these two definitions, we can combine H_0 and H_1 (with $t \in [0, 1]$) to define a time-dependent Hamiltonian given by:

$$H(t) = (1 - t)H_0 + tH_1$$

After a quick examination of the equation above, $H(t)$, it should be relatively easy to see how we move from one to the other. At $t = 0$, $H(t)$ gives only the transverse field (H_0) and at $t = 1$ we get our classical Ising model (H_0). If we change time sufficiently slow (adiabatic evolution) and we start in the ground state of H_0, then we will end up in the ground state of H_1. Here the adiabatic transition ensures that we will stay in the lowest energy solution throughout the change: which is exactly what we are looking for [3].

14.3   Runtime

At this point, you might be wondering, how slow is sufficiently slow. Well, the run time of an adiabatic algorithm scales at worst as a $\frac{1}{\Delta^3}$, at best as $\frac{1}{\Delta^2}$, where Δ is the minimum eigenvalue gap between the ground state and the first excited state of the Hamiltonian (Fig. 14.2).

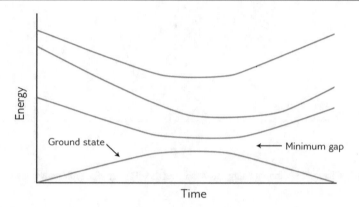

Fig. 14.2 Minimum eigenvalue gap between the ground and the first excited state

Because of the dependence of the run time on the gap, the performance of the adiabatic quantum algorithms is strongly influenced by "the type of quantum phase transition the same system would undergo in the thermodynamic limit" [4]. Every time-step in our transition will have a different gap and our speed limit will be dependent on the inverse of that minimum gap squared $\left(\frac{1}{\Delta^2}\right)$. Therefore, in the instances where the minimum gap is very small, our speed limit can scale exponentially for select NP hard problems. We end up with near infinitely long run times for such problems.

Adiabatic Quantum Computation is somewhat idealized in attempting to solve problems because the minimum gap is often hard to calculate. A less idealized version of Adiabatic Quantum Computation is known as *Quantum Annealing* [5]. Quantum Annealing is a method to solve problems requiring the system to run repeatedly (likely breaking adiabatic conditions) which gives you thousands of different configurations with different energy levels. You can then pick the one with the lowest energy. There is no guarantee that this is the ground state or global optimum for the problem, but this program may still yield a better solution than a classical algorithm. It is also worth mentioning that Adiabatic Quantum Computation assumes a closed system, however, in real life, the quantum computers end up being coupled to the environment through a thermal bath at low temperature. The thermal bath helps to facilitate energy exchange between the processor and the environment but cannot fully isolate the system. Fortunately, the speed limit and thermal exchange should not matter very much while making music.

So how does all the above apply to the creation of music? Below we introduce a piece of software named *Algorhythms*, which was developed for the D-Wave computer.

14.4 The D-Wave Computer

As the D-Wave computer works differently from the other systems used to run the systems presented in this book so far, below is an introduction to its basics.

The D-Wave company was founded in 1999 as a quantum computation company seeking to develop and deliver quantum computing systems, software, and services and is the first commercial supplier of quantum computers [6].

D-Wave uses large Quantum Processing Units (QPUs) to solve problems. Their most recent architecture is called D-Wave Advantage. It has over 5,000 qubits on the QPU. D-Wave also supports a Python-based open-source SDK, Ocean, a package for the development of applications for use on their quantum computers. Advantage and Ocean are both accessible via Leap™, D-Wave's real-time quantum cloud service.

It should be said, however, that D-Wave machines (at least the ones mentioned in this chapter) are not general-purpose computers. They are quantum annealers. This means that they can only solve a set of problems that can be structured as Hamiltonian energy minimizations. For this reason, it is often said that optimization problems are solved best with quantum annealing technology. While there are many proof points of enterprises deriving real business value from these specialized computers, they cannot always outperform algorithms implemented on classical computers. This is the case with most, if not all, quantum computers currently. However, there are areas where they seem to have started to see advantages [7].

So how is this machine created? The D-Wave QPU is a lattice of tiny metal loops, each of which is a qubit with some connection to others via couplers. The QPU is not *fully* connected (Fig. 14.4). The qubits of D-Wave 2000Q and earlier are interconnected with *Chimera* topology while the Advantage QPUs use *Pegasus* topology. In the QPU the set of qubits and couplers that are available for computation is known as the *working graph*. The yield of this working graph is generally less than the total number of qubits and couplers that are fabricated to the QPU. A given logical problem defined on a general graph can be mapped to a physical problem defined on the working graph using what are known as chains. A chain is a collection of qubits bound together to represent a single logical node. The associations between the logical problem and the physical problem is carried out by what is known as minor embedding. When below temperatures of 9.2 K, these loops become superconductors and exhibit quantum-mechanical effects. In the Pegasus topology, qubits are oriented vertically or horizontally (Fig. 14.3).

D-Wave's annealing computers run a more generalized version of the adiabatic algorithm. Annealing is performed using analog lines over a time specified by the user as *annealing_time* and reported out by the QPU as *qpu_anneal_-time_per_sample*. This *annealing_time* is an interval consisting of a constant value plus any additional time specified by the user. The anneal read cycle is also referred to as a sample. The cycle repeats for a specified number of samples and returns one solution per sample [9].

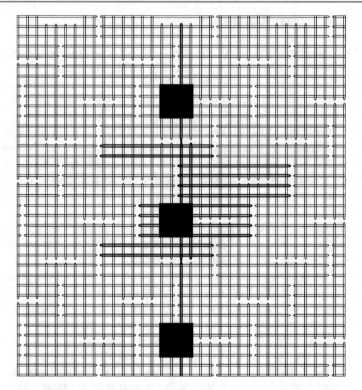

Fig. 14.3 A cropped view of the Pegasus topology [8]

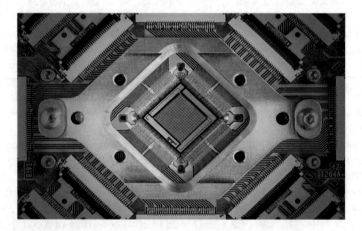

Fig. 14.4 D-Wave's QPU

D-Wave Quantum Annealing processors naturally return low-energy solutions; some applications require the real minimum energy (optimization problems) and others require good low-energy samples (probabilistic sampling problems). The system begins by placing qubits at an absolute minimum. The hardware then slowly alters the system configuration so that the energy landscape represents the problem to be solved. The qubits will return the lowest energy state of the landscape, which in their final state will represent a solution to that problem. The landscape can be shifted further to represent a problem structured as minimization of Hamiltonian energy. The landscapes should look like a set of peaks and valleys, and while there is a chance that the system will get stuck in a valley that is not at the global minimum, the system should be able to take advantage of quantum tunnelling to move out of these valleys. The process is not deterministic and can sometimes stay stuck. However, getting stuck does not always matter because in many cases a solution near the absolute minimum can be worth as much as the true global minimum. In situations where it matters, the problem can be run many times and the solution can be identified by frequency. The computers can also run a method called *reverse* annealing, which has the qubits start at a known minimum: the qubits are released, and the hope is that a qubit will tunnel to a better solution.

There are areas where Quantum Annealing will provide clear advantages in performance. One of the challenges of today is that classical computers will start to have exponential increases in run time as the size of optimization problems increases. The current generation of hardware does not yet have the qubits required to handle all these problems. As a result, a chunk of developers are working on hybrid algorithms. Hybrid algorithms are programs that have some of the work done on a classical computer and other parts run on D-Wave hardware. The software, Algorhythms is hybrid in the sense that the code pushes input and output through a quantum annealer and then turns the output into playable music.

Algorhythms uses both a D-Wave local annealing simulator and D-Wave Leap hybrid solvers. Algorhythms has a built-in command-line interface that allows the user to choose between using the local quantum simulation solver or the actual quantum computers at D-Wave, which are accessible via their cloud service. The interface also allows the user to pick a name, duration, and labels for musical style such as 'happy' or 'sad'. We chose to set up our music as a probabilistic sampling problem.

14.5   Algorhythms

14.5.1   Definition of the Task

Let us set up the problem using a Bayesian network. In this case, we end up with chords or notes defined as nodes connected by probability chains that determine the switch between them. Figure 14.5 shows a song represented as a random walk model; that is, possible sequences of I, ii, iii, IV, V, vi, vii and V7 chords where every node is connected to every other node.

Fig. 14.5 Representation of a song as a random walk model

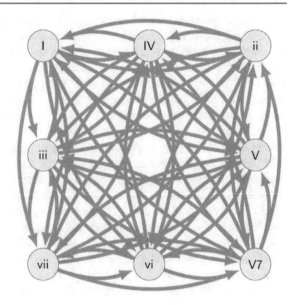

When creating a simple song, it might end up being simpler to establish some constraints; that is establish that some chord progressions be prohibited. An example is shown in Fig. 14.6.

Similarly, a Markov chain is a graph that is used to represent state machines. It consists of nodes, representing states, and edges representing the transitions between those states. The edges can be weighted, and oftentimes represent the conditional probabilities of transitioning from one state to the next (Fig. 14.7).

Markov chains are relevant to music generation because we can encode the desired notes or chords as states, and, using some basic music theory, define edges, and transition probabilities between chords that should be played in succession (Fig. 14.8).

Fig. 14.6 Constrained node connections

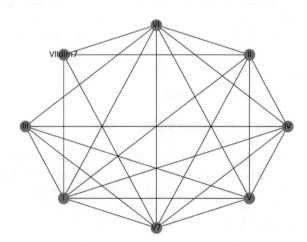

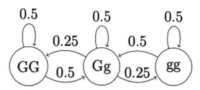

Fig. 14.7 An example of a Markov chain with weighted probabilities

Now, let us see how we can generate music with this Markov chain. We can perform a random walk on the matrix. We start with a given state, and using the transition probabilities, we can determine which state to go to next. This process, however, has no memory: only the current state is ever taken into consideration. Random walks and other algorithms such as Markov Chain Monte Carlo (MCMC) are very powerful for stochastic simulations, and in our case, creating randomized quantum music, but that still abides by the musical rules.

In order to implement a random walk or MCMC using D-Wave's samplers, we have to change our setup just a bit in order to formulate it as an optimization problem. This can be done using Markov Random Fields, which define relationships between and dependencies between vertices, instead of transition probabilities (Fig. 14.9). Converting from a normal Bayesian network (a Markov network with conditional transition probabilities) into a Markov Random Field is a process known as *moralization*. Each edge (a, b) can be one of 00, 01, 10, 11, indicating the binary values of its vertices. Each one of those states is associated with a potential energy, and our objective is now to find the lowest energy state of the entire Markov network.

As a matter of fact, D-Wave has a Python package for the exploration and analysis of networks and network algorithms called *dwave-networkx*. This allows us to create a simple Markov Random Field for the chords I, ii, iii, IV, V, vi, and VIIdim. Defining the potentials with *dwave_networkx* is easy. The desired states are assigned lower potentials. In this example, the lowest energy state assigns 0 to each node in the network (Fig. 14.10).

To benefit from the sampler and introduce stochasticity, we decided to randomly assign potentials, as in the example below with three chords (Fig. 14.11).

Fig. 14.8 Markov chain with chords as nodes

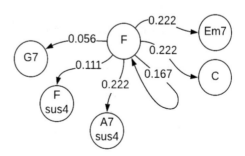

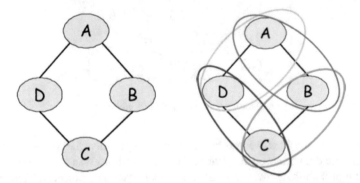

Fig. 14.9 A simple Markov random field with undirected edges and vertex dependencies

```
>>> potentials = {('a', 'b'): {(0, 0): -1,
...                            (0, 1): .5,
...                            (1, 0): .5,
...                            (1, 1): 2},
...               ('b', 'c'): {(0, 0): -9,
...                            (0, 1): 1.2,
...                            (1, 0): 7.2,
...                            (1, 1): 5}}
>>> MN = dnx.markov_network(potentials)
>>> sampler = dimod.ExactSolver()
>>> samples = dnx.sample_markov_network(MN, sampler, fixed_variables={'b': 0})
>>> samples[0]           # doctest: +SKIP
{'a': 0, 'c': 0, 'b': 0}
```

Fig. 14.10 Markov random field potentials

```
{('I', 'II'): {
(0, 0): 10,
(0, 1): -9.720022593351157,
(1, 0): -3.264126577542288,
(1, 1): 10
},
('I', 'III'): {
(0, 0): 10,
(0, 1): -7.664969424108326,
(1, 0): -2.8128625691633147,
(1, 1): 10
}}
```

Fig. 14.11 Randomly assigned chord potentials

We consider the 1 state to be the chord being played. The (0,0) and (1,1) edges were assigned an arbitrarily high potential energy to avoid states where the current note is played again, or two notes are played simultaneously. This is done for each chord. We then encode the chords into a MIDI file, which is returned to the user and can be opened in a music editor software such as MuseScore or Sibelius to play it back and see the score.

Algorhythms uses the Python package Mingus, an advanced cross-platform music theory and notation package with MIDI file and playback support [10]. It can be used to play around with music theory, to build editors, educational tools, and other applications that need to process and/or play music. We also experimented with another Python package called Music21, which provides excellent music functionalities [11].

14.5.2   Music of Algorhythms

Algorhythms produces two kinds of music ('music styles'), referred to as 'happy' or 'sad'. Simply put, for happy music the system uses major chords and for sad music it uses minor chords. We used the diatonic chords of the key of C and C minor. In Fig. 14.12 you can see the arrangements of the diatonic chords for C major and its relative minor.

Algorhythms chooses one of these chords by the Markov Field method described above. The major and minor modes have a hard coded tempo of 100 beats per minute (bpm) and 60 bpm respectively: this can be customized. The melody uses notes from major and minor pentatonic scales. Just as they are good for soloing in a song, the pentatonic scale seemed to be of good use for a safe walk over our diatonic chords. The melody is selected in the exact same way as the chords although the melody selection has no dependence on the chord selection. The first generation of Algorhythms is seeded with the root chord of the input key. A starting example of a generated 'happy' quantum song can be seen in the figure below (Fig. 14.13).

Algorhythms is also hard coded to end with a perfect authentic cadence to try to give a stronger sense of resolution at the end of the generated tune but the lack of voice leading in the chordal structure makes the cadences less powerful. The program has dynamics input for the melody that's scaled randomly from 0 to 127 which changes note volume; this can be expanded to include delay and reverberation effects.

Fig. 14.12 C major (top) and A minor (bottom) diatonic chords

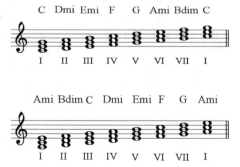

Fig. 14.13 The first eight measures of a song using algorhythms

14.6 Expandability and Applications

So now where can we go from what we already have created? Algorhythms has plenty of room to grow and doing so would be straightforward. For instance, we can add the ability to generate rhythmic variety to the system. Currently, the program is hard coded to generate two chords and four notes per measure. With the implementation of half, eighth, and sixteenth notes we would open the door to passing tones, which would help us move away from the pentatonic constraints. There can also be a specification to have pentatonic tones on the beats and open the nodes of the passing tones to play in between. This can be done with a similar method to how we pick notes and chords. Having a set of nodes in a new Markov field will allow our quantum annealer to pick note durations. We could use the combination of passing tones and rhythmic variety to add ornaments and grace notes. In the same vein, the changing of tempo would be possible with the change of a button. As previously mentioned, the tempo of our 'sad' song is 60 bpm and a 'happy' one is 100 bpm.

The diatonic chord structures we have in the Algorhythms example are fantastic for simple use. However, as we expand our familiarity with the structure of annealing, we could easily increase chordal variety by adding or removing nodes from our chordal Markov field. Changing chordal structures and adding variety could be easily done with the Mingus library. Including different extended chords; e.g., 7ths, add 9, 13, 11, diminished, augmented, and harmonics. Similarly, with the press of a button, we could change the instrumentation because the Algorhythms output is a MIDI file which means it can be translated to any instrument.

Mingus containers allow us to create sections of music with given duration. Most pieces of music have motifs and repetition throughout the song which is part of what makes that song memorable. With our current annealing setup, there is no way to guarantee repeated patterns; they will likely never be seen. However, giving sections a set duration before running the algorithm, and having the program copy and paste MIDI sections post-generation according to the desired structure would not be difficult; it would only require a few extra lines of code.

Algorhythms could be expanded to include as loose or strict parameters as desired. The adiabatic theorem allows for our low energy sampling methods to create everything needed for a great song. Furthermore, the recommendations above are useful for the immediate use of the technology. Looking into the long term we can expect a myriad of applications for quantum technology. Nobody could have accurately predicted many of the ways that we currently use classical computers and in a similar vein, it is incredibly difficult to see how quantum may change our approach to music. Fortunately, quantum theory tells us that uncertainty is not necessarily a bad thing. Quantum unpredictability may become an important option in all sectors of music: whether that be a live performance, mixing, writing, instrumentation, and so on. We may find something far off like a way to make an instrument out of quantum technology or work with something more familiar like a new way to write music using quantum output.

14.7 Concluding Discussion

Adiabatic Quantum Computing is a great way to create music using quantum computers. Although, at the time of writing, Adiabatic Quantum Computing gives no advantage to creating algorithmic music over classical computers. The exploration of Algorhythms has allowed for music to be successfully generated on real quantum computers. Currently, the actual quantum hardware provides a reduced speed in comparison to using a computer-simulated environment due to queue times on the annealers and internet speeds. Of course, this will change as quantum systems continue to become increasingly advanced.

Quantum computing has progressed past just a research experiment and is now becoming a viable source of computational advantage. Quantum computing is on the cusp of transforming a variety of industries such as medicine, where quantum computers have achieved rapid DNA sequencing. Many expect that quantum computing has the capacity to help us unlock a better understanding in biochemistry, curing cancer, cyber security, or any industry where data is an important ingredient. The quantum computing market is expected to increase by a factor of 100 over the next ten years and tech companies, big and small, have been investing heavily into research and development. While quantum computing has a few more years before it can start delivering on some of these expectations, there will be an exponential curve of capabilities as quantum takes off: the time for experimentation and investment is now.

There seems to be an inherent order to science, math, and music. In all the beauty and elegance of the sciences, it is hard to believe that there would not be new developments in music that we are yet to open the door into. Quantum music might very well be the next frontier of musical creation. The program Algorhythms provides a proof of concept that music can be created on quantum computers and can be expanded to create music of almost any variety. We are confident that there are an abundance of applications for this hardware and may become a vital part of the music industry. D-Wave presents ample opportunity to experiment and play with the actual quantum hardware through Leap and Ocean. Algorhythms is available through GitHub at: https://github.com/jchuharski/Algorhythyms.

References

1. Born, M., & Fock, V. A. (1928). Beweis des Adiabatensatzes. *Zeitschrift fur Physik A, 51*(3–4), 165–180. https://doi.org/10.1007/BF01343192
2. Wang, Y., Wu, S., & Zou, J. (2016). Quantum annealing with Markov Chain Monte Carlo simulations and D-Wave quantum computers. *Statistical Science, 31*(3), 362–398. https://doi.org/10.1214/16-STS560
3. Kato, T. (1950). On the adiabatic theorem of quantum mechanics. *Journal of the Physical Society of Japan, 5*(6), 435–439. https://doi.org/10.1143/JPSJ.5.435
4. Tameem, A., & Lidar, D. A. (2018). Adiabatic quantum computation. *Reviews of Modern Physics, 90*, 015002. https://doi.org/10.1103/RevModPhys.90.015002
5. Bachmann, S., De Roeck, W., & Fraas, M. (2017). Adiabatic theorem for quantum spin systems. *Physics Review Letters, 119*, 060201. https://arxiv.org/abs/1612.01505. Accessed 18 May 2022.
6. D-Wave. (2021c). *Meet D-Wave.* www.dwavesys.com/our-company/meet-d-wave. Accessed 18 May 2022.
7. Violaris, M. (2021). D-Wave demonstrates performance advantage in quantum simulation. *Physics World, 14.* https://physicsworld.com/a/d-wave-demonstrates-performance-advantage-in-quantum-simulation/. Accessed 18 May 2022.
8. D-Wave. (2021b). *D-Wave Qpu Architecture: Topologies.* docs.dwavesys.com/docs/latest/c_gs_4.html. Accessed 18 May 2022.
9. D-Wave. (2021a). *D-Wave Quantum Processing Unit: D-Wave User Manual 09-1109A-Y.* D-Wave.
10. (Mingus 2022). *Mingus 0.5.1 Documentation.* https://bspaans.github.io/python-mingus/. Accessed 18 May 2022.
11. Cuthbert, M. S. (2021). *Music21 Documentation.* web.mit.edu/music21/doc/. Accessed 18 May 2022.

Applications of Quantum Annealing to Music Theory

15

Ashish Arya, Ludmila Botelho, Fabiola Cañete, Dhruvi Kapadia, and Özlem Salehi

Abstract

With the emergence of quantum computers, a new field of algorithmic music composition has been initiated. The vast majority of previous work focuses on music generation using gate-based quantum computers. An alternative model of computation is adiabatic quantum computing (AQC), and a heuristic algorithm known as quantum annealing running in the framework of AQC is a promising method for solving optimization problems. In this chapter, we lay the groundwork for music composition using quantum annealing. We approach the process of music composition as an optimization problem. We describe the fundamental methodologies needed for generating different aspects of music including melody, rhythm, and harmony. The discussed techniques are illustrated through examples to ease the understanding. The music pieces generated using D-Wave's quantum

A. Arya
Ira A. Fulton Schools of Engineering, Arizona State University (Online), Kanpur, India

L. Botelho · Ö. Salehi (✉)
Institute of Theoretical and Applied Informatics Polish Academy of Sciences Gliwice, Gliwice, Poland
e-mail: osalehi@iitis.pl

L. Botelho
Joint Doctoral School, Silesian University of Technology, Gliwice, Poland

F. Cañete
Benemérita Universidad Autónoma de Puebla, Puebla City, Mexico

D. Kapadia
Sarvajanik College of Engineering and Technology, Surat, India

Ö. Salehi
QWorld Association, Tallinn, Estonia

© The Author(s), under exclusive license to Springer Nature Switzerland AG 2022
E. R Miranda (ed.), *Quantum Computer Music*,
https://doi.org/10.1007/978-3-031-13909-3_15

annealers are among the first examples of their kind and presented within the scope of the chapter.

Keywords

Quantum annealing · Music composition · D-Wave · Adiabatic quantum computing · Quantum music

15.1 Introduction

Music composition can be thought of, in a very simplistic manner, as a creative process where one puts sounds and silences together that results in a sequence that is aesthetic or pleasant to the ear. Over the years, it has been discovered that music pieces that are soothing and pleasing follow some rules and possess common patterns. Those rules have evolved and solidified up to some extent over the centuries. Yet, there is still certain flexibility keeping open room for creativity.

Being able to identify some rules and common patterns to guide the music composition process is one of the keystones of the field of algorithmic music composition. The seeds of computer-generated music were sown at the end of the nineteenth century by Ada Lovelace, the first computer programmer, who put forward the idea that Babbage's prototype computer, the analytical engine, "might compose elaborate and scientific pieces of music of any degree of complexity or extent" [1]. Yet, this dream was not realized until the 1950s, when the first computer-generated music piece, the *Illiac Suite*, was composed [2]. Following the advancements in computer science, various methodologies have been explored for generating music, including stochastic approaches, rule-based systems, evolutionary algorithms, and machine learning [3]. The emergence of quantum computers heralds a new addition to this sequel.

With quantum computers being an alternative tool for generating music, we are witnessing the growth of a new field referred to as quantum computer music [4]. Although the term comprises using quantum computers to generate, perform, and listen to music, we will focus on music generation harnessing the quantum computing paradigm in the scope of this chapter.

Gate-based computing and adiabatic quantum computing are the two popular computational models in quantum computing. In the gate-based model, states of the qubits are manipulated through unitary operations, the so-called quantum gates. Most of the work undertaken so far on music generation using quantum computing is based on the gate-based model. In [5], a simple algorithm named Gatemel is developed to generate music using IBM quantum computers. A classical-quantum algorithm is introduced in [6], which uses Grover's search and follows a rules-based approach for composing music. In Chap. 3 in this volume, Miranda and Basak use quantum walks and Chap. 13 presents another novel approach, quantum natural language processing to compose music.

Adiabatic quantum computing (AQC) is an alternative to the gate-based model of computation. In AQC, the computation is driven by applying an external magnetic field. We will be particularly interested in quantum annealing (QA) [7,8], a heuristic algorithm based on the AQC model for solving optimization problems. Using QA for creating music requires the formulation of the music creation process as an optimization problem. QA has been previously used to generate harmony by Kirke and Miranda [9] and see also Chap. 14 in this volume.

In this chapter, we develop new methodologies for generating music using quantum annealing. We present the main building blocks for formulating rules-based music generation as an optimization task. We consider the problem from various aspects, including the composition of melody, rhythm, and harmony. Using D-Wave[1] quantum annealers, we generate music pieces that are displayed in the course of the text. The presented material contributes to the field as the first text focusing on the role of quantum annealing for music composition in an extensive manner.

The rest of the chapter is structured as follows. We begin with a review of the classical approaches for music composition in the framework of optimization in Sect. 15.2. In Sect. 15.3, we present a background on optimization problems, quadratic unconstrained binary optimization and integer linear programming formulations, quantum annealing, and Markov random fields. We describe the fundamental techniques and formulations for music composition using quantum annealing in Sect. 15.4. Finally, we conclude with a discussion and suggestions on future work in Sect. 15.5.

15.2 Music Composition as an Optimization Problem

Computational music generation is a field that emerged with the invention of computers in the late 1940s. The first computer to play a music piece was CSIR Mark-1 [10]. In the initial period, most studies focused on playing an existing music piece using computers rather than composing a new music piece. Later with the increase of computational power, the focus of researchers shifted to creating new music with the help of computers [11]. Programs and a set of programming languages known as MUSIC-N were developed by Max Mathews at Bell Laboratories in 1957 [12]. Thus the field of computational music, which is also known as algorithmic music, began [13]. Various tools and techniques for algorithmic music generation have been thoroughly discussed in [14].

Optimization is a widely used technique for computational music generation. As mentioned previously, any piece of music can be seen as a sequence of sounds and rests. These sequences can be identified for their adherence to a particular music style or any other musical property in such a way that if a musical element deviates

---

[1] D-Wave is the company that produces publicly available quantum annealers. https://www.dwavesys.com/.

from that musical style or property, then having that musical element in the generated music piece leads to a cost or penalty. Therefore through the optimization process, a sequence of music elements with minimum cost, i.e., one minimizing the deviation from the pre-identified music style or any other musical property, can be generated. Now, we will briefly summarize some of the techniques used for computational music generation, where the music generation is achieved through optimizing some parameters related to the music piece.

Statistical modelling is a common technique used in computational music generation. Under this technique, the existing music corpus is analyzed and its statistical properties are derived. The new piece of music starts with a given note. Then, the probabilities of having each possible note (pitch) as the next note in the generated music piece are calculated. The note with the highest probability is selected as the next note in the new music piece. Thus, sequentially, the entire new music piece is obtained. Here it is important to note that the newly generated music piece follows the statistical properties of the music piece from which the probabilities were calculated [15]. *Illiac Suite* is considered to be the first musical score generated by a computer in 1957 [2, 16], using a statistical method known as Markov chains. Markov chains as a tool for music generation have been described in detail in Sect. 15.3.3.1. It is an active area of research even to this day [17].

Constraint programming is a programming paradigm where instead of steps to solve a problem, the properties of the solution are specified. These properties are the constraints that the solution is expected to follow. Mainly, it is an expansion of constraint logic programming, which in turn is an expansion of satisfiability problem (SAT) [18]. The set of constraints with a general-purpose search algorithm can solve large practical combinatorial and scheduling problems [19]. Since music composition is a process where at every step, the choices available for the composer are in the form of combinations of notes, chords, or intervals; these combinations are constrained naturally by the rules of music, such as melody or harmony generation rules [20]. This resemblance in the process of music generation and constraint programming has been used in modelling and generation of various musical forms such as counterpoint, harmony, rhythm, form, and instrumentation [21].

Genetic Algorithms (GA) have been claimed to simulate the creative process of music composition through its operators such as *mutation, selection* and *crossover*. GA is an optimization technique inspired by Darwin's theory of natural selection and his observation that in any ecosystem, the species' growth is governed through a process where only the fittest offsprings survive among a huge population, and the surviving ones reproduce and form the next generation. The process of reproduction and the natural selection continues and gives rise to different species. Accordingly, the first step to use GA for music composition is to generate a set (a.k.a *population* in GA terminology) of random solutions. Then the set is updated using the technique of offspring creation or *reproduction* such as *mutation, selection* and *crossover*, and only the potentially feasible solutions which are highly favored based on certain *fitness function* are kept. The cycle of *reproduction* and keeping only the fittest members of the population continues and induces a solution [22]. GA was used in computer-based music generation first in the early 1990s [23]. NEUROGEN was a GA-based program developed in 1991 to produce and combine several musical fragments [24]. Lee Spector and Adam Alpern also used GA to identify deep musical structures and generate music [25]. MusicGenie, developed in 2006, was a music composition program influenced by GA [26].

Machine learning is the latest addition in the quiver of optimization-based techniques for music generation. Neural network-based machine learning methods have been used for music composition since 1988 [27]. As the subsequent notes/chords or any music element depends on the previous music elements in the music sequence, the recurrent neural network and long short term memory networks had been among the favourite choices of neural network researchers for music composition [28,29].

In the cutting edge of computational music generation techniques, deep learning is among the most successful and recent ones. Briot et al. have provided a detailed survey of deep learning-based methods for music generation [30]. Using MuseNet, a deep neural network, a 4-min long music piece with ten different instruments is composed. MuseNet also combines several different musical styles, including those of Mozart, Beatles, and Country music [31]. These techniques are being further refined with the use of generative adversarial networks (GAN) and the development of Generative Pretrained Transformers (GPT-2 and GPT-3) [32].

Integer linear programming (ILP), which is often referred to as integer programming (IP) in the literature, is another main framework for solving combinatorial problems. Though it shares a lot in common with constraint programming, ILP only uses variables with integer values to represent the problem as will be described in the following section. Based on our knowledge, integer programming has not been used extensively in the literature in the scope of music generation. Some works in this line are the following. The natural one-to-one mapping between integers and pitch values of the 12-tonal music system has been exploited by Tanaka et al. [33] for musical motif analysis of existing masterpieces of music. Nailson dos Santos Cunha et al. have generated guitar solo music using integer programming [34].

The bottleneck in the ILP approach to solving a combinatorial problem is the method of optimization used. Therefore, several heuristic methods such as hill-climbing, simulated annealing, ant colony optimization, Hopfield neural networks, and tabu search have been used to reach the solution set [35,36]. The next imperative step would be using quantum methods for solving ILP problems. With this motivation, ILP becomes especially important in the context of this chapter as any ILP formulation can be converted into a form that is suitable for quantum annealing.

15.3 Technical Background

In this section, we present the necessary background on optimization and quantum annealing. Before we move on to the discussion, let us get familiar with some notations that will be useful in the rest of the chapter.

By $\mathbb{Z}$ and $\mathbb{R}$, we denote the set of integers and real numbers respectively. Given that x is a column vector defined over $\mathbb{Z}$ or $\mathbb{R}$, x_i denotes the i'th element of x and

$x^\top$ denotes the transpose of x. When A is a matrix, A_{ij} denotes the element in the i'th row and j'th column of A. By $[n]$, we denote the set of integers $\{1, 2, \ldots, n\}$.

15.3.1 Combinatorial Optimization

Combinatorial optimization aims to minimize or maximize an objective function that is defined over a discrete set. Such problems appear in almost every field of science and engineering, including logistics, supply chain management, transportation, and finance. Many of the well-known problems like the knapsack problem [37], travelling salesperson problem [38], and graph coloring [39] are optimization problems, and they have applications in scheduling, resource allocation, assignment, and planning. All of the mentioned problems belong to the class NP-Complete [40], the class containing the hardest of the problems whose solutions are verifiable in polynomial time, and become easily intractable. A vast number of optimization techniques were developed on classical computers to solve optimization problems, including both exact and heuristic methods. Quantum computing is offering novel approaches for solving optimization problems, as we will discuss in the upcoming subsections.

15.3.1.1 Integer Linear Programming

Most of the time when we optimize a function, the optimization is subject to some constraints. *Integer linear programming* (ILP) is a mathematical model for problems defined over integer variables with a linear objective function and a set of linear constraints. Formally, an integer linear program is defined as

$$\text{minimize} \quad \sum_j c_j y_j$$

$$\text{subject to} \quad \sum_j A_{ij} y_j \leq b_i, \quad i = 1, \ldots, m$$

$$y_j \geq 0, \, y_j \in \mathbb{Z}$$

where $A_{ij} \in \mathbb{R}$, $b_i \in \mathbb{R}$, $c_j \in \mathbb{R}$. ILP problem is known to be NP-Hard. In case the objective function is a quadratic polynomial, then the model is named as integer quadratic programming (IQP). There are exact algorithms, including cutting plane [41] and branch-and-bound methods [42], and heuristic algorithms like simulated annealing [43] and ant colony optimization [44] for solving ILPs.

15.3.1.2 Quadratic Unconstrained Binary Optimization

Quadratic unconstrained binary optimization (QUBO) problems involve an objective function defined over binary variables consisting of linear and quadratic terms. As opposed to ILP, there are no constraints. QUBO formulation has become extremely popular with the advent of quantum annealing, as will be explained in the upcoming subsection. An extensive list of problems and their QUBO formulations are presented in [45].

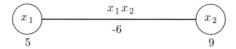

Fig. 15.1 A visualization for the function $f(x_1, x_2)$, where the circles represent the variables, the numbers below the circles are the coefficients of the linear terms, and the label of the edge between is the quadratic coefficient

Mathematically, QUBO formulation is defined as in Eq. 15.1.

$$f(x) = \sum_{i \le j} x_i Q_{ij} x_j, \qquad (15.1)$$

where $x_i \in \{0, 1\}$ and Q is a real square upper triangular matrix. The above sum can be equivalently expressed as $x^\top Q x$ where x is the vector of binary variables. The goal is to find the binary vector x that minimizes $f(x)$.

Let us look at an example involving two variables. Suppose that we aim to minimize the objective function given in Eq. 15.2.

$$f(x_1, x_2) = 5x_1 + 9x_2 - 6x_1 x_2 \qquad (15.2)$$

A visual representation of $f(x_1, x_2)$ is given in Fig. 15.1.

Let us identify matrix Q for the given $f(x_1, x_2)$. Here, $5x_1$ and $6x_2$ are the linear terms. Note that $5x_1 = 5x_1^2$ and $9x_2 = 9x_2^2$ since x_1 and x_2 are binary variables. We will place 5 and 6 to the diagonals of the Q matrix and the 1st row, 2nd column of the matrix is -6 due to the term $-6x_1 x_2$ as shown in Eq. 15.3.

$$\begin{matrix} & x_1 \ \ x_2 & \\ \begin{pmatrix} 5 & -6 \\ 0 & 9 \end{pmatrix} & \begin{matrix} x_1 \\ x_2 \end{matrix} \end{matrix} \qquad (15.3)$$

Observe that $x^\top Q x$ yields us $f(x_1, x_2)$ as displayed in Eq. 15.4

$$\begin{bmatrix} x_1 & x_2 \end{bmatrix} \begin{bmatrix} 5 & -6 \\ 0 & 9 \end{bmatrix} \begin{bmatrix} x_1 \\ x_2 \end{bmatrix} = \begin{bmatrix} x_1 & x_2 \end{bmatrix} \begin{bmatrix} 5x_1 - 6x_2 \\ 9x_2 \end{bmatrix} = 5x_1^2 - 6x_1 x_2 + 9x_2^2 \qquad (15.4)$$

Let us find out the values for x_1 and x_2 that minimizes $f(x_1, x_2)$ analytically. There are four possible cases summarized in Eqs. 15.5–15.7 and 15.8.

$x_1 = 0$ and $x_2 = 0$;

$$f(0, 0) = 5 \cdot 0 + 9 \cdot 0 - 6 \cdot 0 \cdot 0 = 0 \qquad (15.5)$$

$x_1 = 0$ and $x_2 = 1$;

$$f(0, 1) = 5 \cdot 0 + 9 \cdot 1 - 6 \cdot 0 \cdot 1 = 9 \qquad (15.6)$$

$x_1 = 1$ and $x_2 = 0$;

$$f(1, 0) = 5 \cdot 1 + 9 \cdot 0 - 6 \cdot 1 \cdot 0 = 5 \qquad (15.7)$$

$x_1 = 1$ and $x_2 = 1$;

$$f(1, 1) = 5 \cdot 1 + 9 \cdot 1 - 6 \cdot 1 \cdot 1 = 8 \qquad (15.8)$$

The case $x_1 = 0$ and $x_2 = 0$ minimizes the objective function and yields the lowest possible value.

15.3.1.3 Converting ILP/IQP to QUBO

Any ILP or IQP can be converted into QUBO. This conversion is helpful as ILP formulations for many problems are already known, and it is often easier to express optimization problems through constraints. Now, let us explain how ILP and IQP can be processed as a QUBO. The necessary steps are described on the diagram in Fig. 15.2.

As we will see, there are three steps of this process. Let us discuss each step briefly.

1. **Inequality to Equality**: The first step of the conversion is turning inequality constraints into equality constraints by adding so-called *slack* variables. Slack variables compensate the difference between the left-hand side and the right-hand side of the inequality if the inequality is satisfied. Suppose that we have the linear inequality constraint given in Eq. 15.9.

$$\sum_{i=1}^{k} a_i y_i \leq b \qquad (15.9)$$

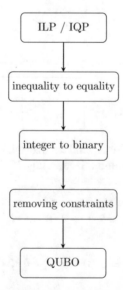

Fig. 15.2 Steps of the conversion from ILP/IQP to QUBO

Table 15.1 A list of linear constraints and equivalent penalties [48]

Constraint	Equivalent penalty
$x_1 + x_2 \leq 1$	$x_1 x_2$
$x_1 + x_2 \geq 1$	$1 - x_1 - x_2 + x_1 x_2$
$x_1 + x_2 = 1$	$1 - x_1 - x_2 + 2x_1 x_2$
$x_1 \leq x_2$	$x_1 - x_1 x_2$
$x_1 + x_2 + x_3 \leq 1$	$x_1 x_2 + x_2 x_3 + x_3 x_1$
$x_1 = x_2$	$x_1 + x_2 - 2x_1 x_2$

Then by adding slack variable ξ, we obtain $\sum_{i=1}^{k} a_i y_i + \xi = b$. Note that when $\sum_{i=1}^{k} a_i y_i = b$, then ξ is 0, which is the lower bound for ξ. The upper bound should be large enough so that the equality is satisfied when $\sum_{i=1}^{k} a_i y_i$ has the lowest possible. Further details can be found in [?].

2. **Integer to Binary**: This step involves expressing each bounded integer variable using a set of binary variables [46]. Suppose y is an integer variable with the lower bound $\underline{y}$ and upper bound $\overline{y}$. Note that y can be equivalently expressed as in Eq. 15.10.

$$\underline{y} + \sum_{i=0}^{k-2} 2^i x_i + \left(\overline{y} - \sum_{i=0}^{k-2} 2^i\right) x_{k-1}, \qquad (15.10)$$

where $k = \lceil \log_2(\overline{y} - \underline{y} + 1) \rceil$, and x_i are the newly introduced binary variables. Hence, we transform our problem into an equivalent one expressed using binary variables.

3. **Removing Constraints** Converting constrained programs into unconstrained ones dates to 1970s [47]. To create a constraint-free formulation, the penalty method is used. The idea is to introduce penalties to the objective function when the constraints are violated. In Table 15.1, a list of linear inequality/equality constraints and how they are incorporated into the objective function is given.

For instance, suppose that the objective function is $f(x_1, x_2) = (x_1 + x_2)^2$ and we have the constraint $x_1 + x_2 \leq 1$ such that x_1 and x_2 are binary variables. The equivalent QUBO formulation is given by $f(x) + Cx_1 x_2$ where C is the non-negative, real, sufficiently large penalty coefficient. Note that the constraint enforces that both x_1 and x_2 are not equal to 1 at the same time. Whenever this is the case, a penalty of C is added to the objective in the QUBO formulation, due to term $Cx_1 x_2$.

Now let us see how to deal with linear constraints of the general form. As we have seen already a method to convert inequalities into equalities, it is enough to consider linear equality constraints only. Suppose we have the minimization problem

$$\begin{aligned} \text{minimize} \quad & f(x) \\ \text{subject to} \quad & g_i(x) = b_i, i \in [n] \\ & x_i \in \mathbb{Z} \end{aligned}$$

where $f(x)$ is a linear or quadratic objective function, $g_i(x) = b_i, i \in [n]$ is a set of linear equality constraints. The equivalent unconstrained formulation is given as

$$\text{minimize} \quad f(x) + \sum_{i \in [n[} C_i(g(x) - b_i)^2$$

where C_i are the associated penalty parameters. The larger the penalty values are, the larger the increase in the energy will be in the case the constraint is violated. If C_i is not large enough, then it is likely that the corresponding constraint is violated in favor of the objective function.

15.3.1.4 Quadratization

Sometimes, one needs to deal with formulations consisting of not only quadratic but also higher-order terms. Such unconstrained formulations defined over binary variables are called higher-order binary optimization (HOBO) problems. By introducing auxiliary variables $y_1, y_2, \ldots, y_m$, it is possible to reduce the problem of minimizing HOBO into the problem of minimizing QUBO. There are several proposed methods for quadratization. We will explain the one by Rosenberg et al. [49].

1. Find two variables x_i and x_j, such that $x_i x_j$ appears in a term with the degree at least 3.
2. Replace all terms that contain $x_i x_j$ with $y_{ij} \in \{0, 1\}$.
3. Add the penalty term $C(x_i x_j - 2x_i y_{ij} - 2x_j y_{ij} + 3y_{ij})$, where C is the penalty coefficient.

15.3.2 Quantum Annealing

Let us now explain the theoretical background behind quantum annealing, and also give insights on solving optimization problems using the publicly available quantum annealers.

15.3.2.1 Motivation

Many interesting questions can be boiled down into optimization problems. Let us consider the travelling salesperson problem, where the aim is to find the route with minimum distance (cost) that passes through each city exactly once and returns to the first city, given a set of cities and the distance between them. Imagine that the salesperson has to visit 50 different cities and return to the starting point. There are 50! different routes that can be taken by the salesperson, and finding the route with the smallest cost by calculating all the possibilities is a costly method in terms of time and energy; and for many complex problems, it is almost impossible.[2] If we consider the 50! possible routes as our search space and call the cost associated with each route the energy, the problem can be framed as an energy minimization problem. Hence, finding the answer is equivalent to looking around the hills and valleys in an energy landscape for the lowest point.

Quantum annealing (QA) is a promising heuristic algorithm for solving optimization problems by taking advantage of properties peculiar to quantum physics like quantum tunneling, entanglement, and superposition [50,51]. This approach for finding the minimum of an objective function is based on the principles of adiabatic quantum computing (AQC). AQC is an alternative to the gate-based computation, and the two computational models are equivalent in terms of power [7,8]. Unlike the gate-based model in which the evolution of the system is discrete and is driven by the application of gates, AQC is a continuous-time process, and it has an analog nature. The computation is driven by the application of a time-dependent external magnetic field. In QA, the evolution takes a restricted form of AQC, and some conditions of AQC, such as the computation taking place in a totally closed system, are relaxed.

Quantum annealing is the quantum counterpart of simulated annealing (SA) [43], a probabilistic technique for optimization. In SA, the exploration of the search space is governed by a temperature parameter that is slowly decreased throughout the process. In the lower temperatures, transitions between states occur less frequently. The term "annealing" originates from a metallurgy technique, where a material is heated and then cooled in a controlled manner to alter its physical properties, analogous to the SA temperature parameter. SA harnesses thermal fluctuations to climb over the valleys and escape from local minima. In QA, this process of moving towards the low energy states is achieved by quantum tunneling. In Fig. 15.3, how the both algorithms move through the energy landscape is depicted.

Quantum annealing is experimentally realizable on commercially available D-Wave quantum processing units (QPUs) [52] and sparked the interest to solve combinatorial optimization problems, with applications ranging from transportation problems [53,54], finance [55], chemistry [56], to scheduling problems [57].

15.3.2.2 Encoding the Problem: The Ising Model and QUBO

In order to describe how quantum annealers can be used for solving problems, it is necessary to know how to formulate and encode them in such a way that can be processed by quantum machines. For this, one needs to know how to map the elements in our search space to certain states, and to energies.

---

[2] Although there are more clever methods than trying all the routes one by one, the best known exact algorithm has still exponential time complexity.

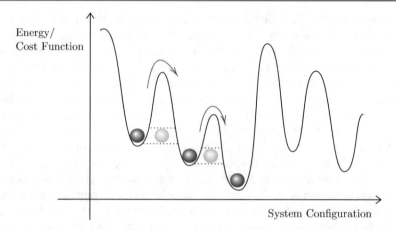

Fig. 15.3 Arrows describe how SA climbs over the valleys through thermal fluctuations while QA uses tunneling effect to move through them as depicted by circles

In quantum mechanics, the energy configuration of the system is driven by the Hamiltonian: an operator that describes the forces to be applied to a single qubit and qubit pairs to move the state of the system into some desired state. The system is initialized with the ground state of a Hamiltonian H_0 whose ground state is easy to prepare. The problem Hamiltonian H_P is introduced gradually to the system, whose ground state encodes the solution to the problem of interest. And then, if H_0 and H_P do not commute and the evolution is slow enough, according to the Quantum Adiabatic Theorem [58], during an annealing time T, the system will remain, ideally, in the minimum energy state throughout the process. In other words, the evolution of the system is described by Eq. 15.11.

$$H(t) = \left(1 - \frac{t}{T}\right) H_0 + \frac{t}{T} H_P \qquad (15.11)$$

Initialized with the ground state of H_0 at time $t = 0$, we obtain the solution to our problem measuring the quantum state at a time $t = T$. Therefore, to solve the problem of interest, we need to design H_P, the problem Hamiltonian. Then, we use the properties of nature as described by Quantum Adiabatic Theorem, to solve the problem.

Consider particles arranged on the nodes of a graph, where each particle can interact with its neighbors. The particles can be either in state -1 or $+1$, called the *spin*. An assignment of -1s and 1s to the spins is known as the spin configuration. A mathematical model called the *Ising model* is used for describing the properties of such physical systems that evolve in time. The interaction force or the coupling strength between the particles is denoted by J_{ij}, and an external force h_i called the qubit bias is applied on each particle. The energy of a configuration is given by Eq. 15.12.

$$H(s) = \sum_i h_i s_i + \sum_{i<j} J_{ij} s_i s_j, \qquad (15.12)$$

where $s_i \in \{-1, +1\}$.

D-Wave quantum annealers also fit this setting. The problem Hamiltonian H_P is encoded through an Ising model, simply by substituting s_i by the Pauli-z operator σ_i^z acting on i'th qubit resulting in Eq. 15.13.

$$H_P = \sum_i h_i \sigma_i^z + \sum_{i<j} J_{ij} \sigma_i^z \sigma_j^z \tag{15.13}$$

The Hamiltonian H_0 for initializing the system is the transverse field Hamiltonian give in Eq. 15.14.

$$H_0 = -h_0 \sum_{i=1}^{N} \sigma_i^x, \tag{15.14}$$

where σ_i^x is the Pauli-x operator acting on the ith qubit so that the ground state of H_0 is the equal superposition of all base states. One should note that the problem of finding the spin configuration which minimizes $H(s)$ is NP-Hard in general [59]. For further information regarding quantum annealing, we refer the readers to [60].

The significance of the ability of the QUBO model to encompass many problems in combinatorial optimization is enhanced by the fact that the QUBO model can be shown to be equivalent to the Ising model. The transformation between QUBO and Ising model can be performed easily using the mapping $x_i \leftrightarrow \frac{1-s_i}{2}$. Hence any problem for which QUBO formulation is known, or that can be expressed using QUBO formulation, can be attempted in principle to be solved using quantum annealing. We would like to remark that it is often more desirable to work with QUBO formulation than Ising model.

15.3.2.3 Running Problems on D-Wave

The D-Wave QPUs are lattices of interconnected qubits. While some qubits connect to others via couplers, the D-Wave QPUs do not have fully connected architectures. Therefore, the variables can not be mapped directly to the physical qubits on the machines. Hence, each variable is represented by a set of qubits called the *chain*, and the qubits in a chain are coupled strongly enough based on a parameter called *chain strength* so that they end up in the same state. The existence of longer chains reduces the quality of the solutions obtained. This process of mapping the variables to the physical qubits is known as the *minor-embedding problem* and can be handled by D-Wave, though we would like to remark that it is an NP-Hard problem itself.

When submitting problems to D-Wave, certain parameters need to be tuned besides the chain strength. This includes the *number of reads* and the *annealing time*. The number of reads is the total number of samples returned by D-Wave. Ideally, the sample with the lowest energy corresponds to the spin/qubit configuration of the ground state. However, due to the limitations of the device and the external noise, the ground state is not always achieved.

Annealing time depends both on the problem and the problem instance that is in consideration. There is a huge effort to detect whether quantum annealing provides any speedup against classical methods [61–64], and there are both supporting and opposing claims in this regard. Anyhow, it is still a field that is expanding and promising with the emergence of quantum-classical hybrid methods [65].

15.3.3 Markov Random Fields

Now, we will explore another tool that can be used to model our problems when using quantum annealing.

15.3.3.1 Markov Chains

Suppose that we want to predict the weather of the following day. Is it more likely that tomorrow will be cold? Or perhaps, will it be rainy? To solve the problem, we could make the following analysis: let us say that the probability of a cold day in our city is 1/4; if today it is cold, the likelihood of tomorrow being cold would be the joint probability of these events, that is, P(today is cold and tomorrow is cold) $= \frac{1}{4} \cdot \frac{1}{4} = \frac{1}{16}$. This probability seems too low, and usually, cold days follow one another in a row. If today is the first cold day in a while, a probability of 1/16 for tomorrow being also a cold day does not reflect our experience entirely.

Markov's revolutionary idea was to approach this problem in a different way; instead of viewing each probability as independent from one day to another, he decided to consider the present state as a necessary piece of information, the only one actually, for calculating the weather of the next day. In our analogy, this is like saying that the probability of being cold tomorrow depends only on the state of today's weather. If today it is cold, the probability of tomorrow being cold should be higher than it would be if today is too hot instead. With this approach, a sequence of weather states can give rise to a chain of events that satisfies what it is called the *Markovian property*.

Consider a discrete-time stochastic process, this is, a sequence of random variables $\{X_{n\geq0}\}$, with state space E. Here, we will consider a countable state space. If for all integers $n \geq 0$ all the states $i_0, i_1, \ldots, i_{n-1}, i, j$ satisfy Eq. 15.15, we say that the process is a *Markov chain*.

$$P(X_{n+1} = j | X_n = i, X_{n-1} = i_{n-1}, \ldots, X_0 = i_0) = P(X_{n+1} = j | X_n = i)$$
(15.15)

In our example, the state space has three states, namely {hot, cold, rainy}. As for the conditional probabilities $P_{i,j} \equiv P(X_{n+1} = j | X_n = i)$ (the probability of j happening tomorrow given that i occurs today), it is customary to arrange them in a matrix called the *transition matrix* as depicted in Table 15.2. For instance, $P_{\text{hot,cold}} = 1/4$ represents the probability of a cold day happening tomorrow, given that a hot day occurs today.

A transition matrix can also be visualized as a graph whose vertices represent the states of E. This graph has an oriented edge from i to j that will appear labeled with the probability $P_{i,j}$. The graph representation for our example is given in Fig. 15.4.

Table 15.2 Transition probabilities for the Markov chain with the state space {hot, cold, rainy}

	Hot	Cold	Rainy
Hot	1/2	1/4	1/4
Cold	1/6	1/2	1/3
Rainy	1/8	3/8	1/2

15.3.3.2 Markov Random Fields

Let's generalize the concept of a Markov chain and introduce the Markov random field. A *Markov random field* (MRF) or *Markov Network* is a set of random variables that form an undirected graph which obeys the Markovian property [66,67]. Random variables are represented by the nodes of the network (the vertices of the graph). Each random variable can take values from a finite set, and an assignment to the variables is called a *configuration*. Any pair of random variables that are not connected are conditionally independent.

In the example visualized in Fig. 15.5, we can observe several fully connected subgraphs of the graph. We denote these subgraphs as *cliques*. A *potential* function is defined over the cliques of the graph, assigning a value to every configuration of the clique. It is important to note though that, these values need not represent actual probabilities, that is, they may not add up to 1.

Concerning the potential functions, these are associated with an energy function. The total energy is defined as the sum over all clique potentials. High energy will indicate a low probability for a certain configuration to happen, and conversely, low energy will suggest that a specific configuration has more chances to occur. Although

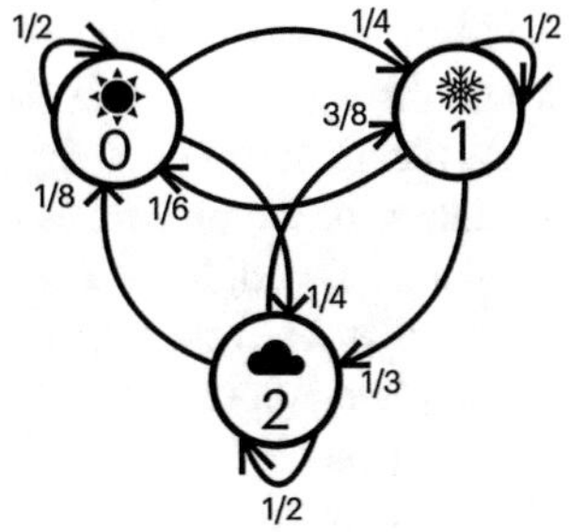

Fig. 15.4 The graph representation for the Markov chain with state space hot, cold, rainy. Each transition is labeled with the appropriate probability

Fig. 15.5 An example of a Markov random Field

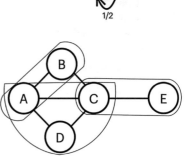

Table 15.3 Potentials for the clique $C_0 = \{C, E\}$ from Fig. 15.5

C	E	$p(C, E)$
0	0	0.3
0	1	0.9
1	0	2.6
1	1	5.0

we do not go into the details of the energy calculation here, we refer interested readers to [68].

From Fig. 15.5, let's choose the clique $C_0 = \{C, E\}$ with $C \in \{0, 1\}$ and $E \in \{0, 1\}$, that is C and E are binary random variables. We can define the potentials for the different configurations of the clique as shown in Table 15.3.

We will be primarily interested in the configuration with the highest probability of occurrence, equivalently the lowest energy. This is where the idea of *optimization* comes into play. The idea here is to encode the states of interest as the nodes of the network and then define the potentials so that using an optimization algorithm the lowest energy configuration is obtained. Markov random fields have been extremely popular for vision and image processing [69].

15.3.3.3 Quantum Annealing and Markov Random Fields

Markov random fields are inspired by the Ising model [68] and can be viewed as an attempt for generalization of the 2-local Ising model traditionally defined over a lattice. From the view of probability theory, the probability that each particle ends up in state -1 or 1 depends only on the spin values of its neighbors, hence satisfying the Markovian property. Therefore, the Ising model is indeed a special case of MRF, where there are cliques of sizes 1 and 2 only, and the state space is $\{-1, 1\}$.

As mentioned previously in this chapter, quantum annealing provides a way to take advantage of the properties of a quantum system to find solutions for optimization problems. Through the use of tools such as the Ocean software development kit provided by D-Wave, one can create a Markov network and use D-Wave machines to sample configurations of the random variables with the lowest energy. This is accomplished by D-Wave, by creating a QUBO model from the potentials of the Markov network as described below.

Given random variables X_1 and X_2 with potentials $\phi_{00}, \phi_{01}, \phi_{10}, \phi_{11}$ where ϕ_{ij} is the potential for $X_1 = i$ and $X_2 = j$, the corresponding QUBO formulation is defined as in Eq. 15.16.

$$(\phi_{10} - \phi_{00})x_1 + (\phi_{10} - \phi_{00})x_2 + (\phi_{11} - \phi_{10} - \phi_{01} + \phi_{00})x_1x_2 + \phi_{00} \quad (15.16)$$

15.4 Music Composition Using Quantum Annealing

In this section, we will explore how one can use quantum annealing to compose different elements of music such as melody, rhythm, and harmony. We will describe how one can model the process of music creation through a set of constraints and an objective function. The codes used in this section to generate the music pieces are available in the form of a Jupyter notebook in [70].

15.4.1 Melody Generation

As described in the previous section, quantum annealing aims to find the optimal solution to an optimization problem. We will start by investigating different ways of formulating the process of melody generation as an optimization problem. When we talk about melody generation, we refer to the generation of the pitches only.

15.4.1.1 Model

Suppose that we want to generate a melody consisting of n notes, where the pitches belong to the set $P = \{p_1, p_2, \ldots, p_k\}$. We will define the binary variables $x_{i,j}$ for $i \in [n]$ and $j \in P$ as in Eq. 15.17.

$$x_{i,j} = \begin{cases} 1 & \text{note at position } i \text{ is } j, \\ 0 & \text{otherwise.} \end{cases} \quad (15.17)$$

The total number of variables required in this formulation is $n|P|$. Note that we aim to generate n notes simultaneously. At the end of the optimization process, we will obtain an assignment to the binary variables $x_{i,j}$, which will indicate the pitch of the note selected for each position.

Next, we will define some constraints which can be included in the objective function using the penalty method described in Sect. 15.3.1. The first rule we need to incorporate is that only one of the variables $x_{i,j}$ is equal to 1 for each position i. The rule is necessary as exactly one pitch should be selected for each time point. This is equivalent to having the constraint defined in Eq. 15.18 for each $i \in [n]$.

$$\sum_{j \in P} x_{i,j} = 1 \quad (15.18)$$

This constraint is the backbone of our formulation, and it should be included in the QUBO using a sufficiently large penalty coefficient as it should never be violated.

Let us go through an example. Let $P = \{C4, D4, E4, G4\}$ and $n = 5$. The QUBO formulation has 20 variables defined through Eq. 15.17 and penalty terms of the form presented in Eq. 15.19 for each $i = 1, \ldots, 5$, that are obtained from Eq 15.18.

$$\left(1 - \sum_{j \in P} x_{i,j}\right)^2 \quad (15.19)$$

Table 15.4 The list of first 5 samples obtained from D-Wave. The columns represent the values of the variables $x_{1,C4}, x_{1,D4}, x_{1,E4}, x_{1,G4}, x_{2,C4}, \ldots, x_{5,G4}$ in the given order

	$i=1$				$i=2$				$i=3$				$i=4$				$i=5$			
Sample 1	0	0	1	0	0	0	1	0	0	0	0	1	0	1	0	0	0	1	0	0
Sample 2	0	1	0	0	0	0	0	1	1	0	0	0	1	0	0	0	0	1	0	0
Sample 3	0	1	0	0	0	1	0	0	0	0	0	1	0	0	0	1	0	0	1	0
Sample 4	0	0	1	0	0	0	0	1	0	0	1	0	1	0	0	0	0	0	0	1
Sample 5	0	1	0	0	0	0	1	0	1	0	0	0	0	0	1	0	0	1	0	0

Table 15.5 The list of note sequences corresponding to the samples given in Table 15.4

Sample 1	E4 − E4 − G4 − D4 − D4
Sample 2	D4 − G4 − C4 − C4 − D4
Sample 3	D4 − D4 − G4 − G4 − E4
Sample 4	E4 − G4 − E4 − C4 − G4
Sample 5	D4 − E4 − C4 − E4 − D4

At this point, any sequence of 5 notes has 0 energy and is equally likely to be produced and there are in total 4^5 such sequences. The list of the first 5 samples obtained from D-Wave as a result of running the QUBO formulation described above is given in Table 15.4.

The energies of all the samples in Table 15.4 are 0 as no constraint is violated, i.e., precisely one of the variables is 1 for each i. The resulting note sequences are given in Table 15.5.

So far, we have only defined a single rule ensuring a single note at each time point. In general, one would like to introduce some more rules while composing a melody as we will discuss next.

15.4.1.2 Rules About Consecutive Notes

Suppose that we want to add a restriction that the note p_l does not appear after the note p_k. This is useful for avoiding particular intervals and amending our model. Such a restriction can be incorporated into the QUBO formulation by adding the term defined in Eq. 15.20 to the objective function multiplied with a suitable penalty coefficient C for each $i \in [n-1]$.

$$x_{i,p_k} x_{i+1,p_l} \tag{15.20}$$

Note that when both variables equal 1 simultaneously, a penalty of C is added to the objective function. Alternatively, we can express the same rule using the constraint defined in Eq. 15.21.

$$x_{i,p_k} + x_{i+1,p_l} \le 1 \tag{15.21}$$

In this case, the inequality should be first transformed into equality by using slack variables and then added to the objective function.

Now let us consider a rule saying that the same note does not appear more than twice in a row. Similar to what we had above, the term $x_{i,p_j} x_{i+1,p_j} x_{i+2,p_j}$ can be added to the objective for each $i \in [n-2]$ and $p_j \in P$. However, this is not a quadratic term, and quadratization is needed to obtain a QUBO. Alternatively, the rule can be expressed by the constraint given in Eq. 15.22, which forces that at most two of the variables are equal to 1 simultaneously.

$$x_{i,p_j} + x_{i+1,p_j} + x_{i+2,p_j} \le 2 \qquad (15.22)$$

Taking the previous example and assuming that $P = \{C4, D4, E4, G4\}$ and $n = 5$, let us also add the rule that G4 does not follow D4 using Eq. 15.20 and include Eq. 15.22 in our formulation as well. The first 5 samples from the experiment results are listed in Table 15.6. All the sequences in the table have 0 energy and obey the rules we have incorporated.

15.4.1.3 Semitones and Augmented Intervals

Now let us investigate the different ways we can choose to set P. We can identify the notes through the number of semitones between the lowest pitch and the pitch in consideration. The binary variables $x_{i,j}$ are defined as in Eq. 15.23 for each $i \in [n]$ and $j \in P$.

$$x_{i,j} = \begin{cases} 1, & \text{note at position } i \text{ is } j \text{ semitones apart from the lowest pitch of the sequence,} \\ 0, & \text{otherwise.} \end{cases}$$

$$(15.23)$$

When P is selected as $\{0, 1, 2, \ldots, 12\}$, then it represents the notes from a chromatic scale. Note that this representation is independent of the key chosen as the result may be interpreted in any key. For instance, if we let $x_{i,0} = C4$, subsequently the resulting P is the set of notes from the chromatic scale of C.

Identifying the notes through semitones, it will be easier for us to model some rules like avoiding particular intervals. Let A be the list of intervals in semitones, that we would like to avoid. This rule can be incorporated by adding the term defined in Eq. 15.24 to the objective function for all $i \in [n]$, $|j' - j| \in A$.

$$x_{i,j} x_{i+1,j'} \qquad (15.24)$$

Table 15.6 The list of note sequences obtained from D-Wave after incorporating constraints given in Eqs. 15.20 and 15.22

Sample 1	G4 − D4 − E4 − G4 − C4
Sample 2	E4 − E4 − C4 − E4 − G4
Sample 3	E4 − D4 − C4 − E4 − G4
Sample 4	D4 − E4 − G4 − D4 − C4
Sample 5	D4 − E4 − G4 − D4 − E4

Fig. 15.6 The sequence of semitones is obtained from D-Wave hybrid solver and it is interpreted in C Major

Alternatively, it translates to the constraint given in Eq. 15.25, so that whenever an unallowed interval is used, we have a penalty.

$$x_{i,j} + x_{i+1,j'} \leq 1 \text{ for all } i \in [n], |j' - j| \in A \qquad (15.25)$$

We are also capable of taking P as a subset of the chromatic scale. For instance, the set $P = \{0, 2, 4, 5, 7, 9, 11, 12\}$ represents the notes from a major scale. Let us also assume that we would like to set the first and the last pitch of the generated music piece as the first degree of the scale. This can be incorporated by simply adding the terms given in Eq. 15.26 to the objective.

$$(1 - x_{1,0}), \quad (1 - x_{n,0}) \qquad (15.26)$$

Let us go over an example. We will let $A = [6, 8, 10, 12]$, so that we would like to avoid the intervals tritone, augmented fifth, augmented sixth, and augmented seventh (octave). Assuming that $P = \{0, 2, 4, 5, 7, 9, 11, 12\}$, $n = 20$ and incorporating rules Eqs. 15.18, 15.22, 15.24, and 15.26, we obtain a QUBO formulation. Due to the increased number of constraints, the solution returned by D-Wave QPU violates some constraints and fails to return the ground state. Using D-Wave's hybrid solver, the obtained melody interpreted in C Major is given in Fig. 15.6. Note that not all the constraints are satisfied in this sample as well. This can be viewed both as a caveat and a feature, as the violation of some constraints introduces some randomness to the process.

15.4.1.4 Diatonic Scale and Tendency Notes

Previously, we investigated how one can identify the notes through semitones. All music pieces have a definite key signature. Therefore it is often more suitable to work with pitches from a particular scale.

For simplicity, let us consider the 8 degrees of a diatonic scale. In this case, the set P consists of $d_1, d_2, \ldots, d_8$ where d_j is the j'th degree of the scale. Instead of defining the variables by the pitches, we will define them through degrees for each $i \in [n]$ and $d_j \in P$ as given in Eq. 15.27.

$$x_{i,j} = \begin{cases} 1 & \text{note at position } i \text{ is } d_j, \\ 0 & \text{otherwise.} \end{cases} \qquad (15.27)$$

As a result of the optimization procedure, we will obtain a degree sequence, which can then be translated into a note sequence based on the chosen scale. Hence, our model is readily adaptable to different scales. Furthermore, the rules described in the previous subsections are still applicable.

Fig. 15.7 The degree sequence is obtained from D-Wave and it is interpreted in `C Major` and `G Minor` (natural) in the presented music scores, respectively

Some notes in the scale are less stable than the others which are known as the *tendency notes* and tend to resolve to the stable ones. Let us examine how to incorporate rules about tendency notes. According to the rule, degrees 2, 4, and 6 resolve down by one step, and degree 7 resolves to the octave. To reflect the rule about tendency notes, for each $i \in [n-1]$, we will add the terms defined in Eq. 15.28 to the objective.

$$x_{i,2}(1 - x_{i+1,1}), \quad x_{i,4}(1 - x_{i+1,3}), \quad x_{i,6}(1 - x_{i+1,5}), \quad x_{i,7}(1 - x_{i+1,8}) \quad (15.28)$$

Using Eqs. 15.26, 15.27, and 15.28 to formulate our model and setting $n = 20$, the degree sequence obtained from D-Wave corresponding to one of the samples with the lowest energy is given in Fig. 15.7. The degree sequence is interpreted for different scales.

15.4.1.5 Objective Function

Having discussed how to incorporate different constraints into the model, we can now explore how we can modify the objective function to differentiate between the feasible solutions. When we have only the constraints, all sequences of notes that do not violate any of the constraints are feasible solutions, and they are equally likely to be sampled since they have the lowest possible energy. Any violated constraint increases the energy value by the penalty value of the constraint. Note that as mentioned earlier, sometimes we would like particular constraints to be never violated (like Eq. 15.18), while a solution in which some constraints are violated can still be desirable (avoidance of particular intervals).

In order to differentiate between the feasible solutions, we can give some "rewards" to a particular sequence of notes, i.e. decrease their energy. For instance, we might give a higher reward for pitch D4 following C4 versus pitch E4 following C4. The way to accomplish this is to have the term given in Eq. 15.29 in the objective function.

$$- \sum_{\substack{i \in [n-1] \\ j, j' \in P}} W_{j,j'} x_{i,j} x_{i+1,j'} \quad (15.29)$$

Here, $W_{j,j'}$ is the weight associated with having note j' after note j. The larger the weight, the higher the reward we have in the objective function. Note that we have a negative sign in front in Eq. 15.29, as we have a minimization problem and want to decrease the energy. The weights can be determined by analyzing some music pieces and forming a transition matrix of weights examining the consecutive notes. Below, we illustrate this idea through a simple music piece.

In Fig. 15.8, an excerpt from Beethoven's Ode to Joy is given. To identify the weights, we count the occurrences of consecutive pairs. To start with, we identify the occurrences of each note and then count the number of times the note is followed by another particular note. For instance, the note F#4 appears at positions 1, 2, 7, 12, 13. It is followed by F#4 and E4 twice, and by G4 once. Hence, we can deduce the weights given in Eq. 15.30.

$$W_{F\#4,E4} = 2, \quad W_{F\#4,F\#4} = 2, \quad W_{F\#4,G4} = 1. \tag{15.30}$$

As the selected music piece is a short one, it does not contain all the notes from P and for those notes i, the corresponding weight $W_{i,j} = 0$ for all j. We would like to remark that having 0 as the weight does not imply that the corresponding note tuple is always avoided but means that we don't give additional rewards to such pairs. The list of all non-zero weights is defined in Eq. 15.31.

$$\begin{aligned}
&W_{F\#4,E4} = 2, \quad W_{F\#4,F\#4} = 2, \quad W_{F\#4,G4} = 1, \tag{15.31}\\
&W_{G4,F\#4} = 1, \quad W_{G4,A4} = 1,\\
&W_{A4,G4} = 1, \quad W_{A4,A4} = 1,\\
&W_{E4,D4} = 1, \quad W_{E4,E4} = 1, \quad W_{E4,F\#4} = 1,\\
&W_{D4,D4} = 1, \quad W_{D4,E4} = 1.
\end{aligned}$$

Note that taking the number of occurrences as the weights, we are also giving rewards to pitches that appear more frequently than the other. For instance, F# appears five times, and the overall reward is higher when more F#'s appear in the sequence.

Now the question is how should we select set P. We can use Eq. 15.27 to define our binary variables as the degrees from a scale. Hence, the matrix W defines the transition weights between the scale degrees. Note that the newly generated music piece mimics the one from which the transition weights are obtained. The longer the music piece, the better estimates are obtained for the weights. Multiple pieces can be selected as well, paying attention that they are from the same scale, or in case considering pieces from different scales, one should take degrees of the scale instead of the pitches when calculating the weights.

We define the QUBO formulation defined through binary variables given in Eq. 15.27 using the constraints defined in Eqs. 15.18, 15.22, 15.26, 15.28 and 15.29 as the objective function with the weights obtained from Eq. 15.31. Note that in this case, one needs to properly set the penalty coefficients; in case the constraint is

Fig. 15.8 An excerpt from Beethoven's Ode to Joy

violated and there is a reward, an increase in the energy due to the penalty should be larger than the decrease in the energy due to reward. The resulting music piece obtained from the D-Wave hybrid solver is given in Fig. 15.9. We interpreted the obtained degree sequence in D Major.

Alternatively, instead of generating weights for the transitions between individual degrees, we can collect statistics about the different intervals used in the music piece and how often they appear. Then accordingly, we can reward the intervals that occur more frequently.

15.4.1.6 Rests

The sets we have considered so far only consisted of the pitches; however, we may want to include rests in the music piece as well. In this case, a rest element can be included in the set P with appropriate rules. For instance, we may want to avoid two consecutive rests, which we can easily accomplish with the rules we have shown for consecutive notes. In addition, we can set the number of rests used in the music piece by introducing the constraint given in Eq. 15.32.

$$\sum_i x_{i,r} = k, \tag{15.32}$$

where k is the total number of rests we want in the music piece and $x_{i,r}$ denotes that note at position i is a rest.

15.4.2 Rhythm Generation

So far, we have discussed generating the pitches of the melody. In this section, we additionally take into account the rhythm.

15.4.2.1 Rhythmic Sequence

When generating a music piece, one option would be to generate the pitch sequence and the rhythmic sequence separately. In such a case, the idea will be similar to what we had previously. The set S will consist of possible durations for the notes, such as whole, half, quarter, etc. The binary variables $y_{i,j}$ for $i \in [n]$ and $j \in D$ will be defined as in Eq. 15.33.

$$y_{i,j} = \begin{cases} 1 & \text{note at position } i \text{ has duration } j, \\ 0 & \text{otherwise.} \end{cases} \tag{15.33}$$

Fig. 15.9 The degree sequence is obtained from D-Wave using the transition weights from Ode to Joy and it is interpreted in D Major

Fig. 15.10 The rhythmic sequence obtained from D-Wave is combined with the pitch sequence obtained in Fig. 15.9

Similarly, the first rule we need to incorporate is that only one of the variables $y_{i,j}$ is equal to 1 for each position i, which is expressed using the constraint given in Eq. 15.34 for each $i \in [n]$.

$$\sum_{j \in D} y_{i,j} = 1 \tag{15.34}$$

For the objective function, the same method can be used. Let us denote half note by H, quarter note by Q, dotted quarter note by DQ and eighth note by E. For the music piece given in Fig. 15.8, we obtain the weights given in Eq. 15.35.

$$W_{Q,Q} = 11, \quad W_{Q,DQ} = 1 \tag{15.35}$$
$$W_{DQ,E} = 1$$
$$W_{E,H} = 1$$

If we only incorporate Eqs. 15.34 and 15.35 in our formulation, then it is very likely that we will have a sequence of quarter notes only, as they have the highest weight. To avoid this, we will make sure that there are at least two notes of each duration using the constraint given in Eq. 15.36 for each $d \in D$.

$$\sum_{i=1}^{n} y_{i,d} \geq 2 \tag{15.36}$$

We generate a rhythmic sequence with the binary variables defines as in Eq. 15.33, using Eqs. 15.34 and 15.36 as the constraints and the transition weights given in Eq. 15.35 to obtain the objective function defined in Eq. 15.29. We combine it with the degree sequence generated in Fig. 15.9 and obtain the music piece given in Fig. 15.10.

We would like to note that in this approach, we are not fixing the total length of the music piece, but we are determining the durations for a given fixed set of notes. To have a fixed music length, what we can do is include a constraint that takes into account the duration of each type of note as given in Eq. 15.37.

$$\sum_{\substack{i \in [n] \\ j \in D}} d(j) y_{i,j} = L, \tag{15.37}$$

where $d(j)$ is the duration of j and L is the total length of the music piece in terms of eighth notes so that $d(E) = 1, d(Q) = 2, d(DQ) = 3$ and $d(H) = 4$. We discretize the durations in terms of eighth notes as it is the note with shortest duration in our example.

15.4.2.2 Rhythm and Pitch Generated Together

Another alternative is to consider pitches together with their durations. If P is the set of possible pitches, and D is the set of possible durations, then overall, there will be $|D||P|$ possibilities for each note. Assuming there are n notes, the number of variables we need significantly increases to $n|D||P|$ in this case. The binary variables for $i \in [n]$, $j \in P$ and $k \in D$ take the form presented in Eq. 15.38.

$$x_{i,j,k} = \begin{cases} 1 & \text{note at position } i \text{ is pitch } j \text{ and has duration } k, \\ 0 & \text{otherwise.} \end{cases} \tag{15.38}$$

The previous rules we defined about the consecutive notes and intervals apply here too. Those constraints are included independent of k, the note's duration. Likewise, we can still take an objective function based on another music piece. This time, we inspect the number of occurrences of consecutive pitch-duration pairs. However, we would like to remark that the performance of the quantum annealers decreases as the number of variables increases. Hence, it is often desirable to have models with a smaller number of variables.

15.4.3 Harmony Generation

We have seen so far how to generate melody and rhythm. Now it is time to discuss harmonization using quantum annealing.

15.4.3.1 Algorhythms

Although it does not directly fit into the scope of harmonization, we would like to discuss a previous work that uses Markov random fields to produce chord progressions. "Algorhythms: Generating Music with D-Wave's Quantum Annealer" project was submitted to the iQuHack 2021 MIT Hackathon [71], and it features a novel example of how one can use a Markov network in order to generate music. It is further discussed in this book, in the chapter authored by Chuharski.

Let us explain the idea briefly. Each node represents one of the chords I, II, III, IV, V, VI, VIIdim. Having realized that chords can represent the states of a Markov random field, the authors created a mechanism that assigned values to the potentials between the nodes in a random manner. The potentials for $(0, 0)$ and $(1, 1)$ are assigned high values to avoid two chords or no chord being selected at a time point. Each run of the algorithm outputs a chord based on the randomly assigned potentials. To get a sequence of chords, the algorithm is called several times. In Fig. 15.11, we can see a song generated with this algorithm.

Each chord is selected from the set of samples that the D-Wave computer outputs. What we are observing is a sequence of states each of which represents the lowest energy state for the given configuration of the potentials. As each chord is generated independently, the progressions do not follow any rules or music style. Next, we will see how we can create a chord progression following some rules.

15.4.3.2   Generating a Chord Sequence Using Markov Random Fields

Consider the chords that can be built taking each note of the major scale as the root of a triad. To generate a chord progression of n notes we need to define our nodes as $\text{I}_i, \text{ii}_i, \text{iii}_i, \text{IV}_i, \text{V}_i, \text{vi}_i, \text{VIIdim}_i$ where $i \in [n]$. For each time point, we have multiple nodes reflecting multiple possibilities. Then, we can employ a more structured chord progression defining the potentials accordingly.

One way to make the result more similar to the musical pieces we are used to listening to is to take into account some rules of musical harmony. For example, there are musical structures that have existed for a long time and remain in force due to the stability they provide when presenting a complete musical idea: the cadences. Harmonic *cadences* are progressions of two or more chords that help complete a musical section by giving resolution to a musical phrase. We have, for instance, the "perfect" cadence formed by the chords V-I. This structure is one of the most used because of its forcefulness, but there are also other cadences that help complete a musical discourse. If we were to encode these structures into our network, we would need to set low energy for the potentials relating, in the case of the perfect cadence, the chords V_{i-1} and I_i. This would ensure that when the system evolves, it would end up in a state that contains this particular progression.

For instance, suppose that we want to generate a sequence of 4 chords that will tend to exhibit the pattern of a perfect cadence. We can start by identifying our binary random variables and defining the couplings between them. Note that in order to avoid having several chords played at the same time, we have to set high values for the potentials that relate to the chords designated for each step of the sequence, i.e, the set of chords that represent the first chord, the second chord, etc. Let us visualize the graph of our problem (Fig. 15.12).

Now, let us define our pairwise potentials. We give some examples in Tables 15.7, 15.8 and 15.9. In Table 15.7, observe that we penalize the configuration that represents having both chords played at the same time. In Table 15.8, we penalize the configuration that represents having the same chord repeated over in the sequence. In Table 15.9, we favor the configuration that represents having the pattern V-I. The rest of the potentials are defined in a similar manner.

This approach is rather different from the one used in the "Algorhythms: Generating Music with D-Wave's Quantum Annealer" project. First, we do not have to run the algorithm several times because we are generating the sequence all at once. Then, observe that we are setting specific values to the potentials and that by doing so, we are encoding some harmony considerations into the model. One of the results we can

Fig. 15.11 A song containing a sequence of chords obtained by "Algorhythms: Generating Music with D-Wave's Quantum Annealer" project [71]

Table 15.7 Values of the potential that associates the chords I_1 and ii_1

I_1	ii_1	(pI_1, ii_i)
0	0	50.0
0	0	50.0
1	0	50.0
1	1	100.0

Table 15.8 Values of the potential that associates the chords I_1 and I_2

I_1	I_2	$p(I_1, I_2)$
0	0	50.0
0	0	50.0
1	0	50.0
1	1	100.0

Table 15.9 Values of the potential that associates the chords V_1 and I_2

V_1	I_2	$p(V_1, I_2)$
0	0	50.0
0	0	50.0
1	0	50.0
1	1	0.0

Fig. 15.12 Markov random field is delineated with the random variables defined for a progression of 4 chords. For simplicity, the dependency relations are shown only for the chord I_1 (1st chord, chord I)

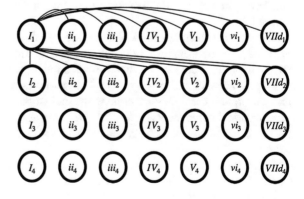

get with this algorithm is given in Fig. 15.13. Observe that the resulting progression satisfies the requirement of showing the pattern V-I.

In conclusion, as we have seen, Markov random fields are tools that prove to be useful when solving optimization problems. Moreover, they also represent new approaches to the task of music generation.

Fig. 15.13 A chord
progression generated using
Markov Random Fields
incorporating the perfect
cadence

15.4.3.3 qHarmony

One of the earlier papers on music composition using quantum annealing is provided by Kirke and Miranda [9]. Taking a music piece from C Major, the qHarmony tool harmonizes the given melody. In this section, we will briefly describe the used technique.

Instead of QUBO formulation, the problem is encoded directly using Ising formulation, taking also into account the embedding to the Chimera graph, the graph representing the topology of the underlying qubits of the D-Wave 2000 QPU. For simplicity, we will not discuss the embedding component as this part can be handled by D-Wave solvers. The set S is defined as {C4, D4, E4, F4, G4, A4, B4, C5}.[3]

Unlike the approach we have followed so far where we were considering a sequence of n notes at a time, only a single chord is generated at a time. The spin variables q_i for $i \in S$ are defined as in Eq. 15.39.

$$q_i = \begin{cases} 1 & \text{note } i \text{ is selected,} \\ -1 & \text{otherwise.} \end{cases} \tag{15.39}$$

The coupling constants are defined as $J_{i,j} = 7 - 2|i - j|$. Note that the smaller the $|i - j|$ is, the larger the value of $J_{i,j}$. Since the annealer tries to minimize the overall energy, the qubits corresponding to the notes that are semitone or tone apart will have a higher coupling constant; thus, the possibility of getting such intervals will reduce.

The external magnetic field h_i's indicate which note is harmonized; it is set as $h_i = -7$, if note i is harmonized, and 1, otherwise. Hence setting q_i as 1 will reduce the energy as expected. Note i will be called the input note.

It is also possible to specify multiple input notes to harmonize by setting more than one h_i value as -7. Furthermore, the tool works in a hybrid manner involving some classical components as well, allowing the user to identify for which notes of the piece, harmony should be generated, and whether it should be a minor or major chord.

There are several drawbacks of the proposed approach. First of all, the provided example works for eight notes, in particular the notes from the scale of C Major. This is not a significant problem as the given example can be generalized for other sets and scales by tuning the coupling constants. Secondly, the generated chords at each time point do not take into account the previously generated ones. Finally, the number of notes that will appear in the chord can not be determined beforehand in

---

[3] In the original text, the set is taken as {c, d, e, f, g, a, b, C} where C denotes the note one octave above c.

this model. Next, we will discuss an alternative approach and try to overcome the mentioned drawbacks.

15.4.3.4 Model

Suppose that we would like to add three-note chords, triads, to a given music piece. The notes appearing in the triads will be restricted to the set of pitches $P = \{1, 2, 3, 4, 5, 6, 7, 8\}$, where the elements represent the degrees of the scale. Our binary variables $x_{i,j}$ for $i \in [n]$ and $j \in P$ are defined as in Eq. 15.40.

$$x_{i,j} = \begin{cases} 1 & \text{chord at position } i \text{ contains note } j, \\ 0 & \text{otherwise.} \end{cases} \tag{15.40}$$

At each time point, we would like to have three notes. Hence, we are going to add the constraint defined in Eq. 15.41 to our model.

$$\sum_{j \in P} x_{i,j} = 3 \tag{15.41}$$

Recall that we had already defined a constraint so that the melody begins and ends with the first degree of the scale. Similarly, we can enforce the first and the last triads to be built upon the first degree of the scale. We can add the terms defined in Eq. 15.42 to the objective function:

$$(1 - x_{1,1}), \quad (1 - x_{1,3}), \quad (1 - x_{1,5}), \quad (1 - x_{n,1}), \quad (1 - x_{n,3}), \quad (1 - x_{n,5}). \tag{15.42}$$

For each time point, one of the pitches in the triad should be the pitch of the melody. Let $N = [p_{1_j}, p_{2_j}, \ldots, p_{n_j}]$ be the note sequence that we would like to harmonize. We assume that each $p_{i_j} \in P$. To enforce that one of the three notes in the triad at time point i is p_{i_j}, we add the term defined in Eq. 15.43 to the objective function for all $i = 2, \ldots, n - 1$. (We are assuming that the first and the last pitch of the note sequence is the first degree of the scale.)

$$(1 - x_{i,p_{i_j}}) \tag{15.43}$$

We want to generate triads either obtained by taking the degrees of the scale as their root or their inversions. We want to avoid consecutive degrees from the scale and the degrees 1–7, 2–8, 1–8 to appear in the same triad by adding the terms defined in Eq. 15.44 to the objective function for all $i = 2, \ldots, n - 1$, $|j - j'| \in \{1, 6, 7\}$.

$$x_{i,j} x_{i,j'} \tag{15.44}$$

Using Eqs. 15.40–15.43, and 15.44 and harmonizing the music piece illustrated in Fig. 15.10, we obtain the music piece presented in Fig. 15.14.

The new method allows more flexibility than the one previously proposed. Yet, it does not take into account any preference between the consecutive chords. For instance, it is more likely that some chords built upon the particular degrees of a scale follow each other, and sometimes it is the opposite case. Furthermore, if one follows 4-part harmony rules, there should be further rules that should be incorporated in the model.

15.5 Conclusion and Future Work

As a follow up to the previous chapter, the main goal of this chapter was to lay the groundwork for music composition using quantum annealing. We introduced various formulations for melody, rhythm, and harmony generation and demonstrated how music rules and styles could be incorporated into the model. Prior to this work, the majority of the studies on music composition focused on gate-based quantum computers. Notwithstanding the previous efforts [9,71], this is the first time quantum annealing is used for melodic music composition.

The presented methodologies will be intriguing for composers, quantum computing researchers, and the community of algorithmic music generation and allow interested readers to build upon the given notions. Being the first comprehensive study on the nascent field of music composition using quantum annealing, we believe that it will foster the development of the area. As a side contribution, a novel application area for quantum annealing is demonstrated within this chapter.

The popularity of quantum annealing relies on the promise that one may gain speedup by exploiting quantum effects when solving optimization problems. We would like to emphasize that creativity is in the foreground instead of potential quantum speedup throughout the chapter. Nonetheless, it is envisaged that it will become possible to solve larger-scale problems and obtain higher quality results faster than the known classical techniques with technological advancements. As the technologies evolve, the ideas discussed here can be leveraged for building larger-scale and more sophisticated models, and it may also be possible to exploit quantum annealing for speedup when composing music.

Markov random fields stand out as an alternative model for music composition using quantum annealing, but they have not been a popular way of composing music in classical computing. As Markov random fields are defined through potentials, they are amenable to reflecting the statistical properties of previously generated music pieces or musical styles. We would like to point out that the statistical approach for music composition using Markov chains relies on randomness, while the optimization aspect is prevalent in Markov random fields.

The study has opened up a vast amount of directions to investigate. First of all, the models can be ameliorated to incorporate further rules. This might be beneficial for harmony generation in particular, as the traditional rules for harmonization have complex structures. In addition, one may adopt the approach we have taken for defining the objection function while generating a melody, for the Markov random fields. The harmonic progressions can be identified from an existing music piece,

Fig. 15.14 The music piece obtained by harmonizing the music piece given in Fig. 15.10

and the potentials can be set in accordance. One may focus on generating specific music types, such as counterpoint music, which heavily depends on rules. As a natural progression, a target problem would be music completion. Music completion refers to the task of replacing the missing notes in a given music piece. It is a suitable candidate problem as it can be defined as the problem of maximizing the likelihood that a sequence of notes is selected to replace the missing ones. Besides music creation, one may consider other problems from the domain of music, such as music arrangement, where the aim is to arrange a given music piece to a given list of instruments by reduction. The list can be expanded to include any problem that can be expressed as an optimization task.

Acknowledgements ÖS and LB have been partially supported by Polish National Science Center under the grant agreement 2019/33/B/ST6/02011. The project was initiated under the QIntern program organized by QWorld, therefore we would like to thank the organizers of the program. We would like to thank Adam Glos and Jarosław Adam Miszczak for their valuable comments.

References

1. Lovelace, A. A. (1843). Sketch of the analytical engine invented by Charles Babbage by LF Menabrea of Turin, officer of the military engineers, with notes by the translator. Bibliotheque Universelle de Geneve.
2. Hiller, L. A., & Isaacson, L. M. (1979). *Experimental music; composition with an electronic computer.* Greenwood Publishing Group Inc..
3. Papadopoulos, G., & Wiggins, G. (1999). AI methods for algorithmic composition: A survey, a critical view and future prospects. In *AISB Symposium on Musical Creativity* (Vol. 124, pp. 110–117).
4. Miranda, E. R. (2020). Quantum computer: Hello, music! arXiv:2006.13849.
5. Kirke, A. (2018). Programming gate-based hardware quantum computers for music. *Musicology, 24,* 21–37.
6. Kirke, A. (2019). Applying quantum hardware to non-scientific problems: Grover's algorithm and rule-based algorithmic music composition. arXiv:1902.04237.
7. Aharonov, D., Van Dam, W., Kempe, J., Landau, Z., Lloyd, S., & Regev, O. (2008). Adiabatic quantum computation is equivalent to standard quantum computation. *SIAM Review, 50*(4), 755–787.
8. Farhi, E., Goldstone, J., Gutmann, S., Lapan, J., Lundgren, A., & Preda, D. (2001). A quantum adiabatic evolution algorithm applied to random instances of an NP-complete problem. *Science, 292*(5516), 472–475.
9. Kirke, A., & Miranda, E. R. (2017). Experiments in sound and music quantum computing. In *Guide to Unconventional Computing for Music* (pp. 121–157). Springer.
10. Doornbusch, P. (2017). Early computer music experiments in Australia and England. *Organised Sound, 22*(2), 297–307.
11. Bogdanov, V., Woodstra, C., Bush, J., & Erlewine, S. T. (2001). *All music guide to electronica: The definitive guide to electronic music.* CMP Media.
12. Manning, P. (2013). *Electronic and computer music.* Oxford University Press.
13. Short history of computer music. http://artsites.ucsc.edu/EMS/Music/equipment/computers/history/history.html. Accessed 15 Dec. 2021.

14. Miranda, E. (2001). *Composing music with computers*. CRC Press.
15. Manaris, B., Roos, P., Machado, P., Krehbiel, D., Pellicoro, L., & Romero, J. (2007). A corpus-based hybrid approach to music analysis and composition. In *Proceedings of the National Conference on Artificial Intelligence* (Vol. 22, p. 839).
16. Funk, T. (2016). *Zen and the art of software performance: John Cage and Lejaren A. Hiller Jr.'s HPSCHD (1967–1969)*. Ph.D. thesis. University of Illinois at Chicago.
17. Conklin, D. (2003). Music generation from statistical models. In *Proceedings of the AISB 2003 Symposium on Artificial Intelligence and Creativity in the Arts and Sciences* (pp. 30–35).
18. Apt, K. (2003). *Principles of constraint programming*. Cambridge University Press.
19. Van Beek, P., & Chen, X. (1999). CPlan: A constraint programming approach to planning. In *AAAI/IAAI* (pp. 585–590).
20. Truchet, C., Agon, C., & Codognet, P. (2001). A constraint programming system for music composition, preliminary results. In *In the Seventh International Conference on Principles and Practice of Constraint Programming, Musical Constraints Workshop, Paphos*.
21. Anders, T. (2018). Compositions created with constraint programming. In R. T. Dean & A. McLean (Eds.), *The Oxford handbook of algorithmic music* (ch. 10). Oxford University Press.
22. Biles, J. A. (2007). Evolutionary computation for musical tasks. In J. A. Biles & E. R. Miranda (Eds.), *Evolutionary computer music*. Springer.
23. Horner, A., & Goldberg, D. E. (1991). *Genetic algorithms and computer-assisted music composition* (Vol. 51). Michigan Publishing, University of Michigan Library.
24. Gibson, P., & Byrne, J. (1991). NEUROGEN, musical composition using genetic algorithms and cooperating neural networks. In *1991 Second International Conference on Artificial Neural Networks* (pp. 309–313).
25. Spector, L., & Alpern, A. (1995). Induction and recapitulation of deep musical structure. *Proceedings of International Joint Conference on Artificial Intelligence, IJCAI, 95*, 20–25.
26. Samadani, R., & Zhang, T. (2007). Music Genie: Interactive, content-based browsing of music based on thumbnail playback. Tech. Rep. HPL-2007-38, HP Laboratories.
27. Todd, P. (1988). A sequential network design for musical applications. In *Proceedings of the 1988 Connectionist Models Summer School* (pp. 76–84).
28. Marinescu, A.-I. (2019). Bach 2.0—Generating classical music using recurrent neural networks. *Procedia Computer Science, 159*, 117–124.
29. Kotecha, N., & Young, P. (2018). Generating music using an LSTM network. arXiv:1804.07300.
30. Briot, J.-P., Hadjeres, G., & Pachet, F.-D. (2020). *Deep learning techniques for music generation* (Vol. 1). Springer.
31. Payne, C. (2019). Musenet. https://openai.com/blog/musenet/. Accessed 15 Dec. 2021.
32. Park, S.-W., Ko, J.-S., Huh, J.-H., & Kim, J.-C. (2021). Review on generative adversarial networks: Focusing on computer vision and its applications. *Electronics, 10*(10), 1216.
33. Tanaka, T., Bemman, B., & Meredith, D. (2016). Integer programming formulation of the problem of generating milton babbitt's all-partition arrays. In *The 17th International Society for Music Information Retrieval Conference*.
34. Cunha, N. d. S., Subramanian, A., & Herremans, D. (2018). Generating guitar solos by integer programming. *Journal of the Operational Research Society, 69*(6), 971–985.
35. Conforti, M., Cornuéjols, G., Zambelli, G., et al. (2014). *Integer programming* (Vol. 271). Springer.
36. Glover, F. (1990). Tabu search-part II. *ORSA Journal on Computing, 2*(1), 4–32.
37. Harvey, C. A. D. K., Salkin, M. (1975). The Knapsack problem: A survey. *Naval Research Logistics, 22*, 127–144.
38. David, V. C., Applegate, L., Bixby, R. E., & Cook, W. J. (2007). *The traveling salesman problem: A computational study*. Princeton University Press.
39. Tommy, B. T., Jensen, R. (1994). *Graph coloring problems*. Wiley-Interscience.

40. Garey, M. R., & Johnson, D. S. (1979). *Computers and intractability* (Vol. 174).
41. Kelley, J. J. E. (1960). The cutting-plane method for solving convex programs. *Journal of the Society for Industrial and Applied Mathematics, 8,* 703–712.
42. Lawler, D. E. W. E. L. (1966). Branch-and-bound methods: A survey. *Operations Research, 14,* 699–719.
43. Kirkpatrick, S., Gelatt, C. D., & Vecchi, M. P. (1983). Optimization by simulated annealing. *Science, 220*(4598), 671–680.
44. Dorigo, M., Birattari, M., & Stutzle, T. (2006). Ant colony optimization. *IEEE Computational Intelligence Magazine, 1,* 28–39.
45. Lucas, A. (2014). Ising formulations of many NP problems. *Frontiers in Physics, 2,* 5.
46. Karimi, S., & Ronagh, P. (2019). Practical integer-to-binary mapping for quantum annealers. *Quantum Information Processing, 18*(4), 1–24.
47. Geoffrion, A. M. (2010). Lagrangian relaxation for integer programming. In *50 years of integer programming 1958–2008* (pp. 243–281). Springer.
48. Glover, F., Kochenberger, G., & Du, Y. (2019). Quantum bridge analytics I: A tutorial on formulating and using QUBO models. *4OR, 17*(4), 335–371.
49. Rosenberg, I. G. (1975). Reduction of bivalent maximization to the quadratic case. *Cahiers du Centre d'etudes de Recherche Operationnelle, 17,* 71–74.
50. Apolloni, B., Carvalho, C., & De Falco, D. (1989). Quantum stochastic optimization. *Stochastic Processes and their Applications, 33*(2), 233–244.
51. Kadowaki, T., & Nishimori, H. (1998). Quantum annealing in the transverse Ising model. *Physical Review E, 58*(5), 5355.
52. Johnson, M. W., Amin, M. H., Gildert, S., Lanting, T., Hamze, F., Dickson, N., Harris, R., Berkley, A. J., Johansson, J., Bunyk, P., et al. (2011). Quantum annealing with manufactured spins. *Nature, 473*(7346), 194–198.
53. Neukart, F., Compostella, G., Seidel, C., Von Dollen, D., Yarkoni, S., & Parney, B. (2017). Traffic flow optimization using a quantum annealer. *Frontiers in ICT, 4,* 29.
54. Domino, K., Kundu, A., Salehi, Ö., & Krawiec, K. (2022). Quadratic and higher-order unconstrained binary optimization of railway rescheduling for quantum computing. *Quantum Information Processing, 21*(2), 1–30.
55. Rebentrost, P., & Lloyd, S. (2018). Quantum computational finance: quantum algorithm for portfolio optimization. arXiv:1811.03975.
56. Perdomo-Ortiz, A., Dickson, N., Drew-Brook, M., Rose, G., & Aspuru-Guzik, A. (2012). Finding low-energy conformations of lattice protein models by quantum annealing. *Scientific Reports, 2*(1), 1–7.
57. Venturelli, D., Marchand, D. J., & Rojo, G. (2015). Quantum annealing implementation of job-shop scheduling. arXiv:1506.08479.
58. Farhi, E., Goldstone, J., Gutmann, S., & Sipser, M. (2000). Quantum computation by adiabatic evolution. arXiv:quant-ph/0001106.
59. Barahona, F. (1982). On the computational complexity of Ising spin glass models. *Journal of Physics A: Mathematical and General, 15,* 3241–3253.
60. McGeoch, C. C. (2014). *Adiabatic quantum computation and quantum annealing: Theory and practice* (Vol. 5). Morgan & Claypool Publishers.
61. Rønnow, T. F., Wang, Z., Job, J., Boixo, S., Isakov, S. V., Wecker, D., Martinis, J. M., Lidar, D. A., & Troyer, M. (2014). Defining and detecting quantum speedup. *Science, 345*(6195), 420–424.
62. Hen, I., Job, J., Albash, T., Rønnow, T. F., Troyer, M., & Lidar, D. A. (2015). Probing for quantum speedup in spin-glass problems with planted solutions. *Physical Review A, 92*(4), 042325.
63. Katzgraber, H. G., Hamze, F., Zhu, Z., Ochoa, A. J., & Munoz-Bauza, H. (2015). Seeking quantum speedup through spin glasses: The good, the bad, and the ugly. *Physical Review X, 5*(3), 031026.

64. Mandra, S., & Katzgraber, H. G. (2018). A deceptive step towards quantum speedup detection. *Quantum Science and Technology, 3*(4), 04LT01.
65. Hybrid solver for constrained quadratic models. https://www.dwavesys.com/media/rldh2ghw/14-1055a-a_hybrid_solver_for_constrained_quadratic_models.pdf. Accessed 15 Dec. 2021.
66. Spitzer, F. (1971). Markov random fields and Gibbs ensembles. *The American Mathematical Monthly, 78*(2), 142–154.
67. Preston, C. J. (1973). Generalized Gibbs states and Markov random fields. *Advances in Applied probability, 5*(2), 242–261.
68. Kindermann, R., & Snell, J. L. (1980). *Markov random fields and their applications*. American Mathematical Society.
69. Blake, A., Kohli, P., & Rother, C. (2011). *Markov random fields for vision and image processing*. MIT press.
70. Salehi, Ö., Cañete., & Miszczak, J. A. (2022). Unconstrained binary models of the travelling salesman problem variants for quantum optimization. *Quantum Information Processing, 21*(2), 1–30.
71. Freedline, A. Algorhythms: Generating music with D-Wave's quantum annealer. https://medium.com/mit-6-s089-intro-to-quantum-computing/algorhythms-generating-music-with-d-waves-quantum-annealer-95697ec23ccd. Accessed 15 Dec. 2021.

Making Sound with Light: Sound Synthesis with a Photonic Quantum Computer

16

Eduardo Reck Miranda, Paul Finlay, and Tom Lubowe

Abstract

This chapter reports on the initial results of the authors' research on developing sound synthesizers with photonic quantum computers. More specifically, it introduces three systems that render sounds from the results of processing photons using Gaussian Boson Sampling (GBS). Essentially, a GBS algorithm normally includes three modules: squeezers, interferometers and photon detectors. In a nutshell, the squeezers prepare the inputs, the interferometer operates on the inputs, and the photon detectors produce the results. Pulses of laser light are input to an array of squeezers. What a squeezer does is crush light into a bunch of photons in a state of superposition, referred to as a squeezed state. Next, squeezed states are relayed to the interferometer. The interferometer provides a network of beam splitters and phase shifters, which are programmed with operations to manipulate the photons. The interferometer is expected to produce highly entangled quantum states encoding the processed quantum information. These are subsequently channelled to detectors that count how many photons are within each stream of squeezed states. The results of the computation are encoded in the statistics of this photon counting. The photon-counting data are used as control parameters for bespoke sound synthesizers.

E. R. Miranda (✉)
ICCMR, University of Plymouth, Plymouth, UK
e-mail: eduardo.miranda@plymouth.ac.uk

P. Finlay · T. Lubowe
Xanadu, Toronto, ON, Canada
e-mail: paul@xanadu.ai

T. Lubowe
e-mail: thomas@xanadu.ai

16.1 Introduction

In this chapter, we report on the initial results of our research on developing sound synthesizers with photonic quantum computers. Specifically, we introduce three systems that render sounds following the preparation, manipulation, and measurement of photons in a process known as Gaussian Boson Sampling (GBS). GBS is a special-purpose model of quantum computing which builds upon the Boson sampling theory introduced by Aaronson and Arkhipov [1].

Essentially, the circuit that implements a GBS algorithm is made up of three stages: *state preparation, manipulation,* and *measurement*. Special quantum-mechanical states of light known as *squeezed states* are injected into an interferometer, which manipulates the light via a sequence of beam splitters and phase shifters. These programmable elements provide a sequence of quantum mechanical gates that operate on the entangled photons and produce a Gaussian state, which is finally read out using photon-counting detectors [3].

While the particulars of the GBS algorithm make this quantum computing platform ideally suited to tackling a variety of interesting, classically intractable problems (ranging from comparing dense sub-graphs to calculating vibronic spectra [12]), in this paper we present a novel application of GBS whereby the resulting photon-counting data are used as control parameters for bespoke sound synthesizers, here referred to as *PhotonSynths*.

The PhotonSynths presented here are based on two types of sound synthesis architectures: *additive synthesis* and *granular sampling* [25]. The additive architecture employs a bank of oscillators, each of which generates a sinusoidal wave. Then, the waves are added to produce the resulting sound. Sinusoidal waves are characterized by their respective amplitudes, frequencies and phases. Varying these characteristics will yield perceptible differences in the timbre of the resulting sound. In contrast, the granular sampling architecture produces sounds by cutting short sections from a given sound and splicing them together to form a new one.

PhotonSynths' GBS engine was implemented on Xanadu's X8 photonic hardware [3]. We developed a technique to interface Xanadu's quantum photonic Python library Strawberry Fields [12,22,32] with the Csound programming language [7]. Csound comes with a comprehensive set of tools for implementing sound synthesis applications. Integrating these two libraries into one application enabled us to develop synthesizers whose parameters are controlled by the outputs of photonics-based quantum mechanical processes in the cloud: Xanadu's computer is housed in Toronto (Canada), whereas the workstation that renders the sounds can be located anywhere with an Internet connection.

The chapter begins with a brief introduction to photonic quantum computers, highlighting how they differ from typical matter-based quantum computers, such as the ones discussed in other chapters in this volume. Then, it presents our GBS engine, followed by the synthesizers. We developed three synthesizers, two of which are additive and one granular. The chapter ends with some concluding remarks.

16.2 Photonic Quantum Computing

There is a variety of quantum computing based implementations. Largely these can be divided into two groups: adiabatic and gate based models. Adiabatic quantum computers rely on the adiabatic theorem which stipulates that a system which is gradually perturbed by external forces updates its formation in such a way as to achieve a global minimum-energy state. This allows for computation to be performed but is arguably not universal, meaning that it cannot compute all problems equally [2]. Having said that, Chaps. 14 and 15 discuss how adiabatic computing can be applied to generate music.

Gate-based models, in contrast, utilize operations introduced externally to a system (gates) to manipulate the system's state in order to perform calculations. This is similar to the implementation of logic gates in classical computing. Gate-based models which offer a universal gate-set would, in principle, enable any form of computation. These are also known as universal gate models of quantum computing [15].

Another key concept is measurement-based computing. This means that the qubit or unit of computation travels through the chip and through a set of physical gates that are turned on or off like in classical computers. We then measure the state of the quantum system following a sequence of operations to understand the outcome of the computation [11].

There is a wide range of technologies which can enable either of the abovementioned paradigms. Josephson Junctions are known as superconducting circuits and are used in both adiabatic and gate based models. Trapped Ions, neutral atoms, nitrogen vacancy centres and photonics are others [13,17,23,31,34]. In all of these technologies, one manipulates fundamental units of physics to enable quantum computation.

In photonic-based quantum computers, the fundamental unit used for computation is light. There are effectively two approaches to implement photonic quantum computing: *discrete* and *continuous variable* (CV). The former uses discrete numbers of photons to carry out computations, very much like the 'qubit' model of computation [6]. The CV model, on the other hand, is a natural fit for simulating bosonic systems (electromagnetic fields, harmonic oscillators, phonons, Bose-Einstein condensates, or optomechanical resonators) and for settings where continuous quantum operators (such as position and momentum) are present.

Continuous-variable photonic quantum computers prepare light in particular quantum states (squeezed states) which are then manipulated with gates for computation. With Xanadu's processor, light is confined to particular regions of phase space (this is referred to as *squeezed light*) until it is in a well-described quantum state. We call this state a *qumode*.

Qumodes are like qubits in that they occupy discrete quantum-mechanical states. But in principle, these states have infinite dimensionality, whereas discrete variable qubits are typically two-level systems. This allows for more flexibility when performing computations, and indeed, for creating sound and music.

In Xanadu's X8 processor four pairs of qumodes are initially prepared and then run through the programmable interferometer, implemented via integrated nanophotonics on-chip. This allows the user to apply transformations in the form of phase shifts and beam splitters to these qumodes. The resulting Gaussian state is then measured on the Fock basis to determine how many photons are in each qumode. Below, we formalize the notions of qumode, Gaussian state and Fock basis.

16.2.1 Qumodes

The most elementary CV system is the bosonic harmonic oscillator, defined via the canonical mode operators $\hat{a}^\dagger$ and $\hat{a}$. The creation operator $\hat{a}^\dagger$ acting on a state will increase the number of particles in that state by 1, while the annihilation operator $\hat{a}$ reduces the number of particles in the state by 1.

It is also common to work with the *quadrature operators*, $\hat{x}$ and $\hat{p}$, which can be expressed in terms of the creation and annihilation operators:

$$\hat{x} := \sqrt{\frac{\hbar}{2}}(\hat{a} + \hat{a}^\dagger),$$

$$\hat{p} := -i\sqrt{\frac{\hbar}{2}}(\hat{a} - \hat{a}^\dagger).$$

where $\hbar$ is Plank's constant. Technically $\hat{x}$ and $\hat{p}$ represent the in-phase and out-of-phase (real and imaginary parts) of the complex amplitude of the electromagnetic mode, respectively. Even though an electromagnetic oscillator does not have a well-defined position and momentum, one can think of $\hat{x}$ and $\hat{p}$ as representing the position and momentum of the harmonic oscillator as these operators behave in a similar way. We can picture a fixed harmonic oscillator mode (say, within an optical fibre or waveguide on a photonic chip) as a single 'wire' in a quantum circuit.

Qumodes are the fundamental information-carrying units of CV quantum computers. By combining multiple qumodes (each with corresponding operators $\hat{a}$ and $\hat{a}^\dagger$) and having them interact via sequences of suitable quantum gates, we can implement general CV quantum computation.

16.2.2 CV States

The difference between qubit and CV systems is clearly seen in the *basis expansions* of quantum states:

Qubit	$\lvert\phi\rangle = \phi_0\lvert 0\rangle + \phi_1\lvert 1\rangle,$
Qumode	$\lvert\psi\rangle = \int dx\,\psi(x)\lvert x\rangle.$

For qubits, we have two basis states, hence the bit nomenclature. Here we used the z-basis (a.k.a. computational basis), though others are possible. For CV systems, however, we can have a continuum. The states $|x\rangle$ are the eigenstates of the $\hat{x}$ quadrature operator, $\hat{x}|x\rangle = x|x\rangle$, with $x \in \mathbb{R}$. These quadrature states are special cases of a more general family of CV states, the Gaussian states.

16.2.2.1 Gaussian States

Starting from the vacuum state $|0\rangle$, a general state $|\psi\rangle$ can be generated via:

$$|\psi\rangle = \exp(-itH)|0\rangle,$$

where H is a bosonic Hamiltonian and t is the evolution time. States where the Hamiltonian is at most quadratic in the operators $\hat{x}$ and $\hat{p}$ are called *Gaussian*.

For a single qumode, Gaussian states are parameterized by two continuous complex variables: a displacement parameter $\alpha \in \mathbb{C}$ and a squeezing parameter $z \in \mathbb{C}$. Gaussian states are so-named because we can identify each Gaussian state through its displacement and squeezing parameters, with corresponding Gaussian distribution. The displacement gives the centre of the Gaussian, while the squeezing determines the variance and rotation of the distribution.

16.2.2.2 Fock States

Complementary to the continuous Gaussian states are the discrete number states $|n\rangle$, $n \in \mathbb{N}$. These states are referred to as *Fock states*. They are the eigenstates of the number operator $\hat{n} = \hat{a}^\dagger \hat{a}$. The number states form a discrete countable basis for the states of a single qumode. Gaussian states can be expanded on a number state basis, and vice versa. For example, an undisplaced squeezed Gaussian state in the Fock basis would be written as:

$$|z\rangle = \frac{1}{\sqrt{\cosh r}} \sum_{n=0}^{\infty} \frac{\sqrt{(2n)!}}{2^n n!} [-e^{i\phi} \tanh(r)]^n |2n\rangle.$$

Note that the undisplaced squeezed state only has an even number of states on its basis. We shall revisit the Fock basis in the CV measurements section below.

16.2.3 CV Gates

Unitary operations can always be associated with a generating Hamiltonian H via the recipe

$$U = \exp(-itH).$$

For convenience, we can classify unitaries by the *degree* of their generating Hamiltonians. We can build an N-mode unitary by applying a sequence of gates from a universal gate set, each of which acts only on one or two modes. We focus on a universal gate set (Table 16.1), which contains two components: *Gaussian gates* and *non-Gaussian gates*.

Table 16.1 A number of fundamental CV gates

Gate	Unitary	Symbol
Displacement	$D_i(\alpha) = \exp(\alpha \hat{a}_i^\dagger - \alpha^* \hat{a}_i)$	—[D]—
Rotation	$R_i(\phi) = \exp(i\phi \hat{n}_i)$	—[R]—
Squeezing	$S_i(z) = \exp(\frac{1}{2}(z^* \hat{a}_i^2 - z\hat{a}_i^{\dagger 2}))$	—[S]—
Beamsplitter	$BS_{i,j}(\theta, \phi) =$ $\exp(\theta(e^{i\phi}\hat{a}_i^\dagger \hat{a}_j - e^{-i\phi}\hat{a}_i \hat{a}_j^\dagger))$	≡[BS]≡
Cubic phase	$V_i(\gamma) = \exp(i\frac{\gamma}{6}\hat{x}_i^3)$	—[V]—

16.2.3.1 Gaussian Gates

One-mode and two-mode gates are quadratic in the mode operators; e.g., displacement, rotation, squeezing, and beamsplitter gates. These are equivalent to the Clifford group of gates from the qubit model [6].

16.2.3.2 Non-Gaussian gates

A non-Gaussian gate is a single-mode gate which is degree three or higher; e.g., the cubic phase gate. These are equivalent to the non-Clifford gates in the qubit model.

We can see that many of the Gaussian states are connected to a corresponding Gaussian gate. Any multimode Gaussian gate can be implemented through a suitable combination of Displacement, Rotation, Squeezing, and Beamsplitter Gates [33], making these gates sufficient for quadratic unitaries.

16.2.4 CV Measurements

As with CV states and gates, we can distinguish between Gaussian and non-Gaussian measurements. The Gaussian class consists of two (continuous) types: *homodyne* and *heterodyne* measurements, while the key non-Gaussian measurement is *photon counting* (Table 16.2).

16.2.4.1 Homodyne Measurements

Ideal homodyne detection is a projective measurement onto the eigenstates of the quadrature operator $\hat{x}$. These states form a continuum, so homodyne measurements are inherently continuous, returning values $x \in \mathbb{R}$. More generally, we can consider projective measurement onto the eigenstates of the Hermitian operator

$\hat{x}_\phi := \cos\phi\,\hat{x} + \sin\phi\,\hat{p}$, which is equivalent to rotating the state by $-\phi$ and performing an $\hat{x}$-homodyne measurement. If we have a multimode Gaussian state and we perform a homodyne measurement on one of the modes, the conditional state on the remaining modes stays Gaussian.

16.2.4.2 Heterodyne Measurements

Whereas homodyne is a measurement of $\hat{x}$, heterodyne can be seen as simultaneous measurement of both $\hat{x}$ and $\hat{p}$. Because these operators do not commute, they cannot be simultaneously measured without some degree of uncertainty. Like homodyne, heterodyne measurements preserve the Gaussian character of Gaussian states.

16.2.4.3 Photon Counting

Photon counting is a complementary measurement method to the "-dyne" measurements, revealing the particle-like, rather than the wave-like, nature of qumodes. This measurement projects onto the number eigenstates $|n\rangle$, returning non-negative integer values $n \in \mathbb{N}$.

Except for the outcome $n = 0$, a photon-counting measurement on a single mode of a multimode Gaussian state will cause the remaining modes to become non-Gaussian. Thus, photon-counting can be used as an ingredient for implementing non-Gaussian gates.

16.3 Gaussian Boson Sampling

In its most general form, Gaussian Boson Sampling (GBS) consists of preparing a multi-mode Gaussian state and measuring it on the Fock basis. It differs from universal photonic circuits only because it does not employ non-Gaussian gates and restricts measurements to the Fock basis.

A GBS circuit with four qumodes is shown in Fig. 16.1. A Gaussian quantum state is prepared from the vacuum state with photon squeezers $\mathbf{S}$ and a linear interferometer [29] comprising rotation gates (i.e., phase shifters) $\mathbf{R(n)}$ and beam-splitters $\mathbf{BS}(\theta_\mathbf{n}, \phi_\mathbf{n})$. Values for the angles δ_n, θ_n and ϕ_n define the interferometer's characteristics. That is, they specify how the interferometer processes the photons. The

Table 16.2 Types of CV measurements, their operators, and values

Measurement	Measurement operator	Measurement values
Homodyne	$|\hat{x}_\phi\rangle\langle\hat{x}_\phi|$	$q \in \mathbb{R}$
Heterodyne	$\frac{1}{\sqrt{\pi}}|\alpha\rangle\langle\alpha|$	$\alpha \in \mathbb{C}$
Photon counting	$|n\rangle\langle n|$	$n \in \mathbb{N}, n \geq 0$

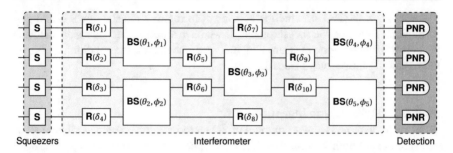

Squeezers   Interferometer   Detection

Fig. 16.1 The sequence of gates that are used to create a Gaussian state and respective measurements

quantum state is subsequently measured by photon-number resolving (**PNR**) detectors in the Fock basis. The measurements reveal the number of photons in each qumode.

GBS offers great versatility in the scope of problems that it can encode. This led to the appearance of several GBS algorithms with applications to quantum chemistry [19], graph optimization [4,9], molecular docking [5], graph similarity [8,10,30] and point processes [20]. The GBS applications layer in Strawberry Fields [22] is built with the goal of providing users with the capability to implement these GBS algorithms using only a few lines of code. Programming the GBS device, generating samples, and classical post-processing of the outputs are taken care of automatically by built-in functions.

16.3.1 GBS Distribution

A general pure Gaussian state can be prepared from a vacuum state by a sequence of single-mode squeezing, multimode linear interferometry, and single-mode displacements. It was shown in [16] that for a Gaussian state with zero mean—which can be prepared using only squeezing followed by linear interferometry—the probability $Pr(S)$ of observing an output $S = (s_1, s_2, \ldots, s_m)$, where s_i denotes the number of photons detected in the i-th mode, is given by

$$Pr(S) = \frac{1}{\sqrt{\det(\mathbf{Q})}} \frac{\text{Haf}(\mathscr{A})}{s_1! s_2! \cdots s_m!},$$

where

$$\mathbf{Q} := \Sigma + I/2$$
$$\mathscr{A} := \mathbf{X}\left(I - \mathbf{Q}^{-1}\right),$$
$$\mathbf{X} := \begin{bmatrix} 0 & I \\ I & 0 \end{bmatrix},$$

and Σ is the covariance matrix of the Gaussian state. The matrix function $\text{Haf}(\cdot)$ is the hafnian [28]. When the state is pure, the matrix $\mathscr{A}$ can be written as $\mathscr{A} = \mathbf{A} \oplus \mathbf{A}^*$ and the distribution becomes

$$Pr(S) = \frac{1}{\sqrt{\det(\mathbf{Q})}} \frac{|\mathrm{Haf}(\mathbf{A}_S)|^2}{s_1! \ldots s_m!},$$

where $\mathbf{A}$ is an arbitrary symmetric matrix with eigenvalues bounded between -1 and 1. Therefore, besides encoding Gaussian states into a GBS device, it is also possible to encode symmetric matrices $\mathbf{A}$. Notably, these may include adjacency matrices of graphs and kernel matrices.

16.3.2 Programming a GBS Device

In GBS without displacements, indicating gate parameters is equivalent to specifying the symmetric matrix $\mathbf{A}$. Employing the Takagi-Autonne decomposition, we can write

$$\mathbf{A} = \mathbf{U} \mathrm{diag}(\lambda_1, \lambda_2, \ldots, \lambda_m) \mathbf{U}^T,$$

where $\mathbf{U}$ is a unitary matrix. The matrix $\mathbf{U}$ is precisely the unitary operation that specifies the linear interferometer of a GBS device. The values $0 \leq \lambda_i < 1$ uniquely determine the squeezing parameters r_i via the relation $\tanh(r_i) = \lambda_i$, as well as the mean photon number $\bar{n}$ of the distribution from the expression

$$\bar{n} = \sum_{i=1}^{M} \frac{\lambda_i^2}{1 - \lambda_i^2}$$

It is possible to encode an arbitrary symmetric matrix $\mathbf{A}$ into a GBS device by rescaling the matrix with a parameter $c > 0$ so that $c\mathbf{A}$ satisfies $0 \leq \lambda_i < 1$ as in the above decomposition. The parameter c controls the squeezing parameters r_i and the mean photon number. Overall, a GBS device can be programmed as follows:

1. Compute the Takagi-Autonne decomposition of $\mathbf{A}$ to determine the unitary $\mathbf{U}$ and the values $\lambda_1, \lambda_2, \ldots, \lambda_m$.
2. Program the linear interferometer according to the unitary $\mathbf{U}$.
3. Solve for the constant $c > 0$ such that $\bar{n} = \sum_{i=1}^{M} \frac{(c\lambda_i)^2}{1-(c\lambda_i)^2}$.
4. Program the squeezing parameter r_i of the squeezing gate $S(r_i)$ acting on the i-th mode as $r_i = \tanh^{-1}(c\lambda_i)$.

The GBS device then samples from the distribution

$$Pr(S) \propto c^k \frac{|\mathrm{Haf}(\mathbf{A}_S)|^2}{s_1! \ldots s_m!}, \quad k = \sum_i s_i$$

The GBS applications layer includes functions for sampling from GBS devices that are programmed in this manner.

16.3.3 GBS Implementation for the PhotonSynths

The circuit of the GBS system that we implemented for the PhotonSynths is depicted in Fig. 16.2, and the Strawberry Fields code is available in Appendix A. The circuit uses non-degenerate spontaneous four-wave mixing to create a squeezed state, which generates two modes at different frequencies in each of four ring resonators, resulting in eight qumodes in total. For historical reasons the qumodes 0, 1, 2 and 3 are referred to as the *signal qumodes* and qumodes 4, 5, 6 and 7 as the *idler qumodes*.

Having four two-mode squeezers enables us to entangle the squeezed light across the interferometer giving us more quantum mechanical properties to leverage for computation than the scheme shown in Fig. 16.1. Here we use two 4×4 unitaries to represent the depth of the circuit. Since it is depth 4, but across eight modes we can have two 4×4 matrices stacked on top of each other.

Strawberry Fields provides a function to generate random $N \times N$ unitary matrices to build interferometers. Random unitary matrices are fit for purpose at this stage. We built two identical random (**U4**) gates, one of which is applied to the signal qumodes and the other to the idler ones. And then, the eight qumodes are read out by performing photon-counting measurements on each of them.

All thee PhotonSynths handle the results from the GBS circuit by bundling measurements from several shots into snapshots. In the case of the examples discussed in this chapter, a snapshot consists of eight shots (Fig. 16.3).

Each snapshot yields parameters for synthesising a sound. In other words, think of each sound corresponding to a snapshot. Thus, for instance, 200 shots will produce 25 sounds. Effectively, each snapshot is represented here as an 8×8 matrix. Then,

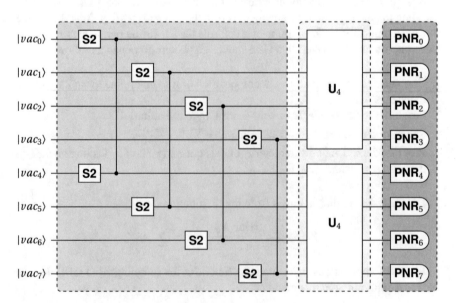

Fig. 16.2 The sequence of gates that are used to create a Gaussian state

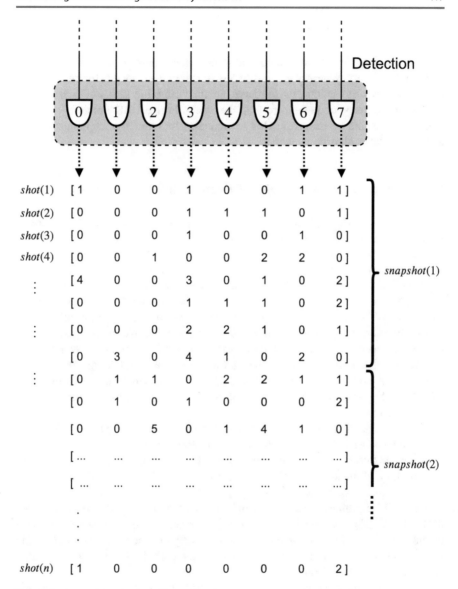

Fig. 16.3 A snapshots consists of a number of shots. In this example, a snapshot is eight shots long

the synthesis parameters to produce a sound are obtained by performing simple operations on this matrix; for instance, by taking the arithmetic mean of the rows, or adding the values of a specific column, and so on.

16.4 The PhotonSynths

This section introduces three sound synthesis systems, named as PhotonSynth 1, 2 and 3, respectively. Whereas the first two systems produce sounds by means of the additive synthesis technique, the third uses granular sampling [25]. For each of them, we developed bespoke methods to map the results from a GBS circuit into control parameters for the synthesisers. This section describes how the mapping methods and the synthesis algorithms work.

16.4.1 PhotonSynth 1: Photon-Driven Additive Sound Spectrum

The synthesisers are implemented in Csound, a programming language for sound synthesis [7]. The Csound Application Programming Interface (API) reference is coded in the programming language C [21]. Thanks to the `ctcsound` Python module, we can run Csound code from within Python, which facilitates direct communication with Xanadu's Strawberry Fields photonic computing programming tool. This Python module wraps the C functions of the Csound API in a class called `ctcsound`. The methods of this class call the corresponding functions of the API.

Briefly, a Csound synthesiser is made of two modules, referred to the *orchestra* and the *score*, respectively. The orchestra contains the specification of the synthesiser's circuit, with the control parameters for its various modules. In Csound terminology, these control parameters are referred to as p-fields; their label starts with the letter 'p' followed by a number. A score contains lists of p-field of values for the orchestra (e.g., Fig. 16.5).

In Csound, the first 3 p-fields will always mean the same thing: `p1` indicates which instrument will make the sound,[1] `p2` indicated the starting time of the sound, and `p3` indicates the duration of the sound in seconds. For all three systems in this chapter, the start time of the next sound is calculated by adding the duration of the previous sound to previous start time: $p2_{t+1} = p2_t + p3_t$.

The additive synthesis technique is informed by the theory of Fast Fourier Transform, or FFT [26]. It is based on the notion that sounds can be characterised as a sum of sine waves, referred to as partials. Thus, PhotonSynth 1 deploys a number of sine wave generators (i.e., oscillators) to produce sound partials. The partials are added up to produce the final result.

A partial is characterised by a frequency value (i.e., speed of its wave cycle) and amplitude value (i.e., the loudness of the wave). In Fig. 16.4, individual partials are represented on the left-hand side of the figure, where a bar on the 'freq' axis (or, frequency domain) has a certain magnitude on the 'amp' axis (or, amplitude domain). The spectrum of the resulting sound is represented on the right-hand side; in this case, it contains eight partials. A schematic representation of the resulting sound in the time domain is also shown.

---

[1] In our case this will always be equal 1 because each orchestra has only 1 instrument.

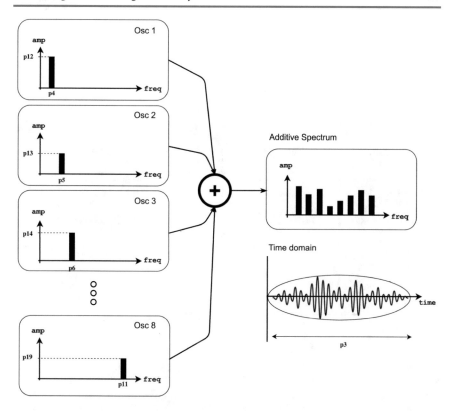

Fig. 16.4 Each oscillator of an additive synthesiser produces a sound partial at a determined frequency with a certain amplitude. The spectrum of the output sound results from the addition of all partials

PhotonSynth 1 comprises eight oscillators (Fig. 16.5), each of which requires a frequency value in Herts (Hz) and an amplitude, whose value varies between 0.0 (silence) and 1.0 (maximum loudness).

The amplitude for each oscillator (osc) is specified through an envelope (env). This is a breakpoint linear function, which takes a small portion of the total time (represented by the p-field p3) to raise the amplitude of the sine wave from 0.0 up to the respective calculated p-field value (p12, p13 ... p19). And then it takes another small portion of time to fade it out. This is done to smoothen the edges of the sound, as depicted in the time domain representation of the resulting sound in Fig. 16.4.

The synthesiser produces stereo sounds. To this end, the oscillators are distributed into two groups of four oscillators each: one to produce the left channel for the stereo sound and the other to produce the right channel. Each channel is submitted to a reverb, which gives an impression that the sound is produced in an acoustic space.

The p-fields for PhotonSynth 1 are listed in Table 16.3. The duration of each sound (p3) is calculated from the number of photons counted by a chosen detector.

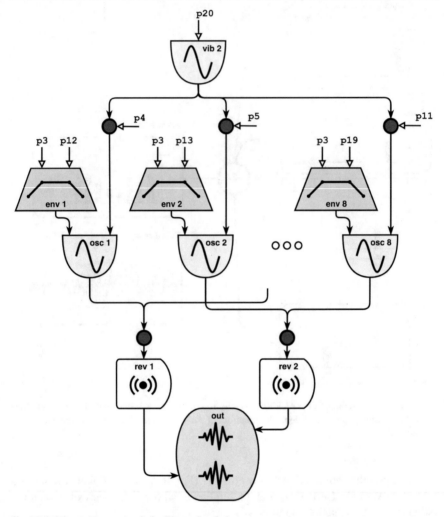

Fig. 16.5 The orchestra-circuit for PhotonSynth 1

For instance, in Fig. 16.3, detector number 3 counted 13 photons. Therefore, the first sound will last for 13 s. The start time (p2) of the next sound is calculated by adding the duration of the previous sound to previous start time: $p2_{t+1} = p2_t + p3_t$.

With respect to the frequencies for the oscillators, the p-fields from p4 to p11 are computed as follows: for each sound, a reference value (ν) is obtained by adding the total number of photons detected in an entire snapshot. Then, the p-field for each of the eight oscillators is calculated by multiplying ν by eight different coefficients: $\{\omega_1, \omega_2, ...\omega_8\}$ (Fig. 16.6). These coefficients come from the arithmetic mean of the number of photons detected per shot across all detectors: $\omega_n = \bar{x}_{shot(n)}, n = \{0, 1, 2, ...7\}$. In Fig. 16.3, for example, $snapshot(1) = 47$

Table 16.3 Parameters for PhotonSyth 1 Csound orchestra

P-field	GBS control	P-field	GBS control
p3	Duration	p12	Sine wave 1 amplitude
p4	Sine wave 1 frequency	p13	Sine wave 2 amplitude
p5	Sine wave 2 frequency	p14	Sine wave 3 amplitude
p6	Sine wave 3 frequency	p15	Sine wave 4 amplitude
p7	Sine wave 4 frequency	p16	Sine wave 5 amplitude
p8	Sine wave 5 frequency	p17	Sine wave 6 amplitude
p9	Sine wave 6 frequency	p18	Sine wave 7 amplitude
p10	Sine wave 7 frequency	p19	Sine wave 8 amplitude
p11	Sine wave 8 frequency	p20	Vibrato frequency

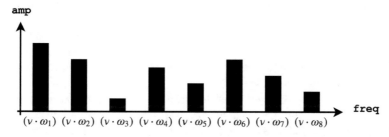

Fig. 16.6 The frequency for each partial is calculated by multiplying a common reference value (ν) by a respective coefficient (ω_n)

photons and $\bar{x}_{shot(1)} = \frac{4}{8} = 0.5$. Thus, the value of p4, for the first oscillator, is calculated as $p4 = 47 \times 0.5 = 23.5$. This value is subsequently normalised[2] to yield the value of $470Hz$ for the first oscillator's frequency. Inevitably, there may be cases with more than one oscillator with a determined frequency. In these cases, their amplitudes will add up in the resulting spectrum because all sine waves have the same phase.

As for the amplitudes, the p-fields from p12 to p19 are calculated by summing the number of photons counted by each detector in a snapshot: detector 0 yields the amplitude for the first oscillator, detector 1 the amplitudes for the second, and so on. In the case of our example, $p12 = 5$, $p13 = 3$, ... $p19 = 7$. As in the case of the frequencies, these values are normalised.

As briefly mentioned earlier, the synthesiser is programmed to accept amplitudes between 0.0 (silence) and 1.0 (maximum loudness). A sound with amplitudes above 1.0 will be distorted. Thus, each oscillator should not have an amplitude higher than 0.125. In order to avoid distortion, the value is scaled by 0.01; e.g., $p12 = 5 \times 0.01 = 0.05$.

---

[2] The normalisation is customisable. For the examples in this chapter it is given as $p4 \times 20$.

Vibrato is a slight variation of the pitch of a sound, which performers make to add expression to musical notes. Vibrato is useful to add naturalness to artificially synthesised sounds. This is achieved here by means of an oscillator (known as Low Frequency Oscillator, or LFO), which modulates the frequencies of the partials (p20 in Fig. 16.5). Normally, this value should not be higher than 10 Hz. It is computed as the sum of the arithmetic mean of photons detected in a shot, over a snapshot. For example, considering Fig. 16.3, the vibrato frequency for the first sound is: $\frac{4}{8} + \frac{4}{8} + \frac{2}{8} + \frac{5}{8} + \frac{10}{8} + \frac{5}{8} + \frac{6}{8} + \frac{10}{8} = 5.75$ Hz.

16.4.2   PhotonSynth 2: Furnishing Dynamics to the Spectrum

The spectrum of sounds produced by acoustic instruments varies while they are produced. This is a characteristic that often distinguishes natural sounds from electronically synthesised ones.

PhotonSynth 2 is an advanced version of PhotoSynth 1, with the add-on ability to produce a varying spectrum. In order to do this, we increased the number of breakpoints on the amplitude envelopes. And each of them can be controlled individually while a sound is produced (Fig. 16.7).

Figure 16.8 illustrates the effect of the envelope on the synthesised spectrum: as the sound evolves in time, the amplitudes of the partials can vary, independently from each other. Figure 16.9 depicts the envelope for the first oscillator. At present, the breakpoints are equally spaced from each other, and the transitions are linear. More sophistication could involve variable spacing and other types of transitions, such as exponential or logarithmic.

The breakpoint values are calculated from the GBS results as follows: each detector yields eight breakpoint values for one envelope. Thus, detector 0 yields the envelope for the first oscillator, detector 1 for the second, and so on. Each shot returns amplitude values for the envelope, which is subsequently normalised, in the same way as in PhotonSynth 1 (i.e., the value is multiplied by 0.01). For instance, given the results in Fig. 16.3 and the envelope in Fig. 16.9, the resulting p-fields for the instrument are: $\{p12 = 0.01, p13 = 0.0, p14 = 0.0, p15 = 0.0, p16 = 0.04, p17 = 0.0, p18 = 0.0, p19 = 0.0\}$ (Table 16.4).

16.4.3   PhotonSynth 3: Granular Sound Sampling

Granular synthesis works by generating a rapid succession of tiny sounds (e.g., 50 milliseconds long each), referred to as *grains*. Metaphorically, this synthesis technique can be compared with the functioning of motion pictures, where an impression of continuous movement is produced by displaying a sequence of slightly different images at a rate above the scanning capability of the eye. But consider that in granular synthesis, 'images' (i.e., grains) may overlap. And there could be various 'movies' streaming simultaneously.

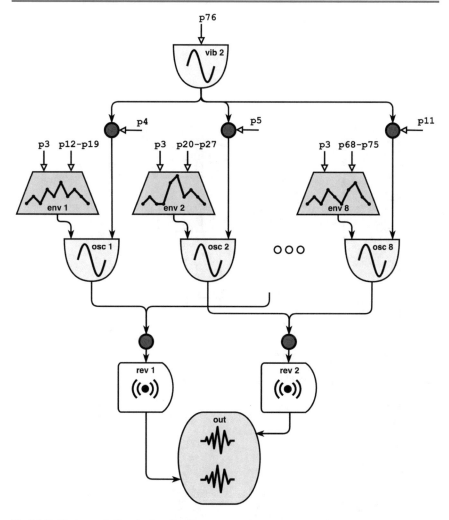

Fig. 16.7 Photonsynth 2 orchestra-circuit

In theory, both PhotonSynth systems introduced above could be turned into granular synthesisers by setting them to produce large quantities of snapshots in order to produce thousands of sounds in the milliseconds' range. However, PhotonSynth 3 does not synthesise sounds by stacking up sine waves from scratch. Instead, it implements a specific granular synthesis technique referred to as *granular sampling*.

Granular sampling employs a granulator device, which creates a new sound by coping tiny sections from a given source sound and pasting them into a 'blank canvas'. The granulator can be controlled in a number of ways. Typically, it is possible to delimit zones on the source where the grains are to be copied from, specify how to scan the source, the size of the grains, and so on. Once extracted, the grains can

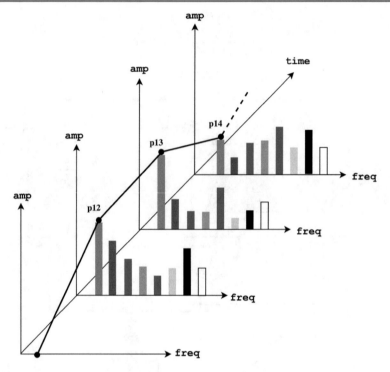

Fig. 16.8 Dynamic additive synthesis with envelope breakpoints

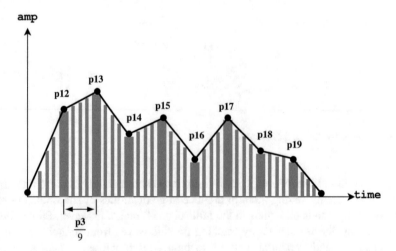

Fig. 16.9 Hypotherical breakpoint for the first oscillator of synthesis in Fig. 16.7

Table 16.4 Parameters for PhotonSynth 2 Csound orchestra

P-field	GBS control	P-field	GBS control
p3	Duration	{p12, ..., p19}	Sine wave 1 amplitude breakpoints
p4	Sine wave 1 frequency	{p20, ..., p27}	Sine wave 2 amplitude breakpoints
p5	Sine wave 2 frequency	{p28, ..., p35}	Sine wave 3 amplitude breakpoints
p6	Sine wave 3 frequency	{p36, ..., p43}	Sine wave 4 amplitude breakpoints
p7	Sine wave 4 frequency	{p44, ..., p51}	Sine wave 5 amplitude breakpoints
p8	Sine wave 5 frequency	{p52, ..., p59}	Sine wave 6 amplitude breakpoints
p9	Sine wave 6 frequency	{p60, ..., p67}	Sine wave 7 amplitude breakpoints
p10	Sine wave 7 frequency	{p68, ..., p75}	Sine wave 8 amplitude breakpoints
p11	Sine wave 8 frequency	p76	Vibrato frequency

Table 16.5 Parameters for PhotonSyth 3 Csound orchestra

P-field	GBS control	P-field	GBS control
p3	Duration of resulting sound	p20	Grains pitch-shift 1
p14	Gap between grains	p21	Grains pitch-shift 2
p16	Size of copied grains	p22	Grains pitch-shift 3
		p23	Grains pitch-shift 4

be modified in a number of ways. And normally, individual grains are subjected to an amplitude envelope, very much like the envelopes used in PhotonSynth 1. The amplitude envelope is of critical importance because they prevent the occurrence of spurious glitches that would otherwise be produced by phase discontinuities between the grains.

Csound provides a granulator device called `granule`, which has 22 control parameters. However, the current version of PhotonSynth 3 uses the GBS results to control only a subset of them, whose respective p-fields are listed in Table 16.5. The other parameters are set with constant values and their role will not be discussed in this chapter.[3] Thus, because `granule` encapsulates a fully-fledged granulator, the orchestra-circuit for PhotonSynth 3 is rather simple (Fig. 16.10): the only add-ons are two reverb units to add reverberation to the resulting sound.

Figure 16.11 shows a schematic representation of how PhotonSynth 3 produces sounds. It pastes the grains copied from the source sound onto 10 tracks, or streams. To begin with, the entire source is demarcated into portions of equal sizes, defined by `p16`. The system loops through the source to copy and paste the demarcated parts to produce a new sound of duration `p3`.

The copied grains are subjected to a few modifications before they are pasted onto a track. The track is chosen by chance. The modifications are as follows:

---

[3] For more details about `granule` the reader is invited to consult [24].

Fig. 16.10 PhotonSynth 3 orchestra-circuit

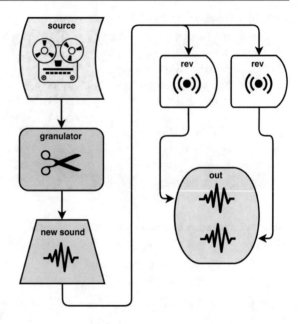

- There is a 50% probability that a grain might be reversed. That is, played back to front.
- To begin with, the size (or duration) of the grain is compressed by a factor of five. For instance, if $p16 = 1.0$ s then $p16' = 0.2$ s.
- Then, the size might be shortened further or enlarged by chance, up to 30%; this is represented in the figure as $\frac{p16'}{5} \times \tau$.
- The pitch of the grain is shifted according to one of four pitch-shift ratios, given by $p20$, $p21$, $p22$, $p23$. The choice of which of the four ratios is applied is random.[4] For instance, a pitch-shift ratio equal to 1.0 maintains the same pitch. And whereas a value equal to 2.0 transposes the pitch one octave upwards, 0.5 transposes one octave downwards.
- An envelope with linear attack and decay is applied to smooth the edges of the grain; hence the trapezoid representation of the pasted grains.

The p-field $p14$ defines a time gap between grains. The system calculates $p14$ from the GBS results by taking the arithmetic mean of the arithmetic mean of the number of photons counted by each detector in a snapshot. For example, in *snapshot*(1) the arithmetic mean for each detector are: {0.625, 0.375, 0.125, 1.625, 0.625, 0.75, 0.75, 0.875}. The arithmetic mean of these values is equal to 0.718. As it happens with a grain duration, a gap is either enlarged or shortened up to 30% by chance; this is represented in Fig. 16.11 as $p14 \times \delta$.

---

[4] That is, pseudorandom because this is done on a classical computer. Essentially, classical computers are deterministic devices.

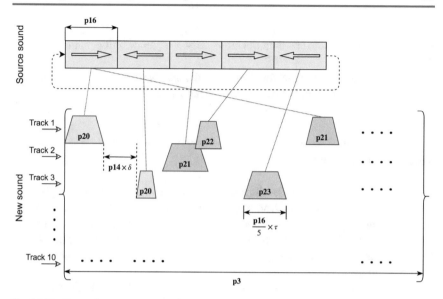

Fig. 16.11 PhotonSynth 3 extracts grains from a source sound and paste them into a blank canvas to create a new sound

Let us assume that at a certain point during granulation $\delta = 0.8$. Therefore the gap between the present grain[5] and the previous is calculated as $0.718 \times 0.8 = 0.574\,\text{s}$, or 574 ms.

The size of the copied grain (p-field $p16$) is obtained by taking the arithmetic mean of the quantity of photons returned by the shot that counted the maximum number of photons in a snapshot. For instance, in $snapshot\,(1)$, $shot\,(5)$ and $shot\,(8)$ detected the highest number of photons: 10. Thus $p16 = \frac{10}{8} = 1.25$. As an example, let us assume the hypothetic case of the first grain on track 1 in Fig. 16.11. And let us assume that $\tau = 2.0$. Thus, the duration of this grain will be $\frac{1.25}{5} \times 2 = 0.5\,\text{s}$, or 500 ms.

The values for the pitch-shift coefficients are established by the number of photons detected by a pair of detectors in a snapshot. The respective value is then normalized by multiplying it by 0.1. The detector pairs are as follows:

- $p20$ detectors 0 and 4
- $p21$ detectors 1 and 5
- $p22$ detectors 2 and 6
- $p23$ detectors 3 and 7.

An an example, consider that a given grain is to be pitch-shifted by $p21$. In this case, detector 1 counted 3 photons and detector 5 counted 6. Therefore, the grain

---

[5] If this happens to be the very first grain, then there is no need to calculate the gap.

will be pitch-shifted by a factor of $(3 + 6) \times 0.1 = 0.9$. So, if the grain's original frequency is, say, 354.56 Hz, then the grain's new frequency will become 354.56 × 0.9 = 319.1 Hz.

And finally, as with the previous two systems, the duration for a new sound (p3) is calculated from the number of photons counted by a chosen detector.

16.5 Final Remarks

Our research is aimed at the development of sound synthesisers based on photonic quantum computing. It stems from the computer music community's avid interest in harnessing the potential of new computing technologies to build new instruments for electronic music [27]. This chapter introduced three systems that render sounds following the preparation, manipulation, and measurement of photons in Gaussian Boson Sampling.

Admittedly, the methods that we developed to calculate the synthesis parameters from the measurement of photons are rather arbitrary. They were defined empirically, by trial and error. The design criteria were the aesthetic preferences of the authors. This is a common practice in creative technology development [14]. Nevertheless, much research is needed to improve affordance. On the one hand, we need to gain a much better understanding of how to harness the interferometer to control, or play, the synthesisers. Values for the angles δ_n, θ_n and ϕ_n for phase shifters $\mathbf{R(_n)}$ and beam-splitters $\mathbf{BS}(\theta_\mathbf{n}, \phi_\mathbf{n})$ define the interferometer's characteristics. However, we have not experimented with different angles to see how they might affect the sound. Instead, we built (pseudo)random interferometers.

Moreover, we need to explore other ways to calculate the parameters for synthesisers. For instance: what would be the effect of defining snapshots with a higher number of shots than eight? Also, the Csound granulator device (granule) used in PhotonSynth 3 has 22 control parameters. Yet, we worked with only a subset of seven of them. There are numerous possibilities to be explored.

And of course, other synthesis methods, such as Frequency Modulation (FM), Amplitude Modulation (AM), and Physical Modelling [25], are waiting to be explored. And further developments from the photonic computing hardware front will certainly provide us with a higher number of qumodes to work with and new methods for generating entangled states.

A Appendix

The Strawberry Fields code for GBS.

```
1  # - - - - - - - - - - - - - - - - - - - - - - - - - - - - - - - - - - - - - - - - - - - - - - - - -
2  # Gaussian Bosson Sampling on Xanadu's Hardware
3  # 17 June 2021
4  # E R Miranda
```

```
5    # ------------------------------------------------------
6    import strawberryfields as sf
7    from strawberryfields import ops
8    from strawberryfields import RemoteEngine
9    from strawberryfields.utils import
         random_interferometer
10   # ------------------------------------------------------
11   # ----------------
12   # Creates Unitary
13   # ----------------
14   U4 = random_interferometer(4)
15
16   # ----------------
17   # Creates program with 8 qumodes
18   # ----------------
19   gbs_prog = sf.Program(8)
20
21   # ----------------
22   # The circuit
23   # ----------------
24   with gbs_prog.context as q:
25       # ----------------
26       # Squeezers
27       # ----------------
28           ops.S2gate(1.0) | (q[0], q[4])
29           ops.S2gate(1.0) | (q[1], q[5])
30           ops.S2gate(1.0) | (q[2], q[6])
31           ops.S2gate(1.0) | (q[3], q[7])
32           # ----------------
33           # Interferometer
34           # ----------------
35           ops.Interferometer(U4) | (q[0], q[1], q[2],
               q[3])
36           ops.Interferometer(U4) | (q[4], q[5], q[6],
               q[7])
37           # ----------------
38           # Detection
39           # ----------------
40           ops.MeasureFock() | q
41
42   # ----------------
43   # Instantiates X8 processor
44   # Runs the program for 2,000 shots
45   # Prints results
46   # ----------------
47   eng = RemoteEngine("X8")
48   results = eng.run(gbs_prog, shots=2000)
49   print(results.samples)
50   # ------------------------------------------------------
```

References

1. Aaronson, S., & Arkhipov, A. (2013). The computational complexity of linear optics. *Theory of Computing, 9*(1), 143–252.
2. Albash, T., & Lidar, D. A. (2018). Adiabatic quantum computation. *Reviews of Modern Physics, 90*(015002).
3. Arrazola, J. M., Bergholm, V., Brádler, K., et al. (2021). Quantum circuits with many photons on a programmable nanophotonic chip. *Nature, 591*, 54–60.
4. Arrazola, J. M., & Bromley, T. R. (2018). Using Gaussian boson sampling to find dense subgraphs. *Physical Review Letters, 121*(3), 030503.
5. Banchi, L., Fingerhuth, M., Babej, T., & Arrazola, J. M. (2019). Molecular docking with Gaussian boson sampling. *Science Advances, 6*(23).
6. Bernhardt, C. (2019). *Quantum computing for everyone*. The MIT Press. ISBN: 978-0262039253.
7. Boulanger, R. (Ed.). (2000). *The Csound book: Perspectives in software synthesis, sound design, signal processing, and programming*. The MIT Press. ISBN: 978-0262522618.
8. Brádler, K., Israel, R., Schuld, M., & Su, D. (2019). A duality at the heart of Gaussian boson sampling. arXiv:1910.04022 [quant-ph].
9. Brádler, K., Dallaire-Demers, P. L., Rebentrost, P., Su, D., & Weedbrook, C. (2018). Gaussian boson sampling for perfect matchings of arbitrary graphs. *Physical Review A, 98*(3), 032310.
10. Brádler, K., Friedland, S., Izaac, J., Killoran, N., & Su, D. (2018). Graph isomorphism and Gaussian boson sampling. *Special Matrices, 9*(1), 166–196.
11. Briegel, H. J., Browne, D. E., Dur, W., Raussendorf, R., & Van den Nest, M. (2009). Measurement-based quantum computation. *Nature Physics, 5*, 19–26.
12. Bromley, T. R., Arrazola, J. M., Jahangiri, S., Izaac, J., Quesada, N., Gran, A. D., Schuld, M., Swinarton, J., Zabaneh, Z., & Killoran, N. (2019). Applications of near-term photonic quantum computers: Software and algorithms. arxiv:1912.07634 [quant-ph].
13. Bruzewicz, C. D., Chiaverini, J., McConnell, R., & Sage, J. M. (2019). Trapped-ion quantum computing: Progress and challenges. *Applied Physics Reviews, 6*(021314).
14. Dorfman, J. (2013). *Theory and practice of technology-based music instruction*. Oxford University Press. ISBN:978-0199323784.
15. Deutsch, D., Barenco, A., & Ekert, A. (2008). Universality in quantum computation. arXiv:quant-ph/9505018 [quant-ph].
16. Hamilton, C. S., Kruse, R., Sansoni, L., Barkhofen, S., Silberhorn, C., & Jex, I. (2017). Gaussian boson sampling. *Physical Review Letters, 119*(170501).
17. Henriet, L., Beguin, L., Signoles, A., Lahaye, T., Browaeys, A., Reymond, G. O., & Jurczak, C. (2020). Quantum computing with neutral atoms. *Quantum, 4*, 327.
18. Horn, R. A., & Zhang, F. (2011). A generalization of the complex Autonne-Takagi factorization to quaternion matrices. *Linear and Multilinear Algebra, 60*(11–12), 1239–1244.
19. Huh, J., Guerreschi, G. G., Peropadre, B., McClean, J. R., & Aspuru-Guzik, A. (2015). Boson sampling for molecular vibronic spectra. *Nature Photonics, 9*(9), 615–620.
20. Jahangiri, S., Arrazola, J. M., Quesada, N., & Killoran, N. (2020). Point processes with Gaussian boson sampling. *Physical Review E, 101*(022134).
21. Kernighan, B., & Ritchie, D. (1988). *The C programming language*. Pearson. ISBN: 978-0131103627.
22. Killoran, N., Izaac, J., Quesada, N., Bergholm, V., Amy, M., & Weedbrook, C. (2019). Strawberry fields: A software platform for photonic quantum computing. *Quantum, 3*, 129.
23. Kjaergaard, M., Schwartz, M. E., Braumuller, J., Krantz, P., Wang, J.I.-J., Gustavsso, S., & Oliver, W. D. (2020). Superconducting qubits: Current state of play. *Annual Review of Condensed Matter Physics, 11*(1), 369–395.
24. Lee, A. S. C. (2000). Granular Synthesis in Csound. In R. Boulanger (Ed.), *The Csound book: Perspectives in software synthesis, sound design, signal processing, and programming* (pp. 283–292). The MIT Press. ISBN: 978-0262522618.

25. Miranda, E. R. (2001). *Computer sound design: Synthesis techniques and programming.* Elsevier Focal Press. ISBN: 978-0240516936.
26. Muller, M. (2015). *Fundamentals of music processing: Audio, analysis, algorithms, applications.* Springer. ISBN: 978-3319357652.
27. Roads, C. (1996). *The computer music tutorial.* The MIT Press. ISBN: 9780262680820.
28. Quesada, N. (2019). *The Hafnian.* https://hafnian.readthedocs.io/en/stable/hafnian.html. Accessed 14 Sep. 2021.
29. Serafini, A. (2017). *Quantum continuous variables: A primer of theoretical models,* Routledge CRC Press. ISBN 978-1482246346.
30. Schuld, M., Brádler, K., Israel, R., Su, D., & Gupt, B. (2020). Measuring the similarity of graphs with a Gaussian boson sampler. *Physical Review A, 101*(032314).
31. Slussarenko, S., & Pryde, G. J. (2019). Photonic quantum information processing: A concise review. *Applied Physics Reviews, 6*(041303).
32. *Strawberry Fields Documentation.* https://strawberryfields.ai/photonics/. Accessed 23 July 2021.
33. Weedbrook, C., Pirandola, S., Garcia-Patron, R., Cerf, N. J., Ralph, T. C., Shapiro, J. H., & Lloyd, S. (2012). Gaussian quantum information. *Reviews of Modern Physics, 84,* 621–669.
34. Zhang, X., Li, H.-O., Cao, G., Xiao, M., Guo, G.-C., & Guo, G.-P. (2019). Semiconductor quantum computation. *National Science Review, 6*(1), 32–54.

Giuseppe Clemente, Arianna Crippa, Karl Jansen and Cenk Tüysüz

Abstract

We explore ideas for generating sounds and eventually music using quantum devices in the NISQ era using quantum circuits. In particular, we first consider a concept for a *Qeyboard*, that is, a quantum keyboard, where the real-time behaviour of expectation values using a time-evolving quantum circuit can be associated to sound features like intensity, frequency and tone. Then, we examine how these properties can be extracted from physical quantum systems, taking the Ising model as an example. This can be realized by measuring physical quantities of the quantum states of the system, e.g. the energies and the magnetization obtained via variational quantum simulation techniques.

17.1 Introduction

With the current acceleration in the development and improvement of quantum technologies, it is conceivable that we shall witness an increasing influence of quantum ideas in everyday life, music included. Public availability and easy access to the Noisy Intermediate-Scale Quantum (NISQ) [1] devices allowed users of different backgrounds (e.g., composers, software developers, video game designers) to experiment with them. Using principles of Quantum Mechanics to generate or manipulate music is gaining popularity in recent years [2,3].

G. Clemente · A. Crippa · K. Jansen (✉) · C. Tüysüz
Deutsches Elektronen-Synchrotron DESY, Platanenallee 6, 15738 Zeuthen, Germany
e-mail: karl.jansen@desy.de

A. Crippa · C. Tüysüz
Institut für Physik, Humboldt-Universität zu Berlin, Newtonstr. 15, 12489 Berlin, Germany

© The Author(s), under exclusive license to Springer Nature Switzerland AG 2022
E. R Miranda (ed.), *Quantum Computer Music*,
https://doi.org/10.1007/978-3-031-13909-3_17

In this chapter, we present two ideas. First, the *Qeyboard*, an attempt to turn a Quantum Computer into a musical instrument, allows the performer to exploit quantum effects such as superposition and entanglement. This opens up new avenues for live performances and musical compositions. The second idea converts the algorithmic process of simulating a quantum system into music, making it possible to hear the properties of the quantum system as it evolves. Both of these ideas are simple enough to be practically realizable with the current technology and little effort; they also allow for straightforward extensions and generalizations for later stages of our line of research.

17.2 Qeyboard: Some Concepts for a Real-Time Quantum Keyboard

The idea of a *quantum instrument*, that is, a device capable of producing sounds as end-products of quantum mechanical processes instead of classical mechanical ones, is starting to take shape in the quantum music community [2]. The "true" nature of the real world is quantum (at least, according to our most accurate description of nature), so any classical musical instrument is already quantum at the fundamental level, but the extent of quantum effects (such as superposition, interference, entanglement) is usually obscured by the macroscopic and incoherent nature of the phenomena involved in the sound production.

In order to harness the full potentiality of quantum processes in the NISQ era, in the following discussion, we will focus on the quantum circuit model as a convenient representation for abstract wavefunctions: a generic quantum state is prepared as a sequence of gates acting on qubits starting from an initial fiducial state (usually the state with all qubits set to 0). Having prepared a specific wavefunction, one can then measure its properties which can in turn be related to sound features to be classically synthesized, according to the pipeline diagram depicted in Fig. 17.1.

In the following sections, we will describe some of the possible choices for each steps of this pipeline, namely:

1. real-time **interface** classical input and evolution of the circuit $\mathcal{U}(t)$ (and therefore $|\psi(t)\rangle$);
2. set of **measurements** on the state $|\psi(t)\rangle$ at each frame;
3. map between measurements (real or binary valued) and sound **features**;
4. **synthesis** of the final sound from different sound sources.

17.2.1 Real-Time Interface for Evolving a Dynamical Parameterized Quantum Circuit

The circuit structure, described abstractly in Fig. 17.1 as a multi-qubit unitary operator $\mathcal{U}(t)$, is time-dependent according to the time dependence of the input data. In

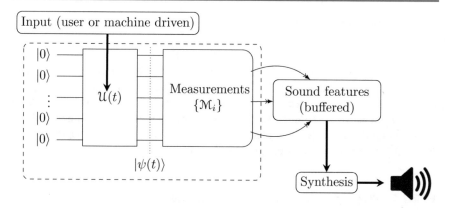

Fig. 17.1 Schematic pipeline diagram of a digital quantum instrument. The dashed box represents the part involving quantum processes: $\mathcal{U}(t)$ is the circuit preparing the state $|\psi(t)\rangle = \mathcal{U}(t)|0\rangle$, while $\{\mathcal{M}_i\}$ is a set of Hermitian operators representing measurements

complete generality, the circuit represented by $\mathcal{U}(t)$ can include time-varying parameterized gates, as well as evolving topologies, where gates are added or removed at any time and at any point of the circuit. Notice also that here we are not making any assumptions on the continuity or differentiability of $\mathcal{U}(t)$ with respect to the time parameter t: this makes possible abrupt changes in the properties of the wavefunction, which in turn allows us to model all possible shapes of ADSR envelopes (attack, decay, sustain and release), which is normally used in sound-synthesis algorithms to shape the amplitude of a sound in time.

From the point of view of a human user, a good level of real-time manipulation of the circuit can be realized by pressing combinations of keys mapped to a finite set of single and double-qubit gates, which are then added to the right end of the circuit. These gates can be parameterless (like Pauli, Hadamard, CNOT or SWAP gates) or parameterized like generic rotations. In turn, the parameters can be changed in real-time using a slider (e.g., operated via mouse). Another possibility, which requires some more work in terms of interface but enhances the level of manipulation expressibility, is to manage the whole circuit with a touch monitor where gates can be added or removed at specific points or their parameters can be changed. This can be realized by simple gestures or even with multiple simultaneous actions.

If one is interested instead in machine-driven execution, the circuit dynamics can be represented by a predetermined *quantum music sheet*, or some other form of input, which drives the circuit changes in full generality and without the limitation of the human user (limited pace and simultaneous actions).

17.2.2 Measurements

Here we discuss the second step in the pipeline of Fig. 17.1, namely the association between properties of the wavefunction produced by measurements on the circuit $\mathcal{U}(t)$ and properties of the sound. Notice that, in practice, it is not possible to run quantum circuits and measurements continuously in t, so we would assume a reasonable sampling rate at discrete times t_i which still allows us to capture the main features of the circuit dynamics without loss of expressibility. The results of measurements can finally be interpolated during post-processing.

17.2.2.1 Playing Qubits as Quantum Strings

In this paradigm, which we named *quantum strings with counts to intensity*, we associate an oscillator with a specific frequency to any qubit register, while the corresponding sound intensity is determined by the average count of measurements with outcome 1. As a concrete example, we can consider a $q = 8$ qubits system associated to the major scale in the octave $C4$–$C5$, so that a circuit could be visually mapped to pentagram lines and spaces. At every time t, one can make n_{shots} measurements in all the qubit registers, which produces in general different states on the computational basis in terms of a dictionary containing the 0–1 bit-string representation of the state and the number of times that have been observed: {"$00\cdots00$" : $c_{00\cdots00}$, "$00\cdots01$" : $c_{00\cdots01}$, $\cdots$}. The intensity associated with the n-th quantum string would then be determined by the ratio between the sum of counts of states with the n-th qubit register set to 1 and the total number of shots:

$$\mathcal{I}_n = \sum_{s \in \mathbb{Z}_2^q \mid s_n = 1} \frac{c_s}{n_{\text{shots}}} \in [0, 1]. \tag{17.1}$$

In this way, in absence of noise and with a trivial circuit $\mathcal{U}(t_i) = I$, only the state with all qubits set to zero would be observed for every shot ($c_0 = n_{\text{shots}}$), so the sound would be silence. A generic (non-diagonal) circuit $\mathcal{U}(t_i)$ would instead be associated to a generic distribution of count ratios c_s^i / n_{shots}. Notice that the addition of noise and a finite number of shots would always introduce fluctuations in the intensity associated with each quantum string at neighbouring times t_i and t_{i+1}, even if the circuit does not change.

17.2.2.2 Expectation Values to Continuous Sound Properties

In this paradigm, the whole wavefunction is associated with different properties of the final synthesized sound. Unlike the previous approach, we will not associate a single qubit register to specific and predetermined frequencies, but instead we will characterize the properties of the sound at each time t_i in terms of expectation values of Hermitian operators (observables). This idea can be implemented in a completely general way, but we will give a simple concrete example. Let us consider a two-qubit system and two Hermitian operators

$$H_f \equiv \frac{1}{2}(I - \sigma^X) \otimes I, \qquad H_i \equiv \frac{1}{2}I \otimes (I - \sigma^Z). \tag{17.2}$$

At any time t, after applying the circuit $\mathcal{U}(t)$, one would then estimate the expectation value of the observables in Eq. (17.2): $\langle H_f \rangle(t) \equiv \langle \psi(t)|H_f|\psi(t)\rangle$ and $\langle H_i \rangle(t) \equiv \langle \psi(t)|H_i|\psi(t)\rangle$, which takes any value in the range $[0, 1]$. Fixing a conventional frequency range $[f_0, f_1]$, the value $\langle H_f \rangle(t)$ can be associated to continuous values of frequency in that range by the linear relation $f(t) = f_0 + (f_1 - f_0)\langle H_f \rangle(t)$, while intensity would simply be $i(t) = \langle H_i \rangle(t)$. These time-dependent frequencies and intensity properties of a single sound will be then synthesized, as discussed in the next section. In the specific example of Eq. (17.2), the two properties are commuting and it is intuitive how the sound can be manipulated by an appropriate rotation in the first or second qubit register. In general, one can associate pairs of Hermitian operators to the frequency and intensity properties for a certain number of sounds N_S; for example, one can build a set of observables by considering all the possible combinations of tensor products of I, and

$$\Pi_j = \frac{1}{2}(I - \sigma^j), \tag{17.3}$$

where σ^j are the Pauli matrices and Π_j is the projector to the eigenstate of σ^j with eigenvalue 1. This set of operators can in principle be used to make a tomography of the wavefunction $\psi(t)$ at any time t in order to extract all possible information from it. This choice would give a wide range of expressivity, since the number of properties could scale as $4^q - 1$, but we recommend the user to select just a few of them or a meaningful combination. We want to stress also that one could add more sophisticated sound properties, like tone, which would require a different preprocessing stage during synthesis.

17.2.3 Synthesis

In this section we will briefly describe how to process the collection of properties $\mathcal{P}(t_i) = \{(f_s(t_i), i_s(t_i))\}_{s=1}^{N_S}$ for each sound at any time t_i collected during the measurement stage (previous section), and synthesize them in order to obtain a single waveform. This can be done using inharmonic additive synthesis [4], since the properties of each sound source are generally time-dependent. First of all, an interpolation step must be performed in order to make the sound properties vary continuously with time $\mathcal{P}(t)$. The interpolation can be linear or higher order with some smoothing factor. The final waveform is then built as follows[1]

$$w(t) = \frac{1}{\mathcal{N}} \sum_{s=1}^{N_S} i_s(t) \sin\left[2\pi f_s(t)t\right], \tag{17.4}$$

where a global normalization $\mathcal{N}$ has been added to make the waveform vary between -1 and 1, so to avoid clipping effects.

---

[1] The phase of an individual sound could be added as a further property, but this would not be perceptible to the listener's ear.

As a first example, we consider a three-qubit system, with the following observables associated with intensity and frequency (fixed for the whole run):

$$H_i = I \otimes I \otimes \Pi_Z \tag{17.5}$$

$$H_f = \left(2\Pi_Z \otimes I + I \otimes \Pi_Z + I \otimes I\right) \otimes I, \tag{17.6}$$

where Π_i are the projection operators, defined in Eq. (17.3). In this case, the intensity can be easily controlled by acting on the rightmost qubit register, for example by applying σ^Y or σ^X, while the first two registers from the left are associated to a frequency, which can take values from 1 to 4. For example, applying the following circuit evolution:

$$\mathcal{U}(t) = \begin{cases} I \otimes I \otimes I, & \text{if } t < 0.5s \\ I \otimes I \otimes \sigma^X, & \text{if } 0.5s < t < 1.0s \\ e^{-i\frac{\pi(t-1s)}{6s}\sigma^X \otimes \sigma^X} \otimes \sigma^X, & \text{if } 1.0s < t < 4.0s \\ e^{-i\frac{\pi(7s-t)}{6s}\sigma^Y \otimes \sigma^Y} \otimes \sigma^X, & \text{if } 4.0s < t < 7.0s \\ I \otimes I \otimes \sigma^X, & \text{if } t > 7.0s, \end{cases} \tag{17.7}$$

the behaviour in Fig. 17.2 is produced, where measurements are interpolated and then synthesized as in Fig. 17.3.

Figures 17.4 and 17.5 show another example of Qeyboard dynamics, again for a three-qubit system, but with six (non mutually commuting) Hermitian operators associated to intensities and frequencies for three sounds. The Qeyboard-driven circuit evolution and the set of observables used in this case are more complicated, so we will not put the specific details of its generation here, but it should be nevertheless possible to appreciate the degree of customizability and expressivity which can be realized using this paradigm.

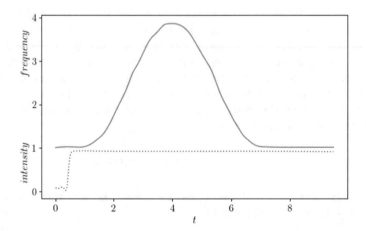

Fig. 17.2 Simple example of circuit synthesis of single sound evolution as described in the text: measurements are taken at every 0.1 s, quantum noise is present and a smoothed interpolation is applied at the post-processing stage, with sampling rate 44100 Hz

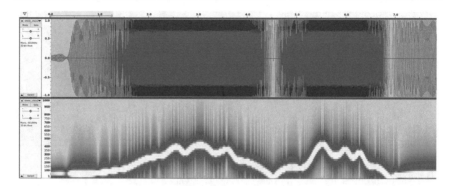

Fig. 17.3 Inharmonic synthesis of the waveform obtained by using Eq. (17.4) with the frequency and intensity functions $f(t)$ and $i(t)$ shown in Fig. 17.2, with a base frequency $f_0 = 523.26$ and $f(t) \equiv f_0 \cdot \langle H_f \rangle(t)$. Due to the presence of sampling noise, and since the synthesis is inharmonic, the spectrogram does not reflect straightforwardly the behaviour in Fig. 17.2

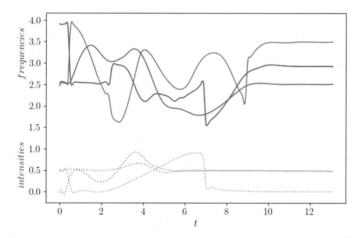

Fig. 17.4 More complex synthesis for three sounds played simultaneously with both evolving frequencies and intensities with some smoothing applied and synthesized with sampling rate 44100 Hz

17.3 The Sound of the Ising Model

In this section, we explore how to use physical systems to make music. To this end, we will employ the spectrum and other properties of a quantum system; here we consider the *Ising model* as a convenient toy system. The energies of the spectrum will be used as frequencies and other quantities such as the magnetization can be used for the intensities. These principles can be actually applied to many other physical systems, which would supply a very broad portfolio of sounds and eventually *quantum music*. The reason is that physical quantum systems can have very different properties showing a variety of phases and corresponding phase transitions.

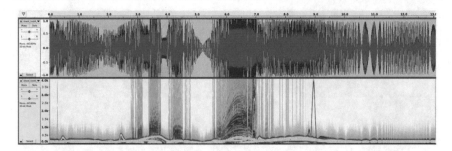

Fig. 17.5 Inharmonic synthesis of the waveform obtained by using Eq. (17.4) with the frequency and intensity functions $f(t)$ and $i(t)$ shown in Fig. 17.4, with a base frequency $f_0 = 523.26$ and $f(t) \equiv f_0 \cdot \langle H_f \rangle (t)$. Due to the presence of sampling noise, and since the synthesis is inharmonic, the spectrogram does not reflect straightforwardly the behaviour in Fig. 17.4

The Ising model is a simple statistical mechanical system, which can be considered as a microscopic model for magnetism exhibiting a quantum phase transition from unmagnetized to a magnetized phase. It consists of discrete two-valued variables that represent the two possible states ($+1$ or -1) of magnetic dipole moments, or *spin*. These spins are defined on a lattice and they interact with their nearest neighbours. The Hamiltonian of the system has two terms

$$H = -J \sum_i \sigma_i^Z \sigma_j^Z - h \sum_i \sigma_i^X, \tag{17.8}$$

the first describes the interaction between neighbouring spins: if $J > 0$, neighbouring spins prefer to be aligned ($\uparrow\uparrow$ or $\downarrow\downarrow$), which denotes a *ferromagnetic* behaviour. If $J < 0$, the preferred combination is anti-aligned ($\uparrow\downarrow$), leading to an *anti-ferromagnetic* behaviour. The second term represents the action of an external magnetic field with amplitude h, which endows an energy advantage to the spins aligned to the magnetic field. If the value of h is sufficiently large ($h = O(1)$) the Ising model undergoes a phase transition where the fluctuations of the spins increase and interesting physics starts to happen. Here also the magnetization, defined in Sect. 17.3.2.3, decreases sharply as a function of the external magnetic field. It is the goal of this section to use the properties of the Ising system to generate also interesting quantum sounds and even quantum music.

The idea is to use a variational approach, such as the Variational Quantum Deflation algorithm [5] (see Sect. 17.3.1) to find pairs of eigenvalues and eigenvectors($\{(E_k, |\psi_k\rangle\}$, $k = 0, 1, \ldots$) of the Ising Hamiltonian, and then convert the properties of the system into audible sounds.

17.3.1 Variational Quantum Algorithms

The Variational Quantum Eigensolver [6] uses a variational technique to find the minimum eigenvalue of the Hamiltonian of a given system. An instance of VQE requires a trial state (ansatz), and one classical optimizer as summarized in Fig. 17.6.

The ansatz is varied, via its set of parameters θ, generating a state $|\Psi(\theta)\rangle$ which allows to measure the energy as the expectation value of the Hamiltonian, $\langle\Psi(\theta)|H|\Psi(\theta)\rangle$. The classical optimizer then gives back a new set of parameters for the next computation of the energy. This procedure is repeated until convergence to the true minimum of the expection value is found.

The VQE can be generalized also for computing excited states, for which the Variational Quantum Deflation (VQD) algorithm is used. The method has the following steps:

1. Apply the VQE method and obtain optimal parameters θ_0^* and an approximate ground state $|\psi_0\rangle \simeq |\Psi(\theta_0^*)\rangle$.
2. For the first excited state define a Hamiltonian:

$$H_1 = H + \beta \left|\Psi(\theta_0^*)\right\rangle\left\langle\Psi(\theta_0^*)\right| \tag{17.9}$$

where β is a real-valued coefficient.
3. Apply the VQE approach to find an approximate ground state of H_1.
4. This procedure can be repeated for higher eigenstates.

17.3.2 How to Play a Quantum System

The aim of this section is to describe different possibilities for extracting sounds from a quantum physical system, such as the aforementioned Ising model. By applying variational techniques we can get access to the observables of a quantum theory at the end of the minimization process and convert them to sounds. We can also measure the observables during the optimization itself and thus 'play' quantum music running the VQE or the VQD algorithms.

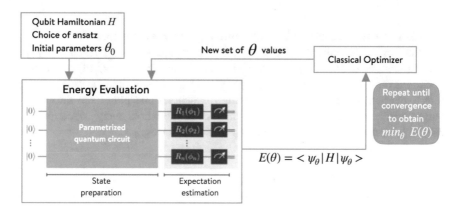

Fig. 17.6 Schematic procedure of the VQE algorithm. *Source* [7]

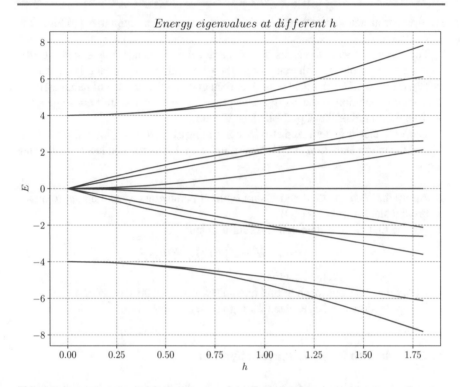

Fig. 17.7 The energy spectrum taken as frequencies and amplitudes h, as time, can be played as audible sounds

Most of these techniques can be generalized to an arbitrary Hamiltonian, such as the one of Quantum Electrodynamics, or even more intricate systems from condensed matter or high energy physics.

17.3.2.1 Convert Energy Eigenvalues E_k Into Frequencies

The first approach applies the VQD algorithm, compute the energy eigenvalues and convert them to audible frequencies. To this end, a suitable interval of the energies is chosen for a given value of the coupling h. Using h as a time variable, we can follow the behaviour of the corresponding frequencies and play them through an output device. Figure 17.7 shows the dynamics of the whole energy spectrum (16 eigenvalues) and can be naturally interpreted as a spectrogram.

17.3.2.2 Use the Callback Results

With this technique, the results for the ground state energy (or generic E_k) are collected during the VQD minimization with the NFT optimizer [8]. The energies are measured now in each step of the optimization procedure and again converted

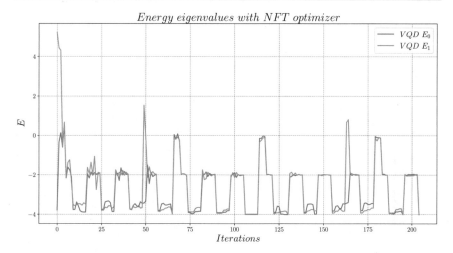

Fig. 17.8 Intermediate values during the optimization for ground state (E_0) and first excited state (E_1) with NFT optimizer

into frequencies. As can be seen in Fig. 17.7, the highly oscillatory behaviour of the energy values can be translated into frequencies. These oscillations are typical of the NFT algorithm but the detailed evolution depends on the physical quantum system under consideration. Playing the frequencies of this hybrid quantum/classical approach can lead to very interesting sounds.

17.3.2.3 Exploring How the Sound Changes Across the Phase Diagram

With this method we include the *magnetization* as an observable measured in the ground state ψ_0 and which is defined as

$$M = \frac{1}{N} \sum_i \langle \psi_0 | \sigma_i^Z | \psi_0 \rangle. \tag{17.10}$$

In Fig. 17.9 we can see that for small h the magnetization is equal to one, this corresponds to a *ferromagnetic*[2] system. When h increases, the magnetic term becomes more relevant and eventually the system reaches a *paramagnetic*[3] behaviour, with $M \sim 0$. In particular, we can observe a quantum phase transition when $h \sim 1$.

The definition of the magnetization in Eq. (17.10) can be generalized for higher excited states

$$M_k = \frac{1}{N} \sum_i \langle \psi_k | \sigma_i^Z | \psi_k \rangle. \tag{17.11}$$

---

[2] Materials with a strong magnetization in a magnetic field. They can turn into permanent magnets, i.e. have magnetization in the absence of an external field.

[3] Materials with a weak induced magnetization in a magnetic field, which disappears when the external field is removed.

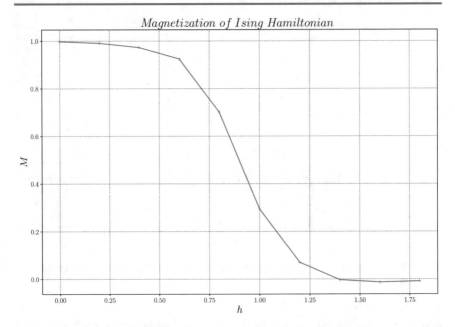

Fig. 17.9 Phase transition of Ising system. Varying the external magnetic field h, we go from a ferromagnetic phase to the paramagnetic phase by crossing a quantum phase transition. This can be clearly seen in the behaviour of the magnetization in Eq. (17.10) measured on the ground state

These eigenstate-dependent magnetizations can be related to the intensity of the sound of the corresponding frequency, defined by the k-energy eigenvalue E_k.

17.4 Summary and Outlook

In this chapter, we have discussed two approaches to generating sounds through quantum devices based on the circuit model. The first idea is to use the quantum computer as an instrument. Here we use a real-time evolution and manipulate the quantum circuit through a (quantum-)keyboard. Measurements during the time evolution are performed to make them audible. The ideas that we described for a quantum instrument are open for customization by the user at different stages of the pipeline and allow for a high degree of flexibility.

The second idea is to use quantum physical systems for generating sound and therefore to be able to actually listen to a true quantum system. Here we followed the approach of assigning the role of 'time variable' to some parameter of the model under consideration. In particular, in the case of the here discusses Ising model, the external magnetic field was chosen. Frequencies can then be computed from the energy eigenvalues and intensities from the magnetization measured in the corresponding eigenstates. In our opinion, using quantum systems to generate sound and eventually quantum music can lead to very interesting effects since such quantum models describe often very complex phenomena and phase diagrams with intricate physical properties. In addition, they exhibit phase transitions where large fluctuations can occur with strong correlations. We believe that these characteristics of quantum systems can be harvested through the quantum mechanical principles of superposition and entanglement possibly leading even to new directions in music.

Some resources (figures and sound files) for the examples that we discussed in this chapter can be found in [9].

Our first step to generating quantum music presented in this chapter manipulates only frequencies and intensities which can be obtained through measurements of specific Hamiltonians or observables such as magnetization. Our approach can be generalized to also generate tones and even more complicated music properties.

References

1. Preskill, J. (2018). Quantum computing in the NISQ era and beyond. *Quantum, 2*(July), 1–20.
2. Putz, V., & Svozil, K. (2017). Quantum music. *Soft Computing, 21*, 1467–1471.
3. Miranda, E. R. (2020). Quantum computer: Hello, music!. arXiv:2006.13849 [quant-ph].
4. Miranda, E. (2002). *Computer sound design: Synthesis techniques and programming.*
5. Higgott, O., Wang, D., & Brierley, S. (2019). Variational quantum computation of excited states. *Quantum, 3*, 156.
6. Peruzzo, A., McClean, J., Shadbolt, P., Yung, M.-H., Zhou, X.-Q., Love, P. J., Aspuru-Guzik, A., & O'Brien, J. L. (2014). A variational eigenvalue solver on a photonic quantum processor. *Nature Communications, 5*(1), 4213.
7. http://openqemist.1qbit.com/docs/vqe_microsoft_qsharp.html.
8. Nakanishi, K. M., Fujii, K., & Todo, S. (2020). Sequential minimal optimization for quantum-classical hybrid algorithms. *Physical Review Research, 2*, 043158.
9. https://github.com/QC-DESY/qeyboard_and_isingsound_resources.

Superconducting Qubits as Musical Synthesizers for Live Performance

18

Spencer Topel, Kyle Serniak, Luke Burkhart, and Florian Carle

Abstract

In the frame of a year-long artistic residency at the Yale Quantum Institute in 2019, artist and technologist Spencer Topel, quantum physicists Kyle Serniak and Luke Burkhart, and producer Florian Carle collaborated to create *Quantum Sound*, a distinctive piece of music created and performed directly from measurements of superconducting quantum devices. Using analogue- and digital-signal-processing sonification techniques, the team transformed GHz-frequency signals from experiments inside dilution refrigerators into audible sounds. The project was performed live at the International Festival of Arts and Ideas in New Haven, Connecticut on June 14, 2019, as a structured improvisation using the synthesis methods described in this chapter. At the interface between research and art, *Quantum Sound* represents an earnest attempt to produce a sonic reflection of the quantum realm.

S. Topel · K. Serniak (✉) · L. Burkhart · F. Carle (✉)
Yale Quantum Institute, Yale University, New Haven, CT, USA
e-mail: kyle.serniak@ll.mit.edu

F. Carle
e-mail: florian.carle@yale.edu

S. Topel
Physical Synthesis, Brooklyn, NY, USA

K. Serniak
Current Address: MIT Lincoln Laboratory, Lexington, MA, USA

L. Burkhart
Current Address: Keysight Technologies, Cambridge, MA, USA

E. R. Miranda (ed.), *Quantum Computer Music*,
https://doi.org/10.1007/978-3-031-13909-3_18

18.1 Introduction

The past several decades have seen breakthroughs in both the theory and the practice of quantum science. The quantum phenomena of superposition and entanglement are now understood as unique resources that can be harnessed to solve computationally intensive problems. Experimental progress has enabled precise control over individual quantum objects, whether naturally occurring microscopic systems like atoms, or carefully designed macroscopic quantum systems whose properties can be engineered.

These advances may soon allow us to perform otherwise intractable computations, ensure privacy in communications, and better understand and design novel states of matter. The emerging discipline of quantum information processing combines physics, electrical engineering, mathematics, and computer science to further the basic understanding of the quantum world, and to develop novel computational devices and other quantum-enabled measurement and sensing technologies.

The speed of development of quantum technologies has dramatically increased over the last few years. The prospect of novel applications of quantum computers has triggered a frenzy of investment and intense development in a race toward the first demonstration of quantum advantage, wherein a quantum computer definitively outperforms a classical computer. But in this race, most people outside of the field of quantum computing are left wondering how this technology works and how it might impact their lives. With the goal of encouraging public conversation about quantum science and to combat scientific reticence, Florian Carle created an Artist-in-Residence program for the Yale Quantum Institute in 2017. This program brings talented artists into the research laboratories to produce artwork in collaboration with quantum physicists. By exploring art as a medium and leveraging the intersectionality of science and the humanities, this program increases public understanding and discourse of quantum physics by seeing this topic through the perspective of a collaborative artist. In building this program, an emphasis was put on connecting the right people with the proper expertise at the right time to make something truly unique and inspiring to a new generation, and to give them the desire to push the boundary of our collective knowledge.

In this chapter, we will focus on the live performance of *Quantum Sound*—a collaborative work of the second Artist-in-Residence, Spencer Topel, who is a co-author on this publication. Spencer is a musician, artist, and researcher working with electromechanical music synthesizers, interactive sound installations, live performances, and recordings. In 2019, Spencer collaborated with Kyle Serniak and Luke Burkhart, two quantum physicists finishing their Ph.Ds at Yale University, and producer Florian Carle, to "play" sounds generated by the operation of prototype quantum processors in the Yale Quantum Institute laboratories, cooled to nearly absolute zero (~ 10 mK), as if they were musical instruments in an orchestra. To the best of our knowledge, this performance was the first of its kind, attracting the interest of scientists in the quantum community due to its technical challenge, and of the public for the novel soundscape that was produced.

In many respects, quantum physicists and electronic musicians speak a similar language, which is why there has been a surge of interest in quantum computer music in the last decade with projects like *Quantum Music* [10, 17] or *Quantum Sound* [24], the creation of quantum-music-centric conferences [11, 12], or even books like this one. Musicians and researchers interact with their instruments thinking in common terms such as frequencies, signals, and standing waves. Furthermore, they must worry about similar problems like electromagnetic interference, noise, and aberrant resonances. Keeping in mind that the advent of personal computing served to democratize electronic music production, it is worthwhile to assess whether quantum technologies will further expand the musician's toolkit. Though we do not address this question directly, our demonstration—working with fundamental technologies being developed in pursuit of larger-scale quantum systems—echoes experimentations with new musical processes from more than a century ago, when Leon Theremin invented instruments and transducers exploiting principles of electromagnetism and recently-invented radio proximity sensors [25]. The most famous of these instruments, the *Theremin*, became the first contactless musical instrument and is still fabricated and performed today.

This chapter discusses a mixture of science and art, as it relates to sonification (the act of expressing inaudible phenomena as sound) and synthesis intended to describe to the reader (in language meant to bridge the two fields) the tools we utilized to create music using measurements taken from quantum systems. Section 18.2 will give an overview of the technology and hardware used to generate the data. Section 18.3 will focus on the synthesizer programming and design, and how the signals were made usable and audible. Section 18.4 will describe the live performance, detail the musical motifs therein, and explain the artists' intentions for the piece.

18.2   Quantum Experiments Used to Generate Sounds

Quantum information processing relies on precise control of quantum systems. In recent years, groundbreaking quantum information experiments have solidified the position of superconducting quantum processors as a viable technology for the Noisy Intermediate-Scale Quantum era and beyond [2, 19] (NISQ, referring to the stage where quantum processors are reaching 100s of qubits and can be utilized for small-scale, specifically tailored algorithms). While atoms and subatomic particles are archetypes of the quantum world, some solid-state systems can also behave quantum mechanically. In the case of superconducting qubits [9, 16] the *quantumness* is observed in the dynamics of collective excitations in the electrical circuits [26] when they are cooled far below the superconducting transition temperature (for aluminium, the most common material used in the field, this transition occurs at ~ 1.2 K, or $\sim -457°$F). In these systems, relevant transition frequencies are in the few GHz range, which translates to energies greater than the

Fig. 18.1 Photograph of Blue, one of the two dilution refrigerators that housed the experiments used as physical synthesizers to perform Quantum Sound, and Luke Burkhart (left), one of the performers

temperature at which experiments are conducted. This is most commonly facilitated by cryogenic systems (commonly referred to as cryostats) called dilution refrigerators (see Fig. 18.1), which nowadays can be purchased commercially and have become a ubiquitous tool for low-temperature physics [5, 18, 28]. These systems can operate at ~ 10 mK, which is nominally cold enough to freeze out all electronic excitations in the superconductor and have enough cooling power to overcome the power dissipation associated with control and measurement of many superconducting qubits.

The qubit devices addressed during the performance of *Quantum Sound* were designed for specific experiments related to superconducting quantum information processing. Each are based on transmon qubits [2], which consist of two circuit elements in parallel: a capacitor and a uniquely superconducting component—the Josephson junction (JJ). In the transmon, the JJ serves as a nonlinear inductor and is crucial to achieving coherent control of the qubit. Transmon qubits are constructed using traditional lithography and deposition techniques, like those used in semiconductor circuit manufacturing (see Fig. 18.2).

Experiments performed using superconducting qubits rely on low-noise electrical signal generation ranging from DC to around 10 GHz, surpassing the audio-frequency range by many orders of magnitude. Passive and active components up to these frequencies are readily available commercially due to vast research and development efforts related to telecommunications and radar. These

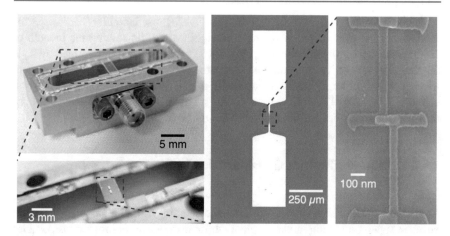

Fig. 18.2 Physical realization of a 3D transmon superconducting qubit. Top left shows a photograph of one half of the 3D waveguide cavity resonator that houses the transmon and is used to read out the state of the qubit (in this case, it was machined from 6061 Al, a superconducting alloy). Zooming in, the bottom left shows the sapphire substrate, upon which the transmon was fabricated, mounted in the centre of the cavity. Zooming in further, the centre panel shows an optical micrograph of the transmon, with large coplanar capacitor paddles. On the right is a scanning electron micrograph (SEM) of an Al/AlOx/Al Josephson tunnel junction fabricated using the "bridge-free" technique [14]. Figure reprinted from Kyle Serniak's Ph.D. Thesis [23]

established technologies facilitate high-fidelity control of qubit states with microwave-frequency drives, which means that experimentalists can prepare the qubit in any superposition of its energy eigenstates with error rates approaching 1 in 10,000 [13].

With the exception of direct qubit control explicitly utilized in Luke's experiment for *Quantum Sound*, the qubit-state readout was responsible for most of the musical choices made in the performance. Whether a qubit is occupying its ground or excited state is determined via a technique called dispersive readout, in which the qubit state is detected via a state-dependent frequency shift of a nearby harmonic oscillator, which is also made from superconducting materials (henceforth referred to as a transmon-cavity system). The qubit's state is encoded in the amplitude and phase (or in Cartesian space, the in-phase and quadrature components) of a microwave signal that interacts with the oscillator. Therefore, by monitoring that signal, one can efficiently determine the state of the qubit. With quantum-noise-limited parametric amplifiers, sufficient signal-to-noise (SNR > 1) for single-shot readout can be achieved with measurement durations of a few hundreds of nanoseconds, the inverse of which sets the maximum sampling rate with which signals in our experiments could be sonified. These signals are mixed down from GHz to ~ 10 s of MHz using standard frequency mixing techniques, then detected with a high-bandwidth analog-to-digital converter and demodulated.

While each experiment discussed here [7, 23] used similar hardware, the motivations for these experiments differed significantly, illustrating the breadth of current research on superconducting qubits. The first experiment performed by Kyle Serniak focused on readout and noise characterization. The second experiment performed by Luke Burkhart focused on high-fidelity qubit control based on classical feedback. The following sections summarize these experiments, whose data provided material for the *Quantum Sound* performances.

18.2.1 Nonequilibrium Quasiparticles in Superconducting Qubits

Kyle Serniak's experiment focused on understanding a particular mechanism of errors in superconducting qubits—namely those from nonequilibrium quasiparticles (QP) excitations [21] QPs are electronic excitations in a superconductor and are why it is so important to operating at very low temperature. So-called BCS superconductors [3], named after the physicists Bardeen, Cooper, and Schrieffer for their development of this theory, are characterized by a phonon-mediated electron–electron interaction that produces an energy gap in the electronic conduction band centred at the chemical potential. This gap serves as the backbone for a plethora of mesoscopic quantum phenomena (in the case of aluminium, this gap around 400 micro-electronvolts) in that it suppresses electronic excitations (the aforementioned QPs) at low energies. At low temperatures, there is an exponentially small occurrence of thermally generated excitations above this gap. In fact, in order to find just one pair of excitations in an otherwise isolated block of aluminium sitting at 10 mK one would *expect* to need a volume of material larger than the Earth! Unfortunately, coupling to external sources of energy such as infrared radiation and radioactive decay products results in an unexpectedly high, *nonequilibrium* population of QP excitations.

These QPs will tunnel across the JJ of the transmon, and when they do, they can induce qubit errors. To characterize the rate of these errors and distinguish them from other error mechanisms, it's possible to monitor other observables in the transmon called the *offset charge* and *charge parity*. The former is a classical voltage difference across the JJ due to spurious charges in the environment that reconfigure on a timescale of a few minutes, and the latter of which is the number parity (even or odd) of QPs that have tunnelled across the JJ (which tunnel on a timescale of a few milliseconds). The goal of this experiment was to characterize the timescale on which QP tunnelling events occurred in transmon qubits, and to do so in a way that is more efficient than previous demonstrations [20–22] Using a single transmon-cavity system, this experiment utilized the same dispersive coupling responsible for qubit-state readout to also measure the charge parity of the transmon. The result was a readout signal from which one could determine not only the state of the qubit (ground or excited), but also the charge parity (even or odd) simultaneously (see Fig. 18.3—Simultaneous measurement of qubit state (ground or excited) and charge parity (the number parity of quasiparticles (QPs) that have tunnelled across the Josephson junction, even or odd) in a transmon qubit [21]. Experimental data is shown with overlaid horizontal lines denoting the signal amplitudes that correspond to each state. Signals such as these were the basis for sounds generated for the performance and sonified using the 4-state synthesizer (see Sect. 18.2.1). Repeated measurements of the system, acquired with a 5–100 kHz sample rate, were used as waveforms to be processed into sound in the *Quantum Sound* performance.

18.2.2 Error-Detected Networking for 3D Circuit Quantum Electrodynamics

The other experiment, performed by Luke Burkhart, aimed at generating quantum entanglement between physically separated but linked quantum systems (see Fig. 18.4) [6]. Although no aspect of this entanglement was explicitly used in the performance, key technological primitives necessary to operate these quantum systems were put to the test in order to create various sonic motifs. The device consisted of two transmon-cavity systems coupled via an auxiliary cavity mode. Each transmon-cavity system was capable of independent readout and control, which was used to musical effect, creating waveforms that were "shaped" by deterministically controlling the state of the qubits. Two examples of this included (1) applying $X(\pi)$-gates to a single qubit conditioned on fast feedback of its own state (practically referred to as state initialization or reset), and (2) applying $X(\pi)$-gates to one qubit conditioned on fast feedback of the other qubit's state. Errors in this feedback protocol (the so-called *Bad Follower* synthesis engine) were introduced by intentionally over- or under-rotating the follower qubit, effectively enacting $X(\theta)$-gates for continuous θ in $[0, 2\pi)$. All measurements were performed in the σ_z basis, and therefore these suboptimal gates effectively simulated imperfect state preparation in the computational basis. Similarly, modulation of the expected qubit-state population as a function of time was achieved by modulating the rotation angle, creating waveforms like those of voltage-controlled oscillators in analog synthesizers, with imperfections induced by the stochastic, digital nature of projective measurements.

18.2.3 Experimental Data as Control Voltages

Measurements of transmon qubits are represented by voltage outputs from analogue-to-digital converters (ADCs). Repeated measurements (potentially with high sample rates up to ~ 1 MHz) strung together sequentially produce signals that can be translated to audio-rate signals relatively simply via resampling. The jumps in these signals represent state changes (see Fig. 18.5), which at the simplest level can be used as markers to select or trigger notes, tones, or other musical events. Alternatively, the amplitude of the signal can be used directly as an equivalent to control voltage (CV) generation in traditional analogue synthesizers.

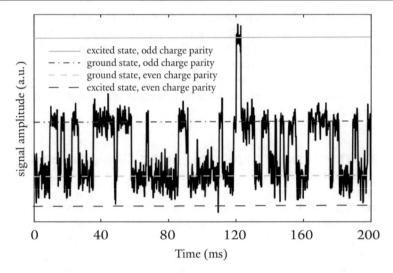

Fig. 18.3 Simultaneous measurement of qubit state (ground or excited) and charge parity (the number parity of quasiparticles (QPs) that have tunneled across the Josephson junction, even or odd) in a transmon qubit [21]. Experimental data is shown with overlaid horizontal lines denoting the signal amplitudes that correspond to each state. Signals such as these were the basis for sounds generated for the performance and sonified using the 4-state synthesizer (see Sect. 18.2.1)

These signals also contain a certain amount of noise from quantum fluctuations, which is detectable due to the use of nearly-quantum-limited parametric amplifiers [4, 15]. While this could be used as a stochastic musical source, it can also be used to modulate oscillators creating pitch vibrato and other kinds of audible musical effects. Using quantum fluctuations as a modulating signal is one example of direct sonification of quantum phenomena.

18.3   A Simple Quantum Synthesizer

In order to sonify the signals acquired from the aforementioned experiments we developed a simple quantum synthesizer utilizing measurement traces as an input. A block diagram that illustrates this synthesizer is shown in Fig. 18.6. Most synthesizer designs used in the performance are variations of this model.

The basic concept is to take the output from the quantum systems and down-sample them to audio rate with a DC offset to center the signal at 0 V, scaled to 2 V pole-to-pole. These processed signals act as an oscillator operating in audible range (kHz) with the qubit-transition information used as a primary control voltage and the quantum noise signal extracted for modulation of the oscillator as a secondary effect.

Cavity 1   Cavity 2
"Leader"   "Follower"

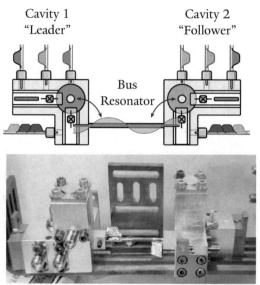

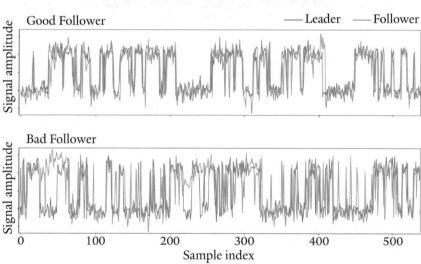

Fig. 18.4 Diagram [7] and photograph of Luke's two qubit-cavity devices (top). Cavity 1 ("leader") is coupled to Cavity 2 ("follower") via a cavity bus. The qubit housed in Cavity 2 can track the state of that in Cavity 1 via high-fidelity control and classical feedback ("Good Follower," top plot). By intentionally introducing errors in the control sequence, the correlation between readout signals can be reduced ("Bad Follower," bottom plot)

A modulation index parameter allows the user to control the amount of modulation applied, which uses the quantum noise encoded in the signal to generate its waveform. An index equal to zero would result in no modulation effect applied, with increasing index corresponding to an increasing modulation effect.

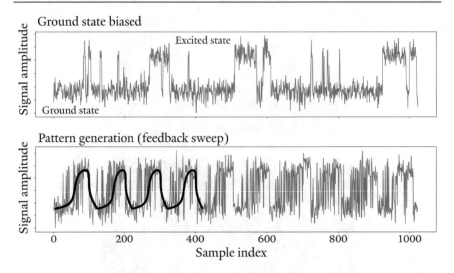

Fig. 18.5 Some synthesis tools/functions created to generate diverse sounds. Top: qubit dynamics with fixed feedback controls, biased toward ground-state occupation. Bottom: sweeping feedback parameters to modulate the expected qubit-state occupation

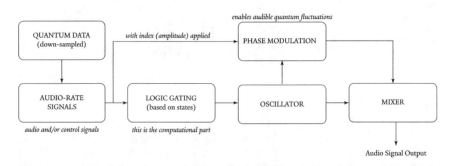

Fig. 18.6 Process block diagram for a simple quantum music synthesizer. The experimental data is first resampled to audio rate, and then utilized to control oscillator parameters selected by the user

For the piece *Quantum Sound,* we designed three synthesizers based on the simple model of the quantum synthesizer described above. In this section, we will discuss each model and the resulting synthesizer design, with considerations for what was included as controls and what could be added in future iterations. The three synthesizers we designed were based on the experiments summarized in Sect. 18.2, and are identified as follows:

1. *2-State* is a two-state synthesizer with selectable waveforms, amplitudes, and frequencies for each state that can be phase modulated with the quantum fluctuations captured in the measurements taken from the aforementioned experiments.

2. **4-State** is a four-state synthesizer with similar features to *2-State:* selectable waveforms, amplitudes, and frequencies for each state that can be phase modulated with the quantum fluctuations captured in the measurements taken from the aforementioned experiments.
3. **Bad Follower** is a leader-follower synthesizer whereby the state-following behaviour is accurate or inaccurate depending on the fidelity of classical feedback controlling the state of the follower qubit based on measurement outcomes of the leader qubit.

In addition to these synthesizers, we also created a synth engine built into both *2-State* and *4-State* that sonifies a measurement of the offset charge in Kyle's transmon qubit as a function of time, which due to its slow time dynamics could be played back at near its native sampling rate. Colloquially we referred to this as drift. The drift synthesis engine used the normalized offset charge as a continuously valued control voltage that determined the pitch of a musical drone produced by a sine-wave oscillator. To reduce the number of interfaces we were performing with, we added the drift sonification to *2-State* and *4-State*, which is read from a separate datafile, though it is worth noting that this sonification process could be a stand-alone synthesizer by itself.

18.3.1 Two-State

The *2-State* synthesizer is a realization of the synthesizer model described above. We created this synthesizer in the Max-for-Live Ableton environment [1] since it is a flexible and fast way to create customized synthesis processes with a high degree of usability. The input to the system is a monophonic audio file containing the experimental data down sampled to audio rate. A latching-filter state assignment is performed, which determines which oscillator is selected. The user can select several standard synthesis parameters for each state/oscillator: waveform type; frequency (in Hz); attack and decay envelope; and modulation amount. The user can also control global parameters such as overall gain output from the synthesizer, data smoothing to reduce noise, and the wet/dry mix which results in either the raw data sonification, the processed data as synthesized tones, or some mixture of the two.

18.3.2 Four-State

4-State expands the number of states from two to four enabling the user to create four-note melodic patterns based on the experimental data described in Sect. 18.2.1. Like *2-State,* the synthesizer is activated through a monophonic audio file containing the experimental data. Both interfaces for *2-State* and *4-State* contain similar user controls shown in Fig. 18.7.

Fig. 18.7 Ableton Max-for-Live virtual device interface for 4-State. The system allows the user to set different waveforms for the four oscillators (sine, saw, square, and noise), the pitches of these oscillators and their basic envelopes (attack and decay). The controls for modulation driven by quantum noise include modulation index and modulation amplitude. A secondary process was performable from this interface, which allowed for the sonification of offset-charge drift (shown bottom right)

18.3.3 Bad Follower

Bad Follower explores experimental methods described in Sect. 18.2.2, whereby the investigators utilize two transmon-cavity devices with independent readout and control producing a leader-follower arrangement, represented as two separate audio signals, left and right respectively. Depending on the parameterization of the system, the state of the follower qubit would either accurately follow or inaccurately follow the state of the leader qubit using fast, classical feedback. The resulting data were converted to audio files, allowing the user to select good, average, or bad following, which is clearly audible when smoothing is applied. Like the other synthesizers described in this section, the user can apply phase modulation to both the data channels. A smoothing parameter can also be applied to both channels to produce a more continuous melodic pattern.

18.4 *Quantum Sound*: Superconducting Qubits as Music Synthesizers

Quantum Sound premiered on June 14, 2019, at Firehouse 12, a jazz concert hall and recording studio during the 24th International Festival of Arts and Ideas of New Haven CT (USA). Spencer, Kyle, and Luke performed two back-to-back 35-min musical sets, preceded by a 15-min introduction to the quantum physics behind the performance, and followed by a 10-min question-and-answer session between the audience and the artists.

During the performance, Kyle and Luke used data acquired (some pre-recorded, some acquired live during the show) from two experimental setups (the dilution refrigerators affectionately named "Blue" and "JPC," located back in the laboratories on the 4th floor of Becton Center), which was processed and performed live (see Fig. 18.8). Spencer, using pre-recorded data, processed and performed that data while mixing the three audio signals like a conductor to create a coherent

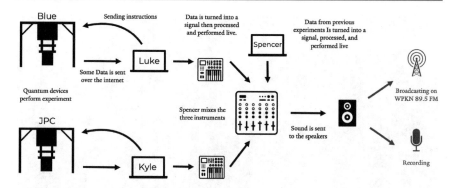

Fig. 18.8 Diagram of data acquisition and process during the live performance to transform quantum signals into an audible musical experience

composition. The second set was broadcast live on WPKN Radio to allow as many people as possible to experience the performance.

It is difficult to illustrate in writing[1] the variety and range of sounds produced by the superconducting instruments. The performance includes moments of intense noise, intercut by melodies that are at different times diatonic, ominous, or almost imperceptible. The audience, safely protected inside the bent-wood cocoon of Firehouse 12, was transported to an eerie and desolate winter landscape, evoking sounds akin to winds blowing through a mountain pass as well as looming storms. At times there is a comforting flutter bringing warmth to the listener, which Spencer calls a wobble, created by the quantum noise that exists within the sonified data. The completed *Quantum Sound* composition resides at the intersection of polyrhythmic electronica and ambient noise music.

Lighting, designed by Florian, played an important role in the performance. Composed of solid and intense colours, the light evolved as the performance (and system) transitioned from a calm section (blue), to a fast-paced one (red) (Fig. 18.9), with a transition period with reds and blues mixing in a superposition of states with shifting pinks, mimicking line-cuts of Wigner quasiprobability distribution diagrams [27]. The intentional lack of green or any natural lighting echoed the nearly complete isolation of superconducting qubits deep inside dilution refrigerators at extremely low temperatures.

18.4.1 From Noise to Meaning

In order to stay true to the notion of scientific outreach via musical performance, it was of utmost importance that the artistic choices taken throughout be relatable back to aspects of the experiments themselves. Unfortunately, the full relation to

---

[1] NOTE: Readers can listen to the album *Quantum Sound* at *QuantumInstitute.yale. edu/Quantum-Sound* as well as watch a mini live performance inside the Yale quantum laboratories next to the quantum computer which generated the data.

Fig. 18.9 Photograph of the live performance at Firehouse 12 in the 3rd sonic section "Crescendo (melodic into danger)," with performers from left to right: Luke Burkhart, Spencer Topel, and Kyle Serniak

experiment was not something that was particularly accessible *during* the performance, but the audience picked up on many motifs that were discussed during the subsequent question-and-answer sessions. Here we seek to explain for the record some of these relations, and how certain motifs were inspired by aspects of the experiments.

As a whole, the structure of the performance can be considered as four distinct sections:

1. Noise (primitive, raw, direct)
2. Rhythmic (randomness into patterns)
3. Crescendo (melodic into danger)
4. Release (ambient resolution).

The first section of the piece is characterized by faithful representation of the collected data as waveforms which are played at the natural sampling rate of the experiment (between 1 and 100 kHz), resulting in an atmosphere of unrecognizable noise. After the three "instruments" are introduced by entry of the performers, artistic liberty was taken to shape the noise into something akin to a conversation between the instruments. Various filtered noise voices enter and exit with movement arising from manual sweeps of filter bandwidth and cutoff frequency. This is not dissimilar to how noise is intentionally filtered via trial and error of different hardware components in experimental setups to achieve optimum performance of the quantum systems. In situ filtering of the noise that decoheres a quantum superposition state, known as dynamical decoupling [8], is another example of noise shaping in experiments.

Discernable pitch is introduced gradually as a transition into the second section of the performance. The simplest approach to creating pitched melodic structure was to feed a synthesis engine with a normalized measurement record where signal amplitude is translated to pitch. With this approach, a given pitch corresponds to a particular quantum state, and vibrato (subtle variations of pitch) was a direct representation of amplified quantum noise. A digital synthesis method was also utilized, whereby a latching-filter state assignment was performed on a qubit measurement trace, discretizing the audible pitches. Examples of these techniques can be heard as many instruments as possible in the second section. A staccato line evocative of Morse code was created from a short snippet of resampled data in which the pitch corresponding to the qubit ground state was inaudibly low, while the excited state was set to around 700 Hz pitch.

Occasional "pings," akin to the way active sonar from submarines is presented in movies, marks the entrance of sustained tones. For these, a resampled and state-assigned measurement trace served as a volume gate in addition to determining pitch. The pings were triggered by occupation of the excited state of the transmon, with two audible pitches denoting the transmon's two charge-parity states. These qubit excitations are relatively rare, as the excited state was only populated $\sim 6\%$ of the time in this experiment.

The second section makes heavy use of this state assignment (both from the charge-parity mapping experiment and the single-qubit control experiment) as a CV to determine the pitch played by each instrument as the pace quickens and a bassline emerges. While the first section of *Quantum Sound* is arguably the truest sonic representation of the data, this second section is truest to the *interpretation* of the data, as experimentalists oftentimes rely on state assignment of single-shot measurements as opposed to continuous-valued voltage measurements. The second section builds in intensity with duplicated passages that are re-pitched and re-filtered to achieve a broader sonic palate.

The third section begins relatively calm, with more state-assigned measurement traces dictating changes in pitch of the *Bad Follower* synthesizer, which is tuned to have a bell-like tonality. The serenity is then disrupted by a droning note that slowly changes pitch (this is created by using measurements of offset charge as a function of time as a CV, as described in Sect. 18.3). This transition brings about an image of an approaching airplane disturbing the peace of a desolate landscape. The drone signal is then also used to modify the base pitch of the *2-state* synthesizer, where the continuous shift in pitch through microtones indicates clearly that something is changing, and not for the better. Suddenly, a short, staccato phrase (a perfect fourth interval, generated by a snippet from the *4-state* synth) sounds the alarm. Noise begins to reenter the sonic landscape, and the alarm sounds more frequently before the entrance of pulsed tones with increased harmonic content and ramped phase modulation, performed manually in a metaphorical battle between the instruments. At this point there is no semblance remaining of the calm from the start of the passage. The opponents fade away as a serene atmosphere generated by the good-follower algorithm rises in amplitude. The plate reverb from Firehouse 12 gives the impression of retreat as one of the combatants lets out a final cry in the distance, signaling the beginning of the fourth and final passage.

Musical motifs from throughout the previous sections are reprised in this final section (excited-state pings, manually-filtered noise, state-assigned pitch synthesis, and the slowly varying offset-charge drone, for example) with Luke's quantum control experiment laying a serene foundation. In the final moments, this tranquility is all that remains.

The listener is encouraged to identify these sonic movements as metaphors for other aspects of experimental physics. For example, we had in mind a coarse representation of the cooldown procedure of a dilution refrigerator. It is at different points both calm and chaotic, eventually arriving at a state of dynamic equilibrium (at least until it's time to warm up and load in a new experiment).

18.5 Conclusions

A primary goal of using transmon qubits as musical-signal generators was to hear what is happening inside these complex experimental systems. While quantum physics is not exactly the most accessible topic, translating its concepts into audible music is a step toward reaching a broader audience. By creating this science outreach project with sound in mind, we sought a natural link between the listener and the quantum devices, and to offer a sonic interpretation of something that had not been heard before.

Shortly after the inception of the project, we realized that one potential challenge would be easily overcome: building a shared language between electronic music and experimental data. It boils down to the fact that signal processing is signal processing, regardless of whether you're working at audio frequencies or in the microwave range. By resampling the experimental signals to an audio rate, the signals were immediately interpretable in a musical context as control voltages and raw audio. This meant that not only were we able to quickly start playing with the raw data as sonic objects, but we were also able to consider new possibilities for control and sound synthesis. As we proceeded into the design of simple synthesizers, we drew inspiration from classic analogue synthesizers which provided all the tools necessary for the translation of experimental data into audio signals.

While the synthesizers built here could be easily generated or simulated using classical systems, the fact that they are constructed from truly quantum systems opens a door to the utilization of uniquely quantum phenomena for audio synthesis. The player can control certain aspects of the musical creation (or more accurately, force the quantum system into a certain state to produce the type of sound desired), while the stochastic nature of the system, the possibility of errors, and the influence of the environment add extra dimensions inherent to the physical implementation of the synthesizer. The authorship of the music is shared with a truly quantum device.

Extensions of this work could utilize quantum correlations in larger arrays of qubits as a step toward truly quantum musical synthesis. This work points toward the future utility of prototype physical devices (quantum or otherwise) as tools for artistic and humanistic applications yet to be imagined.

Acknowledgements The authors thank the Yale Quantum Institute for its financial support of this project, Michel Devoret and Robert Schoelkopf for their constant support and for graciously allowing us to use their labs' experimental systems, Firehouse 12 and their audio engineer Greg DiCrosta for hosting the live performance and the recording, the International Festival of Arts & Idea staff, Martha W Lewis and the WPKN radio station for the broadcasting the live show, and Sang Wook Nam for mastering a recording of the piece for public release.

References

1. Ableton. (n.d.). Max for live. https://www.ableton.com/en/live/max-for-live/. Accessed 15 Feb 2022
2. Arute, F., Arya, K., Babbush, R., Bacon, D., Bardin, J. C., Barends, R., & Biswas, R., et al. (2019). Quantum supremacy using a programmable superconducting processor. *Nature, 574* (7779), 505–510.
3. Bardeen, J., Cooper, L. N., & Schrieffer, J. R. (1957). Theory of superconductivity. *Physical Review, 108*(5), 1175–1204. https://doi.org/10.1103/PhysRev.108.1175
4. Bergeal, N., Schackert, F., Metcalfe, M., Vijay, R., Manucharyan, V. E., Frunzio, L., Prober, D. E., Schoelkopf, R. J., Girvin, S. M., & Devoret, M. H. (2010). Phase-preserving amplification near the quantum limit with a Josephson ring modulator. *Nature, 465*(7294), 64–68. https://doi.org/10.1038/nature09035
5. Bluefors. (n.d.). Dilution refrigerator systems for quantum technology and research. https://bluefors.com/home/. Accessed 14 Dec 2021.
6. Burkhart, L. D., Teoh, J. D., Zhang, Y., Axline, C. J., Luigi Frunzio, M. H., Devoret, L. J., Girvin, S. M., & Schoelkopf, R. J. (2021). Error-detected state transfer and entanglement in a superconducting quantum network. *PRX Quantum, 2*(3), 030321. https://doi.org/10.1103/PRXQuantum.2.030321
7. Burkhart L. D. (2020). Error-detected networking for 3D circuit quantum electrodynamics. Ph.D., United States Connecticut. Yale University. https://www.proquest.com/pqdtglobal/docview/2543746166/911AAD2A72A7441APQ/1.
8. Bylander, J., Gustavsson, S., Yan, F., Yoshihara, F., Harrabi, K., Fitch, G., Cory, D. G., Nakamura, Y., Tsai, J.-S., & Oliver, W. D. (2011). Noise spectroscopy through dynamical decoupling with a superconducting flux qubit. *Nature Physics, 7*(7), 565–570. https://doi.org/10.1038/nphys1994
9. Devoret, M. H., & Schoelkopf, R. J. (2013). Superconducting circuits for quantum information: An outlook. *Science, 339*(6124), 1169–1174. https://doi.org/10.1126/science.1231930
10. Institute of Musicology SASA. (2015). Quantum music. Beyond Quantum Music 2018. http://quantummusic.org/.
11. Institute of Musicology SASA Belgrade, Квантна. (2018). Quantum Music (and beyond)— Music and New Technologies in the 21st Century, 32.
12. Interdisciplinary Centre for Computer Music Research. (n.d.) 1st international symposium on quantum computing and musical creativity. In *1st International Symposium on Quantum Computing and Musical Creativity*. https://iccmr-quantum.github.io/1st_isqcmc/. Accessed 18 Oct 2021.

13. Krinner, S., Lacroix, N., Remm, A., Di Paolo, A., Genois, E., Leroux, C., & Hellings, C., et al. (2021). Realizing repeated quantum error correction in a distance-three surface code. http://arxiv.org/abs/2112.03708.

14. Lecocq, F., Pop, I. M., Peng, Z., Matei, I., Crozes, T., Fournier, T., Naud, C., Guichard, W., & Buisson, O. (2011). Junction Fabrication by shadow evaporation without a suspended bridge. *Nanotechnology, 22*(31), 315302. https://doi.org/10.1088/0957-4484/22/31/315302

15. Macklin, C., O'Brien, K., Hover, D., Schwartz, M. E., Bolkhovsky, V., Zhang, X., Oliver, W. D., & Siddiqi, I. (2015). A near-Quantum-Limited Josephson traveling-wave parametric amplifier. *Science, 350*(6258), 307–310. https://doi.org/10.1126/science.aaa8525

16. Kjaergaard, M., Schwartz, M. E., Braumüller, J., Krantz, P., Wang, J.-J., Gustavsson, S., & Oliver, W. D. (2019). Superconducting qubits: Current state of play | annual review of condensed matter physics. *Annual Review of Condensed Matter Physics, 11*(December), 369–395.

17. Novković, D., Peljević, M., & Malinović, M. (2018). Synthesis and analysis of sounds developed from the bose-einstein condensate: Theory and experimental results. *Muzikologija, 24*, 95–109.

18. Oxford Instruments. (n.d.). Cryogenics—Dry systems. https://nanoscience.oxinst.com/. Accessed 14 Dec 2021.

19. Preskill, J. (2018). Quantum computing in the NISQ era and beyond. *Quantum, 2*(August), 79. https://doi.org/10.22331/q-2018-08-06-79.

20. Ristè, D., Bultink, C. C., Tiggelman, M. J., Schouten, R. N., Lehnert, K. W., & DiCarlo, L. (2013). Millisecond charge-parity fluctuations and induced decoherence in a superconducting transmon qubit. *Nature Communications, 4*(1), 1913. https://doi.org/10.1038/ncomms2936

21. Serniak, K., Diamond, S., Hays, M., Fatemi, V., Shankar, S., Frunzio, L., Schoelkopf, R. J., & Devoret, M. H. (2019). Direct dispersive monitoring of charge parity in offset-charge-sensitive transmons. *Physical Review Applied, 12*(1), 014052. https://doi.org/10.1103/PhysRevApplied.12.014052

22. Serniak, K., Hays, M., de Lange, G., Diamond, S., Shankar, S., Burkhart, L. D., Frunzio, L., Houzet, M., & Devoret, M. H. (2018). Hot Nonequilibrium quasiparticles in transmon qubits. *Physical Review Letters, 121*(15), 157701. https://doi.org/10.1103/PhysRevLett.121.157701

23. Serniak, K. (2019). Nonequilibrium quasiparticles in superconducting qubits. Ph.D., United States—Connecticut. Yale University. https://www.proquest.com/pqdtglobal/docview/2394329051/abstract/5CDA859FE5504556PQ/1.

24. Spencer Topel. (2019). *Quantum Sound: A Live Performance of Superconducting Instruments.* http://QuantumInstitute.yale.edu/Quantum-Sound.

25. Ssergejewitsch, T. L. (1928). Method of and apparatus for the generation of sounds. United States US1661058A, filed December 5, 1925, and issued February 28, 1928. https://patents.google.com/patent/US1661058A/en.

26. Vool, U., & Devoret, M. (2017). Introduction to quantum electromagnetic circuits. *International Journal of Circuit Theory and Applications, 45*(7), 0098–9886.

27. Wigner, E. (1932). On the quantum correction for thermodynamic equilibrium. *Physical Review, 40*(5), 749–759. https://doi.org/10.1103/PhysRev.40.749

28. Zhao, D. Z., & Wang, D. C. (Eds.). (2019). *Cryogenic Engineering and Technologies: Principles and applications of Cryogen-free systems* (1st ed.). CRC Press.

Printed in the United States
by Baker & Taylor Publisher Services